always up to date

The law changes, but Nolo is always on top of it! We offer several ways to make sure you and your Nolo products arc always up to date:

1 **Nolo's Legal Updater**
We'll send you an email whenever a new edition of your book is published! Sign up at **www.nolo.com/legalupdater**.

2 **Updates @ Nolo.com**
Check **www.nolo.com/update** to find recent changes in the law that affect the current edition of your book.

3 **Nolo Customer Service**
To make sure that this edition of the book is the most recent one, call us at **800-728-3555** and ask one of our friendly customer service representatives. Or find out at **www.nolo.com**.

NOLO

please note

11th edition

Patent It Yourself

by Patent Attorney David Pressman

ELEVENTH EDITION   APRIL 2005

Editor   RICHARD STIM

Illustrations   LINDA ALLISON

Book Design   TERRI HEARSH

Cover Design   WOODS + WOODS STRATEGIC DESIGN

Production   SARAH HINMAN

Index   JULIE SHAWVAN

Proofreading   ROBERT WELLS

Printing   CONSOLIDATED PRINTERS, INC.

INTERNATIONAL STANDARD SERIAL NUMBER (ISSN) 1554-9925

ISBN 1-4133-0180-0

Quantity sales: For information on bulk purchases or corporate premium sales, please contact the Special
Sales Department. For academic sales or textbook adoptions, ask for Academic Sales, 800-955-4775. Nolo,
950 Parker Street, Berkeley, CA 94710.

Acknowledgments

My deep thanks go to my clients, and other inventors whose creativity and genius I so greatly admire and envy. My readers have given me much valuable feedback and suggestions, and I am grateful to them as well.

I also thank the staff at Nolo, including Richard Stim, Steve Elias, Patti Gima, Stephanie Harolde, and Ralph Warner for their ideas, contributions, and support, Linda Allison for her clever drawings, and, especially, Terri Hearsh for substantially improving the look and feel of the book.

Finally, I thank my wife Roberta for her unflagging support and contributions.

11th Edition Preface

While this is the 21th anniversary of the Nolo version of *Patent It Yourself*, I actually started writing it in 1977, about 27 years ago. I decided to write a how-to patent guide for the layperson after I came across a book on patenting written by a layman that was full of serious errors. I also saw that Nolo was publishing well-written do-it-yourself divorce and incorporation books by lawyers. So, I decided that there was room for a good accurate book for the layperson on patenting.

It took me two years to write the first version of *Patent It Yourself!* (note the exclamation point) which was published by McGraw-Hill in hardback in 1979. The book was moderately successful but had only about 180 pages and was relatively superficial. When the patent laws and rules became more complicated in the next several years, McGraw-Hill did not want to revise and expand it, since they felt the market was saturated. I disagreed and brought the book to the editors of Nolo, who fortunately shared my opinion and were willing to allow me to expand the book to give the subject a fuller treatment.

The first edition of Nolo's version of *Patent It Yourself* was published in 1983 and was an immediate success. I owe much credit to my editor, Steve Elias, who forced me to put forth my best. Nolo's *Patent It Yourself* turned out to be a huge success, beyond all of our wildest expectations. In fact, it was Nolo's biggest seller and now is in its 11th edition with over 40 printings. I am very gratified, not only because of the book's success, but also because I was able to demystify the patent process for and help so many inventors.

Many people ask me how I got into the patent business. I was an underclassman in my junior year at Penn State's Electrical Engineering School when we started to design circuits. While I always liked science, I found the fine details of circuit design boring. Serendipitously, I found that I could still remain in technology and use my writing ability (and make good money!) by becoming a patent attorney. So after getting my electrical engineering degree, I went to law school. In 1960, I transferred to evening law school and went to work as a patent examiner in what was then the U.S. Patent Office in Washington, DC.

Patent law was much simpler then, with $30 filing and issue fees, no maintenance fees, no small and large entities, no 18-month publications, no complicated amendment formats, and so forth. But, as anyone who has filed a patent application recently knows, things got a lot more complicated and expensive in recent years. I disagree with most of the changes, since they frustrate our goals of empowering the layperson and eliminating the need to hire lawyers. But we have to live with them, so I've had to continually expand and revise *Patent It Yourself* to keep up with the ever more complicated patent world.

To illustrate some of the changes, in 1960 the fees for getting and keeping a patent over its life were just $60 but now they total $4,160 for a small entity (an individual) and twice that for a large entity (corporation with over 500 employees)! We now have many more forms to contend with, a prescribed format for a patent application and amendments, a need to write and amend claims very carefully to avoid the esoteric doctrine of "file wrapper estoppel," to keep the ability to use the "doctrine of equivalents," and Internet, business method, biological, and manual method inventions which can be patented.

On the other hand, some things have greatly improved in many areas due to the advance of technology: we can fax most communications to the U.S. Patent and Trademark Office (PTO), get complete copies of patents almost instantly on the Internet, make rough searches from our computers, make payments by credit card, and, for the truly brave, even file patent applications on the Internet.

It has been very gratifying to have sold so many copies of *Patent It Yourself*, not only for the royalties, but because I know that so many sales indicate that inventors like it and I am helping them. I get a lot of feedback from inventors who have gotten their own patents, and from quite a few who have licensed or are marketing their inventions successfully. Readers have told me that they've patented zippers, a computer mouse, construction laminates, a cello end pin, various board games, a subliminal messaging system, a shower valve, a bicycle handlebar stem, a hair braider, a modeling device, a metronome, a tree stand, a golfer's tool, a bookmark, a flange cutting tool, marine navigation systems, a music graphic system, a sun visor, an electrical plug safety lock, a measuring stick, a lingerie strap retainer, a pruning blade, a power tool holster, a pizza box, a computer processor, chiming mechanisms, and many more.

Patent It Yourself has been endorsed by many, including the late Dr. R. Buckminster Fuller, *The Wall Street Journal*, *Money*, *Forbes*, and many newspapers, including *The New York Times* and *The Denver Post*, which labeled it "The Inventor's Bible." My greatest thrill occurred when I visited Ketchikan, Alaska, in August 2000 and I stopped in the library and found a copy of *Patent It Yourself* in the same bookcase with some books by one of my idols, Robert W. Service, the Bard of the Yukon.

I thank my readers for giving me lots of feedback, which has helped me improve *Patent It Yourself* as I revised it for the various printings and editions. While most inventors think they need help with the claims, I've learned that the biggest stumbling block is the description or specification, which most inventors do not write clearly and completely enough. I've put in checklists to help ensure that they avoid this and other pitfalls. Also I've added chapter summaries to reinforce the main points of each chapter.

In the future, it seems clear that the PTO intends to eliminate most, if not all, use of paper and postal mail. This will present additional challenges, since most of us tend to take less care if our writing doesn't appear on paper. I hope that without paper "prior art" to search, the quality of patents won't suffer. But I'll continue doing my best to revise and improve *Patent It Yourself* to meet whatever challenges we encounter.

Table of Contents

I Introduction

1 Introduction to Patents and Other Intellectual Property

8 How to Draft the Specification and Initial Drawings

9 Now for the Legalese—The Claims

10 Finaling and Mailing Your Application

11 How to Market Your Invention

12 Going Abroad

13 Getting the PTO to Deliver

14 Your Application Can Have Children

15 After Your Patent Issues: Use, Maintenance, and Infringement

16 Ownership, Assignment, and Licensing of Inventions

Appendixes

1 Abbreviations Used in *Patent It Yourself*

2 Resources: Government Publications, Patent Websites, and Books of Use and Interest

3 Glossaries

4 Fee Schedule

5 Mail, Telephone, Fax, and Email Communications With the PTO

6 Quick-Reference Timing Chart

7 Tear-Out Forms

8 Forms Available at the PTO Website

Index

Introduction

What *Patent It Yourself* Does

Patent It Yourself is a guidebook that allows you, the inventor, to patent and commercially exploit your invention by yourself. It provides:

- Instructions for inventing and documenting an invention, including how and when to use the Patent and Trademark Office's (PTO's) Disclosure Document Program, and how and when to file a Provisional Patent Application;
- Step-by-step guidance for obtaining a U.S. patent, together with tear-out, copyable, or downloadable forms that are necessary for each step of the process;
- An overview of the procedures and requirements for getting patent protection abroad and concrete suggestions for finding the necessary resources to help you do this;
- An overview of the alternative and supplementary forms of protection available for inventions, such as trade secrets, copyrights, trademarks, and unfair competition law; and
- Detailed information and advice on how to commercially evaluate, market, and license your invention.

By following the instructions set out here, you'll not only save healthy attorney fees, but you'll be personally involved with every step of the patenting process. We favor this way of proceeding, since you know your invention better than anyone else, and assuming you're willing to wade through a number of patent technicalities, you're the best person to patent it.

I think of the book as a great equalizer, since it provides the know-how to enable the garage-shop or basement do-it-yourselfer to get as good a patent as a large corporation. It provides the legal tools necessary for inventors (whether large or small) to provide first class legal protection for their work. And it especially gives the small inventor the tools to competently and efficiently protect an invention, whether or not he or she can afford a patent attorney.

You Don't Have to Use a Patent Attorney

In this view, many inventors believe that one must use a patent attorney to get a valid patent. This isn't true. First, the laws contain absolutely no requirement that one must have a patent attorney to file a patent application, deal with the PTO concerning the application, or to obtain the patent. In fact, PTO regulations (MPEP, Section 707.07(j)) specifically require patent examiners to help inventors in *pro se* (no lawyer) cases. Second, and perhaps more persuasive, many hundreds of patent applications are filed and successfully prosecuted each year by *pro se* inventors.

A Layperson Can Do a Quality Job

The quality of a patent is mainly dependent upon four basic factors:

1. whether the patent application contains a full, clear, and accurate description that tells how to make and use the invention,
2. whether the reach of the patent (technically covered in the patent "claims") is as broad as possible, given the state of prior developments in the field,
3. whether the application "sells" the advantages of the invention, and
4. how an applicant handles correspondence with the PTO.

Fortunately, it takes no special legal expertise to do an excellent job for these factors.

Using an Attorney

Even if you do choose to work with an attorney, or have one available to you through the process, you'll find that this book allows you to take an active role in the process, do a better job of monitoring your attorney (no trivial consideration), and greatly adds to your understanding of the ways in which the law is willing to protect your invention. No matter how competent an attorney is, the client who understands what's going on will always obtain better service. Indeed, many corporate legal departments use this book to educate their inventors and support personnel to deal with patent attorneys and to protect their inventions more effectively.

Should You Do It Yourself?

The big question is, of course, even though many if not most inventors can file and handle their own patent application, should you do so on your own or hire an expert? After all, you probably hire people to do all sorts of things for you, from fixing your car to remodeling your kitchen, that you could do yourself. The most powerful incentive for patenting it yourself is the amount of money expert help costs. Or put another way, even though most car mechanics make a pretty good living, most of them can't afford to belong to the same country club as patent attorneys. The cost factor alone may dictate your decision for you if you can't afford the $3,000 to $10,000 most attorneys now charge to prepare a patent application on a simple invention.

On the other hand, if you're fortunate enough to be able to afford an attorney and you either don't have enough time to do it yourself, you don't think you'll be able to write a detailed description of your invention in conjunction with drawings (it's easier than you think), you aren't diligent and committed enough to complete projects in a reasonable time, or you don't think you can complete a detailed writing job in a fairly high quality manner, then perhaps you should use an attorney in conjunction with *Patent It Yourself*, to monitor and enhance the attorney's work, as stated above.

The above can be expressed by the following proportion:

$$\text{DIY } \alpha \ \frac{\text{AT} \cdot \text{WA} \cdot \text{D} \cdot \text{DC}}{\text{AF}}$$

which means you should be inclined to *Do It Yourself* in direct proportion to your *Available Time*, your *Writing Ability*, your *Diligence*, and your *Desire to Control* things, and in inverse proportion to your *Available Funds*. While this proportion isn't even an approach at precision, it provides the appropriate criteria and how to use them when making the do-it-yourself v. hire-an-attorney decision.

The best answer for some inventors may be to do some of both. Using this approach, diligent inventors will do much of the patent work themselves, only consulting with an attorney at an hourly rate if snags develop, or to check the patent application before submission.

New Material in the Eleventh Edition

- New law concerning Internet and business method patents
- instructions on preparing claim chart to determine infringement
- additional sources for contingent-fee patient litigation financing

- new websites of interest to inventors
- updated information about online searching facilities
- revised rules regarding drawings, photo submissions, and amendments
- current fee information
- new rules for patent application and amendment formats
- additional tips and techniques for more effective patenting and marketing
- revised listings of foreign filing countries under international conventions

How to Use *Patent It Yourself*

The book is organized primarily for chronological use, starting with an overview of the entire intellectual property field (which includes patents, trademarks, copyright, and trade secret law). Then it sequentially covers the steps most inventors will take to monopolize and profit from their inventions. I strongly recommend that you first read the book all the way through, skimming lightly over the many chapters that actually tell you how to do things.

In this way you'll first get an overview of the patent forest before you return and deal with the individual steps (trees) necessary to fully protect your invention.

Throughout the book I refer to a number of forms and in many instances reproduce them in the text. A tear-out or copyable version of each is also located in Appendix 7 for your use, and all PTO forms can be downloaded from the PTO website. If you don't have Internet access, I recommend that you make photocopies of PTO forms so you'll have ample spares for drafts and extra copies for your records.

Also throughout the book I refer to various statutes and governmental administrative rules, mostly in the patent area. I use standard forms of legal citation; these are interpreted as follows:

    35 USC 102 = Title 35 of the U.S. Code, Section 102

    37 CFR 1.111 = Title 37 of the (U.S.) Code of Federal Regulations, Section 1.111.

Title 35 of the U.S. Code (USC) contains all of the federal patent statutes and Title 37 of the U.S. Code of Federal Regulations (CFR) contains all of the federal administrative rules issued by the Patent and Trademark Office and Copyright Office that deal with patents, trademarks, and copyright matters. Part 1 of 37 CFR is concerned with patents. Thus Patent Rule 111 = 37 CFR 1.111.

In addition to the Patent Rules, the PTO publishes much more information on the patent process in its *Manual of Patent Examining Procedure* (MPEP), which is available online. Both the U.S. Code and the CFR are available in any law library and online as part of the MPEP, as indicated in Appendixes 2 and 5, Resources: Government Publications, Patent Websites, and Books of Use and Interest; and Mail, Telephone, Fax, and Email Communications With the PTO.

I've used many abbreviations throughout *Patent It Yourself* to save space and spare you the tedium of repeatedly reading long phrases. I've tried to define each abbreviation the first time I've used it and again if there is a long break before it is used again. If at any time you need to refresh your memory about a particular abbreviation, please refer to Appendix 1, Abbreviations Used in *Patent It Yourself*.

Appendix 3 provides two dictionaries. The first is a list of technical terms used in the preparation of patent applications (Glossary of Useful Technical Terms). The second list provides definitions for many of the terms used throughout this book (Glossary of Patent Terms).

The law is constantly changing. We try to update the important changes in each printing, but in the meantime you can get updates from the following websites on the Internet:

www.PatentItYourself.com/update.html, and
www.nolo.com.

Welcome to the world of intellectual property! Good luck and successful inventing!

Icons Used in This Book

Look for these icons, which alert you to certain kinds of information.

 The caution icon warns you of potential problems.

 The "fast track" arrow alerts you that you can skip some material that isn't relevant to your case.

 This icon indicates that the information is a useful tip.

 The note icon highlights information which pertains only to a specific patent field.

 This icon refers you to helpful books or other resources.

 This icon lets readers know when they need the advice of an attorney or other expert.

Chapter 1

Introduction to Patents and Other Intellectual Property

Inventor's Commandment #1

Prior to deciding how to proceed with any creation, you should learn and be familiar with the various forms of intellectual property, including utility patents, design patents, trademarks, copyright, trade secrets, and unfair competition, so that you will be able to select and employ the proper form(s) of coverage for your creation.

In this chapter I'll first introduce you to the world of "intellectual property" law including patents, trademarks, etc. Each of the patent-related items discussed here I'll amplify in subsequent chapters, as they relate to the actual process of obtaining and profiting from a patent. I also present an overview of the other forms of "intellectual property," which are potentially available to you. Although you may think that a patent is the only form of protection for your creation, I strongly recommend you become familiar with and consider the alternatives, some of which you can use in addition to or in lieu of a patent.

A. What Is a Patent and Who Can Apply for It?

Before we start, to show the importance of patents to a society, consider the following:

"That reminds me to remark, in passing, that the very first official thing I did, in my administration—and it was on the very first day of it, too—was to start a patent office; for I knew that a country without a patent office and good patent laws was just a crab, and couldn't travel any way but sideways or backways."
—Mark Twain, *A Connecticut Yankee in King Arthur's Court*, Chapter IX, "The Tournament."

Have you ever thought about why the standard of living in the United States is so high? I believe it's due in part to the United States patent system, which stimulates the creative genius in the U.S. As Lincoln said, "The patent system added the fuel of interest to the fire of genius."

What is a patent? It's a right granted by the government to an inventor.

What is the nature of the patent right? A patent gives its owner—the inventor or the person or business to whom the inventor legally transfers the patent—the right to exclude others from making, using, or selling the invention "claimed" in the patent deed for approximately 17 to 18 years, provided three maintenance fees are paid. (See Chapter 9 for more on patent claims, and Chapter 15 for more on maintenance fees.) You can use this right to exclude others by filing a patent infringement lawsuit in federal court.

Important Definitions

While these definitions may seem elementary, I provide them here because many inventors confuse these terms, and so that you will know exactly what I mean when I use these terms later.

An **invention** is any new article, machine, composition, or process or new use developed by a human.

A **patent application** is a set of papers that describe an invention and that are suitable for filing in a patent office in order to apply for a patent on the invention.

A **patent** is a grant from a government that confers upon an inventor the right to exclude others from making, using, selling, importing, or offering an invention for sale for a fixed period of time.

Who can apply for a patent? Anyone, regardless of age, nationality, mental competency, incarceration, or any other characteristic, so long as he or she is a true inventor of the invention. Even dead or insane persons may apply through their personal representative. (See Chapter 16 for more on patent ownership.)

A patent is a form of personal property and can be sold outright for a lump sum, or its owner can give anyone permission to use the invention covered ("license it") in return for royalty payments. More on this in Chapter 16.

B. The Three Types of Patents

There are three types of patents—utility patents, design patents, and plant patents. Let's briefly look at each.

- **Utility Patents:** As we'll see in Chapters 8 to 10, a utility patent, the main type of patent, covers inventions that function in a unique manner to produce a utilitarian result. Examples of utility inventions are Velcro hook-and-loop fasteners, new drugs, electronic circuits, software, semiconductor manufacturing processes, new bacteria, newly discovered genes, new animals, plants, automatic transmissions, and virtually anything else under the sun that can be made by humans. To get a utility patent, one must file a patent application that consists of a detailed description telling how to make and use the invention, together with claims (formally written sentence fragments) that define the invention, drawings of the invention, formal paperwork, and a filing fee. Again, only the actual inventor can apply for a utility (or any other) patent. The front or abstract page of a typical utility patent is illustrated in Fig. 1A.

• **Design Patents:** As discussed in more detail in Chapter 10, a design patent (as opposed to a utility patent) covers the unique, ornamental, or visible shape or surface ornamentation of an article or object, even if only on a computer screen. Thus if a lamp, a building, a computer case, or a desk has a truly unique shape, its design can be design patented. Even computer screen icons and an arrangement of printing on a piece of paper can be patented. The design must be for an article that is different from an object in its natural state; thus a figure of a man would not be suitable for a design patent but if the man is an unnatural position, this can be patented. For an example, see patent Des. 440,263 (2001) to Norman. However, the uniqueness of the shape must be purely ornamental or aesthetic and part of an article; if it is functional, then only a utility patent is proper, even if it is also aesthetic. A good example is a jet plane with a constricted waist for reducing turbulence at supersonic speeds: although the shape is attractive, its functionality makes it suitable only for a utility patent.

A useful way to distinguish between a design and a utility invention is to ask, "Will removing or smoothing out the novel features substantially impair the function of the device?" If so—as in the jet plane with the narrowed waist—this proves that the novel features have a significant functional purpose, so a utility patent is indicated. If not—as in a woodshop wall clock that is shaped like a circular saw blade, or a phone that is shaped like a shoe—a design patent is indicated. Another useful question to ask is, "Is the novel feature(s) there for structural or functional reasons, or only for the purpose of ornamentation?"

Sometimes the state of the art, rather than the nature of the novelty, will determine whether a design or utility patent is proper for an invention. If a new feature of a device performs a novel function, then a utility patent is proper. However, if the state of the art is such that the general nature of the feature and its function is old, but the feature has a novel shape which is an aesthetic improvement, then only a design patent will be proper.

The design patent application must consist primarily of drawings, along with formal paperwork and a filing fee.

• **Plant Patents:** A plant patent covers asexually reproducible plants (that is, through the use of grafts and cuttings), such as flowers (35 USC 161). Sexually reproducible plants (that is, those that use pollination), can be monopolized under the Plant Variety Protection Act (7 USC 2321). Both sexually and asexually reproducible plants can now also be monopolized by utility patent (35 USC 101). Plant patents are a comparatively recent innovation (1930). Luther Burbank, the great California botanist, goaded Congress to act, stating, "We plant inventors cannot patent a new plum, though the man who makes an automobile horn can get a patent and retire to Southern California and wear silk underclothes the rest of his life."

C. The Novelty and Unobviousness Requirement

With all three types of patents, a patent examiner in the Patent and Trademark Office (PTO) must be convinced that your invention satisfies the "novelty" and "unobviousness" requirements of the patent laws.

The novelty requirement is easy to satisfy: your invention must be different from what is already known to the public. Any difference, however slight, will suffice.

Novelty, however, is only one small hurdle to overcome. In addition to being novel, the examiner must also be convinced that your invention is "unobvious." This means that at the time you came up with your invention, it would have been considered unobvious to a person skilled in the technology (called "art") involved in your creation. As we'll see in Chapter 5, unobviousness is best shown by new and unexpected, surprising, or far superior results, when compared with previous inventions and knowledge ("prior art") in the particular area of the invention. (In addition to being novel and unobvious, utility inventions must also be "in a statutory class" and be useful. More on this later.)

United States Patent [19]

Holmes

[11] Patent Number: **4,949,887**

[45] Date of Patent: **Aug. 21, 1990**

[54] **INSULATED MULTI-USE SEAT CUSHION WITH CLOSABLE HAND AND FOOT OPENINGS**

[76] Inventor: **William A. Holmes,** 209 Highland Ave., Piedmont, Calif. 94611-3709

[21] Appl. No.: 132,982

[22] Filed: **Dec. 15, 1987**

Related U.S. Application Data

[63] Continuation-in-part of Ser. No. 867,453, May 28, 1986, abandoned.

[51] Int. Cl.⁵ A61G 1/00
[52] U.S. Cl. 224/151; 224/205; 224/236; 2/66; 2/202; 126/204; 297/188
[58] Field of Search 224/151, 153, 202, 205, 224/257, 206, 207, 236, 237; 2/66, 91, 93, 108, 202, 203; 383/61, 110, 98, 99, 8; 128/382; 190/107, 102; 5/417–421; 297/230, 188, 192, 219; 126/204, 207, 208

[56] **References Cited**

U.S. PATENT DOCUMENTS

273,523	3/1883	Havasy	190/102
1,137,049	4/1915	Bushwick	190/107
2,835,896	5/1958	Giese	2/66
3,460,740	8/1969	Hagen	383/110
3,793,643	2/1974	Kinoshita	2/66
4,423,834	1/1984	Rush	224/151
4,604,987	8/1986	Keltner	5/421

Primary Examiner—Linda J. Sholl
Attorney, Agent, or Firm—David Pressman

[57]   **ABSTRACT**

An insulated hollow cushion has a neck strap (30), an interior portion (72) sufficiently large to accommodate a portable heating source and/or hot and cold foods (74, 76), two side slits through which hands can be inserted for warmth, sealable flaps (16, 20) for closing the side slits when insulation is desired, a slit (36) at the top of the cushion for insertion of items into the cushion's interior, a closeable top flap (28) to seal the top opening for insulation purposes, and a closeable top small flap (56) to insulate the gap between a user's ankles when such user's feet are inserted through the top slit. The side flaps can be insulated so that they can be tucked into the side openings to narrow these openings to provide a tight seal when small hands are inserted into these openings. The insulating layer within the front (10) or the back panel can have multiple perforations (92) over an area thereof and this area can be covered, uncovered, or partially covered by a releasably closable flap (84), thereby to provide a "heat window" which allows maximum transmission of heat (or cold) from an internal hot (or cold) source, or partial transmission, or no more transmission than would occur through an intact insulated wall.

20 Claims, 6 Drawing Sheets

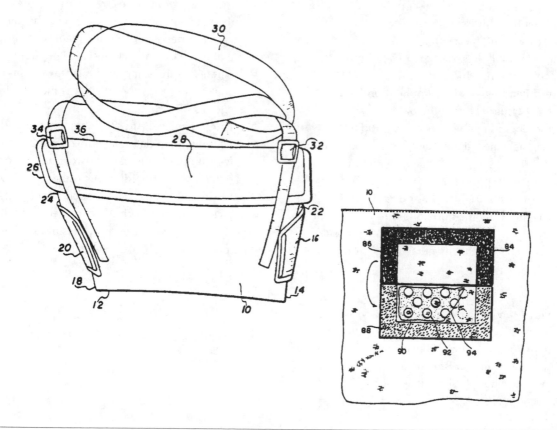

Fig. 1A—Utility Patent Abstract Page

The Life of an Invention

Although most inventors will be concerned with the rights a patent grants during its monopoly or in-force period (from the date the patent issues until it expires (20 years after the filing date)), the law actually recognizes five "rights" periods in the life of an invention. These five periods are as follows:

1. **Invention Conceived but Not Yet Documented:** When an inventor conceives of an invention, but hasn't yet made any written, signed, dated, and witnessed record of it, the inventor has no legal rights whatsoever, only the potential for acquiring rights.

2. **Invention Documented but Patent Application Not Yet Filed:** After making a proper, signed, dated, and witnessed documentation of an invention, the inventor has valuable rights against any inventor who later conceives of the same invention and applies for a patent. An inventor who documents the building and testing of the invention has substantially greater rights than one who merely documents conception. (See Chapter 3, Section E1.) The invention may also be treated as a "trade secret"—that is, kept confidential. This gives the inventor the legal right to sue and recover damages against anyone who immorally learns of the invention—for instance, through industrial spying.

3. **Patent Pending—Patent Application Filed but Not Yet Issued:** During the patent pending period, including the one-year period after a provisional patent application is filed, the inventor's rights are the same as they are in Period 2 above, with one exception noted below.* Otherwise, the inventor has no rights whatsoever against infringers—only the hope of a future monopoly, which doesn't commence until a patent issues. Most companies that manufacture a product that is the subject of a pending patent application will mark the product "patent pending" in order to warn potential copiers that if they copy the product, they may have to stop later (and thus scrap all their molds and tooling) if and when a patent issues. The Patent and Trademark Office (PTO) by law must keep all patent applications preserved in secrecy until the application is published or the patent issues (whichever comes first). The patent pending period usually lasts from one to three years.

4. **In-Force Patent—Patent Issued but Hasn't Yet Expired:** After the patent issues,* the patent owner can bring and maintain a lawsuit for patent infringement against anyone who makes, uses, or sells the invention without permission. The patent's in-force period lasts from the date it issues until 20 years from its filing date, provided maintenance fees are paid. Every patent is guaranteed an in-force period of at least 17 years. In order to assure this 17-year term, the patent will be extended, if necessary, to compensate for delays resulting from failures by the PTO in processing the patent application. Also, once the patent issues, it becomes a public record or publication that can block others who file later from getting patents on the same or similar inventions—that is, it becomes "prior art" to anyone who files after its filing date.

5. **Patent Expired:** After the patent expires (20 years after the filing date, or sooner if a maintenance fee isn't paid), the patent owner has no further rights, although infringement suits can be brought for any infringement that occurred during the patent's in-force period. An expired patent remains a valid "prior-art reference" (as of its filing date) forever.

---

* Under the new 18-month publication statute (see Section Q2), an inventor whose application is published prior to issuance may obtain royalties from an infringer from the date of publication, provided the application later issues as a patent and the infringer had actual notice of the published application.

D. How Long Do Patent Rights Last?

How long can you, the patent owner, exclude others from infringing the exclusive rights granted by your patent? Utility and plant patents expire 20 years from the date of filing while design patents last 14 years from the date of issuance. The terms of patents for certain products whose commercial marketing has been delayed due to regulatory review (such as for drugs or food additives) can be extended beyond the statutory period.

Effective June 2000, every patent is guaranteed an in-force period of at least 17 years. The patent term will be extended for as long as necessary to compensate for any of the following:

- Any delay caused by the PTO failing to examine a new application within 14 months from filing;
- Any delay caused by the PTO failing to take any of the following actions within four months:
  - Reply to an amendment or to an appeal brief,
  - Issue an allowance or Office Action after a decision on appeal, or
  - Issue a patent after the issue fee is paid and any required drawings are filed;
- Any delay caused by the PTO failing to issue a patent within three years from filing, unless the delay was due to the applicant filing a continuation application or buying a delay to reply to an Office Action;
- Any delay due to secrecy orders, appeals, or interferences.

The patent's enforceable monopoly period starts when the patent issues, usually about one to two years after the application is filed. From the date of filing to issuance (termed "pendency period") the inventor has no rights. However, when and if the patent later issues, the inventor will obtain the right to prevent the continuation of any infringing activity that started during the pendency period.

Effective December 2000, an inventor may gain some "provisional" rights against an infringer. Under the new 18-month rule (see Section Q2), an inventor may obtain royalties from an infringer from the date of publication provided (1) the application later issues as a patent; and (2) the infringer had actual notice of the published application. (35 USC 122, 154.)

I provide a time chart in Appendix 6 and "The Life of an Invention" above, to indicate these and other pertinent times.

E. Patent Filing Deadlines

As we'll see in more detail in Chapter 5, in the United States you must file your patent application within one year after you first commercialize, publish, or reveal without restriction

details of the invention. However most foreign countries don't have this one-year grace period, so there's some disadvantage if you sell or publish before filing. For this reason, your safest route is to file a complete U.S. patent application before you publish or commercialize your invention. Under new legislation, you are permitted to file a "provisional patent application" (PPA) describing your invention in detail, in accordance with the instructions in Chapters 3 and 8. (No claims, discussed in Chapter 9, are needed.) This PPA can be used, under most circumstances, to defeat or block a patent application or invention of someone else who may subsequently file a patent application on the same invention. However, to obtain the benefit of the PPA's filing date, a regular patent application must be filed within one year after the PPA's filing date—more on this in Chapters 7 and 8.

F. Patent Fees

How much will it cost to get a patent? Assuming you use this book and don't use any patent attorneys or agents, and not including costs of drawings, typing, photocopying, and postage, the only fees you'll have to pay are government fees.

The amounts of these fees are listed on the PTO Fee Schedule in Appendix 4. As indicated in the Schedule, most PTO fees are two-part: large entity and small entity. The large-entity fees are generally paid by large corporations, while the small-entity fees, which are half the large-entity fees, are generally paid by independent inventors. For more on this, see Chapter 10, Section I. The names of these fees and the circumstances when they're due are as follows:

- **Utility Patents:** To file a provisional patent application, you'll have to pay a *PPA filing fee*. To file a utility patent application, you must pay a *Utility Patent Application Filing Fee*. This fee now has three components—filing fee, search fee, and examination fee—but all three must be paid together. To have the PTO issue your utility patent, you must pay a *Utility Patent Application Issue Fee*. To keep the patent in force for its full statutory term, you must pay the PTO three maintenance fees, as follows:

- *Maintenance Fee I*, payable 3.0 to 3.5 years after issuance;
- *Maintenance Fee II*, payable 7.0 to 7.5 years after issuance;
- *Maintenance Fee III*, payable 11.0 to 11.5 years after issuance.

- **Design Patents:** To file a design patent application, you must pay a *Design Patent Application Filing Fee*. To have the PTO issue your design patent, you must pay a *Design Patent Application Issue Fee*. The law doesn't require maintenance fees for design patents, and there's no PPA for a design patent application.
- **Plant Patents:** To file a plant patent application, you must pay a *Plant Patent Application Filing Fee*. To have the PTO issue your plant patent, you must pay a *Plant Patent Application Issue Fee*. Again, the law doesn't require maintenance fees for plant patents, and there's no PPA for a plant patent application.

G. The Scope of the Patent

The patent right extends throughout the entire U.S., its territories, and possessions. A patent is transferable by sale or gift, by will, or by descent (under the state's intestate succession (no-will) laws). The patent rights can also be licensed, that is, you can own the patent and grant anyone else, including a company, the right to make, use, or sell your invention in exchange for the payment of fees, called "royalties" (more on licensing in Chapter 16). As mentioned, the patent right is granted by the federal government, acting through the Patent and Trademark Office (a division of the Department of Commerce), in Alexandria, Virginia. The patent right is recognized and enforced by the U.S. (federal) courts.

H. How Patent Rights Can Be Lost

The patent right isn't an absolute monopoly for the period that it is in force (from the date of issuance until the expiration date—20 years from date of filing). It can be lost if:

- maintenance fees aren't paid;
- it can be proved that the patent either (a) fails adequately to teach how to make and use the invention, (b) improperly describes the invention, or (c) contains claims that are legally inadequate;
- one or more prior-art references (earlier patents or other publications) are uncovered which show that the invention of the patent wasn't new or wasn't different enough when the invention was made;

- the patent owner engages in certain defined types of illegal conduct, that is, commits antitrust or other violations connected with the patent; or
- the patent applicant committed "fraud on the Patent and Trademark Office (PTO)" by failing to disclose material information, such as relevant prior-art references, to the PTO during the period when the patent application was pending.

In short, the patent monopoly, while powerful, may be defeated and is limited in scope and time.

I. What Rights a Patent Grants and the Prior-Art Reference Value of a Patent

The patent grant gives its owner—one or more individuals, a partnership, corporation, or other entity to which an inventor has "assigned" (legally transferred) the invention— the right to file, maintain, and recover in a lawsuit against any person or legal entity (infringer) who makes, uses, or sells the claimed invention, or an essential part of it. If the patent owner wins the lawsuit, the judge will issue an injunction (a signed order) against the infringer, ordering the infringer not to make, use, or sell the invention any more. Also, the judge will award the patent owner damages— money to compensate the patent owner for loss due to the infringement. The amount of the damages is often the equivalent to a reasonable royalty (say 5%), based on the infringer's sales. However, if the patent owner can convince the judge that the infringer acted in bad faith—for example, infringed intentionally with no reasonable excuse—the judge can triple the damages and make the infringer pay the patent owner's attorney fees.

In addition to bringing in licensing income and enabling a manufacturer to charge more for a unique product, patents also have other uses. Some inventors file for and obtain patents mainly for vanity, or the prestige a patent brings. Others use patents to impress and obtain financing from investors. And many organizations obtain large portfolios of patents simply to assert them as a defense against any company that charges the organization with patent infringement.

The value of patents cannot be overestimated. As Dr. Edwin Land, the inventor and founder of Polaroid, stated, "The only thing that keeps us alive is our brilliance. The only way to protect our brilliance is patents." For a more concrete example, consider that in 2000, the PTO granted over 2,800 patents to IBM, which now holds about 19,000 U.S. patents. These patents generated over $1.5 billion in revenue!

Since the patent defines the invention monopoly very precisely, the patent owner can use the patent only against supposed infringers who make, use, or sell things or processes that fall within the defined monopoly. This means that not everyone who makes something similar to your invention will be an infringer; you can validly sue only those whose products or processes fall within the scope of the claims in your patent. (See Chapters 9, 13, and 15 for more on claims.)

In addition to its above-described use as an offensive weapon, a patent also provides a prior-art reference that will block others from getting a patent on anything disclosed in the patent. In this respect, a patent is like a periodical (magazine) article or book. This dual nature of a patent is illustrated in Fig. 1B.

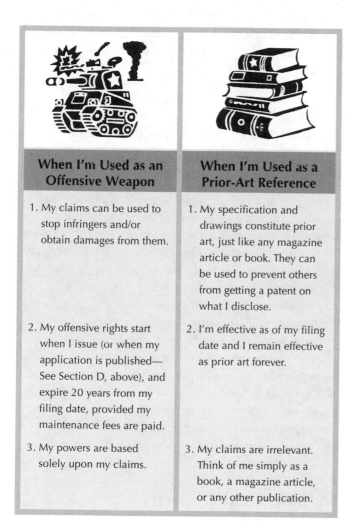

When I'm Used as an Offensive Weapon	When I'm Used as a Prior-Art Reference
1. My claims can be used to stop infringers and/or obtain damages from them.	1. My specification and drawings constitute prior art, just like any magazine article or book. They can be used to prevent others from getting a patent on what I disclose.
2. My offensive rights start when I issue (or when my application is published—See Section D, above), and expire 20 years from my filing date, provided my maintenance fees are paid.	2. I'm effective as of my filing date and I remain effective as prior art forever.
3. My powers are based solely upon my claims.	3. My claims are irrelevant. Think of me simply as a book, a magazine article, or any other publication.

Fig. 1B—A Patent Can Be Used as an Offensive Weapon or as a Prior-Art Reference

J. What Can't Be Patented

You can't patent any process that can be performed mentally. The reason is that the law doesn't wish to limit what people can do essentially with just their brains. The same rule applies to abstract ideas; inventions that aren't reducible to or practicable in hardware form, or inventions that don't involve the manipulation of hardware or symbols (words, letters, numbers) to produce a useful result; naturally occurring articles; business forms and other printed matter per se (not associated with some hardware); scientific principles in the abstract (without hardware); inventions that won't work to produce the result claimed for them (such as perpetual motion machines); abstract algorithms that merely crunch numbers without a useful result; human beings (such as cloned humans); and atomic energy inventions. See Chapter 5.

Computer Program Note. Computer programs, including algorithms, cannot be patented per se. However, if the program, software, or algorithm produces a useful, concrete, and tangible result—for instance, if the algorithm controls a display, a memory, a keyboard, any other hardware or process, or if it processes or analyzes a signal—then it can be patented. If the algorithm merely manipulates numbers, such as calculating π, or merely solves an algorithm, then it can't be patented. Computer programs and algorithms per se (without hardware) can alternatively be protected by copyright, and sometimes by trade secret law. See *Software Development: A Legal Guide,* by Stephen Fishman (Nolo).

With respect to designs, as explained, the PTO won't grant design patents on:
- any design whose novelty has significant functional utility (use a utility patent),
- ornamentation that is on the surface only, rather than forming an integral part of a device, or
- any device which has a shape that exists in nature.

K. Some Common Patent Misconceptions

Over the years that I've practiced patent law, I've come across a number of misconceptions that laypersons have about patents. As part of my effort to impart what a patent is, I want to clear up a few of the most common here at the outset.

Common Misconception: A patent gives its owner the right to practice an invention.

Fact: If you come up with an invention, you may practice (make, use, and sell) it freely, with or without a patent, provided that it's not covered by the claims of another's "in force" patent, that is, a patent that is within its 20-year term.

Common Misconception: Once you get a patent, you'll be rich and famous.

Fact: A patent is like a hunting license: it's useful just to go after infringers. If the invention isn't commercialized, the patent is usually worthless. You won't get rich or famous from your patent unless you or someone else gets the invention into widespread commercial use.

Common Misconception: If a product has been patented, it's bound to be superior.

Fact: Although Madison Ave. would like you to believe this, in reality a patent merely means the invention is significantly different, not necessarily superior.

Common Misconception: If you make or sell a device on which you have a patent, your patent will protect you against the infringement claims of others.

Fact: A patent is for offensive use only and has no value in defending against infringement charges from other patents, except that your patent sometimes will have value in a counterattack if the other patent owner infringes your patent.

Common Misconception: If a product, such as a tooth whitener, says "patented," no one else can make a product with a similar function.

Fact: Most patents cover only one specific aspect or version of a product, rather than the basic function of the product. For instance, the patent on the tooth whitener may cover only a specific composition, and many other compositions that perform the same function (albeit in an inferior—or superior—way) may exist that don't infringe the patent.

L. How Intellectual Property Law Provides "Offensive Rights" (and Not Protection) to Inventors

Many people speak of a patent as a form of "protection." The fact is that, as stated, a patent is an offensive weapon, rather than "protection," which is a defensive shield. To properly benefit from a patent, as we'll see in Chapter 15, the patent owner must sue or threaten to sue anyone who trespasses on the right. The patent doesn't provide any "protection" in its own right and does not give its owner a defense if the inventor infringes an earlier patent. Although the word "protection" is in common usage for all types of intellectual property, it's more accurate to say that a patent—as well as a copyright, trade secret, and trademark—gives its owner "offensive rights" against infringers. In other words the patent, copyright, trade secret, or trademark provides a tool with which you can enforce a monopoly on your creation. The distinction between protection (a defense) and offensive rights is as important in intellectual property law as it is in football or basketball: while a good defense may be valuable, you'll need a powerful offense to win the game or stop the infringer.

To help you keep this distinction in mind, I try consistently to use the term "offensive rights" instead of "protection." However, if I slip up from time to time, please remember that by protection I only mean that inventors have the right to affirmatively come forward and invoke the court's help in preventing infringement by others.

M. Alternative and Supplementary Offensive Rights

As you probably realize, there are several alternative and often overlapping ways to acquire offensive rights on intellectual property. Let's think of these as different roads to the same destination. While the immediate filing of your patent application is one of these roads, it is only one. The purpose of this chapter is to provide you with a map to the other roads and to help you decide which is the best way to travel, given your circumstances.

The value of your invention can sometimes be better monopolized by using one of the other forms of intellectual property and can almost always be enhanced by simultaneously using a patent with one or more of these other forms—such as unique trade dress, a good trademark, and copyright-covered labels and instructions—and by maintaining later improvements as a trade secret.

N. Intellectual Property— The Big Picture

"Intellectual property" (sometimes called "intangible property") refers to any product of the human mind or intellect, such as an idea, invention, expression, unique name, business method, industrial process, or chemical formula, which has some value in the marketplace, and that ultimately can be reduced to a tangible form, such as a computer, a chemical, a software-based invention, a gadget, a process, etc. Intellectual property law, accordingly, covers the various legal principles that determine:

- who owns any given intellectual property;
- when such owners can exclude others from commercially exploiting the property; and
- the degree of recognition that the courts are willing to afford such property (that is, whether they will enforce the owner's offensive rights).

In short, intellectual property (IP) law determines when and how a person can capitalize on a creation.

Formerly, patents were the most overwhelmingly significant part of IP law, so most attorneys who handled trademarks, copyright, trade secrets, and unfair competition, as well as patents, called themselves "patent attorneys." Nowadays, the nonpatent forms of IP law have become far more significant, so most patent attorneys now call themselves IP attorneys. This term has engendered some confusion, since many attorneys who aren't licensed to practice patent law (they only do trademark, copyright, etc.) call themselves IP attorneys. As our society becomes more dependent upon technology and information, the role of IP will continue to expand.

Over the years, intellectual property law has fallen into several distinct subcategories, according to the type of "property" involved:

- **Patent Law** deals with the protection of the mental concepts or creations known as inventions—an example is the flip-top can opener. As indicated earlier, we have three types of patents: utility, design, and plant.
- **Trademark Law** deals with the degree to which the owner of a symbol (for example, a word, design, or sound) used in marketing goods or services will be afforded a monopoly over the use of the symbol (that is, offensive rights against others who try to use it). Examples of trademarks are *Ivory*, *Coke*, *Nolo*, the *Mercedes-Benz* star, and the *NBC* chimes. With regard to advertising slogans, while the courts generally do not regard them as trademarks, they will afford them trademark rights provided their owners have used them consistently as brand names on the goods and not just in the media. Slogans are primarily covered by copyright law and unfair competition (see below).
- **Copyright Law** grants authors, composers, programmers, artists, and the like the right to prevent others from copying or using their original expression without permission and to recover damages from those who do so. Copyright law gives me offensive rights against anyone who copies this book without my permission.
- **Trade Secret Law** deals with the acquisition of offensive rights on private knowledge that gives the owner a

competitive business advantage—for example, manufacturing processes, magic techniques, and formulae. The method of producing the laser light shows and fireworks are trade secrets. Unless its owner makes substantial efforts to keep the knowledge secret, any trade secret rights will be lost.

- **Unfair Competition Law** affords offensive rights to owners of nonfunctional mental creations that don't fall within the rights offered by the four types of law just discussed, but which have nevertheless been unfairly copied by competitors. For example, "trade dress" (such as *Kodak*'s yellow film package), a business name (such as *Procter & Gamble Co.*), a unique advertising slogan (for example, "Roaches check in but they don't check out"), or a distinctive packaging label (such as *Duracell*'s copper-top energy cells) may all enjoy offensive rights under unfair competition principles.

Having covered patent law earlier in this chapter, let's now wade a little deeper into the other forms of intellectual property law, all of which are shown and briefly depicted in Fig. 1C, The Intellectual Property Mandala, below.

* One must obtain a governmental certificate (patent or registration) to enforce any offensive rights.

‡Timing is crucial: application must be filed within one year after public exposure.

Fig. 1C—The Intellectual Property Mandala

Many clients have come to me with an invention or idea, asking if there were some easier and quicker way to protect their invention than the seven methods discussed in the IP mandala, above. Alas, I always have to disappoint them. I have included in this chapter all of the IP techniques that exist. There are no additional weapons in the IP arsenal, so you will have to work with what we have.

O. Trademarks

This is the most familiar branch of intellectual property law. On a daily basis, everyone sees, uses, and makes many decisions on the basis of trademarks. For instance, you probably decided to purchase your car, your appliances, much of the packaged food in your residence, your magazines, your computer, and your watch on the basis of their trademarks, at least to some extent. I believe that trademarks originated in 16th century Britain when silverware makers began putting their initials on their products. Naturally, disreputable competitors seeking to capitalize on a well-known silverware maker's reputation soon came along and counterfeited the "trade mark" on copycat silverware. Judges were called upon to sort out rights in the mark and lo, trademark law was born!

1. Trademarks Defined

In its most literal meaning, a trademark is any word or other symbol that is consistently attached to, or forms part of, a product or its packaging to identify and distinguish it from others in the marketplace. In other words, a trademark is a brand name.

An example of a word trademark is *Kodak,* a brand of camera. In addition to words, trademarks can be other symbols, such as designs or logos (the Nike swoosh), sounds (the NBC chimes), smells, and even colors. For example, the PTO recently granted a trademark registration on a specific color used for a line of dry-cleaning ironing pads. (*Qualitex Co. v. Jacobson Products Co., Inc.,* 115 S.Ct. 1300 (1995).) The shape of an object (such as the truncated, contrasting, conical top of Cross pens) can even be a trademark, provided (1) the shape doesn't provide a superior function, and (2) the shape has become associated in the minds of the purchasing public with the manufacturer (known in trademark terms as "secondary meaning").

Many patented goods or processes are also covered by trademarks. For example, *Xerox* photocopiers have many patents on their internal parts, and also are sold under the well-known *Xerox* trademark. Without the patents, people could copy the internal parts, but *Xerox* would still have a monopoly on its valuable and widely recognized trademark.

The term "trademark" is also commonly used to mean "service marks." These are marks (words or other symbols) that are associated with services offered in the marketplace. The letters *NBC* in connection with the broadcast network are one example of a service mark. Another is the emblem used by *Blue Cross–Blue Shield* for its medical/insurance services. Other forms of marks commonly included within the term "trademark" are "certification marks" (the identifying symbol or name of an independent group, board, or commission that judges the quality of goods or services—such as the *Good Housekeeping* seal of approval), and "collective marks" (an identifying symbol or name showing membership in an organization—for example, the FDIC's symbol to show that deposits in a bank are insured).

An important third category of business identifier that is often confused with trademarks is called a "trade name." In the law, trade name is the word or words under which a company does business, while a trademark is the word or other symbol under which a company sells its products or services. To understand this better, let's use *Procter & Gamble* as an example. The words *Procter & Gamble* are a trade name, while *Ivory* is a trademark, that is, a brand name for *Procter & Gamble*'s white soap. However, the media often refer to trademarks as trade names. Also, many companies such as *Ford,* use the same words as a trade name and a trademark, so the difference sometimes becomes academic.

Trademarks, such as *Ivory,* enjoy offensive rights under both federal and state trademark laws. The trade name *Procter & Gamble,* however, enjoys offensive rights primarily under state law (corporation registrations, fictitious name registrations, and unfair competition law). However, a federal law can also be used to slap down a trade-name infringement as a "false designation of origin" (17 USC 1125).

2. Monopoly Rights of a Trademark Owner

Briefly, the owner of a trademark may or may not be entitled to legal offensive rights depending on how distinctive (or strong) the law considers the trademark. Trademarks that are arbitrary (*Elephant* floppy disks), fanciful (*Double Rainbow* ice cream), or coined terms (*Kodak*) are considered strong, and thus entitled to a relatively broad scope of offensive rights. On the other hand, marks that describe some function or characteristic of the product (such as "*RapidCompute* computers" or "*RelieveIt*" for an analgesic) are considered weaker and won't enjoy as broad a scope of offensive rights. Although the above differences may seem somewhat arbitrary, they really aren't. The courts give fanciful, coined, or other arbitrary marks a stronger and broader monopoly than descriptive marks because descriptive marks come close to words in common usage and the law protects everyone's right to use these. Also, the owner of a "famous" mark can prevent anyone from diluting the mark—that is, blurring or tarnishing its distinctiveness—even if the diluting mark is not used on similar goods or services.

In addition to the strong/weak mark dichotomy, trademark owners may be denied offensive rights if the trademark becomes commonly used to describe an entire class of products, that is, it becomes "generic." For example, "aspirin," once a trademark that enjoyed strong offensive rights, became a generic word (no offensive rights) for any type of over-the-counter painkiller using a certain chemical. Why? Because its owner used it improperly as a noun (such as "Buy *Aspirin*") rather than as a proper adjective (such as "Buy *Aspirin* (brand) analgesic"), and the public therefore came to view it as synonymous with the product it described.

3. Relationship of Trademark Law to Patent Law

As indicated above, trademarks are very useful in conjunction with inventions, whether patentable or not. A clever trademark can be used with an invention to provide it with a unique aspect in the marketplace so that purchasers will tend to buy the trademarked product over a generic one. For example, consider the *Crock Pot* slow cooker and the *Hula Hoop* exercise device. These trademarks helped make both of these products successful and market leaders even though they were not patented. In short, a trademark provides brand-name recognition to the product and a patent provides a tool to enforce a monopoly on its utilitarian function. Since trademark rights can be kept forever (as long as the trademark continues to be used), a trademark can be a powerful means of effectively extending a monopoly initially created by a patent.

4. Overview of How Offensive Rights to Trademarks Are Acquired

Here's a list of steps you should take if you come up with a trademark and you want to acquire offensive rights to it and use it properly. Because this is a patent book, I haven't covered this topic in detail. Probably the best available source for learning how to search for, understand, and acquire offensive rights in your trademarks is *Trademark: Legal Care for Your Business & Product Name*, by Stephen Elias (Nolo).

a. Preserve Your Mark as a Trade Secret Until You Use It

As I explain in Subsection d, below, you must take certain actions before you can acquire offensive rights in a mark. This means that during the developmental stage you must treat your trademark as a trade secret so that others won't adopt your proposed mark and use it first. (See Section Q, below, for an overview of acquiring offensive rights to trade secrets.)

b. Make Sure the Mark Isn't Generic or Descriptive

Ask yourself if the mark is generic or descriptive. A generic mark is a word or other symbol that the public already uses to designate the goods or service on which you want to use the mark. Thus you can't acquire offensive rights on "The Pill" for a birth-control pill, since it's already a generic term. A descriptive mark is similar to a generic mark in that it describes the goods, but hasn't yet gotten into widespread public use. For instance, if you came up with a new electric fork, you cannot acquire offensive rights in the mark *Electric Fork*, since it merely describes the product.

c. Make Sure Your Mark Isn't Already in Use

It's essential to select a mark that is not in use by someone else. The goodwill you develop around the mark may go up in smoke in the event of a trademark infringement contest and you may be liable for damages as well. Even if your proposed mark isn't identical to the already-used mark, the other mark's owner can prevent you from using it if, in the eyes of the law, there is a likelihood of customer confusion. Even if there's no such likelihood, the owner of a famous mark can block a mark that is likely to tarnish the reputation of the famous mark. To determine if your mark is already in use, you'll have to make a trademark search or hire someone to do it for you.

A complete trademark search should cover registered and unregistered (common law) marks. Complete searches of registered and unregistered marks can be ordered through the following three companies:

- *Thomson & Thomson*, (www.thomson-thomson.com), 500 Victory Road, North Quincy, MA, 02171-1545, 800-692-8833;
- *Trademark Research Corporation*, (www.cch-trc.com), 300 Park Avenue South, New York, NY 10010, 800-TRC-MARK;
- *Sunnyvale Center on Innovation, Invention, and Ideas* (SC[i]3; pronounced Sigh-Cubed) (www.sci3.com), 408-730-7290.

The last company mentioned—Sc[i]3—is especially attractive because it's affiliated with the PTO and provides lower prices than most other searching companies. As of

January 2002, Sc[i]3 charged $199 for a complete online analytical search (including state and federal trademark registers and common law sources). As with most trademark search firms, Sc[i]3 doesn't interpret its results; it leaves that to you.

However, you can search all pending and registered trademarks for free at the PTO's website (www.uspto.gov), which contains a searchable database of all pending and registered U.S. trademarks. You can also search all registered marks for free in *The Trademark Register of the United States, CompuMark Directory of U.S. Trademarks* (many libraries), and the PTO's CD-ROMs (any PTDL—see Chapter 6).

An incomplete but free search of unregistered and registered marks can be made on any good Internet search engine such as Google (www.google.com) and in *The Thomas Register* in any library or online at www.thomasregister.com, and in *Gale's Trade Name* (really trademark) *Directory* and *McRae's Blue Book* (most libraries). Further, most libraries have specific trade directories, such as *The Toy Manufacturer's Directory*. For those interested in adopting a World Wide Web site or domain name, Network Solutions, Inc. (InterNIC), has an online search site at www.internic.net.

d.   Use or Apply to Register Your Trademark

The first to actually use or file an intent-to-use (ITU) application to register the trademark owns it—that is, acquires offensive rights against infringers. Actual use means shipping goods or advertising services that bear the trademark (not just use in advertising). If an ITU application is filed, the trademark owner must actually use the mark before it can be registered. As a trademark owner, you can validly sue a person who later uses a similar mark for similar goods in a context that is likely to mislead the public. Contrary to popular belief, trademarks do not have to be registered for offensive rights to be acquired. However, as explained in Subsection e, just below, registration can substantially add to these offensive rights.

e.   Use and Register Your Trademark

If you apply to register your mark federally on the basis of your intent to use it, you will, as stated, eventually have to actually use it on your goods to get it registered. You must thus follow through by actually using it and proving such use as part of your registration application. To federally register a trademark, use the online registration procedures at the PTO website (www.uspto.gov).

If you do adopt and use a trademark on your goods before applying for registration, you should register it in your state trademark office if it's used exclusively in your state, and/or the PTO if it's used across a territorial or international border. Once your mark is federally registered, it will be much easier to sue infringers. The federal registration will cause the court to presume that you have exclusive ownership of the mark and the exclusive right to use it. If you don't register your trademark and it's infringed, you'll have much more difficulty when you go to court.

To register a trademark in your state, call or write to your Secretary of State in your state's capital for a trademark application form and instructions; the cost will be from about $50 to $120.

Trade Group Registration of Trademarks

Instead of (or in addition to) registering your trademark with one or more state trademark offices and the U.S. Patent and Trademark Office (PTO), you can register it with an appropriate specific trade organization. For example, suppose you're an automobile manufacturer and you intend to come out with a new car, the *Zenith,* in a few years. Instead of applying to register it with the PTO, whose requirements are relatively complex, whose procedures are slow, and that will keep an intent-to-use application alive for only three years (at a relatively great expense), you can register your mark with the Automobile Manufacturer's Association under a relatively simple, economical procedure. The AMA-registered mark will be published for all other members of the AMA to see, so that they will know not to use the *Zenith* mark while your registration is alive. Similarly, movie titles can be registered with a movie industry association and websites and domain names for email addresses can be registered with Internet services. So if you intend to use a trademark in a given industry, check with the industry's main association to see if you can register your mark with them as an alternative or in addition to a PTO or state registration.

f. Use Your Trademark Properly

The law considers it very important to use a trademark properly once you've adopted it as a brand name for your goods. Before it's registered, you should indicate it's a trademark by providing the superscript "™" after the mark, for example, LeRoy™ Shoes. If it's a service mark, such as a restaurant name or a name for a service business, use the "SM" superscript—for example, "Alice's SM Restaurant." Once the mark is federally registered, provide the superscript "®" or indicate that the mark is registered in the PTO—such as "Reg. U.S. Pat. & TM. Off."

Word trademarks should always be used as brand names on any literature. That is, they should be used as adjective modifiers in association with the general name of the goods to which they apply, and shouldn't be used as a substitute for the name of the goods. For example, if you're making and selling can openers and have adopted the trademark *Ajax,* always use the words "can opener" after *Ajax* and never refer to an *Ajax* alone. Otherwise, the name can become generic and be lost, as happened to "cellophane" and "aspirin," and as could soon happen to *Xerox.* (Doesn't it somehow feel more natural to use the word "Xerox" than "photocopy," or "Kleenex" rather than "tissue"?)

5. What Doesn't Qualify as a Trademark (for the Purpose of Developing Offensive Rights)

The courts won't enforce trademark offensive rights, nor will the PTO or state trademark offices grant trademark registrations, on the following:

- lengthy written matter (copyright is the proper form of coverage here);
- slogans that are merely informational or laudatory, such as "Proudly made in the U.S.A.";
- trade names not being used as a trademark or service mark;
- immoral, deceptive, scandalous, or disparaging matter;
- governmental emblems, personal names, or likenesses without consent;
- marks that they consider close enough to existing marks as to be likely to cause confusion;
- pure surnames or purely geographical designations;
- generic; or
- descriptive words that do not distinguish a company's products or services.

P. Copyright

A copyright is another offensive right given by law, this time to an author, artist, composer, or programmer, to exclude others from publishing or copying literary, dramatic, musical, artistic, or software works. While a patent can effectively provide offensive rights on an idea per se, assuming it's capable of being reduced to hardware form, a copyright covers only the author's or artist's particular way of expressing an idea. Thus, while a copyright can provide offensive rights on the particular arrangement of words that constitute a book or play, it can't cover the book's subject matter, message, or teachings. Put otherwise, you are free to publish any of the ideas, concepts, and information in this (or any) book, provided that you write it in your own words. But if you copy the specific wording, then you'll infringe the copyright on this book.

Some specific types of works that are covered by copyright are books, poetry, plays, songs, catalogues, photographs, computer programs, advertisements, labels, movies, maps, drawings, sculpture, prints and art reproductions, game boards and rules, and recordings. One yogi has even filed a lawsuit for infringement claiming others have copied his yoga poses. Certain materials, such as titles, slogans, lettering, ideas, plans, forms, useful things, nonoriginal material, and noncreative material (such as a list of names and telephone numbers) can't be covered through copyright. U.S. government publications, by law, aren't covered by copyright and may almost always be freely copied and sold by anyone, if desired.

The 1998 "Digital Millennium Copyright Act" supplements the Copyright Act and provides criminal penalties for those who provide technology that can circumvent copyright protection. (It leaves a "safe harbor" for Internet Service Providers who merely provide access to infringing materials.) It also provides a way to protect original boat hull designs.

While I provide a brief overview of copyright principles in the rest of this section, more complete discussions of this subject are available in *The Copyright Handbook* (for written works), *Copyright Your Software* (for software and computer-related expressions), *The Public Domain,* and *Web & Software Development: A Legal Guide.* Stephen Fishman wrote all of these books (Nolo).

1. What Is Copyright?

Now that we've seen what a copyright covers, what exactly is a copyright? As stated, a copyright is the offensive right that the government gives an author of any original work of expression (such as those mentioned above) to exclude others from copying or commercially using the work of expression without proper authorization.

To obtain copyright rights, the work must be "original," not merely the result of extended effort. Thus, in 1991, the Supreme Court held that a telephone company that compiled, through much work, an alphabetical directory of names and addresses could not prevent another publisher from copying the directory, since it had no originality. (*Feist Publications Inc. v. Rural Telephone Service Co.*, 111 S. Ct. 1282 (1991).) Also, a copyright cannot cover any system, method, process, concept, principle, or device, although it can cover a specific explanation or description of anything.

The copyright springs into existence the instant the work of expression first assumes some tangible form, and lasts until it expires by law (the life of the author plus 70 years, or for works made for hire, 95 years from publication or 120 years from creation, whichever is shorter). A work made for hire is one made by an employee in the course of the employment or by an independent contractor under a written work-made-for-hire contract.

2. Copyright Compared With Utility Patent

The process involved in obtaining a patent differs significantly from that of registering a copyright. A copyright is deemed to exist automatically upon creation of the work, with no registration being necessary. On the other hand, to obtain patent rights, an application must be filed with the PTO, and that office must review, approve, and issue a patent.

If a copyright is registered with the Copyright Office (which technically is part of the Library of Congress) on any copyrightable material, a certificate of registration will be granted without examination as to the work's novelty. The PTO (part of the U.S. Department of Commerce), on the other hand, makes a strict and thorough novelty and unobviousness examination on all patent applications and won't grant a patent unless it considers the invention novel and unobvious.

Finally, with some exceptions, the two forms of offensive rights cover types of creation that are mutually exclusive. Simply put, things that are entitled to a patent are generally not entitled to a copyright, and vice versa. However, it's important to understand that there is a small gray area where this generalization isn't necessarily true. A few creations may be eligible for both types of coverage.

How to Secure Offensive Copyright Rights in a Work

While no longer necessary for works published after March 1,1989, it's still advisable first to place the familiar copyright notice (for example, Copyright © 2005 David Pressman) on each published copy of the work. This tells anyone who sees the work that the copyright is being claimed, who is claiming it, and when the work was first published. (The year isn't used on pictures, sculptures, or graphic works.) This notice prevents an infringer from later claiming that the infringement was accidental.

Next you should register the work with the U.S. Copyright Office. If done in a timely manner, registration makes your case better if and when you prosecute a court action (for example, you can get minimum statutory damages and attorney fees). It's useful to distinguish between steps (a) and (b), placing the copyright notice on the work and actually getting a copyright registration. Thus I suggest that you don't say, "I copyrighted my program," but rather say, "I put a copyright notice on my program," or "I applied for a copyright registration on my program."

3. Areas Where Patent and Copyright Law Overlap

Let's look at these principal areas where you may be able to obtain offensive rights on intellectual property under either patent or copyright coverage, or both.

a.   Computer Software

Computer programs are the best example of a type of creative work that may qualify for both a patent and copyright protection.

Viewed one way, computer programs are in fact nothing more than a series of numerical relationships (termed "routines") and as such cannot qualify for a patent (although they can, of course, be covered under the copyright laws because they have been held to constitute a creative work of expression). However, viewed from another perspective, computer programs are a set of instructions that make a machine (the computer) operate in a certain way. And, in recent years, many patents have been issued on computer programs in association with machinery or hardware that produce a tangible, useful, and concrete result. Simply put, a programmed machine, programmed system, or process using an algorithm to affect some hardware or process that produces a tangible, useful, and concrete result may qualify for a patent, whereas the algorithm per se would not. More on this in Chapter 5, Section C, and Chapter 9, Section G13.

Why patent a program as opposed to simply registering a copyright on it? Because the patent affords up to 20 years of broad, hard-to-design-around offensive rights for the program, even if an infringing program is created independently. What is the drawback? It takes about two years, a considerable amount of work, and a fair amount of money, even if you do it all yourself, to obtain a patent. Because much software becomes obsolete in a much shorter time, your software may not be worth protecting by the time the patent issues. Thus, you often don't need the full term of coverage a patent offers, and money spent on obtaining one may well be wasted.

While copyrighting of programs is relatively inexpensive as well as easy to accomplish, the coverage gained isn't as broad as is offered by a patent. This is so because copyright covers only the particular way the program is written, not what it does. For instance, all major word processing programs accomplish pretty much the same tasks (such as cursor movement, screen and print formatting, search and find functions, and moving text from one location to another) but each does so through a differently expressed program, and thus each is entitled to separate copyright status. Also, a copyright isn't available against independent creators—that is, those who write a similar or even identical program without copying it from the copyrighted program.

So when choosing whether to rely on copyright or a patent for software that produces a tangible, useful, and concrete result, the software author must weigh the broader offensive rights that a patent brings against the expense and time in obtaining one. Likewise, the ease with which copyright is obtained must be counterbalanced by the narrow nature of its coverage.

There is one further drawback to copyright for programs: If you do choose to rely on copyright rather than a patent to cover your program, and you don't bring the program, or a device embodying it in a PROM (Programmable Read-Only Memory), out for a while, you take the risk that someone else may patent it in the meantime.

b. Shapes and Designs

The inventor may also have a choice of utility patent or copyright in areas where an object's shape or design is both functional and aesthetic. Consider, for example, a new alphabet with letters that are attractive, yet which also provide more efficient, unambiguous spelling (such as the efficient alphabet that Shaw used to write *Androcles and the Lion*), or which are easier to read in subdued light. Patent or copyright can be used. The former will afford broader coverage to whatever principles can be identified and the latter will be cheaper, quicker, and easier to obtain, but limited to the specific shapes of the letters. Note that unlike design patents, copyright can be used to cover some aesthetic shapes even if they also have a significant function.

In many areas both forms of coverage can be used together for different aspects of the creation. Thus in parlor games, the game apparatus, if sufficiently unique, can be patented, while the gameboard, rules, box, and design of the game pieces can be covered by copyright. The artwork on the box or package for almost any invention can be covered by copyright, as can the instructions accompanying the product. Also the name of the game (for example, *Dungeons and Dragons*) is a trademark and can be covered as such.

If the invention can also be considered a sculptural work, or if it's embodied or encased in a sculptural work, copyright is available for the sculpture. However, copyright can't be used for a utilitarian article, unless it has an aesthetic feature that can be separated from and can exist independently of the article. This rule, known as the "separability requirement," is very important in copyright law.

Of course, to emphasize my earlier point, both copyrights and patents generally have their exclusive domains. Assuming they don't have any aesthetic components, patents are exclusive for machines, compositions, articles, processes, and new uses per se. On the other hand, copyrights are exclusive for works of expression, such as writings, sculpture, movies, plays, recordings, and artwork, assuming they don't have any functional aspects.

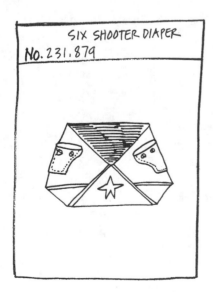

SIX SHOOTER DIAPER
NO. 231.879

c. Copyright Compared to Design Patents

There's considerable overlap here, since aesthetics are the basis of both forms of coverage. Design patents are used mainly to cover industrial designs where the shape of the object has ornamental features and the shape is inseparable from, or meaningless if separated from, the object. For example, a tire tread design, a computer case, and the work-shop sawblade clock (see Section B, above) are perfect for a design patent, but a surface decal, which could be used else-where, is not. In other words, if the work is purely artistic, a design patent is improper. Copyright, on the other hand, can be used for almost any artistic or written creation, whether or not it's inseparable from an underlying object, so long as the aspect of the work for which copyright is being sought is ornamental and not functional. This means copyright can be used for pure surface ornamentation, such as the artwork on a can of beans, as well as sculptural works where the "art" and the object are integrated, such as a statue. For instance, the shape of a toy was held to be properly covered by copyright since the shape played no role in how the toy functioned and since a toy wasn't considered to perform a useful function (although many parents who use toys to divert their children would disagree). The same principle should apply to "adult toys," provided

Design Patent	Copyright
Permissible for All of the Following: The aesthetic aspects of articles of manufacture, such as jewelry, furniture, musical and other instruments, and fabrics.	**Permissible for All of the Following:** Literary and artistic content of written materials, lectures, periodicals, plays, musical compositions, maps, artworks, software, reproductions, photographs, prints, labels, translations, movies, sculpture.
Disadvantages: Must prepare a formal application with ink drawings, must prosecute before the PTO with legal briefs, large filing fee and issue fees, lasts only 14 years, takes a long time (one to three years) to secure rights.	**Disadvantages:** Gives a narrow scope of offensive rights, no doctrine of equivalents, no protection of concepts (only particular form of expression thereof), only good against proven actual copiers (not independent creators).
Advantages: Broader scope of offensive rights, including doctrine of equivalents (see Chapter 15), can cover concepts, good against independent creators.	**Advantages:** Only need fill out a simple form with samples of the actual work, no formal drawings needed, no need for legal briefs, only small filing fee, no issue fee, lasts a very long time (life + 70 years or 95-120 years), instant offensive rights.
Can't Be Used For: Articles where the novel features have a utilitarian function (use utility patent); writings, flat artwork, photos, maps, drawings, programs, prints, labels, movies (use copyright); surface ornamentation, or objects with a shape which appears in nature.	**Can't Be Used For:** Utilitarian articles, unless the aesthetic features are separable from and can exist independently of the article (toys aren't considered utilitarian), machines, processes, systems, concepts, principles, or discoveries.
Recommended For: The aesthetic shape or layout of utilitarian articles.	**Recommended For:** Articles of manufacture that aren't utilitarian, or if utilitarian, have aesthetic aspects that can be separated and exist independently, jewelry, furniture, fabrics, literary content of written materials, lectures, periodicals, plays, maps, musical compositions, artworks, software, reproductions, photographs, prints, labels with artwork, translations, movies, sculpture.

Fig. 1D—Design Patents Compared to Copyrights

they are strictly for amusement and don't have a utilitarian function.

What are the differences in the coverage afforded by design patents and copyright? Design patents are relatively expensive to obtain (the filing fee is higher, an issue fee is required—see Fee Schedule in Appendix 4), a formal drawing is required, a novelty examination is required, and the rights last only 14 years. However, a design patent offers broader rights than a copyright in that it covers the aesthetic principles underlying the design. This means that someone else coming up with a similar, but somewhat changed design would probably be liable for patent infringement.

Copyright, on the other hand, provides relatively narrow offensive rights (minor changes in all of the artwork's features will usually avoid infringement), the government fee for registration is very small (see Fee Schedule), the term is long (the life of the creator plus 70 years, or a flat 95 or 120 years for works classified as made-for-hire). And as no novelty examination is performed, you're virtually assured of obtaining a copyright registration certificate if you file.

It has been said that a design patent is basically a copyright with the teeth of a patent because it can cover similar areas as copyright but provides broader offensive rights.

Because the distinctions between design patents and copyrights are especially confusing, I've provided a comparison chart to summarize the distinctions between these two forms in Fig. 1D.

4. When and How to Obtain Copyright Coverage

If you desire to obtain coverage for a copyrightable invention, program, creation, or for instructions, packaging, or artwork that goes with your invention, you don't need to do anything until the item is distributed or published. This is because, as mentioned, your copyright rights arise when your work is first put into tangible form. And, although there is no requirement for a copyright notice on your work before it's generally distributed to the public, I strongly advise you to put the proper copyright notice on any copyrightable material right away, since this will give anyone who receives the material notice that you claim copyright in it and they shouldn't reproduce it without permission.

When your material is distributed to the public, it's even more desirable (though no longer mandatory for works published after March 1, 1989) that you place a copyright notice on it to notify others that you claim copyright and to prevent infringers from claiming they were "innocent" and thus entitled to reduced damages. This notice should consist of the word "Copyright," followed by a "c" in a circle ©

(or a "p" in a circle for recordings and records), followed by the year the work is first published (widely distributed without restriction), followed by the name of the invention's owner. Thus the original copyright notice on this book appears as "Copyright © 1985 David Pressman. All Rights Reserved."

If anyone infringes your copyright (that is, without your permission someone copies, markets, displays, or produces a derivative work based on your original work) and you want to go to court to prevent this from happening and collect damages, you first have to register your work with the U.S. Copyright Office. Moreover, if you register the work within three months of the time your item is distributed or published, or before the infringement occurs, you may be entitled to attorney fees, costs, and damages that don't have to be proved by you (called "statutory damages"). All things considered, I strongly advise you to register your work as soon as it's published if you think you're entitled to copyright coverage. The Copyright Office, Washington, DC 20559, provides free information and forms on copyright. Tel. No.: 202-707-9100 or website www.copyright.gov.

Q. Trade Secrets

This section provides a basic definition of trade secrets, distinguishes trade secret protection from patents, lists the advantages and disadvantages of trade secret vs. patenting, and tells you how to acquire and maintain trade secret rights.

1. Definition

Thanks to the intensive coverage of the high-tech industry by the media, the term "trade secret" has become virtually a household word. You've probably heard of the recent case where an employee of a biotech (gene splicing) company tried to sell his employer's secrets to some FBI undercover agents.

What are these trade secrets and why are they valuable enough to warrant corporations paying millions of dollars to high-priced attorneys to protect them? In a sentence, a trade secret is any information, design, device, process, composition, technique, or formula that is not known generally and that affords its owner a competitive business advantage.

Among the items considered as trade secrets are:
- chemical formulas, such as the formula for the paper used to make U.S. currency;
- manufacturing processes, such as the process used to form the eyes in sewing needles and the process for

adhering PTFE (sold under the trademark Teflon) to a frying pan;

- "magic-type" trade secrets, such as the techniques used to produce laser light shows and fireworks; and
- chemical recipes that involve both formulas and processes, such as the recipes for certain soft drinks, cosmetics, chemicals, and artificial gems; for example, Chatham, Inc., can actually make precious gems such as rubies, emeralds, and sapphires, and it relies almost exclusively on trade secrets to protect its valuable technology.

Even if the ingredients of a chemical are publicly known, the method of combining the ingredients and their sources of supply can still be a trade secret.

Obviously, since these types of information and know-how can go to the very heart of a business and its competitive position, businesses will often expend a great deal of time, energy, and money to guard their trade secrets.

When I refer to trade secrets in this book, I mean those that consist of technical information, such as in the examples given above. However, virtually every business also owns "business-information" type trade secrets, such as customer lists, names of suppliers, and pricing data. The law will enforce rights to both types of trade secrets, provided the information concerned was kept confidential and can be shown to be nonpublic knowledge and truly valuable.

More so than in any of the other intellectual property categories, the primary idea underlying trade secrets is plain common sense. If a business knows or has some information that gives it an edge over competitors, the degree of offensive rights that the law will afford to the owner of a trade secret is proportional to the business value of the trade secret and how well the owner actually kept the secret. If a company is sloppy about its secrets, the courts will reject its request for relief. Conversely, a company that takes reasonable measures to maintain the information as a secret will be afforded relief against those who wrongfully obtain the information. These central factors underlying trade secrets have profound implications for those who are seeking patents, as I discuss below.

2. Relationship of Patents to Trade Secrets

Assuming that you have kept your invention secret, you can rely on trade secret principles to enforce rights on the invention. If your invention is maintained as a trade secret and you put it into commercial use, you must file a patent application within one year of the date the invention was used commercially. If you wait over a year, any patent that you ultimately obtain will be held invalid if this fact is discovered (and you will lose trade secret protection because your invention will have been published during the application process).

The PTO treats patent applications as confidential, so it is possible to apply for a patent and still maintain the underlying information as a trade secret, at least for the first 18 months of the application period. Effective December 2000, the PTO will publish your patent application 18 months after the earliest claimed filing date, but they will not publish it if, at the time of filing, you file a Nonpublication Request (NPR), stating that that it will not be foreign-filed. (The 18-month publication statute was enacted in order to make U.S. patent laws more like those of foreign countries.) If you don't request nonpublication, your application will be printed verbatim after 18 months and all of your secret "know-how" becomes public and the trade secret status of your application will be lost. If you file an NPR and later decide to foreign-file the application, you must rescind the NPR within 45 days.

If you file an NPR, the information in your patent application will become publicly available only if and when a patent issues.

However, if a patent is refused so that your application is *not* published, the competition will still not know about your invention and any competitive advantage inherent in that fact can be maintained. The trade secret will remain intact. If the PTO allows your patent application, but you wish, instead of getting a patent, to preserve your invention as a trade secret, you can still choose not to pay the issue fee so that no patent will issue.

What happens if your application is not published after 18 months and a patent later issues? This public disclosure doesn't usually hurt the inventor, since the patent can be used to prevent anyone else from commercially exploiting the underlying information.

⚠ If you maintain an invention as a trade secret and put it into commercial use, you *must* file any patent application within one year of the date you first used it commercially. If you wait over a year, any patent that you do ultimately obtain will be held invalid if this fact is discovered. More on the "one-year rule" in Chapter 5, Section E.

The following material discusses the pros and cons of each form of offensive rights.

3. Advantages of Trade Secret Protection

Often I advise people to choose trade secret rights over those afforded by a patent, assuming it's possible to protect the creation by either. Let's look at some of the reasons why:

- The main advantage of a trade secret is the possibility of perpetual protection. While a patent is limited by statute to 20 years from filing and isn't renewable, a trade secret will last indefinitely if not discovered. For example, some fireworks and sewing needle trade secrets have been maintained for decades.
- A trade secret can be maintained without the cost or effort involved in patenting.
- There is no need to disclose details of your invention to the public for trade secret rights (as you have to do with a patented invention).
- With a trade secret, you have definite, already existing rights and don't have to worry about whether your patent application will be allowed.
- Since a trade secret isn't distributed to the public as a patent is, no one can look at your trade secret and try to design around it, as they can with the claims of your patent.
- A trade secret can be established without naming any inventors, as must be done with a patent application. Thus no effort need be made to determine the proper inventor and a company needn't request its inventor-employee to assign (legally transfer) ownership of the trade secret to it, as is required with a patent application.
- A trade secret doesn't have to be a significant, important advance, as does a patented invention.
- A trade secret can cover more information, including many relatively minor details, whereas a patent generally covers but one broad principle and its ramifications. For example, a complicated manufacturing machine with many new designs and that incorporates several new techniques can be covered as a trade secret merely by keeping the whole machine secret. To cover it by patent, on the other hand, many expensive and time-consuming patent applications would be required, and even then the patent wouldn't cover many minor ideas in the machine.
- Trade secret rights are obtained immediately, whereas a patent takes a couple of years to obtain, in which time rapidly evolving technology can bypass the patented invention.

4. Disadvantages of Trade Secret Versus Patenting

Before you stop reading this book, please understand that I spent three years writing it and thousands of hours updating it for a good reason. Or put more clearly, there are many circumstances in which the trade secret rights have important disadvantages. In these contexts, using the rights provided by a patent is essential.

The main reason that trade secrets are often a poor way to cover your work is that they can't be maintained when the public is able to discover the information by inspecting, dissecting, or analyzing the product (called "reverse engineering"). Thus mechanical and electronic devices that are sold to the public can't be kept as trade secrets. However, the essential information contained in certain chemical compositions sold to the public (cosmetics, for example), and in computer programs (assuming they're distributed to the public in object code form), often can't be readily reverse engineered, and thus can be maintained as trade secrets. However, because very sophisticated analytic tools are now available, such as chromatographs, Auger analyzers, spectroscopes, spectrophotometers, scanning electron microscopes, and software decompilers, most things can be analyzed and copied, no matter how sophisticated or small they are. And remember, the law generally allows anyone to copy and make anything freely, unless it is patented or subject to copyright coverage, or unless its shape is its trademark, such as the shape of the Photomat huts, or unless its shape has become so well-known or distinctive as to be entitled to trade dress rights. (See Section R, below.)

Strict precautions must always be taken and continually enforced to maintain the confidentiality of a trade secret. If your trade secret is discovered either legitimately or illegally, it's generally lost forever, although you do have rights against anyone who purloins your trade secret by illegal means. You can sue the thief and any conspirators for the economic loss you suffered as a result of the thief's actions. In practice this amount can be considerable, since it will include the economic value of the trade secret.

Since an individual who steals a trade secret rarely has sufficient assets to compensate for the loss, the trade secret owner will often pursue the thief's new employer or whatever business purchased the secrets—usually an entity with deeper pockets. Under this approach, the trade secret owner must demonstrate the employer or business knew or had a reason to know that the secret was acquired improperly. For example, when some Hitachi employee purloined some

IBM trade secrets, IBM sued Hitachi as well as the individuals concerned and actually obtained millions of dollars in compensation from Hitachi. In addition, a trade secret is more difficult to sue on and enforce than a patent. A patent must be initially presumed valid by the court, but a trade secret must be proven to exist before the suit may proceed.

A trade secret can be patented by someone else who discovers it by legitimate means. For instance, suppose you invent a new formula, say for a hair treatment lotion, and keep it secret. Jane M., who is totally unconnected with you and who has never even heard of your lotion, comes up with the same formula and decides to patent it, which she does successfully. She can legitimately sue and hold you liable for infringing her patent with your own invention!

There is one exception to this principle. If you are charged with infringement of a method patent, but you invented and were commercially using the method as a trade secret at least one year before the effective filing date of a patent, you will have what is known as "prior-user rights," a full defense to the infringement charge. This is also true (and may invalidate the interloper's patent) if you sold a product produced by the method before the patent's effective filing date.

What conclusion should you draw from this discussion? Because offensive rights connected with trade secrets continue as long as the trade secret itself is maintained, and because infringement of patents on "trade-secretable" inventions is difficult to discover, if you have an invention that can be kept as a trade secret for approximately 20 years, you may be better off doing so than obtaining a patent on it.

5. Acquiring and Maintaining Trade Secret Rights

After I explain the differences between trade secret and patents, inventors will often say to me, "I've decided trade secret is the way to go; how do I get one?" The inventor is pleased to learn that as stated, acquiring and maintaining trade secret rights involves only simple, commonsense procedures and doesn't require any governmental or bureaucratic paperwork. All that is necessary is that the inventor take reasonable precautions to keep the information confidential. Also, an employer should have all employees who have access to company trade secrets sign an agreement to keep the information confidential; see Fig. 16A (in Chapter 16) for a typical employment agreement regarding trade secrets and other employer rights. Over the years the courts have devised a number of tests for determining what these reasonable precautions should be and whether a trade secret owner has taken them.

Most states now have a statute that makes the theft of a trade secret a criminal offense as well as a civil action (for instance, the Uniform Trade Secrets Act, California Civil Code 3246 et seq.). Moreover, there is now a federal statute for the same purpose (Economic Espionage Act, 18 USC 1831 et seq.).

If you're interested in further reading on the subject, review Stephen Fishman and Richard Stim's *Nondisclosure Agreements: Protecting Your Trade Secrets & More* (Nolo). Also, see the heading "Books of Use and Interest" in Appendix 2, Resources: Government Publications, Patent Websites, and Books of Use and Interest.

R. Unfair Competition

The area of "unfair competition" is the most difficult to explain. Although anyone who is creative, or is in a competitive business, will encounter unfair competition problems or questions from time to time, any attempts to define this area are necessarily fraught with confusion. And no wonder! The scope of unfair competition law is nebulous in the first place and is regularly being changed by judges who make new and often contradictory rulings.

1. When Unfair Competition Principles Create Offensive Rights

Fortunately, this is a patent book rather than a law school course. And, for the purpose of this book, all you really need to understand about unfair competition law can be summarized in several sentences.

- An unfair competition situation exists when one business either (a) represents or offers its goods or services in such a way as to potentially cause the class of buyers who purchase the particular type of goods or services to confuse them with goods or services offered by another business or (b) is unjustly enriched as a result of using the fruits of the other business's labor or creativity.
- Unfair competition law is usually available only as a source of offensive rights under the federal "false designation of origin" statute (15 USC 1125(a)), or when no offensive rights are available under the trademark, copyright, or patent laws. If a product's design is involved, the purchasing public must associate it with the product's manufacturer, that is, it must have what is known as "secondary meaning." *Wal-Mart Stores, Inc. v. Samara Brothers, Inc.,* 529 U.S. 205 (2000).

- Unfair competition can be used to cover such items as advertising symbols, methods of packaging, slogans, business names, "trade dress" (that is, anything distinctive used by a merchant to package or house its goods, such as the yellow container that has come to be identified with *Kodak* film), and titles. Also, Bette Midler successfully sued an advertising agency for using a singer whose voice sounded like Ms. Midler's. Mother Fuddrucker's restaurants sued a competitor that copied Mother's distinctive restaurant layout. And the owners of the Pebble Beach, California, golf course sued a golf course in Texas for copying Pebble Beach's distinctive layout. In other words, when the characteristics of a product or service aren't distinctive or defined enough to be considered a trademark, then unfair competition may be the appropriate way to cover it.

- If an injured party can prove that a business has engaged in unfair competition, a judge will issue an injunction (legal order) prohibiting the business from any further such activity or defining what the business can and can't do. Further, the court may award compensation (monetary damages) to the injured business (that is, the business that lost profits because of the public's confusion).

2. How Does the Law of Unfair Competition Affect You?

There are several ways in which the law of unfair competition can affect you.

- If you already have a product or service you find has been copied or pirated, and the traditional methods (patents, copyrights, trademarks, and trade secrets) are no help (perhaps because it's not patentable or it's too late to patent it, it doesn't qualify under the copyright or trademark laws, or it doesn't qualify as a trade secret), you still may be able to get relief under the doctrine of unfair competition.

- If you're contemplating coming out with a product or service, try to make it as distinctive as reasonably possible in as many ways as reasonably possible so that you'll easily be able to establish a distinctive, recognizable appearance (termed in the law as "secondary meaning"). For example, you would be wise to use unique and distinctive packaging ("trade dress"), unique advertising slogans and symbols, a unique title, a distinctive business name, and a clever advertising campaign. And the more you advertise and expose your product, and the more distinctive (different) it is, the stronger your unfair competition rights will be.

3. Comparison of Unfair Competition With Design Patents

Some inventors confuse the trade dress area of unfair competition law with design patents. Trade dress refers to the distinctive appearance of a business, a product, or product packaging, where the appearance distinguishes the product or business from other similar products or businesses but isn't significant or specific enough to be

Legal Remedies for Misappropriation of Various Types of Intellectual Property	
Underlying Mental Creation	**Legal Remedy for Misappropriation**
Invention (machine, article, process, composition, new use)—covered by federal utility patent law.	Patent infringement litigation in federal court.
Industrial or aesthetic design—covered by federal design patent law.	Patent infringement litigation in federal court.
Brand name for a good or service; certification or collective mark or seal—covered by common law, or state or federal trademark law.	Trademark infringement litigation either before or after registration in state or federal court.
Writings, music, recordings, art, software, sculpture, photos, etc.—covered by federal copyright law.	Copyright infringement litigation, after registration in federal court.
Confidential technical or business information, not known by competitors—covered by state and federal trade secret law.	Trade secret litigation in state or federal court.
Distinctive trade dress, informative slogans, novel business layout, etc.—covered by common law, state and federal trademark and unfair competition laws.	Unfair competition or trademark litigation in state or federal court.

Acquisition of Offensive Rights in Intellectual Property	
If Your Creation Relates To:	**Acquire Offensive Rights By:**
1. An Invention. The functional aspect of any machine, article, composition, or process or new use of any of the foregoing—such as circuits, algorithms that affect some process or hardware, gadgets, business methods, apparatus, machinery, tools, devices, implements, chemical compositions, and industrial or other processes or techniques that one could discover from final product, toys, game apparatus, semiconductor devices, buildings, receptacles, and vehicles, cloth and apparel, furniture (functional structure), personal care devices, scientific apparatus, abrasives, hardware, plumbing, parts, alloys, laminates, protective coatings, drugs,[1] sporting goods, kitchen implements, locks and safes, timekeeping apparatus, cleaning implements, filters, refrigeration apparatus, environmental control apparatus, medical apparatus, new nonhuman animals, new bacteria, plant (sexually or asexually reproducible), or anything else made by humans where the novel aspects have a functional purpose.	Utility patent (use the rest of this book). File the utility patent application as soon as possible, but within one year of offer of sale or publication, and get a patent.
2. Design. Any new design for any tangible thing where the design is nonfunctional and is part of and not removable from the thing, such as a bottle, a computer case, jewelry, a type of material weave, a tire tread design, a building or other structure, any article, item of apparel, furniture, tool, computer screen icon, etc.	Design patent. File design patent application as soon as possible, but within one year of offer of sale or publication, and get a design patent.
3. Plant. Any asexually reproduced plant.[2]	Plant patent (see PTO Rules 161-167).
4. Trademark. Any signifier whether a symbol, sign, word, sound, design, device, shape, smell, mark, etc., used to distinguish goods (trademark) such as "Ajax"™ tools or distinguish services (service mark) such as FedEx. The signifier cannot be generic, for example, "electric fork," and cannot be descriptive unless adequate sales or advertising demonstrate secondary meaning.	Using it as a trademark with "™" or "SM" superscript and then registering it in state and/or federal trademark offices. Also, you can apply to register federally before using, based upon your intent to use the mark.
5. Copyright. Any book, poem, speech, recording, computer program, work of art (statue, painting, cartoon, label), musical work, dramatic work, pantomime and choreographic work, photograph, graphic work, motion picture, videotape, map, architectural drawing, artistic jewelry, gameboard, gameboard box and game instructions, etc.	Placing a correct copyright notice on the work, e.g., "© 1991 M. Smith"; apply for copyright registration, preferably within three months of publication. (See Section P, above.)
6. Trade Secret. Any information whatever that isn't generally known that will give a business advantage or is commercially useful, such as formulae, ideas, techniques, know-how, designs, materials, processes, etc.	Keep it secret; keep good records so you can prove you kept it secret. Have employees sign "nondisclosure" or "keep-confidential" agreements and identify it as proprietary information or a trade secret, such as "This document contains Ajax Co. confidential information"; or put it on an invention-disclosure–type form (see Chapter 3) and limit its dissemination using appropriate means. (See Section Q, above.)
7. Unfair Competition. Any distinctive design, slogan, title, shape, color, trade dress, package, business layout, etc.	Using it publicly as much as possible, in advertising, etc., so as to establish a "secondary meaning" to enable you to win an unfair competition lawsuit. (See above.)

[1] Orphan drugs (those useful in treating rare diseases) can be covered under the Orphan Drug Act, 21 USC 360; write to the Food and Drug Administration for details.

[2] Sexually reproduced plants can be monopolized under the Plant Variety Protection Act, 7 USC 2321; write to Plant Variety Protection Office, National Agriculture Library, Room 500, 10301 Baltimore Blvd., Beltsville, MD 20705. Also, both types of plants (sexually and asexually reproducible) can be covered by utility patent.

considered a trademark. The coloring of a package or label, or the layout of a business, are good examples of distinctive trade dress.

Patentable designs, on the other hand, relate to the appearance of an article that enhances its aesthetic appeal, which is more than mere surface ornamentation and which is novel and unobvious. Examples are a modernistic lamp design and the pattern of a fabric. While trade dress can be mere coloring, surface ornamentation, or a general appearance, a design patentable invention has to be a shape or appearance of a specific article which is more than a surface appearance, which relates to the overall appearance of the article, and which is different enough to be considered unobvious.

S. Acquisition of Offensive Rights in Intellectual Property—Summary Chart

The chart on the previous page summarizes how an inventor or creator should acquire offense rights in every type of intellectual property.

T. Summary of Legal Remedies for Misappropriation of Various Types of Intellectual Property

Now that you're familiar with all of the types of intangible property, the chart below summarizes how to select the appropriate remedy for any type of intellectual property dispute.

The enforcement of an intellectual property right requires considerable knowledge and experience. For background on intellectual property disputes (and to save money when consulting an attorney), consult the Nolo texts, below.

- **Copyright.** *The Copyright Handbook* or *Copyright Your Software*, both by Stephen Fishman
- **Trademark.** *Trademark: Legal Care for Your Business & Product Name*, by Stephen Elias
- **Trade Secrets.** *Nondisclosure Agreements: Protecting Your Trade Secrets & More*, by Richard Stim and Stephen Fishman.

U. Invention Exploitation Flowchart

To make it easier to use this book, I recommend you follow a five-step procedure after you have invented something. It can be conveniently summarized by the initials RESAM (Record it, Evaluate commercial potential, Search it, Apply for a patent, and Market it). The chart of Fig 1E shows these

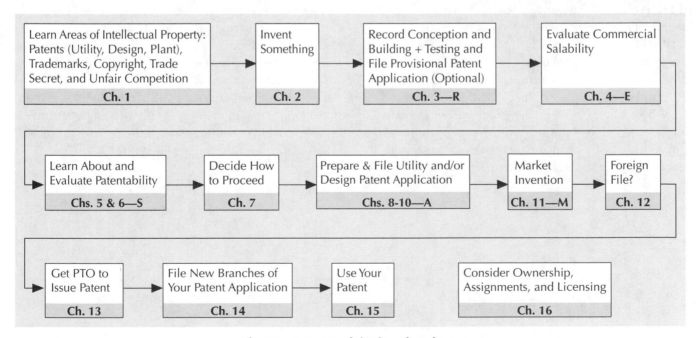

Fig. 1E—Patent Exploitation Flowchart

steps and the other overall steps for exploiting your invention and where the chapter's instructions for these steps are found.

V. Summary

The law recognizes seven ways in which intellectual property can be monopolized or clothed with offensive rights: utility patents, design patents, plant patents, trademarks, copyright, trade secrets, and unfair competition.

Utility Patents provide a government-sanctioned monopoly on utilitarian inventions. The monopoly lasts 20 years from filing, provided three maintenance fees are paid. The U.S. Patent and Trademark Office (PTO) will grant patents only on inventions that are (a) in a statutory class (machines, articles, processes, compositions, and new uses), (b) useful, (c) novel, and (d) unobvious. The PTO charges filing and issue fees and requires a formal description of the invention with drawings, forms, and claims (legal definitions of the invention). Patents provide offensive rights but are not needed to practice one's own invention and do not protect an inventor from infringing patents of others. After a patent expires, its monopoly no longer exists and it becomes part of the vast body of prior art.

Design Patents provide a government-sanctioned monopoly on aesthetic or ornamental inventions; the monopoly lasts 14 years from issuance. No maintenance fees are required. The PTO will grant patents only on designs that are ornamental, involve more than mere surface ornamentation, not a natural object, novel, and unobvious. The PTO charges filing and issue fees and requires a brief description of the design with drawings and forms.

Plant Patents provide a government-sanctioned monopoly on asexually reproduced plants; the monopoly lasts 20 years from issuance. No maintenance fees are required. The PTO will grant patents only on plants that are novel and unobvious. The PTO charges filing and issue fees and requires a brief description of the plant with drawings and forms.

Trademarks are signifiers (such as brand names) for goods or services. Mere use of a mark confers the user with common law monopoly rights, but it's better to register the mark with a state trademark office (intrastate use) or the PTO (interstate use). Before using, make a search of the proposed mark, considering the goods or service and the strength of mark. If confusion is not likely and the mark is not generic, the government will register it. Descriptive marks are registrable provided that the user can demonstrate sufficient sales or advertising. Before federal registration, use the mark with a "TM" superscript (™) and as a proper adjective followed by common name of goods. After registration, use the ® superscript. One can also apply to the federal government for an intent to use the mark, but one must show actual use before the PTO will register the mark.

Copyright covers works of authors, artists, photographers, composers, programmers, etc. Copyright covers only a particular form of expression of an idea, but not an idea per se. Copyright is not good for forms, TMs, slogans, methods, lists, formulae, utilitarian articles (unless artwork is separable from article), etc. On published versions of work, it's desirable to include a © notice. Copyrights last for life of the author plus 70 years, or 95 years from the date of publication in the case of a work made for hire. The work should be registered with the Copyright Office before or after publication to secure full rights.

Trade Secrets: Covers novel information that has some commercial advantage and is not generally known. The information must be kept secret. Trade secret rights will be lost if it is discovered by reverse engineering from the final product. Usually only chemical formulae, industrial and commercial processes, and programs with controlled distribution are covered by trade secrets. Trade secrets have a theoretically perpetual term, incur little cost, and provide definite, immediate rights. Patents are preferable over trade secrets as they can be used against independent creators, can't be avoided by reverse engineering, and enjoy more respect in the business and scientific community.

Unfair Competition: A catchall category based largely on judge-made law and "false-designation-of-origin" statutes to cover trade names, slogans, trade dress, unfair practices, unjust enrichment, "palming off," etc. ■

Chapter 2

The Science and Magic of Inventing

Inventor's Commandment #2

To invent successfully, be aware of problems you encounter and seek solutions. Also, take the time to study and investigate the practicality of new phenomena that occur by accident or flash of insight. Persevere with any development you believe has commercial potential.

Before we get to patents, the primary subject of this book, I provide this chapter to discuss inventions and inventing. Why do this? To begin, you may be a first-time inventor and thus have no experience in the real world of protecting and patenting inventions. I believe that you'll be a better inventor if you understand and become familiar with some successful inventors. Also, I believe that too many first-timers get discouraged without trying hard enough. To inspire you to hang in there, I include here some past success stories. Hopefully, when you see that many other small, independent inventors have found their pot of gold, you'll be stimulated to press on.

Inventing provides things that enhance our lives, making them more interesting, pleasurable, exciting, rewarding, and educational. As the noted Swiss psychologist, Piaget, once said, "We learn most when we have to invent." Remember that everything of significance, even the chair you're probably seated in now, started with an idea in someone's brain. If you come up with something, don't dismiss it; it could turn out to be something great!

Common Misconception: The day of the small inventor is over; an independent inventor no longer has any chance to make a killing with his or her invention.

Fact: As you'll see by the examples given later in this chapter, many small, independent inventors have done extremely well with their inventions. Billions of dollars in royalties and other compensation are paid each year to independent inventors for their creations. In fact 73% of all inventions that have started new industries have come from individual inventors. So, don't be a victim of the "no-use-going-on-with-it-because-surely-someone-has-invented-it-already" syndrome. While I recommend that you don't rush blindly ahead to patent your work without making a sensible investigation of prior inventions and your creation's commercial potential (in the ways I discuss later), I urge you not to quit without giving your invention a fair chance.

Another reason for this chapter is that many inventors come up with valuable inventions, but they haven't developed them sufficiently so that they can be readily sold. If their creations could be improved with further work, they'd have a far greater chance of success. So here I'll also give some hints about such things as improving your inventions, solving problems about workability, and drawbacks.

If you've already made an invention, or are even in the business of inventing, I believe the techniques in this chapter that increase your creativity and provide additional stimulation will help you to make more and better inventions. On the other hand, I also recognize that the information in this chapter may not be particularly helpful to the experienced inventor or the corporate inventor—after all, you're already firmly in the inventing business. If you would rather skip this information for now, go to Chapter 3, where my discussion of record keeping should prove of value to even the most seasoned of inventors.

A. What I Mean by "Invention"

For the purpose of this book, an invention is any thing, process, or idea that isn't generally and currently known; which, without too much skill or ingenuity, can exist in or be reduced to tangible form or used in a tangible thing; which has some use or value to society; and which you or someone else has thought up or discovered.

Note that under this definition, an invention can be a process or even an idea, so long as it can be made tangible in some way, "without too much skill or ingenuity." On the other hand, the definition eliminates fantasies and wishes, such as time-travel or perpetual motion machines, since these obviously (at least to me) can't be made tangible.

An invention must have some use or value to society; otherwise what good is it, and how will you sell it? It must be generally unknown anywhere in the world (at the time you invent it), and it must have been thought up or discovered by you or someone else—otherwise it doesn't really have inventive value.

While you may think that an invention must be a major development to be successful, the truth is that most successful inventions are evolutionary rather than revolutionary. For example, the basic concept of the transistor was invented in the 1930s, but was not feasible enough to be successful until Drs. Brittain, Bardeen, and Shockley made some evolutionary but successful improvements in the late 1940s.

Why do I bother to define the term invention in such detail? So you'll begin to understand it and have a better feel for it, as well as to define the limits of its usage in this book. As you'll see, my primary concern is with inventions that qualify for a patent (that is, patentable inventions). However, nonpatentable inventions can also be valuable as long as society finds them at least somewhat special and useful.

B. Inventing by Problem Recognition and Solution

Now that you know what an invention is, how do you make one? Most inventions are conceived by the following two-step procedure: 1) recognizing a problem, and 2) fashioning a solution.

Although it may seem like duck soup, recognizing a problem often amounts to about 90% of the act of conceiving the invention. "To be an inventor is to perceive need." In these situations, once the problem is recognized, conceiving the solution is easy. Consider some of the Salton products—the home peanut butter maker, for instance, or the plug-in ice cream maker for use in the freezer. In both cases, once the problem was defined (the need for an easy homemade version of a product normally purchased at the store) implementing the solution merely involved electrification and/or size reduction of an existing appliance. Once the problem was defined, any competent appliance designer could accomplish its solution. True, during the implementation of the idea, that is, the design of the actual hardware, designers and engineers often contribute the very aspects of the invention that make it ingenious and patentable. Still, the main ingredient leading to a successful outcome for most inventions consists of recognizing and defining the problem that needs to be solved. Although Edison seemed to contradict this when he said that inventing is 10% inspiration and 90% perspiration, he was referring to the whole experience of inventing, including conception, making a practicable model, and licensing or selling the invention. Here, I'm referring just to the conception part of inventing—what Edison called "inspiration."

Of course, in some contexts, the recognition of a problem plays no part in the invention. Most improvement inventions fall into this category, such as, for example, the improvement of the mechanism of a ballpoint pen to make it cheaper, more reliable, stronger, etc. But in general, you will find it most effective to go about inventing via the two-step process of identifying a problem and solving it. Or, as famed inventor Jacob Rabinow said, "You invent because something bothers you."

Let's look at some simple inventions that were made using this two-step process and which have been commercially implemented. I delineate the problem **P** and solution **S** in each instance. Where I know an Independent Inventor was responsible, I add an "**II**."

1. **Grasscrete. P** Wide expanses of concrete or asphalt in a parking lot or driveway are ugly. **S** Make many cross-shaped holes in the paving and plant grass in the earth below so that the grass grows to the surface and makes the lot or driveway appear mostly green; grass is protected from the car's tires because of its subsurface position.

2. **Intermittent Windshield Wipers. P** In drizzles, the slowest speed of windshield wipers was unnecessarily fast, and merely slowing the wipers was unsatisfactory, since a slow sweep was annoying. **S** Provide a "drizzle" setting where the windshield wipers made normally fast sweeps but paused after each sweep. (Robert Kearns, **II**. Mr. Kearns's brilliantly ingenious yet utterly ingenuous solution, has earned him at least $50 million in royalties thus far.)

3. **Buried Plastic Cable-Locator Strip. P** Construction excavators often damage buried cables (or pipes) because surface warning signs often are removed or can't be placed over the entire buried cable. **S** Bury a brightly colored plastic strip parallel to and above the cable; it serves as a warning to excavators that a cable is buried below the spot where they're digging. (This is a "new-use" invention since the plastic strip per se was obviously already in existence.)

4. **Magnetic Safety Lock for Police Pistols. P** Police pistols are often fired by unauthorized persons. **S** A special safety lock inside the pistol releases only when the pistol is held by someone wearing a finger ring containing a high-coercive-force samarium-cobalt magnet.

5. **Wiz-z-er™ Gyroscopic Top. P** Gyroscopes are difficult to get running: they require the user to wind a string around a shaft surrounded by gimbals and then pull it steadily but forcefully to set the rotor in motion. **S** Provide an enclosed gyro in the shape of a top with an extending friction tip that can be easily spun at high speed by moving it across any surface. (Paul Brown, **II**. Mr. Brown came up with this great invention because, while at a party, he had repeated difficulty operating a friend's son's gyro. His first royalty check from Mattel was five times his annual salary!)

6. **Dolby® Audio Tape Hiss Elimination. P** Audio tapes played at low volume levels usually have an audible hiss. **S** Frequency-selective compounding of the audio during recording and expanding of the audio during playback to eliminate hiss. (Ray Dolby, perhaps the most successful **II** of modern times.)

7. **Xerography. P** Copying documents required messy, slow, complicated photographic apparatus. **S** Xerography—the charging of a photosensitive surface in a pattern employing light reflected from the document to be copied and then using this charged surface to pick up and deposit black powder onto a blank sheet. (Chester Carlson, **II**. When Mr. Carlson, a patent attorney, brought his invention to Kodak, they said it could

EYE PROTECTOR FOR FOWL
No. 620,832

Fig 2.

never be commercially implemented and rejected it. Undaunted, he brought it to The Haloid Co., which accepted it and changed its name to Xerox Corporation; the rest is history.)

8. **Flip-Top Can. P** Cans of beverage were difficult to open, requiring a church key or can opener. **S** Provide the familiar flip-top can. (Ermal Frase, **II**.)

9. **FM, CW, and AGC. P** Information wasn't conveyable by radio due to noisy, limited frequency response and fade-out of AM reception. **S** Provide CW, FM, and AGC circuitry, familiar to all electronic engineers. (Edwin Howard Armstrong, **II**, the genius of high fidelity.)

10. **Thermostatic Shower Head. P** Shower takers sometimes get burned because they inadvertently turn on the hot water while standing under the shower. **S** Provide a thermostatic cut-off valve in the supply pipe. (Alfred M. Moen, **II**.)

11. **VCR Plus. P** Most people are too lazy or too put off by technical matters to learn how to enter a date, time, and channel into their VCR. **S** With VCR Plus, each program is assigned a special code number in the newspaper and the VCR owner need merely enter the number and transmit it to the VCR.

12. **Organic Production of Acetone. P** During WWI, the U.K. desperately needed acetone to make explosives, since its normal source was cut off. **S** Use an anaerobic bacterium to produce acetone from locally available corn mash. (Dr. Chaim Weizmann. This invention helped save one nation and start a new one: It was instrumental in helping the U.K. and the Allies survive WWI and defeat the Germans. The U.K. rewarded Weizmann with the Balfour Declaration, which helped lead to the eventual formation of the State of Israel.)

13. **Grocery Shopping Cart. P** Shoppers in grocery stores used their own small, hand-carried wicker baskets and bought only the small amounts that they could carry in the baskets, thereby necessitating several trips to the grocery and causing sales to be relatively low per customer visit. **S** Provide a "grocery cart," that is, a large wire basket in a frame on wheels so that it can be rolled about and carry a large amount of groceries. (Sylvan Goldman, **II**. When Mr. Goldman first introduced his carts (about 1925), shoppers wouldn't use them and stores wouldn't buy them despite his extensive efforts. He eventually found a way to get his carts accepted: he hired crews of "shoppers" to wheel the carts about and fill them in his store, and also hired a woman to offer the carts to entering shoppers. Goldman then made millions from patents on his cart and its improvements (nesting carts and airport carts). This illustrates the crucial value of perseverance and marketing genius.)

The inventors of these inventions necessarily went through the problem-solution process (though not necessarily in that order) to make their invention. Even if an inventor believes the invention came spontaneously, you'll usually find that problem-solution steps were somehow involved, even if they appear to coalesce.

So, if you either don't have an invention or want to make some new ones, you should begin by ferreting out problem or "need" areas. This can often be done by paying close attention to your daily activities. How do you or others perform tasks? What problems do you encounter and how do you solve them? What needs do you perceive, even if they're as simple as wanting a full month's calendar on your calendar watch? Ask yourself if something can't be done more easily, cheaply, simply, or reliably, if it can't be made lighter, quicker, stronger, etc. Write the problems down and keep a list. Make sure you take the time to cogitate on the problems or needs you've discovered.

Sometimes the solution to the problem you identify will be a simple expedient, such as electrification or reduction in size. Generally, however, it will be more involved, as in some of the examples listed above. But you don't have to be a genius to come up with a solution. Draw on solutions from analogous or even nonanalogous fields. Experiment, meditate, look around. When a possible solution strikes you, write it down, even if it's in the middle of the night. History records a great number of important scientific and conceptual breakthroughs occurring during sleep or borderline-sleep states.

Also, remember that sometimes the "problem" may be the ordinary way something has been done for years, and which no one has ever recognized as a problem. Consider shower heads. Although essentially the same device operated satisfactorily for about 50 years, the inventor of water-massaging shower heads recognized the deficiency of an ordinary constant spray that didn't create any massage effect. He thus developed the water-massaging head that causes the water to come out in spurts from various head orifices, thereby creating the massaging effect.

Don't hesitate to go against the grain of custom or accepted practice if that's where your invention takes you. Many widespread erroneous beliefs have abounded in the past which were just waiting to be shattered. The medical field, in particular, had numerous nonsensical practices and beliefs, such as the use of "poudrage" (pouring talcum powder onto the heart to stimulate it to heal itself), blood-letting, and blistering, and the belief that insanity could be cured by drilling holes in the head to let the demons out.

You'll probably find the going easier if you invent in fields with which you're familiar. In this way you won't tend to "reinvent the wheel." Also, think about uncrowded fields or newly emerging ones where you will find ample room for innovation. But even if you work in an established area, you will find plenty of opportunity for new inventions. For example, more patents issue on bicycles than anything else. Still, you would make millions if you could invent an automatic, continuous bicycle transmission to replace the awkward derailleur. Or how about a truly compactable bicycle (or wheelchair) which could easily be carried onto a train or into the office but worked as well as the standard variety?

The U.S. Government publishes a quarterly list of needed products requiring inventive effort. Write to the U.S. Small Business Administration Office of Technology, SBIR, 409 Third Street, SW, Washington, DC 20416. Phone: 202-205-6450.

Many inventors have discovered problems (and come up with solutions) by observing current events in the media. A few years ago there were problems with medical personnel being stuck and infected by hypodermic needles that slipped or were used against them by disturbed patients. The result—a rash of patents on safety needles. Current problem areas such as terrorism, voting machines, alternative energy, and guerrilla warfare are creating potential markets for inventive individuals. For example, a market exists for a simple, tamper-proof, easy-to-use voting machine. If you have technical ability, another way to invent is to "follow the cutting edge." Biotechnology and nanotechnology are currently hot areas.

One important principle to successful inventing is to remember the acronym KISS (Keep It Simple, Stupid!). If you can successfully eliminate just one part from any machine, its manufacturer (or a competing manufacturer!) will be overjoyed: the cost of the machine will be reduced, it will be lighter, and, of course, it will be more reliable. Another way to look at this is Sandra Bekele's (an inventor-friend) admonition to (figuratively) "eliminate the corners." Or, to quote jazz great Charlie Mingus, "Anybody can make the simple complicated. Creativity is making the complicated simple."

Lastly, says highly successful toy inventor Richard Levy, don't go into inventing for money alone; you've got to enjoy the game and the hunt to make it all truly worthwhile.

C. Inventing by Magic (Accident and Flash of Genius)

When I don't understand how something is done, I some-times call it "magic." Inventions made by "magic" don't involve the problem-solution technique which I just described; rather, they usually occur by "accident" or by "flash of genius." The PTO and the courts really don't care how you come up with an invention, so long as they can see that it wasn't already accomplished and it looks substantially different from what's been done before. In the hopelessly stilted language of the law, "Patentability shall not be negatived by the manner in which the invention was made" (35 USC 103).

Many famous inventions have resulted from accident or coincidence. For example, Goodyear invented rubber vulcanization when he accidentally added some sulphur to a rubber melt. In the late 1800s, a chemist supposedly acci-dentally left a crutcher (soap-making machine) on too long, causing air to be dispersed into the soap mixture. He found that the soap floated when it hardened, thus giving birth to floatable soap bars, such as Ivory® brand. In 1912, another chemist, Jacques Brandenberger, accidentally mixed some chemicals together and spilled them, finding they hardened to a flexible, transparent sheet (later known as "cellophane"). When Alexander Fleming accidentally contaminated one of his bacterial cultures with a mold, he was sufficiently alert and scientifically minded to notice that the mold killed the bacteria, so he carried this discovery for-ward and isolated the active ingredient in the mold, which later was named penicillin. (Unfortunately he didn't patent it, so he got the fame, but not the fortune.)

And in 1948, Georges de Mestral, after taking a walk in the forest of his native Switzerland, noticed some cockleburs had stuck to his pants. Being of scientific mind, he removed and examined them and figured out why they adhered so well. He applied his newly discovered knowledge and as a result invented and made a fortune from hook-and-loop fasteners, which his company sold under the trademark Velcro.

In 1938 chemist Roy Plunkett, while experimenting with refrigerant fluids at a DuPont lab in New Jersey, left some fluorine-based gas in a freezer and came back to find a solid, slippery polymer that was extremely resistant to bonding and to which nothing would stick. Known initially as PTFE, it later earned billions for DuPont under the trademark Teflon.

The law considers the fact that these inventions came about by total accident, without the exercise of any creativity by their "inventors," legally irrelevant. All other things being equal, a patent on cellophane would be just as strong as one on nylon (another former trademark), the result of 12 years' intensive and brilliant work by duPont's now-deceased genius, Dr. Wallace Carothers of Wilmington, Delaware.

Since I don't understand how the "magic" occurs, I can't tell you or even suggest how to invent by accident. Please remember, however, that in case you ever come up with an accidental development, take the time and apply the effort to study, analyze, and try to "practicalize" it. If it has potential value, treat it like any other invention; the law will.

The other type of "magical" invention I'll refer to as the product of a "flash of genius." While "flash of genius" inventions inherently solve a need, the inventive act usually occurred spontaneously and not as a result of an attack on any problem. Some examples of this type are the electric knife and the previously discussed Salton inventions which actually created their own need, the Pet Rock (not a real invention by traditional definitions, but rather a clever trademark and marketing ploy, but highly profitable just the same), Bushnell's "Pong" game, the Cabbage Patch dolls, Ruth Handler's Barbie Dolls, and a client's Audochron® clock, which announces the time by a series of countable chimes for the hours, tens of minutes, and minutes. With these inventions, the inventor didn't solve any real problem or need, but rather came up with a very novel invention which provided a new type of amusement or a means for conspicuous consumption (showing off).

Although I don't understand how the creativity in these types of cases occurs, I suggest in Section E of this chapter several techniques for stimulating and unlocking such creativity. Using these techniques, many inventors have come up with valuable inventions and profitable ideas and marketing ploys.

"Chance favors only the prepared mind"

—Louis Pasteur

D. Making Ramifications and Improvements of Your Invention

Once you've made an invention, write down the problem and solution involved. Then, try to ramify it—that is, to do it or make it in other ways so it will be cheaper, faster, better, bigger (or smaller), stronger, lighter (or heavier), longer- (or shorter-) lasting, or even just different. Why ramify?

1. Most inventors usually find that their initial solution can be improved or made more workable.
2. By conceiving of such improvements first, you can foreclose future competitors from obtaining patents on them.
3. Even if you believe your first solution is the best and most workable, your potential producers or manufacturers may not see it that way. So, it's best to have as many alternatives handy as possible.
4. When you apply for a patent, the more ramifications you have, the easier it will be to make your patent stronger. (See Chapter 8.)
5. Conversely, if the broad concept or initial embodiment of your invention is "knocked out" by a search of the "prior art" (see Chapter 5, Section E1) made by you, your searcher, or the examiner in the Patent and Trademark Office, you'll have something to fall back on, so you'll still be able to get a patent.
6. Ramifications often help you understand your basic invention better, see it in a new light, see new uses or new ways to do it, etc.
7. Ramifications can be held back and introduced later, after the basic invention has been "milked" commercially, thereby prolonging the profits, as duPont did with its Teflon®II. Be sure to try to patent the ramifications as soon as possible, however, to foreclose someone else from doing so.

In some situations, you'll find that you won't be able to ramify beyond your basic conception. But give it a try anyway, and make sure you record in writing any ramifications you do come up with as soon as possible. (See Chapter 3.)

One way to make ramifications is to pretend that a part of your device can't be made due to a law or crucial material shortage and then try to come up with a replacement.

In addition to making ramifications to your invention, you should, after you've finished with filing a patent application or you've gotten it out on the market, try to make improvements—that is, more substantial changes. Why? There are several reasons: (1) To extend your monopoly and keep the gravy flowing longer; (2) To enhance your credibility as an inventor—if you have several patents it will make any infringer look worse in litigation and make it easier for you to win your lawsuit; (3) Improvement patents cut off avenues that another company can use to design around your base patent; (4) A bank or financier will be more likely to lend you money if you have several patents.

E. Solving Creativity Problems

Unfortunately, hardly any invention ever works right or "flies" the first time it's built. You need to build and test it to be aware of the working problems. If you don't, the first builder, whoever it is, will inevitably face them. If this is a corporation to which you've sold or licensed your invention, it's sure to create problems. If your first construction doesn't work, don't be discouraged; expect problems and expect to solve them through perseverance. If you don't believe me, consider Edison's views on this subject:

> *"Genius? Nothing! Sticking to it is the genius! Any other bright-minded fellow can accomplish just as much if he will stick like hell and remember nothing that's any good works by itself. You've got to make the damn thing work!… I failed my way to success."*

If you show your invention to someone and you get static in return, don't necessarily get discouraged; the history of invention abounds with quotes from naysayers who were proved to be disastrously wrong. The enlightening book *303 of The World's Worst Predictions*, by W. Coffey (see Appendix 2, Resources: Government Publications, Patent Websites, and Books of Use and Interest), is full of amusing and insightful erroneous quotes. Here are a few teasers:

> *"Everything that can be invented has been invented."*
> **—U.S. Patent Office Director, urging President McKinley to abolish the Office (1899)**

> *"What, sir? You would make a ship sail against the wind and currents by lighting a bonfire under her decks? I pray you excuse me. I have no time to listen to such nonsense."*
> **—Napoleon Bonaparte to Robert Fulton, after hearing Fulton's plans for a steam engine driven boat**

> *"I think there is a world market for about five computers."*
> **—Thomas J. Watson, IBM President (1956)**

> *"Man won't fly for a thousand years."*
> **—Wilbur Wright to Orville after a disappointing experiment in 1901**

Many have analyzed the creative process, but so far no one has come up with a foolproof recipe or technique for innovating. However, almost all writers recommend that, unless you already have a "flash of genius," you first thoroughly prepare and familiarize yourself with the field, always keeping an open mind. Thereafter, some writers recommend you wait a while (allot an incubation period) to let your mind digest and work on the problem. Following incubation, work on the problem again and insight may come, sometimes in bits and pieces. "To discover something you've never seen before, walk the same path you walked yesterday." R. W. Emerson. Alternatively, some experts recommend that, after preparation, one make a concentrated effort, which may lead to frustration and withdrawal. But be patient, since the insight, which may be an image or a fantasy, will usually come thereafter. Of course follow-through is necessary to implement and profit from the insight or fantasy.

If you have creativity problems, such as how to make that great idea work, here are some specific techniques you can use to enhance your creativity, and hopefully solve that problem.

Frame It Differently: One of the most effective ways to solve a problem is to "frame" the problem properly. Framing is another way of describing the way in which one looks at a situation. A common example of framing a problem occurs when you try to move a bulky sofa through a small doorway. If the first way doesn't work, frame the problem differently by turning the sofa upside down and trying again. Or take another example: If you have an apparatus which includes a lever, and you can't find a design shape for the lever which the machine will accommodate, look at the situation another way; perhaps you can redesign the apparatus to eliminate the lever altogether!

Use Your Right Brain: In the course of trying to solve a problem with an invention, you may encounter a brick wall of resistance when you try to think your way logically through the problem. Such logical thinking is a linear type of process (that is, one step follows another), which utilizes our rational faculties, located in the left side of our brains. This works fine when we're operating in the realm of what we know or have experienced. However, when we need to deal with new information, ideas, and perspectives, linear thinking will often come up short. On the other hand, creativity by definition involves the application of new information to old problems and the conception of new perspectives and ideas. For this you will be most effective if you learn to operate in a nonlinear manner, that is, use your right brain or creative faculties. Stated differently, if you think in a linear manner, you'll tend to be conservative and keep coming up with techniques which are already known. This, of course, is just what you don't want.

One way to engage your right-brain faculties in a search for a creative solution to your quandary is to pose the problem in clear terms and then forget about it and think of something completely different. For example, if you can't fit that lever in your apparatus, think of a different activity, or just take a break (how about a nice boating trip or a hike in the woods). Your subconscious will work on the problem while you're "away." Then come back to the problem and force your different activity onto your problem. In other words, try to think of the apparatus and your boating trip or hike simultaneously. You may find that a solution appears by magic (for example, you may realize a way to design the machine without the lever!).

Let Go of Assumptions: If you adhere to assumptions, you'll never innovate, since innovation, by definition, is the adoption of something new, the embarkation on an untrodden path. As Erich Fromm said, "Creativity requires the courage to let go of [assumed] certainties." So if you've got a problem, try to see what assumptions you're making (they're usually hidden) and then let them go or try to cancel them and see what you come up with.

Meditation: Another way to bring out your creativity is to meditate on the problem or meditate merely to get away from the problem. Either will help. As strange as it seems, some experts say that creativity can be enhanced during reverie by listening to a largo movement from a baroque symphony. At least you'll enjoy it! Also, the use of biofeedback machines can induce or teach deep relaxation with enhanced alpha, or even theta brain waves, a very effective stimulus to creativity.

Dreams: Most creative people find dreams the most effective way of all to solve problems. Or as Edison said: "I never invented anything; my dreams did."

Elias Howe solved the basic problem of his sewing machine in a dream. He saw some tribal warriors who ordered him to come up with a solution or they would kill him. He couldn't make a solution, so the warriors then threw their spears at him. When the spears came close, he saw that each had a hole near its tip. He awoke from the nightmare in terror, but soon realized the symbology: he put a hole near the tip of his bobbin needle and passed the thread through. Again, the rest is history.

Similarly, Mendeleev came up with the periodic table of the elements in a dream.

To stimulate creative dreaming, first immerse yourself in the problem near bedtime. Then forget about it—do some-thing completely different and go to sleep. Your subconscious will be able to work on the problem. You'll most likely have a dream with an inspiration or insight. Then remember the dream and evaluate the insight to find out if it's correct (sometimes it won't be!).

Note that you'll forget most dreams, so keep a dream diary or notebook handy, by your bedside. Also, you'll find a pen with a built-in flashlight is also helpful. Before you go to bed, repeat fifteen times, "I'll remember my dreams." Whenever you do dream, wake up (you'll find it possible to do this if you intend to do so beforehand) and write your dreams down promptly. Once they are written down, forget about them, go back to sleep, and try to figure them out in the morning. Sometimes a week or more will pass before the meanings become clear. Or talk your dreams over with an equally inventive friend and see if he or she can get the meaning—sometimes talking about it helps.

While sleep dreams are usually the most productive, often daydreams will bring valued insight. So, don't dismiss your daydreams either!

Good luck. And pleasant dreams!

Computerized Creating: As strange as it may seem, computers can be used to enhance creativity, solve problems, bust through conceptual roadblocks, and get into the recesses of your memory. Several "mindware" or "CAT" (computer-aided thinking software) programs for this purpose exist, and I believe they can be of significant help in this area. The programs work by first asking you to enter lots of details of your problem or area and then they rearrange the details and suggest lots of modifications and permutations for you to consider. One program is called "The Idea Generator" from Experience In Software, Inc., Berkeley, California, but other programs and services exist in this area.

The Hot Tub Method: This has been used by many creative geniuses, starting with Archimedes who discovered the principle of volumetric measurement while in his tub. It works like this: When you relax in a hot tub for a long period, the heat on your body mellows you out and dilates your blood vessels so as to draw blood from your analytical brain, allowing your creative subconscious to come to the fore.

Unstructured Fanaticism: As "excellence guru" Tom Peters states, structured planners rarely come up with the really great innovations; monomaniacs who pursue a goal with unstructured fanaticism often do. So let yourself go and become an unreasonable madman—it may do the trick!

Group Brainstorming: If all else fails, get a group of friends or trusted associates together (or on a computer network) and throw the problem to the group. For some unknown reason, a group of people working together often come up with more good ideas than the same individuals working separately. This synergistic method is often used in corporations with great success. The use of others to help innovate has been called "leveraging knowledge," since one's knowledge and abilities are multiplied by others in a group.

Increase Self-Confidence: Those with more self-confidence and self-esteem tend to be more venturesome, and hence more creative. If you suffer from low self-confidence or low self-esteem, you may wish to explore local courses or read some of the self-improvement books in Appendix 2, Resources: Government Publications, Patent Websites, and Books of Use and Interest.

20 Questions: Dixie Hammond of Focus Works in Van Nuys, California, suggested 20 questions you can ask to encourage ideas:

1. What if …?
2. Can we improve …?
3. How will a customer benefit?
4. Are we forgetting anything?
5. What is the next step?
6. What can we do better?
7. What do you think about …?
8. How can we improve quality?
9. How can we streamline?
10. What should we modify?
11. What should we replace?
12. What should we add?
13. What should we eliminate?
14. Can we make any new assumptions?
15. What will make it work?
16. What other ideas do you have?
17. What issues should we explore?
18. What patterns can you see?
19. How can we simplify?
20. Why?

Idea Tools: Most inventions don't work well as originally developed. Here are some suggestions for modifying your invention to make it work better:

Divide: Divide it into smaller components or separate functions.

Combine: Combine separate ideas, parts, or functions.

Simplify: Simplify it—for example, by making it smoother, or streamlined.

Substitute: Use different materials, parts, functions, or ingredients.

Add: Add additional parts, movement, color, flavor, sound, functions, textures, or ingredients.

Subtract: Remove parts or steps.

Reverse: Reverse the mode of operation or position, or transpose cause and effect.

Minimize: Make it smaller, lighter, or lower.

Maximize: Make it bigger, stronger, better, higher, in multiples; exaggerate it.

Redesign: Redesign the exterior or interior, change the symmetry, speed, shape, function, or perspective; give it new meaning.

F. Contact Other Inventors

In recent years, many inventors' organizations have developed or sprung up in order to provide inventors with information and ideas, model makers, lists of searchers, speakers, patent attorneys, etc., as well as to sponsor various seminars and trade fairs where inventions can be exhibited. One or more of these organizations may provide you with invaluable assistance in your inventing efforts.

One of the oldest and most well-known groups of inventors is the Minnesota Inventors Congress (www.invent1.org). Inventors' organizations have a reputation for honesty and provide reasonable value for the membership or other fees charged, but check for yourself before investing a significant amount of your time or money. A listing of inventor organizations, can be found at:

- Patent Café (www.patentcafe.com). (Click on "Inventors and Intellectual Property Creators' Resources"), or
- Inventor's Digest Online, www.inventorsdigest.com. (Click on "Inventor Organizations)."

A complete list of all inventors' organizations is also available in *Inventor Assistance Source Directory*, published by Pacific Northwest Laboratory, P.O. Box 999, Mail Stop K8-11, Richland, WA 99352. You can also find inventors' groups in your area by asking the Patent and Trademark Depository Library close to you. You can find a listing of PTDLs in Chapter 6 or by visiting the PTO website (www.uspto.gov) and clicking on "PTDLs" at the bottom of the page.

If you wish to subscribe to an online mailing list in which you can contact other inventors, the InventNet Forum provides an online forum at www.inventnet.com.

G. Beware of the Novice Inventor's "PGL Syndrome"

As highly successful inventor (Whiz-z-er top) Paul Brown has discovered, many novice inventors have a very different attitude from experienced inventors. This attitude can be summarized as the "PGL (Paranoia, Greed, Laziness) syndrome." Let's discuss the components of this syndrome in more detail, since each usually is a significant hindrance for inexperienced inventors.

Paranoia: Extremely common with inexperienced inventors, paranoia (excessive suspicion of other people's motives) makes them afraid to discuss or show their invention to others—some even go as far as refusing to disclose it to a patent attorney. I do advise some measure of caution with unpatented inventions. However, once you record your invention properly (as discussed in Chapter 3), you can and should disclose it to selected persons, provided you take adequate measures to document whom you've disclosed it to and when. Don't be as paranoid as my friend Tom who invented a very valuable stereo movie invention but kept it totally to himself out of fear of theft, only to see it patented and commercialized by someone else.

Greed/Overestimation: Most people have heard fabulous stories of successful inventors who've collected millions in royalties. As a result, some novice inventors think that their invention is worth millions and demand an unreasonably large royalty or lump-sum payment for their creation. This is seldom wise. It is much better to set your sights at a reasonable level (see Chapter 16) so you won't miss out on commercial opportunities.

Laziness: Some novice inventors believe that all they need to do is show their invention to a company, sign a lucrative contract, and let the money roll in. Unfortunately it hardly ever happens so easily. To be successful, you usually have to record your invention properly (Chapter 3), build and test a working model (desirable but not always necessary), file a patent application, seek out suitable companies to produce and market the invention, and work like hell to sell the invention to one of these companies.

H. Don't Bury Your Invention

If you believe that you have what will turn out to be a successful idea, but you have doubts because it's very different, or you get negative opinions from your friends, consider that Alexander Graham Bell was asked by an irate banker to remove "that toy" from his office. The "toy" was the telephone. Or if that doesn't convince you, ponder these words of Mark Twain, Albert Einstein, and John Shedd:

"The man with a new idea is a crank—until the idea succeeds."

—Mark Twain

"For an idea that does not at first seem insane, there is no hope."

—Albert Einstein

"Opportunities are seldom labeled as such."

—John Shedd

And as a recent successful inventor, Nolan Bushnell, *(Pong)* said, "Everyone who's ever taken a shower has an idea. It's the person who does something about it who makes a difference."

Don't forget that, in addition to making money if you're successful, an invention can create jobs, make our lives easier and more interesting, and eliminate drudgery. Consider the Linotype® machine, where each machine eliminated 90 manual typesetters and their arduous task and spawned a new industry and profession. Then came the computer, where each modern computer replaced nine Linotype machines, spawned another new industry and gave almost anyone the ability to create typeset documents. If you still doubt the value of inventors and inventions, consider this: without inventors and their inventions, we would still be living the way we lived 50,000 years ago!

I hope you've received my message in this chapter loud and clear. If you have a worthwhile invention, and you scrupulously follow all the advice and instructions given in this and the succeeding chapters, and persevere, I believe you'll have a very good chance of success.

I. Summary

The day of the lone inventor is not over; many successful inventions and industries have been started by independent inventors.

Most inventions are created after recognizing a problem and finding a solution. However, inventions are also made by "magic" (accident and flash of genius), the process of which is not easily analyzed.

If you make an invention, try to conceive of ramifications to enhance its value. If you have trouble solving invention problems, persevere, frame the problem differently, use nonlinear techniques, let go of assumptions, try meditation, employ your dreams, the computer, use brainstorming, inventors' organizations, and other techniques. Beware of the novice inventors' PGL Syndrome (paranoia, greed, laziness). Above all, persevere! ∎

Chapter 3

Documentation, the DDP, and the PPA

Inventor's Commandment #3

After conceiving of an invention, you shouldn't proceed to develop, build, or test it, or reveal it to outsiders, until you (1) make a clear description of your conception (using ink), (2) sign and date the same, and (3) have this document signed and dated by two trustworthy people who have "witnessed and understood" your creation. (As an alternative to documentary conception in this manner, you can use the PTO's Disclosure Document program, but be aware of the disadvantages and limitations of the DDP.)

Inventor's Commandment #4

(1) Try to build and test your invention (if at all possible) as soon as you can, (2) keep full and true written, signed, and dated records of all the efforts, correspondence, and receipts concerning your invention, especially if you build and test it, and (3) have two others sign and date that they have "witnessed and understood" your building and testing. (As an alternative—or in addition—to documenting, building, and testing in this manner, you can use the PTO's Provisional Patent Application program, but be aware of the disadvantages and limitations of the PPA.)

A. Introduction

It's true in life generally that the better the documentation you keep, the easier it will be for you to retrieve important ideas, information, and, when necessary, proof that something happened. When it comes to inventing, good documentation is even more vital than in most other aspects of our lives. There are two distinct and important reasons why all inventors should document all of their work. The first has to do with the inventing process itself. The second involves the possibility that you will need to prove (1) that you are the inventor, and (2) that you came up with the invention first. Let's examine these reasons in order.

To help you properly document your invention, Nolo publishes *The Inventor's Notebook*. See the back of this book for more information.

B. Documents Are Vital to the Invention Process

It takes more than a good idea to sustain the invention process. It is absolutely essential to keep good, sound records, for the following reasons:

1. Good Engineering Practice

It's good engineering practice to keep a "technical diary," containing accurate, detailed documents of your ideas, work done, and accomplishments. Good engineers and technicians record their developments in chronological order so that they can refer back to their engineering diary at any time—days, weeks, months, or even years later. First, this enables them to avoid running up the same blind alley twice. Second, good records will shed light on subsequent developments, will allow the inventor to find needed data and details of past developments, and will provide a base for new paths of exploration and ramifications, especially if failures have occurred.

2. Psychological Stimulus

Many of us come up with great ideas, especially when we're engaged in some other activity (including dreaming), and we forget to write them down. Later, we may recall that we had a brilliant idea the night before, or during the office party, but because we went back to sleep or were too busy, we forgot it. If we could get into the habit of writing down our thoughts on a piece of paper, later on we'd find that piece of paper there to bug us, almost forcing us to do something about it. So, keep a small pencil or pen and some paper with you at all times, even by your bedside, and in your wallet, and write down your thoughts as soon as they occur. Later on, you'll be glad you did.

3. Analyzation Stimulus

WWII Admiral Raborn once said: "If you can't write it down, you don't really know what you are doing."

Have you ever had an idea, plan, or concept that you really didn't fully understand yourself? I'll bet you discovered that when you tried to write a description of it, you were forced to figure it out, and only then finally realized fully or exactly what you had. Putting a description of your idea in writing forces you to think about it and crystallize it into communicable form. Note that no matter how great your idea, and no matter how much of the work you do yourself, you'll never be able to make a nickel from it until you can communicate it to others, for example, to get a patent, to license it, or to sell the product.

"Writing forces you to think and get your thoughts straight."
—Warren Buffet

C. Documentation Is Vital to Prove Inventorship

If you keep clear, signed, dated, and witnessed documents of your creations, this will prove to others that you made the invention yourself, when you did so, and that you are a methodical, diligent, and reliable person. Who cares about the last point? While you may not be particularly interested in establishing such a reputation, you'll find it invaluable in case you ever get into any dispute over your invention. Also, when you go to license the invention, or undertake any other activity with it, as well as taking any tax deductions for your expenditures (see below), you'll find that having such documents will greatly enhance your standing with anyone who sees, evaluates, or considers your invention, or any aspect of your inventive activity.

There are six reasons why it's legally important promptly and properly to record your conception of your invention:

1. In Case of an Interference

The primary legal reason to record your inventive activities is to counter the claims of others that they invented your invention first. Many valuable inventions are independently and simultaneously conceived and brought to fruition, while others are misappropriated from the true inventor. In either case, for the first and true inventor to prevail, it's important to use the very specific record keeping techniques suggested later in this chapter.

Unfortunately, justice isn't automatic or simple. In the U.S., if two inventors come up with the same invention and file separate patent applications, the first inventor to file will not necessarily get the patent. Instead, the PTO will declare an "interference." The winner of the interference will not be the first to file, but rather the first to invent—the one who can prove they "reduced the invention to practice" (built and tested it or filed a patent application) first, unless the other inventor conceived of it first and was diligent in

reducing it to practice. While this may seem complicated, the main thing that you as an inventor must do is to be prepared. In order to win an interference it is essential that you keep a signed, dated, and witnessed description of the invention. This will prove that you came up with the invention on the date given and that you (and your co-inventor(s), if any) are the actual and true inventor(s) of the creation. As you'll see throughout the rest of the book, dates are crucial in patent law; thus you should date everything you receive or send; you can never tell when you'll need to rely on (prove) any date.

2. Proof in Case of Theft

Similarly, if someone sees or hears about your invention and attempts to "steal" it by claiming it as his or her own invention (in actuality, a rare occurrence), there will probably be a lawsuit or other proceeding in which the true and first inventor must be ascertained. In such a proceeding, the side with the earliest, best, and most convincing evidence will win. 'Nuff said!

3. Proof in Case of Confusion of Inventorship

There's also, commonly, confusion as to who is the actual, true, and first inventor of a particular invention. Often several engineers or friends will be working on the same problem, and if conception isn't promptly recorded, memories fade and there will be confusion as to who is (are) the actual inventor(s). Also, bosses and other supervisors have been known to claim inventorship, or joint inventorship, in an employee's invention. If all inventors promptly recorded their inventions, signed and dated them, and got them witnessed and dated, preferably by coworkers (including bosses), there would be very few cases of such confusion of inventorship.

4. Antedate References

As we'll see later in Chapter 13, if the PTO examiner cites a "prior-art reference" against your application (that is, finds a prior publication that casts doubt on the originality of your invention), you can eliminate that reference as prior art (that is, prevent the examiner from using it) if you filed your application within the year after the reference's publication date and (as in the case of an interference, above) you can prove that you either:

- built and tested the invention prior to the reference's effective date, or
- conceived of the invention prior to the reference's effective date and you were then diligent in "reducing it to practice" (building and testing it, or filing a provisional or regular patent application).

As I'll explain in Chapter 5, Section E, if a reference is a patent, its effective date is its filing date (or the filing date of any applicable PPA). If it's any other publication, such as a magazine article, its effective date is its publication date. This process of antedating a cited reference is called "swearing behind" the reference. Naturally, to be effective and acceptable when swearing behind a reference, your records should be detailed, clear, signed, dated, and witnessed.

5. Supporting Tax Deductions

Once you make an invention and spend any money on your creation, the IRS considers that you are "in business," thus enabling you to file a "Schedule C" or "Schedule E" (Form 1040) with your tax return to deduct all expenditures you made for your invention, from even ordinary income (not investment income) that you received. The IRS will be far more inclined to allow these deductions (assuming you're audited) if you can support them with full, clear, and accurate records of all of your invention activities, including, but not limited to, conception, building, and testing (Form 3-2 in Appendix 7), and expenditures for tools, plastics, other materials, models, etc.

6. Avoidance of Ownership Disputes

Suppose you make an invention in a specific area—say bicycles—and later you go to work for a company engaged in this area—say a bicycle manufacturer. If you haven't already filed a patent application on your bike, you'll have a very hard time proving you already made the invention before your employment with this company if you haven't kept a proper record. In this situation and in many others, the company (or an individual or other organization with whom you deal) will likely claim ownership of your prior invention under your employment (or other) agreement (see Chapter 16, Section D) unless you have the "paper" to prove prior invention.

D. Trade Secret Considerations

In Chapter 1, Section Q, you learned that an invention can qualify as a trade secret, at least for the first 18 months of the patent application period. After 18 months, the PTO will publish the patent application unless the applicant files, at the time of filing, a Nonpublication Request. Applications that are not published after 18 months will remain as trade secrets until the patent issues. The Table "Comparison of PTO's Disclosure Document Program (DDP) With Disclosure (or Notebook) Showing Conception" (in Section H, below) presents the advantages and disadvantages of the DDP compared to Notebook entries. Keeping an invention secret can provide its owner with certain obvious commercial advantages, and the owner may have recourse in the courts against any person who improperly discloses the secret to others.

Making a witnessed record of your invention doesn't conflict in any way with this trade-secret protection. Even if you show your invention to witnesses, this won't compromise the trade-secret status of your invention because of the implied understanding that witnesses to an invention should keep it confidential. However, I recommend that you don't merely rely on this implied understanding, but actually have your witnesses agree to keep your invention confidential. A verbal agreement is good, but a written agreement is far better and will really tie down the confidentiality of your invention. I've incorporated a nondisclosure obligation in the Invention Disclosure (Form 3-2, discussed below), but you can also have your witnesses sign the "Nondisclosure Agreement" (Form 3-1, discussed below) when you give them your lab notebook or disclosure to sign.

Whether your invention is to be patented or kept as a trade secret (you can decide later—see Chapter 7), you should first record it properly so that you can prove that you invented it and that you did so as of a certain date. Since you can keep your notebook confidential, at least for the time being, no loss of any potential trade secret protection will result from your making a proper record of your conception.

Remember that while recording your invention can be vital in the situations outlined above, it provides only limited rights, since it won't give you any weapon to use if anyone independently comes up with your creation, or if anyone copies your invention once it's out on the market. To acquire full offensive rights in these situations, you need to obtain a patent on your invention. As discussed in Chapter 1, only a patent will give you rights against independent creators of your invention and those who copy it once it's out on the market.

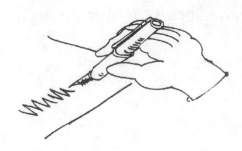

E. Record Conception and the Building and Testing of Your Invention

After you conceive of your invention you should record the conception in a lab notebook or an invention disclosure as explained Section F, below. After recording conception, you should follow my Inventor's Commandment #4 at the beginning of this chapter—that is, try to build and test your invention as soon as you can and keep detailed and adequate records of your efforts.

1. Keep Good Records of Building and Testing Activity

You may now well ask, if I've conceived of my invention and have properly recorded conception, why should I also build and test it? A good question. The main legal reason is in the U.S. patent statutes, specifically part (g) of 102 (35 USC 102(g)), which states:

> "In determining priority of invention there shall be considered not only the respective dates of conception and reduction to practice of the invention, but also the reasonable diligence of one who was first to conceive and last to reduce to practice, from a time prior to conception by the other."

As discussed earlier, the arcane phrase "reduction to practice" (RTP) means building and testing the hardware of the invention (called an "actual RTP") or the filing of a patent application on the invention (called a "constructive RTP," since the law construes this as an RTP). This part of Section 102 (the "first to invent" law) means that if two inventors file patent applications on the same invention, the PTO will award the patent to the one who first "reduced the invention to practice," unless the other inventor conceived of it first and was diligent in reducing it to practice. It also means that if the PTO cites a "prior art" publication having an earlier date than your filing date, you can often "swear behind" the publication if you can prove that you invented before the date of the publication. (More on this in Chapter 13.) So in order to win any possible interference, or swear behind any earlier reference, you should build and test your invention as soon as possible if you aren't going to file on it right away. (But see Section I, below, for a discussion of the new Provisional Patent Application process—a legal alternative to building and testing your invention.)

There are other, nonlegal reasons for building and testing. These are stated in Sections B and C, above. Specifically, it's good engineering practice, it provides psychological stimulus, it helps you analyze the invention, and it is of inestimable aid in case of theft, or confusion of inventorship or ownership. Even more importantly, as we'll learn in Chapter 4, building and testing is vital in evaluating the invention for commercial value, including operability, suitability, usability, etc. In addition, as I'll explain in Chapter 11, if you can build and test a working model of your invention, you can use this to great advantage in selling or licensing it to a manufacturer. So try to build and test it ASAP, if at all possible

Why should you painstakingly record the activities involved in the building and testing of your invention? This is an easy question to answer. All of the reasons discussed for recording the facts of your invention in the first place are applicable here, in spades. This is because the building and testing of an invention can be as (or even more) important than its conception, especially as proof of your invention in case of theft, confusion of inventors, interferences, the need to swear behind references, and the need to establish tax deductions. However, recordation of your efforts to build and test your invention isn't necessary to obtain a patent, unless an interference or other special situation occurs that requires you to prove your development efforts.

To illustrate the value of recordation, I recently prepared a patent application for a client. As she was reviewing it, I got a flyer in the mail from a store listing for sale an item almost identical to that which my client wished to patent! Since the item was being sold and was published before we were able to file the application, the flyer constituted "prior art," which, on its face, would preclude my client's invention from being considered as novel and thus lead to the rejection of her application. But fortunately, my client had read this chapter and built and tested the invention, had made records of her conception and of her building and testing, and had signed and dated these and had gotten them witnessed months before. She could thus go ahead and file without fear, even though the flier was published before her filing date. This is because she could use her records to "swear behind" the flyer. Simply put, by documenting her invention and her efforts to build and test it, my client was still able to obtain a patent. On the other hand, had she failed to properly record her conception and building and testing, her application would have been barred and she would have lost all rights to her invention!

2. Keep Your Building and Testing Activity Confidential

If, as part of the testing of your invention, you have to order any special part or material, or if you have to reveal to or discuss your invention with anyone to get it built, be cautious about how and whom you contact. And when you do make any specific revelation, have the recipient of the information about your invention sign a Nondisclosure Agreement ("NDA") (Form 3-1 in Appendix 7).

Getting the Agreement Signed

Model makers and machine shops are used to signing these agreements. When you make an appointment to show your invention and you wish to have the recipient sign the agreement before viewing, it's only courteous and proper business practice to advise the recipient that you are bringing along a nondisclosure agreement (NDA) before signing. Don't spring the agreement in a surprise manner.

The agreement is completed by specifically identifying the confidential materials (documents or hardware) (the "Confidential Information"), and the name of the recipient (the Receiving Party; you're the Disclosing Party). Have the Receiving Party fill in, sign, and date the bottom of the agreement. I recommend that you give a copy of the signed NDA to the Receiving Party, as well as any extra copies that may be needed if any other persons in the Receiving Party's organization are to sign also.

Note that if you are lending confidential materials to the Receiving Party, the agreement refers to the delivery of materials to the Receiving Party as a "loan." This will give you maximum rights if the Receiving Party makes unauthorized use of or refuses to return the materials.

This agreement will cover almost all situations where you need to disclose your invention or deliver proprietary materials under an NDA. However, it isn't cast in stone: If, for example, you are making more than a loan of the materials, feel free to redraft the agreement, for example, by changing "loaned" to "delivered."

F. How to Record Your Invention

Hopefully, I've managed to sell you on the need to carefully and accurately record your thoughts and activities that normally occur in the course of inventing. There are several ways to do the recording. These are discussed below, together with examples.

1. The Lab Notebook

The best, most reliable, and most useful way to record an invention project (conception, building and testing, marketing, etc.) is to use a lab notebook, such as *The Inventor's Notebook,* by Fred Grissom and David Pressman (Nolo). Specifically designed for use with this book, *The Inventor's Notebook* provides organized guidance for properly documenting your invention. More information about *The Inventor's Notebook* and how to order it can be found at the end of this book.

If you're a prolific inventor, or are employed as an engineer or the like, you will want to record a number of inventions as you make and develop them. The best way to do this is by using a blank or lab notebook. Preferably, it should have a stiff cover, with the pages bound in permanently, such as by sewing or gluing or a closed spiral binding. Also, the pages should be consecutively numbered. Lab notebooks of this type are available at engineering and laboratory supply stores, and generally have crosshatched, prenumbered pages with special lines at the bottom of each page for signatures (and signature dates) of the inventor and the witnesses. As should be apparent, the use of a bound, paginated notebook that's faithfully kept up provides a formidable piece of evidence if your inventorship or date of invention is ever called into question, for instance, in an interference proceeding or lawsuit. A bound notebook with consecutively dated, signed, and witnessed entries on sequential pages establishes almost irrefutably that you are the inventor—that is, the first to conceive the invention—on the date indicated in the notebook. Lab notebooks can be purchased through Fisher Scientific in Pittsburgh, Pa.; call 800-766-7000 (www.fishersci.com) and ask for a reseller near you, or Scientific Notebook Co., Tel. 800-537-3028, (www.snco.com).

If you don't have or can't get a formal lab notebook like this, a standard bound letter-paper-size crackle-finish school copybook will serve. Just number all of the pages consecutively yourself, and don't forget the frequent dating, signing, and witnessing, even though there won't be special spaces for this. Date each entry in the notebook as of the date you and your co-inventor(s), if any, make the entries

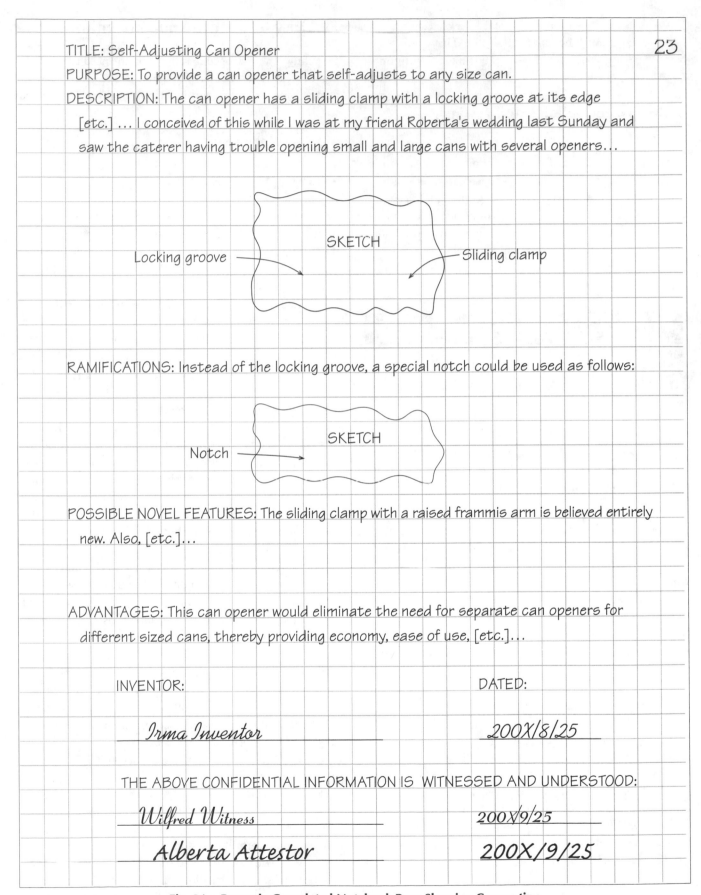

Fig. 3A—Properly Completed Notebook Page Showing Conception

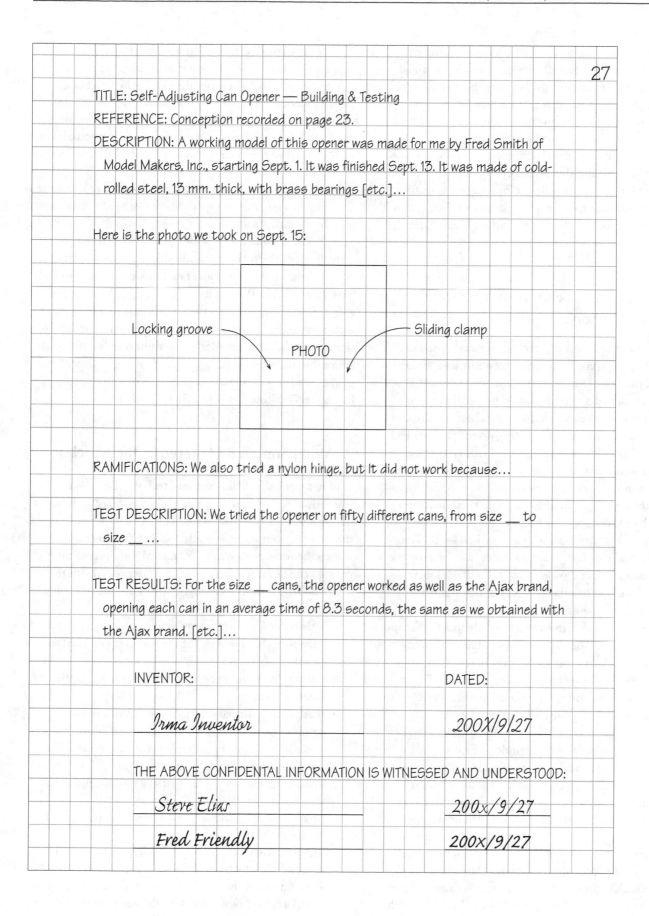

Fig. 3B—Properly Completed Notebook Page Showing Building and Testing

and sign your name(s). If you made the entries over a day or two before you sign and date them, add a brief candid comment to this effect, such as, "I wrote the above on July 17, but forgot to sign and date it until now." Similarly, if you made and/or built the invention some time ago, but haven't made any records until now, again state the full, specific and truthful facts and date the entry as of the date you write the entry and sign it. For example, "I thought of the above invention while trying to open a can of truffles at my sister's wedding reception last July 23 (1995), but didn't write any description of it until now when I read *Patent It Yourself.*"

2. How to Enter Technical Information in the Notebook

Fig. 3A is an example of a properly completed notebook page showing the recordation of conception, and Fig. 3B shows recordation of building and testing.

The sketches and diagrams should be clearly written (preferably double-spaced) in ink to preclude erasure and later-substituted entries. Your writing doesn't have to be beautiful and shouldn't be in legalese. Just make it clear enough for someone else to understand without having to read your mind. Use sketches where possible. Many inventors have told me they put off writing up their invention in a notebook or invention disclosure because they didn't know the proper "legal" terms to use, or had writer's block. However, as indicated, legalese isn't necessary or desirable. There are two very good ways to bypass writer's block:

- Rely mostly on sketches, with brief labels explaining the parts and their functions, or
- Make sketches, describing them orally to a friend, and record your oral description with a tape recorder. Then go back and transcribe your description.

Do not leave any large blank spaces on a page—fill the page up from top to bottom. If you do need to leave space to separate entries, or at the bottom on a page where you have insufficient space to start a new entry, draw a large cross over the blank space to preclude any subsequent entries, or, more accurately, to make it clear that no subsequent entries could have been made in your notebook.

If you make a mistake in an entry, don't attempt to erase it; merely line it out neatly and make a dated note why it was incorrect. The notation of error can be made in the margin adjacent to the correct entry, or it can be made several pages later, provided the error is referred to by page and date. Don't make cumulative changes to a single entry. If more than one change is required, enter them later with

all necessary cross-references to the earlier material they supplement. Refer back to earlier material by page and date.

If possible, make all entries directly in the notebook, or transfer them there from rough notes on the day the notes were made. If this isn't possible, make them as soon as practicable with a notation explaining when the actual work was done, when the entries were made, and why the delay occurred.

If you've made an invention several months ago, and are now going to record it because you've just read this book, you should date the entries in the notebook when you actually write them, but you should also write when you actually made the invention and explain the delay with honesty and candor! Since the notebook is bound, you will have to handwrite the entries in it. Again, don't worry about the quality of your prose—your goal is only to make it clear enough for someone else to understand; use labeled sketches or the tape recorder/transcription techniques given above if writer's block occurs. If handwriting is difficult for you, or if your handwriting is illegible, you can use an Invention Disclosure (see Section G, below).

3. What Should Be Entered in the Notebook

Your notebook should be used as a "technical diary"—that is, you should record in it anything you work on of technical significance, not just inventions. The front of the notebook should have your name and address and the date you started the notebook. When you record the conception of your invention, you and anyone who later sees the notebook will find it most meaningful if you use the following headings:

- Title (what your invention is called)
- Purpose (what purpose the invention is intended to serve)
- Description (a functional and structural description of the invention)
- Sketch (an informal sketch of the invention)
- Ramifications (include all ramifications of the invention that you have conceptualized; If you fail to include a ramification and one of your witnesses thinks of it, the witness may have to be named as a co-inventor if you file a patent application)
- Novel features (include all possible novel features of the invention)
- Closest known prior art (the closest known existing approach of which you're aware), and
- Advantages (of the invention over previous developments and/or knowledge—see the example in Fig. 3A).

Don't forget to sign and date your conception and have two witnesses also sign and date the record of conception. See Section 5, below.

To record the subsequent building and testing of your invention at a later page of the notebook, you will find it most useful to record the following items:

1. Title and Back Reference
2. Technical Description
3. Photos and/or Sketches
4. Ramifications
5. Test Description
6. Test Results
7. Conclusion.

Fig. 3B (above) shows a properly done lab notebook record of the building and testing of an invention. Don't forget to sign and date, and have your witnesses also sign and date, the building and testing record, as well as the conception record. (See Section 5, below.)

If you're skilled enough to conceive, build, and test your invention all at once, just combine all of the items of Figs. 3A and 3B as one entry in your notebook.

I strongly recommend that you record as much factual data as possible; keep conclusions to a minimum and provide them only if they are supported by factual data. Thus, if a mousetrap operated successfully, describe its operation in enough detail to convince the reader that it works. Only then should you put in a conclusion, and it should be kept brief and nonopinionated. For example, "Thus this mousetrap works faster and more reliably than the Ajax brand." Sweeping, opinionated, laudatory statements tend to give an impartial reader a negative opinion of you or your invention. However, it's useful to include the circumstances of conception, such as how you thought it up and where you were. This makes your account believable and helps refresh your memory later.

Word all entries so that they're complete and clear in themselves—that is, so that anyone can duplicate your work without further explanation. While you shouldn't use the lab notebook as a scratch pad to record every calculation and stray concept or note you make or think about, you also shouldn't make your entries so brief as to be of no value should the need for using the notebook as proof later arise. If you're in doubt as to whether to make an entry, make it; it's better to have too much than too little.

Also, you'll find it very helpful to save all of your "other paperwork" involved with the conception, building, and testing of an invention. Such paperwork includes correspondence and purchase receipts. These papers are highly trustworthy and useful as evidence, since they are very difficult to falsify. For example, if you buy a thermometer or have a machine shop make a part for you, you should save receipts and canceled checks from these expenditures since they'll tie in directly with your notebook work.

4. How to Handle Computer Printouts, Large or Formal Sketches, Photos, Charts, or Graphs Drawn on Special Paper

If you have any computer printouts or any other items that by their nature can't be entered directly in the notebook by hand, you should make or enter them on separate sheets. These, too, should be signed, dated, and witnessed and then pasted or affixed in the notebook in proper chronological order. The inserted sheet should be referred to by entries made directly in the notebook, thus tying them in to the other material. Photos or other entries that can't be signed or written should be pasted in the notebook and referenced by legends (descriptive words, such as "photo taken of machine in operation") made directly in the notebook, preferably with lead lines that extend from the notebook page over onto the photo, so as to preclude a charge of substituting subsequently made photos (see Fig. 3B). The page the photo is pasted on should be signed, dated, and witnessed in the usual manner.

If an item covers an entire page, it can be referred to on an adjacent page. It's important to affix the items to the notebook page with a permanent adhesive, such as white glue or nonyellowing (frosty) transparent tape.

If you have to draw a sketch in pencil and want to make a permanent record of it (to put in your notebook) without redrawing the sketch in ink, simply make a photocopy of the penciled sketch: voilà—a permanent copy!

5. Witnessing the Notebook

As I've repeatedly stressed earlier in this chapter, it's important that the notebook entries be witnessed. This is because an inventor's own testimony, even if supported by a properly completed notebook, will often not be adequate for proving an entry date. The witnesses chosen should be as impartial and competent as possible, which means they shouldn't be close relatives or people who have been working so closely with you as to be possible co-inventors. A knowledgeable friend, business associate, or professional will make an excellent witness, provided he or she has the necessary technical ability or background to understand the invention. The witness should also be someone who's likely to be available later. Obviously, a person who's seriously ill, or of very advanced age, wouldn't be a good choice. Don't ask your patent attorney (if you are using one) to perform this function, since the courts and the PTO won't allow an attorney to represent someone and also be that person's witness.

If the invention is a very simple mechanical device, practically anyone will have the technical qualifications to be a witness. But if it involves advanced chemical or electronic concepts, obviously a person with an adequate background in the field will have to be used. The witness need not understand the theory behind the invention, but should be knowledgeable enough to understand what it does and how it works. If called upon later, the witnesses should be able to testify to their own knowledge that the physical and/or chemical facts of the entry are correct. Thus they shouldn't just be witnesses to your signature, so you should not use a notary or a layperson who just witnesses your signature, as do witnesses to a will. Rather the witnesses should actually read or view and understand the actual technical subject material in the notebook, including the actual tests if they are witnessing the building and testing (Fig. 3B). Obviously, then, you should call in your witnesses to observe your final tests and measurements so that they can later testify that they did witness them.

Should You Have Your Notebook Entries or Disclosure Notarized?

Many inventors ask if they should take their notebook or disclosure to a notary and sign it before the notary and have the document notarized. While notarization is slightly better than no witnesses at all, notarization is far inferior to live witnesses. Why? In the U.S. system of jurisprudence, the triers of fact (judge or jury) base their decisions on the testimony of live witnesses, who are subject to cross examination and who understand the document in question and are not merely a "signature witness."

While one witness may be sufficient, the law gives much greater credence to two. If both are available, your case will be very strong. Also having two witnesses will enhance the likelihood of at least one of them being available to testify at a later date. Also, if a dispute occurs between two inventors, the one with the greater number of witnesses will prevail, assuming all other considerations are substantially a wash.

Some notebooks already contain, on each page, a line for the inventor's signature and date, together with the words "Witnessed and Understood" with lines for two signatures and dates. If your notebook doesn't already contain these words and signature lines, merely write them in as indicated in Figs. 3A to 3C. To really tie down the trade secret status of your invention, you should add the words "The above

confidential information is" just before the words "Witnessed and Understood," as has been done on Form 3-2 and on Figs. 3A, 3B, and 3C. You and the witnesses should sign and enter the date on the appropriate lines at the end of your description of the conception of your invention and at the end of your description of your building and testing.

6. What to Do With the Notebook

Now that you've made those nice notebook records of conception and hopefully building and testing, what should you do with the notebook? Basically nothing, except to keep it in a safe place in case it's ever needed (hopefully not!) for one of the six "legal" reasons under Section C, above, and to use it liberally as needed for one of the "invention process" reasons under Section B, above.

G. Another Way to Record Conception or Building and Testing— The Invention Disclosure

Suppose you conclude that for some good reason it's too difficult or inconvenient for you to keep a notebook or technical diary. There's a second, albeit somewhat inferior, way for you to record the conception or building and testing of your invention. This is by using a document called an "Invention Disclosure."

Despite its formidable name, an Invention Disclosure is hardly different from a properly completed notebook entry of an invention. It should be a complete record of your invention, including a title, its purpose(s), advantages, a detailed description of it, in sufficient detail so that one having ordinary skill in the field of your invention will be able to make and use it, possible novel features, ramifications, details of its construction if you built it, and results obtained, if any. While it might better be called an "Invention Record," in the arcane world of patents it's called a "disclosure," since an inventor often uses it to disclose an invention to others to get their opinion, have them develop it, and show what progress is being made. These entries should be made on a separate sheet of paper that has no other information on it except details of your invention and your name and address. For your convenience, Form 3-2 in Appendix 7 provides an Invention Disclosure form, and Fig. 3C illustrates how the form should be completed to record conception.

Since an Invention Disclosure isn't bound, the writing on it can, and preferably should, be printed or typed. But if you do write rather than type, just make sure your hand-

Invention Disclosure

Sheet <u>1</u> of <u>1</u>

Inventor(s): _____ <u>Irma Inventor</u> _____

Address(es): _____ <u>1919 Chestnut St., Philadelphia, PA 19103</u> _____

Title of Invention: <u>Self-Adjusting Can Opener</u> _____

To record **Conception**, describe 1. Circumstances of conception, 2. Purposes and advantages of invention, 3. Description, 4. Sketches, 5. Operation, 6. Ramifications, 7. Possible novel features, and 8. Closest known prior art. To record **Building and Testing**, describe: 1. Any previous disclosure of conception, 2. Construction, 3. Ramifications, 4. Operation and Tests, and 5. Test results. Include sketches and photos, where possible. Continue on additional identical copies of this sheet if necessary; inventors and witnesses should sign all sheets.

1. I thought of this can opener while at my friend Roberta's wedding last Sunday. I saw the caterer having trouble opening small and large cans with several openers. Thinking there was a better way, I recalled my Majestic KY3 sewing machine clamp and how it was adjustable and thought to modify the left arm to accommodate a can opener head.

2. My can opener will work with all sizes of cans and is actually cheaper than the most common existing one, the UR4 made by Ideal Co. of Racine, WI.

3. My can opener comprises a sliding clamp 10, a pincer groove 12, [etc.] as shown in the following sketch:

4. Sketch:

5. Instead of sliding clamp 10, I can use a special notch as follows:

6. I believe that the combination of sliding clamp 10 and pincer groove 12 is a new one for can openers. Also I believe that it may be novel to provide a frammis head with my whatsit.

7. The Acme KZ122 can opener, mfgd. by Acme Kitchenwares of Berkeley, CA, and p. 417 of "Kitchen Tools & Their Uses" (Ready Publishers, Phila. 1981) show the closest can openers to my invention, in addition to the devices already mentioned.

Inventor(s): _____ *Irma Inventor* _____ Date: <u>2002</u> / <u>Jul</u> / <u>6</u>

_____ Date: _____ / _____ / _____

I agree not to disclose the above confidential information. Witnessed and Understood:

Griselda Hammelfarb _____ Date: <u>2002</u> / <u>Jul</u> / <u>7</u>

Neonore Zimla _____ Date: <u>2002</u> / <u>Jul</u> / <u>10</u>

Fig. 3C—Invention Disclosure (Form 3-2 in Appendix 7)

writing is legible. A sheet of professional or personal letter-head (if you have it) is suitable for an Invention Disclosure. Otherwise print your name, address, and telephone number at the top (or bottom, after your signature). Business letter-head is okay if the invention is to be owned by your business. If the disclosure runs to more than one page, you should write the title of your invention on the second and each succeeding page, followed by the word "continued," numbering each page and indicating the total number of pages of the entire disclosure—for example, "Page 1 of 3."

As before, the description of your invention should be signed and dated by you, marked "The above confidential information is Witnessed and Understood," and signed and dated, preferably by two witnesses, who, as before, are technically competent to understand your invention and who actually do understand and have witnessed the subject matter you have entered on your Invention Disclosure. (See Section F5, above.) If you use more than one page, each should be signed and dated by both the inventor and the witnesses.

As with the notebook, if you conceive of an invention on one date and build and test the invention later, you should make two separate invention disclosures—one to record conception and the second to record the building and testing. The second should refer to the first, and both should be signed and dated by you and the witnesses. Refer to Section F, above, to learn how to record building and testing. I haven't provided an example of an Invention Disclosure completed to show building and testing, but it would be similar to the notebook entry to record building and testing (Fig. 3B set out in Section F, above).

Also, as with the notebook, keep the disclosure in a safe place and use it as discussed in Section F6, above.

If you've conceived of or have effectively built and tested your invention on a computer, you must print out a hard copy on paper so that you and your witness can sign it properly. Computer records are too impermanent to be given legal credibility.

EXAMPLE: Nellie Nerdle, while mousing around with a drawing program on her XYZ-98000, puts some triangles, ovals, and bars together and comes up with a new brassiere design. She not only saves it on her hard disk and makes a backup copy, but also makes a paper printout, signs and dates it, writes "Witnessed and Understood:" below her signature, and has her friends, Paul Pocketprotector and Gretchen Guru, sign and date as witnesses so that she'll have a permanent, signed, and dated hard copy of her invention.

If you don't have access to suitable witnesses for your notebook or disclosure—that is, if they are not willing to be a witness, not a close relative, not trustworthy, and not able to understand the invention—you can pay the PTO to be your witness under its Disclosure Document Program (see below).

H. The Disclosure Document Program (DDP)—Or How to Make the PTO Your Witness to Conception

Several years ago the Patent and Trademark Office (PTO) started a program under which it accepts Invention Disclosures and preserves them for two years, or longer if a patent application is filed which refers to the Invention Disclosure. The purpose of this service, for which the PTO charges a small fee (see Appendix 4, Fee Schedule), is to provide credible evidence of the conception date and inventorship for inventors who, for some reason, cannot or don't wish to rely on witnesses. There's no doubt that, in case of an interference or other proceeding where the date of invention or inventorship itself is at issue, the PTO will regard a copy of a PTO-filed Disclosure Document as excellent evidence of conception.

Despite these advantages, I generally recommend that most inventors not use the DDP. Although the PTO's small fee per invention may not seem like much, the methods I've described earlier for recording your invention are free and, in fact, will give you (a) equally good or better evidence of conception and, more importantly, (b) evidence of building and testing. This is because live witnesses can testify to additional facts surrounding conception, and can also testify that they actually saw the building, testing, and operation of your invention. Also, a DDP record isn't as usable in court as a notebook or invention disclosure, since you won't have witnesses to validate the DDP record. Simply put, I hate to see you unnecessarily spend money for an inferior "product."

The table, "Comparison of PTO's Disclosure Document Program (DDP) With Disclosure (or Notebook) Showing Conception" (below) presents the advantages and disadvantages of the DDP compared to Notebook entries.

In the event you do choose to utilize the PTO's DDP, remember several things that I've put into Form 3-3 to remind you: The DDP is not a substitute for filing a patent application or for building and testing the invention. Also, it won't provide you with any "grace period" or any other justification for delaying the filing of a patent application. It's merely an alternative way to get your conception disclosure witnessed. Moreover, even if

Comparison of PTO's Disclosure Document Program (DDP) With Disclosure (or Notebook) Showing Conception	
DDP	**Signed & Dated + Witnessed & Dated Record of Conception**
Plus. Ironclad evidence of date of conception and inventorship	**Negative.** Record may be lost or witness may be unreliable or unavailable
Plus. No need to find or explain invention to witnesses or have them sign	**Negative.** Must find and explain invention to witnesses and have them sign
Plus. Can be used by foreign inventors to establish a "U.S. date"	
Negative. In case of an interference or other trial, must secure testimony of witnesses	**Plus.** In case of an interference or other trial, no need to secure testimony of witnesses
Negative. Must prepare transmittal letter for PTO	**Plus.** No need to prepare any formal papers
Negative. Must send papers with receipt postcard to PTO	**Plus.** No need to send any papers anywhere (but paper records should be preserved)
Negative. Fee (small) required to record (see Section H)	**Plus.** No fee involved
Negative. A patent application must be filed within two years or the DD is destroyed, although the inventor's copy can still be used thereafter	**Plus.** No deadline for filing a patent application

you use the DDP to record your conception, you should still use a lab notebook or separate sheets with proper witnessing to record all the pertinent facts if you build and test your invention. Finally, filing a Disclosure Document with the PTO doesn't allow you to refer to the invention as "Patent Pending" or "Patent Applied For." (It's actually a criminal offense, punishable by a $500 fine, to refer to an invention as "Patent Pending" where no provisional or regular patent application has been filed.)

If you still wish to file a disclosure with the PTO under its Disclosure Document Program, simply send the following four items to Mail Stop DD, Commissioner for Patents, P.O. Box 1450, Alexandria, VA 22313-1450:

1. A letter requesting that the attached disclosure be accepted under the Disclosure Document Program (complete Form 3-3 in Appendix 7)
2. A Credit Card Payment Form (Form 10-4) or check for the specified fee, payable to the Commissioner for Patents. (Regrettably, I can't provide a form for this; you'll have to use your own check!)
3. One copy of your notebook entry (see Section F, above) or Invention Disclosure (completed Form 3-2—see Section G, above)
4. A stamped receipt postcard. The postcard should have your name and address on the front side and a description of your disclosure on the reverse side.

Disclosure Documents may also be filed (by hand or mail delivery) with the Great Lakes Patent and Trademark Center at the Detroit Public Library and the South Central Intellectual Property Partnership at Rice University in Houston. See Fig. 6K.

The disclosure sheets must be numbered and letter size (8.5" x 11") or A4 size (210 mm x 297 mm). You should submit a photocopy of your original signed and witnessed disclosure and keep your original. (You don't have to have an original ink signature, or any signature at all, on the copy of the disclosure that you send to the PTO, but I recommend that you do sign and date your notebook or disclosure to make them more believable in case you ever have to go to court.)

The PTO will stamp all of the papers with the date of receipt and an identifying number and will return the postcard. The date and number on the returned postcard is important and should be carefully preserved.

If you file a Disclosure Document with the PTO and then do nothing else, the PTO will keep the original of your request letter and your disclosure for two years and then destroy them. However, if you later file a patent application on the invention described in your disclosure, you should do so within two years of filing the disclosure. You should also file a separate reference letter in the application, referring to the disclosure (use Form 3-4 in Appendix 7). The PTO will then retain the disclosure indefinitely in case you ever need to rely on it in connection with your patent application. Be sure to file the reference letter within two years of filing the Disclosure Document; otherwise the disclosure will have already been destroyed by the PTO, even if you have filed a patent application. (This is another serious disadvantage of the DDP.)

As I'll discuss in more depth later, in Chapters 11 and 16, many disreputable organizations exist to prey on and exploit inventors. They've even gotten to the DDP. Here are three scams I recently encountered involving the DDP. In one, an inventor was charged $200 by an "invention developer" to file his DDP. In another, a company advertised as follows:

PATENT PROTECTION FOR ONLY $10

A **government sponsored** program requires: Only a $10 registration fee to legally secure your "first priority" filing status for a 2-year period. Conserve your capital. Market NOW— patent later. For application kit send $10 to: xxxxxxxxxxx.

100% GUARANTEED

In a third, an organization advertised that there's no need to search inventions or file patent applications— they're a waste of time and money. An inventor, the ad said, can secure adequate protection for an invention by using a "special government program" whereby the Patent Office will record and preserve any invention for a nominal fee. All the inventor had to do was to sign up and pay the organization about $400 to enter this "special" program.

All three scams indicated that the inventor could "secure priority," "reserve rights," or take advantage of a "grace period" for two years. However, as stated, the DDP is merely a substitute for witnesses to your *conception*—nothing more! If you want to secure proper and full offensive rights on your creation against independent creators and copiers, you *must* patent it. If you want to record conception and/or building and testing to take advantage of the benefits enumerated in Sections B and C, just fill out Form 3-2; you needn't pay anybody anything!

You can now sue scam operators or so-called "Invention Developers" for making false statements or omitting material information from their sales pitch. (35 USC 297.)

Recording Conception by an Online Service

Some online services offer to record computer files for a charge. Although these services use encryption, digital time stamping, and other security measures, I don't favor this type of service because it has not been tested in court or the PTO, and because it's very easy to complete your own invention disclosure using the techniques in this chapter.

I. The Provisional Patent Application— A Substitute for Building and Testing, With Some Disadvantages

⚠ For reasons explained in Section E, above, it's very important to build and test your invention as soon as possible. If you haven't read that section yet, do so now.

Suppose you don't have the facilities, skill, or time to build and test your invention, and you are not in a position to file a complete utility patent application right away. In this case you may file a Provisional Patent Application (PPA) which will serve as a legal alternative to building and testing a utility invention. (The PPA is not available for designs.) Let's explore the PPA and the advantages and disadvantages of using it.

1. What a Provisional Patent Application (PPA) Is

A PPA is a short version of a regular patent application. It is used to establish an early filing date for a later-filed Regular Patent Application (RPA). A PPA must contain:

  a. a detailed description of the invention telling how to make and use it

  b. drawing(s), if necessary to understand how to make and use the invention

  c. a cover sheet and fee transmittal form

  d. a fee (small entity (SE) or large entity—see Appendix 4, Fee Schedule), and

  e. a return receipt postcard.

(The PTO no longer requires a Small-Entity Declaration.)

In actuality the term "PPA" is a misnomer, since it is a simple document deposit, not an application (a request for something). I like to call a PPA a DPED (Domestic Priority Establishing Document) to avoid confusion. Some inventors and publications have improperly referred to it as a "provisional patent." Since a PPA is not even an application, it is not and should never be called a patent.

2. What a PPA Is Not

A PPA is not a regular patent application (RPA) and therefore cannot by itself result in a patent. For those readers already familiar with the regular patent application process described in Chapter 8, the PPA, unlike an RPA, does not require:

- a Patent Application Declaration (PAD)
- an Information Disclosure Statement (IDS)
- patent claims
- an abstract and summary
- a description of the invention's background, or
- a statement of the invention's objects and advantages.

If you don't file an RPA within a year of your PPA's filing date, your PPA will go abandoned and will be forever useless. Also, your PPA cannot provide a filing date for subject matter that is not disclosed in it.

3. What a PPA Accomplishes

You can use a PPA in several ways, but only one use—the substitute for building and testing—is relevant here, so I'll detail only this use now, but will mention the other uses briefly.

If you choose to not build and test your invention right away, or are unable to do so, the next best step would normally be to file an RPA as soon as possible. But this approach can be very costly, especially if you are not sure that your invention will bring in very much money, assuming a patent issues on it. So, assuming you decide that an RPA is not appropriate, your next best step is to file a PPA. Not only are the filing fees associated with a PPA much less than an RPA ($100 as opposed to $500 as of January 2005), but the cost of preparing a PPA is also less than an RPA.

Once you file a PPA, you will be considered to have reduced your invention to practice, even if you've done nothing to build and test it, assuming that:

- an RPA (and optionally one or more foreign patent applications) are filed on the invention within one year, and
- the PPA fully describes the invention claimed in the RPA.

Being able to claim the PPA's filing date as a reduction to practice means you can use that date to:

- overcome the date of any prior art reference that is cited in opposition to your application

- establish your invention's priority in an interference (a procedure conducted by the PTO to decide which of two or more pending patent applications that claim the same invention should receive the patent), and
- antedate any publication of the invention so that any such publication will not be "prior art" to your subsequently filed RPA.

Provisional Patent Application Compared to the Disclosure Document Program

In a way, the PPA program is analogous to the Disclosure Document Program (DDP—Section H, above). The DDP provides a record of conception for those who don't have any witnesses, while the PPA provides the equivalent of an RTP (Reduction to Practice) for any inventors who can't get witnesses to their building and testing, or who aren't able to build and test. In both cases, the filed documents only establish priority over other inventions or prior-art references, and don't themselves lead to a patent or affect its term—for that, a regular patent application is required. To obtain a patent you must file a complete, regular patent application as described in Chapters 8 and 10.

The table below presents the advantages and disadvantages of the PPA compared to Notebook entries showing building and testing.

4. Advantages of a PPA Over Building and Testing

In addition to the benefits of an early filing date, the PPA gives you the right to claim that your invention has "patent pending" status. In common parlance this means that you can publish, sell, or show your invention to others without fear of theft or loss of any domestic rights. (See Chapter 11, Section G.) This is because anyone who sees and steals your invention after you file your PPA would have a later filing date than yours, so you would almost certainly be able to win any interference with the thief. To win, the thief would have to prove conception of the invention before you did, and was diligently attempting to reduce it to practice (by filing a PPA, RPA, or building and testing it) at the very time that you filed your PPA. This would be very hard to prove unless it were true.

Comparison of PTO's Provisional Patent Application (PPA) With Disclosure (or Notebook) Showing Building & Testing	
PPA	**Signed & Dated + Witnessed & Dated Record of Building & Testing**
Plus. Ironclad evidence of date of reduction to practice (RTP) and inventorship	**Negative.** Record may be lost or witness may be unreliable or unavailable
Plus. No need to build and test invention	**Negative.** Must build and test invention
Plus. No need to find or show working invention to witnesses or have them sign	**Negative.** Must find and show working invention to witnesses and have them sign
Plus. A technical article can be used as the PPA, provided it clearly teaches how to make and use the invention	**Negative.** A technical article cannot be used unless it clearly teaches how to make and use the invention and is signed, dated, and witnessed
Plus. In case of an interference or other trial, no need to secure testimony of witnesses	**Negative.** In case of an interference or other trial, must secure testimony of witnesses
Plus. Can call invention "patent pending"	**Negative.** Cannot call invention "patent pending"
Plus. If a patent issues from a regular patent application that is based upon a PPA, the patent will be considered prior art (against later-filed patent applications) as of the PPA's filing date	**Negative.** If a regular patent application (RPA) is filed without being based upon a PPA, the actual filing date of the RPA (not the date of record) will be considered the date of the patent for prior art purposes
Plus. If the PTO finds relevant prior art that is earlier than an RPA, but not earlier than a PPA on which the RPA is based, it will usually not even cite such prior art against the RPA if it finds that the PPA clearly discloses the invention. Even if it cites such prior art, the applicant in the RPA can quickly antedate such art by citing the PPA.	**Negative.** If the PTO finds relevant prior art that is earlier than an RPA, it will cite it against the RPA. The applicant must compile evidence and submit a declaration to prove building and testing of the invention prior to the date of such prior art.
Plus. Can be used by foreign inventors to establish a "U.S. date"	
Negative. Must prepare application or paper with full disclosure teaching how to make and use invention	**Plus.** No need to prepare full disclosure so long as record shows building and testing
Negative. Must prepare transmittal letter for PTO	**Plus.** No need to prepare any formal papers
Negative. Must send papers with receipt postcard to PTO	**Plus.** No need to send any papers anywhere
Negative. Fee required to file (see Appendix 4). (However, a PPA's filing fee is much cheaper than an RPA's.)	**Plus.** No fee involved
Negative. The RPA—and any foreign applications you wish to file—must be filed one year from the PPA's filing in order to obtain the benfit of such date	**Plus.** If the RPA is filed over a year after the date of building and testing, it will still be entitled to such date provided an unreasonable time has not elapsed and the inventor has not abandoned the invention

There are other advantages to using a PPA in place of actually building and testing the invention. These are:

- You need not incur the expense and time usually involved in building and testing an invention in order to reduce it to practice.
- You need not keep meticulous records of whatever building and testing you do accomplish.
- You need not obtain witnesses.
- You can be certain that your PPA will provide excellent proof of inventorship.
- You will be certain that your PPA's early filing date can be relied upon, provided your description of the invention in the PPA is legally sufficient as described below. (To rely on an actual reduction to practice by building and testing your invention, you have to keep adequate records of your building and testing activities and be prepared to prove the validity of these records in a court or in an interference.)
- You can file a technical article (which you might have written anyway) as a PPA. (But remember, the PPA article must fully disclose how to make and use the invention claimed in the RPA. As stated, the RPA must be filed within one year.)
- You can file a PPA, then within one year, file an RPA, which has the practical effect of delaying examination of the RPA and extending—up to one year—your patent's expiration date. In other words a PPA gives you a filing date that does not start your 20-year patent term. Pushing your patent monopoly term ahead a year can be profitable if your invention is ahead of its time and is likely to have its best sales 20 years from now—for example, as often happens with drugs. However, if you have built and tested your invention and made a proper record of this (see Section F3), you can also safely push your monopoly ahead by filing your RPA later. (A PPA can be converted to an RPA (Rule 53(c)(3)) but I advise against doing so since the patent will expire 20 years from the filing date of the PPA rather than 20 years from the filing date of the RPA.)
- If you've filed an RPA and wish to restart your 20-year term, you can do so by converting the RPA to a PPA and then filing a second RPA. To make the conversion, file a petition (a simple request letter will do) with the prescribed conversion fee (see Fee Schedule in Appendix 4) within one year of the RPA's filing date. The PPA will take the first RPA's filing date. Then file the second RPA, also within one year of the first RPA's filing date. The second RPA should claim the benefit of the PPA's filing date. The second RPA will expire 20 years from its own filing date, so you've restarted your 20-year term about a year later, albeit at a price.

- You can refer to your invention as patent pending once you've filed a PPA. This can be a marketing advantage, and some companies will not discuss any invention that is not patent pending.

  Suppose you file a PPA and then, within a year, you file an RPA which claims the benefit of the PPA's filing date. If your RPA issues as a patent it will be effective as a prior-art reference as of its PPA's filing date.
- If you are able to license or sell your invention before it is time to file a PPA, your licensee or buyer will have the opportunity to prepare and file the RPA using their own lawyers.
- Preparing an RPA after you've prepared a PPA will give you a second opportunity to perfect your application.

5. Disadvantages of the PPA

Alas, every silver box seems to contain a cloud: The disadvantages of filing a PPA are as follows:

1. You may tend to forgo building and testing and lose the concomitant advantages, such as determining whether the invention is operable, practical, or useful, and having a working prototype to demonstrate to prospective manufacturers. (See Section E above.)
2. Your PPA may fail to contain a full a description of how to make and use the invention or any embodiment of it. In this case, you won't be able to rely on the PPA's filing date for the invention or any embodiment.
3. You may unintentionally forgo foreign protection. This is because you cannot wait one year after filing the RPA, as is usually done, to foreign file. Instead you must make your foreign filing decision, as well as your regular U.S. filing decision, within one year after your PPA is filed. As I will discuss in Chapter 12, foreign filing is extremely expensive and few foreign filers ever earn their outlay back.
4. You may try to license or interest a manufacturer in your invention in the approximately ten-month period between the time you file the PPA and the time you must begin preparation of your RPA. Since ten months is usually too short a period to license an invention, you may get discouraged and fail to file an RPA and thus give up a potentially valuable invention.
5. If you file an RPA which claims the date of your PPA, and you do not file a Nonpublication Request (see Chapter 10), at the time you file the RPA, your RPA will be published 18 months after you file the PPA, or about six months after you file the RPA. You may not want your application published so early.

6. A PPA's date can be relied upon only if an RPA is filed within one year, while a properly witnessed record of building and testing generally can be relied upon even if the RPA is filed several years later.

7. If you file a PPA and then file an RPA claiming benefit of the PPA, but don't file a Nonpublication Request (see Chapter 10), your RPA will be published about six months after your RPA's filing date. Such a publication will destroy the trade secret status, if any, of your invention at an early date.

6. Should You File a PPA?

For the reasons stated above, I recommend that you file a PPA only if you are not in a position to build and test your invention, properly document your activities, and have your documentation witnessed, and one of the following four reasons applies:

1. you have a good invention on which you wish to file an RPA, but are not currently able to do so due to lack of funds or resources, or

2. you wish to lock in an early date, since you feel your invention is potentially valuable and might be independently developed by others or stolen from you, or

3. a paper or other public disclosure of your invention is going to be made and you don't have evidence sufficient to show that your "date of invention" (Chapter 5, Section E1) antedates the public disclosure, or

4. a paper or other public disclosure of your invention was already made, for example 11.5 months ago, and you don't have time to prepare and file an RPA before the one-year deadline.

7. How to Prepare and File a PPA

Ideally, the more your PPA resembles the RPA you file within the following year, the more you can be assured that you will be able to claim the PPA's filing date. Conversely, the less the PPA resembles the RPA, the more work the patent examiner will have to do to determine whether your PPA fully discloses the invention being claimed in the RPA—which means a greater chance you will be denied the PPA's filing date. And so, my general recommendation is that you follow the basic rules for writing an RPA set out in Chapter 10 (double- or 1½-spacing and with 1" margins, ample headings, short sentences, and a clear description). But, since your PPA will not be examined by the PTO unless and until you file an RPA—and then only to see whether it adequately describes the invention being claimed in the RPA—your description need not:

- be a polished presentation (it should be clearly written and understandable),
- contain claims, or
- be typed in any particular format.

To prepare and file a PPA, you should complete five steps:

1. prepare drawings, if necessary (these need not be polished, but should be understandable)

2. prepare a complete description of the structure and operation of your invention

3. prepare a cover letter and fee transmittal

4. attach a check or credit card payment form for the filing fee and a postcard, and

5. mail all papers to the PTO.

In keeping with my recommendation that you make your PPA look as much like your RPA as is feasible, I recommend that you prepare your drawings and description as I describe in Chapter 8. Although you legally don't need to include the Background, Objects, and Advantages, Description of Drawing Figures, List of Reference Numerals, Summary, Conclusion, or Abstract parts of the specification, it won't hurt if you do, and including these parts will make your PPA that much more effective if it is later examined. Your drawings can be informal drawings; they need not be inked or done carefully with a CAD program, but they (and the description) must be in permanent form (no pencil).

You also don't need to include any claims (Chapter 9). However, if possible, it is a good idea to draft some claims before filing the PPA, since this exercise will help you determine whether your detailed description includes everything necessary about your invention. Also some foreign jurisdictions may require that the application contain a claim to obtain priority.

⚠ Provide a Full Description of Your Invention. While it need not be well written or use any legalese, your "description" MUST comply with the full disclosure requirements—that is, it MUST clearly teach how to make and use the invention and it MUST disclose the best mode or version you currently prefer, if it has several modes or versions. To this end, I suggest you carefully review and follow Chapter 8, Section F, which discusses these requirements in detail.

Your description should be written in as simple terms as possible so that a lay judge can understand it or can be easily taught to understand it. If the invention is technical or abstruse, start your description from ground zero, assuming your reader knows nothing about the field, and then gradually move up to the minimum technical level necessary, defining all technical terms. In addition, your invention must be in a statutory class (see Chapter 5, Section C, for more on statutory classes). For software inventions, this means that the invention must have a tangible, concrete, and useful result and not be a pure algorithm.

If you have several inventions, you can put them all into the PPA, even if they're not related. If you know of several embodiments of any invention, put them all in, even if you have doubts about the operability of any embodiment. The PTO will never read your PPA unless they need to verify that it supports an invention or embodiment that you are claiming in an RPA that you file within one year after you file the PPA. As with the invention disclosure, I recommend that you include as many embodiments of your basic invention as you can think of, even if some may not work. For more information on preparing a provisional patent application, review either *Patent Pending in 24 Hours,* by Richard Stim and David Pressman (Nolo), or *Patent Pending Now,* a software program from Nolo (www.nolo.com) that assists in the drafting of a PPA.

PPAs: The Long and the Short

You can produce an adequate PPA with a minimum amount of work. How little is required? You can fully describe your invention by supplying the information contained in the Description and Operation sections of the Specification in the RPA (and drawings, if necessary). In others words, if you follow the instructions for drafting these two sections in Chapter 8, Section I, you will have an adequate PPA.

For reasons stated in this section, I recommend a richer or more fulsome PPA. This should include information contained in other sections of the RPA (the Background, Objects and Advantages, Drawing Figures, Reference Numerals, Summary, Description, Operation, at least one Claim, and the Abstract). If you follow the instructions for drafting these sections in Chapters 8 and 9, you will have a more-than-adequate PPA.

To give you an idea of the difference between the bare-bones and recommended PPA, I have prepared two PPAs using the same invention (Pat No. 6,018,830, Adjustable Sleeping Bag With Drawcords). Fig. 3E provides an example of the bare-bones approach; while Fig. 3F shows a preferred, fulsome PPA.

After you feel that you've prepared an adequate and full description of your invention—and any necessary drawings—you're ready to prepare the cover letter and fee transmittal. You'll be relieved to learn that this is a simple matter. A cover letter form is provided in Appendix 7 as Form 3-5, and the fee transmittal is Form 10-3; completion is straightforward (the fee is in Appendix 4). First read the cover letter to note all of the disadvantages of the PPA. I put these in the cover letter to warn you of them, as they are significant. If you understand and accept these disadvantages, then simply fill in the name(s) and legal residences of the inventor(s), a title, the number of sheets of specification, and the number of sheets of drawing. The title and name(s) of the inventor(s) are tentative and can be changed later, so long as one inventor named in the PPA is also named in the RPA and that inventor's invention is claimed in the RPA and fully disclosed in the PPA. However, if your RPA contains any essential information that isn't in your PPA, you may not be able to rely on your PPA. So again, be sure your description is adequate and complete.

You are entitled to file as a small entity (SE) if you are an independent inventor, or you don't have an obligation to assign or license the invention to a for-profit organization with over 500 employees. If you file as an SE, you can pay half the fees of a large entity. Complete the "Check or Credit Card" line (the fee schedule is in Appendix 4). If there are co-inventors only one inventor's signature and address is required.

If you want to get an instant filing date, obtain an Express Mail envelope and label from your post office and complete the Express Mail section. (See Chapter 10, Section L.) I recommend that you file your PPA as soon as possible after conception.

Make a complete copy of all papers of your PPA and mount them in a separate "legal" file.

Attach a check or Credit Card Payment Form for the appropriate filing fee and a stamped receipt postcard. Address the front of the postcard to yourself and list on the back all of the papers you're sending for the PPA. Fig 3D provides an example of a completed postcard. If you don't have any postcards, just use a blank 4" x 6" card (preferably colored, so it can be spotted more readily if mixed with other mail) and a postcard-rate stamp.

Provisional Patent Application of Ignatz Inventor and Imogene Inventress for "[Title of Invention]" consisting of ten sheets of specification, three sheets of drawing, cover letter, fee transmittal, $80 check (or Credit Card Payment Form) for filing fee, and receipt postcard filed today.

Fig. 3D—Back Side of Exemplary Receipt Postcard for PPA

Provisional Patent Application of

Robert H. Howe

for

TITLE: ADJUSTABLE SLEEPING BAG WITH DRAWCORDS

DESCRIPTION

FIG. 1 is a perspective view taken from the user's right side of a sleeping bag 11 constructed in accordance with the invention. An upper portion 12 of the bag has a drawcord 14, circumferentially mounted within a fabric casing sleeve 15, and secured by cord lock 16. Such cord arrangements are repeated at each of locations 19, 20, 21, and 22. Each sleeve 15 and each contained drawcord 14 extends only across the upper portion of the bag, from a zipper 17 on the right side of the bag, to a corresponding location 18 (FIG. 2) on the left side. The bottom portion of the bag (not shown) has no drawcords. The drawcords are made of stretchable elastic or nonstretchable material (nylon), while the sleeves are preferably made of the same material as the bag's outer shell, e.g., nylon or rayon. Such sleeves may be sewed, glued, or thermally bonded to the outside of the outer shell.

FIG. 2 is a left perspective view of the bag, showing left-side seam 18 and showing drawcord 14 mounted within sleeve 15 and secured by cord lock 16 at locations 19, 20, 21, and 22. Note that each sleeve 15 and its contained drawcord extends only over the top portion of the bag, from seam 18 to zipper 17.

FIG. 3 is a lateral cross-section through bag 11 at location 19 showing zipper 17, side seam 18, and drawcord 14 relaxed and secured by cord lock 16 while mounted within fabric casing sleeve 15. Sleeve 15 is sewn to outer shell fabric 25. Inner lining fabric 24 and insulation 23 are not compressed since drawcord 14 is relaxed. An occupant 26 of the bag is shown in a horizontal

Fig. 3E—Provisional Patent Application Without Embellishments

2

position; note that the bag fits loosely around the occupant and that there is a lot of air space between occupant 26 and the bag. A conventional underlying insulating pad or mat 27, e.g., of foam is used under the bag.

FIG. 4 is a lateral cross-section through sleeping bag 11 at location 19 with drawcord 14 tightened and secured by cord lock 16. Inner lining fabric 24 and insulation 23 are gathered together where they are surrounded by tightened drawcord 14. Note that the bag now fits relatively closely or tightly around occupant 26 and that there is very little air space left between occupant 26 and the bag. Insulating pad 27 is again shown under the bag.

OPERATION

In operation one uses the bag in a normal manner with insulating pad 27 under the bag. The user can, when desired, increase the warmth of the bag by tightening the drawcords and securing them with cord lock 16 (FIGS. 3 and 4). When the drawcords are tightened, five effects increase the bag's warmth:

(1) Insulating layer 23 and the inner lining fabric 24 surrounding occupant 26 become thicker.

(2) This increase in thickness also makes the bag less susceptible to the user narrowing the insulation by body movement, e.g., by poking the insulation with an elbow.

(3) The surface area of outer shell fabric 25 exposed to cold air is reduced.

(4) Since the drawcord extends only over upper portion 12 of the bag, lower portion 13 does not tend to be raised from pad 27 beneath the bag to be exposed to cold air.

(5) The air space between occupant 26 and the bag is reduced.

When the user wishes to increase the inner volume of the bag to provide greater freedom of movement (at some loss of insulating ability), it is only necessary to relax the drawcords (FIG. 3) and allow the bag to expand.

Fig. 3E—Provisional Patent Application Without Embellishments (continued)

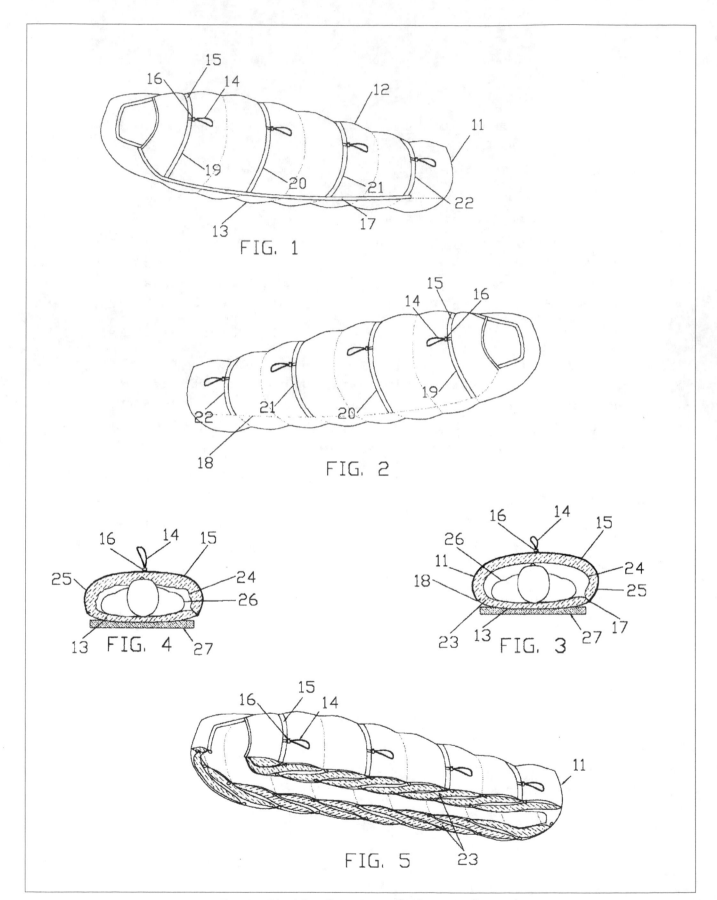

FIG. 1

FIG. 2

FIG. 4

FIG. 3

FIG. 5

Fig. 3E—Provisional Patent Application (Drawings)

Provisional Patent Application of

Robert H. Howe

For

TITLE: ADJUSTABLE SLEEPING BAG WITH DRAWCORDS

CROSS-REFERENCE TO RELATED APPLICATIONS: None.

FEDERALLY SPONSORED RESEARCH: None.

SEQUENCE LISTING: None.

BACKGROUND

This invention relates to sleeping bags, specifically to insulated sleeping bags having means that allow users to adjust the insulating ability and internal volume of the bags. Sleeping bags can be uncomfortable, and when they're uncomfortable, they can deny their users much-needed rest. Sleeping bag comfort is largely a matter of warmth—that is, providing the bag's user with the correct amount of insulation to suit the existing conditions—and a matter of providing the user with adequate freedom of movement. These two aspects of sleeping bag comfort can work against each other. For similarly shaped bags, the more room there is inside a bag, the more freedom of movement its user has. However, the more room inside a bag, the more air space the user's body is required to heat and the more outer bag surface is exposed to the cold. Most sleeping bags provide comfort in only a rather narrow range of temperatures. So, sleeping bag manufacturers have long sought means of effectively adjusting the suitability of sleeping bags to fit a wider range of temperatures.

Both U.S. Pat. No. 2,350,410 to Matthesius (1944) and U.S. Pat. No. 1,583,419 to Perl (1926) show sleeping wraps for infants. These bags have side

Fig. 3F—Provisional Patent Application With Embellishments

2

cords which are tied around the upper portion of each of the wraps after an
infant is placed on top of the wrap and the flat sides of the wrap are folded
around the infant. With both of these wraps the cords are primarily to allow
one to complete closure of the wraps. Therefore, they should not be considered
sleeping bags but rather, what they clearly are—sleeping wraps for infants.
Perl states, "the straps 15 will serve to prevent the possible moving and
kicking of the infant from dislodging the cover portion."

Both wraps are flat, it is presumed, because it is easier and safer to lay
a sometimes struggling, usually writhing infant on a flat surface and fold and
tie the sides around the infant than it is to insert the infant into a bag.
While the cords of these two wraps may be drawn more or less tightly about the
infant before tying, neither wrap is adapted for simple adjustment of its
internal volume.

One method used to optimize the warmth and roominess of a sleeping bag is
shown in U.S. Pat. No. 5,473,779 to Kramer (1995), where nonadjustable, permanently attached bands of elastic material are incorporated into the portion of
the bag surrounding the user's knees and legs. The object is to provide
increased freedom of movement while still reducing the inner volume of the bag
to optimize bag warmth. However the greater freedom of movement is provided
only to the knees and legs. The bag cannot be adjusted to adapt it for cooler
or warmer temperatures.

The lower portions of insulated sleeping bags are typically less insulated
than the upper portions of the same bags because bag manufacturers rely on bag
users to employ well-insulated mats under the sleeping bags. Bag manufacturers
rely on such mats for good reasons—they are cheap, effective, and not as
compressed by the weight of the user as is the insulation contained in the
lower portion of a sleeping bag. If a good insulating mat is not placed under
a sleeping bag, it is likely that more warmth will be lost to the ground by
conduction than will be lost by convection to the air above the sleeper.

However even if a good ground pad is used with the bag shown in U.S. Pat.
No. 4,888,828 to Tatsuno (1989), its effectiveness will be reduced. This is
because Tatsuno uses non-adjustable elastic members that are permanently sewn
into the bag in circumferential rings spaced axially along the bag. These
rings totally encircle the bag and the bag's user and this presents a problem.

Fig. 3F—Provisional Patent Application With Embellishments (continued)

3

By totally encircling the bag, each elasticized member pulls an area of the lower portion of the bag up and away from the underlying insulated pad. Thus, these areas are no longer insulated by full contact with the underlying insulating mat as they would otherwise be, but are instead exposed to cold air.

Roach, in U.S. Pat. No. 4,894,878 (1990) shows a bag with a liner whose circumferential dimension can be reduced by a zipper to create increased overlap of the bag's insulating batts and hence more insulation. However, it is difficult to reach an inside zipper to make the necessary adjustment.

Hunt, in U.S. Pat. No. 3,857,125 (1974) shows an insulated bag with inner and outer shell layers that are differentially cut, except in a small portion of the bag, that provides more freedom of movement for the user's shoulders. This differential cut, Hunt claims, minimizes compression of the insulation when body pressures are exerted against the outer shell. Hunt also claims that the inner shell provides self-adjusting inward lofting of the insulation in the shoulder and chin areas. Hunt's bag provides a hood that surrounds the user's face. Hunt positions the adjustable end of a drawcord used to tighten this hood at one side of the user's face and sews the drawcord to the bag at the other side of the user's face. This, it is claimed, allows the user to independently adjust the tightness of that part of the hood that is above the face. While the effectiveness of providing separate adjustability in areas that are so close together is debatable, one thing is certain: Hunt's bag in no way addresses the need for a bag with adjustability in the fit of the upper insulation.

Demini Sports, of Amsterdam, Holland, has sold a sleeping bag since the early 1970s with drawcords which encircle the bag at spaced locations along the bag. However these bags suffer from the same defect as Tatsuno's, above. I.e., since the means for compressing the bag completely encircle it, they draw the lower portion of the bag away from the underlying insulating ground pad, which, as stated, users normally provide under this type of bag.

In conclusion, insofar as I am aware, no sleeping bag formerly developed provides volume adjustability to a user without the defect of drawing the lower portion of the bag away from the underlying insulating ground pad.

Fig. 3F—Provisional Patent Application With Embellishments (continued)

4

SUMMARY

   The invention, an improved sleeping bag, has adjustable drawcords attached
to the outer shell fabric. These drawcords extend only over the top portion of
the bag. Cord locks are provided to tighten the drawcords to any desired degree
of warmth. The drawcords are encased in drawcord sheaths extending only across
the upper portion of the bag. This allows a user to reduce the inner air space
of the bag without reducing the effectiveness of the insulation of the lower
portion of the bag and without the discomfort of inner encircling drawcords.

   Accordingly several objects and advantages of the invention are to provide
an improved sleeping bag, to provide means of increasing the warmth of a
sleeping bag during cooler weather, to provide a bag with increased freedom of
movement during warmer weather, and to provide a more user-friendly, yet
economical sleeping bag. Still further objects and advantages will become
apparent from a study of the following description and the accompanying drawings.

DRAWINGS

   FIG. 1 is a perspective right-side view of a sleeping bag constructed in
accordance with the invention, showing the upper half of the bag.

   FIG. 2 is a perspective left-side view of the sleeping bag of FIG. 1.

   FIG. 3 is a lateral cross-sectional view of the sleeping bag of FIGS. 1 and
2 with the drawcord relaxed.

   FIG. 4 is a lateral cross-sectional view of the sleeping bag of FIGS. 1 and
2 with the drawcord tightened.

   FIG. 5 is a perspective view of the bag taken from above, showing its
insulation.

DETAILED DESCRIPTION

   FIG. 1 is a perspective view taken from the user's right side of a sleeping
bag 11 constructed in accordance with the invention. An upper portion 12 of
the bag has a drawcord 14, circumferentially mounted within a fabric casing
sleeve 15, and secured by cord lock 16. Such cord arrangements are repeated at
each of locations 19, 20, 21, and 22. Each sleeve 15 and each contained

Fig. 3F—Provisional Patent Application With Embellishments (continued)

5

drawcord 14 extends only across the upper portion of the bag, from a zipper 17 on the right side of the bag, to a corresponding location 18 (FIG. 2) on the left side. The bottom portion of the bag (not shown) has no drawcords. The drawcords are made of stretchable elastic or nonstretchable material (nylon), while the sleeves are preferably made of the same material as the bag's outer shell, e.g., nylon or rayon. Such sleeves may be sewed, glued, or thermally bonded to the outside of the outer shell.

FIG. 2 is a left perspective view of the bag, showing left-side seam 18 and showing drawcord 14 mounted within sleeve 15 and secured by cord lock 16 at locations 19, 20, 21, and 22. Note that each sleeve 15 and its contained drawcord extends only over the top portion of the bag, from seam 18 to zipper 17.

FIG. 3 is a lateral cross-section through bag 11 at location 19 showing zipper 17, side seam 18, and drawcord 14 relaxed and secured by cord lock 16 while mounted within fabric casing sleeve 15. Sleeve 15 is sewn to outer shell fabric 25. Inner lining fabric 24 and insulation 23 are not compressed since drawcord 14 is relaxed. An occupant 26 of the bag is shown in a horizontal position; note that the bag fits loosely around the occupant and that there is a lot of air space between occupant 26 and the bag. A conventional underlying insulating pad or mat 27, e.g., of foam is used under the bag.

FIG. 4 is a lateral cross-section through sleeping bag 11 at location 19 with drawcord 14 tightened and secured by cord lock 16. Inner lining fabric 24 and insulation 23 are gathered together where they are surrounded by tightened drawcord 14. Note that the bag now fits relatively closely or tightly around occupant 26 and that there is very little air space left between occupant 26 and the bag. Insulating pad 27 is again shown under the bag.

REFERENCE NUMERALS

11 sleeping bag

12 upper portion of sleeping bag

13 lower portion of sleeping bag

14 drawcord

15 fabric casing sleeve

16 cord lock

17 zipper

Fig. 3F—Provisional Patent Application With Embellishments (continued)

6

18 side seam

19 sleeve location

20 sleeve location

21 sleeve location

22 sleeve location

23 insulation

24 inner lining fabric

25 outer shell fabric

26 occupant

27 insulating pad

OPERATION

In operation one uses the bag in a normal manner with insulating pad 27 under the bag. The user can, when desired, increase the warmth of the bag by tightening the drawcords and securing them with cord lock 16 (FIGS. 3 and 4). When the drawcords are tightened, five effects increase the bag's warmth:

(1) Insulating layer 23 and the inner lining fabric 24 surrounding occupant 26 become thicker.

(2) This increase in thickness also makes the bag less susceptible to the user narrowing the insulation by body movement, e.g., by poking the insulation with an elbow.

(3) The surface area of outer shell fabric 25 exposed to cold air is reduced.

(4) Since the drawcord extends only over upper portion 12 of the bag, lower portion 13 does not tend to be raised from pad 27 beneath the bag to be exposed to cold air.

(5) The air space between occupant 26 and the bag is reduced.

When the user wishes to increase the inner volume of the bag to provide greater freedom of movement (at some loss of insulating ability), it is only necessary to relax the drawcords (FIG. 3) and allow the bag to expand.

Fig. 3F—Provisional Patent Application With Embellishments (continued)

7

CLAIM

1. A sleeping bag, comprising:

an upper portion which will overlie the body of an occupant when said
   occupant is in a horizontal position in said sleeping bag, and

a lower portion which underlies the body of said occupant, said lower and
   upper portions being joined at opposite sides of said sleeping bag,

at least one drawcord attached to said upper portion of said sleeping bag,
   said drawcord not extending onto said lower portion of said sleeping
   bag, said drawcord having two ends which are attached to said respective
   opposite sides of said sleeping bag,

whereby (a) during cold weather, an occupant of said sleeping bag can
   tighten and clamp said drawcord so that the inner volume and the exposed
   outer surface area of said sleeping bag can be reduced in order to
   better insulate said occupant, (b) contact between said lower portion and
   any underlying flat insulated pad will not be reduced when said drawcord
   is tightened, and (c) said occupant of said sleeping bag can relax the
   tension on said drawcord during warmer conditions and thereby increase
   the volume of air within said sleeping bag adjacent said occupant of said
   sleeping bag in order to give said occupant more freedom of movement.

ABSTRACT

A sleeping bag (11) design for providing adjustability of the inner volume
and outer exposed surface area of the bag comprises sheathed drawcords (14),
preferably elastic, attached only to the top or upper portion of the bag and
secured by cord locks (16). A user of the bag can tighten the drawcords during
cold weather, thereby providing a warmer bag by reducing the inner volume and
the exposed outer surface area of the bag without reducing the thermal protection provided to the lower portion of the bag by an underlying flat insulated
pad, as would be the case with drawcords fully encircling the bag. During
warmer weather, the user can relax the drawcord adjustment, thereby providing
the user with more freedom of movement. Thus a considerably more versatile
sleeping bag is provided—that can be adjusted to provide more warmth during
cold weather or more freedom of movement during warmer weather.

Fig. 3F—Provisional Patent Application With Embellishments (continued)

Mail all papers to the address on the cover letter—that is, Mail Stop Provisional Patent Application, Commissioner for Patents, P.O. Box 1450, Alexandria, VA 22313-1450. If you use Express Mail (advisable), you can consider your PPA filed as soon as you receive the express mail receipt from the postal clerk. About two weeks after you mail the PPA, you'll receive your postcard back, stamped with its date of receipt in the PTO and a serial number that the PTO has assigned to your PPA. If you use regular mail, the date stamped on your postcard will be the filing date of your PPA. Clip your postcard to your PPA cover letter.

About a month later, you'll receive an official filing receipt from the PTO for your PPA. The filing receipt will contain your PPA's serial number, its date, the names of the inventor(s), the title, etc. It will also contain the notation "Foreign Filing License Granted [date]," which means the PTO hasn't classified your invention under military security. After you receive the postcard receipt and filing receipt, you will never hear from the PTO again regarding the PPA. The ball is now in your court to file a timely RPA and to refer to your PPA if you ever need to rely on its date. Mount this in the file with your PPA. Now determine the date that is ten months after your PPA's filing date and mark this date on your calendar to remind you to consider following through with an RPA and possible foreign patent applications. A suitable reminder to write on your calendar is "Consider filing regular and foreign patent applications on PPA filed [filing date of your PPA]." Again, you won't receive any further communication from the PTO about your PPA, and if you don't file an RPA referring to your PPA within a year of your PPA's filing date, the PTO will forever disregard it. (Note, the PTO doesn't require that you file any Information Disclosure Statement (see Chapter 10, Section N,) or prior art in a PPA.)

Even though you've filed a PPA as a substitute for building and testing, you should still try to build and test it if at all possible, for reasons explained in Section E, above.

8. PPA Checklist

If you do decide to file a PPA, here is a checklist to go through before you file it to make sure that you've done everything correctly.

PPA Checklist

☐ 1. The specification and drawings clearly teach how to make and use all embodiments of the invention which you might later want to claim.

☐ 2. Although it's not strictly necessary, I strongly recommend that your PPA be in the format of an RPA, insofar as possible, so that it includes all the parts of an RPA's specification and is written as well and as clearly as an RPA should be. Thus I recommend your PPA comply with the Drawings and Specification checklists in Chapter 8.

☐ 3. Although it's not necessary, I recommend that your PPA contain at least one claim so that you will become familiar with claims and the scope of offensive rights they provide, and also prevent any challenge to your PPA by foreign patent offices for failure to claim the invention as of your earliest filing date. Chapter 9 contains full instructions for drafting claims and checklist for the claims.

☐ 4. PPA Cover Letter completed, including Express Mail section, to avoid possibility of loss in mail and to get an instant filing date.

☐ 5. Return receipt postcard included with all papers being sent listed on back.

☐ 6. Fee Transmittal form completed and included.

☐ 7. Check or Credit Card Payment Form for filing fee. If a check used, payable to "PTO" included. Adequate funds on deposit or adequate credit available.

☐ 8. Parts are assembled in above order and copies made for your file.

☐ 9. Envelope is addressed to
Mail Stop PPA
Commissioner for Patents
P.O. Box 1450
Alexandria, VA 22313-1450

(Again, it is not necessary to file an Information Disclosure Statement or any prior art with your PPA.)

9. PPAs and Foreign Filing

The effect of PPAs on foreign filing is a bit complicated, but not difficult to understand. As we'll learn in Chapter 12, there are two types of foreign jurisdictions in the patent world—those that are members of the Paris Convention and those that are not. If you file a PPA and then file in any Convention jurisdiction (for example, the European Patent Office, Patent Cooperation Treaty (PCT), the U.K., or Japan) within a year, your application in the Convention jurisdiction will be entitled to the priority of your PPA's filing date. Thus, after you file a PPA, you can then freely publish and sell your invention without loss of any rights in any foreign Convention jurisdiction, provided you file in the foreign Convention jurisdiction within a year. Unfortunately, non-Convention countries, for example, Pakistan and Kuwait, do not provide any priority, so you must file in these countries before you publish or offer your invention for sale publicly, as fully explained in Chapter 12.

10. What If You Make Changes to the Invention?

If you make any changes or improvements to the invention after filing a PPA, you should file a subsequent PPA to record these (unless they are minor, such as a change in material). Also, if the date is close to the one-year limit from the filing date of the PPA, it probably isn't worth filing a second PPA; instead, put the changes in the RPA. Your RPA can claim the benefit of more than one PPA and several RPAs may claim the benefit of one or more PPAs. Also, if a PPA contains several inventions, the RPA need not contain them all as well. Conversely, the RPA may contain several inventions even if its PPA contains only one. In this case the RPA will be entitled to the benefit of the PPA's date for only the invention disclosed in the PPA.

J. Don't Use a "Post Office Patent" to Document Your Invention

There's a myth that you can document the date you conceived of your invention (or even protect your invention) by mailing a description of your invention to yourself by certified (or registered) mail and keeping the sealed envelope. In fact, law regards the use of a "Post Office Patent" as tantamount to worthless and no substitute for the signatures of live witnesses on a description of your invention, or even for the PTO's Disclosure Document Program. The PTO's Board of Appeals and Patent Interferences, which has great power in these matters, has specifically said that it gives a sealed envelope little evidentiary value.

K. Summary

Documentation of an invention is vital to protect your legal right to assist in your creation of the invention. You should record conception of the invention, then build and test it, if at all possible, and then record your building and testing. You may record conception and building and testing in a lab notebook or by means of an invention disclosure. In either case you, the inventor, should sign and date the document and have it witnessed and dated. If you lack witnesses, you can use the PTO's Document Disclosure Program, under which the PTO will be your witness for a small fee.

In lieu of or in addition to building and testing, you may also file a provisional patent application (PPA) to obtain patent pending status. The PTO will never read the PPA unless you need to rely on its date later to obtain an earlier date for a regular patent application (RPA). The filing fee for a PPA is relatively small and it need not have claims or the formality of an RPA, but to be effective, the PPA must clearly and fully teach how to make and use the invention. To obtain the benefit of the PPA's filing date, the RPA and any foreign applications must be filed within one year and claim the benefit of the PPA. You may convert an RPA to a PPA and vice versa. Your RPA may claim the benefit of several PPAs. A PPA can contain several inventions, but you can rely on only those that the PPA fully and clearly discloses. You should not use a "post office patent" to document your invention. ■

Chapter 4

Will Your Invention Sell?

Inventor's Commandment #5

To avoid needless expense and effort, don't spend significant time or money on your creation until you have thoroughly evaluated it for commercial potential, including a consideration of all of its advantages and disadvantages.

A. Why Evaluate Your Invention for Salability?

Congratulations! If you've gotten this far, you've made an invention and have properly recorded your conception by a notebook, disclosure, or Disclosure Document Program. I hope you have also built and tested it and/or filed a Provisional Patent Application (PPA) to cement a reduction to practice date.

Now it's time to do two more things before proceeding further: Evaluate it for commercial potential and make a patentability search. While you can do these in any order, I recommend that you do the easier or cheaper one first. Since, for most people, it's the commercial evaluation, I put this chapter first. However, if you live near the PTO, or want to see if your invention is really novel now, then go to Chapters 5 and 6 first. Also, if you're a corporate inventor, the decision as to whether a particular invention is sufficiently marketable to justify applying for a patent may not be yours. In any event I recommend that you at least skim through this material for new ideas that might help you assess your work in a different light before proceeding to Chapters 5 and 6, where I discuss patentability and searching.

The commercial evaluation is so important that I've made it an Inventor's Commandment. Why is a commercial evaluation so important? Because the next steps you take will involve the expenditure of significant money and effort. Specifically, your next step, in addition to searching the invention, is to build and test it for feasibility and cost (if possible), and then to file a patent application on the invention. Naturally, you won't want to take these substantial labor and financial risks unless you feel you have some reasonable chance that your efforts and expenditures will be justified.

Common Misconception: Anyone who gets a patent will be assured of fame and fortune.

Fact: Even if you get a patent, you still may not make any money from the invention. In fact, fewer than one out of ten patented inventions make any money for their owners, mainly because the inventor did not adequately assess the commercial prospects of the inventions at the outset and because the inventor did not promote and market the invention adequately thereafter.

"It is to be remembered, that the pursuit of wealth by means of new inventions is a very precarious and uncertain one; a lottery where there are many thousand tickets for each prize."

—Eli Whitney

The purpose of this chapter, then, is to help you reduce the risk of a "patented failure" by assisting you in checking your invention out for salability. In fact, before you proceed with a search, or the actual filing of a patent application, I recommend that you be reasonably confident that your invention is likely to make you at least $50,000, or at least 20 times the cost of what you plan to spend for searching, building a model, and patenting. Of course if you can do the search easily, or if you're into inventing for the sheer fun of it, or if you want to get a patent to stroke your ego, you can disregard these financial requirements.

Also, if you come up with a technical breakthrough in a high-tech field, or a highly novel invention, you should consider patenting it even though you don't think it has immediate commercial value: it may become very profitable some years later, and your early patent will block later inventors from patenting it.

If after reading this chapter, you're still not sure about the commercial prospects of your invention, you may want to test market it. If you haven't filed a PPA, this can legally be done for up to one year, since you can file a valid patent application up to one year after the invention is first sold or offered for sale. If you have filed a PPA, you still have almost a year to test market it until you have to file an RPA to obtain the benefit of your PPA's date. A test marketing is feasible if you're able to make (or have made) reasonable quantities of your invention cheaply. Obviously, a field or use test of a working model of an invention will tell you much more than the theoretical "paper" evaluation discussed in this chapter. However, unless you have filed a PPA, you must be willing to sacrifice your foreign rights. See Chapter 12, where I explain that you'll lose most of your foreign rights if you sell or otherwise release your invention to public scrutiny before you file for a patent in the U.S.

 If you do decide to test market the invention before filing, you must keep in mind the "one-year rule,"

which I'll also discuss in the next chapter. This rule, contained in Section 102 of the patent statutes (35 USC 102), requires that in order to be valid, a U.S. patent application (regular or PPA) *must* be filed within one year after you first sell your invention (this includes test marketing), offer it for sale, publish, or reveal it to others without restriction. (See Chapter 5, Section E.)

B. Start Small but Ultimately Do It Completely

When you evaluate your invention for commercial potential, try to do it on a small scale at first in order to avoid a large, wasted expenditure. For example, if you make metal parts as part of building a prototype to test operability, try to have them made of wood or cardboard by an economical electric discharge machining (EDM) technique rather than with molds. Similarly, prior to conducting extensive interviews, try to consult with a single expert to be sure you're not way out in left field. If your initial, small-scale investigation looks favorable and you don't run into any serious impediments, I advise that you then do it carefully, completely, and objectively, using the techniques of this chapter.

If after you do the full evaluation your idea looks like it has great commercial potential, but some other factor such as patentability or operability doesn't look too promising, don't make any hasty decision to drop it. Continue to explore the negative areas. On the other hand, if after a careful evaluation you are truly convinced that your invention won't be successful, don't waste any further time on it. Move on.

C. You Can't Be 100% Sure of Any Invention's Commercial Prospects

There's only one question you need to answer in commercially evaluating your invention: If my invention is manufactured and sold, or otherwise commercially implemented (for example, as a process that is put into commercial use), will it be profitable? Unfortunately, no one can ever answer this question with certainty. The answer will always depend on how the invention is promoted, how well it's designed, how well it's packaged, the mood of the market, the timing of its commercial debut, and dozens of other intangible factors. For example, if the Pet Rock came out now, rather than in the 1960s, it might be a complete dud. Similarly, if bottled water was marketed in the '60s, rather than in current times, it probably would not have had as much success. Most marketing experts say that five "P" factors must all be "right" for a new product to make it: Production, Price, Position (its place in the market), Promotion, and Perseverance.

In addition to the "Five Ps," the packaging (outer box as well as the shape of the device itself) can be crucial to its success. Consider a relatively recent invention, the Audochron® clock, which indicates the time by a series of countable chimes. Given this technical feature only, the clock probably wouldn't have sold too well. But a talented designer put the works in a futuristic case shaped like a flattened gold sphere on a pedestal in which a plastic band at the center of the sphere lit with each chime. As a result, it became a status symbol and sold relatively large quantities at a high price; it even appeared in *Architectural Digest*, shown in a photo of a U.S. president's desk!

The trademark you select for your invention can also make a big difference as to whether it's a commercial success. If you doubt this, consider Vaseline's hand lotion. The lotion would very likely have been just another member of the bunch, consigned to mediocre sales, had not some clever marketing person come up with the trademark *Intensive Care*. This helped make it a sales leader. Ditto for the *Hula-Hoop* exercise device and the *Crock Pot* slow cooker, both of which certainly weren't hurt by evocative names. Even something as dull as roach traps were blasted into marketing stardom by the trademark *Roach Motel* and its brilliant ad campaign ("Roaches check in, but they don't check out"). Even something as prosaic as raisins were given a mighty boost with the "dancing raisins" TV campaign thought up by a marketing genius.

D. Take Time to Do a Commercial Feasibility Evaluation

Despite the marketing uncertainties, most experts believe that you can make a useful evaluation of the commercial possibilities of an untested invention if you take the time to do some scientific and objective work in four areas:
- the positive and negative marketing factors attached to your invention;
- consultation with experts, potential users of the invention, marketing people, and others;
- research into prior developments in the same area as your invention; and
- the operability of an actual construction of the invention

Let's take a look at each.

The Positive and Negative Factors Test

Every invention, no matter how many positive factors it seems to have at first glance, inevitably has one or more significant negative ones. To evaluate the positive and negative factors objectively, carefully consider each on the list below. Using Form 4-1, the Positive and Negative Factors Evaluation Sheet (a copy is in Appendix 7), assign a commercial value or disadvantage weight to each factor on a scale of −100 to +100, according to your best, carefully considered estimate. If the factor is irrelevant to your invention, assign a weight of 0.

For example, if an invention provides overwhelming cost savings in relation to its existing counterparts, assign a +80 or higher to the "Cost" factor (#1) in the positive column. But if it requires a high capital expenditure (tooling) to build, a −50 would be appropriate for this factor (#43), and so on.

The following balance scale analogy will help you to understand the positive and negative factors evaluation: Pretend the positive factors are stacked on one side of a balance scale and the negative factors are stacked on the other side, as indicated in Fig. 4A.

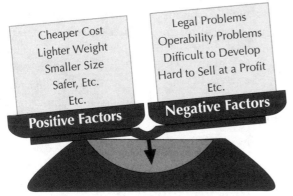

Fig. 4A—Conceptual Weighing of Positive v. Negative Factors

If the positive factors (those given a weight from +1 to +100) strongly outweigh the negative (those from −1 to −100), the arrow would swing to the right and you can regard this as a "go" indication, that is, the invention is commercially viable. Obviously this balance scale is just an analogy. It can't be used quantitatively because no one has yet come up with a way to assign accurate and valid weights to the factors. Nevertheless, you'll find it of great help in evaluating the commercial prospects of your invention.

Before you actually take pen (or word processor) in hand and begin your evaluation, read through the following summary of positive and negative factors.

You should consider each factor carefully, especially if you assign a negative value, even if the negative value is merely due to the need to change or design and produce new production equipment. I've seen inventions and developments that were better in every way than what already existed, but which weren't used solely because the improvement didn't justify the cost of replacing existing production equipment, or the cost associated with manufacturing and promoting the device.

The factors of your invention with negative values are generally more important and require more consideration than do those with positive values, since if your invention fails, it will obviously be one or more of the negatives that causes it.

Factors Affecting the Marketability of Your Invention

1. **Cost.** Is your invention cheaper or more expensive to build or use than current counterparts? An example where making something more expensive to build would be an advantage is a credit or eligibility card; a more expensive card would be more difficult to counterfeit.

2. **Weight.** Is your invention lighter (or heavier) in weight than what is already known, and is such change in weight a benefit? For example, if you've invented a new automobile or airplane engine, a reduction in weight is a great benefit. But if you've invented a new ballast material, obviously an increase in weight (provided it doesn't come at too great a cost in money or bulk) is a benefit.

3. **Size.** Is your invention smaller or larger in size or capacity than what is already known, and is such change in size a benefit?

4. **Safety/Health Factors.** Is your invention safer or healthier to use than what is already known? Clearly there's a strong trend in government and industry to improve the safety and reduce the possible chances for injury, harm, and product liability suits in most products and processes, and this trend has given birth to many new inventions. Often a greater increase in cost and weight will be tolerated if certain safety and health benefits accrue. But beware, some safety devices cause more harm than they prevent: e.g., antilock brakes have caused more skids and accidents than conventional brakes, since users tend to pump them, although they are supposed to be pressed continuously.

5. **Speed.** Is your invention able to do a job faster (or slower) than its previous counterpart, and is such

change in speed a benefit? This advantage, like #6, is important in software inventions.

6. **Ease of Use.** Is your invention easier (or harder) to use (the current buzzword is "ergonomic") or learn to use than its previously known counterpart? An example of a product where an increase in difficulty of use would be a benefit is the child-proof drug container cap. This advantage is especially important if you have a software innovation: if it enables you to use the computer or any other machine more facilely, this counts a great deal.

7. **Ease of Production.** Is your invention easier or cheaper (or harder or more expensive) to manufacture than previously known counterparts? Or can it be mass-produced, whereas previously known counterparts had to be made by hand? An example of something that is more difficult to manufacture yet that is highly desirable is the new credit cards with holographic images: they're far more difficult to forge.

8. **Durability.** Does your invention last longer (or wear out sooner) than previously known counterparts? While built-in obsolescence is nothing to be admired, the stark economic reality is that many products, such as disposable razors, have earned their manufacturers millions by lasting for a shorter time than previously known counterparts.

9. **Repairability.** Is it easier to repair than previously known counterparts?

10. **Novelty.** Is your invention at all different from all previously known counterparts? Merely making an invention different may not appear to be an advantage per se, but it's usually a great advantage: It provides an alternative method or device for doing the job in case the first method or device ever encounters difficulties (such as from government regulation), and in case the first device or method infringes a patent that you want to avoid infringing. It also provides something for ad people to crow about.

11. **Convenience/Social Benefit/Mechanization.** Does your invention make living easier or more convenient? Many inventions with a new function provide this advantage. Although you may question the ultimate wisdom and value of such gadgets as the electric knife, the remote-control TV, and the digital-readout clock, the reality remains that, in our relatively affluent society, millions of dollars have been and are being made from devices that save labor and time (even though the time required to earn the after-tax money to buy the gadget is often greater than the time saved by using it). Even if the invention has one or more serious drawbacks, if it mechanizes a manual operation, it may still fly. Consider the Epilady® leg-hair remover: Even though its rotating

spring ripped out m'lady's leg hairs in an extremely painful manner, it became a great success because it eliminated shaving and depilatories.

Then too, many new industries have been started by making an existing invention easier and convenient to use. Henry Ford didn't invent the automobile; he just produced it in volume and made it convenient for the masses to use. Ditto for George Eastman with his camera. And in modern times, the two Steves (Jobs and Wozniak) did much the same for the computer.

In the software field, especially nowadays, people seem willing to buy almost any program that will computerize a manual task, even if the time required to earn the money to buy the program, learn the program, and use it is much greater than the manual route. Many inventors have told me that they would like to use the PTO's Electronic Filing System, even though it requires lots of paperwork to get qualified and a fairly difficult learning curve to be able to use it.

12. **Reliability.** Is your invention apt to fail less or need repair less often than previously known devices?

13. **Ecology.** Does your invention make use of what previously were thought to be waste products? Does it reduce the use of limited natural resources? Does it produce fewer waste products, such as smoke and waste water? If so, you have an advantage that is very important nowadays and that should be emphasized strongly.

14. **Salability.** Is your invention easier to sell or market than existing counterparts?

15. **Appearance.** Does your invention provide a better-appearing design than existing counterparts?

16. **Viewability.** If your invention relates to eye use, does it present a brighter, clearer, or more viewable image? For example, a color TV with a brighter picture, or photo-chromic eyeglasses that automatically darken in sunlight were valuable inventions.

17. **Precision.** Does your invention operate or provide greater precision or more accuracy than existing counterparts?

18. **Noise.** Does your invention operate more quietly? Does it eliminate or turn unpleasant noise into a more acceptable sound? Noise-canceling headphones fit this bill. Or does it make noise in a desirable situation—for example, a device that produced a warning noise when a VCR cartridge was inserted in the wrong manner would be desirable.

19. **Odor.** Does your invention emanate fewer (or more) unpleasant fumes or odors? The public would benefit by adding an unpleasant odor to a poisonous or harmful substance. For example, public utilities add mercaptan sulphur to heating and cooking gas to warn users when leaks occur.

20. **Taste.** If your invention is edible or comes into contact with the taste buds (for example, a pill or a pipe stem), does it taste better? Like the foul odor above, a foul taste can also be an advantage, such as for poisons to prevent ingestion by children, and for telephone cables to deter chewing by rodents.

21. **Market Size.** Is there a larger market for your invention than for previously known devices? Because of climatic or legal restrictions, for example, certain inventions are only usable in small geographical areas. And because of economic factors, certain inventions may be limited to the relatively affluent. If your invention can obviate these restrictions, your potential market may be greatly increased, and this can be a significant advantage.

22. **Trend of Demand.** Is the trend of demand for your device increasing? Of course you should distinguish, if possible, between a trend and a fad. The first will provide a market for your invention while the second is likely to leave you high and dry unless you catch it in the beginning stages.

23. **Seasonal Demand.** Is your invention useful no matter what the season of the year? If so, it will usually have greater demand than a seasonal invention, such as a sailboat. But sometimes this will be a negative rather than a positive, if the invention is something like skis or a holiday decoration, which does have a seasonal demand, rather than an all-year-around one.

24. **Difficulty of Market Penetration.** Is your device an improvement of a previously accepted device? If so, it will have an easier time penetrating the market and obtaining a good market share than a device that provides a completely new function.

25. **Potential Competition.** Is your invention so simple, popular, or easy to manufacture that many imitators and copiers are likely to attempt to copy it or design around it, or try to break your patent as soon as it's brought out? Or is it a relatively complex, less popular, hard-to-manufacture device, which others wouldn't be likely to produce because of such factors as the large capital outlay required for tooling and production? However, don't assume that something that's easy to copy is not worth patenting, since patents on simple devices are upheld and enforced successfully all the time.

26. **Quality.** Does your invention produce or provide a higher quality output or result than existing counterparts? For example, compact disks provide a much better audio quality than do phonorecords or magnetic tape.

27. **Excitement.** (The Neophile and the Conspicuous Consumer/Status Seeker.) Almost all humans need some form of excitement in their lives: some obtain it by watching or participating in sports, others by the purchase of a new car or travel, and still others by the purchase of new products, such as a 50-inch TV, a laser disk player, or a friendly household robot. Such purchasers can be called "neophiles" (lovers of the new); their excitement comes from having and showing off their new "toy." Purchasers of expensive products, like the Mercedes-Benz or a Rolex watch, are commonly motivated by what Thorsten Veblen has called "conspicuous consumption," and what we now call "status seeking." They enjoy showing off an expensive or unique item which they've acquired. Thus, if your invention can provide consumer excitement, either through sheer newness or through evidence of a costly purchase, it has a decided advantage.

28. **Markup.** If your invention is in an excitement category (that is, if it's very different, novel, innovative, or luxurious), it can command a very high markup, a distinct selling advantage.

29. **Inferior Performance.** Yes, I'm serious! If your invention performs worse than comparable things that are already available, this can be a great advantage, if put to the proper use. Consider the 3M Company's fabulously successful Scotch® Post-It® note pads: Their novelty is simply that they have a strip of stickum that is *inferior* to known adhesives, thus providing removable self-stick notes. Here the invention may not be so much the

discovery of an inferior adhesive as the discovery of a new use for it.

30. **"Sexy" Packaging.** If your invention is or comes in a "sexy" package, or is adaptable to being sold in such a package, this can be a great advantage. Consider the Hanes l'Eggs® stockings where the package (shaped like an egg) made the product!

31. **Miscellaneous/Obviation of Specific Disadvantages of Existing Devices.** This is a catchall to cover anything I may have missed in the previous categories. Often the specific disadvantages that your invention overcomes will be quite obvious; they should be included here, nonetheless.

32. **Long Life Cycle.** If your invention has a potentially long life cycle, that is, it can be made and sold for many years before it becomes obsolete, this is an obvious strong advantage that will justify capital expenditures for tooling and conducting a big ad campaign.

33. **Related Product Addability.** If your invention will usher in a new product line, as did the computer, where many related products, such as disk drives, printers, and software can be added, this will be an important advantage with potentially enhanced profits.

34. **Satisfies Existing Need.** If your invention will satisfy an existing, recognized need, such as preventing drug abuse, avoiding auto collisions, combating terrorism or crime, your marketing difficulties will be greatly reduced.

35. **Legality.** Does your invention comply with, or will its use fail to comply with, existing laws, regulations, and product and manufacturing requirements? Or, are administrative approvals required? If your invention carries legal difficulties with it, its acceptance will be problematic no matter how great its positive advantages are. And if ecological or safety approvals are required (for example, for drugs and automobiles), this will be viewed as a distinct disadvantage by prospective buyers. Also, if the legality of a product is questionable, its manufacturer, distributor, or retailer will have difficulty in obtaining product liability insurance.

36. **Operability.** Is it likely to work readily, or will significant additional design or technical development be required to make it practicable and workable? Usually problems of operability will become abundantly clear when you try to build a working model, which you should try to do as soon as possible, even if you've filed a PPA (Chapter 3, Section I). Many great-looking inventions such as the turbine automobile engine turned out to be "technofizzle" when built and tested. (Don't forget to fill out another copy of Form 3-2 after you build and test it.)

37. **Development.** Is the product already designed for the market, or will such things as additional engineering, material selection, and appearance work be required?

38. **Profitability.** Because of possible requirements for exotic materials, difficult machining steps, great size, and so on, is your invention likely to be difficult to sell at a profit, or at an acceptable price level?

39. **Obsolescence.** Is the field in which your invention is used likely to be around for a long time or die out soon? If the latter, most manufacturers won't be willing to invest money in production facilities.

40. **Incompatibility.** Is your invention likely to be compatible or incompatible with existing patterns of use, customs, and so on?

41. **Product Liability Risk.** Is your invention in a "safe" area, such as a ruler, or in a problem area, such as safety devices, drugs, firearms, contact sports, and automobiles? In the latter area, the risks of lawsuits against the manufacturer, due to product malfunction or injury from use, are likely to be greater than average. For example, a client of mine invented an ingenious, economical, and highly useful device for preventing a revolver from being accidentally fired. But, alas, though he tried everywhere, he couldn't get any company to take it on because they were afraid of product liability lawsuits if the device ever failed.

42. **Market Dependence.** Is the sale of your invention dependent on a market for other goods, or is it useful in its own right? For example, an improved television tuner depends on the sale of televisions for its success, so that if the television market goes into a slump, the sales of your tuner certainly will fall also.

43. **Difficulty of Distribution.** Is your invention easy to distribute, or is it so large, fragile, or perishable that it will be difficult or costly to distribute?

44. **Service Requirements.** Is your invention free from service requirements or will it require frequent servicing and adjustment? If the latter, this is a distinct disadvantage. But consider the first commercial color TVs which, by any reasonable standard, were a service nightmare, but made millions for their manufacturers.

45. **Production Facilities.** Almost all inventions require new production facilities, a distinct disadvantage. This is because the manufacture of anything new requires new tooling and production techniques. But some inventions require only a modest change or no change, a tremendous advantage.

46. **Inertia Need Not/Must Be Overcome.** An example of a great invention that so far has failed because of user inertia is the Dvorak typewriter keyboard, which, although much faster and easier to use, was unable to overcome

the awkward but entrenched Qwerty keyboard. The same goes for the easier-to-use, less confusing, military-European time, or a decimal time system. There's a risk in introducing *any* new product, and when any invention is radically different, potential manufacturers, users, and sellers will manifest tremendous inertia, regardless of the invention's value.

47. **Minor/Great Technical Advance.** In the '60s, I got a client a very broad patent on a laser pumped by a chemical reaction explosion. We were very pleased with this patent. However, it was so advanced at the time that the technology behind it is just now being implemented in connection with the "Star Wars" defense effort. Unfortunately, the patent expired in the meantime. The same goes for the computer mouse patent, which expired in 1980, just before "mice" became popular, and the roller-blade skates, the patent for which expired in 1985, just before the roller-blade craze started. An FRB-Dallas survey found that major innovations like the telephone, radio, dishwasher, color TV, microwave oven, VCR, computer, and cell phone took an average of 11.4 years to be owned by 25% of all U.S. households. The moral? Even if you have a great invention, make sure it can be commercially implemented within about 17 years.

48. **Learning Required.** If consumers will have to undergo substantial learning in order to use your invention, this is an obvious negative. An example: the early personal computers. On the other hand, some inventions, such as the automatically talking clock, make a task even easier to do and thus have an obvious strong advantage.

49. **Difficult/Easy to Promote.** If it will be difficult, expensive, or will require a long time to promote and market your invention, e.g., because it's technically complex, has subtle advantages, or is very expensive, large, or awkward, you've got an obvious disadvantage. But if it solves an omnipresent problem and is cheap and easy to market, this is a clear advantage.

50. **Lack/Presence of Market.** If no market already exists for your invention, you'll have to convince the public that they need it—that is, that you have a "product in search of a market." While not a fatal flaw, and while this type of invention can be most profitable, you (or your licensee) will have to be prepared to expend substantial sums on promotion.

51. **Crowded/Wide Open Field.** If the field is already crowded, you'll have an uphill battle.

52. **Commodities.** If you've invented a new commodity—such as a better plastic, solvent, or grain—you'll face stiff price competition from the established, already streamlined standards.

53. **Combination Products.** If you've invented a "combination product"—that is, a product with two inventions that don't really groove together, like a stapler with a built-in beverage cup holder, people won't be beating a path to your door. On the other hand, the clock-radio was just the ticket.

54. **Entrenched Competition.** Despite its overwhelming advantages, Edison had a terrible time promoting his lightbulb because the gas companies fought him bitterly.

55. **Instant Anachronism.** A clever inventor in Oakland, California, invented a wonderful dictionary indexing device which made it much faster to look up any word. However, he was unable to sell it to any dictionary publisher because the dictionary is being replaced by computerized devices. His clever invention was an "instant anachronism."

56. **Prototype Availability.** Although the presence or absence of a prototype should not affect the marketability or commercial success of your invention, in reality it will! If you have a prototype available, or can make one, you'll find that your invention will be far easier to market, since potential purchasers or licensees will be much more likely to buy something which is real and tangible rather than on paper only.

57. **Broad Patent Coverage Available.** You won't be able to determine whether or not broad patent coverage is likely to be available until you complete Chapters 5 and 6, but keep this factor in mind and come back to it after you evaluate patentability. Obviously, if you can obtain broad patent coverage on your invention, this will affect profitability, because if you're the only source for a device which performs a certain function you'll be able to charge more than you would in a competitive situation. A legal monopoly is a capitalist's dream!

58. **High Sales Anticipated.** If you can anticipate a high sales volume for your invention—for example, for a device like the Hula-Hoop which is relatively simple, cheap, and easy to market—this will be a very positive factor.

59. **Visibility of Invention in Final Product.** If your invention is highly visible in or essentially constitutes the entire final product—for example the sneakers with heels that light up when walking—this will be a distinct marketing advantage to entice buyers who love the new. On the other hand, if the invention is hidden in the final product, such as a stronger frame for an automobile, this factor will not be a plus in marketing.

60. **Ease of Packaging.** If your invention is easy to package—for example, a small gadget that can be put in a cheap blister package—this will be a great aid in marketing. However, if it's difficult and expensive to package, such as a bicycle or hockey stick, this will obviously be a negative factor.

61. Youth Market. Young people have substantial discretionary income and tend to spend more in many product areas than the rest of the population. If your invention is something that will appeal to children or young adults, it may command more sales than something that is not attractive to this age group. In other words, a portable digital music player will sell better than arthritis aids.

62. Part of a Current Fad. If your invention is part of a current fad, such as a low-carbohydrate product, a low-fat product, a spam filter, an identity-theft preventer, a bottled water, and so forth, it will be far easier to sell. For example, a few years ago when the lottery was legalized in California, a spate of lottery-number selection products appeared and sold briskly until the public's interest simmered down.

Now that you have a grasp of the factors that can influence the commercial viability of an invention, complete Form 4-1 by assigning a weight to each listed factor, either positive or negative. Also list and assign weights to any other factors you can think of which I've omitted. Then compute the sum of your factors and determine the difference to come up with a rough idea of a net value for your invention. I suggest that you continue to pursue inventions with net values of 50 and up, that you direct your efforts elsewhere if your invention has a net value of less than 0, and that you make further critical evaluation of inventions with net values between 0 and 50.

The list has many other valuable uses:
- Using the list may cause you to focus on one or more drawbacks that are serious enough to kill your invention outright.
- The list can be used to provide a way of comparing two different inventions for relative value so that you'll know which to concentrate more effort on.
- It can be used to "sell" your invention to the Patent and Trademark Office, a potential licensee, or a judge if your patent is ever involved in litigation.

You now should extract all factors on the list of Form 4-1 that have any value other than 0 and write these factors and their weights on Form 4-2, the Positive and Negative Factors Summary Sheet. (A copy is in Appendix 7.) This sheet, when completed, will provide you with a concise summary of the advantages and disadvantages of your invention. You can use it in at least four valuable ways:
1. To provide you with a capsule summary of your invention for commercial evaluation purposes (this chapter);
2. To help you prepare the "selling" parts of your patent application (see Chapter 8);
3. To help you to sell or license your invention to a manufacturer (see Chapter 11); and

4. To help you to get the PTO to grant you a patent (see Chapter 13).

Don't hesitate to update or redo Forms 4-1 and 4-2 if more information comes to mind.

E. Check Your Marketability Conclusions Using the Techniques of Consultation and Research

Once you reach some tentative conclusions about the commercial viability of your invention, it's time to get a reality check.

1. How to Go About It

If your evaluation of the above positive and negative factors affecting the marketability of your invention gives the positive side the edge, I recommend that you extend your investigation by doing some consultation and research. If you continue to get positive signs, extend your search still further until you've learned all you can about the field of your invention. This knowledge will also be of great benefit when you make your patentability search, prepare your application, market your invention, and deal with the PTO.

In Section 2, below, I suggest a number of procedures to use when you're disclosing your ideas to others so that they won't be stolen and so their trade secret (TS) status will be maintained. Here, I simply warn you at the outset that you shouldn't disclose ideas and information without utilizing appropriate safeguards; otherwise you may lose them to others.

The areas of consultation and research which you should investigate include asking both nonprofessionals and experts in the particular field for an opinion, and researching the relevant literature. As you do this, keep in mind and ask about all of the positive and negative factors listed above. Your consultation efforts and research will almost surely give you more information useful in assessing many of them. If so, again don't hesitate to redo your Forms 4-1 and 4-2.

As indicated, nonprofessionals can often be an excellent source of information and advice, especially if your invention is a consumer item that they are likely to have an opportunity to purchase if it's ever mass-produced. Consult your lay friends and associates, that is, those who have no special expertise in the field in which you are interested, but whose opinion you trust and feel will be objective. Often you may find it valuable *not* to tell them that you are the inventor so you'll get a more objective evaluation. You may also want to inquire as to what price they'd be willing to pay. It's especially helpful if you've built a working model (see Section F, below) so you can show it to them and ask if they'd buy it and for what price.

Experts to be consulted in the particular field of your invention include any and all of the following who can supply you with relevant feedback:
- salespeople and buyers in stores that sell devices similar to yours;
- engineers, managers, or technicians in companies in the field of your invention;
- scholars, educators, or professors who do research in the area of your invention; and
- friends who are "in the business."

Naturally you may not know all of these experts. Getting to them will require the creative use of the contacts you do have so as to arrange the proper introductions. Once you do, however, most people will be flattered that you've asked for their advice and pleased to help you.

If you can afford to pay for an evaluation, you may want to consider using an independent invention evaluation service. Here are two university-based ones that I believe are reputable:
- Wisconsin Innovation Service Center, (www.uww.edu/business/innovate/innovate.htm) 414-472-1365, (about $500), and
- Wal-Mart/WIN/I2 Innovation Network, (www.innovation-institute.com) 417-836-5671, (about $175).

After you show your invention—preferably a working model—note the person's initial reaction. If you hear a "Well, I'll be damned!" or "Why didn't I think of that!" you know you're on the right track. However if a consultant rejects your idea, don't blindly accept the rejection; try to find out the reason and whether it's valid. Some people don't like anything new, so develop a thick skin and an analytical approach. Keep in mind the words of Charles Brower: "A new idea is delicate. It can be killed by a sneer or a yawn; it can be stabbed to death by a quip and worried to death by a frown on the right man's brow."

For your literature search, I suggest that you start by using one or more Internet search engines, locating a research librarian who's familiar with the area of your concern. Large technical and business libraries and those associated with major universities are obvious places to start. The library literature that you should investigate includes product directories, how-to-do-it books, catalogues, general reference books, and patents if they are available. (See Chapter 6.)

Remember that the purpose of the literature search isn't to determine whether your invention is new or patentable, but rather to give you additional background in the field so you can evaluate the positive and negative factors listed above. However, while you're doing your literature search, you may find that your invention was publicly known before you invented it. This is especially likely to occur if you search the patent literature. If so, you'll either have to drop the invention, since you'll know you aren't the first inventor, or try to make a new invention by improving your first effort. You'll be surprised how much better a feel you'll have for your invention once you've done some research and become familiar with the field.

If you work for or have access to a large company, visit its purchasing department and ask for permission to look through its product catalogues. Most companies have an extensive library of such catalogues and you'll often find much relevant and valuable information there that you won't find in even the biggest and best public libraries.

This search isn't the equivalent of the "patent search" that occurs before you apply for your patent. Covered in the next chapter is the more formal patent search, which obviously will provide you with considerably more background in the area of your invention.

2. Precautions to Take During Consultation

If you do show your invention to others or discuss it with them to any extent, a degree of care is mandatory to preserve the trade secret status of your invention and to prevent theft of your ideas, or to prove it in case it occurs. (See Chapter 1, Section Q.) Remember that any of the agreements discussed below are only as good as the parties who have signed them. Thus you shouldn't disclose your invention to anyone you don't trust. Suing someone for breaching a nondisclosure agreement is no substitute for picking a trustworthy person in the first place.

Here are some good alternatives that can be used to protect your invention from being misappropriated by others:

- Have disclosees sign a receipt or logbook entry indicating that they have seen your invention. The logbook entry can be simply a page in your inventor's notebook that says at the top, "The undersigned have seen and understood Tom Brown's confidential [name of invention] as described on pages ___ of this book, on the dates indicated." You may also want to add a "Comments" column to your book to indicate that you value their opinion. Doing this also makes it easier to ask your consultants to sign your receipt page or log notebook.

- Ask those to whom you show your invention to sign and date your disclosure as witnesses. Witnesses can hardly ever claim that they invented independently of you if they're on record as having witnessed your invention. If there are more than two or three witnesses, however, this method won't work as there won't be room in your book for more.

- Get your consultants to sign the Nondisclosure Agreement (Form 3-1). However, it may be difficult for you to ask someone who's doing you a favor to sign this agreement.

- Although inferior to the other devices listed above, send a confirming or thank-you letter before and/or after your consultation so you'll have written, uncontradicted records that you showed your invention to the person on a specific date and that you asked it to be kept confidential. A confirmatory after-the-fact letter can simply say, "Thanks very much for looking at my [name of invention] at your office last Wednesday, July 3. This letter is to confirm that you agreed that the details of my [name of invention] should be maintained in strictest confidence. Thanks for your cooperation. Sincerely, [your name]." Photocopy any such letter and keep a copy for your records.

While care in disclosing your invention is necessary to prevent loss of its trade secret status and theft, don't go overboard with precautions. Many new inventors get such a severe case of "inventor's paranoia" that they're afraid to disclose their brainchild to anyone, or they're willing to disclose it only with such stringent safeguards that no one will want to look at it! In practice, most stolen inventions are taken only after they're out on the market and proven successful. This is because thieves are most interested in sure things. While I don't totally approve, highly successful inventor Paul Brown usually shows his inventions freely: he says, "Let them steal it—they don't know how much work they're in for!"

F. Now's the Time to Build and Test It (If Possible)

Now that you have completed the conceptual process of your invention, it's time to build and test a working model (prototype), or engage someone who will do it for you for a fee.

1. Why Do It?

As stated under #36 in Section D, above, if you haven't already done so, it's very desirable to build and test a working model (prototype) of your invention, if at all possible. The reasons: A working model will give you something real to show your marketing consultants, plus valuable information about operability, cost, technical problems, and most of the other factors on the positive and negative factors list. If it's impractical to build a working model, often a nonworking model, or scale model, will give you almost as much valuable data. It's also possible to build a "virtual prototype" (computer simulation). For an explanation of this process see Jack Lander's article, "Virtual Prototyping: Alive and Well," in *Inventors Digest*, July/August 2003. As stated, don't forget to fill out another copy of Form 3-2 (Invention Disclosure) after you build and test it, in order to have a legal record of your building and testing.

Be Aware of the One-Year Rule. An inventor who offers an invention for sale, sells it, uses it publicly or commercially, or shows it to others without restriction must file a patent application within one year for it to be valid. (See the one-year rule discussed in Chapter 5.) If the public use was for experimentation or if the persons exposed to the use were under an admonition of secrecy, the one-year clock does not start running. Note, the courts have held a patent invalid where an inventor showed her invention to people at a party without restrictions and filed her patent application over a year later. *Beachcombers v. Wildwood Creative Products*, 31 F.3d 1154 (Fed. Cir. 1994). If you show your invention to others and this showing is not for bona fide experimental purposes (see Chapter 5) either file a patent application within one year or have those who saw your invention sign a nondisclosure agreement (see Chapter 3).

2. If You Use a Model Maker, Use a Consultant's Agreement

If you can't build and test it yourself, many model makers, engineers, technicians, and teachers are available who will be delighted to do the job for you for a fee, or for a percentage of the action. If you do use a model maker (consultant), you should take precautions to protect the confidentiality and proprietary status of your invention. There's no substitute for checking out your consultant carefully by asking for references (assuming you don't already know the consultant by reputation or referral).

In addition, have your consultant sign a copy of the Consultant's Work Agreement (Form 4-3 in Appendix 7). Note that this Agreement includes fill-in blanks to describe the names and addresses of the inventor and consultant, the name of the project or invention (such as "New Sweater-Drying Form"), detailed description of the work to be done (such as "build a wire-frame, plastic-covered, sweater-drying collapsible form in accordance with plans in attached Exhibit A—finished form to operate smoothly and collapse to 14" x 23" x 2" (or less) size"), and manner of payment (usually ⅓ at start, ⅓ upon construction, and ⅓ on acceptance by you, the Contractor), and which state's law should govern (pick the state where you reside if the Consultant is out-of-state).

Note that I've provided (see paragraph 7) that any changes in the work to be performed or payment to be made shall be in writing. I've done this because I've been involved in many disputes where the consultant does additional or more difficult work and wants more money, but the parties' memories differ as to what changes were agreed to, if any.

The Agreement also requires the Consultant to perform in a timely manner or you can void the Agreement and pay only 50%, or have the Consultant pay an agreed-upon penalty for every day he or she is delinquent. Finally, the Agreement contains a self-explanatory provision, Item 12, regarding the Consultant's prior inventions.

3. What If the Consultant Invents?

Since many consultants are quite clever, they often come up with patentable improvements, ramifications, or even better versions of the basic invention which they're hired to build, test, or develop. This naturally brings up the issue of who will own and be able to use the consultant's inventions. Having been involved in many disputes in this area, I know that an ounce of prevention—that is, a prior stipulation as to who will own any inventions the Consultant makes—can prevent many misunderstandings, arguments, and even lawsuits later on.

With this end in mind, I've written the agreement to require the Consultant to disclose all innovations made to you, to sign any patent applications which you choose to file on the Consultant's inventions, and also to assign such inventions to you. Note also that the inventions that belong to you (the Contractor) are those that arise out of the Consultant's work under the agreement, even if conceived on the Consultant's own time. This is a customary clause in employment agreements (see Chapter 16) and is provided so that the Consultant won't be able to claim that a valuable invention made under the agreement isn't yours because it was made on the Consultant's time. Generally the Consultant will be a sole inventor (who should be the only one named in the patent application if the Consultant's invention can exist independently of yours), and a joint inventor with you if the invention is closely related to or improves on yours. (More on inventorship in Chapter 10, Section F.) This is because all of the true inventor(s) must be named as inventor(s) in all patent applications no matter who owns the application. I provide an assignment form and a Joint Owners' Agreement in Appendix 7. (See Chapter 16.)

G. The Next Step

Once you've commercially evaluated your invention—that is, garnered all your input and filled out your evaluation and summary sheets with the positive and negative factors—you're in a better position to decide whether or not to go ahead. If you decide to, your next step is to decide whether the invention will qualify for a patent under the patent laws. To do this, you should first learn the basic four legal requirements for getting a patent. (See Chapter 5.) Then, if it meets the first two of these requirements, make a formal patent search (see Chapter 6) to determine if it's sufficiently novel to satisfy the other two requirements. When you make this search, you'll also obtain valuable commercial information about prior developments in the area of your invention. E.g., if you've invented a new electric fork and your search shows 30 patents on electric forks and you've never seen any of these in the market, you should seriously question the commercial feasibility of this concept, even if it's patentable.

If, on the other hand, your commercial evaluation leaves you uncertain, though you feel there's good potential, wait a while before proceeding. The passage of time may give you a new perspective that can make your decision easier. If after a couple of weeks you still can't make up your mind, it's probably best to proceed to the next step (the determination of patentability, including a search). If this determination discloses that your invention is already known or otherwise unpatentable, that's the end of the road. But if it shows that you have a patentable invention, you should probably attempt to patent and market it rather than let a potentially valuable and profitable idea die without being given its day in the sun.

H. Summary

You should carefully evaluate the salability of your invention before filing a patent application, because a patent alone will not make you rich or famous—the invention must also become a success in the marketplace. Test marketing is a valuable activity, but it will destroy your foreign rights if done before filing in the U.S. Also any U.S. application must be filed within one year after the invention is put on the market or shown publicly. Although it can't predict success with certainty, a commercial evaluation can be very valuable. I recommend a study of all of the commercial factors (cost, size, weight, etc.) for their positive or negative aspects and to discover any fatal considerations. Also consult with experts and consumers, but take precautions against invention theft by using the Nondisclosure Agreement and other safeguards. Building a prototype is invaluable for obtaining commercial and technical information, but if you use a model maker, you must also take precautions by using the Consultant's Agreement. ■

Chapter 5

Is It Patentable?

Inventor's Commandment #6

One-Year Rule: Treat the "one-year rule" as holy. You must file your regular or provisional patent application within one year of the date on which your invention (or any product that embodies it) is first published, commercially used, sold, offered for sale, or disclosed to a group of people without restriction. If you wish to preserve your foreign rights and prevent theft of your creation, file your patent application before you publish details of or sell your creation.

Inventor's Commandment #7

To evaluate or argue the patentability of any invention, use a two-step process: a) First determine what novel features (§ 102) the invention has over the closest prior-art reference(s)—novelty can be a new physical (hardware) feature, a new combination or rearrangement of two separate old features, or a new use of an old feature; and b) Then determine if the novelty produces any new and unexpected results or otherwise indicates unobviousness (§ 103).

Here we deal with the specific subject of what's legally patentable and what's not. Over many decades, both Congress and the courts have hammered out a series of laws and accompanying rules of interpretation that the PTO and the courts (and hence you) must use to separate the patentable wheat from the unpatentable chaff. All of these laws and rules are introduced in this chapter and then referred to repeatedly in later chapters.

Because an understanding of the material in this chapter is crucial to the rest of the book and to an understanding of patents in general, I urge you to relax and read it carefully.

A. Patentability Compared to Commercial Viability

If you assessed the commercial potential of your invention, as suggested in Chapter 4, and your invention received a passing grade, your next question probably is, "Can I get a patent on it?" The answer to this question can be crucial, since you're likely to have a difficult time commercially exploiting an invention that isn't patentable, despite its commercial feasibility. Although you may be able to realize value from an invention by selling it to a manufacturer as a trade secret (a difficult sale to make!), or by selling it yourself and using a clever trademark, or (in some cases) by relying on copyright protection and unfair competition laws (as explained in Chapter 1), such approaches are usually inferior to the broad offensive rights that a patent offers. Concisely put, if your invention fails to pass the tests of this chapter, reconsider its commercial prospects and whether other areas of intellectual property will provide adequate offensive rights in the absence of a patent.

You should consider the commercial viability and patentability tests separately, since commercial success and patentability don't always coincide. Most patented inventions are not commercially successful and many inventions, such as the computer, are commercially successful but are not broadly patentable. Your invention should pass both tests before you file a patent application on it.

B. Legal Requirements for a Utility Patent

As you can see from Fig. 5A, the legal requirements for a utility patent can be represented by a mountain having four upward sections, each of which represents a separate test that every invention must pass to be awarded the patent. The PTO is required by statute to examine every utility patent application to be sure it passes each of these tests. If it does, the PTO must award the inventor(s) a patent.

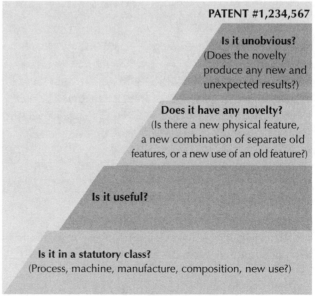

PATENT #1,234,567

Is it unobvious?
(Does the novelty produce any new and unexpected results?)

Does it have any novelty?
(Is there a new physical feature, a new combination of separate old features, or a new use of an old feature?)

Is it useful?

Is it in a statutory class?
(Process, machine, manufacture, composition, new use?)

Fig. 5A—Patentability Mountain
The Four Legal Requirements for Getting a Utility Patent

Design and Plant Patents

Design patent applications must cover a new, original, and ornamental design for an article of manufacture, and are examined in the same way and must pass the same unobviousness test as utility patent applications, except that the "better functioning" tests that are used to evaluate unobviousness (see Section F, below) are not used, since only the aesthetics of a design invention are relevant.

Plant patent applications are subject to the same legal requirements as utility patent applications, except that the statutory class requirement (first test) is obviously not relevant: plants provide their own statutory class. Since plant patents are relatively rare and are of very specialized interest, I won't go into detail except to set forth the additional legal requirements for getting one. They are: (1) the plant must be asexually reproduced; and (2) the plant must be a new variety. These may include cultivated sports, mutants, hybrids, and newly found seedlings, but should not be a tuber, propagated plant, bacterium, or a plant found in an uncultivated state. You may also obtain a monopoly on a sexually reproduced plant under the Plant Variety Protection Act. (For more information, see Chapter 1, Section B.)

Utility patents have been issued for man-made plants (or elements of plants) since the late 1980s. These plants can be reproduced either sexually (by seeds) or asexually (by grafts, cuttings, or other human means).

Utility patents have also been issued for elements of plants, such as proteins, genes, DNA, buds, pollen, fruit, plant-based chemicals, and the processes used in the manufacture of these plant products. To obtain a utility patent, the plant must be made by humans and must fit within the statutory requirements (utility, novelty, and nonobviousness). The patent must describe and claim the specific characteristics of the plant for which offensive rights are sought. Sometimes the best way to meet this requirement is to deposit seeds or plant tissue at a specified public depository. Many countries have International Depository Authorities for such purposes.

Although a utility patent is harder and more time-consuming to acquire than a plant patent, a utility patent is considered to be a stronger form of offensive right. For example, a plant covered by a utility patent can be infringed if it is reproduced either sexually or asexually. By contrast, a plant patent can only be infringed if it is reproduced asexually from the actual plant protected by the patent.

Since the utility patent owner can thoroughly prevent others from making and using the invention, does this mean the buyer of a patented seed cannot sell the resulting plants to the public? No, because according to patent law, the seed's purchaser can sell the resulting plants but cannot manufacture the seed line.

The four requirements and the pertinent respective statutes are:

1. **Statutory Class:** Will the PTO consider that the invention fits into one of five classes established by Congress? (35 USC 101.) Or put specifically, will the PTO regard it as either a:
   - process (method)
   - machine
   - article of manufacture
   - composition, or
   - "new use" of one of the first four.

2. **Utility:** Can the invention properly be regarded as a useful one (or ornamental in the case of designs)? (35 USC 101.)

3. **Novelty:** Will the PTO consider that the invention is novel—that is, does it have an aspect that is different in any way from all previous inventions and knowledge (that is, the relevant prior art)? (35 USC 102.)

4. **Unobviousness:** Will the PTO consider that the invention is unobvious from the standpoint of someone who has ordinary skill in the specific technology involved in the invention—that is, does it provide one or more new and unexpected results? (When dealing with designs, the question becomes: Will the PTO consider the design unobvious in an ornamental or aesthetic sense?) (35 USC 103.)

As Fig. 5A shows, the first three tests are represented by relatively short steps. The last one, unobviousness, is relatively high. This is a real-life reflection of what commonly happens to patent applications before the PTO (or to patents when they're challenged in court). In other words, the PTO will find that most inventions (1) fit within at least

IS IT PATENTABLE?   **5 / 5**

one statutory class, (2) have utility (or ornamentality for designs), and (3) possess novelty. However, most of the patent applications that fail to reach the patent summit (almost half of all patent applications that are filed) are rejected by the PTO because it regards the invention as obvious.

The Patent Laws

Congress derives its power to make the patent statutes from the U.S. Constitution (Art. 1, Sec. 8). The patent statutes passed by Congress can be found in Title 35 of the United States Code (35 USC). Patent statutes are typically referred to by the section of the USC they are put into. So, the statute that creates the five statutory patent classes is referred to as 35 USC 101 or 35 USC § (Sec.) 101. The statutes, in turn, authorize the PTO to issue its Rules of Practice (which are relatively broad, and are termed in the law 37 CFR (Code of Federal Regulations) 1.1, etc.), and its *Manual of Patent Examining Procedure* (MPEP) is relatively specific—see Appendix 2, Resources: Government Publications, Patent Websites, and Books of Use and Interest. Fig. 5B illustrates the relationship between these authorities. The size of each authority varies from one sentence in the Constitution to about 600,000 words in the MPEP, as illustrated below.

Fig. 5B—Patent Authorities

Let's now look at each of these requirements in more detail.

C. Requirement #1: The Statutory Classes

The PTO must consider your invention to fall into one of the five statutory classes in order for it to be patentable. If it does, it's "within a statutory class or category." That is, it's one of the five types of subject matter on which the law authorizes the PTO to grant a patent, assuming the other requirements for a patent are met.

Fortunately, the statutory categories established by the patent laws, although only five, are very comprehensive. Further, the Supreme Court has stated that anything under the sun that is made by humans, except for laws of nature, natural phenomena, abstract ideas, and humans, falls within these classes. *Diamond v. Chakrabarty*, 447 U.S. 303 (1980); *Diamond v. Diehr*, 450 U.S. 175 (1981). So the statutory class requirement is rarely a problem anymore, except as noted below. As we'll discuss below the "abstract ideas" exception is the one which precludes the patenting of abstract software algorithms. Accordingly, you'll usually be able to squeeze most inventions into at least one of them. In many instances an invention will fit into more than one category, since they overlap to some extent. This isn't a problem, since you don't have to specify the one to which your invention belongs when you file your patent application. But you should be fairly sure it does not fall into one of the exceptions below. Otherwise, the PTO may reject it under Section 101 as "nonstatutory subject matter."

Let's discuss the five statutory classes in more detail:

1. Processes, Including Software

Sometimes termed "methods," processes are ways of doing or making things that involve more than purely mental manipulations. Processes always have one or more steps, each of which expresses some activity and manipulates or treats some physical thing. Purely manual processes were formerly regarded as nonstatutory, but now even these are being patented so long as they attain a useful result. Thus patents have recently been granted on a method of gripping a golf club and a method of using a keyboard.

a. Conventional Processes
Examples of conventional processes are heat treatments, chemical reactions for making or changing something, and ways of making products or chemicals. The PTO has even recently granted patents on processes of feeding chickens a special diet that results in better eggs, and combing the hair to cover a bald area, and analyzing essays for plagiarism. To give you an example of an extreme process patent, I repre-

sented one side in a patent lawsuit that involved a patent on a process of attaching a hairpiece to a bald person's scalp by putting suture anchors in the scalp and sewing the piece to the suture anchors. However, although surgical operations can still be patented, it no longer makes sense to do so since new legislation exempts medical practitioners from infringing any patent on a medical procedure per se. See Chapter 15, Section F3.

b.   Software Processes

Since most software-related inventions are claimed as processes, I'll discuss them here. However, be aware that software inventions can also be claimed as machines. As indicated in Chapter 1, algorithms that merely crunch numbers without a tangible, useful, and concrete result can't be patented since they are considered abstract ideas. (An algorithm is a computerized procedure.) However, if the software or algorithm affects some hardware or process, or if it produces a useful, concrete, and tangible result, it falls within a statutory class as a machine or a process. If it merely manipulates numbers or solves an algorithm, then the PTO will not consider it within a statutory class. For example, if the process analyzes EKG, spectrographic, seismic, or data bit signals, controls a milling machine, creates useful images on a computer screen, formats the printing of mathematical formulae, recognizes patterns or voices, or selects stocks that will beat an index, then it is considered to control hardware or a process or produce a useful, concrete, and tangible result and is statutory subject matter. However, if the process merely crunches numbers, generates a non-useful curve, or calculates distances without any practical purpose, then it is considered to be nonstatutory.

However, the main patent court—the CAFC—determined that an algorithm for making a smoother diagonal line on a monitor is Statutory Subject Matter (SSM), probably because smoother diagonal lines look better and are easier to see. (*In re Alappat* 33 F.3d 1526 (CAFC 1994).) Also, the CAFC has held (*In re Lowry* 32 F.3d (CAFC 1994).) that a general purpose computer data structure that organizes information into different categories (selected from an infinite number of categories) is SSM, no doubt because humans can control the selection. And a process for allowing mutual funds to pool their assets into a partnership for administrative and tax advantages was held to be SSM because of its practical utility. *State Street Bank & Trust Co. v. Signal Financial Group, Inc.*, 149 F.3d 1368 (Fed. Cir. 1998), cert. denied 119 S.Ct. 851 (1999).

So if you have an invention involving an algorithm, ask if it produces a useful, concrete, and tangible result, such as the above examples. If so it's probably SSM. If not, such as if it just calculates the value of π, or manipulates numbers or shapes for the fun of it without any practical application, then it's non-SSM.

c.   Internet and Business Method Patents

Until the 1998 court decision in the *State Street* case (see Section C1b), the PTO rarely granted patents for methods of doing business. The PTO reasoned that most business methods were abstract ideas that it traditionally refused to patent. But it gradually started granting patents on business methods and the courts validated this change in the *State Street Bank* case. The court ruled that patent laws were intended to protect *any* method, whether or not it required the aid of a computer, so long as it produced a "useful, concrete and tangible result." Thus with one stroke the court legitimized both software patents and methods of doing business, opening the way for a group of patents that have been categorized as Internet patents and business method patents.

Although the terms "business method patent" and "Internet patent" have been used interchangeably in the media, these patents may deal with mutually exclusive concepts. For example, a patented method of doing business does not have to pertain to an online application. Likewise, a patent for a process used on the Internet may be more accurately described as a software patent than a business method.

Patent attorney Stephen Glazier, in his book, *e-Patent Strategies* (Law & Business), divides these patents into two groups, e-patents and i-patents: e-patents include patents for services enabled by software—these can grant monopolies for new telecom services, new financial services, and new ways of delivering old services; i-patents, according to Glazier, are for Internet applications—for example online commerce applications such as Amazon's "One-Click" system, a method that allows a repeat customer to bypass address and credit card data entry forms when placing an online order (U.S. Pat. No. 5,960,411).

Regardless of their categorization, all of these patents seem to have one thing in common: They expand ways of doing business in new technologies. In the six months following the *State Street* ruling, patent filings for software and Internet business methods increased by 40%. In response to the development of these new methods, the PTO created a new classification for such applications: "Data processing: financial, business practice, management or cost/price determination."

Following the *State Street* case, patents have been issued for business methods such as:

• an online shopping rewards program, referred to as the "ClickReward" (U.S. Pat. No. 5,774,870);

- a system that provides financial incentives for citizens to view political messages on the Internet (U.S. Pat. No. 5,855,008);
- an online auction system by which consumers name the price they are willing to pay and the first willing seller gets the sale (also known as "name your price" or as a "reverse auction" (U.S. Pat. No. 5,794,207); and
- a process that supposedly blocks the auction practices described in the previous patent (U.S. Pat. No. 5,845,265).

Sometimes a business may have been using a particular business method prior to another company acquiring a patent on that method. For example, if Business A files for a business method patent, but Business B can show that it implemented and commercially used the method publicly more than a year prior to the filing. In that case, Business B has a good defense against the patent. This defense was created under a 1999 amendment to the patent law. (35 USC 273(b).)

Many critics contend that patent examiners simply do not have the tools and resources to competently investigate whether an Internet business method is novel or nonobvious. One reason that the PTO is ill-equipped is that when determining novelty, patent examiners have traditionally reviewed past patents and other information in the PTO library. Because the Internet revolution is new, this almost guarantees that the PTO will not detect similar Web-based methods and software process developed recently.

In response to this criticism, the PTO announced in March 2000 that it is adding an additional "layer of review" to business method patent applications and is hiring technology specialists to aid examiners in the areas of finance, e-commerce, insurance, and Internet infrastructure.

2. Machines

Machines are devices or things used for accomplishing a task. Like processes, they usually involve some activity or motion that's performed by working parts, but in machines the emphasis is on the parts or hardware, rather than the activity per se. Put differently, while a process involves the actual steps of manipulation of an item or work piece (the machine that does the manipulation is of secondary import), a machine is the thing that does the manipulating and the steps or manner of its operation, and the process itself, or material worked upon, are of lesser import. I like to classify machines into two categories: conventional and software.

a. Conventional Machines

Examples of conventional machines are cigarette lighters, robots, sewage treatment plants, clocks, all electronic circuits, automobiles, boats, rockets, telephones, TVs, computers, VCRs, disk drives, printers, lasers, photocopiers, and a layout for a bank. The PTO has even issued a patent on an electronic signal, by itself, as a machine (U.S. Pat. No. 5,815,526). Many machine inventions can also be claimed as a process and/or as a machine. For instance, an electric circuit or a weaving machine can be claimed in terms of its actual hardware and/or as a process for manipulating an electrical signal or weaving fabrics.

b. Software Machines

As stated in the previous section ("1. Processes, Including Software"), while most software inventions are claimed and regarded as processes, they can usually also be claimed and regarded as machines. For example, a system for controlling a milling machine according to certain measured parameters of an object can be claimed and regarded either as a process or a machine. As a *process* the system would be regarded and claimed as follows: (a) measuring an object to obtain a set of measurements, and (b) controlling a milling machine according to the set of measurements. As a *machine* the system would be regarded and claimed as follows: (a) means [or an apparatus] for measuring an object to obtain a set of measurements, and (b) means [or an apparatus] for adjusting a milling machine according to the set of measurements.

Note that the first step or "means" (the mensuration or the means for measuring) can be regarded as either an action or as the hardware for performing the action. This applies equally to the second step. Sometimes a software invention can't be regarded as a machine; for example, consider the software inventions defined by the two sample claims in Chapter 9, Sec. G13. The two inventions relate exclusively to process-type inventions and are actually so close to being all mental steps as to be almost (but not quite!) non-SSM.

On the other hand, virtually every machine-type software invention can also be regarded as a process, since each part of a "software" machine always performs some action or step. Insofar as possible, both types of claims can and should usually be provided in a single patent application. As stated in the previous paragraph, it's not important which category (process or machine) you can subsume your software invention under, and it's usually best to claim it both ways.

As I've said, there are no clear lines between the five statutory classes. The important thing to realize is that it doesn't matter as long as your invention fits into at least one of them. Put differently, you needn't be able to tell a machine from a process to qualify for a patent.

3. Manufactures

Manufactures, sometimes termed "articles of manufacture," are items that have been made by human hands or by machines. This excludes naturally occurring things, like rocks, gold, shrimp, and wood, or slightly modified naturally occurring things, like a shrimp with its head and vein removed. But if you discover a new and unobvious use for a naturally occurring thing, such as a way to use the molecules in a piece of gold as part of a computer memory, you can patent the invention as a new use (see below), or as a machine (the gold with the necessary hardware to make it function as a memory).

Manufactures are relatively simple things that don't have working or moving parts as prime features. Clearly, you will see some overlap between the machine and the manufacture categories. Many devices, such as mechanical pencils, cigarette lighters, and electronic circuits can be classified as either. Examples of manufactures are erasers, desks, houses, wires, tires, books, cloth, chairs, containers, transistors, dolls, hairpieces, ladders, envelopes, buildings, floppy disks, knives, hand tools, and boxes. I was recently involved with a patent on a most unusual article—a musical dildo. The PTO has even issued a patent on a vitamin-fortified egg.

Examples of Inventions That Don't Fit Within a Statutory Class

The following are examples of "inventions" that don't fit within any statutory class and hence are nonstatutory subject matter that cannot be patented:
- Processes performed solely with one's mind (such as a method of meditation or a method of speed-reading)
- Naturally occurring phenomena and articles, even if modified somewhat, such as a shrimp with head and vein removed
- Laws of nature, including abstract scientific or mathematical principles (John Napier's invention of logarithms in 1614 was immensely innovative and valuable, but it would never get past the bottom level of the patentability mountain)
- An arrangement of printed matter without some accompanying instrumentality; printed matter per se isn't patentable, but a printed label on a mattress telling how to turn it to ensure even wear, or dictionary index tabs that guide you to the desired word more rapidly, have been patented as articles of manufacture
- Methods that have no practical utility, that is, that don't produce any useful, concrete, and tangible result—for example, a method for extracting π. However, securities trading systems, credit accounting systems, etc., involving account and file postings—have been held patentable
- Computer programs per se, naked computer instructions, or algorithms that don't produce any useful, concrete, and tangible result such as the algorithm for extracting π.
- Ideas per se. Thoughts or goals not expressed in concrete form or usage are obviously not assignable to any of the five categories above. If you have an idea, you must show how it can be made and used in tangible form so as to be useful in the real world, even if only on paper, before the PTO will accept it. For example, an idea for a burping doll can be effectively patented by patenting a doll with a burping mechanism.

4. Compositions of Matter

Compositions of matter are items such as chemical compositions, conglomerates, aggregates, or other chemically significant substances that are usually supplied in bulk (solid or particulate), liquid, or gaseous form. Examples are road-building compositions, all chemicals, gasoline, fuel gas, glue, paper, soap, drugs, microbes, animals (nonhuman), food additives, plastics, and even chicken eggs with high vitamin E (U.S. Pat. No. 5,246,717).

Although, as stated, naturally occurring things such as wood and rocks can't be patented, purified forms of naturally occurring things, such as medicinals extracted from herbs, can be. One inventor even obtained a composition of matter patent on a new element he discovered. And recently, genetically altered plants, microbes, genes, and nonhuman animals have been allowed under this category. Compositions are usually homogeneous chemical compositions or aggregates whose chemical natures are of primary importance and whose shapes are of secondary import, while manufactures are items whose physical shapes are significant, but whose chemical compositions are of lesser import.

5. New Uses of Any of the Above

A new-use invention is actually a new and unobvious process or method for using an old and known invention, whether it be an old and known process, composition, machine, or article. The inventive act here isn't the creation of a new thing or process per se, but the discovery of a new use for something that in itself is old.

If you discover a new and unobvious (unrelated) use of any old invention or thing, you can get a patent on your discovery. For example, suppose you discover that your Venetian-blind cleaner can also be used as a seed planter. You obviously can't get a patent on the physical hardware that constitutes the Venetian-blind cleaner, since you didn't invent it—someone already patented, invented, and/or designed it first—but you can get a patent on the specific new use (seed planting) of the old hardware. In other examples, one inventor obtained a patent on a new use for aspirin: feeding it to swine to increase their rate of growth; one got a patent on the new use of a powerful vacuum to suck prairie dogs out of the ground; and a client of mine got a patent on the new use of a simple strut in a room corner to provide a tool holder. Note, however, that if your invention has any new hardware, your invention probably should be claimed as new hardware, rather than (or in addition to) a new use of old hardware.

New-use inventions are relatively rare and technically are a form of, and must be claimed as, a process. (35 USC 100(b).) However, most patent experts treat them as a distinct category. See Chapter 9 for a discussion of patent claims.

D. Requirement #2: Utility

To be patentable your invention must be useful. Problems are seldom encountered with the literal utility requirement; *any* usefulness will suffice, provided the usefulness is functional, and not aesthetic. But remember, in Chapter 4, I recommend that the usefulness of your invention be relatively great in order to pass the "commercial viability" test. It's hard for me to think of an invention that couldn't be used for some purpose. However, utility is occasionally an issue in the chemical area when an inventor tries to patent a new chemical for which a use hasn't yet been found but for which its inventor will likely find a use later. If the inventor can't state (and prove, if challenged) a realistic use, the PTO won't grant a patent on the chemical. A chemical intermediate that can be used to produce another useful chemical is itself regarded as useful. Software-based inventions usually satisfy the utility requirement, since virtually all software has a utilitarian function, even if used to create aesthetic designs on an idle monitor or to evaluate golf scores or mutual fund assets. The main problem with software-based inventions is that they may not fall (or may not be claimed in a way so that they fall) into a statutory class, as noted in the previous section. (Also see Chapter 9.) Nonetheless, a software invention should be tested for utility just like any other invention just in case it falls into one of the "legally not useful" categories listed below.

Notwithstanding the fact that virtually all inventions are useful in the literal sense of the word, some types of inventions are deemed "not useful" as a matter of law, and patents on them are accordingly denied by the PTO. Let's look at this more closely.

1. Unsafe New Drugs

The PTO won't grant a patent on any new drug unless the applicant can show that not only is it useful in treating some condition, but also that it's relatively safe for its intended purpose. Put another way, the PTO considers an unsafe drug useless. Most drug patent applications won't be allowed unless the Food and Drug Administration (FDA) has approved tests of the drug for efficacy and safety, but drugs that are generally recognized as safe, or are in a "safe" chemical category with known safe drugs, don't need prior FDA approval to be patentable.

2. Whimsical Inventions

Occasionally, the PTO will reject an application for a patent when it finds the invention to be totally whimsical, even though "useful" in some bizarre sense. Nevertheless, in 1937 the PTO issued a patent on a rear windshield (with tail-operated wiper) for a horse (U.S. Pat. No. 2,079,053). They regarded this as having utility as an amusement or gag.

Most patent attorneys have collections of humorous patents. I could easily fill the rest of this book with my collection, but I'll restrain myself and briefly describe just a few.

- a male chastity device (U.S. Pat. No. 587,994—1897);
- a figure-eight-shaped device to hold your big toes together to prevent sunburned inner thighs (U.S. Pat. No. 3,712,271—1973);
- dentures with individual teeth shaped like the wearer's head (U.S. Pat. No. 3,049,804—1962); and
- a dress hanger with breasts (U.S. Pat. No. patent D226,943—1973).

Also, even though the PTO issued U.S. Pat. No. 2,632,266 in 1953 for a fur-encircled keyhole, the censor wouldn't let me show this on a TV show.

3. Inventions Useful Only for Illegal Purposes

An important requirement for obtaining a patent, which Congress hasn't mentioned, but which the PTO and courts have brought in on their own initiative (by stretching the definition of "useful"), is legality. For example, inventions useful solely for illegal purposes, such as disabling burglar alarms, safecracking, copying currency, and defrauding the public, might be incredibly useful to some elements in our society, but the PTO won't issue patents on them. However, most inventions in this category can be described or claimed in a "legal" way. For example, a police radar detector would qualify for a patent if it's described as a tester to see if a radar is working or as a device for reminding drivers to watch their speed.

4. Immoral Inventions

In the past, the PTO has—again on its own initiative—included morality in its requirements. But, in recent years, with increased sexual liberality, the requirement is now virtually nonexistent. Thus the PTO now regularly issues patents on sexual aids, gags, and stimulants.

5. Nonoperable Inventions, Including Perpetual Motion Machines

Another facet of the useful requirement is operability. The invention must appear to the PTO to be workable before they will allow it. Thus, if your invention is a perpetual-motion machine, or a metaphysical-energy converter, or, more realistically, a very esoteric invention that looks technically questionable (it looks like it just plain won't work or violates some well-accepted physical law), your examiner will reject it as lacking utility because of inoperability. In this case you would either have to produce a logical, technical argument refuting the examiner's reasons (you can include affidavits or declarations of witnesses and experts and test results), or bring the invention in for a demonstration to prove its operability.

Operability is rarely questioned, since most patent applications cover inventions that employ known principles or hardware and will obviously work as described. If the examiner questions operability, however, you have the burden of proof. And note that all patent examiners have technical degrees (some even have Ph.D.'s), so expect a very stringent test if the operability of your invention is ever questioned.

Despite the foregoing, the PTO occasionally issues a patent on what appears to be a perpetual-motion-like machine, as they did in 1979 (U.S. Pat. No. 4,151,431). This raises an important point. The fact that a patent is granted doesn't mean that the underlying invention will work. It only means that the invention appears to work on paper (or that the PTO can't figure out why it won't work).

The PTO, however, has recently become more careful about perpetual-energy or perpetual-motion machines, as you may have noted from a recently publicized case where it denied an inventor a patent on an energy machine. The inventor took the case to the courts, but lost after the National Bureau of Standards, acting as a court expert, found the machine didn't have an efficiency of over 100%.

It's a common misconception that the PTO won't "accept" patent applications on perpetual-motion machines: the PTO will accept the application for filing (see Chapter 13), since filing and docketing are clerical functions. However, the examiner (a degreed professional) will almost certainly reject it later as inoperative (giving reasons) after a formal examination.

6. Nuclear Weapons

The invention must not be a nuclear weapon; such inventions aren't patentable because of a special statute. However, if you've invented a doomsday machine, don't be discouraged: you can be rewarded directly by making an application with the DOE (Department of Energy), formerly the Atomic Energy Commission.

7. Theoretical Phenomena

Theoretical phenomena per se, such as the phenomenon of superconductivity, the transistor effect, or the discovery of logarithms aren't patentable per se. You must describe and claim (see Chapter 9) a practical, realistic, hardware-based version of your invention for the PTO to consider it useful.

8. Aesthetic Purpose

If the invention's sole purpose or "function" is aesthetic, the PTO will reject it as lacking utility; such inventions should usually be the subject of a design patent application. A beautiful vase of unique design, a computer case whose unique shape does not make the computer operate better, and a computer program for producing a low-brightness design on an idle computer monitor, where the only novelty is the aesthetic uniqueness of the design, are examples of inventions which the law considers to lack statutory utility. However, if the design of the vase made it easier and safer to lift, if the shape of the computer case made it cheaper to manufacture, or if the computer program produced, on an idle computer monitor, a unique design showing a low-brightness aesthetic conversion of the last file worked on in order to remind the user of that file, then statutory utility would be present.

E. Requirement #3: Novelty

Now let's look at the novelty requirement of a patent. Like "unobviousness" (discussed in Section F), this requirement is often misunderstood.

1. Prior Art

Your invention must be novel in order to qualify for a patent. In order for your invention to meet this novelty test it must differ physically in some way from all prior developments that are available to the public anywhere in the world. In the realm of patent law, these prior developments and concepts are collectively referred to as "prior art." Accordingly,

before I tell you how to determine whether your invention is novel, it's vital to understand what your invention must differ from—that is, how the law defines "prior art."

a.   What Is Prior Art?

According to Section 102 of the patent laws, the term "prior art" means generally the state of knowledge existing or publicly available either before the date of your invention or more than one year prior to your earliest patent application date.

b.   Date of Your Invention

Clearly, in order to decide what prior art is with respect to any given invention, it's first necessary to determine the "date of your invention." Most inventors think it's the date on which one files a patent application. While this date is important, and you can always use it if you have nothing better, under the U.S. patent system you can usually go back earlier than your filing date if you can prove that you conceived of the invention or built and tested it earlier than your filing date. (See Chapter 3.) That is, your date of invention is the earliest of:

- the date you filed your patent application (provisional or regular);
- the date you can prove you built and tested your invention in the U.S. or a country that is a member of NAFTA or the WTO (World Trade Organization). Most industrial countries are members (35 USC 104); or
- the date you can prove you conceived of your invention in a NAFTA or WTO country, provided you can also prove you were diligent thereafter in building and testing it or filing a patent application on it.

So, from now on, when I refer to "your earliest provable date of invention," this will mean the earliest of the above three dates (filing, building and testing, or conception accompanied by diligence) that you can prove.

Reduction to Practice

In the law, the building and testing of an invention is called a "reduction to practice." The filing of a patent application, while not an actual reduction to practice, is termed a "constructive" reduction to practice because the law will construe it in the same way it does an actual reduction to practice. As discussed in Chapter 3, Section I, the filing of a valid Provisional Patent Application (PPA) also qualifies as a constructive reduction to practice.

The kinds of proof that the PTO and the courts typically rely on are the witnessed records of the type I described in Chapter 3. If you follow my recommendations in Chapter 3 about making proper records, you'll be able to go back to your date of conception, which usually will be at least several months before your filing date. More on this in Chapters 13 and 16.

Now that you know what your earliest date of invention is, you also know that the relevant "prior art" is the knowledge that existed prior to that date. More precisely, prior art comprises all of the items in the categories discussed below in Subsection d. Any item in any of these categories can be used against your invention at any time, either by the PTO to reject your patent application, or later on (if the PTO didn't find it or didn't give it adequate weight) to invalidate your patent in court.

c. Your Invention Must Not Be Publicly Known More Than One Year Prior to Your Filing Date— The One-Year Rule

In addition to the six categories under Subsection d, below, prior art is also knowledge about your invention that has become publicly known more than one year prior to the date you file your patent application (either a regular patent application or a valid Provisional Patent Application, as described in Chapter 3, Section I). Known as the "one-year rule," the patent laws state that you must file a patent application within one year after you sell, offer for sale, or commercially or publicly use or describe your invention. If you fail to file within one year of such sale, offer for sale, public or commercial disclosure or use, the law bars you from obtaining a valid patent on the invention, even if you conceived and built and tested it before the sale or publication. Another way to put this, since we're talking about novelty, is that after a year following a sale, offer for sale, public or commercial use, or knowledge about your invention, the PTO will no longer consider it novel. While I've listed this "one-year rule" under the "prior art" heading for the sake of logical placement, it's so important that I've made it Inventor's Commandment #6 at the beginning of this chapter.

Foreign Filing and the One-Year Rule

While you have a year after publication or use to file in the U.S., I advise you not to do so, since most foreign countries aren't so lenient. If you think you may want to foreign file, you shouldn't offer for sale, sell, publicly use, or publish before you file in the U.S. For instance, suppose it's 2005 November 16, and you've just invented a new type of paint. If you have no intention of filing in another country, you can use, publish, or sell your invention now and still file your U.S. patent application (PPA or regular) any time up to 2006 November 16. However, if you think you may eventually want to foreign file on your invention, you should file in the U.S. (PPA or regular) before publicizing your invention. Then you can publish or sell the invention freely without the loss of any foreign rights in the major industrial "Convention" or treaty countries, provided you file there within one year after your U.S. filing date. This is because, under international conventions (agreements or treaties), you'll be entitled to your U.S. filing date in such countries. In "non-Convention" countries (such as Pakistan and Venezuela) you must file before you publicize the invention. (See Chapter 12.)

(The above year-month-day date format is from the International Standards Organization (ISO). It is also commonly used in computerese and trademark applications. I use it because it provides a logical descending order that facilitates calculating the one-year rule and other periods.)

d. Specifics of Prior Art

Now that we've broadly defined prior art, let's take a closer look at what it typically consists of, per 35 USC 102.

i. Prior Printed Publications Anywhere

Any printed publication, written by anyone, and from anywhere in the world, in any language, is considered valid prior art if it was published either (a) before your earliest provable date of invention (see above), or (b) over one year before you file your patent application. The term "printed publication" thus includes patents (U.S. and foreign), books, magazines (including trade and professional journals), Russian (or former U.S.S.R.) Inventor's Certificates, and publicly available technical papers and abstracts. Even photocopied theses, provided they were made publicly available by putting them in a college library, will constitute prior art. The PTO has even used old Dick Tracy comic strips showing a wristwatch radio as prior art!

Computer Tip. While the statute speaks of "printed" publications, I'm sure that information on computer-information utilities or networks would be considered a printed publication, provided it was publicly available.

The "prior printed publications" category is the most important category of prior art and will generally constitute most of the prior art that you'll encounter. And most of the prior printed publications that the PTO refers to (cites) when it's processing your application, and that you will encounter in your search, will be patents, mainly U.S. patents.

ii. U.S. Patents Filed by Others Prior to Your Invention's Conception

Any U.S. patent that has a filing date earlier than your earliest provable date of invention is considered valid prior art. This is so even if the patent issues after you file your application. For example, suppose you conceive of your invention on 2003 June 9, and you file your patent application on 2003 August 9, two months later. Then, six months after your filing date, on 2004 February 9, a patent to Goldberger issues that shows all or part of your invention. If Goldberger's patent was any other type of publication, it wouldn't be prior art to your application since it was published after your filing date. However assume that Goldberger's patent application was filed on 2001 June 8, one day earlier than your date of conception. Under Section 102(e) of the patent laws, the PTO must consider the Goldberger patent as prior art to your application, since Goldberger's application was filed prior to your invention's date of conception. If a patent claims benefits on a PPA, then the PPA's filing date is considered the effective prior-art date for the patent.

A common misconception is that only in-force patents (that is, patents that haven't yet expired) count as prior art. This isn't true. Any earlier patent, even if it was issued 150 years ago, will constitute prior art against an invention. Otherwise, patents would have a lesser status than other publications.

iii. Prior Publicly Available Knowledge or Use of the Invention in the U.S.

Even if there's no written record of it, any public knowledge of the invention, or use of it by you or others in the U.S., which existed or occurred either (a) before your earliest provable date of invention, or (b) over one year before you file your patent application, is valid prior art. For example,

an earlier heat-treating process used openly by a blacksmith in a small town, although never published or widely known, is a prior public use which will defeat your right to a patent on a similar process. It has been held that allowing even one person to use your invention without restriction will constitute public use. With respect to public knowledge, an example would be a talk at a publicly accessible technical society. Recently, even a showing of a kaleidoscope without restriction at a party with 30 attendees was held to be prior public knowledge. Or as one writer commented, "Throw a party and lose your patent rights!"

For still another example of a public use, suppose that you invented a new type of paint and you use it to paint your building in downtown Philadelphia. You forget to file a patent application and leave the paint on for 13 months: it's now too late to file a valid patent application since you've used your invention publicly for over a year. Put another way, your own invention would now be prior art against any patent application you file.

This public-use-and-knowledge category of prior art is almost never used by the PTO since they have no way of uncovering it; they search only patents and other publications. Occasionally, however, defendants (infringers) in patent lawsuits happen to uncover a prior public use that they then rely on to invalidate the patent.

Experimental Exception. If the prior public use was for bona fide (good faith) experimental purposes, it doesn't count as prior art. Thus suppose, in the "painted Philadelphia building" example above, that you painted your building to test the durability of your new paint: each month you photographed it, kept records on its reflectivity, wear resistance, and adhesion. In this case your one-year period wouldn't be initiated (begin to run) until your bona fide experimentation stopped and you left the paint out for nonexperimental purposes.

iv. Your Prior Foreign Patents

Any foreign patent (this includes Russian (or former U.S.S.R.) Inventor's Certificates) of yours or your legal representatives that issued before your U.S. filing date and that was filed over a year before your U.S. filing date is valid prior art. This category is generally pertinent to non-U.S. residents who start the patenting process in a foreign country. If you're in this class, you must file your U.S. application either within one year after you file in the foreign country or before your foreign patent issues. However, if you want to get the benefit of a foreign filing date for your U.S. application, you should file in the U.S. within the one year after your foreign filing date. (See Chapter 12.)

v. Prior U.S. Inventor

If anyone else in the U.S. invented substantially the same invention as yours before your invention's date of conception, and he or she didn't abandon, suppress, or conceal it, then this other person's invention (even though no written record was made) can be used to defeat your right to a patent. However, under a new statute, if your invention clears Section 102 (that is, it is novel) and the prior inventor worked in the same organization as you, then the prior inventor's work won't be considered prior art under Section 103. This prior art problem usually occurs when two (or more) inventors each file a patent application on the same invention. The PTO will declare an "interference" between the two competing applications. (See Chapter 15.)

vi. Prior Sale or On-Sale Status in the U.S.

Under Section 102, the law also considers certain actions by humans to be "prior art," even when no paper records exist. These actions involve the "sale" or "on-sale" category. Suppose you (or anyone else) offer to sell, actually sell, or commercially use your invention, or any product embodying your invention, in the U.S. You must file your U.S. patent application (regular or PPA) within one year after this offer, sale, or commercial use. This is another part of the "one-year rule." This means that you can make sales to test the commercial feasibility of your invention for up to a year before filing in the U.S. Again, however, I advise you not to do so, since this will defeat your right to a patent in most foreign countries, as mentioned above, and as explained in more detail in Chapter 12.

The type of sale or offer of sale that would bar your patent application must be a commercial offer to sell or a sale of actual hardware or a process embodying the invention. Such an offer or sale will start the one-year period running, even if the invention has not yet been built, so long as it has been drawn or described in reasonable detail. On the other hand, an offer to license, or sell, or an actual sale of the inventive concept (not hardware) to a manufacturer will not start the one-year period running.

e. Summary of Prior Art

If these prior-art rules seem complicated and difficult to understand, you're not alone. Very few patent attorneys understand them fully either! Perhaps Congress will simplify Section 102 someday and enact a "first to file" law, like the rest of the world uses. (Write to your Congressperson!) In the meantime, don't worry about it if you can't understand all of the rules. All you really need to remember is that relevant prior art usually consists of:

- any published writing (including any patent) that was made publicly available either (1) before your earliest provable date of invention (see above), or (2) over one year before you can get your patent application on file;
- any U.S. patent whose issue date isn't early enough to stop you but that has a filing or PPA date earlier than your earliest provable date of invention;
- any relevant invention or development (whether described in writing or not) existing prior to the date your invention was conceived; or
- any public or commercial use, sale, or knowledge of the invention more than one year prior your application filing date.

Abandonment

If you "abandon" your invention by finally giving up on it in some way, and this comes to the attention of the PTO or any court charged with ruling on your patent, your application or patent will be rejected or ruled invalid. I've never personally had a case where this happened, but it has occurred.

EXAMPLE: You make a model of your invention, test it, fail to get it to work, or fail to sell it, and then consciously drop all efforts on it. Later you change your mind and try to patent it. If your abandonment becomes known, you would lose your right to a patent. But if you merely stop work on it for a number of years because of such reasons as health, finances, or lack of a crucial part, but intend to pursue it again when possible, the law would excuse your inaction and hold that you didn't abandon.

---

2. Any Physical Difference Whatever Will Satisfy the Novelty Requirement

Any novel feature, no matter how trivial, will satisfy the novelty requirement. For example, suppose you've "invented" a bicycle that is painted yellow with green polka dots, each of which has a blue triangle in the center. Assume (this is easy to do) that no bicycle has been painted this way before. Your bicycle would thus clearly satisfy the requirement of novelty.

Rarely will an investigation into your invention's patentability (called a "patentability search") reveal any single prior invention or reference that could be considered a dead ringer. Of course, if your search does produce a dead-ringer reference for your invention—that is, an actual device or published description showing all the features of your invention and operating in the same way for the same purpose—obviously your patentability decision can be made immediately. Your invention lacks novelty over the "prior art." Another way of saying this is that your invention has been "anticipated" by a prior invention or conception and is thus definitely unpatentable. The concepts of anticipation and prior art are discussed in more detail in Requirement #4—unobviousness.

The law generally recognizes three types of novelty, any one of which will satisfy the novelty requirement of Section 102: (1) physical (hardware or method) difference, (2) new combination, and (3) new use.

a. Physical Differences

This is the most common way to satisfy the novelty requirement. Here your invention has some physical or structural (hardware or method) difference over the prior art. If the invention is a machine, composition, or article, it must be or have one or more parts that have a different shape, value, size, color, or composition than what's already known.

It's often difficult for inventors to distinguish between a physical difference and a new result. When I ask clients, "What's physically different about your invention?" they usually reply that theirs is lighter, faster, safer, cheaper to make or use, portable, and so on. However, these factors are new *results* or *advantages*, not physical differences, and are primarily relevant to unobviousness (see Section F), not to novelty. That is, they won't help your invention satisfy the novelty requirement. Again, a new physical feature must be a hardware (including operational) difference.

Even omitting an element can be considered novel. For example, if a machine has always had four gears, and you find that it will work with three, you've satisfied the novelty requirement.

Also, the discovery of a critical area of a given prior-art range will be considered novel. That is, if a prior-art magazine article on dyeing states that a mordant will work at a temperature range of 100-150 degrees centigrade and you discover that it works five times better at 127-130 degrees centigrade, the law stills consider this range novel, even though it's technically embraced by the prior art.

A physical difference can also be subtle or less apparent in the hardware sense, so that it's manifested primarily by a different mode of operation. Here are some examples: (a) an electronic amplifying circuit that looks the same, but that operates in a different mode—say Class A rather than Class B; (b) a circuit that is the same physically but is under the control of different software; (c) a pump that looks the same, but that operates at a higher pressure and hence in a different mode; and (d) a chemical reaction that takes place at a substantially different temperature or pressure. All of these will be considered novel, even though they appear the same to the eye.

Processes Note. If your invention is a new process, you don't need any novel hardware; your physical novelty is basically your new way of manipulating old hardware. Any novel step or steps whatever in this regard will satisfy the physical novelty requirement.

b. New Combinations

Many laypersons believe that if an invention consists entirely of old components, it can't be patented. A moment's reflection will show that this couldn't be true, since most inventions are made of old components. Thus, the PTO will consider your invention novel if two or more prior-art references (actual devices or published descriptions) together account for all of your invention's physical characteristics. That is, if your invention is a new combination of two old features, the law will consider it novel. For your invention to be considered as lacking novelty and thus subject to rejection under Section 102 of the patent laws, all of its physical characteristics must exist in a single prior-art reference. This is often referred to as the "single document rule"; in other words if two separate documents are necessary to show your invention, it is novel under Section 102. For example, getting back to your bicycle, suppose you now "invent" a bicycle made of one of the recently discovered, superstrength, carbon-fiber alloys. The bicycle per se is old, as is the alloy, but you're the first to "combine" the two old concepts. Your bicycle would clearly be considered novel since it has a new physical feature: a frame that is made, for the first time, of a carbon-fiber alloy. But, remember, just because it's novel, useful, and fits within a statutory class, doesn't mean the bicycle is patentable. It still must surpass the tough test of nonobviousness (covered in the following section).

Another type of new combination which inventors frequently overlook is the new arrangement: If you come up with a new arrangement of an old combination of elements, the PTO will consider this a new combination that will satisfy the novelty requirement. For example suppose you invent an automatic transmission where the torque converter is placed after the gears, rather than before; the PTO will consider that this new arrangement has novelty over the previous arrangement.

"Invention consists in avoiding the constructing of useless combinations and in constructing the useful combinations which are in the infinite minority. To invent is to discern, to choose."

—Henri Poincaré

c.   New Use

As stated in Section C5, above, if you've invented a new use for an old item of hardware, or an old process, the new use will satisfy the novelty requirement, no matter how trivial the newness is. For example, Dorie invents a new vegetable cooker which, after a search, she discovers is exactly like a copper smelter invented by one Jaschik in 1830. Dorie's cooker, even though identical to Jaschik's smelter, will be considered novel, since it's for a different use. (If your invention involves novel physical hardware, technically it can't be a new-use invention.)

If you're the type of person who thinks ahead, you're probably asking yourself, "Why is he bothering with novelty—isn't this requirement inherent in unobviousness—that is, if the invention is found to be unobvious won't it also be found to be novel?" Well, you're 100% correct. If an invention is unobvious, *a fortiori* (by better reason) it must be novel. However, the law makes the determination in two steps (Sections 102 and 103), and most patent professionals have also found it far easier to first determine whether and how an invention satisfies the novelty requirement and then determine if it can be considered unobvious. This two-step process is so important that I've made it Inventor's Commandment #7. See the first page of this chapter.

F.   Requirement #4: Unobviousness

We're now entering what's probably the most misunderstood and difficult-to-understand—yet most important—issue in patent law—that is, is your invention unobvious? Let's start with a "common misconception."

Common Misconception: If your invention is different from the prior art, you're entitled to get a patent on it.

Fact: Under Section 103 of the patent laws, no matter how different your invention is, you're not entitled to a patent on it unless its difference(s) over the prior art can be considered "unobvious" by the PTO or the courts.

Most of the time a patentability search will produce one or more prior-art references that show devices similar to your invention, or that show several, but not all, of the physical features of your invention. That is, you will find that your invention has one or more features or differences that aren't shown in any one prior-art reference. However, even though your invention is physically different from such prior art, this isn't enough to qualify for a patent. To obtain a patent, the physical (or use) differences must be substantial and significant. The legal term for such a difference is "unobvious" or, commonly, "nonobvious." That is, the differences between your invention and the prior art must not be obvious to one with ordinary skill in the field. Because this concept is so important, let's examine it in detail.

1.   Unobvious to Whom?

It doesn't tell anyone much to say an invention must be unobvious. The big question is, unobvious to whom? Under Section 103, you can't get a patent if a person having ordinary skill in the field of your invention would consider the idea of the invention "obvious" at the time you came up with it.

The law considers "a person having ordinary skill in the art to which said subject matter pertains" to be a mythical worker in the field of the invention who has (1) ordinary skill, but who (2) is totally omniscient about all the prior art in his or her field. This is a pure fantasy, since no such person ever lived, or ever will, but realistically there's no other way to come even close to any objective standard for determining nonobviousness.

Let's take some examples. Assume that your invention has to do with electronics—say an improved flip-flop circuit. A person having ordinary skill in the art would be an ordinary, average logic-circuit engineer who's intimately familiar with all prior-art logic circuits. If your invention has to do with chemistry, say a new photochemical process, a typical photochemical engineer with total knowledge of all photochemical processes would be your imaginary skilled artisan. If your invention is mechanical, such as an improved cigarette lighter or belt buckle, the PTO would try to postulate a hypothetical cigarette-lighter engineer or belt-buckle designer with ordinary skill and comprehensive knowledge. If your invention is a design, say for a computer case, the PTO would invent a hypothetical computer-case designer of ordinary skill and full knowledge of all existing designs.

2.   What Does "Obvious" Mean?

Most people have trouble interpreting Section 103 because of the word "obvious." If after reading my explanation you still don't understand it, don't be dismayed. Most patent attorneys, patent examiners, and judges can't agree on the meaning of the term. Many tests for unobviousness have been used and rejected by the courts over the years. The courts have often referred to "a flash of genius," "a synergistic effect (the whole is greater than the sum of its parts)," or some other colorful term. One influential court said that unobviousness is manifested if the invention produces "unusual and surprising results."

Technically (for reasons mentioned below, I stress the term "technically"), none of these tests is used any longer. This is because the U.S. Supreme Court, which has final say in such matters, decreed in the famous 1966 case of *Graham v. John Deere*, 383 U.S. 1, 148 USPO 459 (1966); MPEP 2141, that Section 103 is to be interpreted by taking the following steps:

1. Determine the scope and content of the prior art.
2. Determine the novelty of the invention.
3. Determine the level of skill of artisans in the pertinent art.
4. Against this background, determine the obviousness or unobviousness of the inventive subject matter.
5. Also consider secondary and objective factors such as commercial success, long-felt but unsolved need, and failure of others.

Unfortunately, while in theory the Supreme Court has the last word, in practice it added nothing to our understanding of the terms "obviousness" and "unobviousness"— in the crucial step (#4), the court merely repeated the very terms (obvious and unobvious) it was seeking to define. Therefore, most attorneys and patent examiners continue to look for new and unexpected results that flow from the novel features when seeking to determine if an invention is obvious.

Despite its failure to define the term "obvious," the Supreme Court did add an important step to the process by which "obviousness" is to be determined. In Step #5, the court made clear that objective circumstances must be taken into account by the PTO or courts when deciding whether an invention is or isn't obvious. The court specifically mentioned three such circumstances: commercial success, long-felt but unsolved need, and failure of others to come up with the invention.

So, although your invention might not, strictly speaking, produce "new and unexpected results" from the standpoint of one with "ordinary skill in the art," it still may be considered unobvious if, for instance, you can show that the invention has enjoyed commercial success.

Normally, before you file a patent application you won't be able to consider commercial success as a factor in determining patentability, since I recommend (Chapter 7, Section H) that you don't sell the invention before you file. However, you can argue commercial success later to the examiner during the prosecution phase (Chapter 13, Section F) if your invention is commercially successful by then. Also, you can even consider commercial success before

filing if you disregard my advice and take advantage of the "one-year rule" (Section E, above) by test-marketing your invention before filing.

Under the reasoning of the *John Deere* case, then, to decide whether or not your invention is obvious, you first should ask whether it produces "new and unexpected results" from the standpoint of one skilled in the relevant art. If it does, you've met the test for patentability. However, if there's still some doubt on this question, external circumstances may be used to bolster your position.

If you feel your head spinning, don't worry. It's natural. Because these concepts are so abstract, there's no real way to get a complete and comfortable grasp on them. However, if you take it slowly (and take a few breaks from your reading), you should have a pretty good idea of when an invention is and isn't considered "unobvious." In Section 3, directly below, I discuss examples of "unobviousness" and "obviousness." Then, in Section 4, I cover the types of arguments based on external circumstances (called "secondary factors") that can be made to bolster your contention that your invention is unobvious. I also provide a flowchart (Fig. 5C) that puts it all together in concise form.

3. Examples of Obviousness and Unobviousness

First, for some examples of unobvious inventions, consider all of the inventions listed in Chapter 2: the magnetic pistol guard, the buried plastic cable, the watch calendar sticker, "Grasscrete," the Wiz-z-er top, the shopping cart, etc. These all had physically novel features that produced new, unexpected results—that is, results that weren't suggested or shown in the prior art.

Although generally you must make a significant physical change for your invention to be considered unobvious, often a very slight change in the shape, slope, size, or material can produce a patentable invention that operates entirely differently and produces totally unexpected results.

EXAMPLE: Consider the original centrifugal vegetable juicer composed of a spinning perforated basket with a vertical sidewall and a nonperforated grater bottom. When vegetables, such as carrots, were pushed into the grater bottom, they were grated into fine pieces and juice that was thrown against the cylindrical, vertical sidewall of the basket. The juice passed through the perforations and was recovered in a container but the pieces clung to the sidewalls, adding weight to the basket and closing the perforations, making the machine impossible to run and operate after a relatively small amount of vegetables were juiced. Someone conceived of making the side of the basket slope outwardly so that while the juice was still centrifugally extracted through the perforated side of the basket, the pulp, instead of adhering to the old vertical side of the basket, was centrifugally forced up the new sloped side of the basket where it would go over the top and be diverted to a separate receptacle. Thus the juicer could be operated continuously without the pulp having to be cleaned out. Obviously, despite the fact that the physical novelty was slight—that is, it involved merely changing the slope of a basket's sidewall—the result was entirely new and unexpected, and therefore was considered unobvious.

In general such a relatively small physical difference (changing the slope of the wall of a basket in a juicer) will require a relatively great new result (ability to run the juicer continuously) to satisfy the unobviousness requirement. On the other hand, a relatively large physical difference will need only minor new results for the PTO to consider it unobvious. That is, in Fig. 5A (The Patentability Mountain) the height of the fourth box can be shortened if the height of the third box is increased.

As indicated, new-use inventions don't involve any physical change at all in the old hardware. However, the new use must be (1) a different use of some known hardware or process, and (2) the different use must produce new, unexpected results.

EXAMPLE: Again consider the Venetian blind cleaner used as a seed planter, and aspirin used as a growth stimulant, discussed in Section C5, above. In both instances, the new use was very different and provided a totally unexpected result: thus both inventions would be patentable. Also, in another interesting new-use case, the patent court in Washington, DC, held that removing the core of an ear of corn to speed freezing and thawing was unobvious over core drilling to speed drying. The court reasoned that one skilled in the art of corn processing could know that core removal speeds drying without realizing that core removal could also be used to speed freezing and thawing. Accordingly, the court held that the new result (faster freezing and thawing) was unexpected since it wasn't described or suggested in the prior art.

The courts have held that the substitution of a different, but similarly functioning, element for one of the elements in a known combination, although creating a "novel"

invention, won't produce a patentable one. For example, consider the substitution, in the 1950s, after transistors had appeared, of a transistor for a vacuum tube in an old amplifier circuit. At first blush this new combination of old elements would seem to the uninitiated to be a patentable substitution, since it provided tremendous new results (decreased power consumption, size, heat, weight, and far greater longevity). However, you'll soon realize that the result, although new, would have been entirely foreseeable since, just as in the carbon-fiber/bicycle case, the power reduction and reduced-weight advantages of transistors would have been already known as soon as a transistor made its appearance. Thus, substituting them for tubes wouldn't provide the old amplifier circuit with any *unexpected* new results. Accordingly, the PTO's Board of Appeals held the new combination to be obvious to an artisan of ordinary skill at the time.

A factor that works against inventors is that to most people, many inventions seem obvious once they understand the key ideas. So sometimes we have to convince the patent examiner, a potential licensee, or even a judge, not to use hindsight and to try to view the problem without knowledge of the invention in order to understand why it's actually unobvious.

If you're still a bit misty about all this, put yourself in the shoes of an electronic engineer who, at the time of the replacement of the vacuum tube with the transistor, was skilled in designing vacuum tube circuits and was currently designing a flip-flop circuit. Along comes this newfangled "transistor" that uses no heater and weighs 1/10th as much as a comparable tube, but which provides the same degree of amplification and control as the tube did. Do you think that it wouldn't be obvious to the engineer to try substituting a transistor for the tube in that flip-flop circuit? Similarly, the PTO would consider obvious the substitution of an integrated circuit for a group of transistors in a known logic circuit, or the use of a known radio mounting bracket to hold a loudspeaker enclosure instead of a radio.

The PTO will also consider as obvious the mere carrying forward of an old concept, or a change in form and degree, without a new result. For instance, when one inventor provided notches on the inner rim of a steering wheel to provide a better grip, the idea was held to be obvious because of medieval sword handles that had similar notches for the same purpose. And the use of a large pulley for a logging rig was held nonpatentable over the use of a small pulley for clotheslines. These situations are known as "obviousness by analogy."

On the other hand, one inventor merely changed the slope of a part in a papermaking (Fourdrinier) machine; as a result the machine's output increased by 25%—a dramatic, new, and unexpected result that was held patentable.

In the recipe field it's usually difficult to come up with an unobvious invention, since most ingredients and their effects are known.

> **EXAMPLE:** Lou comes up with a way to make mustard-flavored hot dog buns—admix powdered mustard with the flour. Even though Lou's recipe is novel, the PTO will almost certainly hold it to be obvious since the result of the new combination is entirely foreseeable and expected.

In sum, the PTO will usually hold that substitution of a different material, shape, color, or size is obvious. But if the substitution provides *unexpected* new results, the law will hold it unobvious.

The courts and the PTO will also usually consider the duplication of a part obvious unless it can see new results. For instance, in an automobile, the substitution of two banks of three cylinders with two carburetors was held obvious over a six-cylinder, single-carburetor engine, since the new arrangement had no unexpected advantages. However, the use of two water turbines to provide cross flow to eliminate axial thrust on bearings was held unobvious over a single turbine; again, an *unexpected* new result.

Similarly, making devices portable, making parts smaller or larger, faster or slower, effecting a substitution of equivalents (a roller bearing for a ball bearing), making elements adjustable, making parts integral, separable (modular), or in kit form, and other known techniques with their known advantages, will be held obvious unless new, unexpected results can be shown.

⚠ If you create what you believe to be a valuable invention, but it seems simple and obvious to you, don't assume automatically that it's legally obvious. Some very simple inventions, like the vegetable juicer and the Fourdrinier machine, have been granted very valuable patents!

📝 **Design Patent Tip.** In design cases, the design must have novel features, and the PTO must be able to regard these as unobvious to a designer of ordinary skill. If the design involves the use of known techniques that together don't produce any new and unexpected visual effect, then the PTO will consider it obvious. But if they produce a startling or unique new appearance, then the PTO will hold it to be unobvious. Since only the ornamental appearance and not the function of a design is relevant, the degree of novelty of the design will be the main determinant of unobviousness: a high degree of novelty will always be patentable, while a low degree of novelty will encounter rough sledding unless you can set forth reasons why it has a very different appearance or visual effect.

4. Secondary Factors in Determining Unobviousness

As mentioned, if the new and unexpected results of your invention are marginal, you *may* still be able to get a patent if you can show that your invention possesses one or more secondary factors that establish unobviousness. The PTO and the courts usually give these secondary factors much less weight than the "new and unexpected results" factor, but they still should be considered, especially in close cases. While the Supreme Court listed only three secondary factors in the *John Deere* case, I've compiled a list of 12 basic and nine combinatory secondary factors that the PTO and the courts actually consider. In the real world, these secondary factors must generally be dealt with only if the PTO makes a preliminary finding of obviousness or if your invention is attacked as being obvious. However, when deciding whether your invention is legally entitled to a patent, you'll have a much better idea of how easy or difficult it will be to obtain if you apply these secondary factors to your invention.

➡ If you're sure that your invention is unobvious, feel free to skip this section, Section 5, and Section 6, and proceed directly to Section 7.

Although some of these secondary factors may appear similar, try to consider each independently, since the courts have recognized subtle differences between them. As part of doing this, remember that lawyers like to chop large arguments into little ones so that it will appear that there are a multitude of reasons for their position rather than just one or two. While this approach may seem silly, it's nevertheless a fact (however sad) that the PTO and courts are used to hearing almost exclusively from lawyers (and, in the case of the PTO, from highly specialized patent agents). Accordingly, the general rule is, the more arguments you can use to claim unobviousness, the better your chances will be of getting a patent.

Now let's look at the secondary factors in detail.

Factor 1. Previous failure of others

If the invention is successful where previous workers in the field were unable to make it work, this will be of great help to your application. For instance, many previous attempts were made to use electrostatic methods for making photocopies, but all failed. Chester Carlson (a patent attorney himself) came along and successfully used an electrostatic process to make copies. This greatly enhanced his case for the patentability of his dry (xerographic) photocopying process.

Factor 2. Solves an unrecognized problem

Here the essence of your invention is probably the recognition of the problem, rather than its solution. Consider the showerhead that automatically shuts off in case of excess water temperature discussed in Chapter 2. As the problem was probably never recognized in the prior art, the solution would therefore probably be patentable.

Factor 3. Solves an insoluble problem

Suppose that for years those skilled in the art had tried and failed to solve a problem and the art and literature were full of unsuccessful "solutions." Along you come and finally find a workable solution, such as a cure for the common cold: you'd probably get a patent.

> EXAMPLE: Potato chips used to be sold in relatively expensive, heavy cardboard boxes that manufacturers thought were necessary to protect against chip breakage. Yet, many chips still broke. Someone thought of packaging the chips in plastic bags that were far cheaper, lighter, and actually reduced the amount of breakage.

Factor 4. Commercial success

If your invention has attained commercial success by the time the crucial patentability decision is made, this militates strongly in favor of patentability. Nothing succeeds like success, right?

Factor 5. Crowded art

If your invention is in a crowded field (art)—that is, a field that is mature and that contains many patents, such as electrical connectors or bicycles—a small advance will go farther towards qualifying the invention for a patent than it will in a new, blossoming art, such as monoclonal antibodies.

Factor 6. Omission of element

If you can omit an element in a prior invention without loss of capability, this will count a lot, since parts are expensive,

unreliable, heavy, and labor-intensive. The best example I can think of is the elimination of the inner tube in tires.

Factor 7. Unsuggested modification

If you can modify a prior invention in a manner not suggested before, such as by increasing the slope in a paper-making machine, or by making the basket slope in a centrifugal juice extractor, this act in itself counts for patentability.

Factor 8. Unappreciated advantage

If your invention provides an advantage that was never before appreciated, it can make a difference. In a recent case, a gas cap that was impossible to insert in a skewed manner was held to be patentable since it provided an advantage that was never appreciated previously.

Factor 9. Solves prior inoperability

If your invention provides an operative result where before only inoperability existed, then it has a good chance for a patent. For instance, suppose you come up with a jet fuel additive that prevents huge fires in case of a plane crash; you've got it made, since all previous fire suppressant additives have been largely unsuccessful.

Factor 10. Successful implementation of ancient idea where others failed

The best example I can think of is the Wright Brothers' airplane. For millennia humans had wanted to fly and had tried many schemes unsuccessfully. The successful implementation of such an ancient desire carries great weight when it comes to getting a patent.

Factor 11. Solution of long-felt need

Suppose you find a way to prevent tailgate-type automobile crashes. Obviously you've solved a powerful need and your solution will be a heavy weight in your favor on the scales of patentability.

Factor 12. Contrary to prior art's teaching

If the prior art expressly teaches that something can't be done or is impractical—for example, humans can't fly without artificial propulsion motors—and you prove this teaching wrong, you've got it made.

5. Secondary Factors in Determining Unobviousness of Combination Inventions

Inventions that combine two or more elements known in the prior art can still be held patentable, provided that the combination can be considered unobvious—that is, it's a new combination and it produces new and unexpected results. In fact, most patents are granted on such combinations since very few truly new things are ever discovered. So let's examine some of the factors used especially to determine the patentability of "combination inventions" (that is, inventions that have two or more features that are shown in two or more prior-art references).

The following material is conceptually quite abstract and difficult to understand, even for patent attorneys. I'm presenting it in the interest of completeness. However, if you wish, you can safely skip it for now and proceed directly to Section 7. If the PTO or anyone else suggests that two or more prior-art references, taken together, teach that your invention is obvious, come back and read it then.

Factor 13. Synergism (2 + 2 = 5)

If the results achieved by your combination are greater than the sum of the separate results of its parts, this can indicate unobviousness. Consider the pistol trigger release (Chapter 2) where a magnetic ring must be worn to fire the pistol. The results (increased police safety) are far in excess of what magnets, rings, and pistols could provide separately.

EXAMPLE: For another example, suppose that a chemist combines, through experimentation, several metals that cooperate in a new way to provide added strength without added density. If this synergistic result wasn't reasonably foreseeable by a metallurgist, the new alloy would almost certainly be patentable.

Generally, if your invention is a chemical mixture, the mixture must do more than the sum of its components. For this reason, food recipes are difficult to patent unless an ingredient does more than its usual function or produces a new and unexpected result. Or, if you come up with a new technique of cooking that produces a new and unexpected result—for example, a cookie that is chewy inside and crisp outside—you've got a good chance of prevailing. Similarly, if you combine various mechanical or electrical components, the courts and the PTO will usually consider the combination patentable if it provides more than the functions of its individual components.

As an example of an unpatentable combination without synergism, consider the combination of a radio, waffle iron, and blender in one housing. While novel and useful, this combination would be considered an aggregation and obvious, since there's no synergism or new cooperation: the combination merely provides the sum of the results of its components and each component works individually and doesn't enhance the working of any other component. On the other hand, the combination of an eraser and a pencil would be patentable (had it not already been invented) because the two elements cooperate to increase overall writing speed, a synergistic effect. The same would hold true for mounting loudspeakers in a plastic insulating picnic box, where new cooperation results: the box holds the food and provides a baffle for the speakers.

Factor 14. Combination unsuggested

If the prior art contains no suggestion, either expressed or implied, that the references should be combined, this militates in favor of patentability. Examiners in the PTO frequently are assigned to pass on patent applications for combination inventions. To find the elements of the combination claimed, they'll make a search, often using a computer, to gather enough references to show the respective elements of the combination. While the examiners frequently use such references in combination to reject the claims of the patent application on unobvious grounds, the law says clearly that it's not proper to do so unless the references themselves, rather than an applicant's patent application, suggest the combination.

EXAMPLE: Arthur B. files a patent application on a pastry-molding machine. The examiner cites (or your search reveals) one patent on a foot mold and another on a pastry mold to show the two elements of the invention. It wouldn't be proper to "combine" these disparate references since they're from unconnected fields and thus it wouldn't be obvious to use them together against this invention.

An example of where the law would consider it obvious to combine several references is the case where, as discussed, you make a bicycle out of the lightweight carbon-fiber alloy and, as a result, your bicycle is lighter than ever before. Is your invention "unobvious"? The answer is "No," because the prior art implicitly suggests the combination by mentioning the problem of the need for lighter bikes and the lightness of the new alloy. Moreover, the result achieved by the combination would be expected from a review of existing bicycles and the new lightweight alloy. In other words, if a skilled bicycle engineer were to be shown the new, lightweight alloy, it would obviously occur to the engineer to make a bicycle out of it since bicycle engineers are always seeking to make lighter bicycles.

Factor 15. Impossible to combine

This is the situation where prior-art references show the separate elements of the inventive combination, but in a way that makes it seem they would be physically impossible to combine. Stated differently, if you can find a way to do what appears to be physically impossible, then you can get a patent. For example, suppose you've invented the magnetic pistol release. The prior art shows a huge magnetic cannon firing release attached to a personnel shield. Since the step from a cannon to a small handgun is a large one, physical incompatibility might get you a patent—that is, it would be physically impossible to use a huge cannon shield magnet on a small and very differently shaped trigger finger. Note, however, that sometimes by analogy the large can properly be used on the small if a mere change in size is all that's required.

Factor 16. Different combination

Here your combination is A, B, and C, and the prior-art references show a different, albeit possibly confusingly similar combination, say A', B, and C. Since your combination hadn't been previously created, you've got a good case for patentability even though your creation is similar to an existing one. Again the last analogy holds: a personnel shield for a cannon, even though it has a magnetic firing release, is so far different from a finger ring that the prior-art combination must be regarded as different from that of the invention.

Factor 17. Prior-art references would not operate in combination

Here the prior-art references, even if combined, wouldn't operate properly, such as due to some incompatibility. Suppose you've invented a radio receiver comprising a combined tuner-amplifier and a speaker, and the prior art consists of one patent showing a crystal tuner and an advertisement showing a large loudspeaker. The prior-art elements wouldn't operate if combined because the weak crystal tuner wouldn't be able to drive the speaker adequately; thus a combination of the prior-art elements would be inoperative. This would militate strongly in favor of patentability.

Factor 18. Over three prior-art references necessary to show your invention

While not a very strong argument, if it takes more than three references to meet your inventive combination, this militates in your favor.

Factor 19. References teach away from combining

If the references themselves show or teach that they shouldn't be combined, and you're able to combine them, this militates in favor of patentability. For example, suppose a reference says that the new carbon-fiber alloy should only be used in structural members that aren't subject to sudden shocks, but you were able to make a bike out of the carbon-fiber alloy. If you're able to use it successfully to make a bike frame, which is subject to sudden shocks, you should be able to get a patent.

Factor 20. Awkward, involved combination

Suppose that to make your inventive combination, it takes the structures of three prior-art patents, one of which must be made smaller, another of which must be modified in shape, and the third of which must be made of a different material. These factors can only help you.

Factor 21. References from a different field

If the references show structures that are similar to your invention, but are in a different technical field, this militates in favor of unobviousness and hence of patentability. I used this argument successfully to get a food mold patented over a similarly shaped device for molding a horse's foot.

6. How Does a Patent Examiner Determine "Unobviousness"

Because it's usually helpful to understand how a bureaucracy operates when you're dealing with it over significant issues, let's take a minute to examine how a patent examiner proceeds when deciding whether or not your invention is obvious. When patent examiners turn to the question of whether an invention is unobvious, they first make a search and gather all of the patents that they feel are relevant or close to your invention. Then they sit down with these patents (and any prior-art references you've provided with your patent application) and see whether your invention, as described in your claims (see Chapter 9), contains any novelty (novel physical features, new combination, or new use) that isn't shown in any reference. If so, your invention satisfies Section 102—that is, it is novel.

Next they see whether your novelty produces any unexpected or surprising results. If so, they'll find that the invention is unobvious and allow your patent application. If not (this usually occurs the first time they act on your case), they'll reject your application (sometimes termed a "shotgun" or "shoot-from-the-hip" rejection) and leave it to you to show that your new features do indeed produce new, unexpected results. To do this, you can use as many of the reasons listed above that you feel are relevant. If you can convince the examiner, you'll get your patent.

If a dispute over unobviousness actually finds its way into court, however, (a common occurrence) both sides will present the testimony of patent lawyers or technical experts who fit, or most closely fit, the hypothetical job descriptions called for by the particular case. These experts will testify for or against obviousness by arguing that the invention is (or isn't) new and/or that it does (or doesn't) produce unexpected results.

Again, because the question of whether an invention is unobvious is obviously crucial to whether a patent will issue and because Sections 102 and 103 are widely confused, I have made the two-step evaluation Inventor's Commandment #7 at the beginning of this chapter.

7. Weak Versus Strong Patents

Although in this section I've covered the basic legal requirements for obtaining a patent on an invention, there is, in reality, an additional practical requirement. If the claims in your patent are easy to design around or are so narrow as to virtually preclude you from realizing commercial gain, it's virtually the same as if a patent had been denied you in the first place. I'll come back to this point when I cover how to conduct a patent search (Chapter 6) and how to draft your claims (Chapter 9).

8. The Inventor's Status Is Irrelevant

You may have noticed that in discussing the requirements for obtaining a patent, I didn't mention the inventor's status or personal qualifications (such as, the applicant should be an engineer, over 21, and so on). That is because status and personal qualifications are totally irrelevant. An invention need merely meet the four legal criteria (Section B, above). The applicant must qualify as a true inventor of the invention (discussed in Chapter 10), but his, her, or their age, sex, citizenship, country of residence, mental competence,

health, physical disabilities, nationality, race, creed, religion, state of incarceration, and so on, are irrelevant. The PTO recently issued a patent to a death row inventor (U.S. Pat. No. 6,260,795). Even a dead or insane person can apply (through a legal representative, of course).

The manner of making the invention is also irrelevant, as we'll see by the next Common Misconception.

Common Misconception: If a moron discovers something by accident, the law won't consider it to be as good an invention as if a genius had come up with it through years of hard, brilliant work.

Fact: The manner of making an invention is totally irrelevant to patentability. The invention is looked at in its own right as to whether or not it would be obvious to one skilled in the art; the way it was made or the qualifications or competence of the applicant are never considered by the PTO.

G. The Patentability Flowchart

To get a better grasp of the admittedly slippery concept of unobviousness and the role it plays in the patent application process, consider Fig. 5C—The Patentability Flowchart. This flowchart is like a computer programmer's flowchart, except that all blocks have been made rectangular to use space more efficiently. In addition to presenting all of the criteria used by the PTO and the courts for determining whether an invention is unobvious, the chart also incorporates the first three tests (statutory class, usefulness, and novelty) of Fig. 5A. I strongly advise that you study this chart and the following description of it well, since it sums up the essence of this crucial chapter. Also, you'll want to use this chart when making your search (next chapter) and when prosecuting your patent application (Chapter 13). This chart has been designed to cover and apply to anything you might come up with, so you can and should use it to determine the patentability of any utility invention whatever. I go through the chart using a real invention and real references in Chapter 6, Section H.

Box A (Statutory Class): Assuming that you've made an invention, first determine, using the criteria discussed above, whether you can reasonably classify your invention in one of the five statutory classes indicated. If not, take the "No" output of Box A to the Box X on the left bottom of the chart.

As indicated in Box X, the PTO will probably refuse to grant you a patent, so see if you can gainfully use another form of coverage (such as trade secret, copyright, design

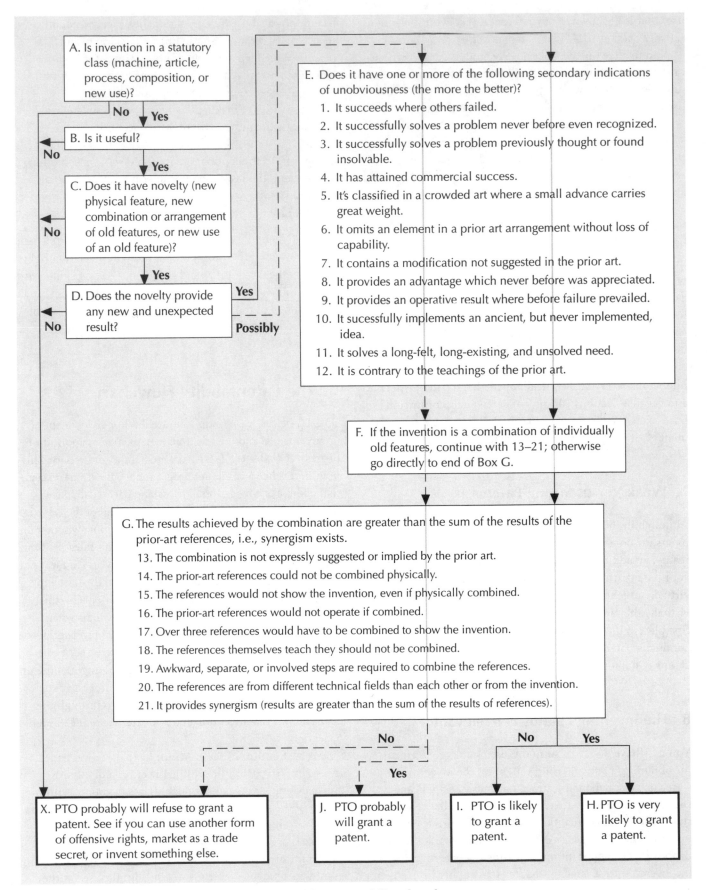

Fig. 5C—The Patentability Flowchart

patent, trademark, or unfair competition, as discussed in Chapter 1). If this possibility also fails, you'll have to give up on the creation and invent something else. If the invention can be classified within a statutory class ("Yes" output of Box A), move on to Box B.

Box B (Utility): Now determine, again using the criteria above, whether the invention has utility, including amusement. If not, move to Box X. If so, move on to Box C.

Box C (Novelty): Here's the important novelty determination. If an invention has any physical features that aren't present in any single prior-art reference, or if it is a new combination or rearrangement of old features, or a new use of an old feature or old hardware, no matter how trivial, it will clear Section 102—that is, it has novelty: take the "Yes" output to Box D. If not, it lacks novelty, so take the "No" output and go to Box X again.

Box D (New and Unexpected Results): This is the heart of the chart. You should now determine whether the novelty of your invention produces any new and unexpected result ("N&UR"). Use the criteria and examples presented in Sections F1 through F4, above. If you definitely feel that your invention does not provide N&UR, take the "No" output from Box D to Box X. On the other hand, if your answer is a clear "Yes" (you're sure you have N&UR), it's likely you'll be able to get a patent. While not mandatory, I recommend that you obtain additional reasons for patentability to boost your confidence by taking the "Yes" output to Box E to consider the "secondary" factors.

If, however, at this point you can't come up with a clear "Yes" or "No" as to N&UR—that is, your invention falls somewhere between these two extremes—it can still qualify for a patent if it has one or more secondary factors. In this case, follow the broken-lined "Possibly" output of Box D to Box E to determine whether your invention qualifies for a patent, even though it doesn't produce any N&UR. From here on, if you took the "Yes" output of Box D, you'll follow a solid-line route, but if you took the Possibility output, you'll follow the broken-line route.

Boxes E, F, and G (Other Factors): No matter whether you take the "Yes" = solid line or "Possibly" = broken line route from Box D, you should next answer all of the questions in Box E. Then move to Box F, which tells you to answer all of the questions in Box G if you have a combination invention, or to go directly to the end of Box G if it's not a combination invention. The more questions in Boxes E and G to which you can answer "Yes," the better your chances will be. No matter how you go through Boxes E to G, there are four possibilities, identified below as 1 (A&B) and 2 (A&B).

1. N&URs exist ("Yes" from Box D—solid-line route):
   A. If you answered "Yes" to Box D and to one or more questions in Boxes E and G (there are

N&URs and one or more secondary unobviousness factors), take the "Yes"/solid-line output from Box G to Box H, where you'll see that the PTO is very likely to grant you a patent.
   B. If you were not able to answer "Yes" to any question in Boxes E and F (there are N&URs, but no secondary unobviousness factors), take the "No"/solid-line output from Box G to Box I, where you'll see that you'll still be likely to get a patent, based on your N&URs (Box D).

2. Possible N&URs ("Possibly" from Box D—broken-line route):
   A. If you answered "Possibly" to Box D and "Yes" to one or more questions in Boxes E and G (you're unsure about N&URs but you have one or more secondary unobviousness factors), take the "Yes"/broken-line output from Box G to Box J, where you'll see that the PTO will still probably grant you a patent.
   B. If you answered "Possibly" to Box D, but were not able to answer "Yes" to any question in Boxes E and G (you're unsure about N&URs and there are no secondary unobviousness factors), take the "No"/broken-line output from Box G to Box X, where you'll see that you probably won't be able to get a patent. Don't give up though, if you still think you might be able to prove some secondary factors later, such as commercial success after it hits the market.

H. Summary

Treat the one-year rule as holy: You must file a regular or provisional application within one year after you publicize, sell, or offer your invention for sale. However to preserve foreign rights, you should file your U.S. application before publicizing the invention.

The law has four requirements for getting a patent: (1) the invention must be in a statutory class—a machine, an article, a process, a composition, or a new use of the first four; (2) it must be useful (safe, not illegal, operable, and not a nuclear weapon); (3) it must be novel—that is, it must be different in some way from every single item or prior art (prior art means any publication, public use, or public knowledge before your date of invention, which is the earliest of the date you file a patent application or provisional patent application); and (4) the novel features must be unobvious to one with ordinary skill in the art—for example, an invention with new and unexpected results. ∎

Chapter 6

Search and You May Find

Inventor's Commandment #8

You should make (or have made) a thorough patent-ability search of your invention before you decide whether to file a patent application, and you should not file a patent application unless you believe your invention has novel features over the prior art which you feel are unobvious.

Since you've learned how to determine patentability from Chapter 5, you can now make a patentability search. The Patent and Trademark Office (PTO) doesn't require a search, but I strongly recommend that all inventors make (or have made) a search prior to deciding whether to file a patent application. Thus I've made the "pre-ex" (pre-examination) patentability search Inventor's Commandment #8. In reality, this chapter is paradoxical, since it tells you how to look for something you hope you won't find! But don't let that affect your search. For the reasons below, you should do the search diligently and thoroughly.

A. Why Make a Patentability Search?

I've come up with 14 reasons for making a patentability search. Let's look at each of them in detail.

1. To Determine Whether You Can Get a Patent

The main reason for making a patentability search of your invention is to discover if the PTO will be likely to grant you a patent on your invention. You may wonder why this should make any difference. After all, why worry about what the PTO will do before it does it? Simply because, if your search indicates that your invention is likely to qualify for a patent, you can go ahead with your development, marketing, and other work on the invention with far more confidence that your efforts will eventually produce positive results. Obviously, if a patent is ultimately granted, you will have a monopoly in the field of the invention for a number of years. Assuming, of course, that your invention has economic value, this will allow you to sell or license it for a reasonable amount, since you'll have at least some assurance that a right to exclude copiers will go with the invention.

If, on the other hand, your patentability search indicates that a patent isn't likely to be granted, you'll have to think long and hard about whether to proceed. The hard truth is that most manufacturers won't want to invest the money in tooling, producing, and marketing something that their competition can freely copy, and perhaps even sell at a lower cost. As we'll see in Chapter 7, however, this isn't always true. While it's somewhat unusual, fortunes have sometimes been made manufacturing and selling unpatentable inventions.

2. To Avoid Needless Expenditures and Work

Another reason to make a patentability search has to do with time and money. It's a lot easier (and cheaper) to make a patentability search than to prepare a patent application that must contain a specification, drawings, claims, a filing fee, forms, etc. It makes sense to do a relatively small amount of work entailing a modest expenditure in order to gain useful information that may well allow you to avoid wasting considerable time and/or spending a relatively large amount of money.

3. To Provide Background to Facilitate Preparation of Your Patent Application

You'll find it far easier to prepare a patent application on your invention if you make a patentability search first. This is because a search will bring out prior-art references (prior publications including patents and literature) in the field of your invention. After reading these, you're almost sure to learn much valuable background information that will make the task of writing your patent application far easier. Patent attorneys almost always routinely review some sample patents from the field of an invention before they begin preparation of a patent application, in order to give them a "feel for the art."

4. To Know Whether to Describe and Draw Components

This reason is closely allied with Reason #3. As we'll see in Chapter 8, a patent application must contain a detailed description of your invention, in sufficient detail to enable a person with ordinary skill in the "art" involved to make and use it. If your invention has certain components with which you aren't familiar, you won't have to take the trouble to draw and describe these in detail if you find them already described in prior-art publications, including patents.

5. To Provide More Information About Operability and Design

When you make a search, you will almost always find patents in the field of your invention, possibly on inventions similar to yours. A reading of these patents will give you valuable technical information about your invention, possibly suggesting ways to make it work better and improve its design, or possibly indicating technical approaches that you should avoid.

6. To Obtain Commercial Information

The patents and other references that you uncover in your search will give you valuable commercial information about similiar developments to your invention, including possible additional advantages and disadvantages, possible new uses, past commercial failures, etc. For instance, suppose you see many patents on inventions that produce the same result as yours, and you know from your familiarity with the field (as a result of your commercial evaluation in Chapter 4 and your preliminary look—see Section D, below) that none of these has attained commercial success. In this event, you might want to reconsider the wisdom of pushing ahead with your own invention. Or you might conclude that you can do better, because the prior inventions were not commercially exploited properly or because they did not operate properly due to lack of proper components, proper materials, etc.

7. To Obtain Possible Express Proof of Unobviousness

Sometimes a search will uncover references that actually "teach away" from your invention—for example, by suggesting that your approach won't work. You can cite such a reference to the PTO to help convince the examiner to regard your invention as unobvious. (See secondary reason #3 in Chapter 5, Section F4.)

For instance, suppose you've invented a bicycle frame made of a new carbon-fiber alloy that makes your bike far lighter and stronger than any previously made. Ordinarily, as discussed in Chapter 5, Section F, the substitution of a known alternative material (here a carbon-fiber alloy for steel) would not be patentable, since the substitution would not provide any *unexpected* results. But suppose during your search you find a prior-art reference (such as an article in *Metallurgic Times*) that states that carbon-fiber should not be used for bicycle frames. If you find that such alloys

can be used successfully, you can cite this reference to the PTO to show that you've turned a past failure into success. Thus you'll have express, positive proof that your invention provides unexpected results and is unobvious.

8. To Define Around the Prior Art to Facilitate Prosecution

By familiarizing yourself with the prior art, you'll be able to tailor and define the general thrust, structure, and advantages of your patent application around such art and its deficiencies. This will save you work and arm you with the proper terminology and support that you may need later in the "prosecution" stage (that is, the stage where you actually try to obtain a patent from the PTO).

EXAMPLE: LeRoy invented a sturdy but edible, baked scoop for dips, including salsa. His search turned up a patent to Minerva on a similarly shaped cereal product, but which was too fragile for scooping dips. As a result of the knowledge gleaned from his search, LeRoy was able to direct his patent application to the novelty of his scoops by knocking the fragility of Minerva's product and explaining and stressing the strength of his scoops with actual (quantitative) performance figures. This enabled him to distinguish over Minerva's invention and get a patent.

More about this in Chapter 13. Also, an international application, discussed in detail in Chapter 12, requires that an invention be defined in a way that distinguishes it from the prior art. Your search will be of great help here.

9. To Learn Your Invention's Novel Features So as to Expedite Prosecution

After making a thorough search of the prior art, you'll be able to find out which of your invention's features are novel (Box C of Patentability Flowchart—Fig. 6E, below). By listing its novel features and their attendant advantages, you'll be able to recite, stress, and direct your patent application to all of those features and advantages. Also, you can tailor your claims to such novel features so as to preclude an early "final action" (see Chapter 13, Section J), expedite the ultimate allowance of your case, and avoid the need to narrow the claims which—under a decision called *Festo v. Shoketsu*—would prevent using the "doctrine of equivalents" to interpret them more broadly. (For more information on *Festo*, see Chapter 9, Section J.)

10. To Facilitate Licensing or Sale of Your Invention

When you attempt to sell or license your invention rights, your potential licensees will want to know if your patent application will be likely to get through the PTO. You can answer their concern, at least partially, by showing them your search results. This will give them confidence in your invention and will save them from having to do their own search, thereby speeding up and facilitating negotiations.

11. To Find Out What You've Really Invented

Yes, I'm serious! From over 30 years' experience I've found that many inventors don't realize or understand exactly what they've invented until they see a search report. Indeed, many inventors get a severe case of "search shock" when their "major advance" turns out to be relatively minor. If this happens, don't give up on your brainchild, since your minor advance may be extremely valuable and vital. On the other hand, occasionally an inventor, believing that the invention is a relatively small advance and that its basic broad idea must have already been invented, is very pleased and surprised to learn from the search results that the invention's a gold mine instead of a nugget!

12. To Get a Stronger Patent

A PTO examiner will usually make a better search than you or a professional searcher will be able to do. Nevertheless, some examiners, at certain times, may miss a highly relevant reference. If anyone uncovers such a reference later, after you get your patent, and brings this reference to the attention of the PTO or any court, it may cast a cloud over, or even invalidate, your patent. However, if you find such a reference in your search, you can (and must) make a record of it in the PTO's file of your patent application, tailor your claims around it (see Chapter 9), and avoid any potential harm it may cause you later, thus making your patent stronger and less vulnerable.

13. To Get Your Patent Application Examined Ahead of Turn

For reasons explained in Chapter 10, Section P, I don't always recommend that you get your patent application issued sooner, but if you really need to speed things up, you'll be entitled to get it examined ahead of its turn if you've made a pre-examination search. (See Chapter 10,

Section P, for more on how to make a patent application "special" in order to speed up examination.)

14. To Determine If Your Invention Will Infringe Any In-Force Patents

The PTO doesn't care one bit about infringement and will allow your patent application even if hardware embodying your claimed invention would infringe ten in-force patents. (Note that a patent application can never infringe anything.) However, you may wish to know if your invention will infringe any existing patents, especially if you're considering manufacturing the invention. A search and study of the claims of all relevant in-force patents will reveal this.

B. When Not to Search

Despite my inventor's commandment about doing a patent search prior to filing, there are at least two situations where you can "skip the search."

If you are dealing in a very new or arcane field with which you're very familiar, obviously a search is highly unlikely to be profitable. For example, if you're a biotech engineer who reads all the journals and keeps abreast of the state of the art, the newness of your field makes it highly unlikely that you will find any early "prior art." Or, if you make semiconductors and have up-to-the-minute knowledge of all known transistor-diffusion processes, and you come up with a breakthrough transistor-diffusion process, a search will probably not produce any reference showing your idea. Before deciding not to search, however, you should be reasonably certain that you or someone else with whom you are in contact knows all there is to know about the field in question, and that you are fairly confident there is no obscure reference that shows your invention.

In addition, if you've made an improvement to an earlier invention that you've already searched, and you feel the search also covered your improvement, there's obviously no need to make a second search.

Designs. Generally I recommend not searching design inventions, since the cost and time required to make the search is greater than the time and cost to prepare a design patent application. However, if you believe that reasons 6, 7, 9, 10, 11, and/or 12 of Section A, above, may be particularly relevant to your situation, you should make a search of your design. Also, you must search your design invention if you want to petition to have your design application examined right away on the "Rocket Docket." See Chapter 10, Section Q.

Common Misconception: It's not necessary to make a patentability search prior to considering whether to file a patent application, since the PTO will make one anyway.

Fact: While it's not necessary to make a search, it's highly desirable, for the 14 reasons given above.

C. The Two Ways to Make a Patentability Search

Basically, there are only two ways in which you can get your search done: have someone do it for you or do it yourself. If you're a conscientious worker and you have the time, and access to a search facility, or you have computer search capability (see below for cautions regarding searching), I recommend that you do the search yourself in order to make sure that it is done thoroughly and in your desired time frame. In addition, this will save you money and enable you personally to accumulate valuable information, as suggested above.

However, you may have very good reasons for hiring a professional searcher—for example, you live far from any search facility or you don't have a computer or enough time. Also, there's the procrastination factor: half the time the only way some of us will ever get a job done, even though we're capable of doing it, is to turn it over to a pro. If for geographical or other reasons you choose to hire a searcher, you'll find advice on choosing one in Section F, below. Even if you do use a searcher, read through the instructions on do-it-yourself searching (Sections I-L, below) in order to understand what you're paying for and to be able to recognize whether the searcher has done a thorough job.

Some inventors, because of the importance of the reasons for searching listed above, prefer to do the search themselves and also have a professional search done, just to double-check their work. I don't recommend this, since I've found that an inventor's diligent search is usually adequate. Still, if you feel insecure about your search, you might want to use a computer search as a rough double check (Section L, below). Don't rely on the computer completely, however, unless your invention is in a new field, such as biotechnology or computers. This is because most computer searches go back only about 25 years. From my experience, most manual searches produce many relevant prior-art references that were published in much earlier periods, some even as far back as the 1800s.

If you do the patentability search yourself, there are three subpossibilities:

1. You can search in the PTO in Alexandria, Virginia (definitely the best place), or

2. You can search in a local Patent and Trademark Depository Library, or even a regular library that has the *Official Gazettes*, or
3. You can do a computer search if your invention involves new technology.

Read through Sections I and K, below, to compare these alternatives.

D. How to Make a Preliminary Search

If you don't live near the PTO in Arlington, Virginia, I recommend that you conduct a brief preliminary search before spending the money or time for a formal search. Sometimes you will quickly "knock out" your invention and save yourself cost and effort. If you haven't made the preliminary search already as part of your commercial evaluation (see Chapter 4), do so now. Look for your invention in two ways:

a. In stores, catalogues, reference books, product directories, etc.: an hour or two in your local library, and perhaps a visit or two to likely stores or suppliers, should be sufficient. For example, if you've invented an automotive add-on product, look in the J.C. Whitney catalogue and some automotive parts stores first.
b. Make a quick, free, Internet search of recent patents. The Internet now has two excellent services which enable one to make a *free* search of all patents issued since 1971 or 1976 using keywords. These services and their addresses (on the World Wide Web) are as follows:
   • The PTO's Patent Server: www.uspto.gov/patft/index.html (for U.S. patents); and
   • The European Patent Office's (EPO's) Server: http://ep.espacenet.com (for foreign and U.S. patents). Presently this site only offers searches of titles and abstracts of patents.

I provide instructions for making a computer search in Section L of this chapter. You can also use any references you uncover with a computer search to work backward to make a reference "tree" to get more patents, as explained in Section L5. Note, however, that all computer searches, while alluring, are incomplete, since they don't go back far enough (except for high-tech inventions), and while they allow you to view patent drawings once you've identified a patent, they don't allow you to search through patent drawings in a subclass rapidly, as you can do in the PTO.

If you don't find anything in your preliminary search, and if your invention doesn't fall into the category discussed under "When Not to Search" (Section B, above), you're ready to make a full search.

E. The Quality of a Patent Search Can Vary

Like anything else, the quality of your patentability search can vary from very bad to near perfect. It can never be perfect since, because of their confidential status, there is no way to search nonpublished pending patent applications. (As stated in the last chapter, a patent application that is based on an RPA or PPA that was filed before your date of invention is valid prior art against your application, even if the patent issues after you file.)

Other reasons why your search may not be perfect are:

- some prior-art references can be missing (stolen or borrowed) from the area you're searching ("class and subclass"—see Section I, below);
- the area in which you're searching may not contain foreign, nonpatent, or exotic references (such as theses, service manuals, magazines, textbooks, etc.);
- very recently issued patents may not have been placed in the search files yet;
- a relevant reference (patent or nonpatent) may not have been classified in the proper class or in a way that conforms to your view of reality—that is, because of human variability, it may be classified where you wouldn't expect it to be; or
- your invention may have either been used publicly (without being published) before your invention, or it may have been previously invented by someone else who did not abandon, suppress, or conceal it.

F. How to Hire a Patent Professional

Suppose you decide to "let the pros handle it." Here are some suggestions for how to find a patent professional and what your role in the process should be.

1. Lay Patent Searchers

Many patent searchers can be located in the Yellow Pages of local telephone directories under "Patent Searchers." Others advertise in periodicals, such as the *Journal of the Patent and Trademark Office Society*, a publication for patent professionals edited and published by a private association of patent examiners, or *Investor's Digest* (see Appendix 2). I have had far better results with patent attorneys and agents than with lay searchers. Attorneys and agents understand the concept of unobviousness (see previous chapter) better and thus dig in more places than might at first appear necessary. However, lay searchers have one big advantage: they charge about half of what most attorneys and agents charge. Nevertheless, before hiring a lay searcher, I would find out about the searcher's charges, technical background, on-the-job experience, usual amount of time spent on a search and where the searcher searches (in the PTO's main search room or in the examining division). Most importantly, I would also ask for the names of some clients, preferably in your city, so that you can check with them. Lay searchers do not have to be licensed by any governmental agency, so you should exercise more care in selecting one and you should be aware that they're not allowed to express opinions on patentability.

2. Patent Agents

A "patent agent" is an individual with technical training (generally an undergraduate degree in engineering) who is licensed by the PTO to prepare and prosecute patent applications. A patent agent can conduct a patent search and is authorized to express an opinion on patentability, but cannot represent you in court, cannot handle trademarks, and cannot handle licensing or infringement suits. All other things being equal, I recommend using an attorney rather than an agent for searching (and patent application work), since most patent attorneys have experience in licensing and litigation which will usually lead them to make wider and stronger searches for possible use in adversarial situations. However, always consider the individual, how much time he or she will spend with you, and how well you get along.

3. Patent Attorneys

A "patent attorney" or "patent lawyer" is licensed to practice both by the PTO and the attorney-licensing authority (such as the state bar, state supreme court, etc.) of at least one state. Thus patent attorneys must be licensed by two authorities. A "general" lawyer licensed to practice in one or more states, but not before the PTO, can handle copyrights and trademarks but is not authorized to prepare patent applications or use the title "patent attorney." An intellectual property attorney handles trademarks and copyrights and may or may not be licensed by the PTO to prepare and file patent applications.

4. Finding Patent Agents and Attorneys

All patent agents and attorneys are listed in the PTO's publication *Attorneys and Agents Registered to Practice Before the U.S. Patent and Trademark Office* (A&ARTP). This is available in all medium- to large-sized public libraries as well as Patent and Trademark Depository Libraries (see Section K, below), government bookstores, and on the PTO's site, www.uspto.gov.

For patent search purposes, you will want to find an attorney or agent in the Washington, DC, area. Most patent attorneys and agents who do searching in the PTO can be found in the District of Columbia section, or the Virginia section of A&ARTP under zip code 22202. Pick one or more of these and then call or write to say you want a search made in a particular field. (Generally, hiring an attorney in your locality to do the search is a very inefficient and costly way to do the job, since the attorney or agent will have to hire an associate in or travel to Arlington to make the search for you. This means you'll have to pay two patent professionals or travel expenses for the search.)

How to Find "Discount" Patent Attorneys and Agents

Active patent professionals (attorneys and agents) are either in private practice (a law firm or solo practice) or employed by a corporation or the government. Most patent professionals in private practice charge about $100 to $500 an hour. But many corporate-employed or semiretired patent professionals also have private clients and charge considerably less than their downtown counterparts. If you want or ever need to consult a local patent professional, you'll save money by using one of these "discount" patent professionals; their services are usually just as good or better than those of the full-priced law firm attorneys. Also, since they have much less overhead (rent, books, secretaries), they'll be more generous with their time (except that patent professionals employed by the federal government are not allowed to represent private clients). Look in the geographical section of the A&ARTP book or search by zip code in the online version on the PTO's site, for corporate-employed or retired (but still licensed) patent professionals in your area; the latter can usually be identified by their corporate addresses or addresses in a residential, rather than a downtown, neighborhood. You can expect to pay substantially more for attorneys in downtown high-rise office buildings.

Of course, finding a good patent professional often involves more than checking a list. The best way is by personal referral. Ask another inventor, your employer, your local inventors' organization, a general attorney whom you like, a friend, etc. Another way to check an attorney or agent is to look at the patents they've prepared. You can find these online on the PTO site (see Section L of this chapter) by entering the attorney's name and reading some of the recent patents with the attorney's name on them. When reading the patent, see if the writing's clear, if the advantages of the invention are stressed, if the invention is explained fully, if ramifications of the invention have been discussed, and if the technical field of the invention is similar to yours. If you do find someone who seems good, make a short appointment to discuss the broad outlines of your problem. This will give you a feel for the attorney, whether the chemistry's good between the two of you, whether the fees are acceptable, etc. Ask what undergraduate degree the attorney has (almost all have undergraduate degrees in engineering or a science); you don't want to use a mechanical engineer to handle a complex computer circuit.

Your next question should be, "Will the professional help you help yourself or demand a traditional attorney-client relationship (attorney does it all and you pay for it)?" Many corporate-employed and retired patent professionals will be delighted to help you with your search, preparation, and/or prosecution of your patent application. Using this approach, you can do much of the work yourself and have the professional provide help where needed at a reasonable cost.

When it comes to fees, you should always work these out in advance. Some patent professionals charge a flat fee for searches (and also for patent applications and amendments); others charge by the hour. If you plan to do much of the work yourself, you'll want hourly billing. If you do agree to hourly billing, be sure to first obtain an estimate of the maximum number of hours and an agreement to notify you in advance if this will be exceeded. Also, be sure it's clear who will pay for other costs associated with prosecuting a patent, such as copies, postage, drafting, filing fees, etc.

When you visit a patent attorney or agent, remember that they're not an oracle of knowledge: don't expect to be able to lay a prototype or sketch of your invention on their desk and say, "What do you think of this?" and have them instantly tell you its commercial value and give you an opinion on patentability. First, they usually are not qualified to do a commercial evaluation. Second, they can't give you an opinion on patentability without making and analyzing a search.

Millie Inventress
1901 JFK Blvd.
Philadelphia, PA 19103

2003 Jan 22
Samuel Searcher, Esq.
2001 Jefferson Davis Highway
Arlington, VA 22202

Patentability Search: Inventress: Napkin-Shaping Ring

Dear Mr. Searcher:

As we discussed on the phone yesterday, you were highly recommended to me as an excellent searcher by Jacob Potofsky, Esq., who is a general attorney here and a cousin of my friend, Shirley Jaschik. You said that you would be able to make a full patentability search on my above invention, including an examiner consultation and a search in the examiner's files to cover foreign and nonpatent references, for $1,000, including patent copies and postage. I have enclosed this amount as full payment in advance, per your request. You said that you would mail the search report (without an opinion on patentability) and references to me within three weeks from the date you receive this letter.

Enclosed are three sheets of drawings from my notebook (I have properly signed, witnessed, and dated records elsewhere); these sheets clearly illustrate my napkin-shaping ring invention. As you can see from the prior-art Figs 1 (A and B), previous napkin rings were simple affairs, designed merely to hold a previously rolled or folded napkin in a simple shape. In contrast, the napkin ring of my invention, shown in Fig 2, and made of metal or plastic, has a heart-shaped outer member 12, an inner leg 14, and two curved-back arms 16. As shown in Fig 3, it is used by introducing a corner 8 of a cloth napkin 10 between an end 4 of leg 4 and the adjacent portion of outer member 12. When napkin 10 is pulled partially through the ring, as indicated in Fig 4, it will be forced to assume the shape of the space between arms 16 and outer portion 12, as indicated.

Thus my napkin-shaping-and-holding ring can be used to make a napkin have an attractive, graceful shape when it is laid flat and placed adjacent to a place setting, as indicated in Fig 5. The extending portion of the napkin can also be folded up and around, as indicated in Fig 6-A, so that the napkin and its ring can be stood upright.

In addition to the specific shape shown, you should of course search the broader concept of my invention, namely a ring-shaped outer member with an inwardly extending tongue or leg that can be used to shape napkins pulled partially through the structure. I believe that I have provided you with sufficient information to fully understand the structure and workings of my invention so that you can make a search, but if any further information is needed, please don't hesitate to call me.

I understand that you will, in accordance with the ethics of your profession, keep all details of my invention strictly confidential, except to consult an examiner.

Most sincerely,

Millie Inventress

Millie Inventress (215-776-3960)
Encs.: $1,000 check, 3 sheets of drawings
(My file: 60:Search.ltr)

Fig. 6A—Inventor's Search Request Letter to Patent Searcher

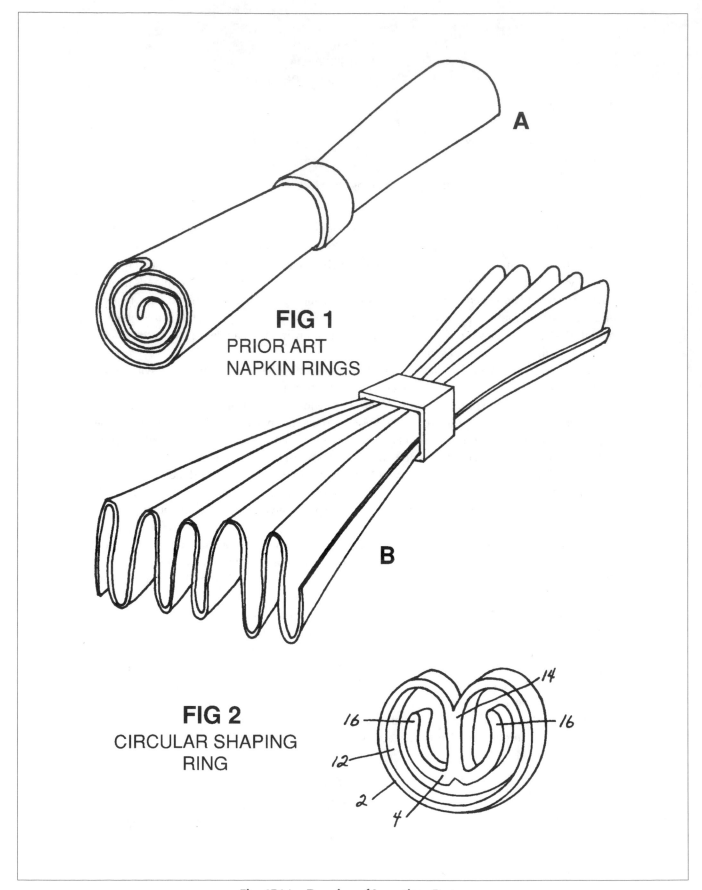

FIG 1
PRIOR ART
NAPKIN RINGS

A

B

FIG 2
CIRCULAR SHAPING
RING

14
16
16
12
2
4

Fig. 6B(a)—Drawing of Invention, Part a

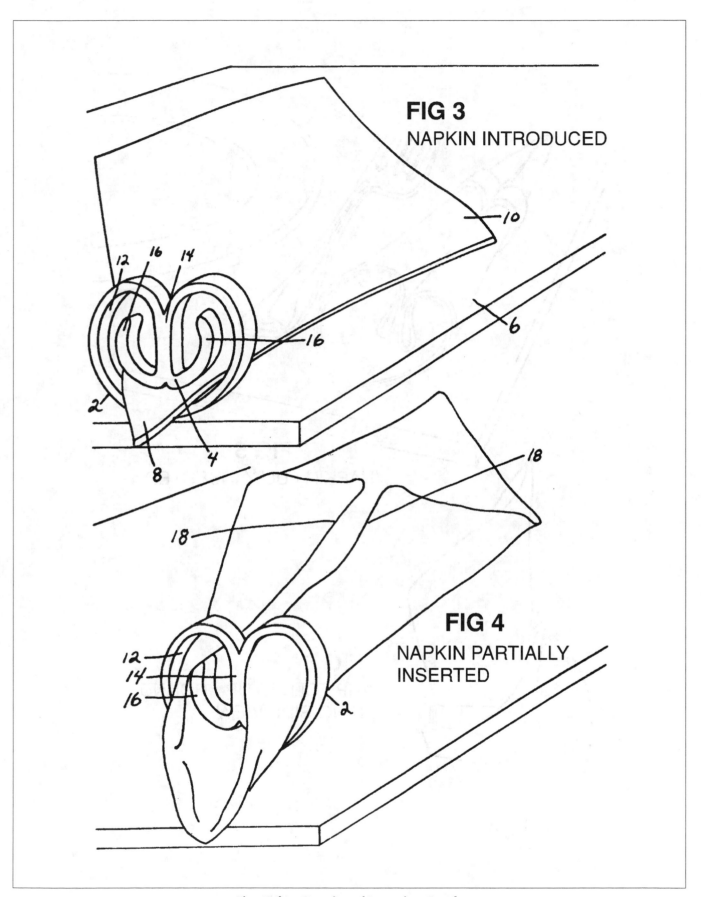

FIG 3
NAPKIN INTRODUCED

FIG 4
NAPKIN PARTIALLY
INSERTED

Fig. 6B(b)—Drawing of Invention, Part b

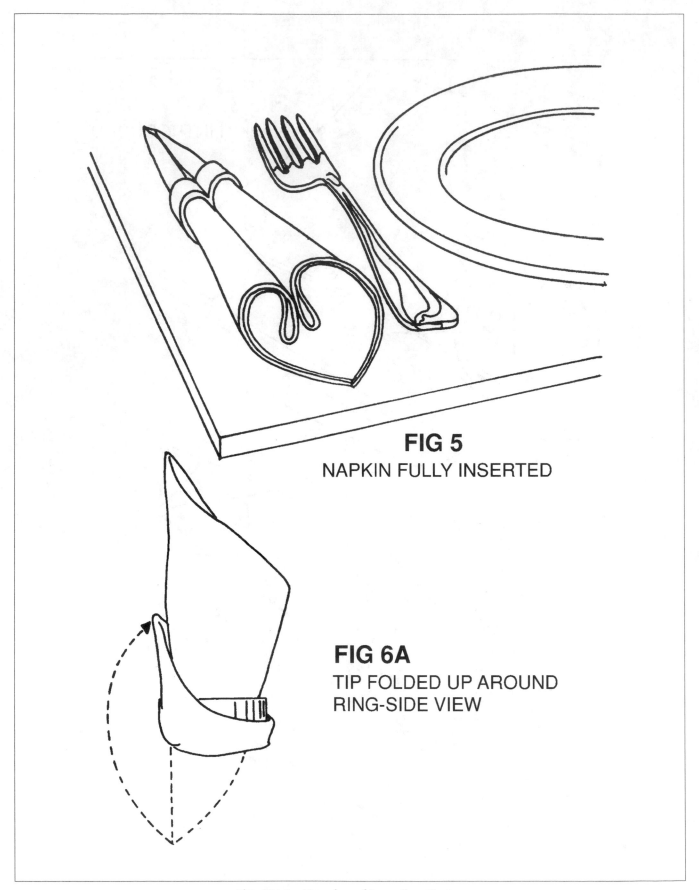

FIG 5
NAPKIN FULLY INSERTED

FIG 6A
TIP FOLDED UP AROUND
RING-SIDE VIEW

Fig. 6B(c)—Drawing of Invention, Part c

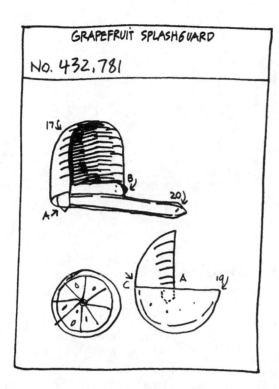

GRAPEFRUIT SPLASHGUARD

No. 432,781

G. How to Prepare Your Searcher

You'll want to use your patent searcher to maximum efficiency. Do this by sending your searcher a clear and complete description of your invention, together with easily understandable drawings. Be sure to disclose all embodiments, variations, and ramifications so that these will be searched. You won't compromise any trade-secret status of your invention by such a letter since by law it's considered a confidential communication. If you wish any type of particular emphasis applied to any aspect of your search, be sure to inform the searcher of this fact. If your notebook record of your invention or your invention disclosure is clear enough, you can merely send the searcher a copy. Whether you send a copy of your notebook entries or a separate disclosure (Form 3-2), I recommend that you blank out all dates on any document you send to anyone: this will make it more difficult for any potential invention thief (extremely rare) who might gain access to your disclosure to antedate you. Fig. 6A is an example of a proper search request letter from an inventor and Figs. 6B (a, b, c) are copies of the attachments to the search request letter of Fig. 6A.

You don't need to have a patent agent or a patent attorney sign a Keep-Confidential Agreement (Chapter 3), since registered (PTO-licensed) patent professionals are strictly bound by the PTO's rules to keep all client communications confidential. However, if you feel insecure, or you are using a layperson to search, you certainly can ask your searcher to sign Form 3-1. In any case, you should always keep a "paper trail" of all disclosures you make to anyone.

H. Analyzing the Search Report

After you send out your search request, the searcher will generally take several weeks to perform the patentability search, obtain copies of the patents and other references that the searcher feels are relevant, and report back. Most search reports have four parts:

1. A description of your invention provided by the searcher to assure you that the searcher has understood your invention and to indicate exactly what has been searched.
2. A list of the patents and other references discovered during the search.
3. A brief discussion of the cited patents and other references, pointing out the relevant parts of each.
4. A list of the classes and subclasses searched and the examiners consulted, if any.

The searcher will enclose copies of the references (usually U.S. patents, but possibly also foreign patents, magazine articles, etc.) cited in the search report and enclose a bill. Most searchers charge separately for the search, the reference copies, and the postage. If you've paid the searcher a retainer, you should be sent a refund unless your retainer was insufficient. In this case, you'll receive a bill for the balance you owe.

EXAMPLES:
- Fig. 6C is an example of a typical, competently done search report sent by Samuel Searcher, Esq., in response to Millie Inventress's letter of Fig. 6A.
- Fig. 6D(a) is a copy of page 1 (the drawing) of the Gabel patent cited in the search report.
- Fig. 6D(b) is a copy of page 2 of Gabel (the first page of Gabel's specification).
- Fig. 6D(c) is a copy of page 1 of the Le Sueur patent cited in the search report.

I haven't shown the other cited patents and the rest of the Gabel and Le Sueur patents, as these aren't necessary for our patentability determination.

You should now read the searcher's report and the references carefully. Then, determine whether your invention is patentable over the references cited in the search report. Let's use Millie's search report as an example of how to do this.

First, note from Fig. 6B that the napkin-shaping ring of the invention has an annular (ring-shaped) outer member with an inwardly projecting leg. The leg has flared-back arms at its free end. When a folded napkin is drawn through the ring, tip first, the arms and annular member will shape the napkin between them in an attractive manner, as indicated in Fig. 6B(c).

SAMUEL SEARCHER
Patent Attorney
2001 Jefferson Davis Highway
Arlington, VA 22202
703-521-3210
2003 Feb 21

Ms. Millie Inventress
1901 JFK Blvd.
Philadelphia, PA 19103

Search Report: Inventress: Napkin-Shaping Ring

Dear Ms. Inventress:

In response to your letter of Jan. 22, I have made a patentability search of your above invention, a napkin-shaping ring comprising an outer portion with an inwardly extending leg and flared-back arms at the end of the leg. I have also searched the broader concept of an annular member with an inward cantilevered leg for shaping a napkin that is drawn there-through. My bill for $900, the total cost of this search, including the references and postage, is enclosed and is marked "Paid"; I thank you for your check and enclose a refund of $100.

I searched your invention in the following classes and subclasses in the actual examining divisions: 40/21, 40/142, D44/20, and 24/8. In addition, I consulted Examiner John Hayness in Group Art Unit 353 regarding this invention. Otherwise, I kept your invention strictly confidential. In my search, I thought the following references (all U.S. Patents) were most relevant, and I enclose a copy of each: **Bergmann,** 705,196 (1902); **Gabel,** 1,771,328 (1930); **Hypps,** 3,235,880 (1966); and **Le Sueur,** 3,965,591 (1976).

Bergmann shows a handkerchief holder that comprises a simple coiled ring with wavy portions.

Gabel is most relevant; she shows a curtain folder comprising a folded metal device through which a curtain (already partially folded) is inserted and then pulled through and ironed at the exit end.

Hypps shows a necktie and holding device.

Le Sueur shows a napkin ring with magnetically attachable names.

I could not find any napkin-shaping devices as such and Examiner Hayness was not aware of any either. However, be sure to consider the Gabel patent carefully, as it appears to perform a somewhat similar function, albeit for curtains.

It was my pleasure to serve you. I wish you the best of success with your invention. Please don't hesitate to call if you have any questions.

Most sincerely,

Samuel Searcher

Samuel Searcher
Encs: $100 Check, Bill, and References

Fig. 6C—Patent Searcher's Search Report

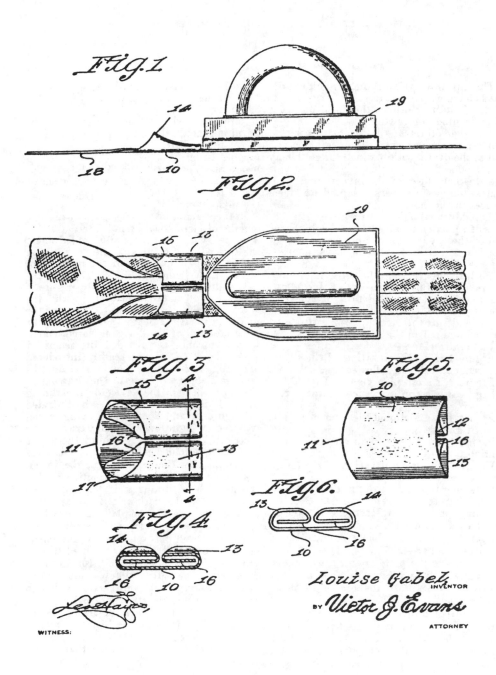

July 22, 1930   L. GABEL   1,771,328

FOLDER

Filed March 16. 1923

Fig. 6D(a)—Drawing of Prior-Art Gabel Patent

1,771,328

UNITED STATES PATENT OFFICE

LOUISE GABEL, OF COLUMBUS, NEBRASKA

FOLDER

Application filed March 16, 1928. Serial No. 262,243.

This invention relates to cloth holding devices and more particularly to a device adapted for holding cloth in the form of plaits while ironing and sewing.

5 An other object of the invention comprehends an enlarged entrance opening in one end of the device within which the cloth may be introduced.

A further object of the invention contem- 10 plates tongue members adapted to form creases in the cloth.

An additional object of the invention consists of a portion removed from the discharge end of the device whereby binding action of 15 a sad iron therewith is obviated while pressing the cloth.

With the above and other objects in view, the invention further consists of the following novel features and details of construc- 20 tion, to be hereinafter more fully described, illustrated in the accompanying drawing and pointed out in the appended claim.

In the drawing:—

Figure 1 is a side elevation of the inven- 25 tion while in use and followed by a sad iron.

Figure 2 is a top plan view of Figure 1.

Figure 3 is a top plan view of the invention per se.

Figure 4 is a sectional view taken on line 30 4—4 of Figure 3.

Figure 5 is a bottom plan view of the invention.

Figure 6 is a front elevation of the invention per se.

35 Referring to the drawing in detail, wherein like characters of reference denote corresponding parts, the reference character 10 indicates a plate member having a curved outwardly projecting forward end 11 and 40 a concaved inner end 12.

The sides of the plate are bent upon themselves upwardly and inwardly upon the plate to provide horizontally disposed guide members 13.

45 As illustrated in Figures 1, 3, 4 and 6, the outermost end, namely 11, is flared to provide an enlarged entrance and to accomplish such construction the outermost ends of the 50 guide members 13 are upwardly flared, as in-

dicated at 14 and concaved, as indicated at 15 upon the foremost edges thereof.

Tongues 16, carri[ed] 13, are extended r[ ] posed in spaced rela[ ] the plate member 1[ ] tongues being also [ ] members. The for[ ] 16 are rounded, as [ ] jected forwardly f[ ] the adjacent ends o[ ]

In the use and o[peration of the invention,] lengths of cloth, such as indicated at 18, o[f] a desired width, are partially folded along the side edges thereof and the strip per se 65 laid upon the upper side of the plate member 10. The folded portions of the strip being adapted to repose upon the upper sides of the tongues 16 and to be projected within the spaces as defined between the tongues and the 70 guide members. Due to the fact that the outermost end of the device is flared, an enlarged entrance is provided by means of which the cloth may be readily introduced and fed. The rounded portions 17 for the 75 tongues also permit ease in the drawing of the cloth through the device or the sliding of the device upon the cloth. As illustrated in Figures 1 and 2 of the drawing, a sad iron, such as indicated at 19, may travel upon 80 the cloth 18 immediately behind the device to press the folded side edges or plaits of the cloth. By the same token, the invention could be used in the formation of different kinds of braids and etc., and to ef- 85 fectively feed the cloth or strip to a sewing machine, in the event the plaits are to be held against displacement from the strip per se.

The concaved portion 12, upon the innermost end of the strip 10, is adapted to pre- 90 vent binding action of the sad iron 19 therewith when the latter closely pursues the plate member. Such construction will also prevent injury to the strip and plaits.

Although I have shown, described and il- 95 lustrated my invention as being primarily adapted for use in the manufacture of plaits, it is to be obviously understood that the invention could be effectively employed for 100

In the use and operation of the invention, lengths of cloth, such as indicated at 18, of a desired width, are partially folded along the side edges thereof and the strip per se laid upon the upper side of the plate member 10. The folded portions of the strip be-

Fig. 6D(b)—Specification of Prior-Art Gabel Patent

United States Patent [19]

Le Sueur

[11] **3,965,591**

[45] June 29, 1976

[54] NAPKIN RING

[75] Inventor: Alice E. J. Le Sueur, Cobble Hill, Canada

[73] Assignee: The Raymond Lee Organization, New York, N.Y. ; a part interest

[22] Filed: Nov. 26, 1974

[21] Appl. No.: 527,216

[52] U.S. Cl.. 40/21 R
[51] Int. Cl.² G09F 3/14
[58] Field of Search.................. 40/142 A, 63, 21 A, 40/21 B, 10; 63/2; 24/8

[56] **References Cited**
UNITED STATES PATENTS
198,065   12/1877   Annin .... 63/1 X

| 2,600,505 | 6/1952 | Jones | 40/142 A |
| 2,653,402 | 9/1953 | Bonagura | 40/21 A |

FOREIGN PATENTS OR APPLICATIONS
1,308,888   10/1962   France 40/142

Primary Examiner—Louis G. Mancene
Assistant Examiner—Wenceslao J. Contreras
Attorney, Agent, or Firm—Howard I. Podell

[57]   **ABSTRACT**

An open cylindrical napkin ring fitted with magnetic means for attaching an identifying name or set of initials in a recess on the outside of the ring.

3 Claims, 4 Drawing Figures

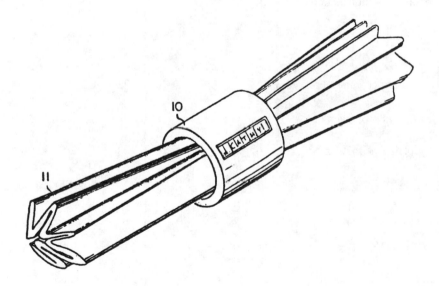

Fig. 6D(c)—Abstract Page of Prior-Art Le Sueur Patent

PATENT DOCUMENT KIND CODES

With new number formats as they appear on documents published on or after January 2, 2001. For a full explanation of document kind codes see WIPO Standard ST.16, available at http://www.wipo.int/scit/en.

New Number Format

US 6,654,321 B1

country code   document number   document code

Document Type	Before Jan. 2, 2001	On or After Jan. 2, 2001	
	Number Format	Code	Number Format
Utility Patents			
Issued patent (no pre-grant publication)	5,123,456	B1	US 6,654,321 B1
Issued patent (with pre-grant publication)	NA	B2	US 6,654,322 B2
Application (first publication)	NA	A1	US 2001/0001111 A1
Second or subsequent republication of an application	NA	A2	US 2001/0002222 A2
Correction of a published application	NA	A9	US 2001/0003333 A9
Plant Patents			
Issued patent (no pre-grant publication)	Plant 11,000	P2	US PP12,345 P2
Issued patent (with pre-grant publication)	NA	P3	US PP12,345 P3
Application (first publication)	NA	P1	US 2001/0004444 P1
Second or subsequent republication of an application	NA	P4	US 2001/0005555 P4
Correction of a published application	NA	P9	US 2001/0006666 P9
Design Patents	Des. 456,789	S	US D654,321 S
Reissue Patents	RE36,543	E	US RE12,345 E
Reexaminations			
Reexamination certificate issued from first reexamination of a patent (utility, plant, design or reissue)	B1 5,123,456 B1 Plant 11,000 B1 Des. 123,456 B1 RE12,345	C1	US 6,654,321 C1 US PP12,345 C1 US D654,321 C1 US RE12,345 C1
Reexamination certificate issued from second reexamination of a patent	B2 5,123,456 etc.	C2	US 6,654,321 C2 etc.
Reexamination certificate issued from third reexamination of a patent	B3 5,123,456 etc.	C3	US 6,654,321 C3 etc.
Other Patent Documents			
Statutory invention registration (SIR) documents	H1,234	H1	US H2345 H

Created: 1/16/01 MJW

Fig. 6D(d)—Patent Document Kind Codes

Of the four previous patents cited, let's assume that only Gabel and Le Sueur are of real relevance. Gabel, a patent from 1930, shows a curtain folder comprising a bent sheet-metal member. A curtain is folded slightly and is drawn through the folder that completes the folding so that the curtain can be ironed when it is drawn out of the folder. Le Sueur, a patent from 1976, shows a napkin ring with a magnetized area for holding the letters of the name of a user.

Now, as part of analyzing this sample search report, we'll use the master flowchart of Fig. 5C. To save you from having to turn the pages repeatedly, I've reproduced it below, as Fig. 6E. If any part of this chart confuses you, reread the part of Chapter 5 that explains each box in detail.

Okay, now let's work our way through the chart:

Box A: Millie's napkin-shaping ring can be classified within a statutory class as an article (or even a machine, since it shapes napkins).

Box B: It clearly has usefulness, since it provides a way for unskilled hostesses or hosts to give their napkins an attractive, uniform shape.

Box C: We must now ask whether the invention is novel—that is, physically different from any single reference. Clearly it's different from Le Sueur because of its inwardly extending leg 14. Also, it's different from Gabel because, comparing it with Gabel's Fig. 6, it's rounder and it has a complete outer ring with an inwardly extending leg, rather than a folded piece of sheet metal. It's important to compile a list of the differences (novel features) that the invention has over the prior-art references, not the differences of the references over your invention.

Box D: The question we must now ask is, Do the novel features (the roundness of the ring, the inwardly extending leg, and the flared-back arms) provide any new and unexpected results? After carefully comparing Gabel with Millie's invention, we can answer with a resounding "Yes!" Note that Gabel states, in her column 2, lines 62 to 66, that the strip of cloth is first partially folded along its side edge and then it is placed in the folder. In contrast, Millie's shaping ring, because of its roundness and leg, can shape a totally unfolded napkin—see Millie's Figs. 3 and 4. This is a distinct advantage, since Millie's shaper does all of the work automatically—the user does not have to specially fold the napkin. While not an earthshaking development or advance, clearly Millie's ring does provide a new result and one that is unexpected, since neither Gabel, Le Sueur, nor any other reference teaches that a napkin ring can be used to shape an unfolded napkin. Thus we take the solid-line "Yes" output of Box D to Box E.

Box E: Although not mandatory, we next check the secondary factors (1 to 21) listed in Boxes E, F, and G.

Reading through these factors, we find first that #2 in Box E applies—that is, the invention solves a problem (the inability of most persons to quickly and neatly fold napkins so that they have an attractive shape) that was never before even recognized. Also, we can provide affirmative answers to factors #8 and #11, since the invention provides an advantage that was never before appreciated and it solves a long-felt, but unsolved need—the need of unskilled persons to shape napkins quickly and gracefully (long felt by the more fastidious of those who hate paper napkins, at least).

Boxes F and G: Since two references are present, and each shows some part of Millie's invention, we have to answer "Yes" to Box F and proceed to Box G to consider the possible effect that a combination of these would have on the question of obviousness ("combinatory unobviousness"). In Box G we see that factors 13, 15, 18, 19, and 21 can reasonably be argued as relevant to Millie's invention. The invention has synergism (#21), since the results (automatic napkin folding) are greater than the sum of the references; the combination of the two references is not suggested (#13) by the references themselves; and even if the two references were combined, Millie's inward leg would not be shown (#15). The references are complete and fully functional in themselves, and hence teach by implication that they should not be combined (#18). And it would be awkward, requiring redesign and tooling, to combine the references (#19). Thus we can with conviction state that several secondary factors are present, so we take the solid-line "Yes" output of Box G to Box H.

Next, (Box H) we see that the PTO is very likely to grant a patent, and our determination on patentability is accordingly positive.

In fact, this exercise is a real case: An examiner initially rejected an application for the napkin-shaping ring as unpatentable over Gabel and Le Sueur. However, he agreed to grant a patent (U.S. Pat. No. 4,420,102) after I filed an argument forcefully stating the above considerations.

Although I've analyzed the search report to determine whether Millie's invention was patentable, it's important to remember that a weak patent isn't much better than no patent. Put differently, a very weak patent and $3.00 will get you a cable car ride in San Francisco. So in addition to reaching a decision on patentability, you should also walk the extra mile to determine whether your patent is likely to be of broad enough scope to make it economically worthwhile. I tell you how to do this in Section J of this chapter.

Note that we have done our own patentability evaluation—the four-part list, above—and that the search report of Fig. 6C didn't include an opinion on patentability. There are several reasons for this.

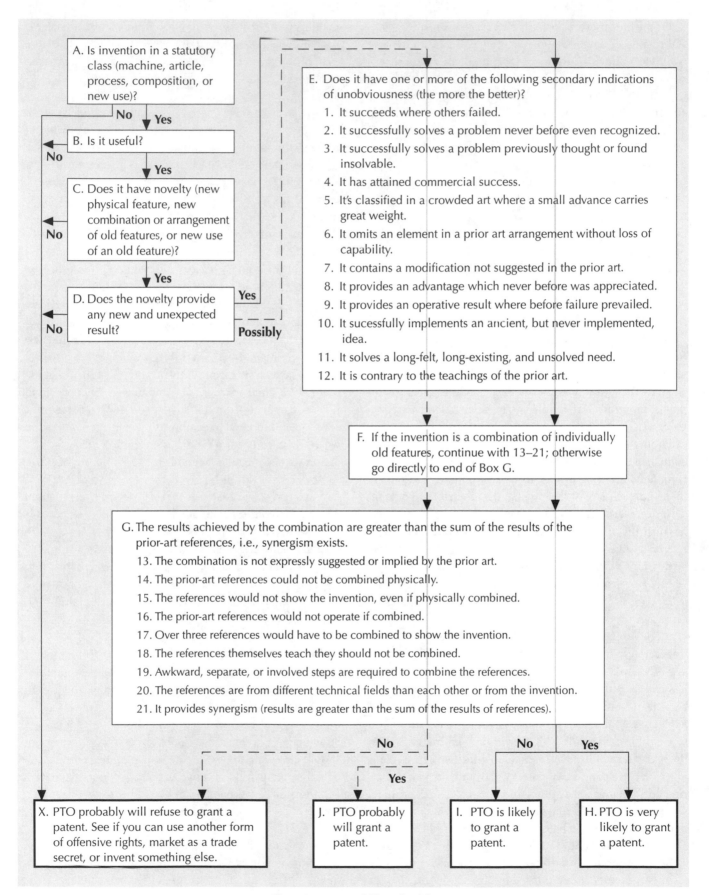

A. Is invention in a statutory class (machine, article, process, composition, or new use)? — **No** → / **Yes** ↓

B. Is it useful? — No / **Yes** ↓

C. Does it have novelty (new physical feature, new combination or arrangement of old features, or new use of an old feature)? — No / **Yes** ↓

D. Does the novelty provide any new and unexpected result? — No / **Yes** / **Possibly**

E. Does it have one or more of the following secondary indications of unobviousness (the more the better)?
1. It succeeds where others failed.
2. It successfully solves a problem never before even recognized.
3. It successfully solves a problem previously thought or found insolvable.
4. It has attained commercial success.
5. It's classified in a crowded art where a small advance carries great weight.
6. It omits an element in a prior art arrangement without loss of capability.
7. It contains a modification not suggested in the prior art.
8. It provides an advantage which never before was appreciated.
9. It provides an operative result where before failure prevailed.
10. It sucessfully implements an ancient, but never implemented, idea.
11. It solves a long-felt, long-existing, and unsolved need.
12. It is contrary to the teachings of the prior art.

F. If the invention is a combination of individually old features, continue with 13–21; otherwise go directly to end of Box G.

G. The results achieved by the combination are greater than the sum of the results of the prior-art references, i.e., synergism exists.
13. The combination is not expressly suggested or implied by the prior art.
14. The prior-art references could not be combined physically.
15. The references would not show the invention, even if physically combined.
16. The prior-art references would not operate if combined.
17. Over three references would have to be combined to show the invention.
18. The references themselves teach they should not be combined.
19. Awkward, separate, or involved steps are required to combine the references.
20. The references are from different technical fields than each other or from the invention.
21. It provides synergism (results are greater than the sum of the results of references).

No / **Yes** / **No** / **Yes**

X. PTO probably will refuse to grant a patent. See if you can use another form of offensive rights, market as a trade secret, or invent something else.

J. PTO probably will grant a patent.

I. PTO is likely to grant a patent.

H. PTO is very likely to grant a patent.

Fig. 6E—Patentability Flowchart

First, if your searcher is a layperson (not a patent attorney or agent), the searcher is not licensed to give opinions on patentability since this constitutes the practice of law.

Second, even if your searcher is an attorney or agent, the searcher usually won't provide an opinion on patentability because most searchers are used to working for other patent attorneys who like to form their own opinions on patentability for their clients.

Third, if the searcher's opinion on patentability is negative, a negative written opinion might be damaging to your case if you do get a patent, sue to enforce it, and the opinion is used as evidence that your patent is invalid. This would occur, for example, if your court adversary (the defendant infringer) obtains a copy of the opinion by pretrial discovery (depositions and interrogatories), shows it to the judge, and argues that since your own search came up with a negative result, this militates against the validity of your patent. However, a negative written opinion can be "worked" in court—that is, distinguished, explained, rebutted, etc.—so if you want the searcher's opinion on patentability in addition to the search, most patent attorney/agent searchers will be glad to give it to you without extra charge, or for a slight additional cost of probably not more than $300 to $600.

Fourth, armed with the knowledge you've gained from Chapter 5, you should be able to form your own opinion on patentability by now; the exercise will be fun, educational, and insightful to your invention.

Fifth, note that there's no certainty in the law. No one can ever say for certain that you'll be able to get a patent before you get it since no search can cover pending patent applications, and human responses (how your examiner will react) are very unpredictable. So take any prediction with a grain of salt.

In any case, don't hesitate to ask any questions about the searcher's practices in advance, and be sure to specify exactly what you want in your search. It's your money and you're entitled to buy or contract for whatever services you desire.

As Elihu Root said, "About half the practice of a decent lawyer consists in telling would-be clients that they are damned fools and should stop."

I. Do-It-Yourself Searching in the PTO

Almost all pre-examination searches should be made primarily in patent files (paper or computer). This is because patents are classified according to a detailed scheme (discussed later in this chapter). Also, there are about ten times as many devices and processes shown in the patent files as in textbooks, magazines, etc., primarily because commercial practicability is not a requirement for patentability. All PTO examiners make their searches in the patent files for these reasons, so you should also. However, if you have access to a good nonpatent data bank, such as a good technical library in the field of your invention, you can use this as a supplement or alternative to your search of the patent files.

Searching is a strange business—it's one of the few times you'll look for something with the hope that you won't find it! Thus, if you do it yourself, you should do it carefully and thoroughly. One professional searcher, Randy Rabin, recommends that for this reason one should not search his or her own invention, or at least do it with the assistance of someone who lacks any ax to grind. Searching is one of the main areas where an ounce of early work can save you pounds of later work and disappointment.

From Arlington to Alexandria: The PTO Has Moved

As of this printing (spring 2005), the PTO has completed most of its move (including the main, public search room) from Crystal City, at 23rd and Jeff Davis Highway in Arlington, Virginia, to the Carlyle Complex at Eisenhower and Duke Streets in Alexandria, Virginia. The new location has a colder, more sterile atmosphere. Certain services, such as the file information unit, where copies of files are ordered, will remain in Crystal City. The PTO has a free shuttle between Alexandria and Arlington.

1. Getting Started at the PTO

As I have said, the best place to make a search of the patent files is in the PTO unless you have access to the files of a large company that specializes in your field. This is because the PTO's search facilities have all U.S. patents arranged by subject matter either in paper form or on computers. For example, all patents that show bicycle derailleurs are grouped together, all patents that show transistor flip-flop circuits are together, all patents to diuretic drug compositions are together, etc. Also, the PTO has foreign patents and literature classified along with U.S. patents according to subject matter. Remember (Chapter 5, Section E1) that foreign patents are valid prior art in the U.S.

All patent-related mail must be addressed to the Commissioner for Patents, P.O. Box 1450, Alexandria, VA 22213-1450. The mail is delivered to the PTO's offices in Alexandria (see "From Arlington to Alexandria: The PTO Has Moved," above). The PTO receives over three million pieces of mail a year, more than any other governmental agency except the IRS.

The PTO is technically part of the Department of Commerce (headquartered in Washington) but operates in an almost autonomous fashion.

The PTO employs about 1,200 examiners, all of whom have technical undergraduate degrees in such fields as electrical engineering, chemistry, or physics. Many examiners are also attorneys. The PTO also has about an equal number of clerical, supervisory, and support personnel. The Commissioner for Patents is appointed by the president, and most of the higher officials of the PTO have to be approved by Congress. Most patent examiners are well paid; a journeyman examiner (ten years' experience) usually makes $75,000 to $100,000 a year.

Assuming you do go to the PTO, here's what you'll find. There are two places you can make the search:
- the public search room, and
- the examiners' search files in the actual examining division.

Most searchers make their search in the public search room because it's more convenient—it's on the first floor, there are search tables, and it's large and well lighted. However, if possible, I recommend putting up with a little inconvenience and going upstairs to the examiners' search files. There are several reasons to do this: The examiners are there to assist you; literature and foreign patents are available; it's much quieter; the patent files are likely to be more intact; and finally, of at least minor importance, the chairs are more comfortable. To get into the search room, you must fill out a form and apply for a user pass, which will take only a few minutes. As of this writing, the PTO plans to make the examiners' search areas more secure, so you will have to wade through some red tape to get upstairs. (I recommend putting up with a little inconvenience and red tape.)

If you need help with your search, you can ask any of the search assistants in the search room or (even better) an examiner in the actual examining division. You won't be endangering the security of your invention if you ask any of these people about your search and give them all the details of your invention. They see dozens of new inventions every week, are quite used to helping searchers and others, and would be fired if they ever stole an invention. Also, the PTO's rules forbid employees from filing patent applications. In theory a PTO employee could communicate an invention to a friend or relative who could file, but it's very unlikely to occur since such a relationship could be easily discovered during patent litigation.

2. How to Do the Search—Paper and EAST Searches

Okay, now that you know something about the PTO and where to search, what do you do next? It used to be that the only way to search at the PTO was with paper patents. However the PTO is in the process of eliminating paper files and patents and is speeding headlong into All-Computer City. Many question the wisdom of this choice, but the PTO claims it lacks the space to store the necessary paper files. In any case, I will cover both types of searches at the PTO here, but bear in mind the following:

1. The PTO's paper files are incomplete because issuing patents have not been placed in the files since 2001 and users have pilfered many paper patents. The PTO has not made integrity checks to replace the missing patents.
2. The PTO's search system, called EAST (Examiner Automated Search Tool) requires some training and skill to use. The PTO has about 250 EAST terminals in the public search room and gives free four-hour training sessions once per month. Also, often a user at an adjacent terminal can help a new user with the basics to get the new user started.
3. The PTO began issuing patents in July 1790, but in 1836 lost all of these early patents in a fire. Some of those 10,000 patents, which were not numbered, have been recovered and are now known as the "X" patents. After the fire, the PTO started numbering patents (patent #1 issued in July, 1836). As of January 2005 the PTO has issued over 6,800,000 patents.

I will discuss the paper and EAST searches, but bear in mind the disadvantages of each.

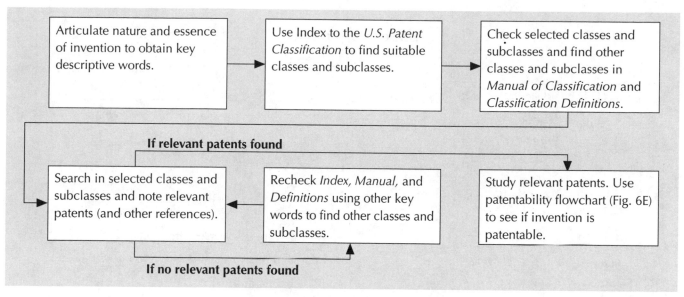

Fig. 6F—Searching Process for Paper Patents

(a) Paper Searching

There are four basic steps to take when conducting a search of paper patents; these are depicted in Fig. 6F and listed below:

Step 1: Articulate the nature and essence of your invention, using as many different terms as you can think of to describe it.

Step 2: Find the relevant classification(s) for your invention.

Step 3: Note relevant prior art (patents and other publications) under your classification.

Step 4: Carefully review the prior art to see whether it anticipates your invention or renders it obvious.

Let's take these one at a time.

Step 1: Write Out the Nature and Essence of Your Invention

As with any other classification or indexing system, your success will depend on the degree to which the words and phrases you use to define your invention coincide with the terms used by the classifier or indexer. For this reason, you should first figure out several ways to describe your invention. Start by writing down all the physical features of your invention in a brief, concise format so that you'll know exactly what to look for when searching.

For example, if you're searching a bicycle with a new type of sprocket wheel, write down "bicycle, sprocket wheel," and briefly add the details. If you're searching an electronic circuit, write down in a series of phrases like the foregoing or, in a very brief sentence, the quintessence of your invention, such as "flip-flop circuit with unijunction transistors" or some other very brief and concise description.

Do the same whether your invention is a mechanical, electronic, chemical, business, Internet, or method invention.

Form 6-1 is a Searcher's Worksheet that you can use to facilitate your searching, and Fig. 6G is a completed version of Form 6-1 that you might produce if you had searched Millie Inventress's invention. Note that the invention description part of the worksheet contains a concise description of the invention for easy reference.

Once you've written a concise description of your invention, think of some alternative keywords or phrases to add to your description. Don't hesitate to define your invention in still additional ways that may come to you during your search. Then, take your worksheet with this brief description and the drawing(s) of your invention to the public search room. Even if you're not going to do your search there, use that room to find out how your invention is classified.

Step 2: Find the Proper Classification for Your Invention

To find the place to search your invention, you'll need its most relevant search classification (called class and subclass). To obtain this, first look at the searcher's "tools" or reference publications, all of which are available in book or CD-ROM form and at the PTO website, www.uspto.gov. (See "CD-ROM Products at PTDLs," in Section K, below.) These consist of:

• the *Index to the U.S. Patent Classification*
• the *Manual of Classification,* and
• the *Classification Definitions.*

Again, let's slow down and look at each of these in detail.

Searcher's Worksheet

Sheet __1__ of __1__

Inventor(s): __Millie Inventress__

Invention Description (use keywords and variations): __Napkin folder—Annular member with inner
leg flared—back arms__

Selected Search Classifications

Class/Sub	Description	Checked	Comments
40-21	Napkin holders	✓	very relevant—the right place
40-142	Misc. tableware	✓	mostly utensils—not too good
044-20	Napkin holders	✓	somewhat relevant
24-8	Shaping devices	✓	N.G.

Patents (and Other References) Thought Relevant

Patent #	Name or Country	Date	Class/Sub	Comment
705,196	Bergmann	1902	40-142	Plain ring
1,771,328	Gabel	1930	40-21	Curtain shaper
3,235,880	Hypps	1966	40-21	Fancy ring
3,965,59	LeSueur	1976	40-21	Ring with magnetic letters

Consulted Examiner
Hayness, John Ext. 353

Searcher: __S. Searcher__

Date: __2002-1-12__

Fig. 6G—Completed Searcher's Worksheet (Form 6-1 in Appendix 7)

Locating PTO Publications Online

If you want to do some of the research yourself before going to the PTO, the *Index to the U.S. Patent Classification*, *Manual of Classification* and *Classification Definitions* can be searched online by accessing the PTO website (www.uspto.gov). Click "Patents," then click "Guidance, Tools and Manuals" under "Patenting Guides." All three publications can be found under "Tools and Manuals."

Index to the U.S. Patent Classification

While bearing an awkward title, this will be your main reference tool. If you want to do some of the research yourself before going to the PTO, the Index can be searched online (see "Locating PTO Publications Online," above). The Index is also published as a paperbound 8.5" x 11" book that alphabetically lists all possible subject areas of invention, from "abacus" to "zwieback," together with the appropriate class and subclass. The Index also lists the classes alphabetically. Let's assume that you've invented a gymnastic exercising apparatus. The first thing to do is to look in the Index under "Gymnastic Devices." Using the hard-copy materials for ease of reference, we come to page 96 (Fig. 6H), a typical page from the Index. It shows, among other things, that "Gymnastic Devices" are classified in class 272, subclass 109.

Manual of Classification

Now that we've found the class and subclass numbers, it's time to turn to the *Manual of Classification*, which lists the classes of invention numerically. The *Manual* can be searched online (see "Locating PTO Publications Online"). (As stated, there are about 430 classes.) In the hard-copy version, each class is on its own page(s), together with about 300 to 400 subclasses under each class heading, for a total of about 140,000 subclasses. The *Manual* lists design as well as utility classes; the classes are not in any logical order. To see where class-subclass 272-109 fits, let's look at the first page that covers class 272. Fig. 6I is a copy of this page. It shows

the first part of "Class 272—Amusement and Exercising Devices." Note that subclass 93 in this class covers "Exercising Equipment," and that subclass 109, which is indented under subclass 93, states "Gymnastic"; thus, class-subclass 272-109 covers gymnastic exercising equipment. Note that under 272-109 are further subclasses that may be of interest; these cover trapezes and rings, horizontal bars, etc.

As I'll explain below, this manual is used as an adjunct to the *Index*, to check your selected classes, and to find other, closely related ones.

Classification Definitions

To check our selected class and subclass still further, we next consult a third source, known as the *Classification Definitions*. The *Classification Definitions* can be searched online (see "Locating PTO Publications Online"). It is also published as a series of loose-leaf books or CD-ROM disks that contain a definition for every class and subclass in the *Manual*. At the end of each subclass definition is a cross-reference of additional places to look that correspond to such subclass.

Fig. 6J shows the classification definition for 272-109. This definition is actually a composite that I've assembled from several pages of the *Definitions*—that is, it includes definitions for class 272 per se and the superior class/subclass 272-93. Note that the class definition (272 per se), as well as many of the subclass definitions (see, for example, 272-110) contain cross-references to other classes and subclasses. You should consider these when selecting your search areas.

Be sure to spend enough time to become confidently familiar with the classification system for your invention. Check all of your subclasses in the *Manual of Classification* and the *Class Definitions* manual to be sure that you've obtained all of the right ones. Usually, two or more subclasses will be appropriate. For example, suppose your gymnastic device uses a gear with an irregular shape. Naturally, you should search in the gear classes as well as in the exercising device classes. Note that the cross-references in the exercising device classes won't refer you to "gears," since this is too specific—the cross-references in the PTO's manuals are necessarily general in nature. It's up to you to consider all aspects of your particular invention when selecting search categories.

	Class	Subclass
Water pistol	222	79
Well tubing perforator	175	2
Y gun	89	1R
Gussets		
Garment	2	275
Pocketbook body construction	150	30
Gut or Gut Treatment	8	94.11
Splitter	83	926A*
Guttapercha	260	709
Gutter	405	119
Eaves trough	52	11
Electric conductor underground structure	174	39
Road and pavement	404	2
Support design	D 8	363
Guy	52	146
Bed spring and frame	52	272
Gymnastic Devices	272	109
Coin controlled apparatus	194	
Gypsum	423	554
Calcining	106	100
Coating or plastic compositions containing	106	109
Alkali metal silicate	106	77
Gyrating		
Reciprocating sifter		
Actuating means	209	366
Horizontal and vertical shake	209	326
Horizontal shake	209	332
Gyratory Crusher		
Jaw crushers rotary component	241	207
Parallel flow through plural zones	241	140
Series flow through plural zones	241	156
Gyro Stabilized		
Article support	248	183
Furniture for ships	114	119
Gyroplane (See Aircraft)	244	17.11
Gyroscope	74	5R
Aerial camera combined	354	70
Aircraft control	244	79
Ammunition digest	102	DIG.3
Direction indicator	33	318
Gimbals	248	182
Gun sight combined	33	236
Gyroscopic compass	33	324
Telemetric system combined	340	870.7
Monorail rolling stock	105	141
Suspended	105	150
Rotors	74	572
Rotors and flywheels	74	
Ship antiroll	114	112
Ship stabilizer	114	122
Ship steering	114	144R
Speed responsive devices	73	504
Torpedo	114	24
Torpedo steering	114	24
Toy	46	50
Transmission	74	64

H

	Class	Subclass
H Acid	260	509
Haberdashery Item	D 2	378
Habitat, Submarine	114	314
Hack Saw	145	31R
Combined	7	149
Design	D 8	96
Hanging	83	783
Hackling		
Combing	19	115R
Decorticating	19	5R
Hacks Tree	30	121
Haemocytometer	356	39
Testing lenses	356	124
Hair		
Artificial furs	428	85
Artificial structure	132	5
Beauty parlor equipment	D28	10
Brush	15	160
Carried hat fasteners	132	60
Clippers	D28	52
Coating compositions	106	155
Curlers		
Curling iron	D28	38
Electrically heated	219	222
Fluid fuel heated	126	408
Cutters	30	
Design	D 8	57
Design clippers	D28	52

	Class	Subclass
For inside ear or nose	30	29.5
Hair planers	30	30
Drying on head		
Apparatus	34	96
Processes	34	3
Supports for	34	101
Dye applicator	D28	7
Dyeing and dyes	8	405
Fasteners	132	46R
Design	D28	39
Fertilizer from	71	18
Hairpiece	D28	92
Inserters	128	330
Jeweled fastener	63	2
Net	132	49
Pins (See hairpins)	132	50R
Planers	30	30
Removing (See notes)	30	32
Burial preparation	27	21
Butchering	17	1D
Coarse or water hair from fur	69	24
Cutters for inside ear or nose	30	29.5
Depilating untanned skins	8	94.16
Depilatories	8	94.16
Electric needle	128	303.18
Electric needle supports	128	303.19
Fiber liberating	19	2
Fur treatment	69	24
Process	17	47
Razors	30	32
Surgical instruments	128	355
Tweezers	128	354
Shampooing apparatus	4	515
Shearing, fur finishing	26	15R
Thinning shears	30	195
Springs	368	175
Strand making		
Covering by spinning etc	57	4
Spinning etc	57	28
Textile spinning etc	57	29
Thinners	30	195
Design	D28	52
Toilet preparations	424	70
Treating process	132	7
Vulcanizable natural hydrocarbon gums with	260	748
Waving	132	7
Hairpin	132	50R
Design	D28	39
Dispenser	132	1A
Hat fastener cord or loop and	132	61
Making	140	87
Packaging	227	25
Half Belts	2	309
Half Wave		
Gas rectifier	313	216
With hot cathode	313	211
High voltage rectifier	313	317
With emissive cathode	313	310
With thermionic cathode	313	310
Rectifier system	363	13
Circuit interrupter for	200	
Dynamoelectric machine	310	10
Electronic tube for	313	317
Gas tube type	363	114
Power packs	307	150
Unidirectional impedance for	357	
Vacuum tube type	363	114
With filter	363	39
With voltage regulator	363	84
Halftone		
Blanks and processes printing	101	401.1
Etching	156	654
X-art	156	905*
Photographic process	430	396
Photographic screens	350	322
Chemically defined	430	6
Printing plates	101	395
Halides (See Material Halogenated)		
Hydrocarbon	570	101
As azeotropes	203	67
Electromagnetic wave synthesis	204	163R
Electrostatic field or electrical discharge synthesis	204	169
Metal	423	462
Electrolytic synthesis	204	94
Nitroaromatic	568	927
Nonmetal inorganic	423	462
Organic acid	260	543
Rubber	260	772

	Class	Subclass
Hydrohalide	260	771
Mixtures containing	260	735
Hall Effect Means in an Amplifier	330	6
Haloamines	564	114
Acyclic	564	118
Hydroxy or ether containing	564	119
Plural difluoramime groups	564	121
Unsaturated	564	120
Alicyclic	564	117
Amidines	564	116
Halogen Compounds (See Material Halogenated)		
Halogenated Carboxylic Acid Esters	560	1
Acyclic acid esters	560	226
Of phenols	560	145
Acyclic amino acid esters	560	172
Acyclic carbamic acid esters	560	161
Acyclic oxy acid esters	560	184
Acyclic polycarboxylic acid esters	560	192
Acyclic unsaturated acid esters	560	219
Alicyclic	560	125
Aromatic amino acid esters	560	47
Aromatic carbamic acid esters	560	30
Aromatic polycarboxylic acid esters	560	23
Oxybenzoic acid esters	560	65
Phenoxyacetic acid esters	560	62
Halogenation (See Halides)	260	694
Halohydrin	568	841
Halowax	570	181
Halter		
Brassiere type garment	128	425
Feed bags supported on	119	66
Harness	54	24
Design	D30	19
Poke with bar and	119	141
Snap releasers	119	114
Hamburger		
Cookers	99	422
Grinders	241	
Molding and shaping (See briquetting meat)		
Hames	54	25
Collar combined	54	18R
Design	D30	23
Traces and connectors	54	30
Tugs	54	32
Hammer	145	29R
Automobile fender straightening	72	705
Burglar alarm	116	88
Claw	254	26
Combined with additional tools	7	143
Design	D 8	75
Drop forging	72	435
Earth boring tool combined	175	135
Firearm	42	
Forging	72	476
Heads for piano actions	84	254
Impact clutch type	173	93.5
Implement combined	81	463
Awl or prick punch	30	358
Internal combustion charge igniter rocking electrode	123	157
Leather compacting	69	1
Magazine	227	133
Making		
Forging dies for	72	470
Processes of	76	103
Metal bending	72	462
Mills	241	185R
Parallel material flow	241	138
Perforated discharge	241	86
Process	241	27
Series material flow	241	154
Musical instruments		
Piano	84	236
Stringed instrument	84	323
Tuning	84	459
Nut cracker	30	120.1
Pile driver	173	90
Punching machine	83	
Riveting	72	476
Road rammer	404	133
Rock drilling	175	135
Rod encircling type	145	30.5
Saw stretching machine	76	26
Scale removing	29	81D
Shoe lasting stretcher and	12	109
Stoneworking combined	125	6
Impact tools	125	40
Tool driving	173	90

Fig. 6H—Sample Page of *Index to Classification*

CLASS 272 AMUSEMENT AND EXERCISING DEVICES

272-1

DECEMBER 1983

1 R	AMUSEMENT	
1 A	..Sand boxes	
1 B	..Water sports	
1 C	..Aircraft simulation	
1 D	..Stick horses and body supported devices	
1 E	..Birling devices	
2	.Houses	
3	.Arenas	
4	..Racing	
5	...Horse	
6	.Elevating devices	
7	..Combined roundabouts	
8 R	.Illusions	
8 M	...Mirrors	
8 N	...Novelties	
8 F	...Fire	
8 D	..Display	
8 P	...Projected light	
8.5	..By transparent reflector	
9	..Stage	
10	...Special projected picture or light effects	
11	...Settings	
12	....Rapid movement	
13	...Mirror	
14	...Sound imitation	
15	...Rain, snow and fire	
16	..Trip simulation	
17	...In passenger-carrying devices	
18	....With projected picture scenery	
19	..Maze or labyrinth	
20	..Pyrotechnic display	
21	.Stage appliances	
22	..Shifting scenery	
23	...Guides, braces and clips	
24	..Aerial suspension devices	
25	..Properties	
26	...Stage tanks	
27 R	.Initiating devices	
27 B	...Blowing and cards	
27 W	...Pins and water jets	
27 N	...Novelties	
28 R	.Roundabouts	
28 S	...Vertical shaft mounting	
29	..Combined with transporting vehicle	
30	..Combined seesaw	
31 R	..Toy	
31 A	....Aircraft	
31 B	....Helicopter	
31 P	....Phonograph driven	
32	..Marine	
33 R	..Occupant propelled	
33 A	....Bowl shape	
33 B	....Bicycle type	
34	..Auto-propelled carriages	
35	..Free carriage	
36	..Vertical and horizontal axes	
37	..Plural vertical axes	
38	..Plural horizontal axes	
39	..Vertical axis only	
40	...Suspended vehicle or rider support	
41	....Circular swings	
42	....With rotating platform	
43	...Rotating vehicle or rider support and stationary track or platform	
44	....Vertically undulating track or platform	
45	....Horizontally undulating track or platform	
46	...Rotating disk, ring or bowl	
47	....Concentric rings or disks	
48	....With vehicle or rider supports	
49	..Horizontal axis only	
50	..Gyrating axis	
51	..Inclined axis	
52	.Hobby horses	
52.5	..Combined or convertible	

53.1	..With actuating means
53.2	..With movable elements
54	.Seesaws
55	..One person
56	..Rocking support
56.5 R	.Slides
56.5 SS	...Ski slopes
85	.Swings
86	..Motor operated
87	..Hand and foot operator
88	..Hand operator
89	...Horizontally reciprocating
90	...Cable grasp
91	....Pulley mounted
92	..Foot operator with separate suspender
93	EXERCISING EQUIPMENT
94	.For head (e.g., jaws, neck, etc.) or foot
95	..Face (e.g., jaws, lips, etc.)
96	..Foot
97	.For simulating skiing
98	.For thrusting a simulated weapon (e.g., fencing foil, etc.)
99	.For improving user's respiratory function
100	.For track or field sports
101	..For jumping, vaulting or hurdling
102	...Cross-bar or support therefor (e.g., hurdle, etc.)
103	....Means to facilitate adjustment of cross-bar height
104	...Vaulting pole or stop therefor
105	..Starting block for track runner
106	..For throwing (e.g., javelin, hammer, etc.)
107	...Discus
108	...Shot put
→ 109	.Gymnastic
61	..Trapezes and rings
62	..Horizontal bars
63	..Parallel bars
64	..Vaulting horses
65	..Projectors
66	...Spring boards
110	..Swinging tower or pole
111	..Balancing bar or rope
112	..For hanging or climbing by the arms
113	..Playground climber (e.g., for use by children)
67	.Hand and wrist
68	..Grips
69	.Tread mill
70	.Walking or skating
70.1	..Stilts
70.2	...Steps
70.3	..Occupant propelled frame
70.4	...Armpit engaging
71	.Swimming
72	.Rowing
73	.Bicycle
74	.Skipping
75	..Ropes
76	.Striking
77	..Striking bags
78	...Supports
114	.For user locomotion (e.g., pogo stick, etc.)
115	..Translatable with user inside
116	.User-manipulated force-resisting mechanism or element
117	..User-manipulated weight
118	...Including guide for vertical array of weights
119	...Worn on user's body
120	...Utilizing user's body weight
121	...Part of user's body
122	...Dumbbell or barbell
123	....Barbell

Fig. 6I—Sample Page of *Manual of Classification*

Date: March 1973   CLASSIFICATION DEFINITIONS   Page 272-1

Class 272, AMUSEMENT AND EXERCISING DEVICES

CLASS DEFINITIONS.

This class is generic for amusement and exercising, and includes devices whose purpose is amusement, recreation, exercising, gymnastics, or athletics, unless by analogy of structure or by other functions they are classified in other classes. It includes apparatus used at amusement parks and in theaters, unless otherwise classified, also houses, arenas, and elevators where the sole function is amusement.

SEARCH CLASS:

9, Boats, Buoys and Aquatic Devices, appropriate subclasses for buoyant structure disclosed, but not claimed with features simulating birds, fish, fowl, etc. See (3) Note in Class Definitions of Class 9 for statement of the line.

46, Amusement Devices, Toys, for species of amusement devices commonly called toys which are principally for the amusement of children.

104, Railways, subclass 53+, for amusement railways.

182, Fire Escapes, Ladders, Scaffolds, subclass 137+, for a body catcher or life net.

187, Elevators, appropriate subclasses, for elevators of general utility.

273, Amusement Devices, Games, for species of amusement devices commonly called games which involve skill or competition.

280, Land Vehicles, appropriate subclasses for various types of land vehicles, particularly subclass 1.1+ for simulations, especially progressive hobby horses; subclass 11.1 for skates; subclass 12+ for sleds; and subclass 47.1 for person supporting bodies connected to wheels so as to effect body rocking as the wheels rotate.

404, Road Structure, Process and Apparatus, subclasses 17+ and 71 for pavement and road structure.

Subclasses.

■ ■ ■

93. Apparatus under the class definition intended to be operated by a user of such apparatus for the purpose of developing the muscles of the user's body by repetitive or continuous activity of the user, such activity being facilitated by such apparatus.

(1) Note. Patents placed into this and indented subclasses clearly show that the disclosed purpose is to condition or develop the user's own body. Apparatus that is used by one person to move another person's body will be found in Class 128, Surgery (see the Search Class Note below). Apparatus that is used for moving a user's body for a purpose other than exercising (e.g., transport) will be found in classes that are exemplified in the Search Class notes found under the definition of this class.

(2) Note. The following terms, used in subsequent definitions of the subclasses hereunder, are defined and explained herein: CONTRACTION (i. e., of a muscle) is the physiological effort of the muscle which produces a force that tends to result in shortening of the muscle tissue. It does not necessarily result in an actual mechanical change in the length of the muscle, but rather in a tendency to change. The effort may result in shortening of the muscle ("concentric" contraction), or may occur during lengthening of the muscle ("eccentric" contraction), or may occur while the muscle is constrained to remain at substantially the same length ("isometric" contraction), but the tendency to shorten the muscle tissue is generally termed "contraction". Force is the result or effect of the effort exerted by a generator of such effort upon an object. As used in this schedule and in the definition of these subclasses, the term "force" replaces the previously-used terms "push" and "pull", because push and pull are easily confused. As commonly used in this context, "push" refers to a force exerted by a person away from the person's body and "pull" refers to a force exerted by a person towards the person's body; however, in a physiological context, all muscles pull when exercised in the sense that they tend to shorten the muscle tissues when contracted. The term "force" also includes a twisting or turning effort, i.e., a torque as well as a push or pull effort.

■ ■ ■

109. Apparatus under subclass 93, wherein significance is attributed to the use of said apparatus for acrobatic purposes.

(1) Note. The terms "gymnastic" and "acrobatic" have come to denote and describe various pieces of equipment such as trapezes, bars, vaulting horses, etc., that are used in the physical activities known by such names. These activities are characterized by extreme movements of the user, who used the equipment as a fulcrum or starting area to launch his/her body through space, or swing therefrom, or perform other such physical activities thereon. As in previously-described athletic activities, the significance of the apparatus is more in the activity for which the apparatus is used than in the structural differences between the apparatus.

110. Apparatus under subclass 109, including an elongated slender rod, of which one end is secured to the ground and the other end serves as a support for the user as his/her body is exercised thereon.

SEARCH THIS CLASS, SUBCLASS:
104, for a structurally similar flexible pole that is used to help launch a pole vaulter over a high bar.

111. Apparatus under subclass 109, including a relatively slender, horizontally-positioned member, on which member a user supports his/her body with the center of gravity of said body above the member while attempting to maintain the body in a state of equilibrium.

112. Apparatus under subclass 109, including equipment that is grasped by a hand or the hands of the user, and from which equipment the user suspends his/her body or ascends the equipment using only his/her arm(s).

Fig. 6J—Sample Page of *Classification Definitions*

Getting Classification From the PTO or a PTDL

You can get a free, informal mail-order classification of your invention for search purposes by sending a copy of your invention disclosure, with a request for suggestions of one or more search subclasses, to Search Room, Patent and Trademark Office, Washington, DC 20231. However, unless you're really stuck in obtaining subclasses, I don't recommend using this method, since you have the interest in and familiarity with your invention to do a far better job if only you put a little effort into it.

Also, to save time if you intend to go to the PTO in Arlington, you can get the search classifications locally, online, or at a PTDL (Patent and Trademark Depository Library) by using its CD-ROM CASSIS (Classification And Search Support Information System). Instructions will be provided at the computer or by the librarian.

Another excellent example of using your imagination in class and subclass selection for searching is given in the paper, "The Patent System—A Source of Information for the Engineer," by Joseph K. Campbell, Assistant Professor, Agricultural Engineering Department, Cornell University, Ithaca, New York, which was presented at the 1969 Annual Meeting of the American Society of Agricultural Engineers, North Atlantic Region. The ASAE's address is P.O. Box 229, St. Joseph, MO 49085. The publication number is NA-64-206. The article costs $7.00. Call 616-429-0300 for more information.

Professor Campbell postulates a hypothetical search of a machine that encapsulates or pelletizes small seeds (such as petunia or lettuce seeds) so they may be accurately planted by a mechanical planter. To find the appropriate subclasses, he first looks in the *Index of Classification* under the "seed" categories. He finds a good prospect, "Seed-Containing Compositions," and sees that the classification is Class 47 (Plant Husbandry), sub 1.

After checking this class/subclass in the *Manual of Classification* to see where it fits in the scheme of things and in the *Class Definitions* to make sure that it looks okay (it does), he would start his first search with Class 27, sub 1. Then, using his imagination, Professor Campbell also realizes that some candies, such as chocolate-covered peanuts, are actually encapsulated seeds. Thus, he also looks under the candy classifications and finds several likely prospects in Class 107: "Bread, Pastry and Confection-Making." Specifically, sub 1.25, "Composite Pills (with core)"; sub 1.7,

"Feeding Solid Centers into Confectionery"; and sub 11, "Pills" look quite promising. Thus he adds class 107, subs 1.25, 1.7, and 11 to his search field. The moral is this: When you search, look not only in the obvious places, but also use your imagination to find analogous areas, as Professor Campbell does.

For another example of searching in analogous areas, consider an automobile steering wheel that you've improved by adding finger ridges to improve the driver's grip. In addition to searching in the obvious area (automobile steering wheels), consider searching in any other areas where hand grips are found, such as swords, tools, and bike handlebars.

Fortunately, the cross-references in the *Class Definitions* manual will be of great help here—note (Fig. 6J) the copious cross-references at the top of Class 272. Also, as stated, the PTO and all PTDLs have the CASSIS system, which will be of great assistance.

Note how Sam Searcher, Esq., has completed the "Selected Search Classifications" section of the search worksheet with appropriate classes to search for prior art relevant to Millie Inventress's invention.

Step 3: Note Relevant Prior Art (Patents and Other Publications) Under Your Classification

After obtaining a list of classes and subclasses to search, find the actual examining division (or location in the search room if you choose to stay downstairs) where these classes and subclasses are actually located. Then go to your search area and look through all the patents in your selected subclasses. The PTO recently implemented several automated search systems; ask the search assistants in the main search room if they have one in your field. If so, you're lucky.

In the public search room, you'll have to remove bundles of patents from slot-like shelves in its huge stack area. Bring them to a table in the main search area, and search them by placing the patents in a bundle holder and flipping through them. In the examiners' search room, the patents are found in small drawers, called "shoes" by the examiners. You should remove the drawer of patents, hold it in your lap, and flip through the patents while you're seated in a chair; generally, no table will be available.

As you flip through the patents, you may at first find it very difficult to understand them and to make your search. I did when as an examiner I made my first search in the PTO. Don't be discouraged! After just a few minutes the technique will become clear and you may even get to like it! You'll find it easier to understand newer patents (see Le Sueur—Fig. 6D(c)), since they have an abstract page up front that contains a brief summary of the patent and the most relevant figure or drawing.

Anticipation v. Infringement

Many inventors have actually asked me, "How can an expired patent block me from patenting my invention?" That is, how can an expired patent be a valid prior-art reference? However, a moment's thought will show that if a patent ceased to be a valid prior-art reference when it expired, then inventors could (a) repatent the same invention approximately every 17 years, (b) patents would have a lower status than other prior-art publications, such as periodicals, which unquestionably remain valid prior art forever, and (c) inventors could patent things that were not new. If a patent ceased to be prior art when it expired then anyone could repatent the wheel, the sewing machine, etc. The misconception that a patent ceases to be a prior-art reference when it expires represents a confusion of *anticipation* with *infringement*. They are entirely separate areas in patent law and should be considered independently.

Anticipation is a situation that occurs when a proposed or new invention is discovered or found anywhere in the "prior art" (prior public use or prior publications, including the specification of any in-force or expired U.S. or foreign patent, any prior book, periodical article, etc.). Since the existence of the prior art proves the invention isn't new, the putative invention is said to be anticipated by the prior art and thus can't be patented. (35 USC 102.)

Infringement is a situation that occurs only when the claims of an in-force patent "read on" a product or process. If so, then the product or process *infringes* (violates) the patent and the patent owner may be able to negotiate licensing royalties from the infringer, or successfully sue the infringer for money damages and/or an injunction ordering the infringer to cease infringing. (35 USC 271.) (Note that a patent application can't infringe anything.)

If an invention is anticipated by a prior-art reference, that does not necessarily mean that it would infringe the reference, since the reference may be (a) a periodical article or book, which can't be infringed, (b) a foreign patent, which can't be infringed by activity in the U.S., or (c) an expired U.S. patent, which can no longer be infringed. Even if an invention is anticipated by an in-force U.S. patent, the invention usually will not infringe the patent. Why? Because the patent's claims usually will not read on the invention, most likely because the patentee was not able to get broad enough claims allowed due to even earlier prior art. The PTO is never concerned with and never takes any action with regard to any infringement; their main concern is to find anticipations to prevent the issuance of patents on old inventions.

EXAMPLE: In the early part of the 20th century, J.A. Fleming invented a two-element vacuum tube—the diode—that rectified alternating current. Then Lee De Forest added a third element—a control grid—to the diode, making a triode, which was capable of amplifying signals. Even though triodes infringed the diode patent, the Patent Office granted a De Forest patent since the PTO is not concerned with infringements. Although De Forest was not able to manufacture his triode without infringing Fleming's diode patent, Fleming was not able to make triodes without infringing De Forest's patent. Cross-licensing solved the problem, enabling each to practice the other's invention.

As was the case with De Forest's triode and Fleming's diode patent, if an invention infringes an in-force U.S. patent, the patent will not necessarily anticipate the invention.

You'll find that the older patents (see Gabel—Fig. 6D(a)) have several sheets of unlabeled drawings and a closely printed description, termed a "specification," after the drawings. However, even with older patents, you can get a brief summary of the patent by referring to the summary of the invention, which is usually found in the first or second column of the specification. Near the end of each patent, you'll find the claims (Chapter 9). See any utility patent, or Fig. 6M, below, for some examples of claims. These are formally worded, legalistic sentence fragments that usually come after and are the object of the heading words "I [or "We"] claim." As mentioned in the last chapter (and as you'll learn in detail in Chapter 9), the claims define the legal scope of offensive rights held by the owner of the patent. I have seen more confusion about claims than perhaps any other area of patent law. If you'll read and heed well the next common misconception, you'll avoid falling into what I call the "claims trap," which technically is known as a confusion of infringement with anticipation. (See "Anticipation v. Infringement," above.)

The PTO recently added "Patent Document Kind Codes" to the numbers of patents and their other publications, in accordance with international practice. Fig. 6D(d) provides a list of these codes.

Common Misconception: If the claims of a prior patent don't cover your invention, you're free to claim it in your patent application.

Fact: The claims of a patent are there solely to define the monopoly or scope of offensive rights held by the owner of the patent. Patent owners use claims mainly in licensing or in court to determine whether the patent is infringed—that is, whether the hardware that an alleged infringer makes, uses, or sells violates the patent. Thus, when you encounter a relevant patent during a search, you should not fall into the "claims trap," that is, you should not read its claims. You should treat the patent like any other publication (book, magazine article, etc.) to see if the patent's specification ("spec.") or drawings disclose (anticipate) your invention, or any part of it. Since the patent's claims merely repeat what's already in the spec. and drawings, they won't contain anything new, so you need not even read the patent's claims to understand the full technical disclosure of any patent. The spec. and drawings will almost always contain more than what is in the claims anyway. So even if a patent's claims don't cover your invention, its spec. and drawings may still disclose your invention. Since the patent is a prior publication as of its filing date, it can thus anticipate your invention, even if it doesn't claim your invention. (If you were free to claim an invention that a prior patent disclosed

but did not claim, that would make patents worth less as prior art than other publications, such as magazine articles!)

Another reason for not reading the claims of searched patents is that they're written in such stilted legalese that they're difficult to understand. Nevertheless, some searchers do like to read claims of patents to get a quick "handle" on the patent's technical content. Also, if you make an *Official Gazette* search in a Patent and Trademark Depository or regular library (see Section K, below), you'll have to rely on claims for the most part, since most of the OGs contain only a single claim of each patent.

If you do read the claims, keep in mind three important considerations:

1. If a prior-art patent shows (that is, describes) but doesn't formally claim your invention, this doesn't mean you're free to claim it.
2. A patent contains much more technical information than what's in its claims; all of this technical information can be used as prior art, just as if the patent were an article in a technical magazine. Thus, you should use the claims only to get a "handle" on the patent; you should not regard them as a summary or synopsis of the patent's disclosure.
3. The scope of coverage you will likely be able to obtain for your invention (see Section J, below) will usually be narrower than the scope of the claims of the closely relevant prior-art patents you uncover. (See Chapter 9 to see how to determine the breadth of claims.)

Common Misconception: If your invention is covered by the claims of a prior patent, you will be liable as an infringer if you file a patent application on the invention.

Fact: Neither a patent application nor its claims can infringe a prior patent. Only the manufacture, use, sale, offer for sale, or importation of an invention in physical form can infringe. And, as previously stated, the PTO has absolutely no concern about patent infringements.

Don't think about obviousness as you search, since this may overwhelm you and detract from the quality of your investigation. Rather, at this stage, try to fish with a large net by merely looking for the physical features of your invention.

As you search, keep a careful record of all patent classes and subclasses you've searched, as indicated in Fig. 6G, above. Probably 95% of the references you encounter when you search will not be relevant. If you find relevant patents or other art, write their numbers, dates, names, or other identification, and order or download copies later. Although you need only the number to order a patent, I recommend that you write the issue date, first inventor's name, and classification as well, to double-check later in case you write down a wrong number.

If you do find an important relevant reference, don't stop; simply asterisk it (to remind you of its importance) and continue your search to the end. When you note a relevant reference, also write down its most relevant features to refresh your memory and save time later.

If you still don't find any relevant patents, double-check your search classes using *Classification Definitions*, the *Manual of Classification*, and some help from a patent examiner or assistant in the search room. If you're reasonably sure you're in the right class and still can't find any relevant references, write down the closest ones you can possibly find, even if they're not relevant. This will establish that you made the search, what the closest art is, and how novel your invention is, and you'll have references to cite on your Information Disclosure Statement (see Chapter 13, Section A) to make the PTO's file of your patent look good; you should never finish any search without coming up with at least several references. If you do consult examiners, write their names in the comments section of the worksheet.

In each subclass, you'll find patents that are directly classified there, and "cross-references" (XRs), patents primarily classified in another subclass, but also classified in your subclass because they have a feature that makes the cross-reference appropriate. Be sure to review the cross-references as well as the regular patents in each subclass.

The public search room has copiers for making instant copies of patents for a per-page fee, but if you don't need instant copies, you can buy a complete copy of any patent for one patent copy coupon, or use two coupons per patent for rush service. To do this, purchase an adequate supply of coupons from the PTO's cashier (see Appendix 4, Fee Schedule); then write down the number of each patent you select on a coupon, add your name and address, and deposit them in the appropriate box in the search room. The patents you request will be mailed to you, generally in a few days if you use one coupon per patent, or in one day if you staple two coupons together per patent. You can also acquire a copy of a patent by:

- downloading a text copy or image copy of the patent from the PTO website (www.uspto.gov); this is the cheapest, fastest, and easiest way;
- ordering the patent from the PTO by phone (703-305-8716), fax (703-305-8759), or letter (Mail Stop Document Services, Commissioner for Patents, P.O. Box 1450, Alexandria, VA 22213-1450) with a list of the patents you want by number and the payment for the price per patent (see Fee Schedule at the PTO website or in Appendix 4) times the total number of patents

you've ordered. The PTO will normally furnish the copies by mail, but will also fax or FedEx them for an additional fee, and they accept credit cards.
- ordering a copy from a private supply company such as MicroPatent (www.micropatent.com) or Thompson-Derwent (www.ThompsonDerwent.com).

Step 4: Carefully Review the Prior Art to See Whether It Anticipates Your Invention or Renders It Obvious

After you've made your search and obtained copies of all the references you thought were pertinent, study them carefully at your leisure. I recommend you write a brief summary of each relevant patent, even if it has an abstract, to force you to really understand it. Then, determine if your invention is patentable over the patents you've found. Follow the steps described earlier in this chapter (Section H) for analyzing the search report when your search is done by someone else.

(b) Computer Searching

In addition to searching the paper files, you can perform a search of your invention on PTO's specialized EAST computer terminals. These terminals are located at the PTO's headquarters—by far the best—and at certain PTDLs. You can also make computer searches on specialized WEST (Web-based Examiner Search Tool) terminals in certain Patent and Trademark Depository Libraries (see Fig. 6K), or on a personal computer connected to the Internet.

EAST is the superior search tool since it can perform a search by class and subclass, similar to the search of paper patents described, above. Users of EAST can also make Boolean or keyword-combination searches back to 1971, or make searches using a combination of both techniques. In terms of speed, it is superior to a paper search because you can flip through patents displayed on the computer monitor faster than you can with the actual paper copies. You can also use EAST to do "forward" searches—that is, if a relevant patent is found, EAST can find and search through all later-issued patents in which the relevant patent is cited (referred to) as a prior-art reference. Further, it can do "backward" searches—that is, it can search through all previously issued patents that are cited as prior art in the relevant patent. You can also use EAST to search European and Japanese patents.

EAST is free to use at the PTO, but the PTO charges for printing out copies of patents. The PTDLs that have EAST charge hourly fees. I do not provide instructions on using EAST in this book since courses are available at the PTO and since most readers will not be able to go to Virginia or an EAST PTDL to use the database.

Hopefully, the capabilities of EAST will be soon be more widely available. In the meantime, if you want to use it you

Reference Collection of U.S. Patents Available for Public Use in Patent and Trademark Depository Libraries

The following libraries, designated as Patent and Trademark Depository Libraries (PTDLs), receive patent and trademark information from the U.S. Patent and Trademark Office. Many PTDLs have on file patents issued since 1790, trademarks published since 1872, and select collections of foreign patents. All PTDLs receive both the patent and trademark sections of the *Official Gazette* of the U.S. Patent and Trademark Office and numerical sets of patents in a variety of formats. Patent and trademark search systems in the CASSIS optical disk series are available at all PTDLs to increase access to that information. It is through the optical disk systems and other depository materials that preliminary patent and trademark searches may be conducted through the numerically arranged collections.

Each PTDL offers reference publications that outline and provide access to the patent and trademark classification systems, as well as other documents and publications that supplement the basic search tools. PTDLs provide technical staff assistance in using all materials.

All information is available for use by the public free of charge. However, there may be charges associated with the use of online systems, photocopying, and related services.

Since there are variations in the scope of patent and trademark collections among the PTDLs, and their hours of service to the public vary, anyone contemplating use of these collections at a particular library is urged to contact that library in advance about its collections, services, and hours.

Partnership PTDLs provide enhanced and expanded services for which fees are charged. They offer online patent text and image searching, online trademark searching, and videoconferencing for examiner interviews and workshops. They accept disclosure documents on site, order file wrappers, assignment documents, and certified copies for their customers, and host a variety of seminars aimed at specific audiences, including practitioners, paralegals, and independent inventors. Currently, partnerships are located at the Great Lakes Patent and Trademark Center (GLPTC) at the Detroit Public Library in Detroit, Michigan, and the Sunnyvale Center for Innovation, Invention and Ideas (SCI³) at the Sunnyvale Public Library in Sunnyvale, California.

For the latest copy of this list, or for Web links to each PTDL, go to the PTO's *Official Gazette* site at www.uspto.gov/web/offices/com/sol/og. Then go to the latest *Official Gazette* and open "Patent and Trademark Depository Libraries."

State	Name of Library	Telephone
Alabama	Auburn University Libraries*	334-844-1737
	Birmingham Public Library	205-226-3620
Alaska	Anchorage: Z.J. Loussac Public Library	907-562-7323
Arizona	Tempe: Noble Library, Arizona State Univ.*	480-965-7010
Arkansas	Little Rock: Arkansas State Lib.*	501-682-2053
California	Los Angeles Public Library*	213-228-7220
	Sacramento: Cal. State Library	916-654-0069
	San Diego Public Library	619-236-5813
	San Francisco Public Library*	415-557-4500
	Sunnyvale Center for Innovation (has APS Image terminals—see Section K)*†△	408-730-7290
Colorado	Denver Public Library	720-865-1711
Connecticut	Hartford Public Library	860-543-8628
	New Haven Free Public Library	203-946-8130
Delaware	Newark: Univ. of Delaware Lib.	302-831-2965
D.C.	Washington: Howard Univ. Lib.	202-806-7252
Florida	Fort Lauderdale: Broward County Main Library*	954-357-7444
	Miami: Dade Public Library*	305-375-2665
	Orlando: Univ. of Central Florida Libraries	407-823-2562

State	Name of Library	Telephone
Florida	Tampa: Campus Library, University of South Florida	813-974-2726
Georgia	Atlanta: Price Gilbert Memorial Library, Georgia Institute of Technology	404-894-4508
Hawaii	Honolulu: Hawaii State Public Library System*	808-586-3477
Idaho	Moscow: Univ. of Idaho Library	208-885-6235
Illinois	Chicago Public Library	312-747-4450
	Springfield: Illinois State Library	217-782-5659
Indiana	Indianapolis: Marion County Public Library	317-269-1741
	West Lafayette: Siegesmond Engineering Library	765-494-2872
Iowa	Des Moines: State Lib. of Iowa	515-242-6541
Kansas	Wichita: Ablah Library, Wichita State Univ.*	800-572-8368
Kentucky	Louisville Free Public Library	502-574-1611
Louisiana	Baton Rouge: Troy H. Middleton Library, Louisiana State Univ.	225-388-8875
Maine	Orono: Raymond H. Fogler Library, University of Maine	207-581-1678
Maryland	College Park: Engineering and Physical Sciences Library, University of Maryland	301-405-9157

* WEST (Web-based Examiner Search Tool—better searching) subscriber.
† Also does fee-based patent searching.
△ EAST (Examiner Assisted Search Tool) subscriber.

Fig. 6K—List of Patent and Trademark Depository Libraries

Reference Collection of U.S. Patents Available for Public Use in Patent and Trademark Depository Libraries (continued)

State	Name of Library	Telephone
Massachusetts	Amherst: Physical Sciences Lib., Univ. of Massachusetts	413-545-1370
	Boston Public Library*	617-536-5400 Ext. 265
Michigan	Ann Arbor: Media Union Library, University of Michigan	734-647-5735
	Big Rapids: Abigail S. Timme Library, Ferris State University	231-592-3602
	Detroit Public Library (has APS Image Terminals*△	313-833-3379
Minnesota	Minneapolis Public Library and Information Center*	612-630-6120
Mississippi	Jackson: Mississippi Library Commission	601-961-4111
Missouri	Kansas City: Linda Hall Library*	816-363-4600
	St. Louis Public Library*	314-241-2288 Ext. 390
Montana	Butte: Montana College of Mineral Science & Tech. Lib.	406-496-4281
Nebraska	Lincoln: Engineering Library, University of Nebraska*	402-472-3411
Nevada	Las Vegas: Clark County Lib.	702-507-3421
	Reno: University of Nevada-Reno Library	702-784-6500 Ext. 257
New Hampshire	Concord: New Hampshire State Library	603-271-2239
New Jersey	Newark Public Library	973-733-7779
	Piscataway: Lib. of Science & Medicine, Rutgers University	732-445-2895
New Mexico	Albuquerque: University of New Mexico General Library	505-277-4412
New York	Albany: New York State Library	518-474-5355
	Buffalo and Erie County Public Library	716-858-7101
	New York Public Library (The Research Libraries)	212-592-7000
	Rochester Public Library	716-428-8110
	Stony Brook: Engineering Lib., State Univ. of New York	631-632-7148
North Carolina	Raleigh: D.H. Hill Library, N.C. State University*	919-515-2935
North Dakota	Grand Forks: Chester Fritz Lib., University of North Dakota	701-777-4888
Ohio	Akron: Summit Cnty Public Lib.	330-643-9075
	Cincinnati and Hamilton County, Public Library of	513-369-6971

State	Name of Library	Telephone
Ohio	Cleveland Public Library*	216-623-2870
	Columbus: Ohio State University Library	614-292-3022
	Dayton: Paul Laurence Dunbar Library, Wright State Univ.	937-775-3521
	Toledo/Lucas County Public Lib.*	419-259-5209
Oklahoma	Stillwater: Oklahoma State Univ. Center for Trade Development*	405-744-7086
Oregon	Portland: Paul L. Boley Law Library, Lewis & Clark College	503-768-6786
Pennsylvania	Philadelphia, The Free Library of*	215-686-5331
	Pittsburgh, Carnegie Library of	412-622-3138
	University Park: Pattee Library, Pennsylvania State University	814-865-6369
Puerto Rico	Bayamón: Univ. of Puerto Rico	787-786-5225
	Mayaguez General Library, University of Puerto Rico	787-832-4040 Ext. 2022
Rhode Island	Providence Public Library	401-455-8027
South Carolina	Clemson University Libraries	864-656-3024
South Dakota	Rapid City: Devereaux Library, S.D. School of Mines & Tech.	605-394-1275
Tennessee	Nashville: Stevenson Science Library, Vanderbilt University	615-322-2717
Texas	Austin: McKinney Engineering Lib., Univ. of Texas at Austin	512-495-4500
	College Station: Sterling C. Evans Library, Texas A & M Univ.*△	979-845-5745
	Dallas Public Library*	214-670-1468
	Houston: The Fondren Library, Rice University*	713-348-5483
	Lubbock: Texas Tech University	806-742-2282
	San Antonio Public Library	210-207-2500
Utah	Salt Lake City: Marriott Library, University of Utah*	801-581-8394
Vermont	Burlington: Bailey/Howe Library, University of Vermont	802-656-2542
Virginia	Richmond: Virginia Commonwealth University*	804-828-1104
Washington	Seattle: Engineering Library, University of Washington*	206-543-0740
West Virginia	Morgantown: Evansdale Library, West Virginia University*	304-293-4695 Ext. 5113
Wisconsin	Madison: Kurt F. Wendt Library, Univ. of Wisconsin, Madison	608-262-6845
	Milwaukee Public Library	414-286-3051
Wyoming	Cheyenne: Wyo. State Lib.	307-777-7281

* WEST (Web-based Examiner Search Tool—better searching) subscriber.

△ FAST (Examiner Assisted Search Tool) subscriber.

Fig. 6K (cont'd)—List of Patent and Trademark Depository Libraries

must make a trip to Arlington or a PTDL with EAST and learn the system there. More information about computer searching is provided in Section L, below.

J. The Scope of Patent Coverage

Although you'd probably like things to be simpler, the determination of whether your invention is patentable will rarely be a "yes" or "no" one, unless your invention is a very simple device, process, or composition. Many inventions are complex enough to have some features, or some combination of features, that will be different enough to be patentable. However, your object is not merely to get a patent, but to get *meaningful* patent coverage—that is, offensive rights that are broad enough that competitors can't "design around" your patent easily. As I've said elsewhere, designing around a patent is the act of making a competitive device or process that is equivalent in function to the patented device but that doesn't infringe the patent.

Often you won't be able to get broad coverage because many "modern" inventions are actually old hat—that is, the basic ideas were known many years before and the real inventions are actually just improvements on old ones. For example, the first computer was a mechanical device invented in the 1800s by Charles Babbage. The ancient Chinese used a soybean mold to treat infections. An inventor, J.H. Loud, received a patent on a ballpoint pen in 1888. The first 3-D film was shown in 1922, and the basic transistor structure was invented in the 1930s!

Simply put, you'll often find a search will indicate that your invention, while valuable, may be less of an innovation than you thought it was. You'll thus have to determine whether or not your invention is sufficiently innovative to get meaningful patent protection. In other words, your scope of coverage will depend upon how close the references that your search uncovers are to your invention—that is, how many features of your invention are shown by the references, and how they are shown. In the end, your scope of coverage will actually depend upon the breadth of the claims that you can get the PTO to allow, but this is jumping the gun at this stage; I cover claims in Chapter 9.

For an example, let's take a simple invention. As stated, in a simple invention patentability will usually be a black or white determination, and you won't have much of a problem about your scope of coverage. Suppose you've just invented a magnetically operated cat door—that is, you provide a cat with a neck-worn magnet that can operate a release on a cat door. Your search references fail to show any magnetically operated pet release door. Thus, the neck magnet and the magnetic door release are the novel features of your invention.

To get a patent, your invention would have to be limited to these specific features, since neither could be changed or eliminated while producing the same result. However, there is no harm in limiting the invention to these features, since it would be difficult for anyone to "design around" them— that is, it would be difficult or impossible for anyone to provide the same result (a cat-operated door release) without using a neck magnet and a magnetic release.

With other inventions, however, your scope of coverage won't be so broad—that is, it won't be as difficult for someone to design around it. For example, suppose you invented the centrifugal vegetable juicer mentioned previously in Chapter 5—that is, a juicer with a sloping side basket permitting the solid pulp to ride up and out so that juicing could continue without having to empty the pulp from the basket.

If the prior art were not "kind" to you—that is, your search uncovered a patent or other publication that showed a juicer with a basket with sloping sides and with a well at the top to catch and hold the pulp—your application would not be allowed if you claimed just the sloping sides (even though it would be superior to the prior art due to the complete elimination of the pulp). To get the patent, you would have to also claim another feature (say, the trough shape). Thus, by having access to the prior art you would know enough to claim your invention less broadly.

Also, suppose you've invented the napkin-shaping ring of Fig. 6B. Suppose further that Gabel did not exist and that your search uncovers only the Le Sueur patent (see Fig. 6D(c)), which shows a plain, circular napkin ring. You'd be entitled to relatively broad coverage, since your novel features are themselves broad: namely, a ring with inner parts that can shape a napkin when it is pulled through the ring.

However, assuming the Gabel patent does exist and your search uncovers it as well as Le Sueur, what are your novel features now? First, your device has a circular ring with a leg extending inwardly from the ring; neither Gabel nor Le Sueur, nor any possible combination of these references, has this combination. Second, your invention has the flaring arms that shape the napkin; these are attached to the end of the inner leg; the references also lack this feature. Thus to distinguish over Le Sueur and Gabel, you'll have to rely on far more specific features than you'd have to do if only Le Sueur existed. Hence your actual invention would be far narrower, since you'll have to limit it to the novel features that distinguish it from Gabel as well as Le Sueur. Unfortunately, this will narrow your scope of coverage, because competitors can design around you more easily than they could do if only Le Sueur existed.

As you've probably gathered by now, your scope of coverage will be determined by what novel features you need to use to distinguish your invention over the prior art and still provide new results that are different or unexpected enough to be considered unobvious. The fewer the novel features you need, the broader your invention or scope of coverage will be. Stated differently, if you need many new features, or very specific features, to define over the prior art and provide new results, it will usually be relatively easy for a competitor to use fewer or alternative features to provide the same results without infringing your patent.

You should make your scope of coverage determination by determining the fewest number or the broadest feature(s) you'll need to distinguish patentability over the prior art. Do this by a repetitive narrowing trial-and-error process: First, see what minimum feature(s) you'll need to have some novelty over the prior art—that is, enough to distinguish under Section 102 (Box C of Figs. 5C and 6E)—and then see if these would satisfy Section 103 (Boxes D, E, and G)—that is, would they provide any unexpected new results?

If you feel that your minimum number of features are enough to ascend the novelty box (pictured in Fig. 5A in Chapter 5), but would not be sufficient to climb the big unobviousness box—that is, you don't have enough features to provide new and unexpected results—then try narrowing your features or adding more until you feel that you'll have enough to make it to the patentability summit.

Common Misconception: If a search shows that your invention is not patentable, you may not manufacture or sell it.

Fact: Even if it's not patentable, you usually still can make and sell it because the prior-art reference(s) which make it not patentable probably are either expired patents or don't claim your invention. For more on how to determine if a prior, in-force patent's claims cover you, see Chapter 15, Sec. K.

This is another one of those aspects of patent law that may have your head spinning. Fortunately, the material covered here under determining the scope of your protection is also discussed in the different context of drafting your claims. (See Chapter 9.) By the time you read this book thoroughly, you will understand all of this a lot better.

After you evaluate your search results, you'll have a pretty good idea of the minimum number of novel features that are necessary to sufficiently distinguish your invention over the prior art. If you're in doubt that you have enough such features, or if you feel that you'd have to limit your invention to specific features to define structure that would be considered unobvious over the prior art, it probably isn't patentable, or even if patentable, it isn't worth filing on,

since it would be easy to design around. One possibility, if you can't make a decision, is to pay for a professional's opinion.

On the other hand, if you've found nothing like your invention in your search, congratulations. You probably have a very broad invention, since, with the six million plus patents that have issued thus far, one or more features of almost all inventions are likely to be shown in the prior art.

K. Searching Paper Patents in a Patent and Trademark Depository Library

If you can't search in the PTO, the next possibility, although somewhat inferior, is to search your invention in one of the Patent and Trademark Depository Libraries listed above in Fig. 6K, all of which currently receive all patents issued by the PTO. Before going to any PTDL, call to find out their hours of operation and what search facilities they have.

Why is searching at a PTDL less useful than searching at the PTO? Simply because not all PTDLs have all patents issued from No. 1 to the present, none have them physically separated by subject matter into searchable classifications as does the PTO, and none have foreign patents or nonpatent literature (books, magazines, etc.). Using a PTDL is therefore more difficult and time-consuming than if you use the PTO. You should carefully balance the large expenditure of your time and the inferiority of the search materials against the $500 to $1,000 or so you would spend for a professional searcher to do the job at the PTO. Of course, as I suggested, the optimum solution is to visit Arlington yourself.

I like to assign percentage values to the various types of searches: I roughly estimate a good examiner's search at 90% (that is—it has about a 90% chance of standing up in court), a good search by a nonexaminer in the PTO at 80%, and a good search in a PTDL at 70%. (Unfortunately, as in business, there's no certainty in the law.) If your invention is

LISTING — CLASS 272 — REEL NO. 7 PAGE 19

105 / *107 / *109 / *109 / *110

	105	*107	*109	*109	*110
80	1,701,026	1,134,008	1,747,352X	3,659,844X	3,754,758
53	1,709,832	1,492,976	1,779,903	3,735,979X	3,834,695
01	1,785,968	1,570,185	1,914,555	3,764,446X	3,837,641X
98X	1,793,898	1,947,025X	1,918,559X	3,778,054X	3,880,422
13X	1,990,497	1,958,807X	1,928,089X	3,785,642X	3,896,858X
28X	2,004,172	2,223,091	2,048,587X	3,825,252X	3,923,302
86	2,144,962	2,640,699X	2,107,377	3,857,561X	4,084,814
22X	2,165,749X	2,864,201X	2,167,696X	3,857,563X	
44	2,323,510	3,312,472X	2,169,710X	3,874,657X	**111**
31	2,341,473	4,121,826X	2,262,761X	3,891,207X	
97	2,505,784		2,324,970X	3,895,795X	D 175,729X
92	2,534,159	**108**	2,496,748	3,912,262	159,301
62	2,890,048		2,572,149X	3,915,451	971,003
16X	2,900,187	450,759	2,595,111X	3,937,461	1,001,300X
18	2,937,871	807,770	2,652,966X	3,947,023X	1,407,642
10X	2,978,692X	1,036,138	2,671,229X	3,966,200	1,419,191X
09	3,010,321X	1,805,121X	2,706,632X	3,969,871X	1,537,686X
22	3,244,421X	1,986,687	2,722,360X	3,971,561X	1,747,721
06	3,400,928	1,997,958X	2,738,189X	3,981,500X	2,000,250
82	3,401,931	2,117,938	2,771,615X	4,014,057X	2,197,600X
91	3,494,615	3,548,420X	2,795,423	4,026,547	2,343,204X
88X	3,608,897	3,759,513	2,829,892X	4,037,834X	2,646,280X
64	3,665,452X	3,884,465X	2,858,132X	4,125,257	2,855,201
64	3,724,843	4,121,826X	2,859,967X	4,137,583X	2,939,704
00X	3,731,298X		2,885,233X	4,147,129X	3,062,542
81	3,746,335	(109)	2,897,013X	4,147,828X	3,083,964
67	3,799,542		2,944,815	4,204,719X	3,173,415X
32	3,809,392X	D 262,394X	2,953,376X	4,210,322	3,339,920
17	4,089,519	RE 25,843	3,006,645	4,216,958	3,404,884
12	4,134,583X	9,695	3,044,773X	4,225,131	3,416,792X
48		174,499	3,085,357	4,274,626	3,485,493X
04	**106**	233,273	3,105,082X	4,275,880X	3,545,747X
24		233,274	3,106,395X	4,325,546X	3,547,435
94X	610,131X	233,541	3,204,259X	4,340,215	3,570,847
16X	649,885	451,411	3,205,888X	4,340,216	3,570,848
80	1,122,157	649,914	3,207,511X	4,344,617	3,580,568
88	1,552,442	664,414	3,211,452X	4,350,721X	3,582,068
68X	1,569,395	802,338	3,242,509X	4,410,175X	3,589,716
34X	1,731,686	811,417	3,251,076X		3,616,126X
	1,994,089	907,075	3,262,134X	**110**	3,658,325
	2,036,524X	932,413	3,284,819X		3,722,881
	2,044,092	932,902	3,319,273X	D 198,923X	3,754,757
66	2,122,023	998,634	3,372,926	D 199,984X	3,781,931X
01	2,180,384	1,003,797	3,379,439X	1,085,505X	3,806,118X
54	2,196,610	1,013,687	3,391,414X	1,100,180X	3,837,644X
26	2,214,464	1,015,208	3,399,407	1,141,292X	3,850,428X
22X	3,163,421X	1,126,082	3,405,939X	1,462,910X	3,944,654
00	3,181,864X	1,128,201	3,409,294X	1,865,095X	3,990,697
78	3,746,334	1,130,813	3,419,270X	1,907,451	4,105,201
65	3,942,793X	1,142,137X	3,432,163	1,916,809X	4,133,524
20X	4,084,813	1,177,473X	3,433,477X	2,198,537	4,183,521X
99	4,333,643	1,204,329X	3,459,611X	2,723,855X	4,197,839X
37X	4,337,940	1,256,734	3,526,911X	2,906,531X	4,204,719X
14X	4,404,053X	1,479,830	3,580,569	2,949,298X	4,258,915
07		1,501,823X	3,598,406X	3,246,893X	4,272,073
70	**107**		3,628,790X	3,250,532	4,278,250X

CLASS 272

112	*113
D 155,940X	D 173,173
D 208,924X	D 176,999
D 212,021X	D 187,138
D 214,572X	D 187,380
239,970X	D 187,381
450,187	D 187,656
775,309	D 198,532
786,672	D 218,455
950,100	D 218,460
1,485,135	D 218,765
1,585,748	D 224,029
1,670,390	D 224,796
1,676,061	D 227,381
2,240,407	D 227,792
2,303,223X	D 231,557
2,365,117	D 232,4..
2,429,939	D 238,694
2,706,632X	D 250,723
2,800,105X	D 250,783
2,838,307	D 250,784
2,929,627	170,495
2,977,118	209,511
3,032,344	7..,550
3,090,617X	796,159
3,156,465	821,391
3,342,484X	1,126,082
3,445,108	1,185,176
3,483,999X	1,351,053
3,501,140X	1,471,465
3,506,261	1,488,244
3,526,399	1,488,245
3,547,435X	1,488,246
3,563,539X	1,707,854
3,598,406X	1,765,361
3,606,315	1,822,786
3,638,602X	1,877,833
3,642,277	1,901,964
3,771,784X	1,917,018
3,782,718	1,929,822
3,794,316	2,126,636
3,837,642X	2,151,403
3,982,754X	2,206,581
4,018,437X	2,222,119
4,077,403X	2,500,425
4,116,433X	2,584,742
4,149,712	2,620,185
4,159,113	2,648,538
4,161,998X	2,648,539
4,272,073X	2,704,667
4,278,250X	2,720,430
4,335,538X	2,723,853
4,355,633X	2,768,823
4,372,552	2,795,423
	2,843,379
113	2,883,192
	2,886,317

Fig. 6L—List of Patents in Class 272-109 From Microfilm Printout

in an active, contemporary field, such as a computer mouse, you should reduce the value of the two nonexaminer types of searches somewhat, due to the fact that patent applications in this field are more likely to be pending.

If you do make a search at a PTDL, you should go through the same four steps given above. First, articulate your invention (in the same manner as before), and second, use the reference tools to find the relevant classes and subclasses. The third step is a review of the patents in the selected classes and subclasses. And finally, you should analyze all relevant prior-art references for their effect on your invention's patentability.

In a PTDL these steps are more difficult than in the PTO. First, you must get a list of the patents and PubPAs in your selected classes and subclasses. (From this point on when I refer to prior-art patents, I am including PubPAs—published patent applications—since these are just as good as prior art as a patent.) Most of the PTDLs have lists of patents in each class and subclass on microfilm or CD-ROM. (See "CD-ROM Products at PTDLs," below.) But if your PTDL doesn't have such a list, you'll have to order one from the PTO in Arlington; this may take several weeks to arrive. The staff will show you how to do this.

Fig. 6L is a typical sample of a microfilm printout—a list of patents that are classified in our old friend, class 272-109, gymnastic devices.

Once you've obtained a list such as this for the first of your selected classes and subclasses, you'll have to locate each patent (or an abstract of it) individually and examine it. There are two ways to access each patent:

1. Look at an abstract of the patent in its *Official Gazette* (OG). The OGs are no longer printed on paper but can be viewed at the PTO's website or on CD-ROMs, or
2. Look at the entire patent in a numerically arranged stack or on microfilm, microfiche, DVD, or at the PTO's website.

The *Official Gazette*

The *Official Gazette (Patents)* is no longer issued weekly in paper (book) form. However, it is still published online. It lists the main facts (patentee, assignee, filing date, classification) plus the broadest claim and main drawing figure of every patent issued that week. It also contains pertinent notices, fees, and a list of all PTDLs (Fig. 6K). The notices are published each week at the PTO's website, under *Official Gazette Notices* and *Electronic OG*, respectively. Also, the complete patents are available online elsewhere on the PTO's website each week.

If you make an OG search (this will be much easier), each patent entry you find will contain only a single claim (or abstract) and a single figure or drawing of the patent, as indicated in Fig. 6M (a typical page from an OG).

Note that for each patent, the OG entry gives the patent number, inventor's name(s) and address(es), assignee (usually a company that the inventor has transferred ownership of the patent to), filing date, application serial number, international classification, U.S. classification, number of claims, and a sample claim or abstract. If the drawing and claim look relevant, go to the actual patent, order or download a copy of it, and study it at your leisure.

Remember that the claim found in the *Official Gazette* is not a descriptive summary of the technical information in the patent. Rather, it is the essence of the claimed invention. The full text of the patent will contain far more technical information than the claim. So, even if a patent's *Official Gazette* claim doesn't precisely describe your invention, the rest of the patent may still be relevant.

EXAMPLE: When recently performing a PTDL search, a client of mine passed over a patent listed in the OG because the single drawing figure appeared to render the patent irrelevant. In fact, another drawing figure in the passed-over patent (but not found in the OG) anticipated my client's invention and was used by the PTO to reject his application (after he had spent considerable time, money, and energy preparing and filing it). The moral? Take an OG search with a grain of salt. Note well that a figure of the patent that isn't shown in the OG may be highly relevant; thus it's best to search full patents.

To make an OG search of the patents in Class 272, subclass 109 (Fig. 6L), start with the first patent in this list, D-262,394X. The "D" means that the patent is a design patent and the "X" means that this patent is a cross-reference. To view patent D-262,394, look on the PTO's website under "Patent Number Searching." You'll find the patent, D-262,394, was issued in 1980. If you find it relevant, print it out and write its identifying data down on your Searcher's Worksheet, Form 6-1.

Currently, 27 of these libraries have WEST (Web-Based Examiner Search Tool) search terminals that can search text of patents back to 1971. (See Section L1.)

The second patent in the list, RE-25,843, is a reissue patent. Reissues are discussed in Chapter 14. For now, all you have to know is that reissues are also available on the PTO's site. Locate the patent, print it out and list it on your worksheet if you feel it's relevant.

All of the rest of the patents in subclass 109 are regular utility patents in numerical and date order. Start with

2824   OFFICIAL GAZETTE   JULY 18, 2000

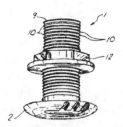

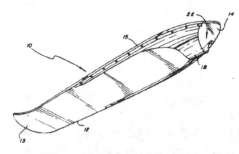

c) at least one groove provided in said flange, said groove facing said opening in said nipple for providing water communication between said groove and said opening in said nipple at an amply low and fairly constant total head; and

d) wherein at some point said groove is narrower than the diameter of said bore.

6,089,934
ENGINE COOLING SYSTEM WITH SIMPLIFIED DRAIN AND FLUSHING PROCEDURE
Timothy M. Biggs, Stillwater; William E. Hughes, Perry; Matthew W. Jaeger, Stillwater; Andrew K. Logan, Stillwater; Robert J. Pitchford, Stillwater, and Charles E. Wright, Stillwater, all of Okla., assignors to Brunswick Corporation, Lake Forest, Ill.
Filed Jul. 26, 1999, Appl. No. 361,370
Int. Cl.[7] B63H 21/10
U.S. Cl. 440—88   20 Claims

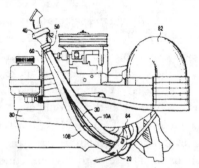

1. An engine cooling system, comprising:
a first opening extending through a first portion of said engine and into said cooling system;
a first flexible conduit having a first end connected in fluid communication with said first opening;
a retainer movably attached to said first flexible conduit and movable between said first end of said first flexible conduit and a second end of said first flexible conduit;
a handle;
a tether attached between said handle and said retainer; and
whereby said second end of said first flexible conduit is movable, in response to manual movement of said handle, from a first position above said first opening to a second position below said first opening.

6,089,935
WATER SKI ATTACHMENT
G. Thomas Fleming, III, 5111 Alta Canyada Rd., La Canada, Calif. 91011
Filed Feb. 6, 1998, Appl. No. 135,511
Int. Cl.[7] B63B 35/81
U.S. Cl. 441—79   10 Claims
1. A water ski comprising:

an upper side, an under side, a front end and a rear end, with an arched fin carried on said ski under side at said ski rear end;
said arched fin having opposed edges adjacent the edges of said ski under side, with said opposed edges joined together adjacent said ski rear end to form an opening for water flow therethrough; and
with said opposed edges tapering forward and upward from said opening to said ski under side, and terminating forward of said ski rear end, the opposing edges of said ski converge toward each other at the rear portion of said ski, and the opposing edges of said arched fin conform to said edges of said ski.

6,089,936
PERSONAL FLOATATION DEVICE
Richard S. Hoffman, 6749 SW. 166 Dr., Pembroke Pines, Fla. 33331
Filed Mar. 5, 1999, Appl. No. 263,350
Int. Cl.[7] B63C 9/08
U.S. Cl. 441—117   26 Claims

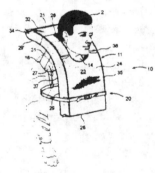

1. A float for a personal flotation device, said float comprising:
a) a front formed of a buoyant material, said front sized to generally correspond and confront a wearer's chest and shoulder region;
b) said front including a neck opening sized and configured to permit passage of the wearer's head therethrough and defining a recess surface about said neck opening;
c) a back formed of buoyant material, said back having a first end, a second end and a body between said ends;
d) said back being movably connected to said front with said first end of said back disposed generally adjacent said recess surface and so as to reduce an inner diameter of said neck opening;
e) said back being movable between a position wherein said neck opening is opened sufficiently to permit the wearer's head to pass therethrough and another position wherein said back confronts the wearer's back region;
f) said body of said back being sized and configured to generally confront the wearer's upper and central back region and to dwell within said neck opening; and
g) said back being movable into another position closing said neck opening.

Fig. 6M—Page of _Official Gazette_ Showing Various Patent Abstracts

patent 9,695, which issued in the middle 1800s. You'll be able to view it easily online, in an old paper OG, or on microfilm or microfiche. Look at the patent in the usual manner to see if it's relevant. If so, write its data on your worksheet.

If your PTDL has full copies of patents readily accessible (each patent usually consists of several pages), you can look at the full text of each patent, one by one, in a similar manner as you looked at their abstracts in the OGs. If you find that the patent is relevant, usually you'll have access to a photocopy machine where you'll be able to make a copy of the whole patent, or just its relevant parts, on the spot.

Alternatively, if you don't want to interrupt the flow of your searching, you can save your patent numbers and order or print out copies later. You can order copies from the PTO online or from a private patent copy sales company. (See Section I2, Step 3, above.)

After you've completed Step 3, the review of patents, then perform Step 4, the analysis and decision, in exactly the same manner as outlined above for the PTO search.

CD-ROM Products at PTDLs

The PTO periodically publishes various CD-ROM disks that contain classification and bibliographic information about patents. All PTDLs subscribe to these disks and have one or more computers with CD-ROM drives for reading the disks. While the disks can't be used to make a true patentability search, they can be used as a searching aid and to provide other information about patents that you may find useful. The two most helpful disks are:

- CASSIS/CLASS disks (go back to 1790) can be used to find the classification of any patent, or the list of patents in any class.
- CASSIS/BIB disks (go back to 1969 for utility patents—number, title, class—and since 1988 also include abstracts) can be used to find the classification of any recently issued patent, to find all patents assigned to any company or individual, to find a list of patents by year of issue, status (expired, reexamined, etc.), all patents by inventor's residence, all recently issued patents with a certain word or words in their title or abstract (this feature can be used to perform a crude search), and to find the field of search (class and subclass) for any type of invention.

L. Computer Searching

Although computer searching is coming of age, you should not yet use a computer search (except for the EAST search system) in place of a full manual search for low-tech inventions. The main reason for this is that the patents in most computer search data banks usually go back to only 1971 (or 1976). Nevertheless, I cover it here because for most high-tech inventions there is no need to search prior to 1971. Also, computer searching does have some advantages that make it useful as a supplement to a manual search. Since I believe that computer searching will eventually virtually replace manual searching, you may be able to avoid a bad case of "future shock" by becoming familiar with computer searching now.

Most basic computer search systems don't show the drawings of any prior patents. However, some services are now offering drawings from the patents being searched. Nor do most computer search systems use the PTO classification system. Instead, they search solely for Boolean combinations of keywords in the texts—specification, claims, abstract, or title—of prior patents. For example, suppose you've invented the bike with a frame made of a certain carbon-fiber alloy. To make a manual search, you would look through the patents in the bike and metallurgical (carbon-fiber alloy) classifications, hoping that if a relevant patent exists, someone would have classified it in either or both of these places. However, to make a computer search, you would select a combination of keywords to describe your invention. Here you should use "bicycle" and "carbon fiber alloy." You then send these words to the computer and tell it to look through its data bank for any patent that contains all of these words. When it finds any patents that contain your keywords in the combination you specify in your search request, it will identify these patents, regardless of their classifications.

If the computer reports too much data for you to conveniently examine—say it's found 200 patents with your words in combination—you should first look at one or two of the patents (the computer will show you the relevant text) to see if your invention is shown in an earlier patent (that is—your invention has been "knocked out"). If so, your search is over. If not, you'll need to narrow your search. This is easy. Simply add one or more additional keywords, say "frame," or some details of the alloy, and redo the search with these increased keywords until you've few enough patents to manually review conveniently. Also, you can narrow the search by using narrower (more specific) keywords.

If you get extremely specific, the computer is likely to report no patents, or just one or two. If this occurs, you'll need to broaden your search. This is just as easy. Merely remove one or more keywords, or broaden your present keywords, and redo the search until you get back what you want. For example, you could eliminate "bicycle" or substitute "frame" for "bicycle" to broaden the search. Note that to broaden your search (pull out more prior art), you should use fewer keywords, and to narrow your search (pull out less prior art), you should use more keywords.

Similarity of Claims to Computer Searches

If you can understand this Boolean-logic concept now (you narrow your search by using additional keywords and/or making your keywords more specific; you broaden your search by using fewer keywords and/or making your keywords more general), you'll have an easy time understanding patent claims (Chapters 9 and 13), since in claims, the more elements that are recited and/or the more specific these elements are, the narrower the coverage.

The data that you search by computer—that is, the texts or claims of patents—is available for free from the PTO and for a fee from several computer search service firms. The latter are private companies that in turn get this data in the form of machine-readable tapes as a by-product of the patent printing process from the Government Printing Office, which prints all patents. As of this writing, one fee-based company, MicroPatent (www.micropatent.com) has used optical character recognition (OCR) to incorporate the data from all patents since 1836 into its data bank (although the U.S. first granted patents in 1790, the patent numbering system did not begin until 1836). While MicroPatent's OCR results are not yet accurate, they do provide the first way to search all patents on the Internet. It doesn't take much imagination to realize what will happen when all patents and possibly other literature are added to the data banks in accurate form and when the computers can also display and print out the drawings of patents. When this occurs—and when more terminals become available in libraries and service centers—computer searching will be faster and more thorough. It will also be independent of the PTO's classification system which is subject to human error and troubled by missing patents.

Presently, the PTO's examiners use computer searching (the EAST search system) almost exclusively. As a result, we're getting better examinations and stronger patents. When computer searching is perfected and completed, I believe that patent application pendency time will be reduced from its present level of about 1.5 to three years to about six months

or less, and that, more importantly, hardly any patent will ever be questioned for validity—that is, almost all patents will be virtually incontestable. (See Chapter 15 for more on patent validity.)

1. Available Computer Search Resources

Now that you get the general idea, how do you go about supplementing your manual search with a computer search? There are two ways to gain access to a computer search service's data bank:

- Via a personal computer (or terminal) with a modem—the PTO's and the EPO's websites are completely free and for others you'll have to make a suitable agreement.
- Via an existing terminal that is dedicated to patent searching, such as at a PTDL, large company, law firm, or the EAST system.

The PTO itself provides free keyword combination searches in bibliographic format (name, title, assignee, city, state, date, etc.) back to 1976 and by patent number and current classification back to 1790. To use this service, visit www.uspto.gov/patft/index.html. To view the actual images of patents (as opposed to simple text versions of the patents) go to the link "How to Access Full-Page Images" and download and install the TIFF viewer AlternaTIFF (www.alternatiff.com) that is available for free. Then use the "Quick Search" or "Advanced Search" links to make the search using the instructions to follow. If you simply want to look up a patent by its number, go to the "Patent Number Search" link.

The EPO (http://ep.espacenet.com) provides Quick and Advanced search capabilities in three languages (English, German, and French), but for patentability searches only the Quick search in English is necessary. Searches can be made in four databases: Worldwide (which covers European countries, EPO, and U.S. patents); Japanese; EP (EPO patents); or WIPO (World Intellectual Patent Organization, which administers the PCT databases. (See Chapter 12 for more on the PCT.) To search all databases, search just the Worldwide and Japanese databases. To make a search, type the appropriate keyword combinations in the keyword box with a suitable connector—for example, bicycle AND plastic OR wood. The dates of the databases vary; see the site for more information.

Delphion (www.delphion.com/simple) offers bibliographic and patentability search services for a fee. The system has several advantages over the PTO. Delphion's database goes back to 1971 for U.S. patents and contains the front pages of Europatents and PCT published patent applications. However, Delphion requires a signup and charges for use and downloading patent images.

Here are several other fee-based organizations that offer computer searching of patent records. Several of the "for fee" databases also provide foreign patent information.

- MicroPatent. (www.micropatent.com), a commercial database of U.S. patents searchable from 1836 to the present. It also includes Japanese and International PCT patent applications from 1983, European patents from 1988, and the *Official Gazette (Patents)*. The U.S. patents before 1971 have been entered into the database by Optical Character Recognition, so expect some errors.

- LexPat (www.lexis-nexis.com), a commercial database of U.S. patents searchable from 1971 to the present. In addition, the LEXPAT library offers extensive prior-art searching capability of technical journals and magazines.

- QPAT (www.qpat.com); Questel/Orbit (www.questel.orbit.com); both commercial services access the QPAT database that includes U.S. patents searchable from 1974 to the present and full-text European A (1987-present) and B (1991-present) patents.

- PatentMax (www.patentmax.com) is another commercial database similar to Questel/Orbit. The site permits batch loading.

- IP Search Engine (www.IPSearchEngine.com) is an expensive service that uses "concept" searching that is more complete than traditional Boolean searching and covers many databases.

- PatBase (www.patbase.com) is a new database that can search back to the 1800s through many nations' patents, and permits batch downloading.

2. Vocabulary Associated With Computer Searches

How do you use a database? Assuming you're going to do the search yourself, first thoroughly study the service's instruction manual so that you'll be able to conduct your search in as little time as possible, thereby minimizing user time charges. While every system is different, and while space constraints preclude coverage of them all, the following usage terms are common to all systems. If you're going to do any patent searching, you should learn these terms now.

- A **File** is the actual name of the patent search database provided by the service; for example LEXPAT is the name and trademark for Mead Data General's patent search database; CLAIMS is Dialog's patent search file.

- A **Record** is a portion of a file; the term is used to designate a single reference, usually a patent within a database.

- A **Field** is a portion of a record, such as a patent's title, the names of the inventors, its filing date, its patent number, its claims, etc.

- A **Term** is a group or, in computerese, a "string," of characters within a field—for example, the inventor's surname, one word of the title of a patent, etc., are terms.

- A **Command** is an instruction or directive to the search system that tells it to perform a function. For example, "Search" might be a command to tell a system to look for some key search words in its database.

- A **Keyword** or a **Search Term** are the words that are actually searched. "Bicycle" and "carbon fiber alloy" are the keywords for our example above.

- A **Qualifier** is a symbol that is used to limit a search or the information that the search displays for your use. Normally no qualifier would be used in novelty searches, but if you're looking for a patent to a certain inventor, you could add a qualifier that limits the search to the field of the patentee's name.

- A **Wild Card Symbol** is an ending (familiar to users of sophisticated word processing programs) that is used in lieu of a word's normal ending in order to broaden a *keyword*. The wild card cuts off immaterial endings so that only word roots are searched. For example, if we were searching Millie's annular napkin-shaping ring, we would want our search to include the words "annular" and "annulus." Thus, instead of using both keywords and the *Connector Symbol* "or" (see below), we might search for "annul*" where "*" was a wild card symbol that tells the computer to look for any word with the root "annul" and any ending.

- **Connector Words** are those (such as "or," "and," and "not") that tell the computer to look for certain defined logical combinations of *keywords*. For instance, if you issued a *command* telling the computer to search for "annulus or ring and napkin," the computer would recognize that "or" and "and" were connector words and would search for patents with the words "annulus" and "napkin," or "ring" and "napkin," in combination.

Obviously, the use of more *keywords* joined by the Boolean "and" connector will narrow your search, since it will add more *keywords* to the search; this will cause the computer to pull out fewer patents, because only patents with all of the *keywords* connected by "ands" will satisfy your search request. However, the use of more *keywords* joined by the "or" connector will broaden your search, since any patent with any one of the *keywords* joined by an "or" will be selected. The "and not" connector is seldom employed, but it can be used to narrow a search when you want to eliminate a certain class of patents that contain an unwanted *keyword*.

(Note that when you get to writing your claims (Chapter 9), "or's" and "not's" are generally verboten.)

- **Proximity Symbols** are those that tell the computer to look for specified *keywords*, provided they are not more than a certain number of terms apart. Thus, if you told the computer to search for "napkin w/5 shaping" it would look for any patent that contained the words "napkin" and "shaping" within five words of each other, the symbol "w/5" meaning "within five words of." If no proximity symbol is used and the words are placed adjacent to each other—such as "napkin shaping"—the computer will pull out only those patents that contain these two words adjacent to each other in the order given. However, if a *connector word* is used—such as "napkin and shaping"—the computer will pull out any patent with both of these words, no matter where they are in the patent and no matter in what order they appear.

3. Think of Alternative Search Terms

Before you even approach the computer, no matter what search system you use, be well prepared with a well-thought-out group of keywords and all possible synonyms or equivalents. Use a thesaurus or a visual dictionary to get synonyms. Thus, to search for Millie's napkin-shaping ring, in addition to the obvious keywords "ring," "annular," "napkin," and "shaping," think of other terms from the same and analogous fields. In addition to napkin, you could use "cloth." Or, in addition to shaping, you could use "folding" or "bending." In addition to "annulus" or "ring," you could try "device," etc.

4. Using the Computer

From here on, simply follow the instructions in the service manual for operating the computer and gaining access to the database. As with the manual search, pull out all relevant patents without any consideration of obviousness. Then later, at your leisure, analyze them as instructed earlier in this chapter. Good luck and smooth searching!

5. Using Computer-Generated References to Work Backward and Forward

After making a computer search and obtaining a group of relevant references generated by the computer, it's possible (and very easy) to use these references to work back and forward and obtain additional, earlier relevant references that antedate the computer's database. How? To work backward, simply look at and/or order each of the "References Cited," which are listed on the abstract page (see Fig. 6D(c)) of each computer-generated patent. These references (usually patents) were cited by the PTO during prosecution of the patent and are usually very relevant. You can even look up the "References Cited" in the additional references to go back even earlier, thereby making a "tree" of references. However, the PTO didn't list the "References Cited" before the '50s, and in earlier patents "References Cited" are listed at the end of the patent.

Another way to work backward, using a hybrid approach, is to find a patent close to your invention using the computer and then find the U.S. Class of the patent (it's 40/21R in Fig. 6D(c)) and then search all patents in this class at a PTDL, or order a list and search them online back to 1971 and in a PTDL for earlier patents.

To work forward, look up any close patent on the Delphion or EAST system and check the "Patents which cite this patent" for each close patent.

M. Problems Searching Software and Business Inventions

Many software experts have recently complained that the PTO has been issuing patents on software and business method inventions that aren't novel and unobvious over the prior art. I believe that there is much validity to this charge—that is, many software and business patents really don't claim a novel and unobvious invention and could be invalidated by a proper search. Part of the problem is due to differences in the PTO's database of software patents. As a result, some people even want to do away with software patents. I strongly disagree with this proposal, since this would be throwing out the baby with the bathwater.

I believe that much, if not most, future technological progress will occur in software, but without the incentive of a patent monopoly, software developers will not have an adequate incentive to innovate. There are many other arguments in favor of software patents, but they're beyond the scope of this book. Suffice it to note that I prefer strengthening the PTO's software search capability.

If you agree and want to support the continued existence of software patents, keep your eyes peeled for any legislative developments and do whatever you can to support the continued existence of software patents. Also if you have a software invention, be aware of the difficulty in doing a good search of your invention. If you search your invention in the PTO database there will be a greater chance that your search will not catch all of the relevant prior art.

One software patent resource is the Source Translation and Optimization patent website (www.bustpatents.com). The STO is directed by Gregory Aharonian, one of the PTO's most vocal critics. The site provides critiques, legal reviews, CAFC rulings, file wrappers, and infringement lawsuits relating to software patents. The STO also offers a free email newsletter.

N. PTO Searches on the Internet

The PTO and Delphion patent searching systems are useful tools for conducting fair-to-good patent searches on inventions using recent technologies and for making free, preliminary searches for inventions in older technologies. If you have a high-tech invention and are willing to spend the time to do a thorough job, you can make a fairly complete search online. However, if you are unwilling or unable to spend the time, or if you have a low-tech invention, I strongly advise you to conduct a more thorough patent search using the techniques and resources described elsewhere in this chapter.

1. The PTO's Search Website With EPO Supplement

The PTO's system can be used to make novelty searches of U.S. patents back to 1976 and U.S. patent applications back to March 2001 when they were first published. You can also use it to make searches by patent number or class and subclass of U.S. patents from 1790 to the present. It cannot be used to make a novelty search of any patents before 1976. The PTO's URL for searching services is www.uspto.gov/patft/index.html. The PTO's servers have been vastly improved, so that you can easily and quickly download, view, and print the images of any patent back to 1790. For example, with a broadband Internet service, you can now view and print the images of a ten-page patent in less than two minutes! Everything is free on the PTO's website, except for orders of patents to be sent by mail. Fig. 6N shows the three types of searches (Quick, Advanced, and Patent Number) that can be made on the PTO's website and Fig. 6O shows the main page of the PTO's search website—note that you can make the three types of searches of either patents or patent applications. In order to view and print the actual images of patents on this website you must download the AlternaTIFF viewer (see Section L, above) or use Patent Logistics' Patent Fetcher (see Section N6, below). You can do a rough extension of your novelty search of U.S. patents back to the 1920s at the EPO's site (http://ep.espacenet.com). In addition, this site also provides a searchable database for some foreign patents.

2. The Delphion Search Website

I prefer the PTO's vastly improved free system to the Delphion (or any other fee-based) system. Nevertheless, some users still prefer Delphion, and since I covered it in previous editions (when it was largely free), I will cover it here. Delphion can be used to make free novelty searches of the front pages of U.S. patents back to 1971, European patents back to 1980, and PCT patent publications back to 1978. You can also use it to make a patent number search (see Fig. 6U). The latter will enable you to freely view the parts of the text (but not the figures) of U.S. patents from 1790 and the texts of foreign countries' patents—for example, Japanese, Swiss, and other foreign patents—from various dates. However, the Delphion service cannot be used to make a novelty search of any U.S. patents before 1971. Delphion requires a membership and charges fees for searching U.S. patents, patent applications, and foreign patents and for obtaining copies of patents with their drawings. Fig. 6P shows the main page of Delphion's search website. (The search terms "bicycle and aluminum" have already been entered in the Quick Text Search box.)

Although this information is accurate as of publication, note that both the PTO and Delphion servers change their features frequently, and this information may no longer be accurate by the time you read this.

3. Limitations of the PTO and Other Systems

The fact that you can only search patents issued since 1971 or 1976 can itself be an extremely important limitation. As I stress in Chapter 5, Section E, all previous inventions (prior art) are relevant when determining whether a new invention qualifies for a patent. Therefore, to be effective, a patent search must cover the earliest prior art that might show your invention. Since novelty searches of the PTO system can be made back only to 1976—and to 1971 for the Delphion system—you can have confidence in your search results only if your invention technology—for example an Internet invention—wasn't around prior to 1971 or 1976. For a low-tech invention that requires searching back beyond the 1971 date (for instance, a bicycle) these systems will only provide a fraction of the total prior art for that invention.

A second limitation is the fact that you must depend on keywords. Traditional patent searching uses a classification scheme to find relevant prior art (see Section I above). This scheme is the result of humans grouping like inventions to-

Delphion Search Site—Main Page
(Fig. 6P)

Patent Number Search Results Page (Fig. 6U)

Boolean Text Search Page (Fig. 6AA)

PTO Search Site—Main Page
(Fig. 6O)

Patent Number Search Results Page (Fig. 6Q)

Boolean Text Search Page (Fig. 6W)

Manual Search Page (Fig. 6Y)

Fig. 6N—Delphion and PTO Search Pages

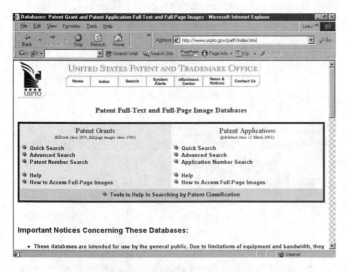

Fig. 6O—PTO Search Site (Main Page)

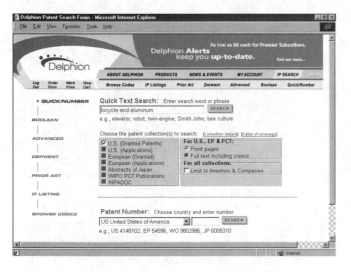

Fig. 6P—Delphion Search Site Main Page

gether and does not depend on the whimsy of which search terms you select. The keyword system, on the other hand, requires you to come up with the right words in your search request. However, patents are often written with legal-sounding terms or technical jargon in place of otherwise ordinary terms. For example, a patent for a telephone may be titled "Full Duplex Voice Telecommunication Device." Such a patent may never be found with "telephone" as the search term. This limitation is inherent in any computerized searching system based on search terms. The disadvantages of the keyword search system can to some extent be overcome by following the tips described in Section 5 below as well as by using the logic implicit in the Boolean search technique (Section 4).

4. The Ways to Search

There are three ways to make a search on the PTO's system (Quick, Advanced, and Patent Number) and two ways (Quick and Patent Number) on the Delphion system.

PTO Patent Number Search

To make a patent number search (better termed a patent lookup by number) on the PTO's website, go to the main search page (Fig. 6O) and click Patent Number Search, which will take you to the Patent Number Search page shown in Fig. 6Q. Then enter the number of the patent you want to view. Note that utility patents need no prefix while design, plant, and reissue patents, and defensive publications (see Chapter 7) and SIRs (see Chapter 13) require the prefixes indicated. By way of example, I have entered the number of a utility patent in the Query box.

Next click "Search," which will take you to the Results page (see Fig. 6R). This shows that the patent is available and gives its title. Next, click the patent number or title, which will take you to the Full Text Display page (see Fig. 6S). This page displays the entire text of the patent and all of its bibliographic data. However, only the first page of this text is shown. Scroll down to see the rest of the patent. Any of the text can be copied and pasted into a word processor for editing. This page does not display any of the drawings of the patent displayed, however.

Finally, assuming that you've downloaded and installed the AlternaTIFF viewer from the link (see Fig. 6O), you can click "Images" at the top of the page and the first (or abstract) page of the actual patent appears (see Fig. 6T). Note that in addition to the first page of the patent, some extraneous information (the PTO's logo and some navigation buttons) also appears at the top and left side of the abstract page. The buttons are used to display other pages of the patent.

Fig. 6Q—PTO Patent Number Search Page

Fig. 6R—PTO Patent Number Search Results Page

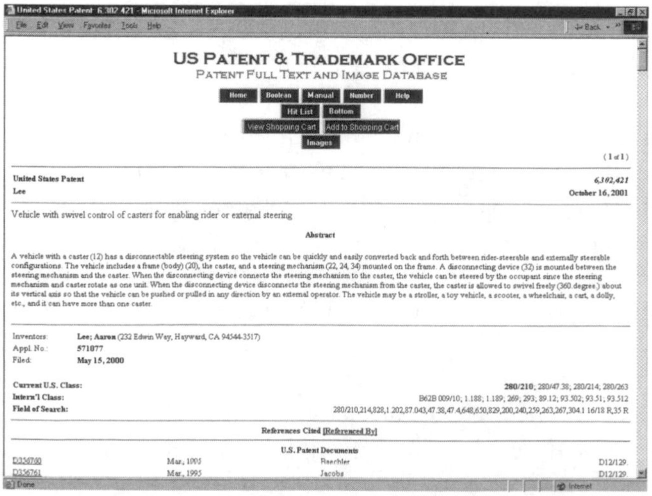

Fig. 6S—PTO Patent Full Text Display (Page 1)

If you need to obtain copies of any patent for sending to the PTO with your Information Disclosure Statement (see Chapter 10, Section N), print out the actual images using this procedure; don't print the text version or the patent page with the extraneous information. To print just the patent images, simply click the printer icon (not shown) at the top of the page just below the patent number. (Don't click "Print" on your computer's toolbar above the page.)

The above procedure can be used to look up patent applications; just use the right-hand side as seen in Fig. 6O. If you do make a patentability search, you should search both patents and published patent applications.

PTO Quick Search

The PTO's "Quick Search" page allows you to enter and search two simple Boolean terms, such as *bicycle* AND *aluminum* (as shown in Fig. 6W). Note that the terms Description/Specification are selected in the Field 1 and Field 2 boxes; this is where you should make all Boolean searches. Also note that the years 1996-2001 are displayed in the Select Years box. In addition to these years, you should repeat the search as necessary, selecting all other year periods so as to cover all years back to 1976. (The Quick Search page and the Advanced Search page can also be used to make bibliographic searches. I will not cover these features, but you will find the use of these intuitive and it is also explained in the Help link.)

Fig. 6X shows the results of the quick search of Fig. 6W. Note that the search yielded 931 patents, which is too large a number to handle, so the search will have to be narrowed by using more specific search terms. Note that Fig. 6X displays the first 16 patents. Scrolling down and visiting subsequent page links can show the rest. To view any patent that looks interesting, click its title or number. Again, the same procedure can be used to search patent applications (use the information on the right-hand side of Fig. 6O).

Also note that in addition to the AND Boolean operator, the operators OR and ANDNOT are available. Further, nested expressions, such as *tennis* AND (*racquet* OR *racket*) are available. If you enter this query, you will retrieve a list of all patents that contain both the terms *tennis* and either *racket* or *racquet* somewhere in the document. For another example, consider the search terms *television* OR (*cathode* AND *tube*). This query would return patents containing either the word *television* OR both the words *cathode* AND *tube*. A third example is the search expression *needle* ANDNOT ((*record* AND *player*) OR *sewing*). This complex query will generate a list of hits that contain the word needle, but not contain any references to sewing. In addition, none of the hits would contain the combination of record AND player.

Fig. 6T—Patent Image (Page 1)

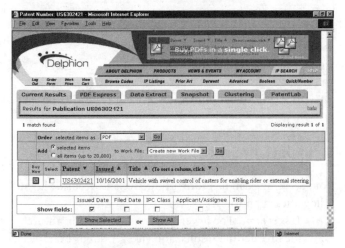

Fig. 6U—Delphion Patent Number Search Results Page

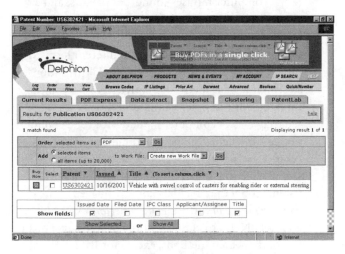

**Fig. 6V—Delphion Patent Partial Text
(Only Abstract and Claims Shown)**

PTO Advanced Search

Despite its name, the "Advanced Search" page (see Fig. 6Y) really doesn't offer any more capabilities than the Quick Search page. The Advanced Search page is simply more difficult to use since it requires that you enter the search query in free form. The field must be manually typed (see Fig. 6Y). Note that the field codes must be typed before the search terms. Fig. 6Z shows part of the results of the advanced search of Fig. 6Y.

Delphion Search

A Delphion search can be made with simple expressions only (such as those listed after "e.g." in Fig. 6P). A search for the term "bicycle and aluminum" was made (see Fig. 6P). This expression is not searched as a Boolean expression, but as a single search term. Thus only patents with the actual expression "bicycle and aluminum" were returned. Patents that contain these terms separate from each other will not be returned. The patents returned from the search of Fig. 6P are partially listed in the results page (see Fig. 6AA). Note, that if you want to study any patent in the results page, you will have to pay Delphion to see the PDF images or go to the PTO's website. Delphion does not provide images of the patents for free, but only some text from the returned patents.

You may now wonder why I am listing Delphion if it can't do Boolean expressions and if they charge. I do this because Delphion goes back to 1971 instead of 1976 and will search European patents and PCT patent applications, if only their front pages. A Delphion search will often return a few more patents than a PTO search will.

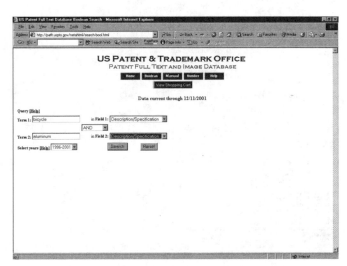

Fig. 6W—PTO Quick Text Search Page

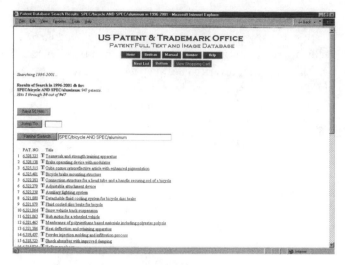

Fig. 6X—PTO Quick Text Search Results Page

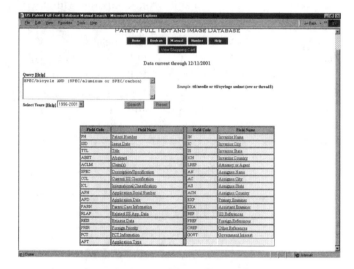

Fig. 6Y—PTO Advanced Search Page

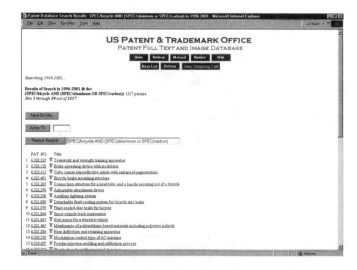

Fig. 6Z—PTO Advanced Search Results (Page 1)

Fig. 6AA—Delphion Quick Text Search Results (Page 1)

5. Important Searching Tips

Your searching can be more productive and accurate if you follow these important tips:

1. *Less is more.* The fewer words used to define a search, the broader the results, and vice versa. For example, a search done with the term "ergonomic computer mouse" found two patents; a search done with the term "computer mouse" found 157 patents; and a search done with the term "mouse" found 3,147 patents (only a maximum of the first 200 can be displayed).

2. *Use alternative terms.* A variety of different terms are often used in patents to describe similar inventions, so search with as many alternative terms as you can think of. For example, a computer mouse is also referred to as a "computer input device" or a "pointing device." Incidentally, a search done using the term "computer input device" found 91 patents, and a search using the term "pointing device" found 475 patents (only the first 200 can be displayed).

3. *Make good use of the Boolean connectors,* AND, OR, and ANDNOT, to connect words or terms in a box in any of the search methods, except for Patent Number

Search. For example, "ergonomic AND mouse" can be entered in the Simple Text Search box. When Boolean connectors are used, multiple-word terms must be enclosed in quotes. For example, "ergonomic AND 'pointing device'" will search for all patents which have the word "ergonomic" AND the expression "pointing device." Boolean connectors can also be used to search for inventions with alternative terms simultaneously. For example, "computer mouse OR 'pointing device'" finds all patents with either the word "ergonomic" OR the expression "pointing device."

4. *Use wild cards.* Use the asterisk * as a wild card to represent any character or characters. For example, John* finds patents by all inventors with the first or last name starting with John, and ending with any character or characters, including John, Johnny, Johnson, and Johnston. Use the question mark ? as a wild card to represent any single character. For example, ?am finds ram, cam, jam, etc.

5. *Inventor Names.* Always enter inventor names last-name first, for example, Edison Thomas.

6. *Class and References.* If you find a relevant patent, click on the Intl. Class and U.S. Class links to display patents for potentially similar inventions, and the U.S. References link to view the patents specifically cited as being similar.

Information on using more advanced search techniques can be found by clicking the search language link in the Advanced Text Search page.

6. Ordering Patent Copies

Although portions of patents are available (see Sections 1 and 2 above) and can be printed directly from the PTO's website free of charge, they must be downloaded and printed one page at a time. To view and print actual patent pages or images (as opposed to an ASCII file of the patent) from the PTO's site, you must first download and install an "Alterna-TIFF" viewer from a link on the main search page (Fig 6O). This viewer provides a bitmapped image with one page per file. If you wish to get numerous patents, this will be a time-consuming process, especially if you have a dial-up Internet service. Instead, you may order copies of the patents and have them delivered to you, but at a cost. To order patents click the title or number of the patent (see the list shown in Fig. 6X) which will produce a full-text view page (see Fig 6S). Then, click "Add To Shopping Cart." Have your credit card ready. Patents can also be ordered from the Delphion website in a similar manner and these

can be delivered online as a PDF, or by fax, or mail. You can also acquire PDF files of patents or published patent applications (one multipage patent per file) at no charge at Patent Logistics (http://free.patentfetcher.com). This service is relatively slow, but there is also a link to a faster, pay-as-you-go service from the same company.

O. Micropatent Patent Searches on the Internet

Because of its unique capabilities, I have included the fee-based MicroPatent service (www.micropatent.com). MicroPatent has the capability to offer full-text search of U.S. patents dating back to 1836. MicroPatent charges approximately $500 for a one-year subscription with unlimited use of their full-text searching facilities of U.S. patents and various foreign patent databases and about $100 for a 24-hour unlimited use subscription. Using the MicroPatent system is easy and intuitive, especially if you've digested the rest of this chapter. However, since the MicroPatent database has been obtained by scanning and OCR-ing the scanned U.S. patents back to 1836, it contains many errors and strange words, so be aware of its limitations before signing up.

P. Summary

There are many good reasons to perform a patentability search for your invention: to save needless work and expenditures; to facilitate patent application preparation prosecution; to learn more about your invention; and to facilitate licensing. To possibly avoid making a full search, make a quick preliminary search yourself in stores and catalogues.

If you hire someone to make a search, hire a competent, experienced searcher, preferably a patent agent or attorney, and prepare your searcher with a full description of your invention. In order to analyze a search report, read the cited patents and other references carefully and determine what novel features your invention has and whether these are unobvious. (Use the criteria given on the Patentability Flowchart in Chapter 5, Section G, to assist you.)

To search yourself, use (a) a Patent Depository Library's computer and/or paper search facilities, (b) the Internet, with a personal computer with the PTO's and the EPO's free services or a fee-based commercial service, or (c) the EAST system or a paper search in the PTO. Computer searches are usually made using the Boolean system by looking for patents with combinations of keywords. You can also search by reviewing all the patents in a particular sub-ject-matter class.

If you make a computer search, be sure to supplement it with a manual search if you have a low-tech invention and the computer's database doesn't extend back beyond 1976 or 1971. ■

Chapter 7

What Should You Do Next?

Inventor's Commandment #9

After making your commercial evaluation and search, carefully consider the following alternatives before proceeding or dropping it: file a utility patent application now, test the market for up to a year and then consider filing, keep it a trade secret, file a design application, use a clever trademark, use copyright coverage, and/or use distinctive "trade dress" for unfair competition coverage.

Now that you have a pretty good idea of the patentability and commercial status of your invention, it is time to make a plan for acquiring the maximum possible offensive rights under the law. While you might think that your next step would be to prepare and file a patent application, you would be wrong in doing so without first considering the information in this chapter. I suggest that your main goal should be to profit from your invention, not to get a patent. Although many inventors have made fortunes from their inventions, their successes are rare and usually an exception to the rule. Be prepared for a difficult task and pursue commercial success diligently. If you don't make it, try to avoid getting disappointed; perhaps you will have better luck in the future. In general, for most inventors my advice is not to give up your day job.

I've provided a Decision Chart (Fig. 7A) to simplify and organize your alternatives. It consists of 23 boxes with interconnecting lead lines. The numbered, light-lined boxes (even numbers from 10 to 40) represent various tasks and decisions on your route to making decisions on available options. The lettered, heavy-lined boxes (A to F and X) represent your actual options.

The numbers in parentheses in the following discussion refer to the boxes on the chart. While there are seven options, several of these can be reached by several routes. Accordingly, the following discussion is divided into more than seven sections.

A. Drop It If You Don't See Commercial Potential (Chart Route 10-12-14-X)

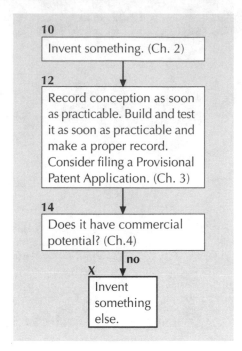

This route has already been covered in Chapter 4, but in order to acquaint you with the use of the chart, I'll review it again.

Referring to the chart above, assuming that you've invented something (Box 10—Chapter 2) and recorded the conception properly (Box 12—Chapter 3), you should then proceed to build and test your invention as soon as practicable, or consider filing a Provisional Patent Application (Chapter 3), provided you're aware of all of the disadvantages of the PPA (Box 12). If building and testing would present appreciable difficulty, you should wait until after you evaluate your invention's commercial potential (Box 14—Chapter 4), or patentability (Box 16—Chapter 5). But always keep the building and testing as a goal; it will help you to evaluate commercial potential and may be vital in the event an "interference" occurs (different persons seek patents for the same invention). What's more, as you'll see in Chapter 11, you'll find a working model extremely valuable when you show the invention to a manufacturer.

Your next step is stated in Box 14—investigate your invention's commercial potential using the criteria of Chapter 4. Assuming you decide that your invention has little or no commercial potential, your answer to the commercial question is "No," and you would thus follow the "No" line from Box 14 to the ultimate decision, Box X, which says "Invent something else," as already covered in Chapter 4. See how easy it is?

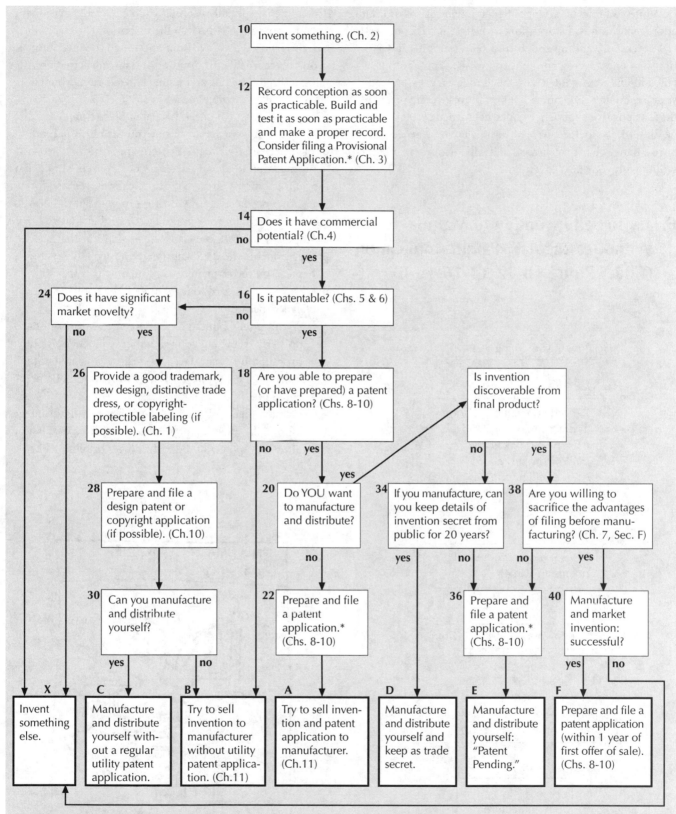

10 Invent something. (Ch. 2)

12 Record conception as soon as practicable. Build and test it as soon as practicable and make a proper record. Consider filing a Provisional Patent Application.* (Ch. 3)

14 Does it have commercial potential? (Ch.4) — **no**

yes

24 Does it have significant market novelty? ← **16** Is it patentable? (Chs. 5 & 6) — **no**

yes

no / **yes** (from 24)

26 Provide a good trademark, new design, distinctive trade dress, or copyright-protectible labeling (if possible). (Ch. 1)

18 Are you able to prepare (or have prepared) a patent application? (Chs. 8-10)

Is invention discoverable from final product?

no / **yes**

28 Prepare and file a design patent or copyright application (if possible). (Ch.10)

20 Do YOU want to manufacture and distribute?

34 If you manufacture, can you keep details of invention secret from public for 20 years?

38 Are you willing to sacrifice the advantages of filing before manu-facturing? (Ch. 7, Sec. F)

no (from 18)

yes (from 20)

30 Can you manufacture and distribute yourself?

22 Prepare and file a patent application.* (Chs. 8-10)

no (20)

yes / **no** (34)

no (38) / **yes** (38)

36 Prepare and file a patent application.* (Chs. 8-10)

40 Manufacture and market invention: successful?

yes / **no** (30)

yes / **no** (40)

X Invent something else.

C Manufacture and distribute yourself with-out a regular utility patent application.

B Try to sell invention to manufacturer without utility patent applica-tion. (Ch.11)

A Try to sell inven-tion and patent application to manufacturer. (Ch.11)

D Manufacture and distribute yourself and keep as trade secret.

E Manufacture and distribute yourself: "Patent Pending."

F Prepare and file a patent application (within 1 year of first offer of sale). (Chs. 8-10)

* If you filed a Provisional Patent Application, you *must* file a regular patent application and any desired foreign convention applications within one year—see Ch.3. (File non-Convention applications before invention is made public or any patent issues on it.)

Fig. 7A—Invention Decision Chart

While you may be disappointed at having spent time and effort recording your invention, investigating its commercial potential, building and testing it, or searching it, your time and effort were definitely not wasted. You haven't failed in any way—unless you failed to learn a lesson from your experience. Edison had 3,000 failures, yet he regarded these as positive experiences since he learned 3,000 things he didn't know before. Armed with what you learned, you'll have a better chance at success and will encounter smoother sailing with your next invention.

B. Try to Sell Invention to Manufacturer Without "Regular" Patent Application (Chart Route 10-12-14-16-18-B)

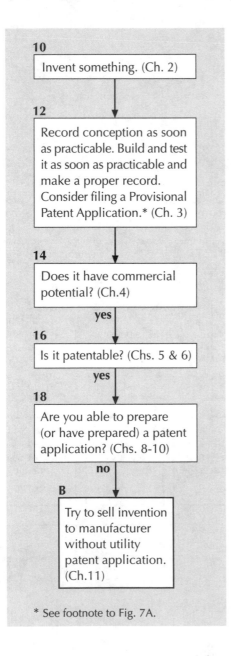

10

Invent something. (Ch. 2)

12

Record conception as soon as practicable. Build and test it as soon as practicable and make a proper record. Consider filing a Provisional Patent Application.* (Ch. 3)

14

Does it have commercial potential? (Ch.4)

yes

16

Is it patentable? (Chs. 5 & 6)

yes

18

Are you able to prepare (or have prepared) a patent application? (Chs. 8-10)

no

B

Try to sell invention to manufacturer without utility patent application. (Ch.11)

* See footnote to Fig. 7A.

This route is especially useful if you've filed a Provisional Patent Application (PPA) on the invention (Box 12), but can also be used if you've built and tested the invention and properly recorded your building and testing activities. After filing a PPA or building and testing and recording your efforts (Box 12), see if the invention has commercial potential (Chapter 4—Box 14) and if it's patentable (Chapters 5 and 6—Box 16). If so, whether or not you're able to prepare—or have prepared—a regular patent application, try to sell your invention to a manufacturer (Box B) in the hope that the manufacturer will have the application prepared for you, either on the basis of your PPA or without the PPA. If you take this route, you should be sure either that your PPA is properly prepared (see Chapters 3 and 8) or that you've properly documented conception, building, and testing (Chapter 3). I recommend this route only if you can't prepare or can't afford to have prepared a regular patent application because:

- if you've only built and tested the invention without properly recording your activities, you run a risk of an unscrupulous manufacturer stealing your invention by filing a patent application on your invention before you do so, and
- if you've filed a PPA, you'll have all of the disadvantages of the PPA. (See Chapter 3, Section I, for a discussion of the advantages and disadvantages of filing a PPA.)

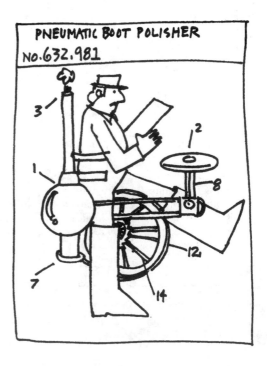

C. File an Application and Sell It to or License a Manufacturer If You See Commercial Potential and Patentability (Chart Route 14-16-18-20-22-A)

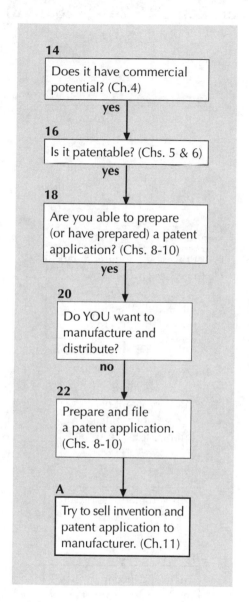

Filing a patent application and selling rights to the invention is the usual route for most inventors. This is because inventors seldom have the capability to establish their own manufacturing and distribution facilities. If (a) your invention has good commercial potential (Box 14), (b) your decision on patentability is favorable (Box 16), (c) you're able to prepare a patent application (Box 18) (or have one prepared for you), and (d) you don't wish to manufacture and distribute your product or process yourself (Box 20), your next step is to prepare a patent application (Box 22). After you prepare

the patent application, you should then try to sell your invention (and accompanying patent application) to the manufacturer, as stated in Box A. Note that if you file a PPA (Box 12), you must file your "regular" patent application, and also any desired foreign convention applications (see Chapter 12) within one year. You should file any desired non-Convention applications before your invention is made public or before any patent issues on it.

Why file a patent application before offering the invention to a manufacturer? A good question, which has four good answers. Let's look at each one individually.

1. Offensive Rights for Your Invention

By preparing and filing a patent application, you've defined your invention and its ramifications in very precise terms, made formal drawings of it, and formally established your claim to it in the PTO. Thus anyone who later sees the invention and wants to steal or adopt it would have to engage in elaborate and (usually) illegal forgeries and other activities. And, the would-be thief will have filed after you, a serious disadvantage. Thus once you file the application, most attorneys agree that you may publish details of your invention freely and show it to anyone you think may have an interest in it (unless you've chosen to maintain your invention as a trade secret while your patent application is pending—see Section F, below).

2. Respect for Your Invention

A manufacturer to whom you show the invention, seeing that you have thought enough of your invention to take the trouble to prepare and file a patent application on it, will treat it, and you, with far more respect and give it much more serious consideration than if you offer an unfiled invention. In other words, if you approach a manufacturer without a patent application, they may not think you're a serious player.

3. You Have Rights Even If You Sign a Manufacturer's Waiver

As you'll see in Chapter 11, most manufacturers to whom you offer an invention will not deal with you unless you first waive (give up) certain potential claims that might arise from the transaction (such as being able to charge the manufacturer with stealing your idea in the event this occurs). Simply put, signing a waiver if you haven't already filed a patent application will put you at the complete mercy of the company to whom you show your invention. Fortunately, however, such waivers do not involve your giving up your rights under the patent laws. Thus, having a patent application on file, in this context, affords you powerful rights against underhanded dealing by the manufacturer (assuming the patent subsequently issues). One inventor, Stephen Key, has said that a patent application levels the playing field, giving an inventor the power to play ball with corporate America.

4. You'll Be Offering More So You'll Get More

Most manufacturers want a proprietary or privileged position —that is, a position that entitles them to a commercial advantage in the marketplace that competitors can't readily copy and obtain. A patent provides a very highly privileged position: a 17- to 18-year (approximately) monopoly. Thus if you have a patent application that already covers your invention, manufacturers may be far more likely to buy your invention (with its covering patent application) than if you offered them a "naked" invention on which they have to take the time and trouble to file a patent application for you themselves.

An Exception. Although, as stated, it's usually best to file your patent application as soon as possible, it may be to your advantage to delay and keep the invention secret or take your chances approaching manufacturers "naked" if your invention is so innovative that it's not likely to be commercialized for many years. Gordon Gould, the inventor of the laser, did this unintentionally when he filed his patent application years late because he mistakenly believed he needed a working model to file. His mistake worked to his great advantage, however, since his delay postponed his monopoly period so that it coincided with the laser's commercial period, thereby turning what would have been a worthless patent into pure gold.

Common Misconception: You shouldn't patent your invention, since someone will see your patent, copy your invention, and make it more cheaply.

Facts: Copiers rarely use patents as a basis for their activities. Usually they copy successful products in the marketplace by reverse engineering. They'll be less likely to do this if it is patented, and a patent will enable you to stop their production or get royalties from them.

Filing before marketing is so important that I've made it part of the Inventor's Commandment at the beginning of this chapter.

D. If You Have Commercial Potential Without Patentability, License or Sell Your Invention to a Manufacturer Without Filing (Chart Route 16-24-26-28-30-B)

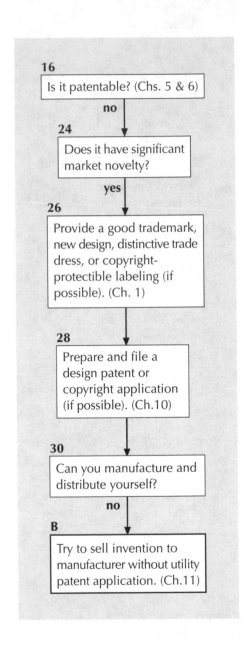

If your invention isn't patentable (that is—the decision in Box 16 is negative), don't give up; there's still hope. Many fortunes have been made on products that weren't patentable. For instance, the Apple computer made its designer-promoters, Jobs and Wozniak, multimillionaires, yet lacked any significant inventive concepts and never was awarded a major patent. Ditto for Henry Ford's automobile and George Eastman's Kodak camera.

Thus you should now decide, on the basis of your commercial potential and patentability evaluations, whether your invention nevertheless possesses "significant market novelty" (Box 24). If so, it may in fact be quite profitable if introduced to the market. Put differently, if your patentability search produces close prior art, but not a dead ringer, this indicates that probably no one has tried your specific, particular idea before, although someone has come close enough to preclude you from getting a patent. However, if you feel, looking back on your commercial-potential and patentability evaluations, that it doesn't have significant market novelty—that is, there's little chance of commercial success—then there isn't much hope and you'll have to try again (Box X).

Assuming that your invention does have significant market novelty (Box 24) but does not qualify for a utility patent, there are several ways that you can use to obtain proprietary rights on your invention and make it more attractive to potential manufacturers. Let's take a closer look at these.

1. Record Conception Properly

While recording conception won't provide you with any rights against independent creators, or "reverse engineers," it will establish (a) you as the inventor, and (b) the date of your invention, so you'll be able to prove that you invented it and when you did so. This will be of great help in stopping any invention thieves who copy it illegally before it's out. (Chapter 3, Section C.)

Recently I came across several layperson "invention gurus" who advocated (for a fee) that inventors "protect" their inventions without a patent application by—and here's the secret—using the PTO's DDP (Chapter 3, Section H). For reasons stated in that section, I recommend not using the DDP. Since it's no better than a witnessed invention disclosure (Form 3-2), it can't document building and testing, and most inventors erroneously think it gives them a two-year grace period.

2. Provide a Clever Trademark

One good way to make your invention more attractive is to provide a clever trademark for it (Box 26). As stated in Chapter 1, Section O, a trademark is a brand name for a product. An excellent type of brand name is one that suggests the function of the product in a very clever way. A clever trademark can be a very powerful marketing tool—

that is, a tool that will greatly enhance the value and salability of your invention and give you added proprietary rights to sell to a manufacturer. Examples of clever, suggestive trademarks are *Ivory* for a soap and *Hushpuppy* for shoes. Also consider *Sunkist* citrus fruit, *Shasta* soft drinks, *Roach Motel* roach traps, *Heavyhands* exercise weights, *Sun Tea* beverage containers, and *Walkman* portable tape players.

If you think the mark is valuable and that you (or a company that will license the product) will be able to offer a product with the mark within several years, then you can file an Intent-to-Use application with the PTO to register the mark. See Chapter 1, Section O, for more on trademarks.

3. File a Design Patent Application

If the invention that fails to qualify for a utility patent is a tangible product, the second trick to obtaining proprietary rights is to give it a distinctive design (Box 26). Then, perhaps, a design patent can be obtained. By distinctive design, I mean a shape or layout that is unique and different from anything you've seen so far. The design, in this case, doesn't mean the function or internal structure of the product, but only its outward, nonfunctional, ornamental, aesthetic shape or layout that makes it distinct visually.

For example, the D-shaped *Heavyhands* weights and Dizzy Gillespie's trumpet with its upwardly bent bell section are excellent examples of valuable design inventions. If you've invented a computer, a new case shape can be a design invention. For a bicycle, a new frame shape design would be a design invention. From abacuses to zithers, from airplanes to zippers, almost every humanly made object under the sun can be redesigned or reshaped in a new way so that it can be covered by a design patent.

However, remember from Chapter 1 that for a design patent to be applicable, the new features must be for aesthetic or ornamental purposes and should not have any significant functional purpose—otherwise the PTO will reject it as nonornamental—that is, only a utility patent will be appropriate. Also, the design must be inseparable from the object and not merely surface ornamentation. In the latter case, copyright is the proper form of coverage. (See Chapter 1, Section P.) For example, the label design on a jar of juice cannot be protected by a design patent, but a new shape for the jar would qualify for one. If you do come up with a distinctive design, you should, of course, record it in the same manner as you recorded your invention. (See Chapter 3.) And as with your invention, you should build a prototype or model as soon as practicable. You should also prepare and file a design-patent application (Box 28) on the ornamental appearance (not workings) of your invention.

As stated in Chapter 6, unless you live near the PTO or a Patent and Trademark Depository Library, it doesn't pay to search a new design beyond the most cursory look in product catalogues. This is because the cost of the search will greatly exceed the cost and effort to prepare and file a design-patent application. As you'll see in Chapter 10, a design-patent application consists simply of a drawing and a few forms that you fill out; it's very easy and economical to prepare.

4. Provide Distinctive "Trade Dress"

If you can't come up with a new design (or even if you can), you can still enhance the proprietary value of your invention by providing it with a distinctive "trade dress," such as a special, uniform color (as Kodak does with its yellow film packages), a special "certificate of authenticity" (if appropriate) as some manufacturers do with their replicas of antique objects, and/or a unique advertising slogan. This type of enhanced uniqueness is not different or special enough to qualify for a utility patent, design patent, copyright, or trademark. However, you can acquire offensive rights, at least before it is made public, under trade secret law. (See Chapter 1, Section Q.) And the law of unfair competition may provide some rights once it is commercially unveiled (Chapter 1, Section R). Be sure to record the trade dress properly (see Chapter 3) before showing it to anyone, and be sure to use it (or have it used) consistently and as much as possible after marketing.

5. Provide Copyrightable Labeling

Look closely at some of the packaged products that you see in your home or on display in a store for a copyright notice, for example, "© 1980 S.C. Johnson & Son, Inc." This copyright is intended to cover either the wording on the label or container, the artwork thereon, or both. While relatively easy to design around (that is—come up with a close but noninfringing alternative), unique labeling with a copyright notice nevertheless provides a measure of offensive rights that is well worth the small effort it takes to invoke. Many market researchers have shown that an attractive label can make all the difference in the success of a product. Accordingly, it can pay, if you're marketing a packaged product, to spend some effort, either on your own or in hiring a designer, to come up with an attractive, unique label, affix a copyright notice, and apply for copyright registration. (See Chapter 1, Section P.)

6. Consider Trade Secret

Keep your invention secret, at least until you file. If you do offer it to any manufacturers, you should apprise them that it can be kept as a trade secret permanently, if it is trade-secretable. More on this in Section F, below.

E. Make and Sell Your Invention Yourself Without a Utility Patent Application (Chart Route 16-30-C)

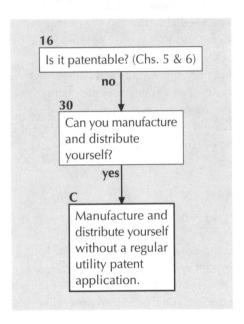

Here we assume again that you have an unpatentable invention. If you can make and distribute it yourself (Box 30), it's better to do so (Box C) than to try to sell it to a manufacturer outright. Even if you have a trademark (even a good one), a design patent application, distinctive trade dress, and/or a unique label, the absence of a utility patent application means a manufacturer does not get a really good privileged position, and so will generally not be as inclined to buy your invention. However, if you decide to manufacture the invention yourself, and you reach the market first, you'll have a significant marketing advantage despite the lack of a utility patent. Also, since you're the manufacturer, you'll make a much larger profit per item than if you received royalties from a manufacturer.

If you're not going to, or won't be able to, bring your invention to the market right away and you want to prevent anyone else from patenting it, consider making a "defensive publication" of it to create prior art on it. See Chapter 14, Section G, for how to make a defensive publication.

F. Manufacture and Distribute Your Invention Yourself, Keeping It as a Trade Secret (Chart Route 20-32-34-D)

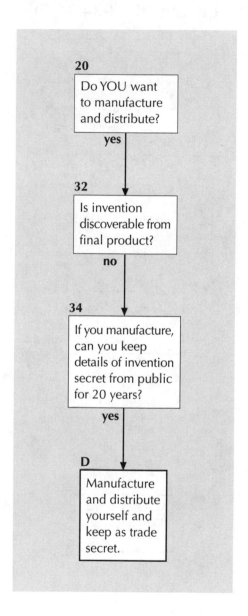

Even though your invention may be commercially valuable and patentable, it isn't always in your best interest to patent it. The alternative, when possible, is to keep an invention a trade secret and manufacture and sell the invention yourself, for example, by direct mail marketing, broadcast or periodical advertising, possibly eventually working your way up to conventional distributors and retailers. As explained in Chapter 1, Section Q, a trade secret has numerous advantages and disadvantages. While an invention can be maintained as a trade secret right up until the time a patent application is published or a patent actually issues, once it does the trade secret is lost. If you file a Nonpublication Request (NPR) at the time of filing, and you don't file for a patent outside the U.S., your application will never be published if it doesn't issue. In that case your invention will remain a trade secret as long as you continue to treat it as one and as long as the invention is not publicly disclosed by others, provided it can't be discovered from the final product (see next paragraph). Your application will not issue if you can't convince the PTO to grant you a patent, or you abandon it—for example, you don't respond to an Office Action or you don't pay the issue fee.

You'll be relieved to learn that it's very easy to keep and protect your invention as a trade secret. You simply identify what the trade secret or secrets are, write them up (use a notebook or invention disclosure as explained in Chapter 3), sign and date the write-up, and get it signed by two witnesses. You should not consider (and you can't protect) every bit of information as a trade secret. You can only protect secret information that has commercial value because it is not known by others. Write up this important information—the crown jewels. After you write it up, take normal precautions to keep the information secret. Keep your documentation safe, don't let anyone see it (or the actual manufacture of the product) unless they have a "need to know" (for example, an employee) and have signed a nondisclosure (keep-confidential) agreement. Also, keep the trade secret information out of any service or instruction manual that goes with the product. You don't need to file any governmental forms or applications for a trade secret.

Remember that you can't maintain trade secret rights on an invention unless it can't be discovered from the final product—even if sophisticated reverse engineering is used. One good example of an invention that was kept as a trade secret is the formula used in the Toni home permanent wave kit. Its inventor, Richard Harris, manufactured and sold the unpatented invention through his own company for many years, making large profits, and thereafter sold his business for $20 million when he decided to retire.

Although not specifically covered on the chart, there is another possibility in the trade secret category. That is, you may sell your invention to a manufacturer who may choose to keep it as a trade secret, provided you've filed an NPR at the time of filing. This may occur with either unpatentable or patentable inventions (Chart routes 16-24-26-28-30-B or 16-18-20-22-A), but you don't have to worry about this alternative since it's the manufacturer's choice, not yours. If you've filed an NPR, the manufacturer can simply allow the patent application to go abandoned so it won't be published, thereby maintaining the trade secret. While you may lose the ego boost of a possible patent, your bulging wallet should provide adequate alternative compensation.

⚠️ One disadvantage of keeping a "hardware" (as opposed to a process) invention as a trade secret is that someone else can validly patent the hardware if they invent it independently and can then sue you for patent infringement, even if you've been using the trade secret commercially for 20 years! However, under a new "prior user's rights" statute (35 USC 273), if someone has a method patent, but you've used the method commercially for over a year before the method patent application was filed, you have a complete defense to any action for patent infringement on the method.

💡 You shouldn't refer to your abandoned patent application in any other application that will issue as a patent, since anyone can gain access to an abandoned application that's referred to in a patent.

G. File Patent Application and Manufacture and Distribute Your Invention Yourself (Trade-Secretable Invention) (Chart Route 20-32-34-36-E)

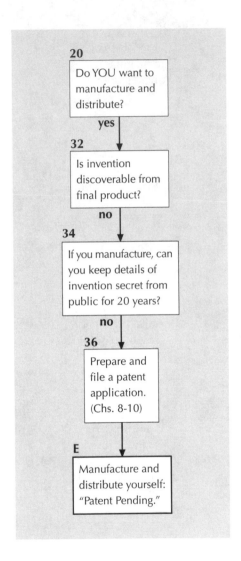

Suppose your invention is not discoverable from your final product (Box 32) so that you can keep it secret for a while, but not for the life of a patent (Box 34). Or, suppose, after evaluating the advantages and disadvantages of a trade secret under the criteria above, you don't wish to choose the trade-secret route, preferring instead to patent your invention. You should then prepare and file a patent application (Box 36) (see Chapters 8 to 10) and then manufacture and distribute the invention yourself with the notice "patent pending" affixed to the invention (Box E).

You may think that preparing and filing a patent application is a lot of hassle (it is), but if you have a patentable invention and a commercially viable product and you don't pay for a patent application now (by hiring an attorney or doing it yourself), you will pay for it later. If you have a successful product on the market, competitors will copy it. If you "go naked" by putting it out with no patent rights, you won't be able to stop the copiers and you'll lose far more market share than what the cost of a patent would have been.

Keep It Secret. While the patent application is pending, you should—provided you've filed an NPR—not publish any details of your invention. That way, if the patent application is finally rejected, you can allow it to go abandoned and still maintain your trade secret. Remember, by law, the PTO must keep your patent application secret until it's published (your application will be published 18 months after filing if no NPR was filed), or until it issues (if it was not published). In practice, the PTO is very strict in this regard. Until pending patent applications are published or they issue, outsiders have no access to them, and PTO personnel must keep patent applications in strict confidence. If you've filed a patent application without an NPR and decide to maintain your invention as a trade secret, you can still prevent the normal 18-month publication of the application by abandoning the application before it's published.

Effect of "Patent Pending" Notice. The patent-pending notice on your product does not confer any legal rights, but it is used by most manufacturers who have a patent application on file in order to deter potential competitors from copying their inventions. The notice effectively warns competitors that the manufacturer may get a patent on the product, so that if they do invest the money and effort in tooling to copy the invention, they could be enjoined from further manufacturing, with a consequent waste of their investment. However, make sure you don't use a patent-pending notice with a product that is not actually covered by a pending application: to do so is a criminal offense.

H. File Patent Application and Manufacture and Distribute Invention Yourself (Non-Trade-Secretable Invention) (Chart Route 20-32-38-36-E)

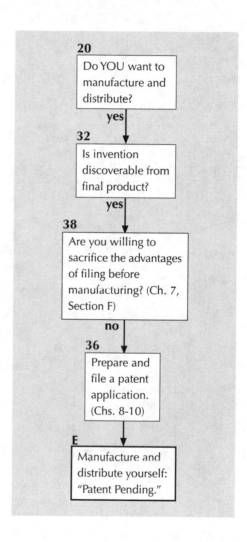

This will be the route followed by most inventors who wish to manufacture their own invention. Assume that the essence of your invention, like most, is discoverable from the final product (Box 32), and assume that it's cheaper to file a patent application than to manufacture and sell products embodying the invention yourself (Box 38). Alternatively, assume that you don't want to sacrifice the advantages of filing before manufacturing. In either case, you should prepare and file a patent application (Box 36) and then manufacture and distribute the invention yourself with the patent-pending notice (Box E).

I. Test Market Before Filing (Chart Route 20-32-38-40-F)

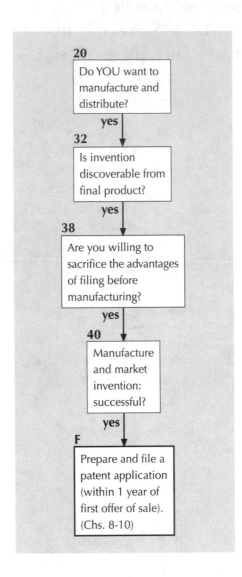

Although I know you'd like to manufacture and test market your invention before filing a patent application on it, I generally don't recommend marketing before filing for patentable inventions because of the following:

1. You have less than one year to do the test marketing because of the "one-year rule" (Chapter 5, Section E).

2. You may get discouraged unjustifiably if you try to market your invention and you aren't successful; that is—you probably will be too discouraged to file a patent application and therefore you'll lose all rights on the invention forever.

3. You'll lose your foreign rights, since most foreign countries or jurisdictions, including the European Patent Office (see Chapter 12), have an absolute novelty requirement, which means that if the invention was made public anywhere before its first filing date, such publication will prevent the issuance of a valid patent.

4. There is a possibility of theft, since anyone who sees it can (assuming it's not trade secretable) copy it and file a fraudulent patent application on it.

5. There are business disadvantages when:
   - the product has a short or seasonal selling period or limited market life;
   - test marketing would disclose an easily copyable product to competitors;
   - the cost of test marketing would be so high as to outweigh the risk of regular marketing;
   - the product is merely a response to competition; or
   - market conditions in the field are changing so fast that the results of a market test would soon be obsolete. (*Wall St. Journal*, 1984 Aug. 27, p. 12.)

So, assuming your invention is discoverable from the final product (Box 32), ask yourself whether it's easier and cheaper to manufacture and test market it than to file a patent application. If it is, and if you're also willing to sacrifice the above five advantages of filing before manufacturing (Box 38), and the above business disadvantages don't apply, you can manufacture and market your invention (Box 40) before filing. While you're test marketing, you can put a warning notice (no legal effect, but possibly a deterrent one) on your product, such as "Patent Rights Reserved," as Federal Express did on its envelopes.

If you discover, within about nine months of the date you first introduce your product, that it is a successful invention and likely to have good commercial success, begin immediately to prepare your patent application (Box F), so that you'll be able to get it on file within one year of the date you first offered it for sale or used it to make a commercial product.

If your manufacturing and market tests (Box 40) are not successful, you should generally drop the invention and concentrate on something else (Box X), although you still have the right to get a patent on your invention. Thus, if the market test is unsuccessful, but you feel that you don't want to give the invention up forever, by all means follow the line, and prepare and file the patent application (regular or PPA) within one year of the first offer of sale (Box F). If you do manufacture and market your invention, and then later file a patent application on it, be sure to retain all of your records and paperwork regarding the conception, building, testing, and manufacturing of your invention; these can be vital if you ever get into an interference. (See Chapter 13, Section K.)

Now that we've covered all possible routes on the chart, I hope you've found one that will meet your needs. If your choice is to file a patent application, move on to Chapters 8 to 10; if you want to try to market your invention first, skip over to Chapter 11. Chapter 10 also covers design patents.

Patent Application Software Now Available

To facilitate and partially automate the preparation of a patent application, a computer program *PatentEase* is now available. This program will take you step-by-step through the entire process of preparing a patent application. The program contains copious examples of every part of a patent application. Further, it automates many tasks associated with the preparation of an application. The *PatentEase* program runs under the Windows™ operating system and is available from Nolo.

J. Summary

After you make your patentability decision and evaluate the commercial potential of your invention, you have a number of possible routes to take. If you feel that your invention lacks commercial potential, drop it and move on to something else. If you feel that it has commercial potential, but you can't prepare a patent application, try to sell it without filing one. If your invention is patentable, file first and then try to sell it to a manufacturer. (You should file first to secure your rights, especially if you sign a manufacturer's waiver form.)

If your invention isn't patentable, you may be able to file a design patent application, secure trademark rights, copyright, or trade dress rights before offering it to a manufacturer. You can make and sell the invention yourself with or without a patent application, and you can keep it a trade secret after putting it on the market if it's the type of invention that can't be reverse engineered. Although test marketing before filing can provide helpful information, it also involves risk of theft and loss of foreign patenting rights. ∎

Chapter 8

How to Draft the Specification and Initial Drawings

Inventor's Commandment #10

The specification and drawings of your patent application must contain a description of your invention in full, clear, concise, and exact terms so that anyone having ordinary skill in the field will be readily able to make and use it. You must also disclose the best mode for carrying out the invention.

Inventor's Commandment #11

In your patent application, you should "sell" your invention to the examiner or anyone else who may read the application. State all the disadvantages of the prior art and all the advantages of your invention in the introduction, the operation sections, and a conclusion.

This and the next two chapters are the heart of this book: they cover the writing and transmittal of your patent application to the Patent and Trademark Office (PTO). This chapter provides an overview of the patent application drafting process and contains specific instructions on drafting a specification and preliminary drawings. Chapter 9 explains how to draft patent claims (sentence fragments that delineate the precise scope of the patent being sought). Chapter 10 explains how to "final" the application as well as the precise steps involved in transmitting it to the PTO. In addition, Chapter 10 covers design patent applications.

Because these subjects can be difficult to understand in the abstract, I use concrete examples throughout. And, at the end of this chapter, you'll find the specification (including the abstract) and formal drawings of a sample patent application. Similarly, at the end of Chapter 9, you'll find the patent claims of this same application. The completed formal papers for this application appear at the end of Chapter 10.

Have you filed a Provisional Patent Application (PPA)? As a result of legislation enacted in 1999, you may now convert the PPA to a regular patent application (RPA) even if the PPA did not include any claims. (35 USC § 111.) I don't recommend converting the PPA to an RPA, because your patent will expire 20 years from the date of your PPA (rather than your RPA).

If you filed a PPA and are ready to file your RPA, I recommend that you file a separate RPA to start the 20-year term from the date of your RPA. To file a separate RPA, follow the instructions in this chapter for preparing an RPA from scratch. You should claim the benefit of the PPA in the RPA. If the one-year anniversary of your PPA falls on a weekend or holiday, you can still get the benefit of the PPA by filing the RPA on the next business day. Remember that your PPA will not be read by any PTO personnel unless you need to rely on its date to predate a reference cited against your claims or in case you're unfortunate enough to get into an interference (a situation in which two pending patent applications by different applicants claim the same invention).

A. Lay Inventors *Can* Do It!

It's a common myth that a lay inventor won't be able to prepare a patent application, or prepare it properly. Having worked with many lay inventors I dispute this vigorously. I have found that lay inventors can and have done very good jobs, often better than patent attorneys, by following this book. To prepare a proper patent application, you should be mainly concerned with three basic, essential considerations:

1. The specification (description and operation of your invention and drawings) should be detailed enough so that there will be no doubt that one skilled in the art will be able to make and use the invention after reading it.

2. The main claims should be as broad as the prior art permits. (More about this in Chapter 9.)

3. You should "sell" your invention by stressing all of its advantages.

If you satisfy these three criteria, you'll be home free. All the other matters are of lesser import and can be fixed if necessary. I'll show you how to satisfy these three main criteria in this and the next chapter. Now let's get started by looking at what's contained in a patent application.

B. What's Contained in a Patent Application

A regular patent application consists of the following parts, which are all sent together to the PTO after assembly in the following order:

1. A self-addressed receipt postcard (see Chapter 10, Section I3)

2. A check or, if paying by credit card, a completed Form PTO-2038 for the filing fee (see Appendix 4, Fee Schedule)

3. A Transmittal Letter and a Fee Transmittal (Forms 10-2 and 10-3)

4. A Nonpublication Request (NPR) (Form 10-7). Send this if you don't want the application to be published 18 months after filing (if it's still pending then) and save the publication fee or if you want to keep your invention secret if it doesn't issue

5. A drawing or drawings of the invention—either formal or informal (see Chapter 10, Sections A-D)

6. A specification containing the following sections:

    a. TITLE* of the Invention (no more than 500 characters)

    b. CROSS-REFERENCE TO RELATED APPLICATIONS*† This is used to refer to and claim priority of any PPA or prior related applications that you've filed.

    c. FEDERALLY SPONSORED RESEARCH*† This is used to indicate that the invention was made under a government contract and that the government has rights in it.

    d. SEQUENCE LISTING OR PROGRAM*† This is used to indicate if the application contains a biotech sequence listing or computer program as an Appendix, on microfiche, or on CD-ROM.

    e. BACKGROUND OF THE INVENTION*—Field of Invention. This indicates the technical field of the invention. Background of the Invention also includes the two subsections below, Prior Art and Objects and Advantages.

    f. Prior Art. This Background section should state any problems that the invention solves and discuss and criticize the relevant prior art (previous relevant developments in the same technological areas).

    g. Objects and Advantages. This Background section should list all the positive aspects of your invention.

    h. SUMMARY* The Summary should briefly describe the invention as claimed.

    i. DRAWINGS*†—Figures. This is a brief listing of the Drawing figures and may include the subsection below, Reference Numerals.

    j. Reference Numerals (optional but desirable). These are the Drawing numbers that designate the respective parts of your invention, such as 10 motor, 12 shaft, etc.

    k. DETAILED DESCRIPTION*—Preferred Embodiment—Figs 1-X. This is a narrative description of the structure of the invention's main embodiment.

If the invention contains a program listing which is not extensive (over about ten pages), include it here or in the drawings. If it is long enough to be put on microfiche, put it in a microfiche appendix or on a CD-ROM. Detailed Description also includes the three subsections below, Operation—Preferred Embodiment, Description—Additional Embodiment, and Operation—Additional Embodiment.

    l. Operation—Preferred Embodiment. This portion of the Detailed Description explains how the main embodiment of the invention works or operates.

    m. Description—Additional Embodiment—Figs Y-Z. This portion of the Detailed Description describes the structure of an alternative embodiment, if you have one.

    n. Operation—Additional Embodiment. This portion of the Detailed Description describes the operation of the alternative embodiment. (Repeat sections l. and m., above, for all additional embodiments.)

    o. Conclusion, Ramifications, and Scope. This part again summarizes the invention's advantages, the alternative physical forms or uses it can take, and a broadening paragraph to remind any judge that it shouldn't be limited to the particular form(s) shown.

7. CLAIMS* These are precise sentence fragments that delineate the exact nature of your invention—see Chapter 9.

8. SEQUENCE LISTING*† Include this heading only if a nucleotide or amino acid sequence is part of the invention and you provide it on paper.

9. ABSTRACT* This is a brief summary of the entire specification. It is technically considered part of the specification.

10. A completed Patent Application Declaration (PAD) form. The PAD is a statement under penalty of perjury that you're the true inventor and that you acknowledge a duty to keep the PTO informed of all material information and prior art related to your invention. (A Small-Entity Declaration is no longer needed.)

11. A Disclosure Document Reference Letter (Form 3-4). This ties your application to any disclosure document you previously filed.

12. An Information Disclosure Statement, List of Prior Art Cited by Applicant (Forms 10-5 and 10-6), and copies of such prior art. Technically, these aren't part of the patent application, but since they're supposed to be sent to the PTO with or soon after the application, I've included them here. These inform the PTO of relevant prior art or any circumstances known to you

---

* This should appear as a section heading in all capital letters without boldface or underlining.

† If this section is not applicable, the phrase "not applicable" should follow the heading.

that may potentially affect the novelty or obviousness of your invention.

Note that a printed patent contains additional data, such as references cited, field of search, and so on. You should *not* include this additional data in your patent application. The PTO will add this data when they print the patent.

A Provisional Patent Application (PPA) must include some, but not all, of the parts just listed for a regular patent application. The parts that must be included for a PPA are:

- items 1-3, and 5 (postcard, payment, transmittal letter, fee transmittal, and drawings)
- items 6a (title), 6i (drawing figures), 6k (description— main embodiment), 6l (operation—main embodiment), and 6m and n (description and operation— alternative embodiments).

Note that the PPA uses a different transmittal letter (Form 3-5) and has a different fee. (See Appendix 4, Fee Schedule.)

The PTO's Rule 77 (37 CFR 1.77) states that the elements of a patent application should be arranged in the above order with the above headings in capital letters. I thus recommend that you use this format for smoothest sailing of your application through the PTO. However, since the headings are rather broad and don't break your application into enough easily digestible parts—as this book does—I recommend you add the additional headings in the above list which are in first letter capitals. I also recommend that you add any further headings you think would be useful, especially if your application is long or technically complex.

C. What Happens When Your Application Is Received by the PTO

When your application arrives at the PTO, it will go to the OIPE (Office of Initial Patent Examination) whose clerical personnel will deposit your check or process your credit card payment. They'll put all of your papers in a folder (termed a "file wrapper"), assign a filing date and serial number to your application, put this information onto your postcard, and return it. Then they'll send you an official filing receipt and forward your file to the drafting department, where your drawings will be reviewed for formal requirements. A drawing objection slip will be put in your file if your drawings have any formal errors, such as blurred lines. They may send you a notice stating that your application will not be examined until you file replacement drawings; if so, file corrected drawings in the time allotted. Once your drawings are approved, your file will be sent to an appropriate examining division.

Within a few months to a year, your application will be reviewed by an examiner who will usually send you an "Office Action." (Examiners rarely allow an application upon first review.) The Office Action will do one or more of the following:

- object to one or more aspects of your specification
- reject some or all of your claims because of imprecise language, or
- reject some or all of your claims because of unpatentability over the prior art.

To overcome these objections and/or rejections, you'll have to submit an "Amendment" (Chapter 13) in which you:

- make changes, additions, or deletions in the drawings, specification, or claims; and/or
- convince the examiner that the Office Action was in error.

Your application will be published 18 months from your earliest claimed filing date, unless you filed an NPR at the time of filing. If you filed the NPR, the information in your patent application will become publicly available only if a patent eventually issues. If you file the NPR and later decide to foreign file (see Chapter 12), you must rescind your NPR (use Form 10-7) within 45 days.

If the examiner eventually decides to allow the application (either as originally presented or as amended), you'll be sent a Notice of Allowance which gives you three months to pay an issue fee, a publication fee if applicable, and fix any drawing errors. Your specification and claims, along with certain other information (your name, address, and a list of all prior art cited by the examiner), will then be sent to the U.S. Government Printing Office. There they'll be printed verbatim as your patent. From filing to issuance, the process usually takes somewhere between six months to three years, but sometimes longer.

 Model of Invention. You never have to furnish or demonstrate a working model of your invention. However, in rare cases, if the examiner questions the operability of your invention, such as if you claim a perpetual motion or energy machine, one way for you to prove operability is by demonstrating a working model. Working models are also useful to enable the examiner to understand and appreciate the commercial or intrinsic value of your invention.

D. Do Preliminary Work Before Preparing Your Patent Application

Before you begin the actual writing of your patent application or prepare any of the forms that go along with it, it's wise to make thorough preparations. Having worked on many patent applications, I can tell you that if adequate preparations are made beforehand, the actual writing of the application will go far more smoothly and will rarely take more than several partial days. Here are the basic preparatory steps:

1. Review the Prior Art

Assemble all your prior-art references, including any references gleaned from textbooks, magazines, or journals you've searched or discovered that are relevant to your invention or to the field of your invention. Read each of these references carefully, noting the terms used for the parts or steps that are similar to those of your invention. Write down the terms of the more unusual parts and, if necessary, look them up in your prior-art patents, textbooks, magazine articles (see Appendix 3, Glossary of Useful Technical Terms), or a visual dictionary (see Appendix 2, Resources: Government Publications, Patent Websites, and Books of Use and Interest). In this way you'll be familiar with the term for every art and its precise meaning. Also, note the way the drawings in these prior-art references are arranged and laid out. Pay particular attention to what parts are done in detail and what parts need be shown only very roughly or generally because they are well known or are not essential to the invention.

If you see any prior-art patent whose specification contains words, descriptions, and/or drawing figures that you can use in your application, feel free to plagiarize! Patents are not covered by copyright and it's considered perfectly legal and ethical to make use of them.

2. Review Your Disclosure

In Chapter 3, I strongly advised that you prepare a description (with sketches) of your invention and have this signed and witnessed, either in a laboratory notebook or on a separate piece of paper, called an invention disclosure. Review this now to be sure you have all of the details of your invention drawn or sketched in understandable form and that the description of your invention is complete. If you haven't done this yet, do it now, referring to Chapter 3 when necessary.

3. Ramifications

Write down all of the known ramifications (potentially different uses and methods of operation) and embodiments (other forms which the invention can take). That is, record all other materials that will work for each part of your invention, other possible uses your invention can be put to, and other possible modifications of your invention. Think of ways in which its size or shape can be altered, parts (or steps in its manufacture) that can be eliminated, and so on. If your invention is a process or method, other ramifications and embodiments can be different materials that your inventive process modifies, variations of your process, and different environments in which the process can be used.

The more ramifications and embodiments you can think of, the broader your patent claims will be interpreted, and the more you'll be able to block others from obtaining patents either on devices similar to your invention or on improvements to it. Also, you'll have something to fall back on if your main or basic embodiment is "knocked out" by prior art that your search didn't uncover or that surfaced after your search.

For instance, suppose your invention is a delaying device that you use to close the lid of a box automatically a few moments after the lid is opened. Another embodiment that could make advantageous use of the delaying device might be in a "roly-poly man" toy to make the man stand up again automatically a few moments after he's tipped over. If you have a process or software-related invention on a process for categorizing investments, alternative embodiments might be the use of the process to categorize inventory hardware or recipes.

Several Related Inventions. If you have two or more related inventions, such as a car radio mount and a housing for the same radio, you may show, describe, and claim both in the same application. The examiner may allow both inventions at once and you'll save fees and effort. However, you're allowed only one invention per filing fee, so the examiner may require you to restrict your application to one invention (Chapter 13, Section M). If so, you can easily file a divisional application (Chapter 14, Section D) on the other inventions before the original application issues and still get the benefit of your original application's filing date. However, under the GATT law, passed Dec. 1994, your original application and any divisionals you file will expire 20 years from the filing date of your original application. Keep this in mind and don't file your divisionals long after your original filing date. The advantage of filing a divisional later is that you postpone the second filing fee a year or two, and you'll avoid paying it altogether if you find the invention hasn't panned out and you decide to drop it. (In any case, don't include several inventions on one application if they're from different inventors.)

4. Sources of Supply

Suppose your invention contemplates the use of an exotic or uncommon material or component, or involves unusual manufacturing steps. In this case you must obtain the names and addresses of potential suppliers and/or identify textbooks or other references outlining how one should obtain or make such unusual elements or procedures. Describe these unusual dimensions, materials, or components in detail.

For example, with an electrical circuit, you generally don't have to include the technical values or identifications of components. However, if the operation of the circuit is at all unusual, or if any component values are critical, or if it contains a possibly novel feature, write down their names or identifications. With a chemical invention, write down the source or full identification of how to make any unusual or possibly novel components or reactions. With a mechanical invention, if any unusual or possibly novel parts, assembly steps, or materials are required, be sure you provide a full description and reference as to where to obtain or how to perform them.

The reason why you will need the full details of any special aspects of your invention is simple. Section 112 of the patent laws (35 USC 112) mandates that the specification must be a "full, clear, concise, and exact" description of the invention such that anyone skilled in the art can make and use it without too much effort. In addition, if any feature is possibly novel, you may have to claim it specifically, so you will want to provide adequate terminology in the specification to support your claim language.

5. Advantages/Disadvantages

List all disadvantages of the relevant prior art that your invention overcomes, referring to the checklist in Chapter 4 (Form 4-2) to make sure your listing is complete. Then list all the advantages of your invention over the prior art, and all of your invention's general disadvantages.

Now that we have reviewed these vital preliminary steps, let's turn to writing the specification.

E. Flowchart

To get you oriented, I've provided, in Fig. 8A below, a self-explanatory flowchart of the entire application preparation process. Steps A to O are covered in Chapter 8, Steps P to T in Chapter 9, and Steps U to W in Chapter 10.

F. Writing Your Patent Specification to Comply With the Full Disclosure Rules

In writing the specification of a patent application, including a PPA, your goal is to disclose clearly everything you can think of about your invention. In case of doubt as to whether or not to include an item of information, put it in. The statutory provision that mandates the inclusion of all this information in your patent application is Section 112 of the patent laws, paragraph 1, which reads as follows:

"The specification shall contain a written description of the invention, and of the manner and process of making and using it, in such full, clear, concise and exact terms as to enable any person skilled in the art to which it pertains, or with which it is most nearly connected, to make and use the same, and shall set forth the best mode contemplated by the inventor of carrying out the invention."

As part of doing this, it may help if you keep well in mind the "exchange theory" of patents. The government grants you a patent (that is, a monopoly on your invention) for a term of 17 to 19 years in exchange for your disclosing to the public the full details of your invention (how to make and use it). In this way the public will get the full benefit of your creativity after your patent expires. Complete disclosure involves disclosing how to make and use the invention and at least one "best mode" of the invention as presently contemplated by you, the inventor. So, if you have several different embodiments of your invention, make sure you identify the one you currently favor. If you can't decide which embodiment is the best, it's okay to list each embodiment and tell its relative advantages and disadvantages. For example, in the delay device referred to above, its use to close a box lid after a few minutes might be your presently preferred embodiment, and the delayed "roly-poly man" might be an alternative embodiment. In this case you need merely state that the box is your preferred practical application of the delay device.

Another reason for disclosing as much as you can about your invention is, as stated, to block others from getting a subsequent improvement patent on your invention. Suppose you invent something and disclose only one embodiment of

Review
A. Review your invention disclosure and all prior art thoroughly.

Rough Sketches
B. Make rough CAD or penciled sketches of invention in separate, numbered Figs. Show every aspect of invention and ramifications, mainly in perspective views.

Name Parts
C. Pencil a suitable name or names adjacent to every part in the drawings—for example "lever," "pivot," etc.

Title *
D. Type a meaningful title that includes some novelty of the invention—for example, "Chair With Water-Filled Seat."

Cross-Reference to Related Applications*
E. Under this heading provide a cross-reference to any parent applications and a claim to priority of any PPA that you've filed.

Federally Sponsored Research *
F. Put in the statement required by your gov't contract or "nonapplicable."

Sequence Listing or Program*
G. Indicate if the application contains a sequence or program or type "non-applicable."

Background of the Inventions*
H. Indicate field of invention. One sentence is adequate—for example, "This application relates to bicycles, particularly to a derailleur."

Background of the Invention * —Prior Art
I. Under this heading indicate the problems of the prior art, if any, and describe and knock all prior art.

Background of the Invention* —Objects and Advantages
J. State the objects and advantages of your invention and add a general O and A statement.

Summary *
K. Prepare a brief summary of your claimed invention. The summary can be a simple paraphrase of your main claim.

Drawings*—Figures
L. Type a "Drawing Figures" section. Use one brief sentence to describe each Fig. without details of the invention.

Drawings *—Reference Numerals
M. While doing Step M, list your reference numbers on Form 8-1 and write them at appropriate places on the drawing Figs., using lead lines. Later insert this list after Drawing Figures.

Detailed Description *— Preferred Embodiment
N. Type a "Description—Fig(s) 1-X" section. Describe overall structure of main embodiment, then structure and function of parts and their inter-connections. Number each part (10, 12, etc.).

Operation—Fig(s) 1-X
O. Write an "Operation—Fig(s) 1-X" section. Describe in detail the operation, use, and advantages of the structure in these Figs.

Repeat Steps M, N, and O
P. Repeat Steps M, N, and O as necessary for all other sets of figures and embodiments.

Conclusion, Ramification, Scope
Q. Type a "Conclusion, Ramifications, and Scope" section. Repeat advantages, describe less important ramifications, and add broadening paragraph.

Claims *—I/We Claim
R. Type first independent claim: type name of invention, then describe essential parts and their interconnections. Then broaden by eliminating as many parts as possible and generalizing remaining parts.

Dependent Claims
S. Type a set of dependent claims. Each must add feature(s) ["The widget of claim 1, further including"] or recite existing features more specifically ["The widget of claim 1 wherein"].

Second Main Claim
T. Type an additional independent claim, phrased differently than the first one.

Second Set of Dependent Claims
U. Type a second set of dependent claims, if possible. These can be similar to the first set of dependent claims.

More Sets of Claims
V. Repeat Steps T & U if possible. Don't exceed three independent or 20 total claims, unless justified.

Sequence Listing *
W. If applicable, type a sequence listing, starting on a separate sheet.

Abstract
X. Type Abstract: describe essence of structure and operation of invention and ramifications. Add reference numbers in parentheses.

Final Drawing (Chapter 10)
Y. On drawings, remove part names (unless unusual), combine Figs. on same sheet, as possible, and neaten or final.

Final Application
Z. Insert claims after "Conclusion..." and before Abstract. Start claims and abstract on new pages. Use consecutive numbers. Final specification and claims.

Final Check & Formal Papers
AA. Check all reference numbers and part names and proofread carefully. Do formal papers. Mail application with check and receipt postcard.

Fig. 8A—Steps in Preparing a Patent Application
* This word or words should appear as a section heading in all capitals without boldface.

it, or only one way to do it. If you get a patent that shows only that one embodiment, someone may later see your patent and think of another embodiment or another way to do it that may be better than yours. This person will then be able to file a new patent application on this "improvement invention" and thereby, assuming a patent is issued, obtain a monopoly on the improvement. If this occurs, you won't be able to make, use, or sell the improvement without a license from the person who owns that patent. This is so even though you have a patent on the basic invention.

"New Matter" May Not Be Added After Filing

What happens if you don't put enough information in about your invention to enable "one skilled in the art" to make and use it without undue effort? Either your entire application can be rejected under Section 112 on the grounds of "incomplete disclosure," or it may be later invalidated if an infringer challenges it when you try to enforce it. Also, if your patent application is rejected because of incomplete disclosure, usually there is nothing you can do since you aren't allowed to add any "new matter" (additional technical information) to a pending application. (See Chapter 13, Inventor's Commandment 24.) In other words, "You must get it right the first time." While many inventors object to and rail against the "no-new-matter rule" ("Why can't I add improvements to my application?"), a moment's thought will convince you that the rule has a good purpose. Without the rule, an applicant could continuously add improvements and modifications, so that the filing date would be meaningless.

As mentioned earlier, you must provide enough information in your patent application to enable anyone working in the field of your invention to be able to build and use it, without undue effort. That is, anyone in the field must be able to make a working version of your invention from the information contained in your patent application. However, to comply with this section, you ordinarily don't have to put in dimensions, materials, and values of components, since the skilled artisan is expected to have a working knowledge of these items. However, as described above, dimensions, materials, or components that are critical to the performance of your invention, or that are at all unusual, *must* be included. If in doubt, include this specific information.

Finally, having reviewed many patent applications prepared by laypersons, I find that the most common error in preparing the specification of a patent application is a failure to include enough detail about the invention, or enough ramifications. Thus, if you "sweat the details" like a good professional does, you'll seldom go wrong.

Common Misconception: A patent specification should not include details of the invention since this will limit the invention to such details.

Fact: The scope of the invention is determined by the claims; so including details in the specification will not limit its scope.

Software Note. If your invention includes a microprocessor and an application program for it, either in software or in firmware, you should either include a source or object code listing of the program with your patent application, or a detailed flowchart. The flowchart should be detailed enough so that a programmer having no more than ordinary skill would be able to use your chart to write the program and debug it without undue effort or significant creativity—even if the task would take several months.

Biotechnology Note. If your invention requires a microorganism or a fusion gene that is not widely available, you must make a deposit of your "special" bug or plasmid in an approved depository. See MPEP (*Manual of Patent Examining Procedure*), 608.01(p)(c), and Chapter 2400, referred to in Appendix 2. If your application contains a nucleotide or amino acid sequence, you must describe your sequence according to the PTO's sequence rules. See MPEP 2420 et seq. for the rules and availability of a program called "PatentIn" for submitting the sequence in electronic form. Applicants can now file program listings and biotech sequence lists on a CD-ROM (in duplicate for program listings, see Rule 52(e)). When a program has 300 lines or fewer (72 characters per line), you can submit it on drawing sheets or in the specification. (If it has more than 60 lines, put it at the end of the specification.) When it has more than 300 lines, it *must* be on a CD-ROM.

Trademarked Chemical Note. If your invention uses a trademarked chemical—such as "Ajax developer"—and you don't know its composition, see if any other similar chemicals will work. If so, you can just refer to the chemical by its generic name, with a reference to a suitable manufacturer—for example, "developer, preferably Ajax brand, sold by Ajax Chemical Company, Inverness Park, California." If the trademarked chemical is critical, try your best to find its generic constituents—for example, by contacting the company or doing research. One clever inventor found the composition by calling a Poison Control Center hotline. If you can't find the constituents, you'll have to refer to the chemical by its trademark and manufacturer, but this can limit your invention severely.

Formula Note. You can enter formulas in the text the same way you would do if you were writing a college paper or textbook. However, it's best to avoid formulas, Greek letters, and subscripts, if at all possible: the printer may get them wrong, and if your patent ever gets into court, they'll turn off a lay judge. Remember, the "KISS" rule (Keep It Simple, Stupid!).

G. Software, Computer-Related Inventions, and Business Methods

Many inventors have asked me if I planned to write a separate book on how to patent software. I always answer in the negative. This is because I believe there is no need for such a book: patent applications for software and other computer-related inventions are prepared under the same rules and with the same general considerations as for any other invention.

The same is true for business method and Internet-related patents (see Chapter 5, Section C1c). While all of these inventions are new, iconoclastic to established practice, and difficult to search, they must be described and claimed in the same manner as any "old-fashioned" invention.

The main consideration applicable to these inventions is in meeting the full disclosure requirement. As stated in the preceding section, a patent application must contain a sufficiently detailed description of the invention so that one having ordinary skill in the art to which it pertains, or to which it is most nearly connected, will be able to make and use the invention without undue effort. In practice, the PTO and courts strictly enforce this requirement when software, computer-related inventions, or business method inventions are involved, since the newness of the field makes most people less comfortable with it. So if you're preparing a patent application on a software, computer-related invention, or business method invention, be absolutely sure that no one will ever be able to challenge it for "incomplete disclosure." That is, make absolutely sure it contains a "full, clear, concise, and exact" description of the invention and how to make and use it.

How should you fulfill this requirement in practice with software inventions? Virtually every software invention uses a computer program of some sort, whether it's in a PROM (programmed read-only memory) or a separate program on a disk which is used with a general-purpose computer. To fulfill the complete disclosure requirement, it is essential that you disclose either a listing of the program or a detailed flow-chart of the operations and steps involved with the invention that a programmer can use to create a working version.

If you've already written the program, the easiest way to provide the necessary disclosure is to supply the listing as part of the patent application. (See "Computer Programs Note" in Section I, below, for how to do this.) The listing can be in machine-readable form (object code) only; you *don't* have to supply the listing in humanly readable form (source code), since the requirement says you need merely disclose how to make and use it; you do not have to enable the public to modify it.

You should explain in the specification how to implement the listing and any special instructions which may be necessary to implement the invention without undue experimentation. The explanation should detail how to configure the computer to perform the required function and interrelate with any other elements to yield the claimed invention. For instance, you should state what programming language the listing is in (for example, "C++"), how to use it to control the computer or microprocessor, what type of computer or microprocessor to use it with (for instance, "a Pentium chip"), and what hardware should be connected to the computer, both on the input and output sides as necessary (for instance, "a MIDI interface" and "a laser printer").

Of course you can also provide the source code and a flowchart, but to frustrate potential competition, I recommend you supply only the object code. The program should be free of any serious bugs and should not have too many minor bugs (virtually no program is 100% bug free). In other words, no one should be able to say your listing wouldn't function according to its specifications. (The PTO won't test your program, but if you get a patent and later seek to enforce it during license negotiations or in court, your adversary will!)

If you choose to provide only a flowchart, make sure it's complete and detailed enough to enable any reasonably skilled programmer to write a program, using only routine skills. The flowchart will be adequate even if it would take a programmer several months to write the program, so long as only routine skill and not extraordinary effort will be involved. In this connection, I like to think of a flowchart like the plans for a building: if the plans are adequate for an ordinary builder to construct the building, they will be adequate, even if it will take the builder several months, or

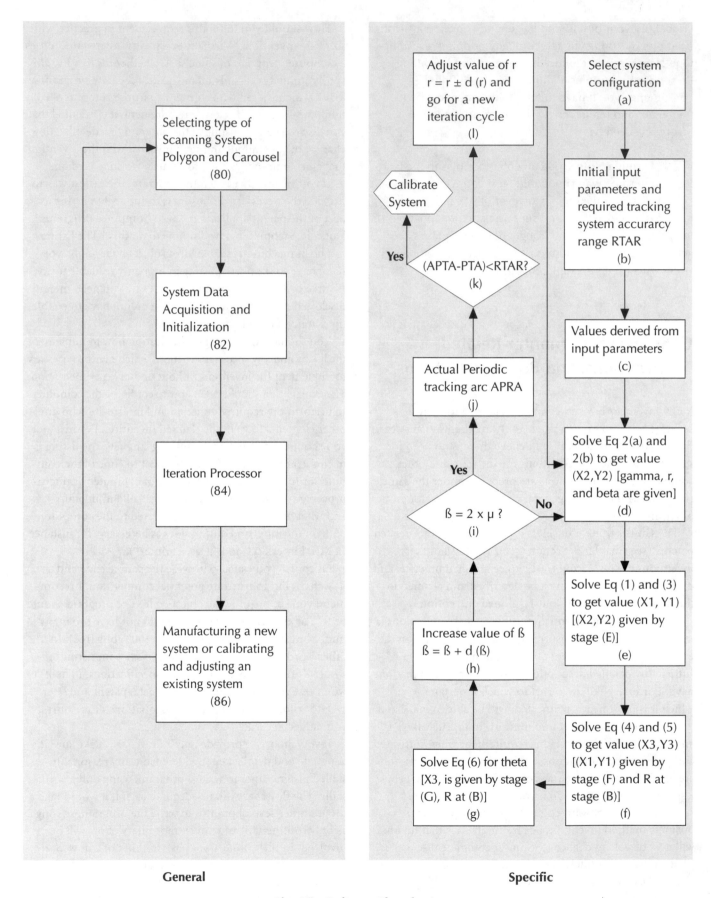

General   **Specific**

Fig. 8B—Software Flowcharts

even a year or more. However, if the plans are rough and sketchy, so that the builder has to hire an architect to complete them, or has to use a lot of imagination to fill in gaps, then they're inadequate. Fig. 8B shows adequately detailed flowcharts (from U.S. Pat. No. 5,170,279, 1992 Dec 8) in two parts: general and specific. The associated explanation in the specification (not provided) discusses each block in detail, lists the equations referred to in the blocks, and explains exactly how to implement the flowchart. Applicants can now file program listings and biotech sequence lists on a CD-ROM (in duplicate for program listings, see Rule 52(e)). When a program has 300 lines or less (72 characters per line), you can submit it on drawing sheets or in the specification. (If it has more than 60 lines, put it at the end of the specification.) When it has more than 300 lines, it *must* be on a CD-ROM.

H. First Prepare Sketches and Name Parts

Before you even begin the actual nuts and bolts preparation of your specification, you should make (or have made for you) penciled sketches of your invention. These will form the basis of the drawings you'll eventually send to the PTO along with your patent application. (See Chapter 10, Section A). Your sketches will also be the foundation of your application. In other words, you'll build from these as you write your specification and claims.

The main reason I discuss sketches at this point is that you have to do your sketches prior to drafting the specification, as well as the other parts of the application. You don't have to worry about planning any layout of your figures on the drawing sheets, or the size of the figures—yet. This will be covered in detail in Chapter 10. For now, merely complete a set of sketches showing all of the aspects of your invention without worrying about size or arrangement; these sketch-figures can even be done very large and on separate sheets. Later on they can be reduced and compiled onto the drawing sheets as part of the "finaling" process (Chapter 10).

After you've completed your sketches, write down a name for each part adjacent to such part in each sketch, such as "handlebar," "handgrip," "clamp," "bolt," etc. Write the names of the parts lightly in pencil so that you can change them readily if you think of a better term. Use lead lines to connect each name to its part if the parts are crowded enough to cause confusion. If you have any difficulty naming any part, refer to the Glossary of Useful Terms (Appendix 3), your prior-art patents, or a visual dictionary such as *The Firefly Visual Dictionary* by Corbeil and Archambaul (Firefly Books,

2002) or the *Visual Dictionary of Science* (DK Publishing, 1998).

Your drawing should be done in separate, unconnected figures, each one labeled ("Fig. 1," "Fig. 2," etc.) so that all possible different views and embodiments of your invention are shown. Use as many views as necessary. Look at a relevant prior-art patent to get an idea as to how it's done. The views should generally be perspective or isometric views, rather than front, side, and top, engineering-type views. If you have trouble illustrating a perspective view, take a photo of a model of your invention from the desired angle and draw the photo—perhaps by enlarging and tracing it. Alternatively you can use a "see and draw" copying device of the type employing a half-silvered mirror in a viewing head on a pedestal; these are available in art supply stores and through gadget mail-order houses. Hidden lines should be shown in broken lines, as shown in Fig. 8C. For complicated machines, exploded views are desirable as shown in Fig. 8D.

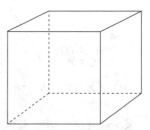

Fig. 8C—Isometric View With Hidden Lines

You can use any reasonable symbols for mechanical, electronic/electrical, and chemical parts; the PTO has no requirements in this area, except that the symbols not be outrageous. I suggest you use conventional symbols, such as those approved by the ANSI (American National Standards Institute), those used in conventional texts, or those used in your prior-art patents. In lieu of graphical symbols, labeled boxes are also acceptable, so long as the part represented by the box is standard or conventional.

If you have an electronic system, a block diagram with each block labeled (for example, "Schmitt Trigger," "flip-flop," "inverter") is fine. If any block represents a non-conventional circuit, however, be sure that you explain clearly what's in the block or provide a reference to a suitable publication. If any block represents a programmed microprocessor or computer, remember that you must provide a listing of the program or a software flowchart to provide a complete disclosure. (See Section F, above.)

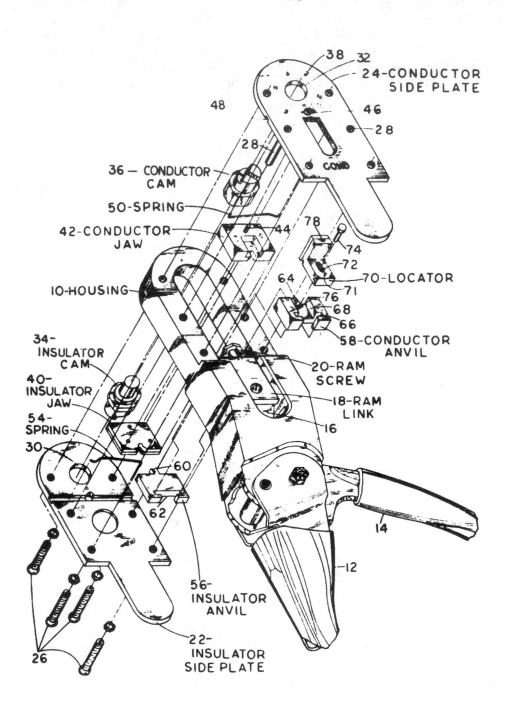

3,751,963

1/2

38 32
24-CONDUCTOR SIDE PLATE
48
46
28
28
36 — CONDUCTOR CAM
COND
50-SPRING
42-CONDUCTOR JAW
44
78
74
72
70-LOCATOR
64
71
10-HOUSING
76
68
66
58-CONDUCTOR ANVIL
34- INSULATOR CAM
20-RAM SCREW
40- INSULATOR JAW
18-RAM LINK
54- SPRING
16
30
60
62
14
56- INSULATOR ANVIL
12
26
22- INSULATOR SIDE PLATE

F I G. 1

Fig. 8D—Isometric Exploded View

If possible, one figure of your drawing should be comprehensive enough to show the basic idea of the invention and to be suitable for inclusion in the *Official Gazette* (OG). If the PTO grants your patent, they will publish one figure, the main claim, and the bibliographic details of your patent in the OG. See Chapter 6, Section K, for more on the OG. The other figures can be fragmentary or partial views; you don't have to show the same details more than once.

Different colors and different shades of gray can be shown with different types of shading lines, but provide a suitable decoding legend in a separate figure. For more information, see Nolo's *How to Make Patent Drawings*, by Jack Lo and David Pressman.

If your invention is related to a prior-art device, you may want to illustrate the prior-art device in the first figure of drawings so that you can explain it and its drawbacks. This Fig. must be labeled "Prior Art."

1. Machine Sketches

If your invention is a machine or an article, your sketches should contain enough views to show every feature of the invention, but you don't have to show every feature that's old and known in the prior art. For example, if you've invented a new type of pedal arrangement for a bicycle, one view can show your pedal arrangement in gross view without detail. Other views can show your pedal arrangement in detail, but you don't have to include any views showing the bicycle itself in detail, since it isn't part of your invention. If one figure of your drawing shows a sectional or side view of another figure, it is customary to provide cross-section lines in the latter figure; these lines should bear the number of the former figure. Look at prior-art patents to see how this is done. See the example in Fig. 8E.

If your machine is complicated, you should show an exploded view of it, as in Fig. 8D.

2. Chemical Composition Sketches

If your invention is a chemical composition, the PTO won't generally require drawings unless your invention is a material that has a nonhomogeneous composition (internally differentiated through layering, for example), in which case you should show it in cross-section detail. Also, if a step-by-step process is involved, the PTO will require a flowchart, even though the process is fully described in your specification (see the next section). The reason: so examiners, judges, and future searchers will be able to understand your patent more rapidly. Benzene rings and other molecular diagrams can usually be presented in the specification.

3. Computer, Chemical, or Mechanical Process Sketches

If your invention includes a process of the electronic-computer, chemical, or mechanical type, you should, as stated, provide a flowchart (or a program listing for software inventions—see Section G above). This flowchart must show the separate steps involved, each described succinctly in a different block. If your blocks are connected, they should all be labeled as one figure; if disconnected, they should be labeled as separate figures. As before, each figure should be labeled—for example, Fig 1, Fig. 1A, Fig. 1B, Fig. 2, Fig. 3, etc.

If you desire, you can try providing a short title after each figure, giving a general description of the part of your invention shown in the figure, just as you would do if you were writing a scientific article for an engineering magazine or textbook. However, PTO drafting personnel often object to such titles for some unknown reason. If this occurs, you'll have to delete the titles, which is easy to do by whitening out the titles on the originals of your drawing and sending in new photocopies.

If you believe it will help in understanding your invention, you may (and should) include a drawing of the prior art as one figure of your drawings. This figure must be labeled "prior art" to indicate that it isn't part of your invention.

I. Drafting the Specification

Once you've reduced your invention to sketches, it's time to begin drafting the specification portion of your patent application. Review the specifications of your prior-art patents—or the sample "spec." at the end of this chapter—to find out how they're written. Your specification should be written as one continuous document with separate sections, each with a heading, the way this book is written.

1. Drafting Tips

Here are some general rules to keep in mind when drafting your specification.

Avoid Legalese
As I'll discuss in more detail below, you should *not* try to write like a lawyer or use legalese. Such syntax is forbidden by PTO rules and is undesirable, since it only makes your writing stilted and less clear. Nothing reads as awkwardly as when a layperson tries to use legalese. The only legal requirements for a patent specification are that it be a full,

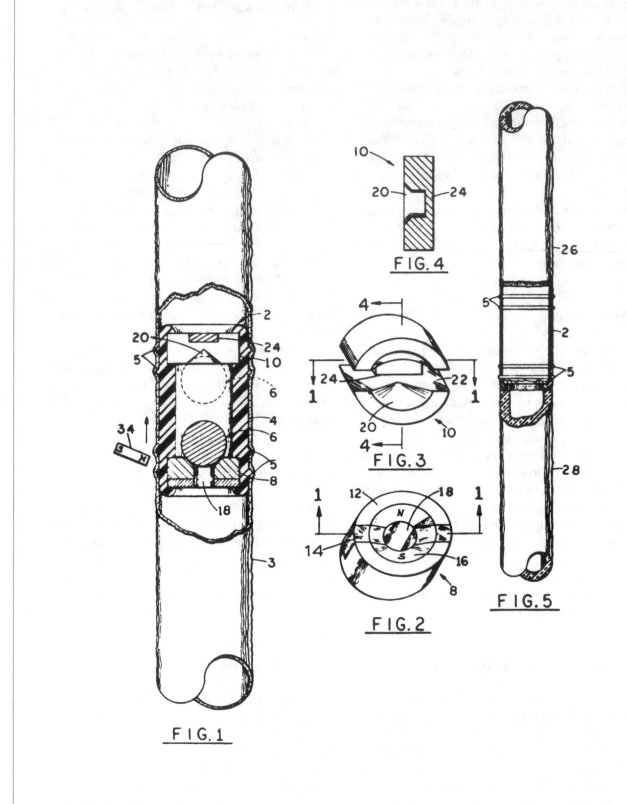

FIG. 4

FIG. 3

FIG. 2

FIG. 1

FIG. 5

Fig. 8E—Views With Cross-Section Lines

clear, concise, and complete description of how to make and use the invention. (The claims, however, should be written with extreme clarity and precision, and to do this you may have to use a few "saids" and "wherebys," but I'll explain this fully in Chapter 9.)

No Need for Legal Terms

I've been told countless times by inventors that they couldn't possibly prepare their own patent application because they don't know "the correct legal terms to use." However, the PTO specifically prohibits legal terms in a specification. Why? So that the specification will be easy to read and understand. Legal terminology was created by lawyers to make their writing less understandable and more obscure, so as to befuddle and confuse laypersons. This makes the law seem esoteric and impenetrable to all but the properly anointed. Happily, the law is moving away from these practices and is opening its doors to laypersons. So don't let any imaginary legal barriers deter you.

> *"Two things are required from every specialized treatise: it should clarify its subject and, more importantly, it should tell us how and by what methods we can attain it and make it ours."*
>
> **—Longinus**

Use Short and Simple Sentences

It's best to write your description in short, simple sentences, with short paragraphs. Each paragraph should generally be shorter than 200–250 words, or one page (double-spaced), and should relate to one part or subpart of your invention. The Cybernetics Institute has found that short sentences communicate best. Also, they found that 50% of adults can't understand a sentence longer than 13 words anyway. Don't worry about the quality or style of your writing or the beauty of your language. Your main goal is to include all points of substance of your invention and make your description clear and understandable. There's an especially good legal reason for this: If a disclosure isn't clear, a court will interpret it narrowly. If you get stuck and don't know how to phrase a description of a part or an operation, here's a helpful trick: Simply pretend you're describing your invention aloud to a close friend. Remember what you said (or make an audio recording) and write it down or use voice recognition software to get a written record. Then go back and polish the language. If you attack the job in small chunks or in piecemeal fashion, it usually will go much easier.

Use Copious Headings

Also, if you use copious subheadings (such as "Fig. 1— Description of Handlebar Attachment"; "Fig. 2—Front Fork Detail"; "Fig. 10—Operation of Derailleur"; etc.)

throughout your specification (as I've done in this book), most people will find it far easier to read. This allows them to take in the information in separate, small, inviting chunks that are easy to digest one at a time. Refer to the specification at the end of this chapter (Fig. 8G) to see examples of headings in an application.

> *"Getting started is the worst part."*
>
> **—Roberta Pressman**

If you have trouble getting started, don't worry; many writers have blocks from time to time, and lots of inventors initially (and erroneously) lament, "I could never write my own patent application." The words of Lao-Tse will encourage you:

> *"A journey of a thousand miles begins with a single step."*

An anecdote that will help is the children's story of a newly manufactured clock that couldn't bring itself to start when told it would have to tick 31,536,000 times per year; it was too daunting a job. However, when its maker cleverly pointed out to it that it would have to tick only once per second, it didn't seem so bad. So the clock started and has been going ever since.

If you still feel daunted, it will help you to know that virtually all inventors who have trouble getting started suffer from *lack of will*, not *ability*. I had a client who came to the U.S. from Hong Kong with little money or English, but with a great invention and tremendous drive. He wrote and filed his own application and got a valuable patent, after I fixed his English. If he could do it, surely you, with probably a much better command of English, can do so also.

> *"Your "I will" is more important than your I.Q."*
>
> **—Marva Collins**

If you feel that you can't write adequately, I suggest that you give it your best shot and then have a writer, college English major, high school English teacher, etc., edit your draft.

 Avoid Negative, Restrictive, or Wishy-Washy Statements That Could Be Used Against You Later. When you write, be especially careful not to include anything that an adversary could later use against you to invalidate or narrow your patent. For example, never say that any novel part of your invention is similar to something that is already known, or that the novelty of your invention is solely in a certain part. If your patent is ever involved in litigation, any adversary will use such statements against you in court.

Common Misconception: If you put any specific feature of your invention, such as a preferred size, a preferred material, a preferred shape, etc., in your specification, the scope of your invention will be limited to this feature, so any device that does lacks this specific feature will not infringe.

Fact: The scope of an invention is determined almost entirely by the claims and not by specifics that are included in the specification. If you do recite any specific feature in a claim, that claim will be limited to this specific feature, but if the specific feature is stated in the specification, it will help provide an adequate disclosure. The patent laws, rules, court decisions, and practitioners actually require and recommend that the specification include as many specifics of the invention as possible, especially in critical areas, so no one will ever be able to validly attack the adequacy of the specification for failure to teach how to make and use the invention. However when stating the specifics of an invention in the specification, it's important to (1) state that these are what you presently prefer, and (2) include as many variations as you can envision. E.g., "I presently prefer that the lever have a rectangular cross section 2 mm by 4 mm and be 4 cm long and made of austenitic steel. However it can have different cross sections, such as oval, triangular, circular, etc., and different sizes and materials, such as high-carbon steel, titanium, polycarbonate, etc."

Now let's get to the nitty-gritty of preparing the specification portion of a patent application.

Make an Outline Before Starting

Prior to starting, in order to guide your path, you will find it helpful first to make an outline, which should be the same as the headings set out below. However, you may want to make the Description and Operation headings more specific and/or break them into several more specific headings each, in accordance with your figures and specific situation. I have provided a skeleton patent application in Fig. 8F which you should copy into a word processor to get you started.

2. The Parts of the Specification

There are also some commonsense rules governing the best presentation of each of the separate parts of your specification. I'll briefly discuss each of these. Only the sections with a "PPA" superscript are needed to file a Provisional Patent Application. (See Chapter 3.) The asterisked (*) words are mandatory under Rule 77 and should be typed in all capitals without boldface.

a.   TITLE * PPA

Have your title reflect the essence of your invention without being too long (about 500 characters maximum) or so specific that it's narrower than your invention's full scope. On the other hand, don't pick a title so broad—such as "Electrical Apparatus"—as to be essentially meaningless. A look at some recently issued patents in your field should give you a good idea of how specific to make your title.

b.   CROSS-REFERENCE TO RELATED APPLICATIONS*

In this section refer to any PPA that you've filed, to any parent applications (see Chapter 14), or to any technically related application. For example, if you've filed a PPA, type, "This application claims the benefit of PPA Ser. Nr. xx/xxx,xxx, filed 200x xxx xx by the present inventors." If the application is a continuation-in-part of an earlier application, type, "This application is a CIP of Ser. Nr. xx/xxx,xxx, filed 2000x xxx xx by the present inventor." If you want to refer to a technically related case, type—for example— "This application uses the frammis vane disclosed in my patent x,xxx,xxx, granted xxxx xxx xx."

c.   FEDERALLY SPONSORED RESEARCH

If your invention was made under a government contract, include the required contract clause here.

d.   SEQUENCE LISTING OR PROGRAM

If you've included a microfiche appendix to provide a program listing, refer to it here. State the number of microfiche pages and frames. If your invention uses a biological sequence, refer to it here and state where it can be found.

e.   BACKGROUND OF THE INVENTION— Field of Invention

Your first sentence should be a brief, one-sentence paragraph stating the general and specific field in which your invention falls. For example, the sentence might read, "This invention relates to bicycles, specifically to an improved pedal mechanism for a bicycle." The field of your invention should be the technical, product, subject, or scientific area with which it's most nearly connected, such as bicycles, kitchenware, lasers, medical instruments, drugs, or skiing. Don't state any details of your invention here.

f.   BACKGROUND—Discussion of Prior Art

Here, discuss how the problem that your invention solves was approached previously (if it was approached at all), and then list all the disadvantages of the old ways of doing it. For example, you can start as follows: "Originally bicycles were made with a fixed transmission ratio. This made

Patent Application of

_____

for

TITLE: _____

CROSS-REFERENCE TO RELATED APPLICATIONS _____

FEDERALLY SPONSORED RESEARCH _____

SEQUENCE LISTING OR PROGRAM _____

BACKGROUND OF THE INVENTION--FIELD OF INVENTION

   This invention generally relates to _____, specifically
to _____.

BACKGROUND OF THE INVENTION--PRIOR ART

   Previously _____ _____.

BACKGROUND OF INVENTION—OBJECTS AND ADVANTAGES

   Accordingly, several objects and advantages of the invention are _____.

   Further objects and advantages will become apparent from a consideration of the ensuing description and drawings.

SUMMARY

   In accordance with the invention, _____.

DRAWINGS--FIGURES

   Fig 1 is _____.

DRAWINGS--REFERENCE NUMERALS

   10 _____.

DETAILED DESCRIPTION--PREFERRED EMBODIMENT--FIGS. ____

OPERATION--PREFERRED EMBODIMENT--FIGS. ____

DESCRIPTION--ALTERNATIVE EMBODIMENT--FIGS. ____

OPERATION--ALTERNATIVE EMBODIMENT--FIGS. ____

CONCLUSION, RAMIFICATIONS, AND SCOPE

   Accordingly the reader will see that, according to the invention, I have provided
_____.

   While the above description contains many specificities, these should not be construed
as limitations on the scope of the invention, but as exemplifications of the presently
preferred embodiments thereof. Many other ramifications and variations are possible
within the teachings of the invention. For example, _____.

   Thus the scope of the invention should be determined by the appended claims and their
legal equivalents, and not by the examples given.

.... page break ....

CLAIMS:

   1. _____

.... page break ....

SEQUENCE LISTING:

.... page break ....

ABSTRACT: _____

Fig. 8F—"Skeleton" Patent Application

pedaling up hills difficult. This problem has been partially solved by the implementation of derailleur mechanisms, but these had and still have significant problems." Then list the derailleurs that were used in the past and their disadvantages. Again, look at prior-art patents to get an idea of what was done. If you can, tell why prior-art people failed to solve the problem and why a solution is needed.

While the PTO doesn't want needlessly derogatory remarks about the inventions of others, you should, as much as possible, try to "knock the prior art" here in order to make your invention look as good as possible. Keep your statements factual (for example, "The derailleur in patent 3,456,789 to Prewitt, 1982 May 3, had a limited number of discrete gear ratios") and not opinionated (don't say, "Prewitt's derailleur was an abject failure"). If applicable, tell why prior-art people didn't think of any solution before and why a solution is needed. Do not discuss any detailed structure or operation of any prior art in this section (unless you provide a suitable figure—see next paragraph), since detailed mechanical discussions without the benefit of drawings will be incomprehensible to most people. Occasionally, you may have such a completely unique invention that there's really no prior art directly germane to your invention. If so, just state the general problem or disadvantage your invention solves.

If you've provided a prior-art figure, you can discuss (and knock!) it here. Use reference numerals to refer to the individual parts of the prior-art device. Alternatively you may discuss (and knock) your prior-art figure in the "Description of Invention" section.

If your invention doesn't solve a specific problem—for example, it's a new game or toy—you won't be able to state any problem that your invention solves. However, you still can discuss the closest prior games or toys and mention some faults or disadvantages of them.

g. Objects and Advantages

In the patent field, the term "objects" means "what the invention accomplishes" and "advantages" means "the things that it does better than before." Thus, you should list here all the things your invention accomplishes and its advantages over the prior art. You can start this section as follows: "Accordingly, several objects and advantages of my invention are…." Then, include just the objects or advantages of your invention that are the converse of the disadvantages of the prior art.

For example, if in your prior-art section you stated that derailleurs were complex and unreliable, you should state now that your invention provides a simpler and more reliable derailleur. Then, in a separate section, starting with, for example, "Other objects and advantages are," add any additional objects and advantages of which you're aware

that are not the converse of the prior art you've cited in your prior art section.

You already know all of the advantages and disadvantages of your invention from your commercial evaluation. (See Chapter 4 and Form 4-2.) Keep in mind you're still selling your invention—to the examiner, to a potential licensee, and possibly to a judge!

Don't include any objects that are so broad that your invention doesn't support them. For example, if you've invented a paper cup that provides better thermal insulation only, don't include an object that states that your cup is stronger, lighter, or cheaper.

Avoid very narrow objects, such as "it is one object to provide a 14.5 mm carbon fiber lever," since these can be used to limit your invention. Similarly avoid objects that can't be accomplished, such as, "it is one object to provide a totally safe bike," since this can also be used against you.

At the end of this section, add a catch-all paragraph reading as follows: "Further objects and advantages of my invention will become apparent from a consideration of the drawings and ensuing description."

Your Objects and Advantages section should be like an ad or sales brochure for your invention: It should tell why someone should buy it, but without any technical details or operational descriptions that wouldn't be meaningful to a new prospective buyer. Your O & A section should not be longer than about 1½ pages, double spread.

It may seem needlessly repetitious to state the disadvantages of the prior art in the "Background" section and then repeat the converse of these in the "Objects" section. However, you'll soon find that this is but one instance of many where repetition is used in a patent application. For instance, the objects are effectively repeated again (a third time!) in the concluding paragraph of the specification, and still again (a fourth time!) in the whereby clauses at the end of the main claims. Moreover, the parts of the invention are actually repeated five times, under "Description," under "Operation," in the Claims, in the Abstract, and in your list of reference numerals.

Why is repetition used so much? Because it's one of the keys to effective communication. There's an apropos old saying:

> *"To communicate effectively to someone, you should first tell your listener what you're going to say, then actually say it, and finally tell the listener what you said."*

h. SUMMARY*

The PTO's Rule 73 requires that the specification contain a summary of the claimed invention, and Rule 72 requires an abstract of the entire specification. In practice, many patent attorneys have omitted the summary, since the abstract, as well as the claims, already provides one. However, Rule 77 requires one. Also a summary will describe the forest before you describe the trees and program your examiner to more readily understand what follows. Your summary can simply paraphrase your main claim (see Chapter 9) or can be a short description (one or two sentences) of the essence of your invention. Your summary should not be longer than about ¾ page, double spaced.

i.   DRAWINGS* PPA

Here, provide a series of separate paragraphs, each *briefly* describing a respective figure of your drawing—for example, "Fig 1 is a perspective (or plan, side, exploded, or rear) view of my invention"; or, "Fig 2 is a view in detail of the portion indicated by the section lines 2-2 in Fig 1." Do not include any reference numerals, specific parts, or any other details in this section—just a brief overall description of each figure.

j.   DRAWINGS—List of Reference Numerals

Although the PTO doesn't require or even recommend a separate list of the reference numerals and the names of their respective parts in an application, I strongly advise that you include such a list in a separately headed section. (I've provided one sample specification at the end of the chapter.) Why? There are three very important reasons for providing the list:

- to help you to keep your reference numerals straight—that is, to avoid using the same number for different parts
- to help you to keep your nomenclature straight—that is, to avoid using different terms for the same part
- to provide a very visible and easy-to-find place where examiners, searchers, and others who read your application or patent can go to instantly identify any numbered part on your drawings.

I find it helpful to compile this list in a separate word-processing window or on a separate sheet of lined paper as I write the patent application, and then incorporate the list in the text. I've provided a suitable worksheet as Form 8-1 in Appendix 7. Also, to keep confusion at a minimum, I advise that you never use single-digit reference numerals, and that you begin your numbers with a number higher than your highest-numbered drawing figure. For example, if you have Figs 1 to 12 of drawings, begin your reference numerals with number 20.

One inventor I know uses three-digit reference numbers throughout. The first digit represents the figure number, so that the parts of Fig 1 would be 110, 112, etc. The parts in Fig 2 would be 210, 212, etc. If Fig 2 has a part that is also in Fig 1, the reader would instantly know that this part (that is, part 110) was first introduced in Fig 1. Also this enables any reader of the specification to go directly to the drawing figure where this part is introduced.

Lastly, I advise that you use even-numbered reference numerals when you write the application. In this way, if you later have to add another reference number, you can use an odd number and put it between two logically related even numbers. (See the list in the sample specification at the end of the chapter.)

k.   DETAILED DESCRIPTION * PPA
—Preferred Embodiment—Figures 1-xx

Here you should describe in great detail the static physical structure of your invention (not how it operates or what its function is). If your invention is a process, describe the procedures or machinery involved in it. Begin by first stating what the figure under discussion shows generally—for example, "Fig 1 shows a perspective view of a basic version of my widget." Then get specific by describing the main parts and how they're connected. (These main parts can form the basis for your claims, as we'll see in Chapter 9.) Then get more specific: describe each main part in detail and all of the sub- or component parts in detail.

Start with the base, frame, bottom, input, or some other logical starting place of your invention. Then work up, out, or forward in a logical manner, numbering and naming the parts in your drawing as you proceed. Use the part names that you previously wrote on your sketches.

To number the parts, write a number near each part and extend a lead line from the reference number to the part to which it refers. Don't circle your reference numerals, since a PTO rule prohibits this. The lead lines should *not* have arrowheads—for example, a bicycle grip might be designated "22———." However, to refer to a group of parts as a whole—for example, a bicycle, use an arrowhead on the lead line, thus, " 10———>." If you have several closely related or similar parts, you can give them the same reference number with different letter suffixes or primes to differentiate, such as "arms 12a and 12b," "arms 12L (left) and 12R (right)," or "arms 12 and 12'."

Although you may think that the patent examiner won't need to have parts that are clearly shown in the drawing separately described in detail, all patent attorneys provide such a description. This is part of the previously mentioned repetition technique that is used to familiarize the examiner with the invention and set the stage for the operational description and the claims (Chapter 9). When you mention each part twice, once in the description and again in the operation discussion, the first mention will initially program your reader to relate to the part so that the reader will really understand it the second time around, when it counts. This is the same technique as is used in the lyrics of blues songs, where the first two lines are always restated to enhance communication.

Another good technique is to use several different equivalent names for a part the first time you refer to it in order to provide one with which your reader will be familiar—for example, "connected to base 10 is a strut, pylon, or support 12." Then pick one name and use it consistently thereafter.

As stated, before you begin a description of any figure, refer to it by its figure number—for example, "Fig 1 shows an overall view of the can opener of the invention." Then as you come to each part or element, give it a separate reference number—for example, "The can opener comprises two handle arms 10 and 12 that are hinged together at a hinge 14." It is essential always to keep your reader apprised of which figure you are discussing.

Where several figures show different views of an embodiment of your invention, you can refer to several figures at once—such as "Figs 1 and 2 show plan and elevational (front) views of a scissors according to the invention. The scissors comprises first and second legs 12 and 14, the second leg being best shown in Fig 2." However, don't refer to too many figures at once, and again, always keep your reader advised as to which figure is under discussion.

Cover every part shown in your drawings and be sure to use consistent terminology and nomenclature for the parts in the drawing. For example, if gear 44 is shown in Fig 8 and also in Fig 11, label it with the reference numeral "44" in both figures. However, if the gear is even slightly different in Fig 11, it must have a different reference numeral, such as, "44a," "44," or "44bis." Fill out the Drawing Reference Numerals Worksheet (Form 8-1) as you write, to keep your numerals and nomenclature consistent. If you use a word processor, I suggest you refer to each part by a number only and then, consistent part names—such as, you can write "44 is connected to 36" and later change "44" to "widget 44" and "36" to "base 36" throughout your specification.

Lastly, be sure to detail all the interconnections or mountings between parts—for example, "Arm 14 is joined to base 12 by a flange 16."

Dem Bones. To understand the technique commonly used to describe the parts and their interconnections, think of the song, "Dem Bones." The song details virtually every bone-to-bone connection in the body in logical order—for example, "The knee bone's connected to the thigh bone, the thigh bone's connected to the hip bone." In a similar manner, your description should also detail every part-to-part interconnection, even if you think the reader would find it obvious from your drawing.

 Don't Be Secretive. Suppose your invention uses some special or exotic parts, techniques, or relationships, but you don't want to describe these because such information is valuable and you want to keep it as a trade secret and not give it away to potential copiers and competitors. Unfortunately, you can't be secretive. You must include complete detailed descriptions of these, including dimensions, relationships, materials, and sources of supply, as applicable, in this section in order to comply with the "full disclosure" statute (35 USC 112). Putting in such specifics will not limit your invention in any way since the claims (next chapter) will determine its scope. However, failing to include these specifics can render your patent application fatally flawed if they are necessary for one skilled in the art to make and use the invention.

Including details and dimensions at crucial places can also prove vital later if you have to rely on these in order to support and distinguish your claims over a close prior-art reference cited by the examiner. Thus, it's almost axiomatic in patent law that you should make your specification as long, specific, and detailed as possible, and your main (independent) claims as short, broad, and general as possible. If you're tempted to skip the details, remember that a few strokes on a keyboard now can save you from losing many thousands of dollars later. Be especially sure to expand your discussion in the areas where you feel that your invention is novel over the prior art.

Use of "A," "The," and "Said"

Although the articles "a" and "the" are two of the most common and elementary words in the American language, many writers often use them improperly.

The articles "a" and "an" are indefinite articles, i.e., they do not refer to any definite or already known thing. Example: "I bought a car."

The articles "the" and the legal word "said" are definite articles, i.e., they refer to a definite or already known thing. Example: "I bought the car that we saw yesterday."

When you first introduce something, your reader is not familiar with it, so always introduce it with an indefinite article. Example: "The device has a handle 10 that is connected to an ax head 12."

When your specification refers again to something that has already been introduced, your reader is familiar with it, so always use a definite article "the." For example, if the parts have already been introduced, say, "The lever and the handle are made of plastic."

If you are referring to the parts by their number, or if they're plural, you often don't need to use "the." Examples: "Lever 10 and handle 12 are made of plastic." or "Levers such as this are well known."

In claims (see Chapter 9) the same rules apply, except that you should use "the" to refer to a part that has not been expressly mentioned but is implied and "said" to refer to a part by the exact name by which it has already been recited. For example, if the claim has already recited a tabletop comprising a flat sheet and four elongated legs, say, " … said legs being attached to the underside of said tabletop."

Never use "a" to refer to an already-introduced part. For example, if a lever has been introduced, do not subsequently say, "A lever is connected to the handle."

Never introduce something with "the." For example, if a lever has not been introduced, do not say, "The lever is made of plastic."

Common Misconception: If you put a specific feature of your invention, such as a preferred size, a preferred material, a preferred shape, etc., in your specification, the scope of your invention will be limited to this feature, so any device that lacks this specific feature will not infringe.

Fact: The scope of an invention is determined almost entirely by the claims and not by specifics that are included in the specification. If you do recite any specific feature in a claim, that claim will be limited to this specific feature, but if the specific feature is stated in the specification, it will help provide an adequate disclosure. The patent laws, rules, court decisions, and practitioners actually require and recommend that the specification include as many specifics of the invention as possible, especially in critical areas, so no one will ever be able to validly attack the adequacy of the specification for failure to teach how to make and use the invention. However when stating the specifics of an invention in the specification, it's important to (1) state that these specifics are what you presently prefer, and (2) include as many variations as you can envision—for example, "I presently prefer that the lever have a rectangular cross section 2 mm by 4 mm and be 4 cm long and made of austenitic steel. However it can have different cross sections, such as oval, triangular, circular, etc., and different sizes and materials, such as high-carbon steel, titanium, polycarbonate, etc."

Trademarks

If any material, substance, or component of your invention is a trademarked product, you should refer to it by its generic name, without using the mark—unless the mark is necessary for full identification. For example, if you have a hook-and-loop fastener, you can say, "hook-and-loop fastener 20 holds tab to base 14." It is not necessary to use either of the marks *Velcro* or *Latchlok*, since H&L fasteners are well known. The same holds true for the trademark *Teflon*—use PTFE instead. However, if the product is not common, you can use its mark, provided you use it properly. This means capitalizing the mark, identifying it as a trademark, using the mark as an adjective with a generic descriptor, and identifying the owner of the mark—such as "Ajax™ developer, manufactured by Goldberger Graphics of San Francisco." If the trademarked product is crucial and you're going to recite it in your claims, and you don't know its composition, see "Trademarked Chemical Note" in Section F, above. (If you have your own (new) trademark for your invention, you should not use it in your specification.)

Avoid technical language, insofar as possible, but if you use any technical terms, be sure to define them for any lay judge or young examiner who may read your application. One patent litigator has suggested drafting all patent applications for a judge with a degree in political science,

English, or government—that is, try to make your description as nontechnical as possible, without eliminating any crucial details. If you do have a technical invention, such as a computer, biotechnical, electronic, chemical, medical, or complex mechanical invention, start your explanation from zero, assuming your reader, who may be a new examiner or a judge with a degree in political science, knows nothing about the field. Then explain the field of the invention, the problem you solve, and any technical information your reader will need to understand it. You don't need to write a complete textbook (and the learning curve can be steep), but you should provide a full guide from zero to the level of the invention.

Computer Programs Note. As stated in Section G above, if your invention involves a computer program, include a program listing or a detailed flowchart with a detailed explanation as to how to configure the computer to perform the required function and interrelate with any other elements to yield the claimed invention. If the listing is 300 lines or less (72 characters per line), it can be submitted as part of the specification, or as part of the drawings. In either case, the listing should be a very black, camera-ready copy. If the printout is to be submitted on drawing sheets, these should be of the proper size (U.S. or international; see Chapter 10), with each sheet including a separate figure number (Fig 1, Fig 2, etc.; or Fig 1-A, Fig 1-B, etc.). If the printout is to be submitted as part of the specification, it must be on the same size sheets. The printout should be positioned just before the claims if it has more than 60 lines of code. If your program is longer than 300 lines, it must be submitted on a CD, as an appendix. It will not be printed with the patent, but will be referred to in the patent. The standards for the microfiche are contained in Rule 52(e) (37 CFR 1.52e)—(see Appendix 2, Resources: Government Publications, Patent Websites, and Books of Use and Interest), available at all Patent and Trademark Depository Libraries and over the PTO's website (see Appendix 5, Mail, Telephone, Fax, and Email Communications With the PTO) or in any law library.

Briefly, the CD should be submitted in duplicate on a CD-ROM or CD-R with all files in ASCII format. Each CD should be in a hard case in an unsealed, unpadded, mailing envelope, accompanied by a transmittal letter. The letter (and a separate paragraph in the specification) must list the machine format (IBM-PC, Macintosh, etc.), the operating system compatibility (MS-DOS, MS-Windows, Macintosh, Unix, Linux, etc.), a list of files on the CD (including their names, size in bytes, dates of creation, etc.). The disks must be labeled "Copy 1" and "Copy 2" and the letter must state that the disks are identical.

l. Operation of Invention [PPA]

After you complete the static description of your main or preferred embodiment, you should then describe in extensive detail the operation or function of the parts covered in your description. Refer to each part by its name and reference numeral, and be sure to include the working or function of every part. Your invention may be of such a nature that it may not be possible to include a physical description and an operational description in separate sections. However, you'll find that this mode of description works generally for most inventions, and you should try to adhere to it since it will force you to be complete and comprehensive. Your operation section should not introduce any part or use any reference numeral that was not introduced in the description section. Again, always keep your reader apprised as to which Figure is under discussion. At the end of or in the Operation section, stress the advantages of your invention—for example, "Thus, since the lever is bent, it avoids the jamming that prior-art couplings experienced."

m. Description and Operation of Alternative Embodiments [PPA]

If your invention includes several embodiments and ramifications, you should first fully describe the structure of the most preferred or most basic embodiment. Then, describe its operation in a separate section immediately following the structural description. In this way, your reader or examiner will get a full understanding of the invention, including its operation.

Then describe each additional important embodiment—those embodiments that you feel have a good chance of being commercially implemented. Describe these additional embodiments in the same manner, but more briefly, since you only need detail the differences over the first embodiment. Thus, several sets of description/operation sections will result. For example, "Fig. 1—Description of Motor," "Operation of Motor," "Fig. 2—Description of Hand Version," "Operation of Hand Version." You must include a highly detailed description of each and every part of your invention, together with a highly detailed description of the operation of each part and its relation to the other parts.

I emphasize that you should describe, draw, and claim specifically all reasonably important embodiments and ramifications so that you'll have more support for broader claims (see Chapter 9). Also, if an infringer is making or selling a ramification, you'll be able to show the judge that you specifically showed that ramification in your application. Infringement is supposed to be determined mainly by the wording of your claims. However, as a practical matter, judges are psychologically influenced in your favor if your specification and drawings show and discuss the very embodiment that is being infringed.

If you are aware of less important embodiments and ramifications, you can describe these in the Ramifications section, discussed below, without drawing or claiming them specifically.

Theory of Operation

If your invention operates by utilizing an interesting or unusual theory, you can include this also, either before or after describing the operation. If you're not sure about the correctness of your theory, you can state this—for example, "While I believe the reaction occurs because of a catalytic effect of the platinum, I don't wish to be bound by this." You are not required to give any theory of operation in your application, since this isn't necessary to enable one skilled in the art to make or use the invention. However if you can include any theory of operation, you should, since it will make your invention more interesting, believable, and likable to your readers (such as your patent examiner or a judge).

Medical Devices and Drugs. If your invention is a medical device or drug, you don't need to supply proof of efficacy if it's obvious that it will work and be safe. For instance, if your invention is a drug that is close or analogous to an existing drug that is already recognized as safe and efficacious, you don't need further proof. But if your invention is a drug that is substantially different from anything on the market, and it's not apparent that the drug will be safe and efficacious, you must be prepared to prove those things. Applications for patents on drugs often are referred to the FDA, which has its own requirements, but in cases where the drug or device isn't radically different, declarations by experts regarding safety and efficacy will usually be accepted by the PTO.

n. Conclusion, Ramifications, and Scope of Invention

After you finish your detailed description of the invention's operation, add a "Conclusion, Ramifications, and Scope of Invention" section to sum things up and to remind the judge who sees your patent that the claims control. Here's an example:

"*Thus the reader will see that the can opener of the invention provides a highly reliable, lightweight, yet economical device that can be used by persons of almost any age. [Keep selling it!]*

[Some inventors have provided arguments for unobviousness here, but I advise against this. Just state the advantages without discussing unobviousness.]

While my above description contains many specificities, these should not be construed as limitations on the scope of the invention, but rather as an exemplification of one preferred embodiment thereof. Many other variations are possible. For example [then continue with brief description of possible variations that aren't important enough to show as ramifications in the drawing].

Accordingly, the scope of the invention should be determined not by the embodiment(s) illustrated, but by the appended claims and their legal equivalents."

In the first paragraph quoted above, the objects and advantages of the invention are restated and summarized to hammer home the great value of your invention. In the "for example" portion of the second quoted paragraph, include a brief description of any alternative embodiments you can think of and that (as stated) you didn't consider important enough to show in the drawing and describe in detail in your description. I usually put exotic, untested embodiments, as well as minor variations in color, size, and materials in the broadening paragraph. It's desirable to include as many ramifications as possible in order to get any means clauses in your claims interpreted as broadly as possible. (See Chapter 9 on drafting claims for a discussion of "means clauses" and their relationship to the specification.)

Thus you should go through the entire application and, for each element of the inventive device or method, state in the ramifications paragraph whether that element can be:

- eliminated or duplicated
- changed in size (made smaller or larger)
- made of a different material
- made in a different shape
- made of a different color
- connected or associated with its adjacent elements in a different manner
- given a different mode or function of operation—for example, suction rather than blowing, or
- made integrally or separately (modular or in sections).

It's very important to be as comprehensive as possible when describing ramifications because recent decisions of the Court of Appeals for the Federal Circuit (the sole patent appellate court) have tended to interpret claims narrowly, unless the infringed device is described or mentioned in the specification.

Look at the sample specification at the end of this chapter to see how this is done.

That's just about all there is to drafting the specification portion of your application. What's left, you ask? The small matter of "Claims," that's what. I'll tell you how to write these in the next chapter.

o. SEQUENCE LISTING* PPA

If you provide a sequence listing of a nucleotide or amino acid sequence on paper, you should include this heading and the listing on a separate sheet after your claims and before your abstract. If you have no sequence listing, don't include the sheet or this heading.

p. ABSTRACT*

Your abstract should be drafted on a separate sheet, after the claims. However, it will be printed on the first page of your patent and appears right after the sample specification of Fig. 8G, since the claims have been saved for the next chapter. The abstract is relatively easy to do once you've done the specification, and since it's very closely related to the specification, I'll cover it here.

The abstract should be put on a new page with the heading "ABSTRACT." To do the actual abstract, write one paragraph providing a concise summary of the specification in no more than 150 words. Spend enough time writing the abstract to make it concise, complete, and clear. This is because the abstract is usually the part of an application that's read first and most frequently consulted. Look at the abstracts of several of your prior-art patents to get an idea of what's involved. To be concise, your abstract should not include throat-clearing phrases like "This invention relates to," but rather, should get right into it and state—for example, "An improved bicycle pedal mechanism having…, etc." If you think you may file the application in other countries, you should include reference and figure numbers in the abstract (with each one in parentheses) to comply with the international rules. International filing is covered in Chapter 12. It's also desirable to include the main advantages of the invention in the abstract.

J. Review Your Specification and Abstract Carefully

After you've completed your draft, review it carefully to be sure you've included everything about your invention you can think of. Also, be sure that there is no possible ground for anyone to say that you haven't included enough to teach one skilled in the art how to make and use your invention. You may have to go through two, three, or more drafts to get it right. Be sure to compare your specification with those of other patents in the field so that yours is at least as complete as theirs. Allow yourself plenty of time—for example, a few days to do the drawings, a few days to write the introductory parts of your specification, and a few days to do the static description. In this way you won't feel pressured and thus you'll be able to do a better, more readable, more legally adequate job.

"Don't do your work in haste. Later on, the public won't ask whether it was completed in three days, but whether it's accurate and complete."
—**Anon.**

"The secret of joy in work is contained in one word—

excellence. To know how to do something well is to enjoy it."
—**Pearl S. Buck**

⚠️ Many prior-art patents are not properly described under today's demanding standards, so don't absolutely rely on them as a standard. Instead, follow the guidelines of this chapter. After you complete the draft of your specification, I recommend that you show it to a coworker, relative, or friend. Have them double check that: It clearly teaches how to make and use the invention, it sells your invention and states all of its advantages, it is logical, free of errors (grammatical and technical), and it is clearly written.

If You Use an Attorney

If you're fortunate enough to be able to hire an attorney (or agent) to prepare your patent application, don't blindly accept whatever the attorney gives you to sign, since even the best attorneys make mistakes and omit important things at one time or another. All attorneys do better work when they have a critical client. Carefully review an attorney's work in detail, making sure the application is well and clearly written, clearly teaches how to make and use the invention, discloses all possible ramifications, contains broad main claims, and has a spectrum of claims. (I discuss claims in the next chapter.) You're paying the attorney a lot of money, so you deserve a high-quality product.

K. Checklist for Your Patent Application Draft

After reviewing many patent applications prepared by laypersons, I've come up with three lists of the most common errors and areas generally needing improvement. The first list (in two parts) follows; it covers the preliminary drawings and draft specification. Before you go on to the claims (Chapter 9) or to the finaling process (Chapter 10), I suggest that you check this list carefully and make any needed corrections in your work. The specification checklist includes many grammar and punctuation rules that I see inventors violate frequently.

Checklist for Preliminary Drawings

☐ D01. Every significant part in the drawings has its own reference numeral.

☐ D02. Every unique part has a different reference numeral—that is, the same reference numeral is never used to indicate different parts. (Suffixed numbers (10, 10'; 10A, 10B, etc.) can be used for different parts.)

☐ D03. The same reference numeral is always used to indicate the same part when such part is shown in different Figs; that is, two different numerals are never used to indicate the same part.

☐ D04. Arrowheads are not used on any lead line, unless it refers to an entire assembly of elements.

☐ D05. The drawings show enough details of your invention to enable it to be fully and readily understood by a lay judge.

☐ D06. The reference numerals start with a number higher than your highest Fig number.

☐ D07. Even reference numerals (10, 12, etc.) are used so you can add more numerals in sequence later, if needed.

☐ D08. The Fig details and reference numerals are large enough to be easily read.

☐ D09. A descriptive label is placed on or near each component whose function is not apparent.

☐ D10. The drawings show every part and modification that you intend to include in your claims. (See Chapter 9.)

☐ D11. No dimensions are used on drawings (unless essential for the invention).

☐ D12. Each figure has a separate number. Suffixed figure numbers (Fig 1-A, Fig 1-B; Fig 1, Fig 1') are okay.

☐ D13. Separate figures are not connected by any line.

☐ D14. Separated parts of any figure are joined by projection lines (see Fig 8D) or a large bracket.

☐ D15. Exotic or special parts are labeled—for example, "saturated transistor"; "gray water"; "electric conduit."

☐ D16. Perspective (isometric) views, rather than engineering (top, side, bottom) views, are used wherever possible.

☐ D17. Any figures that show a prior-art device are so labeled.

☐ D18. A reference number is not used for an entire figure.

☐ D19. A sectional view is indicated by two arrows with crossbars on the main view, numbered with the number of the sectional view.

Checklist for Draft of Specification

Writing Generally

☐ W01. No sentence is over about 13 words (unless really necessary or unless two independent clauses are used).

☐ W02. No paragraph is longer than about 150-200 words or about half a page.

☐ W03. A heading is supplied for approximately every two pages of discussion.

☐ W04. Each discussion relates to and explains only its heading.

☐ W05. Adjacent paragraphs are connected by transitions, and no paragraph is longer than about one page, double spaced.

☐ W06. Every sophisticated term is defined clearly.

☐ W07. The description is written in simple, nontechnical terms, insofar as possible, so that a lay judge can understand it.

☐ W08. All writing is clear, reads smoothly, and is logical.

☐ W09. Male personal pronouns (he, his, etc.) aren't used exclusively; your examiner may be a woman.

☐ W10. No sentence is started with a number.

☐ W11. Every reference numeral is preceded by a noun ("lever 21").

☐ W12. A comma isn't used between subject and verb. (Wrong: "Lever 24, is connected to brace 26.")

☐ W13. A comma is used at all natural pauses.

☐ W14. Don't omit "Oxford" comma: "He ate bread, ham, and eggs." (Comma indicates the ham and eggs aren't mixed.)

☐ W15. All possessives are apostrophized, except "its."

☐ W16. Loose, informal writing isn't used.

☐ W17. A descriptive noun ("lever") rather than a general term ("part") is used for every element.

☐ W18. A group of words serving as a single adjective is hyphenated—for example, "impact-resistant glass."

☐ W19. No sentence fragments are used. (Wrong: "Because the gear is made of nylon.")

☐ W20. Writing is proofread carefully.

☐ W21. The indefinite article "a" (rather than "the") is used to introduce parts in the specification.

☐ W22. The definite article "the" isn't used to refer to a part by its name and reference numeral.

☐ W23. Already introduced parts are not referred to with the article "a."

☐ W24. Every part is referred to by a consistent name throughout.

☐ W25. Your writing does not contain "flab" phrases such as "It will be noted that." (Flab slows reader's pace and detracts from drama and strength of work.)

☐ W26. The writing doesn't change voices (active to passive, or vice versa) in a paragraph, and you use the active voice as much as possible.

☐ W27. The discussion discusses one Fig at a time, insofar as possible, and doesn't jump from figure to figure too much.

☐ W28. Your reader is always kept clearly advised which figure is under discussion.

☐ W29. "Fig" (rather than figure) is used throughout to speed reading.

Specification

☐ S01. The title indicates the essence of your invention without being longer than 500 characters.

☐ S02. The Background—Field of the Invention section is not longer than one sentence.

☐ S03. The Background—Prior Art section does not mention your invention.

☐ S04. All detailed technical discussions refer to a drawing Fig (most humans can't comprehend abstract technical discussions).

☐ S05. Each prior-art approach you discuss is knocked.

☐ S06. When any patent or prior-art reference is referred to, the inventor's or author's name(s), the patent #, or publication and page, and its issue date are included.

Checklist for Draft of Specification (continued)

☐ S07. The Objects and Advantages section states all advantages of your invention but does not state any details of the invention. These include the converse of every disadvantage in the Prior-Art section and the advantage of every possible noble feature of your invention. The Objects and Advantages section also concludes with a general reference to other objects and advantages that will become apparent from the specification and drawings.

☐ S08. The Drawing Description section has just one short sentence for each Fig.

☐ S09. A List of Reference Numerals section is included.

☐ S10. Every reference numeral on the drawings is used in the specification and every reference numeral in the specification is on the drawings.

☐ S11. The same reference numeral is not used for two different parts. (Suffixed numerals—10, 10A, 10' for different parts—are okay.)

☐ S12. The description and the operation of the invention are discussed in separate sections.

☐ S13. Overall or main parts and overall operation are described before describing details of parts and operation.

☐ S14. If any part mentioned in the specification isn't shown in the drawings (for example, because it's conventional), state this. (For example, "Output 24 of generator 22 is connected to a conventional storage battery (not shown).")

☐ S15. You don't refer to your device as an "invention"; you're specific. (Wrong: "My invention thus …" Right: "My can opener thus…")

☐ S16. Ramifications are discussed after the basic version is explained and a preferred embodiment is indicated.

☐ S17. A separate "Summary" section is provided.

☐ S18. Wishy-washy descriptions ("a plastic brace might work here") are eliminated; all descriptions are firm, sure, and positive.

☐ S19. The dimensions, preferred materials, relationships, and/or sources of supply are stated for all exotic or critical parts.

☐ S20. For ease of reading, a shorter term is used when you refer again to a part with a long name. For example, First time: "A liquid-overflow check valve 12." Second time: "Valve 12."

☐ S21. Generic terms, rather than trademarks, are used. Each trademark used is identified as such, typed in caps, used with a generic noun, and its owner is indicated.

☐ S22. No legal words, such as "said" or "means," are used in the specification or abstract.

☐ S23. Metric (or metric followed by British) dimensions are used.

☐ S24. All possible novel features of your invention are discussed in great detail with dimensions, materials, shapes, interconnections, etc., so as to provide language to support any claims that might be directed to this feature.

☐ S25. The Description and Operation sections contain enough detail to enable your invention readily to be built and used. Every part of the invention is discussed, its purpose is stated, and the overall operation of the invention is explained.

☐ S26. The application does not contain any statements that could be used against you by any adversary to narrow or invalidate your invention.

☐ S27. The Operation section does not introduce any part.

☐ S28. A Conclusion, Ramifications, and Scope section is provided at the end of the specification to repeat the advantages, discuss all possible alternatives (less important embodiments and ramifications), and to indicate that the claims control.

☐ S29. The Abstract is technical and terse, without listing too many advantages.

☐ S30. The Abstract has a reference numeral in parentheses "(12)," after each named part, for possible foreign filing.

☐ S31. You have had another person check the draft for completeness, accuracy, and clarity.

L. Specification of Sample Patent Application

The following application is reproduced in final form, ready for filing in the PTO. However, your application will be in draft form after completing Chapter 8.

A2-KoppeLam.SB   your disc and file # (optional)

8-9 cm top margin on p. 1

Note: Dimensions and layout are indicated for typing or printing on letter-size paper (8.5" x 11") so that, if foreign filing is later desired (see Chapter 12), photocopies made directly on A4 paper will have the proper format for foreign filing. If foreign filing is not likely to be desired, legal or letter-size paper with the usual margins (always provide at least a 1" top margin for hole punching), 1-1/2 or double line spacing, and page numbers at bottom or top can be used.

Patent Application of

Lou W. Koppe

for

2.5 cm left margin

TITLE: PAPER-LAMINATED PLIABLE CLOSURE FOR FLEXIBLE BAGS

Printout should have minimum 1.5 line spacing (4 lines/inch) but is shown with denser spacing since this example is shown on a reduced scale.

CROSS-REFERENCE TO RELATED APPLICATIONS

This application claims the benefit of provisional patent application Ser. No. 60/123,456, filed 2003 Aug 9 by the present inventor.

FEDERALLY SPONSORED RESEARCH   Not Applicable

2.8–3.8 cm right margin on 8.5" x 11" paper

SEQUENCE LISTING OR PROGRAM   Not Applicable

BACKGROUND OF THE INVENTION--FIELD OF INVENTION

one sentence for field of invention

This invention relates to plastic tab closures, specifically to such closures which are used for closing the necks of plastic produce bags.

BACKGROUND OF THE INVENTION--PRIOR ART

description of and knocking of prior art

Grocery stores and supermarkets commonly supply consumers with polyethylene bags for holding produce. Such bags are also used by suppliers to provide a resealable container for other items, both edible and inedible.

type almost to bottom of page so A4 copies can be made with proper bottom margin

Originally these bags were sealed by the supplier with staples or by heat. However, consumers objected since these were of a rather permanent nature:

Fig. 8G—Specification of Sample Patent Application

2.5 cm top margin above header

Patent Application of Lou W. Koppe for "Paper-Laminated
Pliable Closure for Flexible Bags" continued
Page 2

the bags could be opened only by tearing, thereby damaging them and rendering them impossible to reseal.

continue
knocking
the prior art

Thereafter, inventors created several types of closures to seal plastic bags in such a way as to leave them undamaged after they were opened. U.S. patent 4,292,714 to Walker (1981) discloses a complex clamp which can close the necks of bags without causing damage upon opening; however, these clamps are prohibitively expensive to manufacture. U.S. patent 2,981,990 to Balderree (1961) shows a closure which is of expensive construction, being made of PTFE, and which is not effective unless the bag has a relatively long "neck."

Thus if the bag has been filled almost completely and consequently has a short neck, this closure is useless. Also, being relatively narrow and clumsy, Balderree's closure cannot be easily bent by hand along its longitudinal axis. Finally, his closure does not hold well onto the bag, but has a tendency to snap off.

Although twist closures with a wire core are easy to use and inexpensive to manufacture, do not damage the bag upon being removed, and can be used repeatedly, nevertheless they simply do not possess the neat and uniform appearance of a tab closure, they become tattered and unsightly after repeated use, and they do not offer suitable surfaces for the reception of print or labeling. These ties also require much more manipulation to apply and remove.

Several types of thin, flat closures have been proposed—for example, in U.K. patent 883,771 to Britt et al. (1961) and U.S. patents 3,164,250 (1965), 3,417,912 (1968), 3,822,441 (1974), 4,361,935 (1982), and 4,509,231 (1985), all to Paxton. Although inexpensive to manufacture, capable of use with bags having a short neck, and producible in break-off strips, such closures can be used only once if they are made of frangible plastic since they must be bent or twisted when being removed and consequently will fracture upon removal. Thus, to reseal a bag originally sealed with a frangible closure, one must either close its neck with another closure or else close it in makeshift fashion by folding or tying it. My own patent 4,694,542 (1987) describes a closure which is made of flexible plastic and is therefore capable of repeated use without damage to the bag, but nevertheless all the plastic closures heretofore known suffer from a number of disadvantages:

Fig. 8G (cont'd)—Specification of Sample Patent Application

Patent Application of Lou W. Koppe for "Paper-Laminated
Pliable Closure for Flexible Bags" continued
Page 3

(a) Their manufacture in color requires the use of a compounding facility
for the production of the pigmented plastic. Such a facility, which is needed
to compound the primary pigments and which generally constitutes a separate
production site, requires the presence of very large storage bins for the
pigmented raw granules. Also, it presents great difficulties with regard to
the elimination of the airborne powder which results from the mixing of the
primary granules.

(b) If one uses an extruder in the production of a pigmented plastic—
especially if one uses only a single extruder—a change from one color to a
second requires purging the extruder of the granules having the first color by
introducing those of the second color. This process inevitably produces, in
sizeable volume, an intermediate product of an undesired color which must be
discarded as scrap, thereby resulting in waste of material and time.

(c) The colors of the closures in present use are rather unsaturated. If
greater concentrations of pigment were used in order to make the colors more
intense, the plastic would become more brittle and the cost of the final
product would increase.

(d) The use of pigmented plastic closures does not lend itself to the
production of multicolored designs, and it would be very expensive to produce
plastic closures in which the plastic is multicolored—for example, in which
the plastic has stripes of several colors, or in which the plastic exhibits
multicolored designs.

(e) Closures made solely of plastic generally offer poor surfaces for
labeling or printing, and the label or print is often easily smudged.

(f) The printing on a plastic surface is often easily erased, thereby
allowing the alteration of prices by dishonest consumers.

(g) The plastic closures in present use are slippery when handled with wet
or greasy fingers.

(h) A closure of the type in present use can be very carefully pried off a
bag by a dishonest consumer and then attached to another item without giving
any evidence of such removal.

Fig. 8G (cont'd)—Specification of Sample Patent Application

Patent Application of Lou W. Koppe for "Paper-Laminated
Pliable Closure for Flexible Bags" continued
Page 4

BACKGROUND OF INVENTION--OBJECTS AND ADVANTAGES

reverse of disadvantages of prior art = praise of your invention

Accordingly, besides the objects and advantages of the flexible closures described in my above patent, several objects and advantages of the present invention are:

(a) to provide a closure which can be produced in a variety of colors without requiring the manufacturer to use a compounding facility for the production of pigments;

(b) to provide a closure whose production allows for a convenient and extremely rapid and economical change of color in the closures that are being produced;

(c) to provide a closure which both is flexible and can be brightly colored;

(d) to provide a closure which can be colored in several colors simultaneously;

(e) to provide a closure which will present a superior surface for the reception of labeling or print;

(f) to provide a closure whose labeling cannot be altered;

(g) to provide a closure which will not be slippery when handled with wet or greasy fingers; and

(h) to provide a closure which will show evidence of having been switched from one item to another by a dishonest consumer—in other words, to provide a closure which makes items tamper-proof.

Further objects and advantages are to provide a closure which can be used easily and conveniently to open and reseal a plastic bag, without damage to the bag, which is simple to use and inexpensive to manufacture, which can be supplied in separate tabs en masse or in break-off links, which can be used with bags having short necks, which can be used repeatedly, and which obviates the need to tie a knot in the neck of the bag or fold the neck under the bag or use a twist closure. Still further objects and advantages will become apparent from a consideration of the ensuing description and drawings.

Fig. 8G (cont'd)—Specification of Sample Patent Application

Patent Application of Lou W. Koppe for "Paper-Laminated
Pliable Closure for Flexible Bags" continued
Page 5

SUMMARY

In accordance with the present invention a bag closure comprises a flat body having a notch, a gripping aperture adjacent the notch and a layer of paper laminated on its side.

DRAWINGS--Figures

In the drawings, closely related figures have the same number but different alphabetic suffixes.

Figs 1A to 1D show various aspects of a closure supplied with a longitudinal groove and laminated on one side with paper.

Fig 2 shows a closure with no longitudinal groove and with a paper lamination on one side only.

Fig 3 shows a similar closure with one longitudinal groove.

Fig 4 shows a similar closure with a paper lamination on both sides.

Fig 5 shows a similar closure with a paper lamination on one side only, the groove having been formed into the paper as well as into the body of the closure.

Figs 6A to 6K show end views of closures having various combinations of paper laminations, longitudinal grooves, and through-holes.

Figs 7A to 7C show a laminated closure with groove after being bent and after being straightened again.

Figs 8A to 8C show a laminated closure without a groove after being bent and after being straightened again.

DRAWINGS--Reference Numerals

10	base of closure	12	lead-in notch
14	hole	16	gripping points
18	groove	20	paper lamination
22	tear of paper lamination	24	corner
26	longitudinal through-hole	28	neck-down
30	side of base opposite to bend	32	crease

Fig. 8G (cont'd)—Specification of Sample Patent Application

[margin note: summary paraphrases main claim]

[margin note: one short sentence for each figure]

Patent Application of Lou W. Koppe for "Paper-Laminated
Pliable Closure for Flexible Bags" continued
Page 6

DETAILED DESCRIPTION--FIGS. 1A AND 1B—PREFERRED EMBODIMENT

**static
description
of figures**

A preferred embodiment of the closure of the present invention is illustrated in Fig 1A (top view) and Fig 1B (end view). The closure has a thin base
10 of uniform cross section consisting of a flexible sheet of material which
can be repeatedly bent and straightened out without fracturing. A layer of
paper **20** (Fig 1B) is laminated on one side of base **10**. In the preferred embodiment, the base is a flexible plastic, such as poly-ethylene-tere-phthalate
(PET—hyphens here supplied to facilitate pronunciation)—available from Eastman
Chemical Co. of Kingsport, TN. However, the base can consist of any other
material that can be repeatedly bent without fracturing, such as polyethylene,
polypropylene, vinyl, nylon, rubber, leather, various impregnated or laminated
fibrous materials, various plasticized materials, cardboard, paper, etc.

At one end of the closure is a lead-in notch **12** which terminates in gripping points **16** and leads to a hole **14**. Paper layer **20** adheres to base **10** by
virtue either of the extrusion of liquid plastic (which will form the body of
the closure) directly onto the paper or the application of heat or adhesive
upon the entirety of one side of base **10**. The paper-laminated closure is then
punched out. Thus the lamination will have the same shape as the side of the
base **10** to which it adheres.

The base of the closure is typically .8 mm to 1.2 mm in thickness, and has
overall dimensions roughly from 20 mm x 20 mm (square shape) to 40 mm x 70 mm
(oblong shape). The outer four corners **24** of the closure are typically beveled
or rounded to avoid snagging and personal injury. Also, when closure tabs are
connected side-to-side in a long roll, these bevels or roundings give the roll
a series of notches which act as detents or indices for the positioning and
conveying of the tabs in a dispensing machine.

A longitudinal groove **18** is formed on one side of base **10** in Fig 1. In
other embodiments, there may be two longitudinal grooves—one each side of the
base—or there may be no longitudinal groove at all. Groove **18** may be formed by
machining, scoring, rolling, or extruding. In the absence of a groove, there
may be a longitudinal through-hole **26** (Fig 6L). This through-hole may be
formed by placing, in the extrusion path of the closure, a hollow pin for the
outlet of air.

Fig. 8G (cont'd)—Specification of Sample Patent Application

Patent Application of Lou W. Koppe for "Paper-Laminated
Pliable Closure for Flexible Bags" continued
Page 7

Operation--Figs 1, 6, 7, 8

operational description of figures

The manner of using the paper-laminated closure to seal a plastic bag is identical to that for closures in present use. Namely, one first twists the neck of a bag (not shown here but shown in Fig 12 of my above patent) into a narrow, cylindrical configuration. Next, holding the closure so that the plane of its base is generally perpendicular to the axis of the neck and so that lead-in notch **12** is adjacent to the neck, one inserts the twisted neck into the lead-in notch until it is forced past gripping points **16** at the base of the notch and into hole **14**.

To remove the closure, one first bends it along its horizontal axis (Fig 1C—an end view—and Figs 7 and 8) so that the closure is still in contact with the neck of the bag and so that gripping points **16** roughly point in parallel directions. Then one pulls the closure up or down and away from the neck in a direction generally opposite to that in which the gripping points now point, thus freeing the closure from the bag without damaging the latter. The presence of one or two grooves **18** or a longitudinal through-hole **26** (Fig 6L), either of which acts as a hinge, facilitates this process of bending.

The closure can be used to reseal the original bag or to seal another bag many times; one simply bends it flat again prior to reuse.

As shown in Figs 1C, 7B, and 8B (all end views), when the closure is bent along its longitudinal axis, region **30** of the base will stretch somewhat along the direction perpendicular to the longitudinal axis. (Region 30 is the region which is parallel to this axis and is on the side of the base opposite to the bend.) Therefore, when the closure is flattened again, the base will have elongated in the direction perpendicular to the longitudinal axis. This will cause a necking down **28** (Figs 1D, 7C, and 8C) of the base, as well as either a tell-tale tear **22**, or at least a crease **32** (Figs 7A and 8A) along the axis of bending. Therefore, if the closure is attached to a sales item and has print upon its paper lamination, the fact that the closure has been transferred by a dishonest consumer from the first item to another will be made evident by the tear or crease.

Figs 7A and 8A show bent closures with and without grooves, respectively. Figs 7C and 8C show the same closures, respectively, after being flattened

Fig. 8G (cont'd)—Specification of Sample Patent Application

Patent Application of Lou W. Koppe for "Paper-Laminated
Pliable Closure for Flexible Bags" continued
Page 8

out, along their longitudinal axes, paper tear **22** being visible.

Figs 2-5--Additional Embodiments

Additional embodiments are shown in Figs 2, 3, 4, and 5; in each case the paper lamination is shown partially peeled back. In Fig 2 the closure has only one lamination and no groove; in Fig 3 it has only one lamination and only one groove; in Fig 4 it has two laminations and only one groove; in Fig 5 it has two laminations and one groove, the latter having been rolled into one lamination as well as into the body of the closure.

Figs 6A-6B--Alternative Embodiments

There are various possibilities with regard to the relative disposition of the sides which are grooved and the sides which are laminated, as illustrated in Fig 6, which presents end views along the longitudinal axis. Fig 6A shows a closure with lamination on one side only and with no groove; Fig 6B shows a closure with laminations on both sides and with no groove; Fig 6C shows a closure with only one lamination and only one groove, both being on the same side; Fig 6D shows a closure with only one lamination and only one groove, both being on the same side and the groove having been rolled into the lamination as well as into the body of the closure; Fig 6E shows a closure with only one lamination and only one groove, the two being on opposite sides; Fig 6F shows a closure with two laminations and only one groove; Fig 6G shows a closure with two laminations and only one groove, the groove having been rolled into one lamination as well as into the body of the closure; Fig 6H shows a closure with only one lamination and with two grooves; Fig 6I shows a closure with only one lamination and with two grooves, one of the grooves having been rolled into the lamination as well as into the body of the closure; Fig 6J shows a closure with two laminations and with two grooves; Fig 6K shows a closure with two laminations and with two grooves, the grooves having been rolled into the laminations as well as into the body of the closure; and Fig 6L shows a closure with two laminations and a longitudinal through-hole.

Advantages

From the description above, a number of advantages of my paper-laminated closures become evident:

Fig. 8G (cont'd)—Specification of Sample Patent Application

Patent Application of Lou W. Koppe for "Paper-Laminated
Pliable Closure for Flexible Bags" continued
Page 9

(a) A few rolls of colored paper will contain thousands of square yards of a variety of colors, will obviate the need for liquid pigments or a pigment-compounding plant, and will permit the manufacturer to produce colored closures with transparent, off-color, or leftover plastic, all of which are cheaper than first quality pigmented plastic.

(b) With the use of rolls of colored paper to laminate the closures, one can change colors by simply changing rolls, thus avoiding the need to purge the extruder used to produce the closures.

(c) The use of paper laminate upon an unpigmented, flexible plastic base can provide a bright color without requiring the introduction of pigment into the base and the consequent sacrifice of pliability.

(d) The presence of a paper lamination will permit the display of multi-colored designs.

(e) The paper lamination will provide a superior surface for labeling or printing, either by hand or by machine.

(f) Any erasure or alteration of prices by dishonest consumers on the paper-laminated closure will leave a highly visible and permanent mark.

(g) Although closures made solely of plastic are slippery when handled with wet or greasy fingers, the paper laminate on my closures will provide a non-slip surface.

Figs 7A and 8A show bent closures with and without grooves, respectively. Figs 7C and 8C show the same closures, respectively, after being flattened out, along their longitudinal axes, paper tear 22 being visible.

Conclusion, Ramifications, and Scope

repeat advantages— keep selling it!

Accordingly, the reader will see that the paper-laminated closure of this invention can be used to seal a plastic bag easily and conveniently, can be removed just as easily and without damage to the bag, and can be used to reseal the bag without requiring a new closure. In addition, when a closure has been used to seal a bag and is later bent and removed from the bag so as not to damage the latter, the paper lamination will tear or crease and thus give visible evidence of tampering, without impairing the ability of the

Fig. 8G (cont'd)—Specification of Sample Patent Application

Patent Application of Lou W. Koppe for "Paper-Laminated
Pliable Closure for Flexible Bags" continued
Page 10

additional ramifications

closure to reseal the original bag or any other bag. Furthermore, the paper
lamination has the additional advantages in that

• it permits the production of closures in a variety of colors without
requiring the manufacturer to use a separate facility for the compounding of
the powdered or liquid pigments needed in the production of colored closures;

• it permits an immediate change in the color of the closure being produced
without the need for purging the extruder of old resin;

• it allows the closure to be brightly colored without the need to pigment
the base itself and consequently sacrifice the flexibility of the closure; it
allows the closure to be multicolored since the paper lamination offers a
perfect surface upon which can be printed multicolored designs;

• it provides a closure with a superior surface upon which one can label or
print;

• it provides a closure whose labeling cannot be altered or erased without
resulting in tell-tale damage to the paper lamination; and

• it provides a closure which will not be slippery when handled with wet or
greasy fingers, the paper itself providing a nonslip surface.

broadening paragraph

Although the description above contains many specificities, these should
not be construed as limiting the scope of the invention but as merely providing
illustrations of some of the presently preferred embodiments of this invention.
For example, the closure can have other shapes, such as circular, oval, trape-
zoidal, triangular, etc.; the lead-in notch can have other shapes; the groove
can be replaced by a hinge which connects two otherwise unconnected halves,
etc.

Thus the scope of the invention should be determined by the appended claims
and their legal equivalents, rather than by the examples given.

**[CLAIMS FOLLOW, STARTING ON A NEW PAGE, BUT
ARE PRINTED IN THE NEXT CHAPTER]**

Fig. 8G (cont'd)—Specification of Sample Patent Application

start abstract on new page, after
claims and sequence listing, if supplied

Patent Application of Lou W. Koppe for "Paper-Laminated
Pliable Closure for Flexible Bags" continued
Page 14

ABSTRACT: A thin, flat closure for plastic bags and of the type having at one edge a V-shaped notch (**12**) which communicates at its base with a gripping aperture (**14**). The base (**10**) of the closure is made of a flexible material so that it can be repeatedly bent, without fracturing, along an axis aligned with said notch and aperture. In addition, a layer of paper (**20**) is laminated on one or both sides of the closure. The axis of the base may contain one or two grooves (**18**) or a through-hole (**26**), either of which acts as a hinge to facilitate bending.

**inset reference numerals in parentheses
for possible foreign filing**

**if there is sequence listing, then insert
it on a separate page titled,**
"SEQUENCE LISTING"

Fig. 8G (cont'd)—Specification of Sample Patent Application

see Fig.10B for permitted drawing sizes

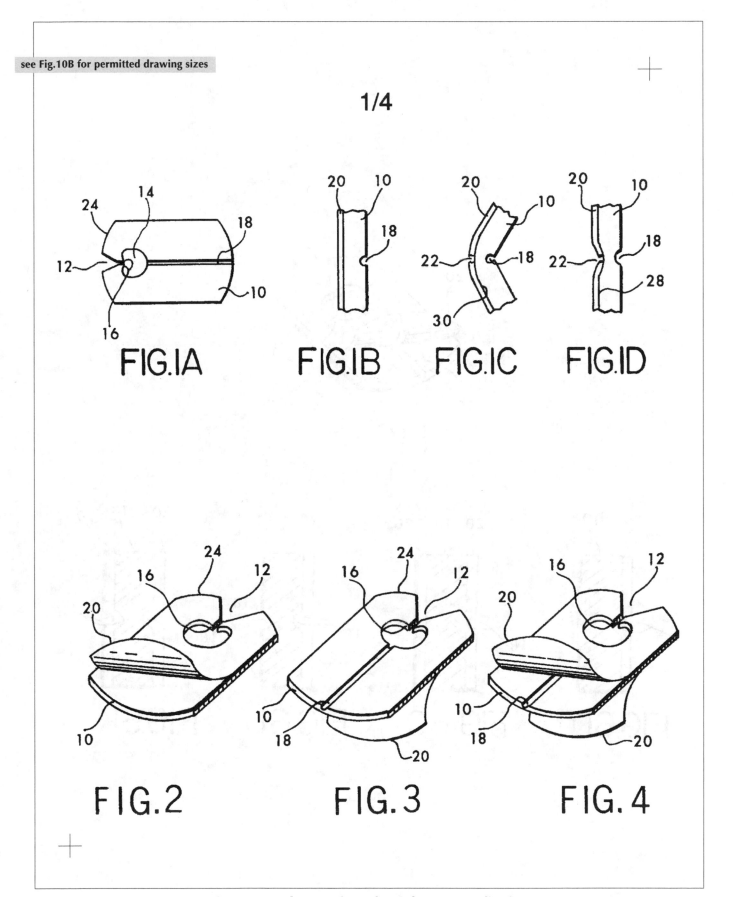

Fig. 8G (cont'd)—Drawings of Sample Patent Application

2/4

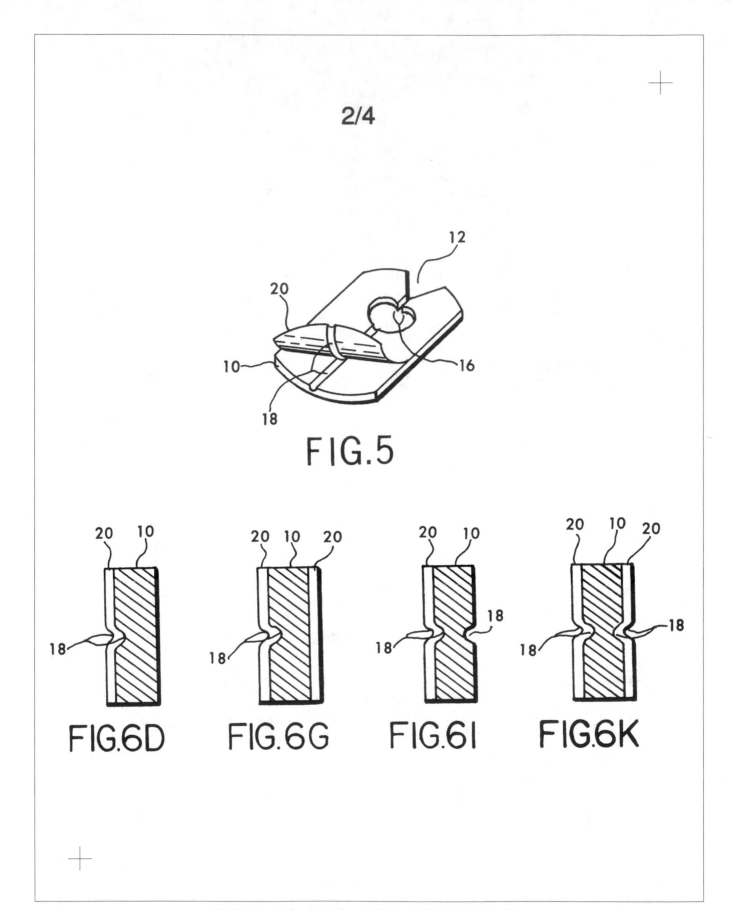

FIG.5

FIG.6D   FIG.6G   FIG.6I   FIG.6K

Fig. 8G (cont'd)—Drawings of Sample Patent Application

3/4

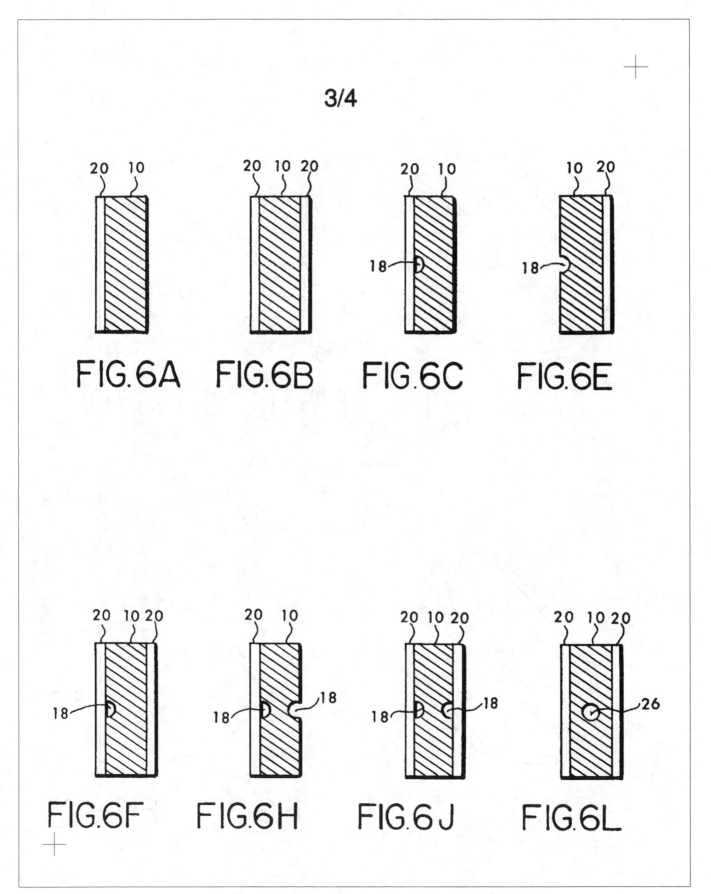

Fig. 8G (cont'd)—Drawings of Sample Patent Application

4/4

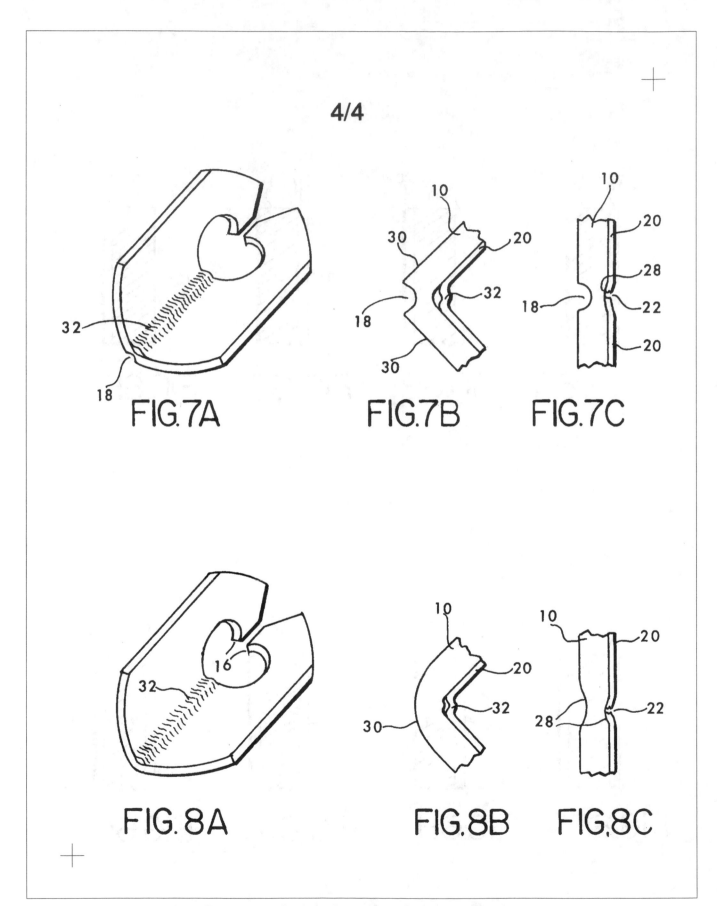

FIG.7A   FIG.7B   FIG.7C

FIG.8A   FIG.8B   FIG,8C

Fig. 8G (cont'd)—Drawings of Sample Patent Application

M. Summary

The specification must describe how to make and use the invention in full, clear, concise, and exact terms. The patent application should also "sell" the invention by stressing and repeating its advantages in the Objects, Operation, and Conclusion sections.

Any layperson who can write a detailed description in conjunction with drawings will be able to write a competent patent application. A patent application should contain certain prescribed headings and additional informative headings.

When your application is received in the PTO it will be processed and put in a file by clerical personnel and later reviewed by drawing reviewers and then an examiner.

Prior to doing your drawings and writing the application you should review your papers and make full preparations. For inventions that use software, the application should have a detailed flowchart or a listing. Do rough drawings first and provide a name for every part. Then draft the specification according to an outline and without legal terms, using short, simple sentences.

Provide a static description of each embodiment before describing its operation and sell the invention throughout. Follow the checklists for the preliminary drawings and specification draft. ■

Chapter 9

Now for the Legalese—The Claims

> ## Inventor's Commandment #12
>
> In your patent application, write at least one main (independent) claim. Make this claim as broad as the prior art permits by (1) reciting as few elements as you can, and (2) using the broadest possible terms for such elements, to make it as difficult as possible for others to avoid infringing such claim.

> ## Inventor's Commandment #13
>
> In your patent application, write (1) one or two alternative independent claims, making these as broad as possible, and different from your first independent claim, and (2) follow each independent claim with as many dependent claims as necessary to recite all of the significant additional features of your invention, thereby providing backup for each independent claim and a range of coverage.

A. What Are Claims?

If you don't yet know what patent claims are, or have never read any, you're in for a surprise. The word "claim" in the patent context is definitely a term of art. A "claim" is not what the common dictionary definitions recite—it's not a demand for something due, a title to something in the possession of another, or that which one seeks or asks for. Rather, a "claim," in the arcane world of patents, is a very formally worded sentence fragment contained in a patent application or patent. Claims recite and define the structure, or acts, of an invention in very precise, logical, and exact terms. They serve as tools to determine whether an invention is patentable over the prior art, and whether a patent is infringed. Just as a deed recites the boundary of a real estate parcel, and a criminal statute defines what acts are punishable by fine or imprisonment, patent claims recite the "bounds" or scope of an invention for the purposes of dealing with the PTO and possible infringers. In other words, claims are the nitty-gritty of patents. While the specification must teach how to make and use the invention, the claims must define its scope.

While claims are literally sentence fragments, they are supposed to be the object of the words "I [or We] claim."

They are actually interpreted, when in a patent application, as saying to the examiner, "Here is my definition of my invention. Please search to see whether my invention, as here defined, is patentable over the prior art." In a patent, claims are interpreted as your own little statutes that say to the public, "The following is a precise description of the elements of this invention; if you make, use, or sell anything that has all of these elements, or all of these elements plus additional elements, or that closely fits this description, you can be legally held liable for the consequences of patent infringement."

Since there are only five statutory classes of inventions (see Chapter 5), every claim must define something that is classifiable into one of these five classes. Thus there are: (1) process or method claims; (2) machine claims; (3) article or article of manufacture claims; (4) composition of matter claims; and (5) claims reciting a new use of any of the previous four statutory classes. Again, the line between (2) and (3) is blurred. Fortunately, as mentioned in Chapter 5, you don't have to do the classifying unless the PTO decides that your invention doesn't fit within any class at all.

If all of this sounds a bit formidable, don't let it throw you; it will become quite clear as we progress, after you see some examples. What's more, when it comes to claims, every layperson who "prosecutes" (handles or controls) a patent application has a safety net: So long as you can convince the patent examiner that you have a patentable invention, the examiner is required by law to write at least one claim for you, for free. I discuss this, along with several aids to claim drafting, in Section G of this chapter.

But a word of caution. If you're tempted to skip this chapter and solely rely on the examiner, you can't. You must provide at least one claim in your application to obtain a filing date. In addition, familiarity with the information I provide here is essential to securing the strongest and broadest possible patent on your invention. So I urge you to approach this chapter as if there were no safety net. Take this chapter as I present it, in small, easy-to-digest chunks, and you'll have no trouble. If you don't understand something the first time, go back again so you'll be farther down on the learning curve where you'll see things much more clearly.

B. The Law Regarding Claims

The law (statutes and PTO rules) concerning claims is written in only the most general and vague terms. Accordingly, I'll be turning to the real world of everyday practice to help you understand the actual requirements for drafting claims. Before I do, however, let's at least take a brief look at the statutes and rules.

1. Legal Requirements for Patent Claims

The only pertinent statute comprises the last five paragraphs of our old friend, Section 112 of the patent laws (35 USC 112), which states:

(2) The specification shall conclude with one or more claims particularly pointing out and distinctly claiming the subject matter which the applicant regards as the applicant's invention.

(3) A claim may be written in independent or, if the nature of the case admits, dependent form.

(4) Subject to the following paragraph, a claim in dependent form shall contain a reference to a claim previously set forth and then specify a further limitation of the subject matter claimed. A claim in dependent form shall be construed to incorporate by reference all the limitations of the claim to which it refers….

(5) A claim in multiple dependent form shall contain a reference, in the alternative only, to more than one claim previously set forth and then specify a further limitation of the subject matter claimed. A multiple dependent claim shall not serve as a basis for any other multiple dependent claim. A multiple dependent claim shall be construed to incorporate by reference all the limitations of the particular claim in relation to which it is being considered.

(6) An element in a claim for a combination may be expressed as a means or step for performing a specified function without the recital of structure, material, or acts in support thereof, and such claim shall be construed to cover the corresponding structure, material, or acts described in the specification and equivalents thereof.

Paragraph (2) is the one that mandates the use of claims in patents. It also means that the claims must be specific enough to define the invention over the prior art ("particularly pointing out") and also should be clear, logical, and precise ("distinctly claiming"). This sentence is the most important part of Section 112 and is referred to by patent examiners almost daily because of the frequency with which they reject claims for lack of clarity or for some other similar reason.

Paragraphs (3) to (5) define independent and dependent claims (more on this later) and make it clear that a dependent claim incorporates all the limitations of the claim to which it refers. Paragraph (5) refers to multiple dependent claims, but since they require a stiff surcharge and since examiners don't like them, I recommend that you don't use them.

Paragraph (6) was enacted to overrule two famous Supreme Court decisions (*G.E. v. Wabash*, 304 U.S. 371

(1938) and *Halliburton v. Walker*, 329 U.S. 1 (1946)). These decisions held certain claims invalid on technical grounds, specifically for "functionality at the point of novelty" because they expressed the essence of an invention in terms of its novel function, rather than reciting the specific structure that performed the novel function. In other words, they contained a broad expression such as "means for hardening latex" rather than a specific expression like "a sulfur additive." Congress enacted this paragraph to enable patent applicants to continue to claim their inventions more broadly. Under paragraph (6), if a claim uses the word "means" for performing a function, it must be construed to cover the structure, material, or acts described in the specification, and their equivalents. That is, if a claim recites "means for conveying rotational energy from said pedals to said rear wheels" and the specification describes a link chain for performing this function, the "means" claim will be construed by the PTO and the courts to cover the link chain and any equivalents, such as a driveshaft, a gear train, etc. (*In re Donaldson Co., Inc.*, 29 USPQ 2d 1845 (CAFC 1994)).

2. Rules of Practice

In addition to Section 112, claims are governed by the PTO's "Rules of Practice." PTO Rule 75 (37 CFR 1.75), parts (b), (d)(1), and (e) to (i) add these additional requirements:

(b) More than one claim may be presented provided they differ substantially from each other and are not unduly multiplied….

(d)(1) The claim or claims must conform to the invention as set forth in the remainder of the specification and the terms and phrases used in the claims must find clear support or antecedent basis in the description so that the meaning of the terms in the claims may be ascertainable by reference to the description….

(e) Where the nature of the case admits, as in the case of an improvement, any independent claim should contain in the following order: (1) a preamble comprising a general description of all the elements or steps of the claimed combination that are conventional or known, (2) a phrase such as "wherein the improvement comprises," and (3) those elements, steps, and/or relationship that constitutes that portion of the claimed combination that the applicant considers as the new or improved portion.

(f) If there are several claims, they shall be numbered consecutively in Arabic numerals.

(g) The least restrictive claim should be presented as claim number 1, and all dependent claims should be grouped together with the claim or claims to which they refer to the extent practicable.

(h) The claim or claims must commence on a separate sheet.

(i) Where a claim sets forth a plurality of elements or steps, each element or step of the claim should be separated by a line indentation.

Part (b) requires that the claims differ substantially from each other and not be too numerous. In practice, minimal differences will suffice. The rule prohibiting numerous claims is more strictly enforced. If more than about 20 claims are presented, there should be some justification, such as a very complex invention or numerous embodiments. Also, there are substantial charges for each independent claim over three and each claim (independent or dependent) over 20—see Appendix 4, Fee Schedule.

Part (d)(1), enforced only sporadically, requires that the terms in the claims should correspond to those used in the specification. It has often been said that the specification should serve as a dictionary for the claims.

Part (e), a newcomer, was introduced to require that claims be drafted, insofar as practicable, in the German or "*Jepson*" style (from a famous decision of that name). The *Jepson*-type claim is very easy for examiners to read and understand. It puts the essence of the invention into sharp focus by providing in the first part of the claim an introduction that sets forth the environment of the invention—that is, what is already known, and in the second part, or body of the claim, the essence of the invention—that is, the improvement of the current invention. In practice, I've never seen this part of Rule 75 enforced.

Parts (f), (h), and (i) are self-explanatory and part (g) means that the broadest claims should be number 1, all dependent claims should be together and under their independent claim, and the elements or steps of a claim should be in separate paragraphs. More information is provided in Section J of this chapter.

C. Some Sample Claims

As mentioned, claims boil the invention down to its essence. In their broadest sense, they eliminate everything nonessential to the invention. In fact, many inventors first realize what their invention truly is when they write or see a claim to it, especially after the claim has been rejected in the patent prosecution process. Conversely, you won't be able to draft an adequate claim unless you have a clear understanding of your invention. Although not a patent attorney, the great theatrical producer David Belasco showed that he

understood the principle behind claims well when he said, "If you can't write your idea on the back of my calling card, you don't have a clear conception of your idea."

And claims are difficult to write just because they are so short. Blaise Pascal once concluded a letter to a friend as follows: "I have made this letter a little longer than usual because I lack the time to make it shorter." Nevertheless, don't get discouraged; if you follow the step-by-step, four-part procedure I give later, you'll find that writing claims is not too much more difficult than writing the specification.

In the following sections, I provide some hypothetical simple claims and some actual ones. Patent applications containing the hypothetical claims would now be rejected since the "inventions" they define are obviously old and in the public domain. A few of the claims—the "method of putting" and the "new use" claim—are from patents.

1. Process or Method Claims: Conventional Process, Software Process, Business Method, and Manual Method

In this section, you'll see examples of various method claims—one to a conventional process, one to a software-based process, one to a business method, and one to a manual method. Note that these claims recite a series of steps (or individual operations), rather than a series of hardware elements as in an article claim. Note also that the software, business method, and manual method claims are similar in construction, which shows you that these processes are generally claimed the same way as any other process.

a. Conventional Process
For the conventional process, assume that you just invented sewing and want to claim the process. Here's how you'd do it.

A method for joining two pieces of cloth together at their edges, comprising the steps of:
a. providing said two pieces of cloth and positioning them together so that an edge portion of one piece overlaps an adjacent edge portion of the other piece, and
b. passing a thread repeatedly through and along the length of the overlapping portions in sequentially opposite directions and through sequentially spaced holes in said overlapping adjacent portions, whereby said two pieces of cloth will be attached along said edge portions.

Note that the first part of this claim contains a title, preamble, or genus, which states the purpose of the method but doesn't use the term "sewing," because sewing is the invention and is assumed to be new at the time the claim is drafted. The claim contains two steps, (a) and (b), that state in sequence the acts one would perform in sewing two pieces of cloth. Note that each clause begins with an "—ing" word. The claim also contains an optional "whereby" clause at the end to point out to the examiner or a judge the advantage of the process.

b.   Software Process

For the software process, assume that you've just invented a word processor and want to claim the word insertion feature (which we now all take for granted) as a method. Here's how you'd do it.

A method of inserting additional characters within an existing series of characters on a display, comprising:

> *(a) providing a memory which is able to store a series of characters at an adjacent series of addresses in said memory,*
>
> *(b) providing a character input means which a human operator can use to store a series of characters in said memory at said respective adjacent series of addresses,*
>
> *(c) storing said series of characters in said memory at said adjacent series of addresses,*
>
> *(d) providing a display which is operatively connected to said memory for displaying said series of characters stored in said memory at said adjacent series of addresses,*
>
> *(e) providing a pointer means which said operator can manipulate to point to any location between any adjacent characters within said series of characters displayed on said display,*
>
> *(f) providing a memory controller which will:*
>
>> *(1) direct any additional character which said operator enters via said character input means to a location in said memory, beginning at an address corresponding to the location between said adjacent characters as displayed on said display, and*
>>
>> *(2) causing all characters in said series of characters which are stored in said memory at addresses subsequent said location in said memory to be transferred to subsequent addresses in said memory so that said additional character will be stored in said memory at said location and before all of said subsequent characters,*
>
> *whereby said display will display said additional character within said series of characters at said location between said adjacent characters, and a writer can add words within existing body of text and the added words are displayed in an orderly and clean fashion without having to reenter said existing body of text.*

Note that the preamble of this claim states the purpose of the method. The series of steps in the body of the claim first state or lay out the hardware of the computer (the memory, the display, etc.) as a series of "providing" clauses, since a method claim is not supposed to state hardware directly, that is, if this claim recited simply "a memory," rather than "providing a memory," the examiner in the PTO would object to it as an improper hybrid claim because it recited both hardware and method steps. More on this later. Finally, note that the end of this claim also contains a first optional "whereby" clause which states the internal function of the claimed method, and a second "whereby" clause which states an overall, external, and meaningful result or function of the method. The two whereby clauses help sell the method to the examiner, as well as to any judge who has to decide on the validity or infringement of this claim.

c.   Business Method

For the business method, assume that you've just invented a procedure for checking the "creditworthiness" of a customer. Now you want to write a claim to this as a business method. Here's how you might write a suitable claim for a credit-checking process:

A method of passing on the creditworthiness of a customer comprising:

> *(a) providing a form for said customer to complete, said form having spaces in which said customer must indicate a plurality of credit accounts and a plurality of credit references,*
>
> *(b) investigating each of said credit accounts and credit references and compiling a score from 1 to 100, for each account and reference, with 1 indicating a minimal credit rating and 100 indicating a maximal or excellent credit rating,*
>
> *(c) averaging all of said scores to compile an overall average,*
>
> *(d) rejecting said customer if said overall average is below a predetermined value and accepting said customer if said overall average is above said pre-determined value.*

d.   Manual Methods

A golfer invented a new way of putting that emphasizes the golfer's dominant hand and claimed this as a manual process (U.S. Pat. No. 5,616,089). Here's how he did it.

A method of gripping a putter comprising the steps: gripping a putter grip with a dominant hand;

> *(a) placing a non-dominant hand over an interior wrist portion of the dominant hand behind a thumb of the dominant hand;*

(b) *resting a middle finger of the non-dominant hand on the styloid process of the dominant hand;*

(c) *pressing a ring finger and a little finger of the non-dominant hand against the back of the dominant hand;*

(d) *pressing the palm of the non-dominant hand against a forward surface of the putter grip as the non-dominant hand squeezes the dominant hand.*

A cat owner invented a new way of exercising a cat using a laser. Some opined that this invention is ridiculous and obvious. Evidently the examiner didn't think so (U.S. Pat. No. 5,443,036). Here's the main claim:

A method of inducing aerobic exercise in an unrestrained cat, comprising:

(a) *directing an intense coherent beam of invisible light produced by a hand-held laser apparatus to produce a bright, highly focused pattern of light at the intersection of the beam and an opaque surface, said pattern being of visual interest to a cat; and*

(b) *selectively redirecting said beam out of said cat's immediate reach to induce said cat to run and chase said beam and pattern of light around an exercise area.*

2. Machine Claims—Conventional and Software Machines

Here are examples of two machine claims, one to a conventional machine and one to a software-based machine. Note that both claims recite a series of hardware elements, rather than a series of steps as in the process claims. Note also that both claims are similar in construction, indicating again that a software machine is generally claimed the same way as any other machine.

a.   Conventional Machine
For the conventional machine, assume now that you've just invented the automobile. Here's how to claim it.

A self-propelled vehicle, comprising:

a.   *a body carriage having rotatable wheels mounted thereunder for enabling said body carriage to roll along a surface,*

b.   *an engine mounted in said carriage for producing rotational energy, and*

c.   *means for controllably coupling rotational energy from said engine to at least one of said wheels,*

   whereby said carriage will be self-propelled along said surface.

This claim again contains a title in the first part. The second part or body contains three elements, the carriage, the engine, and the transmission. These elements are defined as connected or interrelated by the statement that the engine is mounted in the carriage and the transmission (defined broadly as "means for controllably coupling …") couples the engine to at least one wheel of the carriage. Again, the "whereby" clause recites the advantage of the hardware elements of the preamble and clauses a., b., and c.

b.   Software Machine
For the software machine, let's make it easy and continue to assume that you've just invented a word processor and want to claim the word insertion feature as a machine. As I'll explain below, to obtain maximum coverage, it's best to provide both method and machine claims for an invention, if it's possible to do so. Here's the machine claim to the word processor:

A machine for inserting additional characters within an existing series of characters on a display, comprising:

(a) *a memory which is able to store a series of characters at an adjacent series of addresses in said memory,*

(b) *a character input means which a human operator can use to store a series of characters in said memory at said adjacent series of addresses,*

(c) *a display which is operatively connected to said memory for displaying said series of characters stored in said memory at said adjacent series of addresses,*

(d) *a pointer means which said operator can manipulate to point to any location between any adjacent characters within said series of characters displayed on said display,*

(e) *a memory controller which will:*

(1) *direct any additional character which said operator enters via said character input means to a location in said memory, beginning at an address corresponding to the location between said adjacent characters as displayed on said display, and*

(2) *cause all characters in said series of characters which are stored in said memory at addresses subsequent to said location in said memory to be transposed to subsequent addresses in said memory so that said additional characters will be stored in said memory at said location and before all of said subsequent characters,*

   whereby said display will display said additional characters within said series of characters at said location between said adjacent characters, and a writer can add words within the existing body of text and the added words are displayed in an orderly and clean fashion without having to reenter said existing body of text.

Note that this machine claim is essentially the same as the above method claim on word processing, but our machine claim contains only directly recited hardware elements and no method steps. It's simply an alternative way of reciting the word processing invention. As I'll discuss below, it's desirable to provide as many different ways to claim an invention as possible, just as it would be desirable to go into battle with as many different weapons as possible (rifle, pistol, knife, grenade, destroyer, fighter plane, guided missile, etc.), since you never know which one will help you win the battle.

3. Article of Manufacture Claim

You've done it again! Here's a claim to the pencil you've just invented.

A hand-held writing instrument comprising:
   a.   elongated core-element means that will leave a marking line if moved across paper or other similar surface, and
   b.   an elongated holder surrounding and encasing said elongated core-element means, one portion of said holder being removable from an end thereof to expose an end of said core-element means so as to enable said core-element means to be exposed for writing,

   whereby said holder protects said core-element means from breakage and provides an enlarged means for holding said core-element means conveniently.

This claim, like the machine claim, contains a preamble and a body with two elements: (a) the "lead" and (b) the wood. As before, the elements of the body are associated; here the wood ("elongated holder") is said to surround and encase the lead ("elongated core"). The "whereby" clause at the end of the claim states the purpose and advantage of the lead and its holder.

4. Composition of Matter Claim

Now, great inventor that you are, you've come up with concrete. Here's your claim.

A rigid building and paving material comprising a mixture of sand and stones, and a hardened cement binder filling the interstices between and adhering to sand and stones, whereby a hardened, rigid, and strong matrix for building and paving will be provided.

This claim, although not in subparagraph form, still contains a preamble and a body containing a recitation of the elements of the composition (sand, stones, and cement binder), plus an association of the elements (sand and stones are mixed and binder fills volume between and adheres to sand and stones). Again, the whereby clause drives home the advantages of the components.

The height of claim brevity was reached (and will never be exceeded) in two composition of matter patents in 1964 when the PTO issued patents 3,156,523 and 3,161,462 to the late Dr. Glenn T. Seaborg, on two new elements, *americium* and *curium*. The claim for U.S. Pat. No. 3,156,523 (americium) read simply,
   1.   Element 95.
The claim for U.S. Pat. No. 3,161,462 (curium) read,
   1.   Element 96.

5. New Use Claim

Someone discovered that pigs put on weight faster if aspirin is added to their diet. Here's how to claim it.

A method for stimulating the growth of swine comprising feeding such swine aspirin in an amount effective to increase their rate of growth.

This claim recites the newly discovered use of aspirin and the purpose of the new use in a manner that defines over and avoids the known, old use of aspirin (analgesic). Note that it is a method claim (as all new-use claims must be). This is because aspirin per se is old and thus must be claimed more narrowly, as a new use.

Now that you've read a few claims, I suggest you try writing a practice claim or two of your own to become more familiar with the process. Try a simple article or machine with which you are very familiar, such as a table, chair, pen, etc. Write the preamble and then the body. To write the body, first list the elements or parts of the article or machine, and then associate or interconnect them. Don't worry too much about grammar or style, but try to make the claim clear and understandable.

D. Common Misconceptions Regarding Claims

In my experience, inventors' misconceptions about claims are more widespread than in any other area of the patent law, except possibly for the misconception regarding the

"Post Office Patent" explained in Chapter 3. Consider some of the following:

Common Misconception: The more claims that the PTO (Patent and Trademark Office) allows in your patent application, the broader your scope of coverage.

Fact: The scope of your monopoly is determined by the wording of your claims, not their number. One broad claim can be far more powerful than 50 narrow claims.

Common Misconception: If you want to get broad coverage on a specific feature of your invention, you should recite that specific feature in your claims.

Fact: If you recite a specific feature of your invention in a claim, that claim will be limited to that feature as recited, and variations may not be covered—for example, if you have a two-inch nylon gear in your apparatus and you recite it as such in a claim, the claim may not cover an apparatus that uses a one-inch gear, or a steel gear. The best way to cover all possible variations of your gear is to recite it simply as a "gear," or better yet, "rotary transmission means."

Common Misconception: To cover a specific feature of your invention per se, you need merely recite it in a dependent claim.

Fact: As stated in the statute quoted in Section B, above (35 USC 112, ¶ 4), a dependent claim is construed (and reads) as if it incorporated all of the limitations of the claim to which it refers. Thus if your independent claim (#1) recites a telephone having a connecting cord and your dependent claim reads, "The telephone of Claim 1 wherein said connecting cord is coiled," the dependent claim doesn't claim the coiled cord per se, but rather the coiled cord in *combination with the telephone*. More on this later in Section J, Drafting Dependent Claims.

Common Misconception: If a claim doesn't recite a specific feature of your invention, then this feature is necessarily not covered. For example, if your invention includes a two-inch nylon gear and you fail to recite it specifically in a claim, then anyone who makes your invention with this gear can't infringe your patent.

Fact: The fact that a feature isn't recited doesn't mean that it isn't covered. An absurd example will make this clear. Suppose your invention is a bicycle and you show and describe it with a front wheel having 60 spokes. You don't mention the spokes at all in a claim; you simply recite a "front wheel." Any bike that has all of the limitations of the claim will infringe it. Thus a bike that has any "front wheel" will infringe, whether it has zero or 600 spokes.

As I'll explain from time to time, to infringe a claim, an accused apparatus must have at least all of the elements of the claim; if it has more elements than recited in the claim, it still infringes, but if it has fewer, then it doesn't infringe. Claim limitations are thus interpreted using Boolean logic, similar to computer search terms, as explained in Chapter 6, Section L.

Common Misconception: The more features of your invention you recite in a claim, the broader that claim will be. (Stated differently, the longer a claim is, the broader it is.)

Fact: As will be apparent from the previous misconceptions, the less you recite in a claim—that is, *the fewer the elements you recite—the broader the claim will be*. This seeming paradox exists because an accused infringing device must have all the elements of a claim to infringe. Thus, the fewer the elements specified in a claim, the fewer the elements an accused infringing device needs to have to infringe. Put differently, infringement is generally easier to prove if a claim is made shorter or has fewer elements. "To claim more, you should recite less" is a Boolean concept that is difficult for most inventors to absorb, but that you should learn well if you want to secure the broadest possible coverage. Again, see Computer Searching in Chapter 6, Section L, for further clarification of this point.

E. One Claim Should Be as Broad as Possible

As stated in Inventor's Commandment #12, there are two ways to make a claim broader: (1) *minimize* the number of elements; and (2) *maximize* the scope of these elements. Let's see how this works.

1. Minimize the Number of Elements

Take our automobile claim, above, which recites three elements, a, b, and c—that is, the wheeled carriage, the engine, and the transmission. If an accused machine contains just these three elements, it will, of course, infringe.

If it has these three plus a fourth, such as a radio, which we'll label d, it will still infringe.

But if our accused machine contains only elements a and b, the carriage and engine, it won't infringe, since it simply doesn't contain all of the claimed elements, a, b, and c.

If a claim contains many, many elements, say a to m, only devices with all 13 elements, a to m, will infringe. If the maker of the device eliminates just one of the 13 elements, say g, the device will *not* infringe. Thus, it's relatively easy to avoid infringing a claim with many elements.

If a claim contains only two elements, a and b, any device with these two elements will infringe, no matter how many other elements the device has. The only way to have the device avoid infringement is to eliminate either element a or element b, a relatively difficult task.

Thus, it should be very clear that the *fewer the elements in a claim, the harder the claim will be to avoid*, that is, the broader it will be and the more devices it will cover. Therefore, when drafting a main or independent claim to your invention, it will behoove you to put in as few elements of your invention as possible. (You do have to include sufficient elements so that the claim recites an operative, complete assemblage that is novel and unobvious over the prior art. More on this in Sections F and G, below.)

2. Recite Each Element as Broadly as Possible

With regard to the second way of broadening a claim, that is, reciting existing elements more broadly, consider a few examples. Suppose an invention involves a chair. The chair can be drafted broadly as "a seat" or narrowly as a four-legged maple chair with a vinyl-covered padded seat and a curved plywood back. Obviously, a three-legged plastic stool would be "a seat," and it would infringe the broadly recited element, but would miss the narrowly recited maple chair by a country mile. In electronics, "controllable electron valve" is broader than "vacuum tube" or "transistor." In machinery, "rotational energy connecting element" is broader than "helically cut gear" or "V-belt."

One way of reciting elements broadly is to take advantage of paragraph 6 of Section 112 by reciting an element, wherever possible, as "means" plus a specific function. In this way, any device or means that performs the function and is the equivalent of the supporting structure in the specification would infringe. For example, "means for conveying rotational energy" is broader than a drive belt and covers gears, pulleys, and drive shafts if these are the equivalent of a belt, which they will be determined to be if you've mentioned them in the specification. "Amplifying means" is broader than and covers such items as transistor amplifiers, tube amplifiers, and masers.

If you do use the word "means" in a claim, Section 112 requires that the claim recite a "combination"—that is, two or more elements or parts. Claims that recite a single element are not supposed to use the word "means" to describe the single element, since this is considered too broad—for example, "17. Means for providing a continuously variable speed/power drive for a bicycle" would be an example of a prohibited "single means" claim. However, you can effectively obtain practically the same breadth of coverage by adding an immaterial second element to the claim to make it a combination claim. Thus, "17. In combination, a bicycle having a pedal mechanism and means for providing a continuously variable speed/power drive for coupling rotational energy from said pedal mechanism to a wheel of said bicycle" would satisfy Section 112.

Courts have recently been construing "means" clauses narrowly, so you should also include claims with "structural" (nonmeans) clauses; these clauses can be expanded under the "doctrine of equivalents" (Chapter 15, Section J).

To sum up, while you should write your specification as specifically and with as much detail as possible (Chapter 8), you should make the substance of your main claims as general (broad) as possible by (1) eliminating as many elements as is feasible and (2) describing (reciting) the remaining elements as broadly as possible. In other words, make your specification specific and long and your main claims general and short.

F. The Effect of Prior Art on Your Claim

Now that you've learned how to make your claims as broad as possible, it's time for the bad news. What is "possible" has generally much less breadth than you'd like. This is because each claim must define an invention that is patentable over the prior art. Remember the issues of novelty and unobviousness? Well, they (especially unobviousness) are an ever-present factor always to be considered in claim drafting.

1. Novelty

Let's go back to Section 102, which deals with novelty (Chapter 5). A claim must define an invention that is novel in view of the prior art. It must recite something that no single reference in the prior art shows—that is, it must contain something new or novel. Your claim must recite novel hardware (or a novel process step) in a positive, structurally supported, unequivocal manner. For example, reciting "a wheel for providing lateral stabilization" won't adequately define over a prior-art wheel that doesn't provide lateral stabilization, since the function isn't supported by novel structure. The remedy: recite the novel structure that does provide the stabilization—such as a guideway for the wheel, or a "means" for providing stabilization.

Just as a claim can be made broader by eliminating elements and reciting the existing elements more broadly, it can be made narrower in order to define novel structure (1) by adding elements, or (2) by reciting the existing elements more narrowly.

For an example of adding elements, suppose a prior-art reference shows a machine having three elements—A, B, and C, and your claim recites these three elements A, B, and C. Your claim would be said to lack novelty over the prior art and would be rejectable or invalid under Section 102. But if you added a fourth element, D, to the claim, it would clear the prior art and would recite a novel invention (but not necessarily a patentable one, because of the unobviousness requirement). (If the prior art were an in-force patent that *claimed* elements A, B, and C, and your *device* had elements A, B, C, and D, it *would* infringe for reasons given in Section E1, above. However, the PTO is never concerned with infringements, so you don't need to worry about this issue in a patent application.)

For an example of reciting existing elements more narrowly, suppose the prior art shows a machine having the same three elements—A, B, and C. You could also clear this prior art and claim a novel invention by reciting in your claim elements A, B, and C′, where C′ would be the prior-art element C with any change that isn't shown in the prior art. For example, if the prior art shows element C as a steam engine, and you recite a gasoline engine (C′), you've obviated any question of lack of novelty (though probably not obviousness).

In sum, although you'd like to be able to eliminate as many elements as possible and recite all of your elements as broadly as possible, you will usually have to settle for less because there will always be prior art there to make you toe the line of novelty.

2. Unobviousness

As I've stressed, novelty isn't enough. Under Section 103 the claims must define an invention that in addition to being novel, must also be unobvious to one having ordinary skill in the art. Or to use the paraphrase of the law from Chapter 5, the novel feature(s) of the invention defined by each claim must have one or more new features that are important, significant, and produce valuable, unexpected new results. Thus, when you have to narrow a claim to define over the prior art, you must do so by adding one or more elements or by reciting existing elements more narrowly, and you must be sure that the added or narrowed elements define a structure or step that is sufficiently different from the prior art to be considered unobvious. More on this in Chapter 13.

For the last bit of bad news, note that if the wording of a claim has several possible interpretations, the examiner is entitled to use any one, including the one least favorable to you, in determining whether the claim clears the prior art.

Now that I've given you the bad news, I suggest you ignore it at this stage. You should try to write your main claim(s) as broadly as possible while keeping in mind the prior art that you've uncovered. In case of doubt, you should err on the side of too much breadth, since you can always narrow your claims later if your examiner thinks they're too broad. Conversely, if your examiner allows your narrow claims on your first office action (rare), you'll find it very difficult to broaden them later.

ANTI-SNAKE BITE PANTS
No. 5049

G. Technical Requirements of Claims

As stated, in addition to defining adequately over the prior art, each claim must also be worded in a clear, concise, precise, and rational way. If the wording of a claim is poor, the examiner will make a "technical" (non–prior-art) rejection under Section 112. It is this technical aspect of drafting claims that most often serves as a stumbling block to the layperson. To put it candidly, claims, like laws, are not written to be easily understood; they should be written so they cannot be misunderstood. Yet claim drafting really won't be that hard if you:

• Study the sample claims listed later in this chapter, plus those of a few patents, to get the basic idea;

- Use the four-step method (preamble-element-interconnections-broaden) set out in Section H, below; and
- Are conversant with the appropriate terminology associated with your invention's elements.

Remember also that you needn't write perfect claims when you file the application. Why? Because if you have a patentable invention, you can have the examiner write them for you. A provision of the *Manual of Patent Examining Procedure*, Section 707.07(j), states:

> *"When, during the examination of a pro se [no attorney] case, it becomes apparent to the examiner that there is patentable subject matter disclosed in the application [the examiner] shall draft one or more claims for the applicant and indicate in office action that such claims would be allowed if incorporated in the application by amendment.*
>
> *"This practice will expedite prosecution and offer a service to individual inventors not represented by a registered patent attorney or agent. Although this practice may be desirable and is permissible in any case where deemed appropriate by the examiner, it will be expected to be applied in all cases where it is apparent that the applicant is unfamiliar with the proper preparation and prosecution of patent applications."*

You do have to at least give it a try, since you must file at least one claim with your application to get a filing date. But, as indicated, this claim need not be well written or narrow enough for patent coverage. Instead, during the ensuing prosecution stage, you can ask the examiner to write claims for you pursuant to this section if you feel yours aren't adequate. The examiner is bound to do so if your invention is patentable.

If you do choose this option, be sure the examiner's claims are broad enough, since it isn't in the examiner's own interest to write broad claims for you. As with any other claim, ask yourself if any elements of the examiner's claim can be eliminated or recited more broadly and still distinguish adequately over the prior art. If so, amend it as I suggest in Chapter 13, Section E.

Also remember that many patent attorneys and agents will be willing to review your specification and drawings or draft your claims at their regular hourly rates. But use this as a last alternative, since most patent attorneys in private practice charge $100 to $300 per hour. If possible, you should choose a company-employed patent attorney or a retired patent attorney who works at home, since such attorneys' rates will usually be one-half to one-third of those charged by their downtown counterparts. See Chapter 6, Section F, for how to find patent attorneys and agents.

Now that you know there's help out here, let's look at some of the basic rules covering the drafting of claims.

1. Use Proper Antecedents and Be Precise

Your claims must be precise, logical, and determinate. One of the most common reasons for claim rejections is the improper use of articles, such as "a," "the," and "said." Generally, the first time you recite an element, use the indefinite article "a," just as you would if you were speaking to someone who is not familiar with your device—for example, "I just bought a car." If you refer to the same element again using exactly the same words to describe it, use the extremely definite article "said"—for example, " … said car has a burglar alarm." "Said" actually means, in patent law, "the following part, which in this claim (or its parent claim) is previously recited in exactly the following words:" If you refer to an aspect of an element by using different, but implicitly clear words, use the definite article "the" just as you would do in ordinary speech—for example, "The auto was expensive." Here's an example showing how "a," "said," and "the" are properly used in a claim to a table:

> *An article of furniture for holding objects for a sitting human, comprising:*
> (a) *__a__ sheet of rigid material having sufficient size to accommodate use by a human being for writing and working,*
> (b) *__a__ plurality of elongated support members of equal length,*
> (c) *__said__ support members being joined perpendicularly to __the__ undersurface of __said__ sheet of rigid material at spaced locations so as to be able to support __said__ rigid member in __a__ horizontal orientation.*

Note that the first time any element is mentioned, the article "a" is used, but when it's referred to again by its original designation, "said" is used. When another aspect of it is referred to with a different (but clear) designation—that is, the undersurface of the table—"the" is used.

In addition to being precise in the use of articles, you should avoid ambiguous or missing references. For example, if "said elongated lever" is used in a claim and no "elongated lever" has previously been recited in these exact words, a non sequitur has occurred and the PTO will reject the claim for indefiniteness due to a "missing antecedent." Or, if the same element is positively recited twice, such as "a lever" … "a lever," the claim is unclear. The solution is to change the second "a lever" to "said lever."

In a dependent claim (see Section J, below), the antecedent can be provided in the dependent claim itself, the referent claim which the dependent claim depends from (whether independent or dependent), or any lower-numbered referent claim which the first referent claim depends from. Thus, if claim 3 is dependent on claim 2, which is in turn dependent on claim 1, an antecedent for "said lever" in claim 3 can be provided in either claims 1 or 2.

Computer Hint. To help provide proper antecedents, it's very helpful to use a computer and a word-processing program with a "windows" function so that you can display the first part of your claim (or your main claim if you're writing dependent claims) in one window and the latter part of your claim (or the dependent claim you're writing) in a second window. In this way, you'll be able to refer continuously to the higher-numbered (referent) claim to make sure your current writing corresponds.

Vagueness and indefiniteness can also occur if you use abbreviations—such as, "d.c." (say "direct current"); relative terms without any reference—such as, "large" (say "larger than…" or "large enough to support three adults"), or vague, casual language, such as "strong," "suitable," "standard," etc.

2. Use Only One Capital, One Period, and No Dashes, Quotes, Parentheses, Trademarks, or Abbreviations

Amateurs violate this rule so often that a friend who has a foreign patent translation agency and who wants to show he's professional includes the following blurb in his ad flyer: "We promise never to include more than one period or capital letter in any translated claim, no matter how long it is." While it may be hard for you to accept, and while it may seem silly, the rules are that the only capital letter in a claim should be the first letter of the first word, the claim should contain a period only at its end, and there should be no dashes, quotes, or parentheses, trademarks, or abbreviations. (You may use capitals, periods, and parentheses for the lettered subparagraphs of a claim, for instance, "A." or "(A)"; also, hyphens ("hand-held") are okay, but dashes ("—" or "--") are not. (The PTO will allow a second capital in a dependent claim when the word "Claim" is capitalized.)

3. Use Means Clause to Avoid Functionality of Claim

The technical error of "functionality" occurs when elements of the claim are recited in terms of their advantage, function, or result rather than in terms of their structure. The remedy is to recite the elements of the claim as "means" or a "device" for performing the function or achieving the result.

For example, here are some typical improper functional claims actually written by a layperson:

> 7. *An additive for paints that makes the paint dry faster.*
> 8. *A belt buckle that does not tend to snag as much.*

Both of these claims would be rejected under Section 112 because they don't particularly point out and distinctly claim the invention since they recite what the invention *does* rather than what it *is*.

The remedy: use "means" or "device" clauses and also recite the general composition or structure of the additive or buckle. But remember that the claim must be to a combination; a single "means" claim won't pass muster. Thus, even if Claim 7 were written as follows, it would violate Section 112:

> 7. *Additive means for paints for making them dry faster.*

Here's how the above two claims can be properly re-written to pass muster under Section 112:

> 7A. *A paint composition comprising:*
> (a) *a paint compound comprising an oil-based paint vehicle and a suspended pigment in said vehicle, and*
> (b) *additive means admixed with said vehicle for decreasing the drying time of said paint compound and*
> (b') *a volatile solvent admixed [etc.].*

> 8A. *A belt buckle comprising:*
> (a) *a catch comprising two interlocking rigid parts that can be attached to opposite ends of a belt, and*
> (b) *anti-snag means for preventing said interlocking parts from snagging on cloth when placed adjacent said interlocking parts and*
> (b') *a shield for preventing [etc.].*

A moment's reflection will show you that claiming your invention in terms of its unique structure, rather than its results, effects, or functions, makes logical sense. This is because a monopoly, to be precise and to have reasonable limits, must be defined in terms of its structure, rather than the result such structure produces. In other words, if you recited "a belt buckle that doesn't snag" you would be claiming a result only, so that any belt buckle that fulfilled this result would infringe, regardless of its structure. This "functional" type of claim would accordingly be considered unreasonably broad and therefore would have to be narrowed and made more explicit by the addition of some additional structure or a means clause in order to make it more commensurate with the invention.

However, there's now a downside to using "means plus function" clauses: Under the pertinent statute (35 USC §112, ¶ 6) and court decisions, a means plus function clause is supposed to be interpreted according to the corresponding structure or material described in the specification and the equivalents of such structure or material. Thus, a means plus function clause is not supposed to be interpreted literally to cover every possible means which fulfills the function of the means, but only according to the corresponding structure or material in the specification and its equivalents. Thus, in addition to a means plus function claim, it's best to include one or more independent nonmeans claims which are as broad as possible without using means plus function language.

Using Means Clauses in Software Claims

If you use any means clauses in your claims, it is necessary to identify and describe in the specification what structure or material supports the means. If you have a software invention, this requirement is particularly important under the PTO's guidelines (MPEP 2181 et seq.). While it's not necessary to use the term "means" in the specification, the specification should clearly describe an element or structure using the same words used in the claims to recite the function of the means. That is, if your claim recites a "means for displaying the three-dimensional structure of a compound," your specification should clearly describe specific software, for instance, a specific code segment or object, that you employ, and it should also state that this segment or object configures a general-purpose microprocessor to display the three-dimensional structure of the compound.

Of course, while both of the above claims (as I revised them) would pass Section 112, they would not be novel or patentable under Sections 102 or 103, since they recite nothing new according to our present state of knowledge.

4. Be Complete

Each claim must stand on its own—that is, it must recite enough elements to make a working, complete device in accordance with its recognized status in its art. For example, you can recite a lightbulb per se (without reciting the entire lamp) since lightbulbs are a well-known item of commerce. But a claim to just the glass envelope of a lightbulb would

probably be rejected as incomplete, since it won't do anything on its own and isn't a recognized item of commerce. The remedy for failing to include enough elements is simply to add the needed elements. Examiners and attorneys frequently disagree as to whether a claim is incomplete, the examiner wanting the claim narrowed by the addition of elements and the attorney wanting it to remain broad, that is, not to add any more elements.

5. Keep Language Straightforward and Simple

Properly drafted claims use a minimum number of words to delineate the essence of the invention. Excess wordiness of a claim, termed "prolixity" by the PTO, is a frequent error committed by beginners. The remedy is to reword the claim in more compact language.

6. All Elements of Invention Must Logically Interrelate

Each of the elements in a claim must be logically related and connected to the other elements. When the elements of an invention don't appear to cooperate and to be connected in a logical or functional sense, the PTO will reject the claim. This is a more substantive type of rejection, since it's often directed at the underlying invention rather than simply the way the claim is drafted. For example, if you claim the combination of a waffle iron and tape recorder, these elements don't cooperate and hence your claim would be rejected as drawn to an aggregation. But the elements don't have to work at the same time to cooperate; in a typewriter, for example, the parts work at different times but cooperate toward a unitary result.

7. Old Combination and Aggregation

Formerly, claims drafted in terms of an old or well-known combination, such as an automatic transmission and an automobile, where the invention was in the transmission, were rejectable on the ground of "old combination," but this rejection has been eliminated. However claims drafted to a combination of elements which don't cooperate toward a common end, such as a washing machine and a telephone, can be rejected on the ground of aggregation. But the elements do not have to function simultaneously to cooperate: a typewriter is a good example of elements (keys) that don't function simultaneously but do cooperate.

8. Use Only Positive Limitations

In the past, all negative limitations (for example, "non-circular") were verboten, but now only those that make the claim unclear or awkward are proscribed. However, because many examiners still wince when they see negative limitations in claims, it's best to avoid them by reciting what the invention is, rather than what it isn't. For instance, instead of saying, "said engine connected to said wheels without any transmission," say "said engine connected directly to said wheels." You are permitted to recite holes, recesses, etc.; see "Voids" in the Glossary of Useful Technical Terms for a list of "hole-y" words.

9. Use Proper Alternative Expressions

Most disjunctive expressions—that is, those using "or" or the like—were formerly considered indefinite, but under MPEP 2173.05(h) are now permissible, even if two different things are meant. Thus the following expressions are acceptable: "wherein R is A, B, or C"; "made entirely *or* in part of"; and "iron, steel, *or* any other magnetic material."

Markush Group Claims

Another, sophisticated way to write a claim for an invention with two or more elements is to recite the disjunctive elements by using a *Markush* group. A Markush (from a decision with that name) group is a series of related elements joined by "and" which follows these magic words: *"selected from the group consisting of."* Thus, a tube or a transistor could be recited in one claim as follows: "said amplifying circuit containing a device *selected from the group consisting of* tubes and transistors."

10. Avoid Too Many Claims

If you've put in too many similar claims, even though you've paid for them, you'll have to eliminate some to make the examiner's job easier. If you ever have more than 20 claims, the invention should be complex enough or have enough ramifications to justify them and the claims should differ substantially.

11. Make Sure Claims Correspond With Disclosure

First, the literal terms or words of the claim must be present somewhere in the specification. If they aren't, the remedy is to amend the specification by adding the exact terms used in your claims, or to amend the claims by eliminating those terms that aren't literally in the specification. Second, any operation, structure, or result recited in a claim must be clearly and completely described in the "spec."

12. Make Sure Claims Are Supported in Drawing

Under Rule 83, the drawings must show every feature recited in the claims. If they don't, amend either the drawing or the claims. A broad recitation in a claim, such as "fuel atomizing means," can be supported by specific hardware, such as a carburetor, in the drawings. But remember that you can't add any new matter to an application once it's on file. So be sure to include all possibly relevant details of your invention in your drawings and spec. before you file. For example, if an examiner rejects a claim that recites "fuel atomizing means" for lack of support in the drawings, you can overcome this rejection by adding a box labeled "fuel atomizing means" to the drawings. You can't add a carburetor unless your spec. mentions a carburetor, since this would be verboten new matter.

13. Claim Computer Program as Providing a Useful, Practical Result

If your invention involves (or actually is) a computer program or algorithm—that is, a set of instructions for a computer—you must claim it to indicate some practical, useful, concrete, and tangible result, and not just as a set of steps for manipulating data or numbers.

Here's an example of some "program" claims drafted to recite enough practical results to pass muster; these claims go about as far as one can go in claiming programs.

9. *A process of operating a general purpose data processor of known type to enable said data processor to execute formulas in an object program comprising a plurality of formulas, such that the same results will be produced when using the same given data, regardless of the sequence in which said formulas are presented in said object program comprising the steps of:*

(a) *examining each of said formulas in a storage area of said data processor to determine which formulas can be designated as defined*

(b) *storing, in the sequence in which each formula is designated as defined, said formulas that are designated as defined, and*

(c) *repeating steps (a) and (b) for at least undefined formulas as many times as required until all said formulas have been designated as defined and have been stored; thereby producing the same results upon sequential execution of said formulas stored by said process when using the same given data, regardless of the order in which said formulas were presented in the object program prior to said process.* (Pardo & Landau, U.S. Pat. No. 4,398,249; 1983.)

10. *A method for evaluating Boolean expressions in a computer system, comprising:*

forming a first constant from the expression to specify rearrangement of the variables,

setting said first constant into a work area,

translating said first constant in said work area using the variables as a translate table,

forming a second constant from the expressions where the second constant functions to change the values of the variables to position numbers having values one less and two less than the position number of the variable and where the second constant changes the zeros between variables into position numbers that point to previous positions in the result string containing values of previously evaluated subexpressions,

logically combining said translated first constant with said second constant using an exclusive OR operation, and

translating the result of said exclusive OR operation using the result as the translate table as the result is changing during the translation, the result from last translation in the result being the value of the Boolean expression being evaluated. (Berstis, U.S. Pat. No. 4,417,305; 1983.)

Note that in both patents, the claims recite an algorithm itself, but the algorithm performs useful and practical computer functions.

Here's another program claim that was held to be Statutory Subject Matter (SSM):

A method of using a computer processor to analyze electrical signals and data representative of human cardiac activity by converting said signals to time segments, applying said time segments to a high-pass filter, using said computer processor to determine the amplitude of said filter's output, and comparing said amplitude to a predetermined value.

In all claims above, the claimed process or hardware is more than an algorithm per se. This is because claiming an algorithmic function per se would cover an abstract idea. However, the courts have held that the mere fact that a claim contains or is directed to an algorithm will not make it objectionable so long as the algorithm produces a useful, concrete, and tangible result.

Finally, here's a claim that was held to be Statutory Subject Matter, even though it merely recited a computer programmed to manipulate mutual fund price data, since such manipulation produced a useful, concrete, and tangible result:

1. *A data processing system for managing a financial services configuration of a portfolio established as a partnership, each partner being one of a plurality of funds, comprising:*

(a) *computer processor means* [a personal computer including a CPU] *for processing data;*

(b) *storage means* [a data disk] *for storing data on a storage medium;*

(c) *first means* [an arithmetic logic circuit configured to prepare the data disk to magnetically store selected data] *for initializing the storage medium;*

(d) *second means* [an arithmetic logic circuit configured to retrieve information from a specific file, calculate incremental increases or decreases based on specific input, allocate the results on a percentage basis, and store the output in a separate file] *for processing data regarding assets in the portfolio and each of the funds from a previous day and data regarding increases and decreases in each of the funds' assets and for allocating the percentage share that each fund holds in the portfolio;*

(e) *third means* [an arithmetic logic circuit configured to retrieve information from a specific file, calculate incremental increases and decreases based on specific input, allocate the results on a percentage basis, and store the output in a separate file] *for processing data regarding daily incremental income, expenses, and net realized gain or loss for the portfolio and for allocating such data among each fund;*

(f) *fourth means* [an arithmetic logic circuit configured to retrieve information from a specific file, calculate incremental increases and decreases based on specific input, allocate the results on a percentage basis, and store the output in a separate file] *for processing data regarding daily net unrealized gain or loss for the portfolio and for allocating such data among each fund; and*

(g) *fifth means* [an arithmetic logic circuit configured to retrieve information from specific files, calculate that information on an aggregate basis, and store the output in a separate file] *for processing data regarding aggregate year-end income, expenses, and capital gain or loss for the portfolio and each of the funds.*

The bracketed portions of this claim did not form part of the claim, but were added by the court to show the corresponding parts of the specification that each means was construed to represent, pursuant to the *Donaldson* decision, in Section B, above. *(State Street Bank and Trust Co. v. Signature Financial Group, Inc.* (Boes U.S. Pat. No. 5,193,056; 1993), Court of Appeals for the Federal Circuit, July 1998.)

Note that even if a claim recites a computer with a storage medium, the claim will not be regarded as statutory subject matter unless the claim also recites some unique computer hardware or some programming which produces a useful, concrete, and tangible result, as did the above Boes patent claim.

Being in a Statutory Class Is Not Enough

Even though a claim recites statutory subject matter, it still must pass the other tests to be patentable. That is, claims still have to particularly point out and distinctly claim the invention, be supported by the specification, and define novel and unobvious subject matter. Also, all "means plus function" language still must have clear supporting structure in the specification.

14. Recite Each Element Affirmatively as Subject of Its Clause

For maximum clarity, the elements of your invention should be affirmatively and directly recited; don't bring them in by inference or incidentally—for example, say "A transmission comprising: (a) a gear, (b) a shaft, (c) said gear being mounted on said shaft" [etc.], and not "A transmission whose gear is mounted on its shaft." In other words, each significant element of the claim should be recited for the first time (introduced) in a positive, affirmative manner, preferably with the word "a," so it's the subject of its clause, and not with wording that makes it part of the object or assumes that the reader already knows that it's there. This rule is especially important for do-it-yourselfers to follow in order to write clear and understandable claims.

15. Include Structural Support in Recitation of Operation

Assume a claim recites "a lever connected to move said pendulum to and fro at the same rate as said lights flash." The movement of the pendulum at this special rate is too much for the lever to do all by itself. In other words, there's not enough structural support for the operation recited. The remedy? Recite either (a) enough structure to do the job or (b) use a "means" clause. Here are examples of both methods:

(a) *a photoresponsive electromechanical circuit terminating in a lever that is connected to said pendulum and is arranged to move said pendulum at the same rate as said lights flash.*

(b) *means, including a lever connected to said pendulum, for moving said pendulum at the same rate as said lights flash.*

16. Recite Each Element Affirmatively, Followed by Its Shape or Function

Do not follow any element with the function of any other element.

RIGHT:
a container for holding said beans

RIGHT:
a container having a cylindrical shape

WRONG:
a container which receives said beans individually at a speed of 40 cm/second or greater.

RIGHT:
a container having a cylindrical shape,

means for shooting said beans individually at a speed of 40 cm/second or greater into said container.

17. Format

As stated in PTO Rule 75(i) (37 CFR 1.75(i), quoted above), if the claim has several elements or steps, each should be in a separate paragraph with the first line hanging out to the left (see the claims in Section 13 above) or indented.

18. Precede Every Function by an Affirmative Recitation of the Element That Performs That Function

Don't recite any function without preceding the function with an affirmative recitation of the element that performs the function.

WRONG:

> *said beans being shot individually at a speed of 40 cm/second or greater into said container.*

RIGHT:

> *means for shooting said beans individually at a speed of 40 cm/second or greater into said container.*

or

> *a gun for shooting said beans individually at a speed of 40 cm/second or greater into said container.*

H. Drafting Your Main (Independent) Claim

As indicated above, there are two basic types of claims: "independent" and "dependent." "Independent claims" are those that don't refer to any preceding claim; they stand alone. Examples of independent claims are all of those given in the preceding sections of this chapter. Note that these claims don't refer back to any preceding claim and each defines a complete, operative invention by itself.

"Dependent claims," which will be covered in the next section, refer back to a preceding or "parent" claim (this preceding claim can either be independent or dependent). A dependent claim recites narrower subject matter than its preceding claim in either of the two standard ways—that is, either by adding an additional element(s) or defining one or more elements of the preceding claim more narrowly.

The reasons for providing dependent claims will be covered in the next section also; the main point to remember here is that your independent claims are the important ones, since they're the basic and broadest definitions of your invention. If a dependent claim is infringed, its independent or parent claim(s) must also be infringed. If an independent claim is infringed, however, that's enough to win the case. You don't have to worry about your dependent claims.

To draft an independent claim, the easiest and most direct way to do it is to follow these four basic steps:

1. Write a preamble giving the name or title of the invention, or the problem which it solves.
2. List the elements (or steps) of the claim.
3. Interconnect the elements or steps.
4. Broaden the claim.

The claim can be structured so that the elements of the claim appear together, followed by the interconnections. Or, each element can appear in conjunction with its interconnection(s) to adjacent element(s). Most patent attorneys use the latter method—see Claims (2), (3), and (4) in Section C, above, for examples—but you may find it easier to recite the interconnections separately. An exception is process claims, where you'll find it easier to directly associate each step with its predecessor.

Start by writing your first claim without regard to breadth—that is, just get a preamble written, set down the elements of the invention, and interconnect them, paying no attention to how broadly you can recite the invention. In other words, just define your invention as you believe necessary to "get it all down" in a complete manner.

Then, see how many elements (or steps) you can eliminate and how many remaining elements you can broaden so that the result maintains sufficient structure and yet does not tread on the prior art too much. Remember that the broadest way of defining any element is by using "means-plus-a-function" language. Don't forget to refer to your prior-art patents for examples.

To provide a real example that everyone can understand, let's assume you've just invented a table. Since you've already written your specification, you have a name for each part of your invention, so that chore is already behind you. (If you believe your part names leave something to be desired, you can get additional part names from your prior-art search patents, the Glossary of Useful Technical Terms at the end of this book, or any visual dictionary (see Appendix 2, Resources: Government Publications, Patent Websites, and Books of Use and Interest), or in a thesaurus (in a book or computer). All that remains now is to provide a title or preamble. List the parts, interconnect them, and then broaden your claims.

1. The Preamble

To write the preamble, pick a name or title for the whole unit or the problem which it solves, remembering that you can't use the word "table" since it hasn't been invented until now. Try to put it in a class to which it belongs. Since a table is "an article of furniture," these words would be fine. You could also use any other suitable class, such as a "work station device," a "support for holding objects to be handled by a sitting human," etc. I've used "an article of furniture" and I've added the modifier "for holding objects for a sitting human, comprising" to narrow the field a bit and to make my title more meaningful.

2. The Elements

Next, to list the parts of the table, I'll start with the largest, most visible part, the top, and then add the smaller, less apparent parts, the legs. Since the table's just been invented, we'll assume that the words "top" and "legs" are still unknown, but even if they were, it's not wise to use "top" anyway, since it's a notoriously vague homonym (it can mean anything from a hat to a bottle cap to a toy). To define the top, then, we need a more meaningful term or phrase. Let's suppose we've made a model of our invention and have used a large sheet of chipboard for the top. All we need to do at this stage is to say so; thus our first and most basic element becomes "(a) a large sheet of chipboard."

Suppose our model table has four legs and we've made them of six-cm diameter circular oak dowels, each 65 cm long. Then our legs would be recited simply as "(b) four oak dowels, each having a circular cross section 6 cm in diameter and each 65 cm long." Our elements are now all recited—wasn't that easy!

3. Interconnections

Lastly, we have to interconnect the legs to the top, an easy task. Suppose our legs are joined at the underside of the top using four metal flanges, attached at the four corners of the top with each having a cylindrical portion with female threads, and with the top sections of the legs having mating male threads that are screwed into the respective flanges so that the legs extend at right angles to the top. Merely recite the flanges positively and add an interconnection clause as follows:

(c) *four flanges, each having means for attachment to one side of said sheet of chipboard and each having a cylindrical portion with female threads, and*

(d) *said four flanges being attached to one side of said sheet of chipboard at four respective corners thereof and said four oak dowels having male threads on a top section thereof and being screwed into the cylindrical portions of said respective flanges so that said dowels extend from said sheet of chipboard at right angles.*

Eureka! It's done. You've written a complete independent claim.

Here's how it looks:

11. *An article of furniture for holding objects for a sitting human, comprising:*
    (a) *a large sheet of chipboard,*
    (b) *four oak dowels, each having a circular cross section 6 cm in diameter and each 65 cm long, and*
    (c) *four flanges, each having means for attachment to one side of said sheet of chipboard and each having a cylindrical portion with female threads, and*
    (d) *said four flanges [etc.].*

Note, that I always recite the elements and their interconnections in lettered subparagraphs. The PTO now requires this format, since it's easier to analyze than a continuous paragraph. Also, I format paragraphs with a hanging indent style, just as the claims are printed in patents. You can easily "hang" a paragraph in Microsoft Word for Windows by placing your cursor bar in the paragraph and pressing Control-T.

Is there anything wrong with this claim? Yes! As you probably will have realized by now, this claim is far too narrow—that is, it has many elements and each of these is recited too specifically. In fact it even recites specific dimensions, which you don't generally even need in the specification. Thus the claim as written would be easy to avoid infringing: all that an infringer would have to do is to use plywood instead of chipboard, use four pine dowels instead of oak, etc. Let's broaden it then.

Remember, you broaden a claim by (1) eliminating elements where possible, and (2) reciting the remaining elements as broadly as possible.

Going through the claim to eliminate elements, we see that the top can't be eliminated since it's an essential part. However, we don't need to recite four legs—we can eliminate one of these since three legs will support the top. But better yet, we can even use the word "plurality" since this covers two or more legs. (The term "plurality" means more than one. Used here, it is an example of how you'll sometimes need to search for a word or phrase that most broadly describes a particular element. Even though two may not be sufficient to support a top, the PTO will usually not object to this word in this context. We could even go further and eliminate the recitation of legs entirely by reciting "support means," but this would include solid supports, such as in a chest or bureau, which would not be suitable for table-type uses.) Lastly, we can eliminate the flanges, since these aren't essential to the invention and since there are many other possible ways of attaching legs to a table top.

Next, let's go through the claim to see which elements can be recited more broadly. First, the top. Obviously "a large sheet of chipboard" is a very narrow recitation since plywood, solid wood, metal, and plastic tops would avoid infringement. A broad recitation would be "a large sheet of rigid material," but, as stated above, the word "large" is frowned upon by the PTO as too vague to satisfy Section 112. So let's make the top's size more specific. Since we're interested in providing a working surface for humans, let's merely specify that the top is "a sheet of rigid material of sufficient size to accommodate use by a human being for writing and working."

Next the legs. Obviously, the recitation of four circular oak dowels with specific dimensions is very limiting. Let's eliminate the material, shape, and dimensions and recite the legs as merely "a plurality of elongated support members of substantially equal length." This covers square, round, triangular, and oval legs, regardless of their length or material.

Lastly, instead of the flanges (that we've eliminated as unnecessary) to join the legs to the top, let's use "means" (to make it as broad as possible) as follows: "means for joining said elongated support members at right angles to the underside of said top at spaced locations so as to be able to support said top horizontally."

The result would look like this:

11. *An article of furniture for holding objects for a sitting human, comprising:*
    (a) *a sheet of rigid material of sufficient size to accommo-date use by a human being for writing and working*
    (b) *a plurality of elongated support members of equal length, and*
    (c) *means for joining said elongated support members at right angles to the underside of said sheet at spaced locations so as to be able to support said sheet horizontally.*

Obviously, Claim 11 is now far broader than our first effort. Your first independent claim should be as broad as possible, but of course, you can't make it so broad that it lacks novelty or unobviousness. Thus, when you eliminate as many elements as possible, and when you broaden the remaining elements in the manner just described, keep in mind that you must leave enough structure or acts to define your invention over the prior art.

Put differently, writing claims is like walking on a fence: you can't sway too far on the side of specificity or you'll fall onto the side of worthlessness and you can't sway too far onto the side of breadth or you'll fall onto the prior art. To obtain the broadest possible coverage, you should not draft your main claim primarily to cover your invention; rather draft it as broadly as possible with at least some thought of clearing the prior art, then go back and make sure that it at least covers your invention.

Some patent attorneys compare the writing of their first claim to passing through a wall of fire. However, I have found that if I follow the above four steps—(1) write a preamble, (2) recite the elements, (3) interconnect them, and (4) broaden the claims—the going is relatively painless. In case of doubt, err on the side of breadth at this stage, since you can always narrow your claims later, but you may not be able to make them broader if the application's allowed on the first Office Action.

I. Other Techniques in Claim Writing

Now that you understand the basics, here are some other tricks you may want to use when writing your claims. Obviously, not all apply all of the time, but you will probably find that at least several can be used to improve your claim writing.

- **Weasel Words.** Use "weasel" words like "substantially," "about," or "approximately" whenever possible—that is, whenever you specify a dimension or any other specific parameter—to avoid limiting your claim to the specific dimension specified. The renowned judge, Learned Hand, who wrote many famous patent decisions, once opined that judges should read the modifier "substantially" into every claim, even if it's not already cited. However, I strongly recommend that you don't rely on a judge to broaden your claim for you, but rather do it yourself when you first write the claim.

- **Antecedents.** Provide a proper antecedent in the beginning of your claim for every term you use in the latter part of the claim. For example, in Claim 11 in the preceding part, the clause "the underside of said sheet" near the end of the claim has no clear antecedent in the beginning of the claim and thus might be objected to by some examiners. The claim would be better if clause (a) were amended by adding, "said sheet having an undersurface" to provide unequivocal support for the underside phase later.

- **"Whereby" Clause.** At the end of your claim, I recommend adding a "whereby" clause to specify the advantage or use of the invention to hammer home to the examiner, or anyone else who reads your claim, the value of your invention. Thus in Claim 11, above, you should add at the end of this claim, "whereby a human can work, eat, and write in a convenient seated position." "Whereby" clauses don't help to define over the prior art, but they do force the examiner to consider the advantages (Section 103 features) of your invention and thus help to get the claims allowed.

- **Reference Numbers.** You may put the drawing's reference numerals in your claims after the appropriate elements, but this is seldom done unless the elements of the claim aren't clear.
- **Recesses.** If your invention has an opening, hole, or recess in its structure, you may, as stated, recite the hole directly as such, even though it isn't tangible. For example, the recitation "said member having a hole near its upper end" is permissible. See Appendix 3 (Glossary of Useful Technical Terms) for a list of recesses.
- **No Preamble.** Sometimes, instead of using the preamble-elements-interconnections approach, it's desirable to omit the preamble, especially if you feel the preamble will be too restrictive, that is, if the elements of the body of the claims can be used for another function. For example, if we recited "A working surface comprising" as a preamble in the above claim and someone used the actual structure claimed, but turned it upside down and used the legs for a quoit game, it would not infringe since it isn't being used as a working surface. In this case simply start the claim, "In combination:" or "A process comprising:" and then recite the elements or steps and their interconnections.
- **_Jepson_ Claims.** With regard to the rarely enforced Rule 75(e) (quoted in Section B2, above) requiring the use of the _Jepson_ style (a preamble containing old elements and body of claims containing improvements of your invention), most patent attorneys recommend that claims _not_ be cast in this style unless the examiner requests it or unless the examiner is having trouble understanding exactly what your inventive contribution is. The reason for this is that a _Jepson_ claim isolates and hence minimizes your improvement, making it easier to invalidate. If you do claim in the _Jepson_ format, draft your preamble so that it includes all the elements or steps and their interconnections that are already known from the prior art; then add a "cleavage" clause such as "the improvement comprising" or "characterized in that"; and then recite the elements of your invention and their interconnections.
- **Predetermined.** Use the word "predetermined" to indicate that something has a size, thickness, length, quality, etc., without limiting the claim to any specific dimension or quality. For example, "said member having a predetermined cross-sectional shape" and "said valve arranged to open when a predetermined gas pressure is developed."
- **Consisting v. Comprising.** A claim that recites a group of elements can be made "open" or "closed." An open claim (the normal case) will cover more elements than it recites, whereas a closed claim is limited to and will cover only the elements it specifically recites. To make a claim open, use "includes" or "comprising"—for example, "said machine _comprising_ A, B, and C." In this case, a machine with four elements A, B, C, and D will infringe. To make a claim closed (rarely done), use "consist" or "having only"— for example, "Said machine _consisting_ of A, B, and C." In this case, a machine with elements A, B, C, and D will not infringe, since, in patent law, the word "consist" is interpreted to mean "having only the following elements."
- **A Plurality Of.** Also, whenever you recite several units of anything, preface your recitation with "a plurality of"—such as, "a plurality of holes in said hose."
- **Less Is More.** Remember that, because of the Boolean "less is more" rule in interpreting claims, it's not necessary to recite a specific feature in your main claim in order to cover that feature in combination with the other elements of your invention. For example, once I drafted a claim for a client where one embodiment of her invention had a fingerlike support. Not seeing the finger in the main claim, she asked me, "Did you claim the finger?" I then explained to her that the main claim was broad enough to cover her invention with or without the finger.
- **Is It Sketchable?** After drafting your claim, you or a friend should be able to make enough sense out of it to sketch your invention. If this isn't possible, the claim is unclear and needs to be reworked.
- **Special Terms.** You can use any technical or descriptive terms that you feel are reasonably necessary to define or describe your invention—the claim does not have to be limited to any special "legalese." One patent attorney I know had a devil of a time defining (to the satisfaction of the examiner) a convex transistor structure with a nubbin on top until he simply called it "mammary-shaped."
- **Method Claim.** If possible, provide a method claim to cover your invention; you usually can do this if there's any dynamic operation involved in the invention. Most machines and electrical circuits can be claimed in terms of a method. Method claims are usually broader than apparatus claims, since they're not limited to any specific hardware.
- **Gerunds in Method Claims.** Each substantive clause of a method claim must usually start with an "—ing" word, such as "attaching," "heating," "abrading," etc. If you want to recite some hardware in a method claim, use "providing"—such as, "providing a central processor." (Don't say "comprising the steps of" in a method claim since claims that recite "step" may tend to be interpreted less broadly.)

• **Label Means.** If you do recite any "means," it's desirable to label the means with a nonfunctional adjective in order to provide a mnemonic aid in case you need to refer to the means later. For example, "first means," "second means," etc. Also, the "means" must be followed by or be modified by a function or some structure. For example, "first means for printing" (means plus function); "second means comprising a doctor blade" (means plus structure).

• **Padding.** Lastly, many patent attorneys recommend that a claim not be too short. A claim that is short will be viewed adversely (as possibly overly broad) by many examiners, regardless of how much substance it contains. Thus, many patent attorneys like to "pad" short claims by adding "whereby" clauses, providing long preambles, adding long functional descriptions to their means clauses, etc. The trick here, of course, is to pad the claim while avoiding a charge of undue prolixity under Section 112.

You'll find that a well-written claim is like a well-written poem. Each has a beautiful symmetry and order that gives pleasure and gratification to anyone who appreciates words and logic.

J. Drafting Dependent Claims

In Section H, I pointed out that there are two basic types of claims—independent claims (these stand on their own) and dependent claims (these incorporate an entire preceding claim, which can be an independent or dependent claim). A dependent claim is simply a shorthand way of writing a narrower claim—that is, a claim that includes all the elements of a preceding claim, and/or recites one or more additional elements or recites one or more elements of the preceding claim more specifically.

Patent Attorney Words

If you get stuck and don't know how to phrase something, usually one of the "patent attorney words" below will help.

a (used to introduce a part)

about (used to fudge a specific quantity)

at least (used to hammer home that more elements can be used)

contiguous (used to indicate elements are touching)

device for (interpreted like "means for")

disposed (used to indicate a part is positioned in a particular place)

further including (used in dependent claims to add additional parts)

heretofore (used to refer back to something previously recited)

indicium (used to recite something that a human can recognize, such as a mark or a sound)

means for (used to claim something broadly, in terms of its function, rather than specific hardware)

member (used to recite a mechanical part when no other word is available)

multitude (used to recite a large, indefinite number)

pivotably (used to indicate that a part is rotatably mounted)

plurality (used to introduce more than one of an element)

predetermined (used to state that a part has a specific parameter)

providing (used to recite a part in a method claim)

respectively (used to relate several parts to several other parts in an individual manner)

said (used to refer to a previously recited part by exactly the same word)

sandwiching (used to indicate that one part is between two other parts)

selected from the group consisting of (used in a *Markush* claim to create an artificial group)

slidably (used to indicate that two parts slide with respect to each other)

so that (used to restrict a part to a defined function)

substantially (used to fudge a specific recitation)

such that (used to restrict a part to a defined function)

surrounding (used to indicate that a part is surrounded)

the (used to refer to a previously recited part by a slightly different word)

thereby (used to specify a result or connection between an element and what it does)

thereof (used as a pronoun to avoid repeating a part name)

urging (used to indicate that force is exacted upon a part)

whereby (used to introduce a function or result at the end of a claim)

wherein (used in a dependent claim to recite an element (part) more specifically)

(For names of components, see Glossary of Useful Technical Terms in Appendix 3.)

1. Reasons for Writing Dependent Claims

If an independent claim is broader, you may wonder why you need dependent (narrower) claims—especially since the independent claim must be infringed if its dependent claim is infringed. Below are eight good answers to that question:

1. **Backup.** Dependent claims are by definition always narrower than the claims on which they depend. You may accordingly be wondering, "If my broad independent claim covers my invention, why do I need any more claims of narrower scope?" True, if all goes well, your broad claim will be all you'll need. However, suppose you sue an infringer who finds an appropriate prior-art reference that neither you nor the PTO examiner found and that adversely affects the validity of ("knocks out") your broad claim. If you've written a narrower claim you can then disclaim the broad claim and fall back on the narrower claim. If the narrower claim is patentable over the prior art, your patent will still prevail. Thus the dependent claims are insurance in case of broad claim invalidity. Each claim, whether independent or dependent, is interpreted independently for examination and infringement purposes. If the claim is dependent, it's interpreted as if it included all the wording of its parent (incorporated) claim or claims, even if the incorporated claim is held invalid.

2. **Reification of Broad Claims.** Dependent claims are useful to explain and reify (make real) some of the broad, abstract terms in your independent claims. For instance, if you recite in a claim "additive means," many judges may not be able to understand what the "additive means" actually covers, but if you add several dependent claims that state, respectively, that the additive means is benzine and toluene, they'll get a very good idea of what types of substances the additive means embraces. If your main claim recites a new parlor game, adding a dependent claim that recites that the game is simulated on a computer will make it clear that the main claim covers computer simulation as well as board versions. (Don't forget to show the computer version in your drawings and discuss it in your specification.)

3. **Provide Spectrum of Coverage.** Narrower claims can be used to provide a range, spectrum, or menu of proposed coverage from very broad to very narrow so that your examiner can, by allowing some narrower claims and rejecting the broader ones, indicate the scope of coverage the examiner's willing to allow.

4. **Prevent Premature Final Action.** Providing dependent claims of varying scope and approaches forces the examiner to make a wider search of your invention on the first examination. This will prevent the examiner from citing new prior art against your application on the second office action, which usually must be made "final." (See Chapter 13.) Thus, you should include every possibly novel feature (or novel combination of features) of your invention in your dependent claims.

5. **Provide Broader Base for Infringement Damages.** By providing dependent claims that add more elements, you define your invention (in these claims) as a more comprehensive structure, thereby providing a broader base upon which a judge can calculate infringement damages.

6. **Provide a Specific, Descriptive Recitation.** This reason is slightly different than Item 2 above. If the recitation in the independent claim is broad and abstract, such as, "urging means for …," I strongly recommend that you provide dependent claims with a descriptive, definite recitation (for example, "wherein said urging means is a coil spring") to hit the nail on the head, or provide a specific hardware recitation so a judge won't have to use his or her imagination.

7. **Preserve Right to Rely Upon Doctrine of Equivalents.** Traditionally patent owners have been able to rely on a "Doctrine of Equivalents" (DoE) to effectively expand a claim beyond its literal wording if it didn't cover an infringing device. However, the U.S. Supreme Court in *Festo v. Shoketsu*, 122 S.Ct. 1831 (2002), held that a patentee who amended (narrowed) a claim when it was before the PTO may no longer be able to rely on the DoE. (See Chapter 13 for a more detailed explanation.) To preserve your right to rely on the DoE, draft as many dependent claims as possible to cover all aspects of your invention. In this way you'll have some claims that won't have to be amended (narrowed) if the PTO cites relevant prior art against these claims, and thus you'll preserve your right to use the DoE to expand these claims if necessary.

8. **Litigators Prefer Them.** Litigators prefer narrower and more specific claims (provided they cover the infringing device) because they provide a broader base for infringement damages—see Item 5 above—and are more difficult to invalidate since they read on less prior art. Furthermore, it's easier for a litigator to prove infringement since the claim is less abstract and recited the specific structure that is infringed—see Item 6 above.

2. The Drafting

For the reasons above, when you're satisfied with your first, basic, and broadest independent claim, you should write as many dependent claims as you can think of. Each dependent claim should begin by referring to your basic claim, or a previous dependent claim, using its exact title.

EXAMPLE:

Independent claim:

1. *A cellular telephone having a hinged body and a coiled antenna.*

Improper dependent claim:

2. *The hinged body of claim 1 wherein said hinge has five knuckles.* [The preamble or beginning of the claim does not correspond with claim 1 and there's no antecedent for "said hinge."]

Proper dependent claim:

2. *The cellular telephone of claim 1 wherein said hinged body includes a hinge with five knuckles.*

If the dependent claim recites one or more elements of the independent claim more narrowly, it should use the word "wherein"—for example, "The bicycle of Claim 1 wherein"—and then continue by reciting one or more elements of the independent claim.

Note that a dependent claim does not affect or narrow the scope of any previous claim from which it depends; it merely provides an alternative, narrower recitation in a shorthand manner.

If the dependent claim recites additional elements, it should use the words, "further including"—for example, "The bicycle of Claim 1, further including..."—then continue by reciting the additional feature(s) of your invention. The additional features can be those you eliminated in broadening your basic claims and all other subsidiary features, including all combinations and permutations of such features of your invention you can think of. The features recited more narrowly or the additional elements recited by the dependent claims can be specific parameters (such as materials and temperatures) or other specifics of your invention (such as specific shapes, additional elements, or specific modes of operation). Refer to your prior art patents for guidance on how to draft these.

Note that a dependent claim must either recite the elements of its parent claim more specifically, or recite additional elements. It may not change any element to a different type or kind. Thus if the parent claim is an apparatus claim, each of its dependent claims must recite additional structure or recite some previously recited structure more specifically. If the parent claim is a method claim, each of its dependent claims must recite an additional step or recite a previously recited step (or structure in such a step) more specifically. For example, if your parent claim recites "1. A house made of red bricks," its dependent claim can say "2. The house of Claim 1 wherein said bricks are made of clay" (recites bricks more specifically) or "2. The house of Claim 1, further including a layer of paint over said bricks" (recites additional structure). The dependent claim can't say "2. The house of Claim 1 wherein said bricks are yellow."

Here are some dependent claims for Claim 11 (set out in Section H, above). Note that each dependent claim either recites an additional element or recites an already recited element more specifically.

11. *An article of furniture (etc.).*
    12. *The article of furniture of Claim 11 wherein said sheet of rigid material is made of wood.*
        13. *The article of furniture of Claim 12 wherein said sheet of rigid material of wood is made of chipboard.*
            14. *The article of furniture of Claim 13 wherein said sheet of chipboard has a rectangular shape.*
    15. *The article of furniture of Claim 11 wherein said means for joining comprises a set of flanges, each of which joins a respective one of said support members to the underside of said sheet of rigid material.*
        16. *The article of furniture of Claim 15 wherein each of said flanges is made of iron and includes a cylinder with female threads and wherein one end of each of said elongated members has male threads and is threadedly mated with the female threads of a respective one of said flanges.*
    17. *The article of furniture of Claim 11, further including a layer of a rigid plastic laminate bonded to a top side of said sheet of rigid material.*

Note that a dependent claim may be dependent upon the parent claim or another dependent claim. A dependent claim should be numbered as closely as possible to the number of its parent claim. Note also how I've made a physical indication of claim dependency by indenting (nesting) each dependent claim under its parent claim(s) as shown above. This is optional, but makes things clearer for you and the examiner. Also, you should always skip a line between claims (we didn't do it here in order to conserve space).

Multiple Dependent Claims

A dependent claim may actually be made dependent upon several previous claims (called "multiple dependent claiming" and common in Europe), but I recommend that you do *not* include multiple dependent claims (e.g., *"3. The widget of claims 1 or 2 wherein…"*) since the PTO's examiners dislike the practice, there's a stiff surcharge for the privilege, and for fee purposes each MDC counts as the number of claims to which it refers. (See Appendix 4, Fee Schedule.)

A dependent claim will be read and interpreted by examiners and judges as if it incorporated all the limitations of its parent claim(s). Thus suppose your independent and dependent claims read, respectively, as follows:

18. *A rifle having an upwardly curved barrel.*
    19. *The rifle of Claim 18 wherein said barrel is made of austenitic steel.*

The dependent claim (19) will be treated independently, but with Claim 18 incorporated, so that it effectively reads as follows:

19. *A rifle having an upwardly curved barrel, said barrel being made of austenitic steel.*

Use Only Significant Limitations. You can make your dependent claims as specific as you want, even to reciting the dimensions of the tabletop, its color, etc. However, extremely specific limitations like this, while possibly defining an invention that is novel over the prior art (Section 102), do not recite unobvious subject matter (Section 103), so they'll be of little use to fall back on if you lose your independent claim. Thus, you should mainly try to use *significant* limitations in your dependent claims—that is, limitations that an infringer might use if he or she made your invention.

You should draft dependent claims to cover all possible permutations of the subsidiary features of your invention. For example, suppose you've invented a telephone and some of the dependent features are that it has (a) a musical ringer, (b) a coiled cord, and (c) a stand. You can provide three dependent claims with features (a), (b), and (c), respectively. Then write four more dependent claims with features (a) and (b), (a) and (c), (b) and (c), and (a), (b), and (c), if you think these combinations are feasible.

You should try to draft at least one dependent claim with as many parts as possible so as to provide as broad a base as possible for maximizing infringement damages. Also try, insofar as possible, to draft at least one claim to cover parts of the invention whose infringement would be publicly verifiable, rather than a nonverifiable factory process or machine.

As with independent claims, you should not make your dependent claims purely "functional"—that is, each dependent claim should contain enough physical structure to support its operational or functional language. Here are some examples:

WRONG:

17. *The bicycle of Claim 16 wherein said derailleur operates with continuously variable speed-to-power ratios.* [This claim has no structure to support its operational limitation.]

RIGHT:

17. *The bicycle of Claim 16 wherein said derailleur contains means for causing it to operate with continuously variable speed-to-power ratios.* [The "means" limitation is a recitation of structure that supports the operational limitation.]

RIGHT:

17. *The bicycle of Claim 16 wherein said derailleur contains a cone-shaped pulley and a belt pusher for causing it to operate with continuously variable speed-to-power ratios.* [The pulley and pusher constitute structure that supports the operational limitation.]

If your independent claim recites a means plus a function, your dependent claim should modify the means and not the function. For example, assume an independent Claim 20 recites, "variable means for causing said transmission to have a continuously variable gear ratio." Here are the right and wrong ways to further limit this "means" in a dependent claim:

WRONG:

21. *The transmission of Claim 20 wherein said continuously variable gear ratio ranges from 5 to 10.*

RIGHT:

21. *The transmission of Claim 20 wherein said variable means is arranged to provide ratios from 5 to 10.*

Common Misconception: If a dependent claim recites a specific feature of your invention, say a two-inch nylon gear, your invention will be limited to this gear, so that if any copy of the invention uses a one-inch gear, or a steel gear, it won't infringe on your patent.

Fact: Although the copy won't infringe the dependent claim, it will infringe the independent claim so long as it isn't limited to this specific feature. And as long as even one claim of a patent is infringed, the patent is infringed and you can recover as much damages (money) as if 50 claims were infringed.

Common Misconception: The limitations in a dependent claim will narrow its independent claim.

Fact: The independent claim is interpreted independently of its dependent claims and the latter never narrow the former.

If you still don't get the principle of broad and narrow claims, here are three simple claims that everyone can understand:

1. A house that has a sloping roof with a gable.
   2. The house of Claim 1 wherein said gable has a dormer.
      3. The house of Claim 2 wherein said dormer has eight panes of glass.

Claim 1 is very broad: it will cover any house that has a sloping roof with a gable. Thus it may cover, say 30 million houses in the United States. Claim 2 is of intermediate scope; since it incorporates all of Llaim 1 and has additional verbiage, it's longer than Claim 1. However Claim 2 is narrower in scope since it is limited to houses with sloping roofs that have a gable with a dormer. Thus it will cover fewer houses, say ten million in the U.S. Claim 3 is still longer than Claim 2, but is far narrower since it is limited to houses with sloping roofs that have a gable with a dormer with eight panes of glass. Thus it will cover fewer houses still, say one million houses in the United States.

Note that I made the number of the independent claim (#1) bold and I indented the dependent claims to indicate the dependency so that each dependent claim is nested under its referent claim. This is optional but desirable since it makes the claims clearer. As indicated above in Section G1, if you're working on a computer, use its "windows" function (if available) to keep your independent claim displayed while you write your dependent claims.

K. Drafting Additional Sets of Claims

After you've written your first independent claim (IC) and all the dependent claims you can think of (all numbered sequentially), consider writing another set of claims (an IC and a set of dependent claims) if you can think of a substantially different way to claim your invention. See the prior-art patents and the sample set of claims at the end of this chapter (Fig. 9A) for examples of different independent claims on the same invention. Your second set of dependent claims can be similar to your first set; a word processor with a block copy function will be of great aid here. Writing more sets of claims will not always give your invention broader coverage, but will provide alternative weapons to use against an infringer. That is, writing a second set of claims is like going into battle with a sword as well as a gun. Also, writing more sets of claims will give your examiner additional perspectives on your invention. That is, your chances of getting your examiner to bite will be increased if you present many flavors to choose from.

In the example above (Claim 11), I might start my second IC with the legs instead of the top and I might try to define the top and legs differently—for example, instead of "elongated members," I might call the legs "independent support means." Instead of calling the top a "sheet of rigid material," I might call it a "planar member having paralleled, opposed major faces."

Claims of Different Scope

The concept of claims of different scope (independent and dependent) is confusing to most inventors. Here's another way of explaining it, if you still don't understand.

An *independent claim* (IC) is one that *doesn't* refer back to any previous claim. For example, *"1. A telephone comprising (a) a base, (b) a handset, and (c) a rotary dial,"* is an example of an IC.

To write another independent claim like Claim 1 (C1), but which is narrower than C1 by reciting a base of black plastic, simply repeat all of Claim 1 and add that the base is black plastic. For example, *"2. A telephone comprising (a) a base of black plastic, (b) a handset, and (c) a rotary dial,"* is an example of a second IC which is narrower than C1.

However, there's an easier, shorter, and cheaper way to avoid repeating all of C1 each time: Simply write a claim that refers to the IC (#1) so as to incorporate all of it by reference, and then state one or more additional elements, and/or recite one or more elements of the incorporated claim more specifically. Such a shorthand claim is called a *dependent claim* (DC). A DC is thus one that refers back to and incorporates all of a preceding claim and adds or modifies one or more limitations to recite the invention more narrowly. For example, *"2´. The telephone of Claim 1 wherein said base is made of black plastic,"* is a dependent claim which has the same scope as C2. C2´ will be interpreted as if it included *all* of the subject matter of C1, *together with the additional subject matter in C2´.*

It follows that to infringe a DC, a device must have all of the elements of the DC, *plus all of the elements of the incorporated claim.*

Thus, adding a DC to recite a specific feature of your invention won't broaden or narrow your coverage; it will just provide another, yet more precise, missile. The eight reasons for including DCs are in Section J.

Also note that a DC can refer back to a preceding claim, and the preceding claim can in turn refer back to a further preceding claim. To infringe such a *third-level DC*, the device must have *all* of the elements of *all three claims* in the chain.

Here are still other ways to write a different IC: (1) Rewrite one of the dependent claims from your first set in independent form; (2) wait a few days and write an IC again, with independent thought; (3) write the IC by reciting the elements of the first IC in reverse or inverse order; and (4) if your first IC has any "means" clauses, make your next IC a structure (apparatus) claim (no means clauses), or vice versa; (5) If your invention uses any unique supplies, blanks, or starting elements, or accessories, it is wise to provide claims to these also. For example, if you've invented a unique paper cup which is made from a unique starting blank, provide independent claims to both the cup and the blank.

Another valuable way to write a different IC is to provide a method (process) claim if your first IC is an apparatus claim, or vice versa; you're allowed to have both method and apparatus claims in the same case. You should always include an independent method claim if possible, since a method claim is usually not limited to specific hardware and thus affords broader coverage. Every step of each independent method claim must be an action step, for instance, "providing..." or "heating...." If your invention is a product and the process of making it is novel, or if it uses an intermediate construction in the process, you should claim the process and the intermediate construction.

Your filing fee entitles you to up to three ICs and 20 total claims. I generally try to use up my allotment by writing three ICs and three sets of five to seven dependent claims each. However, if I feel that I can write a fourth, substantially different IC and the cost can be borne by my client, I will add it, plus more dependent claims. The PTO now charges a substantial additional fee for each IC over three, and for each claim (independent or dependent) over 20.

On the other hand, for relatively simple inventions, I may not be able to think of any substantially different ways to write an IC, so I may submit only one, plus a few dependent claims. I advise you generally not to submit more than the number of claims permitted for your basic filing fee—that is, three ICs and 20 total claims—unless the complexity of your invention justifies it, or you have some other good reason. Don't make your case like one published application (U.S. Pat. No. 20030100451): it has 7,215 claims!

As with the specification, be sure to review your claims very carefully after you've written them.

L. Checklist for Drafting Claims

Here's the second part of the application checklist that I started in Chapter 8. As before, I suggest you go through this list carefully and make any needed corrections in your claims before going on to Chapter 10.

Checklist for Draft Claims

☐ C01. Grammatical articles are used properly in the claims:

"a" or "an" to introduce any singular part,

"the" to refer to a part a second time when using a different (but clearly implied) term as before, and,

"said" only to refer to a part using the IDENTICAL term as before.

☐ C02. Two articles together, such as "the said," aren't used.

☐ C03. Every part and feature in every claim is shown in the drawings and discussed in the specification.

☐ C04. No claim uses any disjunctive ("or") expression (except to recite two equivalent parts or a disjunctive function of a machine).

☐ C05. No claim uses any naked functional clause; all claims contain a structural recitation or "means" to support every functional recitation.

☐ C06. A memory aid is recited adjacent each "means," for example, "first means"; also, each "means" is followed by function or structure.

☐ C07. For each unique "means" followed by a function in the claims, the specification describes some hardware or an element which implements or provides the function for such means, using the same words as used in the claim to describe the function.

☐ C08. "Consisting" isn't used in any claim (except if you want to say "having only").

☐ C09. No claim uses any abbreviation, dash, parentheses, or quote.

☐ C10. No term is used for the first time in any claim.

☐ C11. The subparagraph form is used in long claims for ease of reading.

☐ C12. Each claim has just one capital letter (two if "claim" is capitalized in a dependent claim) and one period (except lettered paragraphs), and no parentheses (except lettered paragraphs, quotes, abbreviations, or trademarks).

☐ C13. All significant parts are affirmatively recited in the claims as the subject and not the object of a clause.

Checklist for Draft Claims

☐ C14. The main (independent) claim is made as broad as possible by reciting minimum number of elements and by generalizing existing elements (without reading on prior art).

☐ C15. No vague, loose, or casual language is used in any claim.

☐ C16. Space between adjacent claims is greater than space between adjacent lines of a claim.

☐ C17. No dependent claim recites an additional function unless "means" or structure is specified to support such structure.

☐ C18. All parts recited in claims are connected.

☐ C19. All claims recite enough parts to provide a complete assemblage.

☐ C20. You haven't submitted over 20 total or over three independent claims unless the case is very complex or extra claims are justified.

☐ C21. No independent claim refers to any other claim and all dependent claims refer to a previous claim in line 1 or line 2.

☐ C22. You've filed enough dependent claims to cover all features and permutations and you've filed second and third sets of claims (with differently phrased independent claims) if possible.

☐ C23. You've included an independent method claim and a set of dependent method claims, if possible.

☐ C24. If the invention involves novel hardware, that is, it's not a pure method, you've included one or more structural independent claims, that is, the claims contain no means plus function clauses (means plus structure clauses are okay).

☐ C25. Every dependent claim starts with either:

"The _____ of Claim x wherein..." to provide an alternative recitation of the element(s) in the parent claim in a narrower fashion, or

"The _____ of Claim x, further including..." to provide an alternative recitation of the element(s) in the parent claim plus one or more new element(s).

☐ C26. No dependent claim is used to substitute a different part for any part recited in its parent claim; each dependent claim either narrows or adds to the existing parts of its parent claim.

☐ C27. No dependent claim recites a method limitation if its parent claim is an apparatus claim, and vice versa.

☐ C28. The same element isn't recited more than once in any claim unless the second and later recitations use "said" before the element.

☐ C29. You've included a set of claims (one independent and several dependent) with means plus function clauses and a set without means plus function clauses.

☐ C30. Each independent claim has a set of several dependent claims to provide backup.

☐ C31. Every possible novel or significant feature of the invention is recited in the claims to (hopefully) provide some claims that will not have to be canceled or narrowed.

☐ C32. At least one dependent claim has as many elements or parts of the inventive apparatus as possible, providing a larger base for infringement claims and greater damages.

Patent Application of Lou W. Koppe for "Paper-Laminated
Pliable Closure for Flexible Bags" continued
Page 11

Printout should have
minimum 1.5 line spacing
(4 lines/inch) but is shown
with denser spacing since
this example is shown on a
reduced scale.

start claims on new page

first
independent
claim

CLAIMS: I claim:

Number of
each
independent
claim is bold

1. In a bag closure of the type comprising a flat body of material having a
lead-in notch on one edge thereof and a gripping aperture adjacent to and
communicating with said notch, the improvement wherein said closure has a
layer of paper laminated on one of its sides.

Skip a line
between claims—
omitted here to
conserve space.

2. The closure of claim 1 wherein said body of material is composed of
polyethyleneterephthalate.

3. The closure of claim 1 wherein said body is elongated and has a
longitudinal groove which is on said one side of said body and extends
the full length of said one side, from said gripping aperture to the
opposite edge.

optional
indent for
dependent
claims

4. The closure of claim 3 wherein said groove is formed into and along
the full length of said lamination.

5. The closure of claim 1 wherein said body is elongated and has a
longitudinal groove which is on the side of said body opposite to said
one side thereof and extends the full length of said one side, from
said gripping aperture to the opposite edge.

6. The closure of claim 1 wherein said body is elongated and has two
longitudinal grooves which are on opposite sides of said body and
extend the full lengths of said sides, from said gripping aperture to
the opposite edge.

7. The closure of claim 6 wherein the groove on said one side of said
body is formed into and along the full length of said lamination.

8. The closure of claim 1 wherein said body has a paper lamination on both
of said sides.

9. The closure of claim 8 wherein a groove is on one side of said body
and extends the full length of said one side, from said gripping
aperture to the opposite edge.

10. The closure of claim 8 wherein two grooves, on opposite sides of
said body, extend the full lengths of said sides, from said gripping aperture to the opposite edge.

11. The closure of claim 10 wherein said grooves are rolled into and
along the full lengths of said laminations, respectively.

Fig. 9A—Claims for Sample Patent Application

Patent Application of Lou W. Koppe for "Paper-Laminated Pliable Closure for Flexible Bags" continued – Page 12

12. The closure of claim 1 wherein said paper lamination is colored.

13. The closure of claim 1 wherein said body is elongated and has a longitudinal through-hole.

second independent claim, phrased differently than first

14. A bag closure of the type comprising a flat body of material having a lead-in notch on one edge thereof, a gripping aperture adjacent to and communicating with said notch, characterized in that one of its sides has a layer of paper laminated thereon.

15. The closure of claim 14 wherein said body of material is composed of polyethyleneterephthalate.

16. The closure of claim 14 wherein said body is elongated and has a longitudinal groove on said one side of said body and which extends the full length of said one side, from said gripping aperture to the opposite edge.

17. The closure of claim 14 wherein said body is elongated and has a longitudinal groove which is on the side of said body opposite to said one side thereof and extends the full length of said one side, from said gripping aperture to the opposite edge.

18. The closure of claim 14 wherein said body is elongated and has two longitudinal grooves which are on opposite sides of said body and extend the full lengths of said sides, from said gripping aperture to the opposite edge.

19. The closure of claim 14 wherein said body has a paper lamination on both of said sides.

20. The closure of claim 19 wherein a groove is on one side of said body and extends the full length of said one side, from said gripping aperture to the opposite edge.

21. The closure of claim 19 wherein two grooves, on opposite sides of said body, extend the full lengths of said sides, from said gripping aperture to the opposite edge.

22. The closure of claim 14 wherein said paper lamination is colored.

23. The closure of claim 14 wherein said body is elongated and has a longitudinal through-hole.

Fig. 9A (cont'd)—Claims for Sample Patent Application

Patent Application of Lou W. Koppe for "Paper-Laminated Pliable Closure for
Flexible Bags" continued – Page 13

   24. A method of closing a plastic bag, comprising:

      (a) providing a bag closure of the type comprising a flat body of
          material having a lead-in notch on one edge thereof, a gripping
          aperture adjacent to and communicating with said notch, and a layer
          of paper laminated on one of its sides,

      (b) providing a plastic bag and inserting contents into said plastic
          bag,

      (c) twisting said plastic bag so that it forms a neck portion to hold
          said contents from falling out of said plastic bag,

      (d) inserting said bag closure onto said neck portion of said plastic
          bag so that said neck portion of said plastic bag passes said lead-
          in notch and into said gripping aperture,

   whereby said bag closure can be easily marked to identify and/or price
      said contents in said plastic bag.

   25. The method of claim 24 wherein said flat body of material is com-
       posed of polyethyleneterephthalate.

   26. The method of claim 24 wherein said layer of paper is colored.

Third independent claim is a method claim.

abstract follows on new page—see Ch. 8

Fig. 9A (cont'd)—Claims for Sample Patent Application

M. Summary

Claims define the invention in logical and precise terms. They are sentence fragments beginning with the words "I claim" and are provided at the end of a patent application.

The patent statute and rules regarding claims require that they (a) be clear and unambiguous, (b) be independent or dependent, (c) must use terms from the specification, and (d) should be phrased in a two-part form (prior art plus improvement). Claims can also have elements expressed in "means-plus-function" form.

Every claim should be classifiable into one of the five statutory classes of invention: machine, article, composition, process (method), or new use. Software or business claims are usually process claims, but can be machine claims. The number of claims is not as important as their breadth and the specific features of the invention need not be recited in a claim to be covered.

For a device to infringe a claim, it must meet all of the elements of the claim. Claims can be made broader by eliminating elements or broadening existing elements, but each claim should define a novel and unobvious invention over the prior art. When an element is first introduced in a claim, the article "a" should be used, but when the element is referred to again the article "the" or "said" should be used.

A "means clause" in a claim covers the hardware in the specification and its equivalents. A patent application should have means, nonmeans (apparatus), and method independent claims, if possible.

Each independent claim should be followed by a set of dependent claims. Each dependent claim must recite additional element(s) or recite the existing elements more broadly. Claims must be logical, complete, unambiguous, and every element in every claim must be shown in the drawings. Computer program claims must claim a concrete, practical, and useful program. ■

Chapter 10

Finaling and Mailing Your Application

Inventor's Commandment #14

Before signing any document, whether in the patent field or elsewhere, read, understand, and be sure you agree to it fully. After signing, obtain and be sure to save an identical copy of what you signed.

Inventor's Commandment #15

Avoid Fraud on the PTO: In addition to making a full disclosure, promptly tell the PTO, in Information Disclosure Statements, about any pertinent "prior art" or other material facts concerning your invention of which you are aware or of which you become aware.

Inventor's Commandment #16

Fax: Except for the actual application, you can and should fax all papers to the PTO to avoid loss in the mail. When you fax to the PTO, be sure all blanks on all forms are completed, all forms and documents are signed, a Credit Card Payment Form is included, if needed, all pages are present, and the document is timely faxed. If you mail any papers, follow the admonitions for faxing (you may pay by check as well as a credit card) and always include a receipt postcard addressed to you with all of the paper(s) listed on the back of the card.

Inventor's Commandment #17

Orderly File: Prepare and maintain file folders for (1) Official Papers and (2) Correspondence. Include a copy of every paper you send to or receive from the PTO in the Official Papers file. Include a copy of every paper you send to or receive from anyone other than the PTO in the Correspondence file. Write the date received on every incoming paper and date every outgoing paper.

Now that you've drafted your patent application, it's time to put it in final form. Since the PTO places great emphasis on thoroughness, this chapter is, accordingly, filled with many picky details. In the event you want to rebel and sim-

ply pass over those requirements that are inconvenient, remember that the PTO has many rules with which you must comply. If you fail to comply with certain rules—for example, you forget to enclose a declaration or a check—the PTO will impose substantial monetary penalties. Also your patent examiner has discretion to approve or reject your application. An application that fully meets the requirements and standards of the PTO will have much smoother sailing than one that doesn't.

Fortunately, while you must pay attention to detail, meeting the PTO's requirements and standards is relatively easy if you've followed my suggestions in the previous chapters. Because you've reviewed a number of patents in the same field as your own, you'll be familiar with the standards for writing the specification and claims (Chapters 8 and 9). Because you've prepared preliminary drawings (Chapter 8) in basic conformance with the rules for final drawings, putting them in final form will not involve great difficulty. Because you've analyzed all relevant prior art known to you and can distinguish it from your invention, you are in a good position to follow through with your application to a successful completion (Chapter 13).

A. The Drawing Choices

You have two basic choices for your drawings. You can file the application with:

- *Formal drawings* (generally CAD drawings or other computer-created drawings or xerographic copies of ink drawings done with instruments on Bristol board or Mylar film and in accordance with all the rules), or
- *Informal drawings* (generally xerographic copies of good pencil or ink sketches, which include all the details of the invention).

Further, in each case the drawings can be filed in either:

- The U.S. letter size (8.5" x 11"), or
- The A4 international size (210 mm x 297 mm).

Should you submit formal or informal drawings? I strongly recommend that, if at all possible, you submit formal drawings. However, if cost and time are important considerations, you can file informal drawings. If you do, the PTO usually will require you to file formal drawings before they will examine your application. In any case, when the application is allowed (see Chapter 13, Section I), you will have to pay an issue fee and file any required corrected drawings within three months. Also, if you want to file abroad, you'll have to prepare formal drawings approximately 11 months after filing.

As far as the choice of the U.S. or international sizes is concerned, if you have any serious thoughts about filing abroad, it's better to use the international (A4) size, since you can make good photocopies, file these for your U.S. application, and later use the originals (or another good set of copies) for the international application. (I discuss foreign filing in Chapter 12.) If you do use the U.S. size and later decide to foreign file, you can still make A4 copies by using a photocopier or a patent drawing service in the Arlington, Virginia, area (about $20 a sheet).

If necessary to illustrate the invention properly—that is, if color is an essential part of the invention—color photos or color drawings may also be used. File three sets of color photos or drawings in one of the two permitted sizes with:

1. a petition explaining why color is necessary; use the format of the petition of Fig. 10R (Form 10-9 in Appendix 7) but change the title. For example, write "Petition Explaining Why Color Is Necessary" and change the body of the form to provide an explanation;

2. the petition fee (see Appendix 4, Fee Schedule), and

3. a statement in the specification just below the title reading as follows: "The file of this patent contains at least one color drawing. Copies of the patent with color drawings will be provided by the PTO upon payment of necessary fee."

Black and white photos may only be used for patent drawings, if necessary to illustrate the invention, for example, to show a photomicrograph of a composite material. File one set of B&W photos in one of the two permitted sizes on double-weight photographic paper or mounted on Bristol board. You must also file a petition explaining why black and white photos are necessary. No fee is needed.

All photos must be of sufficient quality that all details can be reproduced in the printed patent and the photos must illustrate all features of the invention, just as ink or CAD drawings must do.

B. PTO Rules for Drawings

The PTO has a number of rules for preparing formal drawings. Even if you plan to submit informal drawings, the rules should be followed as much as possible so that much of the work will already be done in the event you later need to submit formal drawings (they are required if your patent application is allowed). For step-by-step instructions and examples on how to implement these rules, see *How to Make Patent Drawings*, by Jack Lo and David Pressman (Nolo).

When your drawings arrive at the PTO, whether with your application or after allowance, your drawings are inspected by the PTO's drawing inspectors, who are themselves draftspersons. If they find that any of your drawings are informal or in violation of any of the above rules, they will fill out and insert a drawing objection sheet in your file.

A copy of this (shown in Fig. 10A) will be sent to you before or with your first Office Action or after allowance. (See Chapter 13.) You must correct the drawings before the patent will be examined or before a patent can issue; the drawings are "corrected" by substituting new drawings. Thus, you should keep the originals of your drawings and send in good photocopies. Then if you have to correct the drawings, you can correct your originals and then send in new photocopies.

The most common drawing defects are listed on the drawing inspector's sheet (Fig. 10A). These and other frequently encountered defects are as follows:

- Lines are pale
- Paper is poor
- Numerals are poor
- Lines are rough, blurred, or matrixy (zig-zag)
- Copier marks are on the drawing
- Shade lines are required
- Figures must be numbered
- Heading space is required
- Figures must not be connected
- Criss-cross or double line-hatching is objectionable
- Arrowheads are used on lead lines for individual parts
- Parts in section must be hatched
- Solid black is objectionable
- Figure legends are placed incorrectly (for example, inside figure or vertically when drawing is horizontal)
- Drawing has mounted photographs
- Drawing contains extraneous matter
- Paper is undersized or oversized
- Margins are too small
- Lettering is too small
- Figures contain dimension lines
- The sheets contain wrinkles, tears, or folds
- Both sides of the sheet are used
- Margin lines have been used
- Sheets contain too many erasures
- Sheets contain broken lines to illustrate regular parts of the invention
- Sheets contain alterations, interlineations, or overwritings
- Sheets contain unclear representations
- Sheets contain freehand lines
- Sheets contain figures on separate sheets that can't be assembled without concealing parts
- Sheets contain reference numerals that aren't mentioned in the specification
- Sheets contain the same reference numeral to designate different parts
- Figures aren't separately numbered
- Drawings contain dimensions.

Rcd 95028

Form PTO 948 (Rev. 10-93)   U.S. DEPARTMENT OF COMMERCE - Patent and Trademark Office   Application No. 07/883567

NOTICE OF DRAFTSPERSON'S PATENT DRAWING REVIEW

PTO Draftpersons review all originally filed drawings regardless of whether they are designated as formal or informal. Additionally, patent Examiners will review the drawings for compliance with the regulations. Direct telephone inquiries concerning this review to the Drawing Review Branch, 703-305-8404.

The drawings filed (insert date) 9/27/95 are
A.____ not objected to by the Draftsperson under 37 CFR 1.84 or 1.152.
B. ✓ objected to by the Draftsperson under 37 CFR 1.84 or 1.152 as indicated below. The Examiner will require submission of new, corrected drawings when necessary. Corrected drawings must be submitted according to the instructions on the back of this Notice.

1. DRAWINGS. 37 CFR 1.84(a): Acceptable categories of drawings:
Black ink. Color.
____ Not black solid lines. Fig(s)_____
____ Color drawings are not acceptable until petition is granted.

2. PHOTOGRAPHS. 37 CFR 1.84(b)
____ Photographs are not acceptable until petition is granted.

3. GRAPHIC FORMS. 37 CFR 1.84 (d)
____ Chemical or mathematical formula not labeled as separate figure. Fig(s)_____
____ Group of waveforms not presented as a single figure, using common vertical axis with time extending along horizontal axis. Fig(s)_____
____ Individuals waveform not identified with a separate letter designation adjacent to the vertical axis. Fig(s)_____

4. TYPE OF PAPER. 37 CFR 1.84(e)
____ Paper not flexible, strong, white, smooth, nonshiny, and durable. Sheet(s)_____
____ Erasures, alterations, overwritings, interlineations, cracks, creases, and folds not allowed. Sheet(s)_____

Transparent objectionable Figs 1,3

5. SIZE OF PAPER. 37 CFR 1.84(f): Acceptable paper sizes:
21.6 cm. by 35.6 cm. (8 1/2 by 14 inches)
21.6 cm. by 33.1 cm. (8 1/2 by 13 inches)
21.6 cm. by 27.9 cm. (8 1/2 by 11 inches)
21.0 cm. by 29.7 cm. (DIN size A4)
____ All drawing sheets not the same size. Sheet(s)_____
____ Drawing sheet not an acceptable size. Sheet(s)_____

6. MARGINS. 37 CFR 1.84(g): Acceptable margins:

Paper size	
21 cm. X 27.9 cm. (8 1/2 X 11 inches)	21 cm. X 29.7 cm. (DIN Size A4)
2.5 cm. (1")	2.5cm.
.64 cm. (1/4")	2.5 cm.
.64 cm. (1/4")	1.5 cm.
.64 cm. (1/4")	1.0 cm.

Margins do not conform to chart above.
Sheet(s)_____
____Top (T) ____ Left (L) ____Right (R) ____Bottom (B)

7. VIEWS. 37 CFR 1.84(h)
REMINDER: Specification may require revision to correspond to drawing changes.
____ All views not grouped together. Fig(s)_____
____ Views connected by projection lines. Fig(s)_____
____ Views contain center lines. Fig(s)_____
Partial views. 37 CFR 1.84(h)(2)
____ Separate sheets not linked edge to edge. Fig(s)_____
____ View and enlarged view not labeled separately. Fig(s)_____
____ Long view relationship between different parts not clear and unambiguous. 37 CFR 1.84(h)(2)(ii) Fig(s)_____
Sectional views. 37 CFR 1.84(h)(3)
____ Hatching not indicated for sectional portions of an object. Fig(s)_____
✓ Hatching of regularly spaced oblique parallel lines not spaced sufficiently. Fig(s)_____
____ Hatching not at substantial angle to surrounding axes or principal lines. Fig(s) 3
____ Cross section not drawn same as view with parts in cross section with regularly spaced parallel oblique strokes. Fig(s)_____
____ Hatching of juxtaposed different elements not angled in a different way. Fig(s)_____
Alternate position. 37 CFR 1.84(h)(4)
____ A separate view required for a moved position. Fig(s)_____

____ Modified forms. 37 CFR 1.84(h)(5)
Modified forms of construction must be shown in separate views. Fig(s)_____

8. ARRANGEMENT OF VIEWS. 37 CFR 1.84(i)
____ View placed upon another view or within outline of another. Fig(s)_____
____ Words do not appear in a horizontal, left-to-right fashion when page is either upright or turned so that the top becomes the right side, except for graphs. Fig(s)_____

9. SCALE. 37 CFR 1.84(k)
____ Scale not large enough to show mechanism without crowding when drawing is reduced in size to two-thirds in reproduction. Fig(s)_____
____ Indication such as "actual size" or "scale 1/2" not permitted. Fig(s)_____
____ Elements of same view not in proportion to each other. Fig(s)_____

10. CHARACTER OF LINES, NUMBERS, & LETTERS. 37 CFR 1.84(l)
✓ Lines, numbers & letters not uniformly thick and well defined, clean, durable, and black (except for color drawings). Fig(s)_____

11. SHADING. 37 CFR 1.84(m)
____ Shading used for other than shape of spherical, cylindrical, and conical elements of an object, or for flat parts. Fig(s)_____
____ Solid black shading areas not permitted. Fig(s)_____

12. NUMBERS, LETTERS, & REFERENCE CHARACTERS. 37 CFR 1.84(p)
____ Numbers and reference characters not plain and legible. 37 CFR 1.84(p)(1) Fig(s)_____
____ Numbers and reference characters used in conjuction with brackets, inverted commas, or enclosed within outlines. 37 CFR 1.84(p)(1) Fig(s)_____
____ Numbers and reference characters not oriented in same direction as the view. 37 CFR 1.84(p)(1) Fig(s)_____
____ English alphabet not used. 37 CFR 1.84(p)(2) Fig(s)_____
____ Numbers, letters, and reference characters do not measure at least .32 cm. (1/8 inch) in height. 37 CFR(p)(3) Fig(s)_____

13. LEAD LINES. 37 CFR 1.84(q)
____ Lead lines cross each other. Fig(s)_____
____ Lead lines missing. Fig(s)_____
____ Lead lines not as short as possible. Fig(s)_____

14. NUMBERING OF SHEETS OF DRAWINGS. 37 CFR 1.84(t)
____ Number appears in top margin. Fig(s)_____
____ Number not larger than reference characters. Fig(s)_____
____ Sheets not numbered consecutively, and in Arabic numerals, beginning with number 1. Sheet(s)_____

15. NUMBER OF VIEWS. 37 CFR 1.84(u)
____ Views not numbered consecutively, and in Arabic numerals, beginning with number 1. Fig(s)_____
____ View numbers not preceded by the abbreviation Fig. Fig(s)_____
____ Single view contains a view number and the abbreviation Fig. Fig(s)_____
____ Numbers not larger than reference characters. Fig(s)_____

16. CORRECTIONS. 37 CFR 1.84(w)
Corrections not durable and permanent. Fig(s)_____

17. DESIGN DRAWING. 37 CFR 1.152
____ Surface shading shown not appropriate. Fig(s)_____
____ Solid black shading not used for color contrast. Fig(s)_____

ATTACHMENT TO PAPER NO. 9   REVIEWER CBR   DATE 10/25/95

Applicant's Copy

Fig. 10A—Draftsperson's Drawing Objection Sheet
Although the PTO form still refers to four sizes of paper, new rules only allow two sizes: 8½" x 11" and A4.

Summary of PTO Drawing Rules

1. **Need for Drawings:** Drawings (or only a single drawing) must be filed whenever necessary to understand the invention.

2. **Flowcharts:** Flowcharts should also be included whenever useful for an understanding of the invention.

3. **Must Show Features Claimed:** The drawings must show every feature recited in the claims.

4. **Conventional Features:** Conventional features that are not essential for an understanding of the invention, but are mentioned in the description and claims, can be shown by a graphical drawing symbol or a labeled rectangular box. For example, a motor can be shown by an encircled "M," and a CPU in a computer can be shown by a rectangle labeled "CPU."

5. **Improvements:** When your invention consists of an improvement in an old machine, the drawing should show the improved portion disconnected from the old structure with only so much of the old structure as is necessary to show how your improvement fits in. For example, if you've invented a new taillight for a bicycle, show the bicycle itself with the new taillight (without detail) in one figure labeled as "prior art." Then show just the portion of the bike where the taillight is mounted in detail in another figure, together with details of the mounting hardware.

6. **Paper:** The filed drawings (xerographic copies) should be on paper that is flexible, strong, white, smooth, nonshiny, and durable. Ordinary 20# bond is acceptable. (You should do the originals on Mylar film, vellum, or hard, rather than soft, Bristol board; this is available in most good art supply stores. Strathmore Paper Co. makes excellent patent drawing boards in both U.S. and A4 sizes (about $1/sheet), but you can get your sheets more economically by buying larger sheets of hard Bristol board and cutting them to the proper size. If you're using CAD, do the originals on regular bond and, since additional originals are so easy to make, send the originals to the PTO. (Keep your disk copy and a backup of your drawing file!)

7. **Lines:** The main requirement for all drawings is that all lines must be crisp and perfectly black. A good photocopy on good quality bond paper is usually used, but the lines should be crisp and sharp. A good xerographic copy from a dark-penciled original will be accepted. Jagged slant lines from a dot matrix printer or bitmapped drawing program are verboten for formal drawings.

Lines the PTO Recognizes on Drawings:

Normal Lines: Use a solid thin line (_____) to show regular parts and a thick solid line (▬▬▬▬) to show a shadowed edge—see Rule #14—or hatching a cross-section.

Hidden Lines: This is a dashed line (– – – – – – – –) to show a part behind another part—see Fig. 8C.

Projection Lines: This is composed of alternating long dashes and dots (— · — · — ·) and is used to connect exploded parts—see Fig. 8D.

Phantom Lines: Similar to a projection line, but which uses two dots instead of one (— ·· — ·· — ··); this is used to show an alternate position of a movable part, or on an adjacent structure which is not part of the invention.

8. **White Pigment:** The use of white pigment (for example, White Out™, Liquid Paper™) to cover lines is now acceptable, provided all lines are sharp and black.

9. **Uniform Size:** All drawing sheets in an application must be exactly sized in the same U.S. letter or A4 size. Fig. 10B shows these two sizes.

10. **Invisible Margins:** The margins must not contain any lines or writing; all writing and lines must be in the remaining "sight" (drawing area) on the sheet. Margin border lines are forbidden, but crosshairs (about 1cm long) should be drawn over two opposite (cater-corner) margin corners.

11. **No Holes:** The drawing sheets should not contain any holes.

12. **Instrument Work:** All lines must be made with drafting instruments or a laser printer and must be very dense, sharp, uniformly thick, and black. Fine or crowded lines must be avoided. Solid black areas are not permitted. Freehand work must be avoided unless necessary.

13. **Hatching:** Parts in section must be filled with slanted parallel lines (hatching) that are spaced apart sufficiently so that they can be distinguished without difficulty. Crisscross and double-line hatching is forbidden.

14. **Shading:** Objects can be shaded with surface and edge shadings so that the light appears to come from the upper left at a 45-degree angle. Thus the shade sides of all objects (the right and bottom) should be done with heavier lines. Surface shading should be open. On perspective views, the closest edges should be made heavier. Edge and surface shading is mandatory in design patent applications.

15. **Scale:** The scale should be large enough to show the mechanism without crowding when the drawing is reduced to ²/₃ of its original size for reproduction. Detailed parts should be shown on a larger scale, and spread out over two or more sheets if necessary, to accomplish this, but the number of sheets should not be more than necessary.

16. **Figures:** The different views should be consecutively numbered figures, for example, "Fig. 1A," "Fig. 1B," "Fig. 2," etc. Each figure should be separate and unconnected with any other figure. If possible, you should number the figures consecutively on consecutive sheets. However, if you want to arrange the figures in nonconsecutive order to use space efficiently, that's okay, albeit less desirable.

17. **Reference Numerals and Lead Lines:** Numbers must be plain, legible, carefully formed, and not encircled. They should be at least 3.2 mm (¹/₈") high. When parts are complex, they should not be placed so close that comprehension suffers. They should not cross or mingle with other lines. When grouped around a part, they should be placed around the part and connected by lead lines to the elements to which they refer. They should not be placed on hatched or shaded surfaces unless absolutely necessary; if then, they should be placed in a blank space in the hatching or shading. (Numerals are preferred to letters.) Arrowheads should not be used on lead lines, but if a numeral refers to an entire assembly or group of connected elements, its lead line can have an arrowhead, or it can be underlined to distinguish it from the lead lines of numerals that refer to a single part.

18. **No Duplication of Reference Numerals:** The same part in different figures must always be designated by the same reference numeral. Conversely, the same reference numeral must never be used to designate different parts. Numbers with primes and letter suffixes are considered different numbers.

19. **Graphic Symbols:** These can be used for conventional parts, but must be defined in the specification. For instance, if you use an encircled "M" for a motor, the specification should say, for example, "A motor, represented in Fig. 2 by an encircled 'M.'" Conventional symbols, such as those approved by the IEEE, ASA, etc., or from any standards or symbols book, can be used. Arrows should be used to show direction of movement, where necessary.

20. **Descriptive Matter:** The rules state that descriptive matter on the drawings is not permitted. I vehemently oppose this rule, since the use of descriptive matter on drawings makes them far more meaningful, and since textbooks, magazine articles, etc., all use drawings with ample descriptive matter. Unfortunately, this rule is being enforced now, so just put the figure number and nothing else under each figure—for example, "Fig. 1," and not "Fig. 1—Apparatus in Ready State."

    The Rules do permit (and even require) legends to be used within rectangular boxes, on flowcharts, piping (plumbing) lines, or wherever else additional clarity is highly desirable. If used, the descriptive matter lettering should be as large as, or larger than, the reference numerals.

21. **Views:** The drawings should have as many views (figures) as is necessary to show the invention. The views may be plan, sectional, exploded, elevational, or perspective; detailed larger-scale views of specific elements should be employed. Engineering views (such as front, side, bottom, or back) should not normally be used if perspective views can adequately illustrate the invention. If exploded views are used, the separated parts of the same figure must be joined by assembly lines or embraced by a bracket. (See Fig. 8D.)

    A large machine or schematic or flowchart can be extended over several sheets, but the views should be arranged to be easily understandable and so that the sheets can be assembled adjacent each other to show the entire machine. Never place one figure within another.

22. **Sectional Views:** The plane upon which a sectional view is taken should be illustrated in the general view by a broken line, the ends of which should be designated by numerals corresponding to the figure number of the sectional view with arrows indicating the direction in which the sectional view is taken. For example, suppose your Fig. 1 shows a left-side front view of your carburetor and Fig. 2 shows a cross-sectional front of the back half of the carburetor on a plane vertically bisecting the carburetor into front and back halves. In this case, Fig. 1 should contain a broken vertical line spaced halfway from left to right with arrows pointing to the right at the top and bottom of this line; the arrows should each be labeled "2" to indicate the section is shown in Fig. 2.

Summary of PTO Drawing Rules (Cont'd)

23. **Moving Parts:** To show two positions of a movable part, show its main position in full lines and its secondary position in phantom lines, provided this can be done clearly. If not, use a separate view for the secondary position. (See Item 7, above, for how to do a phantom line.)

24. **Modifications:** Show modifications in separate figures, not in broken lines.

25. **No Construction Lines:** Construction lines, center lines, and projection lines connecting separate figures are forbidden. However, projection lines to show the assembly of parts in an exploded view in one figure are permitted. (See Fig. 8D.)

26. **Position of Sheet:** All views (figures) on a sheet must have the same orientation, preferably so that they can be read with the sheet upright (that is, in portrait orientation with its short side at the top) so the examiner won't have to turn the sheets or the file to read the drawing. However, if views longer than the width of the sheet are necessary for the clearest illustration of the invention, the sheet can be turned to a landscape orientation, that is, on its side so that its short side and the appropriate top margin is on the right-hand side. The orientation of any lettering on a sheet must conform with the orientation of the sheet, except that the sheet number and number of sheets separated by a slash (1/2) must always be at the top. (See Fig. 10B.)

27. **OG Figure:** One figure should be a comprehensive view of the invention for inclusion in the *Official Gazette*, a weekly publication of the PTO that shows the main claim and drawing figure of every patent issued that week.

28. **No Extraneous Matter:** No extraneous matter—that is, matter that is not part of the claimed invention or its supporting or related structures—is permitted on the drawings. However, you can (and should) place additional matter, such as a hand on a special pistol grip, if necessary to show use or an advantage of the invention. Also, you should put the sheet number and total number of sheets ("1/4, 2/4," etc.) below the top margin, in centered numerals that are larger than the regular reference numerals. If the center space is occupied, the sheet number should be placed to the right.

29. **No Wrinkled Sheets:** The sheets should be sent to the PTO with adequate protection so that they will arrive without wrinkles or tears. You should send the sheets flat, between two pieces of corrugated cardboard within a large envelope, but they can also be rolled and sent in a mailing tube, provided they don't wrinkle. Never fold patent drawing sheets or typed sheets of the specification.

30. **Phantom Lines:** Parts that are hidden, but that you want to show, for example, the inside of a computer, should be shown in phantom lines—that is, broken lines. (See #7 above.) Reference numeral lead lines that refer to phantom parts should also be broken, in accordance with standard drafting practice. Broken lines must never be used to designate a part of the actual invention, unless to illustrate a phantom part or a moved position of a part.

31. **Identification on Back:** So that the PTO can identify and utilize the drawings in case they get separated from the file, you should include the title of the invention, and the first inventor's name and telephone number on the back of each sheet, at least 1 cm down from the top. Use a label or sticker if necessary to prevent this information from showing through to the front.

C. Doing Your Own Drawings

Many inventors sensibly choose to prepare their own patent applications instead of hiring a patent attorney or agent to do it for them. However, these same inventors frequently conclude that preparing the drawings is beyond their ability and turn the job over to a professional draftsperson. This can be costly. The typical draftsperson charges $75 to $150 per sheet of patent drawings (each sheet may contain several figures or separate drawings). Since most patent applications have between two to ten sheets of drawings, an inventor can sometimes shell out up to $1,500 for drawings.

Fortunately, patent drawings, like the application itself, are frequently susceptible to a self-help approach. To be sure, you'll need to learn some PTO rules and a certain learning curve is involved. However, the result will not only save you a lot of money over many patent applications, but also:

- You will be able to prepare promotional brochures for marketing your invention to prospective manufacturers or customers.
- You will be able to render your invention more accurately than a hired professional, because you know your invention best. By doing your own drawings, you do not have to take the time to make someone else understand your invention, or have to send the drawings back and forth for corrections.
- You will have the great satisfaction of properly completing the entire patent application by yourself—an impressive accomplishment for an inventor.

How to Make Patent Drawings, also published by Nolo, provides detailed guidance on making the drawings yourself. There are two methods for making patent drawings: pen and ruler, and computer-aided drafting (CAD). (You may not use photos unless necessary to illustrate fine details of the invention.)

You can file your application with either informal or formal drawings, as stated in Section A above. If you are submitting "informal" drawings, the copies need not be perfectly clean and neat, but if you choose the formal route, the copies must be very clean and neat, and all lines must be sharp and black. Full details about both U.S. and A4 sizes and the margin requirements are shown in the diagrams of Fig. 10B, below. (The typed specification sheets must have different margins—see Section E, below.)

If you decide to use international-size drawings, you'll find that some copiers now have A4 size paper and settings. If the copier does accommodate A4 paper, make copies on legal size sheets and trim them to A4 size (210 mm x 297 mm) ($8\frac{1}{4}$" x $11\frac{11}{16}$"). To get the margins right, you'll probably have to experiment a bit with the position of your original on the copier platen. (What's the basis of the system which includes the A4 size? This international standard, used by most of the world except the United States, is based on the principle that the height-to-width ratio of all pages is the square root of two. If you cut one sheet parallel to its shorter side into two equal pieces, then the resulting page will have again the same width/height ratio. This system makes for more efficient cutting of paper and matching of dimension of the pages.) The odd dimensions of A4 paper occur because an A1 sheet is purposely made one square meter in area (841 x 1189 mm with the $1{:}\sqrt{2}$ ratio) and after 4 bisecting cuts as above, the pieces each become 210 x 297 mm.

Even if you file informal drawings, you must include everything necessary in your drawings, since you won't be able to add any "new matter" (any new technical information that is not present in your original sketches) after you file. Be sure to study the drawings of the patents uncovered in your patentability search (Chapter 6) to get an idea of what's customarily done for your type of invention, and to better understand the PTO rules.

I recommend that you make your drawings as comprehensive and meaningful as possible, almost to the point that most people can fully understand the invention by looking at the drawings alone. This is because most people are picture, rather than word, oriented and thus can understand an invention far more readily from drawings because they are a lower level of abstraction than text.

For example, in electronic schematics, try to arrange the parts so that:

- the signal progresses from left to right
- the input sources and output loads are clearly indicated
- transistor states are indicated (that is, NNC = normally nonconductive; NC = normally conductive)
- signal waveforms are shown, and
- circuits are labeled by function (for example, "Schmitt Trigger").

In chemical and computer cases, I suggest you use a flowchart, if possible. In mechanical cases, I suggest you use exploded views, perspective views from several directions, and simplified perspective "action" views, showing the apparatus in operation and clearly illustrating its function. In other words, do the drawings so completely that they "speak" to their reader.

1. Making Drawings Manually

a. Informal Drawings

To make informal drawings, I recommend that you select from and use the techniques in Subsection b (Formal Drawings) below, except that everything is done in pencil, preferably on Mylar film, since this can be repeatedly and easily erased without damaging the film. (Vellum is a less-preferable alternative and Bristol board is a third alterna-

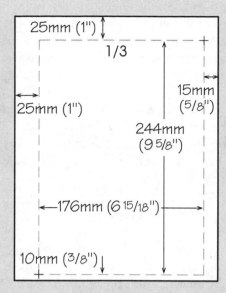

U.S. Letter Size
(8.5" x 11" or 216 mm x 269 mm)

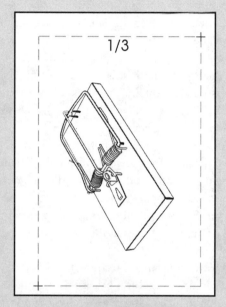

Layout for Landscape Orientation
(Not Preferred)

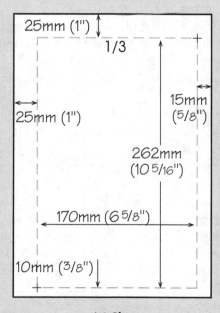

A4 Size
(8¼" x 11¹¹/₁₆" or 210 mm x 297 mm)

Note: Margin lines should *not* be used but are shown as broken lines to indicate the margin and "sight" sizes. Visible crosshairs (targets) should be put in either pair of opposite corners and should be about 1.5 cm (0.5") long. (The crosshairs are shown on these two sheets in the lower left and upper right corners.)

Fig. 10B—The Two Permitted Drawing Sizes

tive.) After you've made your penciled drawings (be sure to include all details, since, as stated, you can't add any new matter later), make photocopies on 20- or 24-pound bond to include with your patent application. Keep the penciled originals, since you'll need these to make your formal drawings later, which the PTO usually will require you to file before examination or after it allows your application.

b. Formal Drawings

The traditional or old way of making formal patent drawings is manually, with pen, ruler, and other instruments. A set of instruments can be assembled relatively inexpensively, and making simple drawings is fairly easy. However, pen and ruler allow little room for mistakes, because, except for very small marks, it is very difficult to correct misplaced ink lines. Nevertheless, with careful planning of drawing positioning (layout), and great care in laying down ink lines, drawing with pen and ruler is still a viable technique. However, few professional patent draftspersons still make drawings this way.

The necessary tools include pencils for preliminary sketches, ink drafting pens (also known as technical pens) for drawing ink lines, straight rules for drawing straight lines, triangles for drawing angled lines, templates for drawing certain standard shapes, French curves for drawing curves, an optional drafting table, and Mylar (best) or Vellum film or Bristol board. Pen and ruler may be used to make patent drawings in the following ways:

i. Drawing From Scratch

You can draw an object by visualizing in detail what it should look like, carefully sketching that image on the film or board with a pencil, correcting it until it looks about right, and finally inking over the pencil lines. The sketch of a telephone is illustrated in Fig. 10C. You must have some basic drawing skills to draw from scratch.

ii. Tracing

Tracing is much easier than drawing from scratch. An obvious method is to trace a photograph of an object that you wish to draw, as shown in Fig. 10D. You can also trace an actual, three-dimensional object by positioning a transparent drawing sheet on a transparent sheet of glass or acrylic, as shown in Fig. 10E, looking at the object through the glass, tracing the lines of the object on the film, and photocopying the tracing onto a sheet of paper. Tracing requires very little skill other than a steady hand.

iii. Drawing to Scale

You can also draw by scaling—that is, measuring and then reducing or enlarging—the dimensions of an actual object to fit on a sheet of paper, and drawing all the lines with the scaled dimensions. For example, if an object has a height of 50 cm and a width of 30 cm, you can reduce those dimensions by 50%, so that you would draw it with a height of 25 cm and a width of 15 cm to fit on the paper, as shown in Fig. 10F. All other dimensions of the object are scaled accordingly for the drawing. Making a drawing that looks right is easier by drawing to scale than by drawing based on only a mental image.

After making your ink drawings on film or Bristol board, make good photocopies on good-quality 20- or 24-pound bond paper for submission to the PTO. Keep the originals in case you have to make changes later.

2. Drawing With a Computer

CAD (computer-aided drafting or design) allows you to produce accurate drawings even if you consider yourself to have little or no artistic ability. In fact, no drawing skills in the traditional sense are needed at all. Furthermore, CAD enables you to correct mistakes as easily as a word processor enables you to edit words in a document. Even if you discover a mistake after you've printed a drawing, you can easily correct the mistake and print a new copy. To use CAD, you will need some computer skills, but if you know how to type letters on your computer, you can easily learn how to draw with it.

You will need either a PC (IBM-compatible) or a Mac, an ink jet or laser printer, a CAD program, an optional scanner, and an optional digital camera. A computer may be used to make patent drawings in the following ways:

a. Tracing

If you have a scanner, you can scan a photograph of an object, import (load) the scanned image into a CAD program, and trace it easily, as shown in Fig. 10G, a photo of an aircraft (the black outlines are the tracing lines which are difficult to see in a black-and-white book). If you have a digital camera, you can take a photograph of the object and download (transfer) the image directly into your computer through a cable, without having to print and scan the photograph. Once it is in your computer, tracing the image is very easy. Since you use a mouse instead of an ink pen, you don't even need a steady hand.

b. Drawing From Scratch

A 3-D (three-dimensional) CAD program enables you to construct an accurate, 3-D representation of your invention within the computer, such as the pipe fitting shown in Fig. 10H. A 3-D model is typically built by using and modifying basic geometric building blocks, such as boxes, cylinders, planes, and custom-defined shapes. You may create each part with specific dimensions, or you may simply draw a

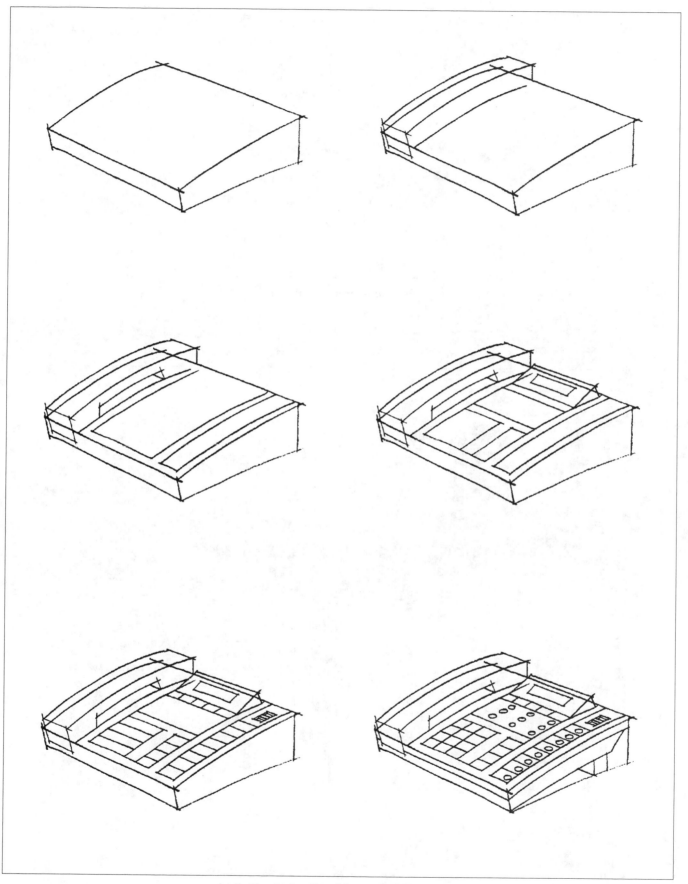

Fig. 10C—Sketching Techniques

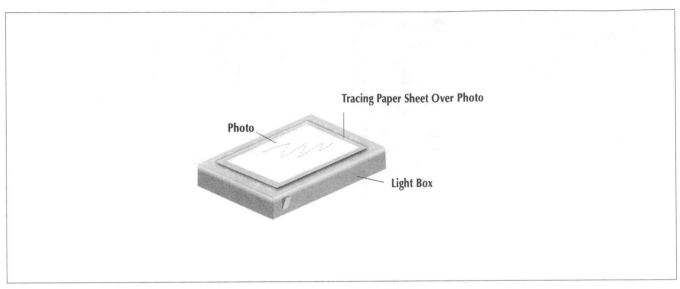

Photo

Tracing Paper Sheet Over Photo

Light Box

Fig. 10D—Tracing a Photo

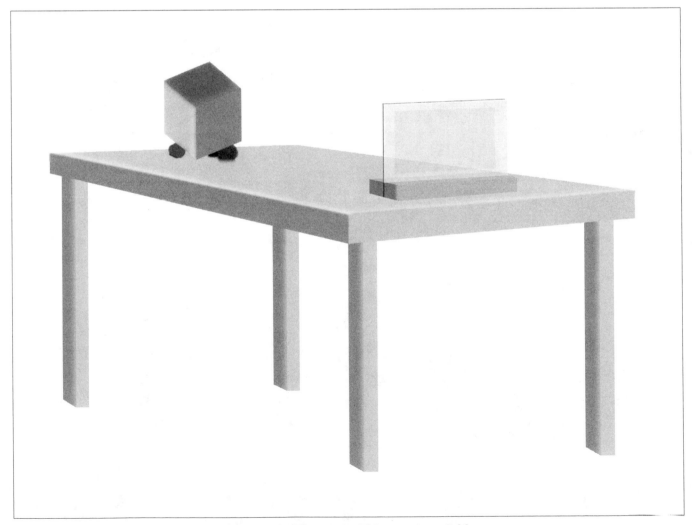

Fig. 10E—Tracing Large Object on Long Table

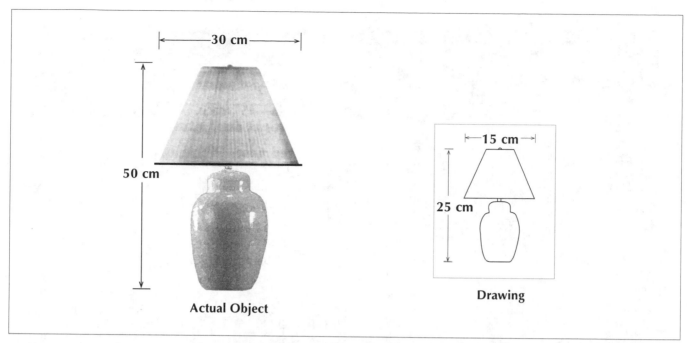

Fig. 10F—Drawing to Scale

Fig. 10G—Tracing a Photo on a Computer

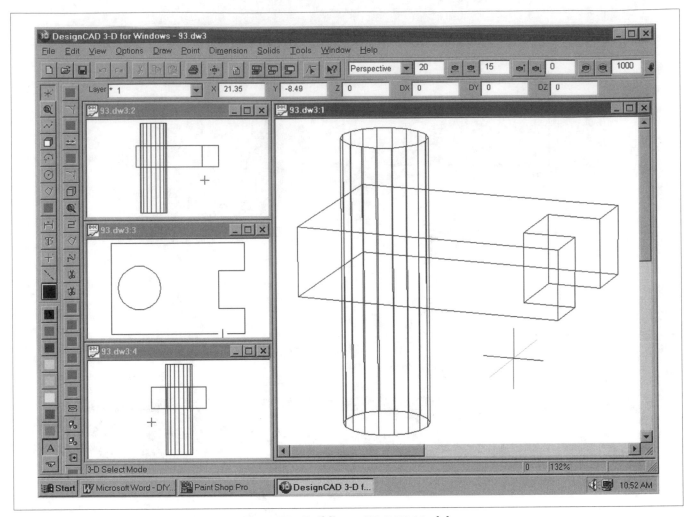

Fig. 10H—Building a 3D CAD Model

shape that looks about right. You can easily rotate the finished model to see it from any angle. You can also easily zoom in or out to adjust the viewing distance. Once you are satisfied with the view, you can print it as a line drawing (a drawing of dark lines on a light background). Therefore, you can make professional-looking drawings with a computer, even if you consider yourself to be a terrible artist.

3. Photography

Almost everyone has some degree of familiarity with photography. Obviously, a camera can take an accurate photograph or "drawing" of an object. While photographs may no longer be submitted as patent drawings (except in rare cases—see Section A above), they may be converted into acceptable line drawings by tracing them, by scanning them, or with a digital camera, their images may be copied directly into and manipulated and cleaned up with a CAD

program. Although photography spares you from having any drawing skills, you must have some photographic skills to take clear pictures, including a basic understanding of lighting and exposure. To take an accurate photograph, you will need a 35 mm camera with a selectable aperture, zoom and macro (close-up) lenses, and a tripod.

D. Consider Using a Professional Patent Draftsperson

If you don't feel competent to do your own drawings, you'll want to hire someone to do them for you. You can locate people who specialize in preparing patent drawings by letting your fingers do the walking through the nearest metropolitan area Yellow Pages. Look under the heading "Drawing Services," which should list several patent drafters. While expensive (about $30 to $50 per hour, or $75 to $150 per sheet), these people should do the job correctly the first time with CAD or in India ink on Bristol board. Also, you can use a "starving artist" who's proficient in the medium to be used (such as India ink or CAD), and reads and understands the rules thoroughly. Finally, if you don't mind working with someone at a distance, you can find many professional patent draftsmen in inventor magazines and in the *Journal of the Patent and Trademark Office Society*.

E. Finaling Your Specification, Claims, and Abstract

Before putting them in final form, you (and perhaps an acquaintance of yours) should reread your specification, claims, and abstract, to make sure your writing is clear, complete, understandable, and free of grammatical and spelling errors. Again, make sure that the main substantive requirements (as discussed in Chapters 8 and 9) are satisfied.

Try to do a perfect job with your patent application, because doing so will make a better impression on the examiner and anyone else, such as a judge or potential licensee, who reads it. Remember that any flaws or faults in the application will be seized upon by the examiner, whose job is to find flaws. The less excuse you give your examiner to find objections, the smoother will be the sailing of your application in the PTO.

Another, albeit nonlegal reason for striving for perfection was well stated by Pearl S. Buck:

"The secret of joy in work is contained in one word— excellence. To know how to do something well is to enjoy it."

As with your drawings, you must type your specification, claims, and abstract on either U.S. or A4-size paper. All sheets must be of the same size, free of holes, and have 2 cm top, bottom, and right margins, and a 2.5 cm left margin. Use 1.5 or double spacing and number the sheets at the top or bottom, inside the margin. (All correspondence that you send to the PTO at any time should always be 1.5 or double-spaced; never use single spacing and never type on both sides of a sheet.)

If you think you may later want to file corresponding foreign applications, it's easiest to type your application on U.S. letter-size paper with proper margins, so that if photocopied onto A4 size paper it will have the proper A4 margins. To do this print out or type the application on letter-size or computer paper (8½" x 11" after removal of the selvage or carrier strip). Use a 1" left margin, 6.2" line width, 1" top margin (3" on p. 1), and a bottom margin of

0.3", so that the last line is almost at the bottom of the page. The sample specification in Chapter 8 (Fig. 8G) is typed this way, except that the 1" top margin has been omitted. Save the original for possible later use in making an A4 version for an international application. Use a conventional typeface (do not use script) in at least 12-point type. Dot matrix printers are okay so long as the printout, or its photocopy, is clearly readable. You should not justify (line up the right margin of) your typing, since unjustified printing (as in this book) is much easier to follow. Alternatively, if you don't want to bother with aligning the typing for A4 now, just save the computer file of the application and then format it for A4 later (see "Typing and Filing Application on A4 Paper," below) if and when you foreign file.

You must start your claims and abstract on new pages, with the abstract on the last sheet, *after* the claims. The title should go on the first page. Don't submit an application on easily erasable paper, or on paper that has white pigment covering any typewritten lines, since these are not considered permanent, unaltered records. If you're not a good typist, and you don't have a word processor, one solution is to type your application on easily erasable paper or regular paper, cover the errors with white pigment, type in the corrections, and then make bond paper photocopies of your typewritten original for submission to the PTO.

If, after putting your specification in final form, you find you must make a few minor changes (one or two words in a few places), it's okay to do so, provided you make these changes neatly in ink—in handwriting—and date and initial the margin adjacent to each change *before* you sign the application.

Typing and Filing Application on A4 Paper

Alternatively, you can type and file your U.S. application on A4 paper, following the proper requirements for such matters as margins and line spacing (the abstract page). A4 paper (Hammermill #10303-6) can be obtained from a printer's supply house. Also, you can cut it yourself or have it cut for you. If you cut it yourself, the sheets should be 210 by 297 mm (11¹¹⁄₁₆" x 8¼") in size, with top margins 2 to 4 cm, left margins of 2.5 to 4 cm, and bottom and right margins of 2 to 3 cm, with sheets numbered consecutively at the top and typed with 1.5 line spacing—that is, four lines per inch or per 2.5 cm. Keep the originals and file an A4 xerographic copy. As stated, the PTO isn't very strict about format, but if you later file a PCT application (discussed in Chapter 12) these measurements must be followed to comply with WIPO (and EPO) requirements.

You don't have to file your drawings and your typewritten papers on the same size sheets; the drawings can be on A4 paper and the typewritten pages on U.S.-size paper, or vice versa. However, all drawing sheets must be the same size, as must all typed sheets. Never use both sides of a sheet, either for drawings or for the specification. A neatly typed specification will certainly make a very favorable impression on your examiner. If you can do your application with a laser printer with larger heading fonts, the result will be most impressive. As mentioned earlier, if you don't own a laser printer, consider using one at a copy center.

Some inventors have prepared their applications to look like patents, complete with narrow, single-spaced columns and cited references. Don't do this; your application should look like the sample in Chapter 8. When it issues the patent, the PTO will supply and print the list of references cited, your name, and all other data that normally goes on the abstract page.

The PTO suggests that you number all paragraphs (not including headings) of your application as follows: [0001], [0002], etc. (Include the brackets; don't use parentheses.) Since any changes must now be done by replacing entire paragraphs, such numbering will facilitate amendments. Fortunately, this is optional.

 Minimize the potential for disaster by not placing cups of coffee or other beverages at your desk while handling your final papers.

F. Name All True Inventors and Only True Inventors

In several different parts of your application, you're required to name the applicants or inventors. For example, the first page of the application lists the names, and Form 10-1 (Patent Application Declaration) must be signed by the inventors (see Figs. 10I (A & B) discussed below.)

While anyone can apply for a patent, the named applicant(s) must be the true inventor(s) of the invention. So, if you discover an invention abroad or that your deceased uncle invented, you aren't allowed to apply to patent it in your name. If you've conceived the invention (as defined by the claims) entirely on your own, there are no co-inventors. If you've invented it with someone else, both of you should be named as "joint inventors." But be sure that both of you actually are joint inventors. If somebody other than you played a significant role in conceiving the invention, review Chapter 16, Section B, for a more detailed discussion on inventorship.

PTO Rule 45 states that each joint inventor must have contributed something to at least one claim of the application. However, joint inventors need not have worked together or at the same time, their contributions need not be equal, and each need not have contributed to every claim of the application. Under no circumstances should you name your financier, your boss, or anyone else who was not an actual inventor. If you are not a U.S. citizen or are living outside the U.S., your rights are as good as a U.S. citizen-resident. The PTO will correspond with you in any country.

If joint inventors receive a patent, under Section 262 of the patent statutes, each joint patentee or owner of a patent can practice the invention without accounting to the other owners. Since this can be unfair, I have provided a Joint Owners' Agreement (Form 16-2, discussed in Chapter 16, Section C) to protect each owner. I strongly recommend that all joint owners sign this form to prevent injustice later.

Also, under PTO Rule 48, if the claims are changed or cancelled so that the original joint inventorship is no longer correct, the inventor who is improperly listed should be removed from the application. To record and preserve the contributions of the respective inventors, I have provided a Statement of Respective Contributions form as Form 16-1 (also discussed in Chapter 16, Section C). All joint applicants should fill out this form and sign and keep a copy so that inventorship can be changed with confidence later.

G. The Essential and Optional Parts of Your Application

A basic patent application consists of a set of minimal but necessary parts. However, for the reasons indicated below, you may wish to file additional or optional parts with your application. The following is a list of the minimal and necessary parts and also the additional and optional parts to get you familiar with them before I discuss them in detail later.

Minimal and Necessary Parts
- **Receipt Postcard.** This is stamped by the PTO and returned to you to let you know when your application was filed and its serial number.
- **Patent Application Transmittal Letter.** This tells the PTO what parts you're sending for your patent application.
- **Fee Transmittal.** This makes it easy for the PTO to compute and verify your filing fee.
- **Credit Card Payment Form, Check, or Money Order.** This pays your fees to the PTO.
- **Drawings.** These are required if the invention can be illustrated with a drawing.

- **Specification, Claims, and Abstract.** These parts are discussed in detail in Chapters 8 and 9.
- **Patent Application Declaration.** This states who the inventors are, that they've read the application, that they will disclose all material information, and that they understand that they can be charged with perjury if they lie on this form.

Additional and Optional Parts

- **Disclosure Document Reference Letter.** This refers to any Document Disclosure (DD) that you've filed and instructs the PTO not to discard the DD.
- **Request for Claim Drafting by Examiner Under MPEP 707.07(j).** This asks the examiner to draft claims for you if your application contains allowable subject matter.
- **Nonpublication Request (NPR).** This instructs the PTO not to publish your application (all applications are normally published 18 months after filing unless they've issued before then) so as to save you the publication fee and preserve your trade secret rights. If you foreign file the application, you must file a revocation of the NPR within 45 days.
- **Assignment and Transmittal.** This transfers ownership of your application to another individual or company.
- **Information Disclosure Statement, PTO Forms PTO/SB/ 08 (A and B), and Copies of Any Non-U.S. Patent References.** This cites prior art of which you are aware.

This book provides copies of actual PTO forms, most of which are now available in editable PDF format and can be completed and printed on your computer. (The PTO prefers that inventors use PTO forms.)

⚠️ Although the PTO forms provided in PDF format can be completed and printed on your computer, the free Adobe Acrobat Reader program which you need to show and complete these forms currently does not permit saving any completed PDF forms. Therefore, you should always print out any PDF forms you have prepared, since the information you enter on the forms will be lost once you turn off your computer.

H. Completing the Patent Application Declaration

Each patent application must be accompanied by a patent application declaration (PAD), which is a written statement under oath. Since the PAD is essential, I'll discuss it first, even though it's placed after the application when it's transmitted to the PTO. The other forms are important, but not abso-lutely essential, so I'll discuss them below. A PAD form is provided as Form 10-1, and a completed example is provided below in Fig. 10I (A & B).

While completing the PAD is a straightforward process, you should not treat it lightly. Rather, you should read and review it very carefully before you sign. If anyone can prove that you signed the declaration knowing that any of its statements were false, your patent can be held invalid. In fact, I've seen so many inventors sign PADs without reading or keeping a copy that I've provided Inventor's Commandment #14 at the beginning of this chapter. This advises you to read, make sure you agree with, and keep a copy of all documents you sign.

You can view and complete the PAD on your computer, a typewriter, or with a pen (do it neatly). If you want to use the computer, go to the PTO's forms website (www.uspto .gov/web/forms/index.html), open the editable version of Form PTO/SB/01, and refer to Fig 10I (A&B). Complete the form as follows:

Attorney Docket Number. No entry is needed, but if you prefer you may use any reference characters or names you wish to help you locate your patent application file.

First Named Inventor. Type the name of the sole inventor or the first inventor if there's more than one.

Leave the Application Number, Filing Date, Art Unit, and Examiner Name blank.

Declaration Submitted With Initial Filing. Check this box.

Title of the Invention. Type the title in this large box.

Under "the specification of which," check the box before "is attached hereto."

Leave all other blocks on the first page (Form 10-1) blank.

Complete the second page of Form 10-1 (Fig 10I-B) as follows:

If you want the PTO to correspond with someone other than an inventor, check the box after "direct all correspondence to" and the box before "Correspondence address below." In the next four lines, complete the name, address, phone, and fax (if any) of any noninventor who is to receive correspondence. (If you have several applications on file at the PTO, you may want to get a Customer Number, which enables you to use a number instead of your address. You can apply for a Customer Number using PTO Form SB125.)

If you want the PTO to correspond with an inventor, check the box after "Correspondence address below" and the PTO will send all correspondence to Sole or First Inventor.

While every joint inventor must sign most papers that are sent to the PTO, the PTO will correspond with one inventor only. Therefore you should list the inventor who is most available (or who has best access to a photocopier or scanner) in the Sole or First Inventor section of the form.

PTO/SB/01 (09-04)
Approved for use through 07/31/2006. OMB 0651-0032
U.S. Patent and Trademark Office; U.S. DEPARTMENT OF COMMERCE
Under the Paperwork Reduction Act of 1995, no persons are required to respond to a collection of information unless it contains a valid OMB control number.

DECLARATION FOR UTILITY OR DESIGN
PATENT APPLICATION
(37 CFR 1.63)

Attorney Docket Number	Goldberger-Briskin
First Named Inventor	M. Goldberger
COMPLETE IF KNOWN	
Application Number	
Filing Date	
Art Unit	
Examiner Name	

[✓] Declaration Submitted With Initial Filing   **OR**   [ ] Declaration Submitted after Initial Filing (surcharge (37 CFR 1.16 (e)) required)

I hereby declare that:

Each inventor's residence, mailing address, and citizenship are as stated below next to their name.

I believe the inventor(s) named below to be the original and first inventor(s) of the subject matter which is claimed and for which a patent is sought on the invention entitled:

Food chopper with convoluted blade.

(Title of the Invention)

the specification of which

[ ]   is attached hereto

OR

[✓]   was filed on (MM/DD/YYYY) [_____] as United States Application Number or PCT International

Application Number [_____] and was amended on (MM/DD/YYYY) [_____] (if applicable).

I hereby state that I have reviewed and understand the contents of the above identified specification, including the claims, as amended by any amendment specifically referred to above.

I acknowledge the duty to disclose information which is material to patentability as defined in 37 CFR 1.56, including for continuation-in-part applications, material information which became available between the filing date of the prior application and the national or PCT international filing date of the continuation-in-part application.

I hereby claim foreign priority benefits under 35 U.S.C. 119(a)-(d) or (f), or 365(b) of any foreign application(s) for patent, inventor's or plant breeder's rights certificate(s), or 365(a) of any PCT international application which designated at least one country other than the United States of America, listed below and have also identified below, by checking the box, any foreign application for patent, inventor's or plant breeder's rights certificate(s), or any PCT international application having a filing date before that of the application on which priority is claimed.

Prior Foreign Application Number(s)	Country	Foreign Filing Date (MM/DD/YYYY)	Priority Not Claimed	Certified Copy Attached? YES	NO
			[ ]	[ ]	[ ]
			[ ]	[ ]	[ ]
			[ ]	[ ]	[ ]
			[ ]	[ ]	[ ]

[ ]   Additional foreign application numbers are listed on a supplemental priority data sheet PTO/SB/02B attached hereto.

[Page 1 of 2]

This collection of information is required by 35 U.S.C. 115 and 37 CFR 1.63. The information is required to obtain or retain a benefit by the public which is to file (and by the USPTO to process) an application. Confidentiality is governed by 35 U.S.C. 122 and 37 CFR 1.11 and 1.14. This collection is estimated to take 21 minutes to complete, including gathering, preparing, and submitting the completed application form to the USPTO. Time will vary depending upon the individual case. Any comments on the amount of time you require to complete this form and/or suggestions for reducing this burden, should be sent to the Chief Information Officer, U.S. Patent and Trademark Office, U.S. Department of Commerce, P.O. Box 1450, Alexandria, VA 22313-1450. DO NOT SEND FEES OR COMPLETED FORMS TO THIS ADDRESS. **SEND TO: Commissioner for Patents, P.O. Box 1450, Alexandria, VA 22313-1450.**
If you need assistance completing the form, call 1-800-PTO-9199 and select option 2.

Fig. 10IA—Completed Declaration for Patent Application (Form 10-1 in Appendix 7)

PTO/SB/01 (09-04)
Approved for use through 07/31/2006. OMB 0651-0032
U.S. Patent and Trademark Office; U.S. DEPARTMENT OF COMMERCE
Under the Paperwork Reduction Act of 1995, no persons are required to respond to a collection of information unless it contains a valid OMB control number.

DECLARATION — Utility or Design Patent Application

Direct all correspondence to:	☐ The address associated with Customer Number:		OR ☑	Correspondence address below

Name
Mildred Goldberger

Address
1901 Kennedy Blvd.

City	State	ZIP
Philadephia	PA	10103

Country	Telephone	Fax
US	215-555-0362	

I hereby declare that all statements made herein of my own knowledge are true and that all statements made on information and belief are believed to be true; and further that these statements were made with the knowledge that willful false statements and the like so made are punishable by fine or imprisonment, or both, under 18 U.S.C. 1001 and that such willful false statements may jeopardize the validity of the application or any patent issued thereon.

NAME OF SOLE OR FIRST INVENTOR: ☐ A petition has been filed for this unsigned inventor

Given Name (first and middle [if any])	Family Name or Surname
Mildred	Goldberger

Inventor's Signature	Date
Mildred Goldberger	11/11/2003

Residence: City	State	Country	Citizenship
Philadelphia	PA	US	US

Mailing Address
1901 Kennedy Blvd.

City	State	Zip	Country
Philadelphia	PA	19103	US

NAME OF SECOND INVENTOR: ☐ A petition has been filed for this unsigned inventor

Given Name (first and middle [if any])	Family Name or Surname
Nathan	Briskin

Inventor's Signature	Date
Nathan Briskin	11/11/2003

Residence: City	State	Country	Citizenship
Philadelphia	PA	US	US

Mailing Address
1919 Chestnut St.

City	State	Zip	Country
Philadelphia	PA	19103	US

☐ Additional inventors or a legal representative are being named on the _____ supplemental sheet(s) PTO/SB/02A or 02LR attached hereto.

[Page 2 of 2]

Fig. 10lB—Completed Declaration for Patent Application (Form 10-1 in Appendix 7)

In the middle section of the form, complete the given name, family name, city (or county), state, and country of legal residence, citizenship, and mailing address of the sole or first inventor. Leave the date blank (unless you know the date it will be signed). Non-U.S. citizens have the same rights as U.S. citizens. The PTO will correspond with them no matter where they are and they don't have to be represented by an attorney in the U.S.

Complete the bottom section of the form for any second inventor in the same manner.

If there are more than two inventors, complete an additional sheet—Form PTO/SB/02A.

Note the wording on the first page of the PAD, which states that you have read and understand the specification and claims. If you haven't written the specification and claims, you should carefully read and understand them. Failure to do this can cause you embarrassment and may even result in fines for perjury.

The next sentence on page 1 of the PAD states that you acknowledge a duty to disclose information of which you are aware and that is material to the examination of the application. This provision is designed to impress upon inventors their duty to disclose (to the PTO) any information that could affect the examination or validity of the application. This means you must disclose to the PTO all relevant prior art that you have uncovered, any disadvantages of your invention of which you are aware, or any other act you think the examiner would want to be aware of when examining the application. Normally, all of this information will be provided in your Information Disclosure Statement (see Section N below). This disclosure requirement is very important and courts have, as mentioned, held patents invalid for "fraud on the PTO" when inventors have neglected this duty. Thus I've made it Inventor's Commandment #15.

Finally, note the statement in the middle of page 2 of the PAD. This states that everything on the form is true and that you are liable for perjury, and the patent application and any resulting patent may be held invalid, if you knowingly lie. Each inventor should then sign and date the appropriate "Inventor's Signature" spaces in the middle and bottom sections of page 2 of the PAD.

Claiming the Benefit of a PPA

If you have filed a Provisional Patent Application (PPA) and wish to claim the benefit of its filing date, you *must* do so in the "CROSS REFERENCE TO RELATED APPLICATIONS" section of your specification—as I have done in the sample specification included in Chapter 8.

The PTO rules are very strict in requiring that you should not sign the PAD until the entire application is completed. If the PTO finds out that you signed it before it was completed, or if you made any changes to the application after you signed the PAD, your application can be stricken or rejected entirely. If you need to make any changes to the application after it's finaled, you can do so neatly in ink, provided you date and initial each change and you do this before you sign the PAD. You can also make changes by amendment(s) after the application is filed (see Chapter 13), provided you don't add new matter to the application.

I. Complete the Transmittal Letter and Fee Transmittal, Payment, and Postcard

Now it's time to prepare the routine paperwork necessary to actually send your patent application to the PTO. Here's how to do it.

1. Prepare the Transmittal Letter

The transmittal letter (Form 10-2; PTO/SB/05) should be completed as follows (see Fig. 10J for an example of a completed form):

Attorney Docket No. and **First Inventor:** Complete as you did with the PAD (see Section H, above).

Title: Complete as you did with the PAD (see Section H, above).

Express Mail Label: If you use Express Mail (I strongly recommend it—see Section L, below) to mail your application, type or write the Express Mail number from the Post Office's Express Mail Label here.

Box 1: Check Fee Transmittal Form and complete this form (Form 10-3) as explained below.

Box 2: Check this Small Entity Box if you qualify for a Small Entity (SE) fee. An individual or individuals qualify

PTO/SB/05 (09-04)
Approved for use through 07/31/2006. OMB 0651-0032
U.S. Patent and Trademark Office. U.S. DEPARTMENT OF COMMERCE
Under the Paperwork Reduction Act of 1995, no persons are required to respond to a collection of information unless it displays a valid OMB control number.

UTILITY PATENT APPLICATION TRANSMITTAL

(Only for new nonprovisional applications under 37 CFR 1.53(b))

Attorney Docket No.	Goldberger-Briskin
First Inventor	M. Goldberger
Title	Food Chopper with Convolute Blade
Express Mail Label No.	DP123456789US1US

APPLICATION ELEMENTS
See MPEP chapter 600 concerning utility patent application contents.

ADDRESS TO: **Commissioner for Patents**
P.O. Box 1450
Alexandria VA 22313-1450

1. ☑ **Fee Transmittal Form** (e.g., PTO/SB/17)
   (Submit an original and a duplicate for fee processing)
2. ☑ **Applicant claims small entity status.**
   See 37 CFR 1.27.
3. ☑ **Specification**   [Total Pages ___12___]
   Both the claims and abstract must start on a new page
   (For information on the preferred arrangement, see MPEP 608.01(a))
4. ☑ **Drawing(s)** *(35 U.S.C. 113)* [Total Sheets ___2___]
5. **Oath or Declaration**   [Total Sheets ___2___]
   a. ☑ Newly executed (original or copy)
   b. ☐ A copy from a prior application (37 CFR 1.63(d))
      (for continuation/divisional with Box 18 completed)
      i. ☐ DELETION OF INVENTOR(S)
         Signed statement attached deleting inventor(s)
         name in the prior application, see 37 CFR
         1.63(d)(2) and 1.33(b).
6. ☐ **Application Data Sheet.** See 37 CFR 1.76
7. ☐ **CD-ROM or CD-R** in duplicate, large table or
   Computer Program *(Appendix)*
   ☐ Landscape Table on CD
8. **Nucleotide and/or Amino Acid Sequence Submission**
   (if applicable, items a. – c. are required)
   a. ☐ Computer Readable Form (CRF)
   b. Specification Sequence Listing on:
      i. ☐ CD-ROM or CD-R (2 copies); or
      ii. ☐ Paper
   c. ☐ Statements verifying identity of above copies

ACCOMPANYING APPLICATION PARTS

9. ☐ **Assignment Papers** (cover sheet & document(s))
   Name of Assignee_____
   _____
10. ☐ **37 CFR 3.73(b) Statement**   ☐ **Power of**
    (when there is an assignee)   **Attorney**
11. ☐ **English Translation Document** *(if applicable)*
12. ☑ **Information Disclosure Statement** (PTO/SB/08 or PTO-1449)
    ☐ Copies of citations attached
13. ☐ **Preliminary Amendment**
14. ☑ **Return Receipt Postcard** (MPEP 503)
    (Should be specifically itemized)
15. ☐ **Certified Copy of Priority Document(s)**
    (if foreign priority is claimed)
16. ☑ **Nonpublication Request** under 35 U.S.C. 122(b)(2)(B)(i).
    Applicant must attach form PTO/SB/35 or equivalent.
17. ☐ Other:_____
    _____

18. If a CONTINUING APPLICATION, *check appropriate box, and supply the requisite information below and in the first sentence of the specification following the title, or in an Application Data Sheet under 37 CFR 1.76:*

☐ Continuation   ☐ Divisional   ☐ Continuation-in-part (CIP)   of prior application No.: ....

Prior application information: Examiner _____   Art Unit: _____

19. CORRESPONDENCE ADDRESS

☐ The address associated with Customer Number: [_____]   **OR**   ☑ Correspondence address below

Name	Mildred Goldberger
Address	1901 Kennedy Blvd.

City	State	Zip Code
Philadelphia	PA	19103
Country	Telephone	Fax
USA		

Signature	*Mildred Goldberger*	Date	23 MAR 2005
Name (Print/Type)	Mildred Goldberger	Registration No. (Attorney/Agent)	

This collection of information is required by 37 CFR 1.53(b). The information is required to obtain or retain a benefit by the public which is to file (and by the USPTO to process) an application. Confidentiality is governed by 35 U.S.C. 122 and 37 CFR 1.11 and 1.14. This collection is estimated to take 12 minutes to complete, including gathering, preparing, and submitting the completed application form to the USPTO. Time will vary depending upon the individual case. Any comments on the amount of time you require to complete this form and/or suggestions for reducing this burden, should be sent to the Chief Information Officer, U.S. Patent and Trademark Office, U.S. Department of Commerce, P.O. Box 1450, Alexandria, VA 22313-1450. DO NOT SEND FEES OR COMPLETED FORMS TO THIS ADDRESS. **SEND TO: Commissioner for Patents, P.O. Box 1450, Alexandria, VA 22313-1450.**
If you need assistance in completing the form, call 1-800-PTO-9199 and select option 2.

Fig. 10J—Utility Patent Application Transmittal (Form 10-2 in Appendix 7)

Use latest fees—See Appendix 4, Fee Schedule

for SE fees if they haven't assigned (transferred) or licensed the invention (and they have no obligation to assign or license the invention) to a for-profit company with over 500 employees. (The PTO no longer requires that you file SE declarations.)

Box 3: "Specification" is used here in the statutory sense, meaning the specification (written description), including the claims and abstract (See Chapters 8 and 9). Check this box and type the total pages of all of these parts of your application.

Box 4: Check this box (unless your application has no drawings) and indicate the total number of drawing sheets.

Box 5: Oath or Declaration. Type the number of pages of your declaration. Your declaration should be two pages unless you have additional sheets for more than two inventors. Check Box A, since you're submitting a new application.

Box 6: Application Data Sheet. As of this printing, the PTO has not provided an Application Data Sheet form, so I haven't provided one. Although the PTO would like you to submit one, it's optional.

Boxes 7, 8, 10, to 11, 13, 15, and 18: Leave these blocks blank unless you're providing a computer program on a CD, a biosequence, a translation, a preliminary amendment, a certified copy based on a foreign filed application, or a continuing application (see Chapter 14).

Box 9: If you're filing an assignment with the application—see Section O below—check this box.

Box 12: If you're supplying an Information Disclosure Statement with the application (see Section N), check this box. Otherwise you must file your IDS within three months. If your IDS cites any foreign or nonpatent references, check the "Copies of citations attached" box. You don't have to send U.S. patent references to the PTO.

Box 14: Check this box and don't forget to complete and include a return receipt postcard—see Section 3.

Box 16: Nonpublication Request (NPR). I recommend that you file an NPR (Form 10-7; PTO/SB/35) and check this box, unless you definitely will be foreign filing or unless you want an early publication of your application to be able to use against infringers (see Chapter 15). If you check this box but later decide to foreign file, be sure to revoke your NPR within 45 days—use Form PTO/SB/36. If you don't file an NPR, your application will be published electronically 18 months after filing (if it hasn't issued by then), or sooner if you request it, and you will have to pay a stiff publication fee (see Appendix 4, Fee Schedule) when you pay the issue fee. The fee can be particularly unfair if, as sometimes happens, the patent issues within a few weeks of publication. If you check the NPR box and later file abroad and you don't revoke your NPR and notify the PTO of such foreign filing within 45 days (use Form PTO/SB/36), your application will be regarded as abandoned unless you pay a stiff fee and declare that delay was unintentional. To fill out the NPR, merely fill in the name of the first inventor, the title, the docket number, and the date. The first inventor should sign it and print their name under the signature. You must file the NPR with the application; if you file it later it will be in vain.

Box 17: Other: If you attach any other documents, check this box. For example, if you've filed a DDP (see Chapter 3), check this box and type in "DDP Reference Letter" after "Other:" and enclose the Reference Letter (Form 3-4).

If you're not sure your claims are entirely proper and would like the examiner to write claims for you if they find allowable subject matter, type "Request Under MPEP Section 707.07(j)" and file the Request (Form 10-8). (I recommend this.)

Box 19: Check the box before "Correspondence address below" and complete the next four lines as you did with the PAD (see Section H, above).

In the next-to-last line type the name of the inventor who is to receive correspondence from the PTO. This inventor should sign and date the bottom lines.

PPA: The form does not contain any box to refer to any PPA that you've filed. (Do not use Box 18 to refer to a PPA.) You should claim the benefit of any PPA that you've filed in the "CROSS REFERENCE TO RELATED APPLICATIONS" section of the specification, as explained in Chapter 8, Section I. Be sure to include the serial number and filing date of your PPA. You must file your regular patent application (RPA) within one year of your PPA's filing date if you want to claim the benefit of your PPA. If the last day of the one-year period falls on a weekend or holiday, you may file your Regular Patent Application (RPA) on the next business day after the weekend or holiday. The RPA must name at least one inventor who has been named in the PPA. If you file the application without a PPA claim in your specification, you must amend the specification within four months from your RPA's filing date or 16 months from your PPA's filing date.

2. Fill Out Fee Transmittal and Pay by Credit Card or Check

Fill out the Fee Transmittal (Form 10-3 or PTO/SB/17) by completing the name of the first (or only) inventor and docket number at the top right. Form 10-3 includes the fees as of December 2004, which should be good until October 2005. If you're filing after that date, the fees are likely to be higher. You can still use Form 10-3, but first check the fees on the PTO's website and change them if necessary. The PTO will change its form PTO/SB/17 after October 1, 2005.

Approved for use through 07/31/2006. OMB 0651-0032
U.S. Patent and Trademark Office; U.S. DEPARTMENT OF COMMERCE
Under the Paperwork Reduction Act of 1995, no persons are required to respond to a collection of information unless it displays a valid OMB control number

Effective on 12/08/2004.
Fees pursuant to the Consolidated Appropriations Act, 2005 (H.R. 4818).

FEE TRANSMITTAL
For FY 2005

[✓] Applicant claims small entity status. See 37 CFR 1.27

TOTAL AMOUNT OF PAYMENT   ($)   700.00

Complete if Known

Application Number	
Filing Date	
First Named Inventor	M. Goldberger
Examiner Name	
Art Unit	
Attorney Docket No.	Goldberger-Briskin

METHOD OF PAYMENT (check all that apply)

[ ] Check   [✓] Credit Card   [ ] Money Order   [ ] None   [ ] Other (please identify): _____

[ ] Deposit Account   Deposit Account Number: _____   Deposit Account Name: _____

For the above-identified deposit account, the Director is hereby authorized to: (check all that apply)

[ ] Charge fee(s) indicated below   [ ] Charge fee(s) indicated below, **except for the filing fee**

[✓] Charge any additional fee(s) or underpayments of fee(s)   [ ] Credit any overpayments
under 37 CFR 1.16 and 1.17

WARNING: Information on this form may become public. Credit card information should not be included on this form. Provide credit card information and authorization on PTO-2038.

FEE CALCULATION

1. BASIC FILING, SEARCH, AND EXAMINATION FEES

Application Type	FILING FEES Fee ($)	Small Entity Fee ($)	SEARCH FEES Fee ($)	Small Entity Fee ($)	EXAMINATION FEES Fee ($)	Small Entity Fee ($)	Fees Paid ($)
Utility	300	150	500	250	200	100	500.00
Design	200	100	100	50	130	65	_____
Plant	200	100	300	150	160	80	_____
Reissue	300	150	500	250	600	300	_____
Provisional	200	100	0	0	0	0	_____

2. EXCESS CLAIM FEES

Fee Description	Fee ($)	Small Entity Fee ($)
Each claim over 20 (including Reissues)	50	25
Each independent claim over 3 (including Reissues)	200	100
Multiple dependent claims	360	180

Total Claims	Extra Claims	Fee ($)	Fee Paid ($)	Multiple Dependent Claims Fee ($)	Fee Paid ($)
24 - 20 or HP =	4	x 9.00 =	36.00	_____	_____

HP = highest number of total claims paid for, if greater than 20.

Indep. Claims	Extra Claims	Fee ($)	Fee Paid ($)
4 - 3 or HP =	1	x 42.00 =	42.00

HP = highest number of independent claims paid for, if greater than 3.

3. APPLICATION SIZE FEE

If the specification and drawings exceed 100 sheets of paper (excluding electronically filed sequence or computer listings under 37 CFR 1.52(e)), the application size fee due is $250 ($125 for small entity) for each additional 50 sheets or fraction thereof. See 35 U.S.C. 41(a)(1)(G) and 37 CFR 1.16(s).

Total Sheets	Extra Sheets	Number of each additional 50 or fraction thereof	Fee ($)	Fee Paid ($)
_____ - 100 =	_____ / 50 =	_____ (round **up** to a whole number) x	_____ =	_____

4. OTHER FEE(S)   **Fees Paid ($)**

Non-English Specification, $130 fee (no small entity discount)   _____

Other (e.g., late filing surcharge): _____   _____

SUBMITTED BY

Signature	*Mildred Goldberger*	Registration No. (Attorney/Agent)		Telephone 215-555-0362
Name (Print/Type)	M. Goldberger			Date 11/11/2003

This collection of information is required by 37 CFR 1.136. The information is required to obtain or retain a benefit by the public which is to file (and by the USPTO to process) an application. Confidentiality is governed by 35 U.S.C. 122 and 37 CFR 1.14. This collection is estimated to take 30 minutes to complete, including gathering, preparing, and submitting the completed application form to the USPTO. Time will vary depending upon the individual case. Any comments on the amount of time you require to complete this form and/or suggestions for reducing this burden, should be sent to the Chief Information Officer, U.S. Patent and Trademark Office, U.S. Department of Commerce, P.O. Box 1450, Alexandria, VA 22313-1450. DO NOT SEND FEES OR COMPLETED FORMS TO THIS ADDRESS. **SEND TO: Commissioner for Patents, P.O. Box 1450, Alexandria, VA 22313-1450.**

If you need assistance in completing the form, call 1-800-PTO-9199 and select option 2.

Fig. 10K—Fee Transmittal (Form 10-3 in Appendix 7)

to indicate its fees for 2006. See Fig 10K for an example of a completed Fee Transmittal.

A. Fill out the First Named Inventor and Attorney Docket No. boxes in the upper right corner as before.

B. Check "Applicant claims small entity status" box if you qualify. You qualify for small entity status if you haven't assigned or licensed (or are not obligated to assign or license) the invention to a for-profit company with over 500 employees. See PTO Rule 27 (37 CFR 1.27).

C. Fill in the Total Amount of Payment" box. (Do this last after you calculate the total.)

D. Check the appropriate Check, Credit Card, or M.O. box.

   1. Basic Filing, Search, and Examination Fees: Add the Small Entity fees in the "Utility" line and type the total ($500 on this form) in the rightmost column.

   2. Excess Claim Fees: The Basic Filing Fee entitles you to file up to three independent claims and 20 total claims, assuming that each dependent claim refers back to only one preceding claim (independent or dependent). If you don't have more than 20 total and three independent claims, you can leave this section blank.

   If you're filing over 20 total claims, three independent, or a multiple dependent claim (not recommended) fill out these blanks. Enter the total number of claims (independent and dependent) in the blank under "Total Claims." Subtract 20 from this figure, enter the difference under "Extra Claims," and type the fee for each extra total claim over 20 (Large or Small Entity) from the list in the upper right of this section under "Fee ($)," and type the product under the "Fee Paid ($)." If you have more than three independent claims, enter the total number of independent claims under "Indep. Claims," subtract 3 from this figure, enter the difference under "Extra Claims," type the fee for each extra independent claim over three (Large or Small Entity) from the list in upper right part of this section under "Fee ($)," and type the product under the "Fee Paid ($)."

   I recommend that you do not file any Multiple Dependent Claims (MDCs) since the fee is high and examiners don't like them. However, if you do file any MDCs, enter the fee from the right side of this section in the MDC boxes. The fee is also in Appendix 4 and at the PTO's website.

   3. Application Size Fee: If your specification and drawings exceed 100 pages, fill in the boxes in this section.

   Note that the fees for extra claims and MDCs are very high now.

   4. Other Fee(s): Normally you won't have any additional fees at this stage, so you won't have to enter anything in the Other Fees section. However, if you want to obtain a somewhat speedier processing of your application, file a "Petition to Make Special" (see Section P below). If your petition requires a fee, type "Pet. Special" after "Other Fee" and include the amount in the "Other" box. If you're enclosing an assignment (see Section O below), type "Asgt. Recordal." on the blank line.

Total the amounts in Sections 1 to 4 and enter the sum in the "Total Amount of Payment" box at the top left of the form.

Finally, sign and print the corresponding inventor's name and phone number in the next-to-last line of the form and enter your phone number and sign and type the date on the last line.

The PTO accepts payment by credit card, check, or M.O. If you pay by credit card, use the PTO's Credit Card Payment Form (CCPF—Form 10-4 in Appendix 7 or PTO Form 2038) in conjunction with the Fee Transmittal. The PTO will not accept debit cards or check cards that require the use of a personal identification number as a method of payment. Complete the CCPF as in Fig 10L. Fill in all credit card information, including the amount to be charged to your credit card and your signature. Complete the Credit Card Billing Address. That information is required for verification of your credit card account. Under "Request and Payment Information," complete the "Description of Request and Payment Information" with a short statement of what you are paying for. In the present case, since you're paying a patent filing fee, write "Patent Application Filing Fee." Circle "Patent Fee" and write your docket number.

If paying by check or money order, make payment to Commissioner for Patents for the total amount, and attach it to the transmittal letter.

⚠ Be sure you have enough credit reserve in your credit card account or money in your checking account to cover the charge. If your payment bounces, you'll have to pay a stiff surcharge. (Note that if the PTO makes any fee or other errors, they are never penalized.)

Unfortunately, the PTO does not discount its fees for the needy, handicapped, or aged, or allow such individuals to postpone their fees.

PTO-2038 (02-2003)
Approved for use through 02/28/2006. OMB 0651-0043
United States Patent and Trademark Office; U.S. DEPARTMENT OF COMMERCE

Under the Paperwork Reduction Act of 1995, no persons are required to respond to a collection of information unless it displays a valid OMB control number.

United States Patent and Trademark Office
Credit Card Payment Form
Please Read Instructions before Completing this Form

Credit Card Information

Credit Card Type: ☑ Visa   ☐ MasterCard   ☐ American Express   ☐ Discover

Credit Card Account #:   2175-3210-1497-3218

Credit Card Expiration Date: 05/2006

Name as it Appears on Credit Card: Mildred Goldberger

Payment Amount: $ (US Dollars):   700 (The PTO may change this amount if incorrect)

Cardholder Signature: *Mildred Goldberger*   Date: 2003 Nov 11

Refund Policy: The Office may refund a fee paid by mistake or in excess of that required. A change of purpose after the payment of a fee will not entitle a party to a refund of such fee. The office will not refund amounts of $25.00 or less unless a refund is specifically requested, and will not notify the payor of such amounts (37 CFR § 1.26). Refund of a fee paid by credit card will be issued as a credit to the credit card account to which the fee was charged.
Service Charge: There is a $50.00 service charge for processing each payment refused (including a check returned "unpaid") or charged back by a financial institution (37 CFR § 1.21 (m)) .

Credit Card Billing Address

Street Address 1:   1901 Kennedy Blvd.

Street Address 2:

City: Philadelphia

State/Province: PA   Zip/Postal Code: 19103

Country: US

Daytime Phone #:   215-555-0362   Fax #:

Request and Payment Information

Description of Request and Payment Information:

Patent Application Filing Fee

☑ Patent Fee	☐ Patent Maintenance Fee	☐ Trademark Fee	☐ Other Fee
Application No.	Application No.	Application No.	IDON Customer No.
Patent No.	Patent No.	Registration No.	
Attorney Docket No. Goldberger-Briskin		Identify or Describe Mark	

If the cardholder includes a credit card number on any form or document other than the Credit Card Payment Form, the United States Patent and Trademark Office will not be liable in the event that the credit card number becomes public knowledge.

Fig. 10L—PTO's Credit Card Payment Form (Form 10-4 in Appendix 7)

New—Electronic Filing and Patent Status Retrieval

The USPTO now provides software that will facilitate filing patent applications via the Internet. The PTO's Electronic Filing System (EFS) will assemble all application components (including figures) and calculate fee information and then transit the completed application to the PTO via a digitally encrypted secure system. In addition to electronic filing, the PTO also provides electronic access to status information for pending applications via a new Patent Application Information Retrieval (PAIR) system.

In order to perform electronic filing and use PAIR, you must obtain a customer number, a digital certificate, and the EFS software that will be available for download from the Electronic Business Center (EBC) website at www.uspto.gov/ebc/index.html. Although the EFS is in operation as of this edition (spring 2005), and although it will enable you to pay a slightly reduced filing fee, I don't recommend that you use it unless you plan to file many applications. I say this primarily because it will take you much more time and effort—particularly for the initial procedures—than using the mail. Most of the bugs in the EFS system have been resolved, but as with all new software installations, be sure to back up all files before proceeding.

Patent application of Mildred Goldberger and Nathan Briskin for "Food Chopper With Convolute Blade" consisting of two sheets of drawing, 12 pages of specification, claims, and abstract, Patent Application Declaration (2 pp., signed 2003 Nov 11), Patent Application Transmittal, Fee Transmittal, Credit Card Payment Form, Nonpublication Request, and Information Disclosure Statement received for filing today:

Fig. 10M—Completed Back of Receipt Postcard to Accompany Patent Application

3. Postcard

As stated in Inventor's Commandment #16 at the beginning of this chapter, you should enclose a receipt postcard with every paper you send to the PTO. All attorneys use receipt postcards because the PTO receives many thousands of pieces of mail each day and occasionally loses some. It may be months before you receive any reply to a paper you've sent to the PTO, so you'll want to be assured it arrived safely.

Fig. 10M indicates how an application receipt postcard should be completed. Note that the back of the card contains the inventors' names, title of invention, the number of sheets of drawing, the number of pages of specification, claims, and abstract, the Patent Application Declaration, including the number of pages and date it was signed, the Patent Application Transmittal, the Fee Transmittal, CCPF or the check number and amount, and the NPR. Leave space at the bottom of the back of the card for the PTO to affix its date and Serial Number sticker. Occasionally, receipt postcards get lost because of their size and inconspicuous color. I have had better results by using colored (bright red) postcards.

The PTO will affix a sticker to your application postcard receipt with the date your papers arrived and the serial number assigned to your application and mail it back to you as soon as they open your letter (which can take two weeks).

If you're filing from abroad, be sure that your return postcard has sufficient U.S. postage. You can confirm the postcard postage to any nation at the U.S. Postal Service website (www.usps.gov) and you can usually buy U.S. stamps abroad at a philatelic store.

J. Maintain an Orderly File

I often consult with "pro-se" inventors (that is, those who have prepared and filed their own patent applications). Usually they bring me their "application" in the form of a sloppy, loose stack of mixed-up—and occasionally missing—papers. You'll avoid this problem, and the serious trouble it can get you into, if you'll heed Inventor's Commandment #17, shown at the beginning of this chapter, which admonishes you to mount all official papers (those sent to and received from the PTO) in a separate folder. It's good practice to write the date received on every paper you receive connected with your invention and also date every outgoing paper.

You should have a two-part folder or jacket for (a) your application, and (b) correspondence to and from the PTO, and (c) correspondence to the PTO. Keep your prior-art

Final Checklist

☐ (a) Return Receipt Postcard addressed to you with all papers listed on back.

☐ (b) If you are paying the filing fee by a check or money order, make it out for the correct filing fee (basic fee plus fee for any excess claims). Make sure you have adequate funds on deposit or available on your credit card.

☐ (c) Transmittal Letter and Fee Transmittal properly completed and signed.

☐ (d) If you are paying the filing fee using a Credit Card Payment Form, be sure it is made out for the correct filing fee (basic fee plus fee for any excess claims). Make sure your credit limit is not in jeopardy.

☐ (e) Drawing sheets all present; drawings clear, complete, and understandable. Drawings show every feature in claims. The sheet number and total number of sheets (e.g. "1/3") is on the front (below top margin) and your name is on the top back. Originals of drawings (or disk file if CAD used) kept in safe place.

☐ (f) Specification, Claims, and Abstract included; description of invention clear and complete, all reference numbers, dates, spelling, and grammar double-checked, and claims drafted per Chapter 9.

    ☐ (i) Typing is clear and readable and 1.5 or double-spaced; use any normal font, 12-point minimum size.

    ☐ (ii) Application is prepared in form for making proper A4 copies later if foreign filing contemplated (optional).

    ☐ (iii) Top (above page numbers) and left margin is at least 2.5 cm on all pages.

    ☐ (iv) No sentence is longer than about 13 words, paragraphs are not longer than about $1/2$ page, and a heading is supplied for about every two pages.

    ☐ (v) Claims are separated by an extra line.

    ☐ (vi) Claims and abstract start on new pages.

    ☐ (vii) No changes made after application signed.

☐ (g) Patent Application Declaration (PAD) completed, signed, and dated in ink. (The PTO will accept a PAD, or virtually any other document which has a photocopy of your signature. However, you must always be able to produce the ink-signed original.)

☐ (h) Parts are assembled in above order and copies are made for your file.

☐ (i) Information Disclosure Statement, Forms 10-5 and 10-6 (A & B) with references attached if you're filing it with your application (see Section N below). Otherwise IDS must be sent within three months.

☐ (j) Petition to Make Special, Form 10-9 and Supporting Declaration (optional to speed application processing; see Section P below).

☐ (k) Assignment and transmittal letter (optional—see Section O below).

☐ (l) Disclosure Document Reference Letter (Form 3-4) if you previously filed a Disclosure Document.

☐ (m) Envelope addressed to:

Mail Stop Patent Application
P.O. Box 1450
Alexandria, VA 22313-1450

☐ (n) If there are joint inventors, all should complete, sign, and date multiple copies of a Joint Owners' Agreement (Form 16-2; Chapter 16, Section C) and each inventor should keep an original. Do not file this with the PTO.

☐ (o) Have another person check your papers for compliance with these rules.

references in a large envelope loose inside the folder. To avoid confusion, I recommend that you keep other nonofficial papers concerning your invention in a separate folder.

K. Assembly and Mailing of Your Application—Final Checklist

Congratulations. You're now ready to mail your patent application to the PTO, unless you want to include an Information Disclosure Statement (Section N), an Assignment (Section O), and/or a Petition to Make Special (Section P). If you do want to include any of these with your application (optional), consult the indicated sections, complete your paperwork, and then come back to this point.

Assemble in the following order—and carefully check—the following items, which are the third part of the checklist I started in Chapter 8; please do this carefully and methodically, as "haste makes waste," especially when applying for a patent.

I suggest that you file a good photocopy of your signed application and keep the original of your application. In this way you can make copies later if the application is lost in the mail, or if you need to send them to manufacturers when you market your invention. (See Chapter 11.)

Staple the pages of the specification, claims, abstract, and declarations together. Attach the drawings with a paper clip or other temporary fastener. Only one copy need be filed.

If you mail the application by Express Mail, the papers should be transmitted in an Express Mail envelope. If the application doesn't have more than about eight pages, you should include one or two sheets of cardboard or internal envelopes to protect the drawing from bending.

You may send the application to the PTO by first-class mail, but if it's lost in the mail, you will lose your filing date I strongly recommend that you use Express Mail (see next section).

L. Using Express Mail to Get an Instant Filing Date

I strongly recommend you send your application to the PTO by Express Mail (EM). This will provide strong protection against loss of your application, secure full legal rights in case it is lost, give you an "instant" filing date (the date you actually mail your application), and will enable you to make absolutely sure your application is on file before the one-year period expires if a PPA was filed or the invention was

put on sale, sold, or published. You must use "Express Mail Post Office to Addressee" service and you must indicate that you're using this service by completing the EM section at the top of your transmittal letter (Form 10-2/Fig. 10J). Type the EM number in the box at the top right, fourth line of Form 10-2.

The PTO's Rule 10 (37 CFR 1.10) states, in effect, that mailing any paper to the PTO by EM, with the EM number on the transmittal letter, is the same as physically delivering the paper directly to the PTO. Thus you can consider and call your application "patent pending" as soon as the postal clerk hands you the EM receipt, and your filing date will be the date on this receipt, provided all papers of the application are present and are properly completed. Since postal clerks often don't press hard enough when they date the EM receipt, I recommend you ask the clerk to stamp the receipt also with their rubber date stamp. If you've followed the final checklist above, your application will now be properly on file, i.e., patent pending.

You should NOT send your application by registered mail, certified mail, or private courier (Federal Express, etc.) and you should NOT use any "Certificate of Mailing" (Chapter 13). This is because Rule 10 does not give applicants any advantages if they use these methods of transmission. If you use any of these, your filing date will be the date the application is actually received at the PTO and you'll have no rights if your application is lost.

M. Receipt That Application Was Received in PTO

About two to four weeks after you send your application to the PTO, you'll get your postcard back, with the filing date of your application, and also with a sticker indicating an eight-digit serial number (for example, "10/123,456") that has been assigned to your application. Within about a week to a month after that (sometimes longer), you should get an official filing receipt back from the PTO indicating that your application has been officially filed. Check the information on the filing receipt carefully and let the OIPE (Office of Initial Patent Examination) know if there are any errors.

If for any reason your application is incomplete or deficient, the PTO will not regard it as officially "filed" but rather as "deposited." The OIPE (Office of Initial Patent Examination) of the PTO will send you a letter stating the deficiency in your application and telling you to promptly remedy it. However, if you follow all the instructions in this chapter, including the checklist in Section K, carefully, you'll get your filing receipt in due course.

Once you get the filing receipt, your application is officially "patent pending." As discussed in Chapter 7, unless you want to keep your invention a trade secret, (in case your patent application is eventually disallowed), you may publish details of your invention or market it to whomever you choose. You will not lose any legal rights in the U.S. or Convention or treaty countries (see Chapter 12). If you manufacture anything embodying your invention, you should mark it "patent pending" and keep your application, serial number, and filing date confidential to preserve rights in non-Convention countries and prevent access by potential copiers. As stated, if you mailed your application by Express Mail and you faithfully followed the checklists, you may refer to your invention as "patent pending" as soon as you get the EM receipt.

N. File the Information Disclosure Statement Within Three Months

The PTO's rules impose on each patent applicant a "duty of candor and good faith" toward the PTO. This means that all inventors (and attorneys) have a duty to disclose to the PTO information (prior art and any other information such as relevant litigation) of which they are aware. The information must be of the type that might influence the patent examiner in deciding on the patent application. (This duty is embodied in Inventor's Commandment #15, and discussed in Section I above.) To comply with the "prior art" part of Inventor's Commandment #15, the PTO asks all applicants to submit an Information Disclosure Statement (IDS) at the time of filing the application or within the following three months. It's not enough to cite the prior-art references in the Prior Art section of your specification. You must cite them on a PTO/SB08 form and supply copies of non-U.S. patent references to the PTO.

Even if it weren't required, it's to your advantage to file an IDS and to list as many relevant prior-art references as possible in order to have them considered and noted by the examiner. In this way they will be listed as "References Cited" in the patent. This creates a presumption that the claims of your patent are patentable over these references— that is, you'll have put these references behind you. I suggest that you use the option to file afterward; this will prevent overload while preparing your basic application.

The IDS actually consists of an IDS cover letter (Form 10-5 or PTO form SB21) and the actual IDS (Form 10-6 (A&B) or PTO/SB/08 (A&B), on which you list the prior art. A filled-in sample is provided in Figs. 10O, 10P, and 10Q.

The IDS should list all prior-art references known to the inventors (and any assignees) that are relevant to the patentability of the application. These should include all the references you discovered in your patentability search (see Chapter 6), plus any other prior art of which you're aware, including even your own papers. In addition, the inventors must include with the IDS a copy of each cited non-U.S. patent reference and a discussion of the relevance of any non–English-language references to the invention. You must cite all references even if you discussed them in the prior-art section of your patent application. (If you aren't aware of any prior art, don't file an IDS.) You should remove all marks and notes from any references that you send to the PTO. If you have compiled a very large number of references, list only those that are truly relevant (about 20 or so) and don't include any cumulative (duplicative) references.

As mentioned, you can send the IDS with your application instead of taking advantage of the three-month grace period. In this event, the names of the inventors and title of your invention are the only information you need to put at the top of Form 10-5. Don't fill out the Certificate of Mailing at the bottom of the form. If you send it after your application is filed, you'll know the serial number, filing date, and group art unit, and can insert them. Also, you should fill out the Certificate of Mailing at the bottom of the form. You normally won't know the examiner's name unless you've received a first "Office Action" from the PTO.

The blanks in Forms 10-5 and 10-6 are self-explanatory. Information about the Art Unit (requested in the upper right-hand corner of Form 10-6) is on your filing receipt. Before each patent number in the Foreign Patent Documents section, you may use a two-letter international country code, as indicated. The most common county codes are FR (France), JP (Japan), CN (China), GB (United Kingdom), CA (Canada), EP (Europe), and DE (Germany). In the right-hand column, headed "Pages, Columns …," you can list any places in the document that you feel are particularly relevant, but this is optional since the pertinent rules (Rules 97 and 98) require that you merely cite the documents.

If you include any non–English-language reference on Form 10-6, Rule 98(a)(3) requires that you also provide a concise explanation of its relevance on a separate paper or in the specification. I recommend that you also state how your invention, as claimed, differs physically from this reference(s). State the relevance of any non-English references, and any discussion as to how your invention differs, on Form 10-5. Fig. 10O provides an example.

If you send in the IDS with the application, note this on the postcard and transmittal letter that you send with your

In the United States Patent and Trademark Office

Serial Number: _____09/123 456_____

Appn. Filed: _____2001 Nov 11_____

Applicant(s): _____M. Goldberger & N. Briskin_____

Appn. Title: _____Food cutter with convolute Blade_____

Examiner/GAU: _____/ 3240_____

Mailed: _____2003 Dec 13, Thu_____

At: _____Philadelphia, PA_____

Information Disclosure Statement Cover Letter

Commissioner for Patents

P.O. Box 1450

Alexandria, VA 22313-1450

Sir:

Attached is a completed Form PTO/SB/08(A&B) and copies of any non-U.S. patent references cited thereon. Following are comments on any non-English-language references pursuant to Rule 98:

    Rasmussen shows a fruit peeler with a bent guide for controlling the thickness of the fruit as it is being peeled. **Gillet** shows a knife mounted parallel to a space with knife that can be tilted out or in to adjust the spacing of its edge.

    None of the references shows a knife for making a cut of controlled depth wherein a flat-bladed knife with an elongated sharpened edge with an outward protrusion attached to the blade that is spaced back from the edge for limiting the depth of cut that can be made by said edge when it is used to **cut** in a direction **perpendicular** to the plane of the blade, as it is recited in independent claims 1 and 17, and hence their dependent claims 2 to 11 and 18 to 20.

    To the contrary, all of the references show guides that are mounted generally parallel to the blade for limiting the thickness of the **peel** that can be cut by the blade when it is used to peel in a direction **parallel** to its plane.

    Also, none of the references show any blade having a substantially right-angle bend parallel to its direction of elongation, as it is recited in independent claim 12 and its dependent claims 13 to 16.

Very respectfully,

Applicant(s): _____Mildred Goldberger_____

_____Nathan Briskin_____

Enc.: PTO/SB/08(A&B)

c/o: _____M. Goldberger, Applicant Pro Se_____

_____1901 Kennedy Blvd._____

_____Philadelphia, PA 19103_____

Telephone: _____215-555-0362_____

Certificate of Mailing

I certify that this correspondence will be deposited with the United States Postal Service as first class mail with proper postage affixed in an envelope addressed to: "Commissioner for Patents, P.O. Box 1450, Alexandria, VA 22313-1450" on the date below.

Date: 200__3 Dec 3__   _____Mildred Goldberger_____, Applicant

Fig. 10N—Completed IDS Cover Letter (Form 10-5 in Appendix 7)

Substitute for form 1449/PTO

INFORMATION DISCLOSURE STATEMENT BY APPLICANT
(Use as many sheets as necessary)

Complete if Known	
Application Number	09/123,456
Filing Date	2001 Nov 11
First Named Inventor	M. Goldberger
Art Unit	3240
Examiner Name	
Attorney Docket Number	Goldberger-Briskin

Sheet 1 of 2

U. S. PATENT DOCUMENTS

Examiner Initials*	Cite No.[1]	Document Number Number-Kind Code[2] (if known)	Publication Date MM-DD-YYYY	Name of Patentee or Applicant of Cited Document	Pages, Columns, Lines, Where Relevant Passages or Relevant Figures Appear
	A	US- 21,695	10-15-1858	Oot	
	B	US- 602,758	11-11-1898	Landers	p4, 11.21-22
	C	US- 2,083,368	8-9-1937	Gambino	
	D	US- 2,968,867	10-11-1961	Wolff	
		US-			
		US-			
		US-			
		US-			
		US-			
		US-			
		US-			
		US-			
		US-			
		US-			
		US-			
		US-			
		US-			
		US-			
		US-			
		US-			

FOREIGN PATENT DOCUMENTS

Examiner Initials*	Cite No.[1]	Foreign Patent Document Country Code[3]-Number[4]-Kind Code[5] (if known)	Publication Date MM-DD-YYYY	Name of Patentee or Applicant of Cited Document	Pages, Columns, Lines, Where Relevant Passages Or Relevant Figures Appear	T[6]
	E	DK-69,640	5-22-1949	Rasmussen	p2, ll. 13-17	
	F	FR-1,029,924	3-23-1953	Gillet		

Examiner Signature		Date Considered	

Fig. 10O—Information Disclosure Statement (Form 10-6A in Appendix 7)

PTO/SB/08B (08-03)
Approved for use through 07/31/2006. OMB 0651-0031
U.S. Patent and Trademark Office; U.S. DEPARTMENT OF COMMERCE
Under the Paperwork Reduction Act of 1995, no persons are required to respond to a collection of information unless it contains a valid OMB control number.

Substitute for form 1449/PTO	**Complete if Known**	
INFORMATION DISCLOSURE STATEMENT BY APPLICANT *(Use as many sheets as necessary)*	Application Number	09/123,456
	Filing Date	2001 Nov 11
	First Named Inventor	M. Goldberger
	Art Unit	3240
	Examiner Name	
Sheet 2 of 2	Attorney Docket Number	Goldberger-Briskin

NON PATENT LITERATURE DOCUMENTS

Examiner Initials*	Cite No.[1]	Include name of the author (in CAPITAL LETTERS), title of the article (when appropriate), title of the item (book, magazine, journal, serial, symposium, catalog, etc.), date, page(s), volume-issue number(s), publisher, city and/or country where published.	T^2
	G	Phillips, Food Comminuting, Restaurant News, April 1959, Food Press, Willow Grove, PA	

Examiner Signature		Date Considered	

*EXAMINER: Initial if reference considered, whether or not citation is in conformance with MPEP 609. Draw line through citation if not in conformance and not considered. Include copy of this form with next communication to applicant.

1 Applicant's unique citation designation number (optional). 2 Applicant is to place a check mark here if English language Translation is attached.
This collection of information is required by 37 CFR 1.98. The information is required to obtain or retain a benefit by the public which is to file (and by the USPTO to process) an application. Confidentiality is governed by 35 U.S.C. 122 and 37 CFR 1.14. This collection is estimated to take 2 hours to complete, including gathering, preparing, and submitting the completed application form to the USPTO. Time will vary depending upon the individual case. Any comments on the amount of time you require to complete this form and/or suggestions for reducing this burden, should be sent to the Chief Information Officer, U.S. Patent and Trademark Office, P.O. Box 1450, Alexandria, VA 22313-1450. DO NOT SEND FEES OR COMPLETED FORMS TO THIS ADDRESS. **SEND TO: Commissioner for Patents, P.O. Box 1450, Alexandria, VA 22313-1450.**

If you need assistance in completing the form, call 1-800-PTO-9199 (1-800-786-9199) and select option 2.

Fig. 10P—Information Disclosure Statement (Form 10-6B in Appendix 7)

application and don't fill out the Certificate of Mailing at the bottom of Form 10-5. If you send it in after the application is filed, send it with a separate postcard and fill out the Certificate of Mailing. Again, address the front of the card to you; the back should read as in Fig. 10N.

If you haven't followed my instructions in Chapter 6—that is, you haven't made a search and are not aware of any prior art—as stated, you don't have to file an IDS. The PTO won't deny or delay your application if you don't file an IDS. However, if they (or an infringer whom you later sue for patent infringement) discover that you knew of relevant prior art and didn't file an IDS, your patent application or patent can be held invalid for "fraud on the PTO." This is so even if the examiner discovers the reference you withheld and cites it in a regular Office Action. (See Chapter 13, Fig. 13-A/4.)

Suppose you are aware of information other than prior art that may be material to patentability—for example relevant litigation, an assertion by another person claiming to be an inventor, or a sale of a product embodying the invention before the filing date (but not before your date of invention). You have a duty to disclose this information also. You can do this with a narrative statement on a form such as Form 10-5. Also, be sure to state why the information does not negate the patentability of your invention.

Information Disclosure Statement, Form PTO/SB/08 (A and B), and *[insert number]* References in patent application of *[insert name(s) of inventor(s)]*, Serial No. _____, Filed _____ received for filing today:

Fig. 10Q—Back of Postcard for Sending IDS After Filing

O. Assignments

As I mentioned, a patent application must be filed in the name or names of the true inventor or inventors of the invention claimed in the patent application. The inventors then become the applicants for the patent, and the law considers that they automatically own equal shares of the invention, the patent application, and any patents that may issue on the application (Chapter 16, Section B). However, inventorship can be different from ownership. Often all or part of the ownership of the invention and the patent

application must be transferred to someone else, either an individual or a legal entity, such as a corporation, a partnership, or an individual. To make this transfer, the inventor(s) must "assign" (legally transfer) their interest. The assignment transfers ownership (or part of it) from the inventor(s) to another entity. However, inventorship remains the same after an assignment is made. (Directions and forms for completing the assignment are in Chapter 16, Section E.)

If you have assigned the application to another and you want to send the assignment to the PTO for recording (highly advised), you can either send it in with the patent application or at any time afterward. I prefer to send in assignments later, after I get the postcard receipt back, when I know and can add the serial number and filing date of the application to the assignment. This will make the two documents (the assignment and the application) correspond to each other more directly. In this case, you can add the serial number and filing date to the assignment in the spaces indicated. Then prepare an Assignment "Recordation Form Cover Sheet" (Form 16-3B or PTO 1595). In space 1, the conveying parties are the inventor applicants. In space 2A, the receiving party is the assignee—the person or organization to whom you're assigning the application. The Internal Address is the mail stop or apartment number if any, in the assignee's building. In Space 3, the Conveyance is an assignment and the execution date is the date you signed the assignment. In Space 4, the Application Number is the Serial Number of your patent application. I recommend that you also type the filing date. If you don't know these numbers yet, just fill in the execution (signing) date of your PAD. If you're assigning a patent, fill in the patent number and issue date in Space 4B. "Additional numbers attached [ ] Yes [ ] No" should be checked to indicate whether or not you've listed additional cases on an attached sheet. The remaining blocks are self-explanatory. Make sure to include the recordation fee (see Appendix 4, Fee Schedule).

If you wish to send the assignment in with your patent application, complete the Recordation Form Cover Sheet (Form 16-3B), check the "Assignment Papers" (box 9 on Form 10-2), and on Form 10-3 type "Assignment Recordal" after "Other" in Section 3. Include the fee on this line and in your total at the top of the form.

If an assignment of a patent application has been recorded and it is referred to in the issue fee transmittal form (see Chapter 13), the PTO will print the patent with the assignee's interest indicated. However, even if you fail to indicate the assignment on the issue fee transmittal, so that the patent doesn't indicate the assignment, the assignment will still be effective if it has been recorded.

If an assignment has been made, and as a result there are two or more owners of the patent application, then the

In the United States Patent and Trademark Office

Serial Number: __09/123,456__

Appn. Filed: __2001 Aug 9__

Applicant(s): __Goldberger, David__

Appn. Title: __Wind Generator Using Stratus Rotor, Etc.__

Examiner/GAU: __Hayness / 654__

Mailed: __2003 September 20__

At: __San Francisco__

Petition to Make Special

Commissioner for Patents

P.O. Box 1450

Alexandria, VA 22313-1450

Sir:

Applicant hereby respectfully petitions that the above application be made special under MPEP Sec. 708.02 for the following reason; attached is a declaration in support thereof:

I. ☐ Manufacturer Available;*		VII. ☐ Recombinant DNA Is Involved;*	
II. ☐ Infringement Exists;*		VIII. ☐ Special Procedure: Search Was Made;*	
III. ☐ Applicant's Health Is Poor;		IX. ☐ Superconductivity Is Advanced;	
IV. ☐ Applicant's Age Is 65 or Greater;		X. ☐ Relates to HIV/AIDS or Cancer;*	
V. ☒ Environmental Quality Will Be Enhanced;		XI. ☐ Counters Terrorism.*	
VI. ☐ Energy Savings Will Result;			

* ☐ Also attached, since reason I, II, VII, VIII, X, or XI has been checked, is the $_____ Petition Fee pursuant to Rules 102 and 17(i).

Very respectfully,

Applicant(s): __David Goldberger__

Attachment(s): Fee if indicated and supporting Declaration

Applicant(s): _____

c/o: __David Goldberger__

__119 Walnut St.__

__San Francisco, CA 94123__

Telephone: __415-722-0362__

Certificate of Mailing

I certify that this correspondence will be deposited with the United States Postal Service as first class mail with proper postage affixed in an envelope addressed to: "Commissioner for Patents, P.O. Box 1450, Alexandria, VA 22313-1450" on the date below.

Date: 200__3 December 2003__   __David Goldberger__ , Applicant

Fig. 10R—Completed Petition to Make Special (Form 10-9 in Appendix 7)

In the United States Patent and Trademark Office

Appn. Number: 09/123,456
Filing Date: 2001 Aug. 9
Applicant(s): Goldberger, David
Examiner: Hayness / GAU 654

Mailed: 2003 Sep 20
At: San Francisco

Declaration in Support of Accompanying Petition to Make Special
Reason V—Enhancement of Environmental Quality

In support of the accompanying Petition to Make Special, applicant declares as follows: *

1. I am the applicant in the above-identified patent application.

2. The invention of the above application will materially enhance the quality of the environment of humankind by contributing to the restoration or maintenance of the basic life-sustaining natural elements of air and water in the manner described below.

3. Specifically, the invention of the above application is an improved electrical power generator employing wind energy. It provides a more efficient wind power generator than heretofore available because it uses a highly efficient stratus rotor in combination with a Loopis vane, thereby intercepting an average of 25% more of the wind energy passing therethrough than prior-art conventional fan-blade wind turbines, as described in full detail on pages 3 to 5 of the specification.

4. By more efficiently using wind power, it enables the installed cost per average kilowatt of generated wind power on a yearly basis to be materially lowered. This will make wind power generators more economical, cost-effective, and attractive to investors, individual power consumers, and power companies. As a result, more utilization of wind power generation will occur, causing less dependence on and less utilization of conventional power plants using fossil-fuel sources such as coal and oil, or nuclear fission, thereby resulting in less air and water pollution due to reduced effluents in the air and waterways from such conventional power plants. Thus thermal and other pollution of such air and waterways will be reduced so that air and water quality will be maintained and will actually be restored due to natural self-purification.

5. I further declare that all statements made herein of my own knowledge are true and that all statements made upon information and belief are believed to be true, and further that these statements were made with the knowledge that willful false statements and the like so made are punishable by fine or imprisonment, or both, under Section 1001 of Title 18 of the United States Code, and that such willful false statements may jeopardize the validity of the application and any patent issuing therefrom.

Very respectfully,

David Goldberger
David Goldberger

1919 Chestnut Street
Philadelphia, PA 19103
215-237-6639

Fig. 10S—Completed Declaration to Accompany PTMS
*This (and all other papers sent to the PTO) should always be typed with 1.5 or double spacing.

owners should consider signing a Joint Owners' Agreement (Form 16-2). See the reasons for the JOA in Chapter 16, Section C.

P. Petitions to Make Special

If you do need to have your patent issue sooner than in the normal course (one to three years) or want to have it examined sooner for any reason, you can have it examined ahead of its normal turn by filing a "Petition to Make Special" (PTMS—Form 10-9), together with a Supporting Declaration (SD). This can be filed with the application or at any time after. An example of a properly completed PTMS and an SD are shown above in Figs. 10R and 10S.

Before you get excited about filing a Petition to Make Special, however, please consider this. Unless you have a specific need for the early examination or issuance of a patent—for example, an infringement is occurring, you need a patent to get capital for manufacturing the invention, the technology is rapidly becoming obsolete, or you're contemplating foreign filing—most patent professionals agree that you will not gain much of an advantage in filing a PTMS. Why? From experience, filing a PTMS usually advances the examination only a few months. This is likely to be reduced under the new "20-year from filing" patent term, since more applicants will be likely to file a PTMS to extend the period of time their patent is in force.

Also, once a patent issues, the technology is made public (remember, the patent application must teach clearly how to make and use the invention), so that potential competitors can see the patent and start copying its technology and designing around it.

Lastly, most potential licensees (companies that you'd like to license under your patent) would prefer to sign the license while the patent application is still pending and hence kept in secrecy in order to get an edge on the competition. As stated in the next chapter, you should try to license your invention as soon as your patent application is filed and not wait until the patent issues.

As you'll note on the PTMS, an application can be made special, and hence examined ahead of turn, for any of 11 reasons. Those reasons marked with an asterisk (*), reasons 1, 2, 7, 8, 10, and 11, will require a petition fee (for large or small entities). (See Appendix 4, Fee Schedule.) If you use any of the other reasons (numbers 3 to 6 and 9) you won't have to pay any fee, since these are "favorable public policy" (nonmercenary) reasons. Here are the 11 reasons:

1. **Manufacturer Available:** A manufacturer is available —that is, a person or company exists that will manu- facture the invention provided the patent application is allowed or a patent issues.*

2. **Infringement Exists:** Someone is making, using, or selling the invention covered by the patent application and you need a patent to sue the infringer or get the infringer to pay you royalties.*

3. **Applicant's Health Is Poor:** You're in such poor health that your normal life span is likely to be short- ened and you want to get the fruits of your invention before you depart this life.

4. **Applicant's Age Is 65 or Greater:** Self-explanatory.

5. **Environmental Quality Will Be Enhanced:** Your invention conserves natural resources and/or keeps the air, water, or landscape pristine. (See Fig. 10S.)

6. **Energy Savings Will Result:** The invention provides a way to use energy more efficiently, thereby also conserving natural resources.

7. **Recombinant DNA Is Involved:** Public policy favors the full and rapid exploitation of recombinant deoxyribonucleic acid.*

8. **Search Was Made:** If you've made a search and submitted an Information Disclosure Statement—as you're supposed to do anyway (see Section N above) —you can get the case made special, since the examiner's task is made easier by your search.*

9. **Superconductivity Is Advanced:** Public policy favors the exploitation of this phenomenon.

10. **Relates to HIV/AIDS or Cancer:** Self-explanatory.*

11. **Counters Terrorism:** You have a counter-terrorism invention, such as an explosive detector, an aircraft security system, or a vehicle barrier or disabler.*

The supporting declaration that accompanies the PTMS should be in the format of Fig. 10S with the introductory paragraph (paragraph 1) and the last paragraph left intact. The remaining paragraphs must be tailored to your situa- tion and give detailed facts (MPEP 708.02) in support of the reason for the petition. Here are some suggestions:

• If reason 2 is applicable (infringement exists), you should state in your Supporting Declaration (SD) that you've made a rigorous comparison of the claims of your application with the infringer's device and find that the claims "read on" such device (that is, your claims apply to it). You should attach a two-column claim table, listing the elements of one of your claims as separate paragraphs in the left column and explaining in detail how each element "reads on" the infringing device in respective paragraphs in the right column.

• If reason 4 (senior citizen) is applicable, you need merely state in your SD that you're over 65 and give your birth date.

US00D404074S

United States Patent [19]

Sarriugarte et al.

[11] **Patent Number:** **Des. 404,074**

[45] **Date of Patent:** **★★Jan. 12, 1999**

[54] **CARD, PLACARD, OR RIGID PICTURE HOLDER**

[76] Inventors: **Jon Sarriugarte; Sina Hanson**, both of 2601 Adeline St., Oakland, Calif. 94607

[**] Term: **14 Years**

[21] Appl. No.: **69,268**

[22] Filed: **Mar. 21, 1997**

[51] LOC (6) Cl. **19-02**

[52] U.S. Cl. **D19/90**; D20/43; D19/86; D6/313

[58] **Field of Search** D6/313; D11/121; D20/43; D19/65, 75, 78, 86, 87, 90, 91, 95, 99, 100; 211/69.1–69.9, 181.1; 40/606, 659, 642.02; 248/229.26, 175, 475.1, 623; 5/246, 252, 256

[56] **References Cited**

U.S. PATENT DOCUMENTS

D. 26,320	11/1896	Arkin	D19/86
D. 27,364	7/1897	Hill et al.	D20/43
D. 32,692	5/1900	Muth	D20/43
D. 178,356	7/1956	Galef	D19/86
D. 203,185	12/1965	Leaboldi	D19/87
D. 247,265	2/1978	Ledebuhr	D20/43
3,474,555	10/1969	McCaffrey	40/659
3,721,414	3/1973	Yoder	248/175

Primary Examiner—Martie K. Holtje
Attorney, Agent, or Firm—David Pressman

[57] **CLAIM**

The ornamental design for a a card, placard, or rigid picture holder, as shown and described.

DESCRIPTION

FIG. 1 is a front elevational view of a card, placard or rigid picture holder showing our new design, the rear view being substantially a mirror image thereof;
FIG. 2 is a right side elevational view;
FIG. 3 is a left side elevational view;
FIG. 4 is a top plan view; and,
FIG. 5 is a bottom plan view thereof.

1 Claim, 3 Drawing Sheets

Fig. 10T—Sample of Design Patent

• If reason 7 or 9 (DNA or superconductivity) is involved, refer to your application and tell how it involves DNA or superconductivity.

• If reason 8 is applicable, state that an IDS has been filed or is enclosed, and state where (that is, class and subclass) and by whom the search was made.

• If any of the other reasons is involved, give detailed facts or reasoning in support of your main reason, as I have done in Fig. 10S. Attach photocopies of such documents as letters and advertisements to your SD if they are relevant.

• Label each document with a sequential exhibit number—for example, Exhibit A, Exhibit B—and explain it in detail in the declaration.

If you file your PTMS with the application, you should refer to it in your transmittal letter and your postcard receipt. In this case, you won't be able to include the PTO's filing data on the PTMS. Don't fill out the Certificate of Mailing at the bottom of the form. If you file it later, fill out the Certificate of Mailing and add the application filing data to the PTMS, as I have done in Fig. 10R. As always, don't forget the postcard receipt.

If your PTMS is accepted, you'll receive a letter from the PTO stating that your petition has been granted and the examiner in charge of your application has been instructed to examine it ahead of turn.

You should then receive an Office Action (see Chapter 13) several months sooner than normal. If your PTMS isn't accepted, you'll also receive a letter telling you why. Usually the rejection will be because your facts and reasons in the Supporting Declaration aren't detailed enough. In this case, file a revised Declaration, beefing up your facts and reasons.

Q. Filing a Design Patent Application

As I've indicated in Chapter 1, Section B, a design patent covers the ornamental external appearance, rather than the internal structure, function, composition, or state of an invention. Fig. 10T shows an example of the front (abstract) page of a design patent. You may file both a design patent application and a separate utility patent application on the same device, but of course, they should not cover the same feature of the device. The utility patent application should cover only the structure (or a method) that makes the device or invention function or operate. The design patent application should cover an entirely separate "invention," namely, the ornamental (aesthetic) external (nonfunctional) appearance of something. For example, you can file a utility patent application on a computer program (provided it's associated with some hardware), its circuitry, its keyboard mechanism, or its connector structure, and a design patent application on the shape of the computer's case.

You'll be relieved to know that design patent applications are very easy to prepare. A design patent application consists simply of the following:

• DESIGN PATENT APPLICATION TRANSMITTAL (Form 10-10 or PTO/SB/18)

• FEE TRANSMITTAL (Form 10-3 or PTO/SB/17)

• The fee by check, M.O., or CCPF (see Form 10-3, Appendix 4, Fee Schedule, or check the PTO website)

• A Specification having the following elements:

• PREAMBLE (should state the nature and intended use of the design)

• CROSS-REFERENCE TO RELATED APPLICA-TIONS*† (should state any related applications you have (or will) file)

Design Patent Application—Preamble, Specification, and Claim

Mail Stop Design
Commissioner for Patents
P.O. Box 1450
Alexandria, VA 22313-1450
Sir:

PREAMBLE:

The petitioner(s) whose signature(s) appear on the declaration attached respectfully request that Letters Patent be granted to such petitioner(s) for the new and original design set forth in the following specification. The filing fee of $_____170_____, __3__ sheets of drawings, a patent application declaration, fee transmittal, a credit card payment form, and a return receipt postcard are attached.

SPECIFICATION:

The undersigned has (have) invented a new, original, and ornamental design entitled "_____

_____Clothes Hanger_____" of which the following is a specification. Reference is made to the accompanying drawings which form a part hereof, the figures of which are described as follows:

CROSS-REFERENCE TO RELATED APPLICATIONS: None

STATEMENT REGARDING FEDERALLY SPONSORED RESEARCH: None

DRAWING FIGURES:

    Fig. 1 is a front, elevational view of my new clothes hanger
    Fig. 2 is a left side view of the clothes hanger
    Fig. 3 is a perspective view of the clothes hanger
    Fig 4 is a rear view of the clothes hanger.

FEATURE DESCRIPTION: My clothes hanger is characterized by a gradually sloping back with flaring ends and a drooping blade under the back.

CLAIM: I (We) Claim:
The ornamental design for a _____Clothes hanger_____

_____, as shown and described.

Express Mail Label # (EH160200231US) ; Date of Deposit 200_3_ _Sept 8_____

Fig. 10U—Completed Design Patent Application (Form 10-10 in Appendix 7)
Use latest fees—see Appendix 4, Fee Schedule.

- STATEMENT REGARDING FEDERALLY SPONSORED RESEARCH*† (used when the design was made under a government contract)
- DRAWING FIGURES* (describe each drawing figure briefly)
- FEATURE DESCRIPTION* (describes the design's features briefly#)
- CLAIM* (state "I claim the ornamental design for (title of your design) as shown and described.")
- PAD (Form 10-1 or PTO/SB/01)
- The receipt postcard.

* This should appear as a section heading in all capital letters.

† If this section is not applicable, the phrase "Not Applicable" should follow the heading.

\# Although the rules require a Feature Description, the PTO has recently been objecting to the use of any Feature Description since the drawing speaks for itself. I have called the PTO about this, but have not been able to obtain any resolution. I thus recommend that you omit this section, but if you do include it, be prepared to delete it if the PTO objects to it.

A design application form with the first six elements above is provided as Form 10-10 and a completed version is provided as Fig 10U.

If you believe that your invention has a unique ornamental appearance that is significantly different from anything heretofore designed, you can file a design patent application on it.

Although not 100% kosher, some inventors file a design application on the external appearance of a utility invention that is unpatentable in the utility sense, and that has unfinalized or trivial novelty in the design sense. They do this mainly to be able to truthfully and legally state for a few years that the invention is "patent pending."

The first step in completing a design application is to prepare drawings in the same format as for a regular patent application. (See Section A, above.) However, the drawings for the design application should show only the exterior appearance of your invention; no interior parts or workings should be shown and no reference numerals are used. The drawings of a design patent application, whether formal or informal, must be done with good surface and edge shading; see Fig. 10T.

If your invention is a computer-generated symbol (such as an icon like a trash can or a type font), you can file a design patent application on it, but you must show more than just the symbol per se. This is because the pertinent statute (35 USC 171) requires that the design be "an article of manufacture" and the PTO does not consider a computer symbol, per se, as an article. The solution? Simply include a computer display (monitor or display panel) in your drawing and show the computer-generated symbol on the display. Both the symbol and the display should be drawn in solid lines.

Usually only one embodiment of a design is permitted. If you have several embodiments or versions of your design, you can include these all in one application. But if the examiner feels they don't all relate to the same inventive concept, you'll be required to restrict the application to one embodiment. In this case, you can file a divisional application(s) on the other embodiment(s), provided you do so before the original application issues. (See Chapter 14 for divisional applications.)

It's important to remember that drawings of your design application should have enough figures to show all of the details of the external surface of your design. A company I once worked for had an important design patent on a TV set held invalid because the design patent's drawings failed to show the rear side of the TV set.

Once you've made your drawings (in formal or informal form) fill out Form 10-10 as indicated in Fig. 10U. The title of your design can be very simple and need not be specifically directed toward your invention. For example, "Bicycle" is sufficient. Each view of the drawing should be separately indicated. For example, "Fig. 1 is a front perspective view of my bicycle. Fig. 2 is a side view," etc.

Note that the design application has one claim only, and to write that claim you need merely fill in the blank on Form 10-10 with the title of your design. Fill out the fee transmittal (Form 10-3) (the amount is on the form, in Appendix 4, and the PTO's website). Also complete the PAD (Form 10-1). (The SED Statement is on the fee transmittal.) No transmittal letter is needed since Form 10-10 inherently provides a transmittal letter

The design application with the drawings, form, declaration, and receipt postcard should be sent to the PTO in the same manner as your regular patent application. Be sure to keep an identical copy of your design application, including its drawings.

Design Patent Applications. Design patent applications, declarations, drawings, and receipt postcards should be sent to the PTO using the following address:

Commissioner for Patents
P.O. Box 1450
Alexandria, VA 22313-1450

The same address should be used for subsequent communications with the PTO regarding your application.

You'll receive your receipt postcard back in a week or two, and you'll receive a filing receipt a month or so thereafter. If you're aware of any prior art, don't forget to file an Information Disclosure Statement (see Section N, above)

PTO/SB/18 (09-04)
Approved for use through 06/30/2003. OMB 0651-0032
U.S. Patent and Trademark Office; U.S. DEPARTMENT OF COMMERCE
Under the Paperwork Reduction Act of 1995, no persons are required to respond to a collection of information unless it displays a valid OMB control number.

DESIGN PATENT APPLICATION TRANSMITTAL

(Only for new nonprovisional applications under 37 CFR 1.53(b))

Attorney Docket No.	Briskin-Goldberger
First Named Inventor	N. Briskin
Title	Food Chopper Package
Express Mail Label No.	XY1234567890US

ADDRESS TO:
Commissioner for Patents
P.O. Box 1450
Alexandria, VA 22313-1450

DESIGN V. UTILITY: A "design patent" protects an article's ornamental appearance (e.g., the way an article looks) (35 U.S.C. 171), while a "utility patent" protects the way an article is used and works (35 U.S.C. 101). The ornamental appearance of an article includes its shape/configuration or surface ornamentation upon the article, or both. Both a design and a utility patent may be obtained on an article if invention resides both in its ornamental appearance and its utility. For more information, see MPEP 1502.01.

APPLICATION ELEMENTS
See MPEP 1500 concerning design patent application contents.

1. [✓] Fee Transmittal Form (e.g., PTO/SB/17) (Submit an original, and a duplicate for fee processing)
2. [✓] Applicant claims small entity status. See 37 CFR 1.27.
3. [✓] Specification [Total Pages _____] (preferred arrangement set forth below, MPEP 1503.01)
   - Preamble
   - Cross References to Related Applications
   - Statement Regarding Fed sponsored R & D
   - Description of the figure(s) of the drawings
   - Feature description
   - Claim (only one (1) claim permitted, MPEP 1503.03)
4. [✓] Drawing(s) (37 CFR 1.152) [Total Sheets _____]
5. Oath or Declaration [Total Pages _____]
   a. [✓] Newly executed (original or copy)
   b. [ ] A copy from a prior application (37 CFR 1.63(d)) (for continuation/divisional with Box 16 completed)
      DELETION OF INVENTOR(S)
      i. [ ] Signed statement attached deleting inventor(s) named in the prior application, see 37 CFR 1.63(d)(2) and 1.33(b)
6. [ ] Application Data Sheet. See 37 CFR 1.76

ACCOMPANYING APPLICATION PARTS

7. [ ] Assignment Papers (cover sheet & document(s))
8. [ ] 37 CFR 3.73(b) Statement (when there is an assignee) [ ] Power of Attorney
9. [ ] English Translation Document (if applicable)
10. [✓] Information Disclosure Statement (IDS) PTO/SB/08 or PTO-1449
    [ ] Copies of foreign patent documents, publications, & other information
11. [ ] Preliminary Amendment
12. [✓] Return Receipt Postcard (MPEP 503) (Should be specifically itemized)
13. [ ] Certified Copy of Priority Document(s) (if foreign priority is claimed)
14. [ ] Request for Expedited Examination of a Design Application (37 CFR 1.155) (NOTE: Use "Mail Stop Expedited Design"
15. [ ] Other:

16. **If a CONTINUING APPLICATION,** check appropriate box, and supply the requisite information below and in the first sentence of the specification following the title, or in an Application Data Sheet under 37 CFR 1.76:

[ ] Continuation [ ] Divisional [ ] Continuation-in-part (CIP) of prior application No.: _____

Prior application information: Examiner _____ Art Unit: _____

17. CORRESPONDENCE ADDRESS

[ ] The address associated with Customer Number: _____   OR [✓] Correspondence address below

Name	Nathan Briskin
Address	2401 Pennsylvania Blvd.

City	Philadelphia	State	PA	Zip Code	19103
Country	US	Telephone	21-776-1234	Fax	

Signature *Nathan Briskin*   Date 8 JAN 2005
Name (Print/Type) Nathan Briskin   Registration No. (Attorney/Agent)

This collection of information is required by 37 CFR 1.53(b). The information is required to obtain or retain a benefit by the public which is to file (and by the USPTO to process) an application. Confidentiality is governed by 35 U.S.C. 122 and 37 CFR 1.11 and 1.14. This collection is estimated to take 12 minutes to complete, including gathering, preparing, and submitting the completed application form to the USPTO. Time will vary depending upon the individual case. Any comments on the amount of time you require to complete this form and/or suggestions for reducing this burden, should be sent to the Chief Information Officer, U.S. Patent and Trademark Office, U.S. Department of Commerce, P.O. Box 1450, Alexandria, VA 22313-1450. DO NOT SEND FEES OR COMPLETED FORMS TO THIS ADDRESS. **SEND TO: Commissioner for Patents, P.O. Box 1450, Alexandria, VA 22313-1450.**
If you need assistance in completing the form, call 1-800-PTO-9199 and select option 2.

Fig. 10V—Completed Design Patent Application Transmittal (Form 10-11 in Appendix 7)

within three months of your filing date. You must attach copies of any non-U.S. patent references. If the prior art is not in English, the IDS should merely discuss how the appearance of your design differs from such prior art. If the prior art is in English, the IDS need not discuss such prior art.

Expediting a Design Application: The Design Rocket Docket

An applicant can now get a design application expedited rapidly under the PTO's new "Rocket Docket" procedure, but at a stiff price. I recommend that you buy a design rocket docket procedure only if you are selling or are about to sell at least $50,000 worth of something which has a valuable design and you expect it to have a short life in the marketplace. You must first make a thorough preliminary search. Then prepare the application as usual, being sure to include formal drawings and include the IDS forms and references. Then add a completed Rocket Docket Form ("Request for Expedited Examination of a Design Patent Application," Form 10-12 or PTO/SB/27) and the petition fee. The fee is on Form 10-3 and also in Appendix 4 and at the PTO website. The blanks on Form 10-12 are self-explanatory. On the three lines in the middle of the form, type the classes and subclasses where you made the search. On the "Related Applications" line in the middle of the form type the serial numbers and filing dates of any related design applications or patents you own. Send everything to Box: EXPEDITED DESIGN, Commissioner for Patents, P.O. Box 1450, Alexandria, VA 22313-1450.

Plant Patent Applications. I haven't covered plant patent applications, since they're extremely rare and specialized. If you do want to file a plant application, it will be easy to do if you familiarize yourself with this chapter and PTO Rules 161 to 167 (37 CFR 1.161-7).

R. Summary

Use either the U.S. or A4 paper size when finaling the drawings. File formal drawings if possible, since the PTO requires formal drawings before it will examine the application. The drawing rules require that every figure be in clear black lines with proper margins and numbered figures and a reference numeral for every part. The drawings should show every feature of the invention you intend to claim. Ideally, the drawings should almost explain the invention itself, so as to communicate your invention better to the examiner or a judge. Nowadays it is possible to do your own drawings using computer-assisted drawing (CAD) software. (Formerly drawings had to be done in India ink, which was difficult to use.) Professional patent drafters are also widely available. One way to make CAD drawings is to use a digital photo and trace the outline.

The specification, claims, and abstract can be typed on A4- or U.S.-size paper. Strive for perfect work, since that will create fewer obstacles as your application moves through the PTO.

Only the actual and correct inventors should be named in the application. The essential parts of the application are the Postcard, Transmittal Letter, Fee Transmittal, Check or Credit Card Payment Form, Drawings, Specification, Claims, and Abstract, and Patent Application Declaration. You may also wish to file a Disclosure Document Reference Letter, a Request for Claim Drafting by the Examiner, a Nonpublication Request, an Assignment and its Cover Sheet, and/or an Information Disclosure Statement (IDS), the PTO/SB/08 form, and copies of the references.

Take the Declaration seriously. No changes should be made after it's signed.

A patent application can be filed electronically, but the work and possible difficulties in qualifying are generally not worth the effort.

Always include a receipt postcard with the application, which the PTO will return with the Filing Date and Serial Number. It's best to mail your application by Express Mail to get an instant filing date and have protection in case of loss in the mail.

If you are aware of prior art and circumstances relevant to patentability, be sure to file the IDS (with attachments) within three months to advise the PTO of that information. If the application will be owned by anyone other than the inventor(s), prepare and file an assignment. You can petition to make any application special (examined ahead of turn) if you fulfill any of eleven possible bases. Usually there's not much advantage in doing so.

Design patent applications are easy to prepare, once the drawings are completed. Any applicant can have a design application examined quickly under an expedited procedure ("Rocket Docket") by submitting a special petition with a stiff fee and copies of a search. ∎

Chapter 11

How to Market Your Invention

Inventor's Commandment #18

Try to market your invention as soon as you can after filing your patent application; don't wait until your patent issues. Favor successful companies that are close to you and small in size, and that already make and sell items as close to yours as possible.

Inventor's Commandment #19

If you want your invention to be successful, pursue commercial exploitation with all the energy that you can devote to it, and use every avenue available.

Inventor's Commandment #20

Never pay any money to any invention developer unless the developer can prove to you that it has a successful track record—that is, most of its clients have received more income in royalties than they have paid the developer in fees.

The Project Team Approach

If you already know how your invention will be marketed, or you work for a corporation that plans to handle this task, you can skip this chapter and continue reading about obtaining patent coverage. Also, if you would rather spend all your time at your workbench and not have to deal with marketing, a good way to go is to put together a "project team," as suggested by Richard White in *The Entrepreneur's Manual.* Your project team should consist of several persons with diverse skills, such as an inventor, a manufacturing expert, a marketing expert, a person to handle the legwork, a model maker, etc. Chapter 12 deals with obtaining patents in other countries and Chapter 13 with getting the U.S. PTO to grant your patent.

In this chapter I make an important detour from the central task covered by this book—obtaining a valid and effective patent on your invention. The reason for this sudden turn is simple. In the usual course of events, you'll have an interval (six months to two years) after you file your patent application before you need to either consider foreign filing or reply to an Office Action from the PTO. I strongly recommend that you use this interval to get your invention out on the market. This advice is so important that I've included it as Inventor's Commandment #18 at the beginning of this chapter.

 For more information on licensing your invention, consult *License Your Invention,* by Richard Stim (Nolo.)

"Out on the market?" you ask. Shouldn't you keep your invention, and the fact that you've filed the application, secret? The answer is, "No." In fact, once you file a patent application (including a Provisional Patent Application; see Chapter 3, Section I) on your invention, you may show it to whomever you think might be interested in buying or licensing it with minimal risk of having someone scoop you on your invention.

This is because it would be very difficult for someone to steal your invention when you're the first to file a patent application on it. A patent thief would have to:

- file another application (the filing date would necessarily be substantially later than yours due to the preparation time), and
- get into a patent contest with you (called an "interference"—see Chapter 13, Section K), and be able to win it. It's unlikely that this will happen, because the later filing date would make the thief a "junior party" with a large burden of proof. You would also be able to prove that the thief "derived" the invention from you if you keep records of those to whom you reveal your invention. Moreover, the thief would have to commit perjury (a serious felony) by falsely signing the Patent Application Declaration (Chapter 10). Of course, if you plan to maintain the invention as a trade secret, you should take the proper precautions (Chapter 1, Section Q). At any rate, inventions are seldom stolen in their early stages, before they're commercially successful.

Your next question might be, why try to sell or license your invention before a patent has been issued? While there are advantages to selling an already-patented invention, generally it's best to try to sell or license your invention as soon as possible after filing your patent application. This is because prospective corporate purchasers of your invention will want time to get a head start on the competition and to have the time the patent is in force coincide with the time the product's actually on the market. Also, you'll be able to offer the manufacturer the right to apply for foreign patents;

this right will be lost once your patent issues. The lack of prestige that a pending patent has as compared to an already issued patent can be compensated for by a favorable search report showing that there's no strong prior art—that is, that a patent is likely to issue on your invention.

A. Perseverance and Patience Are Essential

As Paul Sherman, then N.Y. Asst. Attorney General, said in his excellent article, "Idea Promoter Control: The Time Has Come" (*Journ. Pat. Off. Soc.*, 1978 April, p. 261), "It is a failing of our system that there are no recognized avenues for amateur inventors to have their ideas evaluated and presented to manufacturers." Even if you get a patent, it will almost certainly be totally worthless unless it covers a commercially exploited invention. In fact, millions of patents have issued on inventions that were never successfully commercialized. None of these patents ever yielded a nickel to their owners.

To get your invention into commercial production, you'll have to persevere. There's no magic solution to the invention marketing process. As noted toy inventor Paul Brown says, "You almost have to be obsessed with your invention to get it going." Or put another way, Emerson's famous adage about building a better mousetrap would have been better written, "If you build a better mousetrap, you'll still have to beat a path to many doors to get it sold." This brings us to Inventor's Commandment #19, regarding perseverance, which you should now reread.

Even though you believe you've got the greatest thing since sliced bread, the money won't start flowing in that quickly in most cases. It takes time to develop, market, and sell a product. Chester Carlson, a patent attorney and the inventor of xerography, may have exaggerated somewhat, but he wasn't too far off base when he said:

> "The time scale of invention is a long one. Results do not come quickly. Inventive developments have to be measured in decades rather than years. It takes patience to stay with an idea through such a long period.
>
> "In my case, I am sure I would not have done so if it were not for the hope of the eventual reward through the incentives offered by the patent system."

Unfortunately, the marketplace is not rational or linear. An inferior product can be successful and a superior product can be a failure, depending upon how it's promoted.

B. Overview of Alternative Ways to Profit From Your Invention

As you can see from the chart of Fig. 11A, there are seven main ways or routes for the independent inventor to get an invention into the marketplace and profit from it—Routes 1 to 7. These choices involve increasing difficulty and work for you. Before we go on, I recommend you study this carefully to become familiar with the various possible routes to success. I also recommend that most inventors use Route #3, and have accordingly highlighted this route.

1. Route 1: Using a Contingent-Fee Intermediary

Starting at the top, Route 1 involves getting a contingent-fee invention broker or intermediary to find a suitable manufacturer/ distributor for you and then using the broker to represent you in the sale or license of your invention.

Sometimes termed "invention developers," "invention marketers," "invention promoters," and the like, these contingent-fee brokers are firms that will represent you and try to market your invention by selling or licensing it for a percentage of your rights, the "contingent-fee basis." Unlike fee-based inventor-exploiters (or FBIEs; see "Don't Use a Fee-Based Inventor-Exploiter") these firms do not charge a fee for their services. They are generally considered to be reputable and to provide a legitimate service for a fair form of compensation. Most of the invention brokers are reputable and honest, and provide a legitimate service for a fair fee.

Obviously, Route 1 is the easiest possible path, since the broker will do all of the work for you. However, it's neither that difficult to find suitable manufacturer/distributors (Section D, below) if they exist, nor to present your invention to them once you locate them (Section G, below). Thus, I recommend that you consider handling this task yourself. No one can sell an invention as sincerely and with as much enthusiasm and conviction as you, the true inventor. Also, you'll get 100% of the benefits and won't have to share the fruit of your creativity with a salesperson. Finally, companies will respect you more if you approach them directly; if you approach them through an intermediary, they'll think less of you and your invention. Why? They may think that you don't have the ability or initiative to approach them yourself.

If you do use an invention broker, you should be concerned about two main possibilities for harm:

1. Loss of your invention rights through theft or communication to a thief, and

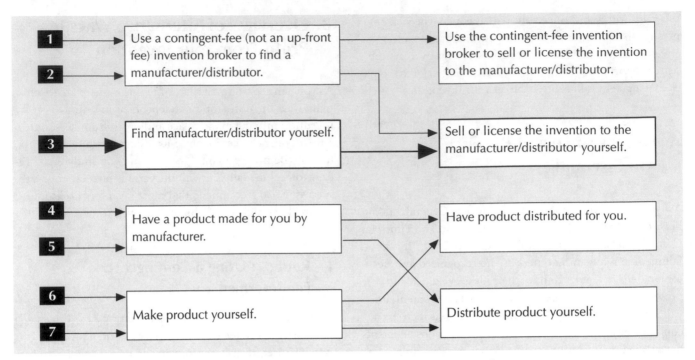

Fig. 11A—Alternative Ways to Profit From Your Invention

2. Loss of time and hence other opportunities.

The first possibility isn't great because you've already got a patent application on file. However, the second possibility is very real, and you should accordingly verify the efficacy of any promoter beforehand. Unfortunately, about the only surefire way to do this is by word-of-mouth. Check with a patent attorney (Chapter 6, Section F), an inventors' organization (Chapter 2, Section F), or some of the intermediary's clients if your own associates are unable to provide you with a lead.

Once you're satisfied with the promoter's honesty and references, you should next investigate the contract you are offered by the promoter to be sure you don't lose time needlessly. Thus, the contract should specify that the promoter will perform substantial services, such as identifying the prospective manufacturers, preparing an invention presentation or demonstration, building and testing the invention, submitting your invention to the prospects, negotiating a license or sales agreement for you, etc. And most important, the agreement should set a time limit for the promoter to succeed—that is, get you a firm offer to buy, license, or get your invention on the market in product form. I feel that a year is reasonable; 18 months is about the maximum you should ever consider. Make sure that if the promoter fails to succeed in the allotted time, all of your rights will be returned to you, together with all of the promoter's research, presentation documents, models, etc.

Several companies that currently market inventions on a contingent-fee basis are AmericaInvents.com and BigIdeaGroup.net, but I cannot vouch for the legitimacy of any marketing firm and urge you to check out any firm carefully before signing. You can find other invention marketing firms through inventors' organizations. (For a listing of inventor organizations, go to www.InventorsDigest.com/connect/orgs.html.)

In addition, many universities now have invention marketing departments that exist primarily to market the technology developed in the universities' research labs, but they also take ideas from outsiders on a contingent-fee basis. Check with your local colleges.

2. Route 2: Partial Use of an Intermediary

Route 2 (a seldom-used path) is the same as Route 1, except that here you use a broker to find prospects and then you take over and do the selling. Contingent-fee brokers won't accept this type of arrangement, since they'll want to control the sales negotiations. However, there are many inventor assistance companies that will provide you with product evaluation, illustration, advertising, packaging design, market research, and product testing services for a fee; one such organization is Synergy Consultants, 2915 LBJ, Suite 254, Dallas, TX 75234. If you feel that your strong suit is in presenting and selling, and that sales research is for someone else, you can pay a broker or market researcher (either contingent-type or fee-based) to research possible purchasers. Then go out and present your invention yourself.

Don't Use a Fee-Based Inventor-Exploiter

There are other firms, which I call fee-based inventor-exploiters (FBIEs), that you should generally avoid like the plague. Paul Turley of the FTC reported that of 30,000 people who paid such FBIEs a fee, not one ever received any payback. These companies or organizations run ads in newspapers, magazines, radio, and TV, stating something like "Inventions and Ideas Wanted!" They will commonly first send you an "inventor's kit" that includes a disclosure form similar to my Form 3-2 and that promises to "evaluate" your invention for free or for a relatively small fee (say $200 to $600). The evaluation almost always is glowingly positive. Then they'll ask for a relatively large fee—$1,000 to $5,000 and up—using very high-pressure sales tactics. They'll promise to do "market research" and try to sell your invention or have it manufactured. They sometimes also take a percentage (for example, 20%) of your invention.

Generally, FBIEs will do little more than write a brief blurb describing your invention and send it to prospective manufacturers in the appropriate fields. Their efforts are virtually 100% unsuccessful, as reported in the article "Patent Nonsense," in the *Wall Street Journal*, 1991 Sept 19, and on the TV program "20/20" on 1995 Jun 6. In other words, FBIEs make their money from inventors, not inventions (S.P. Gnass). For this reason I recommend you not use an invention promoter unless you find one that can establish a successful track record—that is, a record of bringing a significant percentage of its clients royalties in relation to the fees it charged them.

As a result of federal legislation, FBIEs must now make certain disclosures to prospective customers. If they don't, they can be sued for false statements or material omission. The invention promoter must disclose to you in writing:

- the total number of inventions evaluated by the FBIE for commercial potential in the past five years, as well as the number of those inventions that received positive evaluations; and the number of those inventions that received negative evaluations;
- the total number of customers who have contracted with the FBIE in the past five years, not including customers who have purchased trade show services, research, advertising, or other nonmarketing services from the invention promoter; or who have defaulted in their payment to the FBIE;
- the total number of customers known by the FBIE to have received a net financial profit as a direct result of the invention promotion services provided by such invention promoter;
- the total number of customers known by the FBIE to have received license agreements for their inventions as a direct result of the invention promotion services provided by such invention promoter; and
- the names and addresses of all previous FBIE companies with which the invention promoter or its officers have collectively or individually been affiliated in the previous ten years.

In other words, these requirements should tell you about the experience, track record, volume of services, and the effectiveness of the firm.

Note that the PTO does not investigate complaints or participate in legal proceedings against invention promoters. The PTO will accept complaints, forward these complaints to the FBIEs, and make the complaints and responses publicly available on the PTO's Independent Inventor website.

To learn what you will need to file a complaint, visit the PTO website (www.uspto.gov/web/forms/2048a.pdf) for a complaint form (PTO Form SB/2048). Complaints should be mailed to the following address:

United States Patent and Trademark Office
Mail Stop 24, P.O. Box 1450
Alexandria, VA 22313-1452

If you still are thinking of using an FBIE, I strongly suggest you first read some of the complaints about them posted by inventors at the PTO's complaint posting site.

To learn more about FBIEs, go to www.inventnet .scam.html or www.inventorfraud.com.

3. Route 3: Finding a Manufacturer and Distributor Yourself

Route 3 is the path I most favor and which most independent inventors use. Here you do your own research and selling. If you succeed, you'll get 100% of the rewards and you'll control the whole process, yet you won't be bothered with manufacturing or distributing.

4. Route 4: Having Your Invention Manufactured and Distributed for You

Route 4 is a viable alternative for some relatively uncomplicated products. Here you have your invention manufactured for you—a Far-Eastern manufacturer will usually be cheapest—and then use U.S. distributors to sell the product. Of course, you have the headaches of supervising a manufacturing operation, including such items as quality control and red tape associated with importing. But, if you succeed, you'll keep much of the manufacturing profit for yourself.

5. Route 5: You Distribute

In Route 5, you handle distribution as well as supervising manufacturing. More profit, but more headaches and work.

6. Route 6: You Manufacture

In Route 6, you really get into it; you have to do the manufacturing yourself, with all of its headaches (see Section J), but you'll get a lion's share of the profits, if there are any.

7. Route 7: You Manufacture and Distribute

Last, and most difficult, in Route 7 you do it all yourself—manufacturing and distributing. While you get all of the profits, you'll have all of the headaches, as explained in Section J. Successful inventor Robert G. Merrick advocates this route in his excellent book, *Stand Alone, Inventor!* (Lee).

Because, as I said, Route 3 makes the most sense for most independent inventors, I devote the bulk of this chapter to finding a manufacturer/distributor to build and market your patent. (If you want to pursue the possibility of manufacturing and distributing your invention, I've included an overview of potential resources in Section J, below, to help you do this.)

C. Be Ready to Demonstrate a Working Model of Your Invention to Potential Customers

Assuming that you choose Route 3, the best way to get a manufacturer or others to "buy" your invention is to demonstrate an actual working model. Pictures and diagrams may convey an idea and get a message across, but the working model is the thing that will make believers out of most people and show them that your invention is real and doable, and not just chicken scratchings on paper. So, if you haven't made a model before, do your best to make one now, even if it has to be made of cardboard or wood. One essential is to make your model or prototype as simple as possible. Simplicity enhances reliability, decreases cost, decreases weight, and facilitates salability, both to a manufacturer and to the public.

If you're not handy, hopefully you can afford to have a professional model maker or artisan build the model, or you may have a handy friend or relative. Where can you find model makers? Ask your local inventors' organization. (See Chapter 2, Section F.) If that fails, an inventor's magazine, *Investors Digest* (see Appendix 2, Resources: Government Publications, Patent Websites, and Books of Use and Interest), has ads in every issue from model makers. Another obvious place is in your nearest metropolitan area Yellow Pages under "Model Makers." Also try "Machine Shops" and "Plastics—Fabricating, Finishing, and Decorating."

In addition, your local college or community college may have a design and industry department that may be able to refer you to a model maker. If you live near an industrial plant that employs machinists or model makers, perhaps you can get one of these employees to moonlight and do the job for you—put a notice on the plant's bulletin board, call, or ask around.

If you do use a model maker and you disclose critical information, including dimensions, materials, suppliers, or other data you consider to be proprietary (a trade secret), it is best to have the model maker sign a Consultant's Work Agreement (Form 4-3) before you turn over your drawings or other papers. Follow the instructions in Chapter 4 to fill out this form. I also suggest that you add a confidentiality legend to any drawings or descriptions you turn over to your model maker. Such a legend can be made in rubber-stamp or sticker form or can be typed on the drawings, should read as follows:

This drawing or description contains proprietary information of [your name] and is loaned for use only in evaluating or building an invention of [your name] and must be returned upon demand. By acceptance hereof, recipient agrees to all of the above conditions. © 200_ [your name]."

After you've made a working model, you should take at least one good photograph of it. The photograph should be of professional quality—if you are not a good photographer, have a professional do it, and order several views if necessary. Have at least 50 glossy prints made of the photo, possibly with several views on one sheet. Then write a descriptive blurb about your invention, stating the title or the trademark, what it is, how it works, its main advantages and selling points, plus your name, address, telephone number, and the legend "Patent Pending." Don't get too bogged down in detail, however. In other words, make your write-up snappy and convincing. Then have it typed or printed and have at least 50 copies made to go with the photographs.

If you can't build a real working model, you can build a "virtual prototype" (computer simulation). For an explanation of this process see Jack Lander's article, "Virtual Prototyping: Alive and Well," in *Inventors Digest,* July/August 2003.

D. Finding Prospective Manufacturers/Distributors

The next step is to compile an initial listing of manufacturers who you believe could manufacture and distribute your invention profitably. You should keep your marketing notes, papers, and correspondence in a separate file from your patent application (legal) file. Your initial list should comprise all the manufacturers who meet the following four criteria:

• they're geographically close to you
• they already manufacture the same or a closely related product,
• they're not too large, and
• they're anxious to get new products out.

Nearby or local manufacturers who already work in your field are best. If they manufacture your invention, you can monitor their progress, consult with them frequently, and take any needed action more easily if anything goes wrong. Obviously, it's a big help to deal with a company that has experience with devices similar to yours. They already know how to sell in your field, are aware of competitive pricing policies, can make your invention part of their existing product line—which allows them to keep sales costs low—and presumably want new models related to their existing

products in order to keep ahead of the competition. If the manufacturer is not in a closely allied line, both the seller and the product will be on trial, so why start with two strikes against you?

The reasons for avoiding giant manufacturers are these:

1. Smaller manufacturers are more dependent on outside designers. In other words, most don't have a strong inbred prejudice against inventions they did not invent themselves (see the "NIH" Syndrome in Section E, below).

2. You can contact the decision makers or the owners of the company directly, or more easily.

3. Decisions are made more rapidly because the bureaucracies are smaller.

4. You are less likely to be required to sign a waiver form (see "The Waiver," in Section F, below).

5. Giant companies have more access to patent lawyers and, hence, a greater tendency to try to "get around" your invention by investigating and trying to invalidate your patent or trying to avoid infringing it. Medium and small companies, on the other hand, will be more interested in your invention's profit potential and its effect in the marketplace.

Obviously, you shouldn't use companies that are so small that they don't have enough money to finance the manufacture of your invention or market it adequately. Companies with sales of about $10 million to $100 million are best (unless you have enormous market potential).

To find companies meeting the above criteria, start by first considering people you know. Which one of them is likely to have contacts in the field of your interest? Put them to work for you and you may be amazed that with a few phone calls you can get just the introduction you need.

If this doesn't work, try looking in your appropriate local stores for manufacturers of closely allied products that are already on the shelves. You'll know for sure that these companies have a successful distribution and sales system or operation.

Inventors' magazines, such as *Inventors Digest* (see Appendix 2, Resources: Government Publications, Patent Websites, and Books of Use and Interest), and *The Patent Café* (www.patentcafe.com) have ads from and list companies seeking new products from inventors; be on your guard for scams, however.

Also, check the library for books listing local manufacturers (such as the *California Manufacturers Register*) and check national resources such as the *Thomas Register* or *Dun's Million Dollar Directory.* In addition, check the ads in pertinent trade and hobby magazines. Lastly, stock advisory services, such as *Value Line Investment Survey, Standard &*

Poor's, and *Moody's,* supply excellent information about companies. Get the names of the company presidents, vice presidents, directors of engineering, marketing, etc. Find out all you can about each company you select; know its products, sales and corporate history, profitability, and factory location(s).

If your invention is in the gadget category and you believe it would appeal to the affluent, try Hammacher Schlemmer, a specialty store and mail-order house at 147 East 57th Street, New York, NY 10022, or The Sharper Image, 650 Davis St., San Francisco, CA 94111, Attn: New Products Committee. These outfits develop and sell a wide variety of gadget exotica, both through their catalogues and over the counter. They each receive thousands of ideas for inventions each year, accept some of these, and arrange to have them produced by manufacturers. Many items that they financed and had manufactured, or first sold as strictly luxury gadgets, have become commonplace in American homes. For example, the steam iron, the electric razor, the pressure cooker, the blender, the humidifier, the electric can opener, the high-intensity lamp, the microwave oven, the automatic-drip coffee maker, the nonfogging shower mirror, the electrostatic air purifier, etc., were first introduced by these firms. Another firm is JS&A, but they don't develop or manufacture any products. Also, trade fairs or shows—such as The Gift Show—are good places for you to wander about, looking for prospective manufacturers. Talk to the people who run the exhibits to get a feel for the companies, whom to contact, and what their attitude toward outside inventions is.

If your invention is a new automotive tool, Lisle Corp., 807 East Main St., Clarinda, IA 51632, actively seeks such inventions. Write them for their Invention Disclosure Agreement. The Sharper Image, 415-445-6125, is hungry for new products in the "executive gadget" category, while Homax Products, www.homaxproducts.com, 800-729-9029, wants home improvement inventions. Kraco Enterprises, Inc., 505 E. Euclid Ave., Compton, CA 90224, 800-678-1910, is looking for new automotive products. Hog Wild Toys, 107 SE Washington St., Portland, OR 97214 (contact Dana Cuellar at dana@hogwildtoys.com), is looking for novel toys and gifts. The Bohning Co., Ltd., 7361 North 7 Mile Rd., Lake City, MI 49651 (contact Karen Abrahamson at abrhamsn@freeway.net), is seeking new plastic products to manufacture. If you have a new exercise or fitness machine, consider NordicTrack, 104 Peavey Rd., Chaska, MN 5538.

If you can't find any U.S. companies, try foreign ones. Sadly, there has been a recent trend in many U.S. firms to become complacent or tight. They've refused to undertake new ventures that foreign firms have jumped at, which can work to your advantage as an inventor.

E. The "NIH" Syndrome

Before presenting your invention to any manufacturer, two possible impediments should be kept in mind:
- the "NIH" (Not Invented Here) syndrome, and
- the common insistence that you give up many of your legal rights by signing a waiver (Section F, below).

Generally, the larger the manufacturer, the greater the chances of encountering one or both of these impediments.

The NIH syndrome is an unwritten attitude that handicaps inventors who submit their ideas to a company, no matter how meritorious such ideas may be. Put simply, many companies have a bias against any outsider ("the enemy") or any outside invention because it was "not invented here." This attitude prevails primarily because of jealousy. The job of the corporate engineering department is to create new and profitable products for their company. If an engineering department were to recommend an outside invention, it would almost be a tacit admission that the department had failed to do its job in solving a problem and coming up with the solution the outside inventor has found.

How can you overcome the NIH syndrome? First, realize that it's more likely to exist in larger companies, or companies with extensive engineering departments. Second, when forced to deal with engineering departments or any department in a company where the NIH syndrome may be present, always remember that the more your invention appears to be a logical extension of ideas already developed within the company, the better your chances of acceptance will be.

F. The Waiver and Precautions in Signing It

Most inventors affected with the paranoia part of the "Paranoia/Greed/Laziness Syndrome" (see Chapter 2, Section G) are afraid to show their invention to anyone, even after they've filed a patent application. The truth is, however, that most companies are far more afraid of you suing them for taking your invention than they are interested in stealing it. Most companies with access to legal advice will require you to sign their agreement (called a "waiver"), under which you give up a number of important rights that you would otherwise possess under the law. The reason for this

waiver is that many companies have been sued by inventors claiming violation of an implied confidentiality agreement, or an implied agreement to pay if all or any part of the invention is used. Even though the company's own inventor may have come up with the invention independently of the outside inventor, many companies have lost these suits or were forced to compromise because of the uncertainties and expenses of litigation.

The waiver itself usually requires you to give up all your rights, except those which you may have under the patent laws. Specifically, the waiver typically asks you to agree that:

1. The company has no obligation to pay you if they use your idea.
2. The company isn't bound to keep your idea in confidence.
3. The company has no obligation to return any paper you submit.
4. The company has no obligation whatever to you, except under the patent laws.

Many companies add many other minor provisions, which are not significant enough to discuss here. The effect of the waiver is that you have no rights whatever against the company if they use your invention, except to sue them for patent infringement if and when you get a patent.

The usual procedure, if you send a letter mentioning your idea to the company, is for the company to route your letter to the patent or legal department, which will send you a form letter back stating their policy and asking you to sign the waiver before they agree to review your idea. Once you do so, the patent or legal department will approve your submission for review and send it to the appropriate engineering manager of the company.

Since you may not get a patent, since the company may use a variation of your idea that may not be covered by any patent you do get, and since you would like to have the company keep your submission in confidence, it's best to avoid signing any waiver if at all possible. For this reason, you should, at least initially, concentrate on smaller companies. The smaller the company, the less likely they are to make you sign a waiver. In fact, the best sort of relation you can have with a company to which you submit your ideas is to have them sign an agreement that you have drafted. Many small companies actually want to review outside inventions and are willing to sign a proprietary-submission agreement.

If the company is willing, or if you can swing it (say, by touting the commercial potential of your invention, being dramatic, establishing a rapport with the research people, etc.), have the company sign a Proprietary Submission Agreement such as the following:

Proprietary Submission Agreement

X Company agrees to review an invention from *[your name]* for a new and improved *[describe invention]*, to keep in confidence such invention and all papers received, to return upon request all papers submitted, and to pay *[your name]* a reasonable sum and royalty to be settled by future negotiation or arbitration if X Company uses or adopts such invention.

If a company won't sign the above agreement, you can make it a bit more palatable by eliminating the last clause regarding the payment of a reasonable fee and royalty. Even with the last clause eliminated, you're in a very good position if you've gotten them to sign. If the company still refuses to sign your agreement, you can add the following clause:

The forgoing shall not obligate X Company with respect to any information which X Company can document (a) was known to it prior to receipt from me, either directly or indirectly, or (b) which is now or hereafter becomes part of the public domain from a source other than X Company.

If you can't get them to sign even this, you're still in a pretty good position legally if you can get them to review your invention without any agreement being signed by either side.

If all else fails and you do have to sign a waiver before the company will look at your invention (that's what will usually happen), it's not all that bad, since you do, at least, have a pending patent application. And most companies are far more afraid of you suing them (for taking your invention) than they are interested in stealing your invention. Now you can understand why I emphasized the need to file your patent application before submitting your invention to any company. If you sign the waiver, your position won't be seriously jeopardized if your patent issues. However, if you're submitting an invention to a company without having first filed a patent application (Block B of the Invention Decision Chart from Chapter 7), it's very important that you try to get the company to sign the above Proprietary Submission Agreement or, failing that, try to submit it without signing their waiver.

If you do have to sign a waiver, try to make sure the company is a reliable and fair one. Also, it's important to insist, by means of a separate letter, that the company make its decision within a given time, say six months, or else return all of your papers to you. This is because many companies, especially large ones, can take many months or years to make a decision if you let them, which may interfere with your efforts to market the invention to others.

To the extent you are uncertain about whether signing a waiver is a good idea under the circumstances, a consultation with a patent attorney might be wise. On the other hand, don't let the waiver prevent you from showing your invention to a reputable manufacturer that promises to give you a decision in a reasonable time. As long as your patent is pending and eventually issues, you'll have reasonably strong rights.

G. The Best Way to Present Your Invention to a Manufacturer

The best and most effective way to sell your invention to a manufacturer is personally to visit the decision maker in the company you elect and demonstrate a working model or prototype of your invention (or present drawings of it if you have no working model). To accomplish this, write a brief, personal, friendly, and sincere letter to the president of the company, saying that you have a very valuable invention you believe would be profitable for the company's business and that you would like to make an appointment when convenient to provide a brief demonstration. You can disclose the general area of your idea, but don't disclose its essence until you can present it properly. Keep the initiative by stating that you will call in a few days. Follow through accordingly. Here's an example:

Mr. Orville Billyer
President, Billyer Saw Co.
[etc.]

Dear Mr. Billyer:

I'm employed as an insurance agent, but in my spare time I like to tinker. While building a gun rack, I thought of and have perfected a new type of saw fence which I believe can be produced at 60% of the cost of your A-4 model, yet which can be adjusted in substantially less time with greater accuracy. For this reason, I believe that my fence, for which I've applied for a patent, can be a very profitable addition to your line. I'll call you in a few days to arrange a demonstration of my invention for you in your plant.

Most sincerely,
Marjorie Morgenstern
Marjorie Morgenstern

When you come to the demonstration, be prepared! Set up your presentation well in advance. Practice it on friends. Explain the advantages of your invention first: how it works, how it will be profitable for their business, and why it will sell. Make sure your model works. Also, prepare appropriate and attractive written materials and photos for later study by the decision maker.

In your presentation and written material, it's wise to cover the "Three Fs"—Form, Fit, and Function.

Form is the appearance of your invention. Stress how it has (or can have) an attractive, enticing appearance.

Demonstrate how your invention fits with other products, or with the environment in which it is to be used. If your invention is a highly functional device, such as a saw fence, show and tell how it fits onto a table saw. If it's a clock, show (or present attractive pictures showing) how it looks attractive on a desk or coffee table.

Function is what your invention does, how it works, what results it attains. Demonstrate and discuss its function and its advantage here. Mention all of the advantages from your Positive and Negative Factors Evaluation (Form 4-1, Appendix 7). In addition, be prepared to discuss such items as cost of manufacture, profit, retail price, competition, possible product liability, and product life. Review all of the positive and negative factors from the list in Chapter 4 to be sure you've covered all possible considerations.

During the verbal part of your presentation, it's wise to use diagrams and charts, but keep your model, written materials, and photos hidden from view. Otherwise, the people you're trying to sell to will be looking at these instead of listening to you. Then, at a dramatic moment, bring out your model and demonstrate how it works. Don't apologize if your model is a crude or unattractive prototype, but radiate enough confidence in yourself and your invention that they will overlook any lack of "cosmetics." If you can't bring or show them your model for any reason, a videotape, filmstrip, drawing, diagram, or slide presentation that shows the three F's will be a viable, though less desirable way, to show the invention.

If possible, make them think that the invention is basically their idea. You can do this by praising their related product line and then showing how your idea compliments theirs, or by enthusiastically endorsing any reasonable suggestion they make for your idea.

At the end of your verbal presentation, produce your written materials and pictures for study (either then and there or at a later time). If they're interested in the invention, be prepared to state your terms and conditions. (See Chapter 16, Section G.) If they're really serious and ask for it, you can show them your patent application without your claims, but only with the understanding that it won't be copied and will be returned to you. You shouldn't offer the claims, prior art from your search, serial number, or filing date, unless you're asked. If you're relying on a Provisional Patent Application for your patent pending status, then you won't have drafted your claims yet, and you also may not have conducted a patentability search.

If you've done your best and still get a rejection, don't accept it blindly and walk away with your tail between your legs, but turn it into an asset for next time. Talk to the executives about it and learn exactly why they decided not to accept your idea so that in the future you'll be better prepared to answer and overcome the disadvantage that blocked your initial acceptance.

Assuming the company is interested, you shouldn't blindly or automatically accept it as your patron. Rather, you should evaluate the company to which you're demonstrating your invention just as they're evaluating you and your invention. For example, if the company seems to lack energy or vision, don't go with them. Also, you should check out the company with their local Better Business Bureau to see if they have a clean record. After all, you're risking a lot, too, when you sign up with a company. If the company doesn't promote your invention enthusiastically and correctly, it can fail in the market, even if it's the greatest thing to come down the pike in 20 years.

Don't Be Afraid of Simultaneous Submissions. If you're aware of several prospective companies that you feel might be interested, I recommend that you approach all of the companies simultaneously; otherwise, you'll waste too much time. If several companies "bite" concurrently, you'll be in the enviable position of being able to choose your licensee. (Some companies do ask that you not submit your invention to anyone else while they're looking at it; you should honor this request.)

H. Presenting Your Invention by Correspondence

Another way to present your invention is by correspondence. Because letters are easy to file and forget, and because any salesman will tell you a personal presentation is a thousand times more likely to make a sale, I strongly advise against submitting an invention to a manufacturer by correspondence if you can avoid it. Try your utmost to arrange a personal demonstration with a working model as described in the previous section. Nevertheless, if you do have to resort to correspondence, don't let your efforts slacken.

Your letter should always be addressed to a specific individual. Find the president's name from the directories mentioned in Section D above. If you receive an expression of interest from the company, you will probably be faced with the waiver question. My comments in the previous discussion cover how to handle this problem. Before you send a model, get an advance written commitment from the company that they'll return it within a given time. You should send your model by certified, insured mail, return receipt requested, and make follow-up phone calls as appropriate.

I. Making an Agreement to Sell Your Invention

If you sell your invention to a manufacturer/distributor, the next step is to sign an agreement of some sort with the manufacturer. The question thus arises, what will be the terms of the agreement, exactly what will you sell them, and for how much? There are many possibilities. These are covered in Chapter 16, which deals with ownership and transfer of patents rights.

J. Manufacturing and/or Distributing the Invention Yourself

For reasons stated earlier, manufacturing and/or distributing a product embodying your invention—unless you already have manufacturing experience, a plant, and/or distribution facilities—is very difficult. Besides, you can spend your time more effectively selling your invention or patent application, rather than dealing with manufacturing and product-marketing problems.

If you do plan to manufacture and/or distribute your invention yourself (Routes 6 or 7), I strongly suggest that you learn about the subject thoroughly beforehand so you will know what is involved and which pitfalls to avoid. The best place to obtain literature and reading material is your local SBA (Small Business Administration) office, which has scads of literature and aids available to apprise you of the problems and pitfalls. They even have a service that allows you to obtain the advice of an experienced executive free; ask for a "Counseling Request from Small Business Firm" form. Nolo publishes an excellent book, *How to Write a Business Plan*, by Mike McKeever, which tells potential businesspeople how to assess the costs of a proposed business, how to draft a business plan, and how to obtain sufficient start-up money.

1. Financing the Manufacture of Your Invention

Financing any manufacturing venture of your own is a separate and formidable problem. If you have an untried and unsold product, most banks will not lend you the money to go ahead. However, if you can get orders from various local firms, the bank may lend you the money. Thus a local test-marketing effort on a limited scale may be desirable.

For obtaining money to finance untried products, a money lender who's willing to take more risk is needed. Such a person is usually termed a "venture capitalist" (VC). A VC will lend you money in exchange for shares or a portion of your enterprise. Pratt's *Guide to Venture Capital Sources* (listed in Appendix 2, Resources: Government Publications, Patent Websites, and Books of Use and Interest) is the most popular source of VCs, but most libraries have other VC resources. A comprehensive list of venture capital resources and related information can be found at the Venture Capital Resource Library (www.vfinance.com) and at Clickey.com (www.clickey.com) where you should search using the term "venture capital." Also the Venture Capital Hotline, 408-625-0700, will provide you with a list of suitable VCs for a fee (about $75). However, VCs won't lend you money on the same

terms a bank would. Because of the higher risks they take, they demand a much larger return—namely a piece of the action. Also, they'll want to monitor your company and exercise some degree of control, usually by putting their people on your board of directors. A thorough discussion of the pros and cons of working with venture capitalists can be found in the Nolo book, *How to Write a Business Plan*, mentioned earlier. While most VCs are companies or partnerships, sometimes wealthy individuals finance inventions, so if you have a rich uncle or know of a suitable patron, include them on your list.

A recent development in the VC field is the "Incubator VC." This is a VC that provides several different inventors with offices, labs, and/or a manufacturing area in a special building, called an "innovation center." Also the VC may provide technical, financial, and marketing consultation, as well as other services, until each nurtured enterprise is ready to leave the "nest." The sources in the preceding paragraph, as well as inventors' organizations (Chapter 2, Section F), will give you the names of Incubator VCs; they are sponsored by academia, state and federal governments, and private organizations.

2. Prepare a Business Plan

To obtain venture capital to start a business based on your invention, you'll have to prepare a business plan—a presentation that tells all about your invention, the market for it, and how you plan to use the money. You can get an excellent booklet from a national accounting firm gratis, which will tell you how to prepare your business plan. This is *Financing Business Growth* , available free from any office of Deloitte & Touche LLP. This practical guide tells how to write and present your business plan. Again, *How to Write a Business Plan* is also recommended for this purpose.

3. Distribution Through Mail Order or the Internet

Mail order is often an easy way for an individual to distribute an invention, whether the inventor makes it or has it made. An excellent guide is *How I Made $1,000,000 in Mail Order*, by E. Joseph Cossman (Prentice-Hall). Once your mail order operation starts bringing in some cash, you can branch out and try to get some local, then regional, then state, and then (hopefully) national distributors who handle lines similar to yours.

There are two principal ways to contact your potential customers:

* magazine/media advertising, and

• direct mail advertising.

If you're interested in the latter, order the *Dunhill Marketing Guide to Mailing Lists* from Dunhill International List Company, Inc., 444 Park Avenue South, New York, NY 10016.

You can also try to use a mail order distributor. Many mail order houses will, if you send them a production sample and they like it and feel you can meet their demand, buy your production. There are 15,000 mail order houses in the U.S. and they depend upon novelty and Mom-and-Pop suppliers, as well as large manufacturers. They'll put in their own ads, manufacture, and distribute their own catalogue, and thus are valuable intermediaries for many garage-shop manufacturers. Walter Drake & Sons, Colorado Springs, CO 80940, is one of the largest, but you can obtain the names of many others by looking for ads in *Redbook, House Beautiful, Better Homes and Gardens, Apartment Life, Sunset, Holiday,* etc. These mail order firms are always looking for new gadgets, and most of their products come from small firms. While many of them will purchase quantities of your product outright, some will want to take them on consignment, which means they do not pay you until and unless they sell it themselves.

The Internet also provides a vast marketplace for marketing a device, but getting potential customers to your site can be difficult. One solution is to offer your device on eBay or to set up a store at Yahoo.com or Msn.com. See Section 5, Publicity, below, for other ideas.

4. Utilize Government Services

If your invention is or can be used in a product that the federal government might purchase, write to the General Services Administration, Federal Supply Service, 1734 New York Avenue, NW, Washington, DC 20406, telling them that you're offering a product that you feel the government can use. They'll send you appropriate forms and instructions. Also, don't neglect your corresponding state and local purchasing agencies.

If you have an energy-related invention, the Department of Energy may give you a research grant if the National Bureau of Standards gives it a favorable evaluation. Write for an Energy-Related Inventions Program brochure from the U.S. Department of Energy, Office of Technical and Financial Assistance, Forrestal Building, CE-50, 1000 Independence Ave., SW, Washington, DC 20585.

5. Publicity

Publicity will sometimes be of great aid to you before you get your invention into production, and is invaluable once it's on the market. Assuming it's not yet on the market and you're either looking for a manufacturer, distributor, or thinking of manufacturing or distributing it yourself, publicity can cut both ways. As stated, many manufacturers like to get a secret head start on their competition and thus won't be too interested if your invention has already been disseminated to the public.

If you're going to make and sell it yourself, I believe you should wait until you've got the product out before you try to publicize it. Why? The public's memory span is short, so they'll be likely to forget about your product by the time you get it on sale. My advice is to not seek publicity until a product with your invention is almost or actually on the market, unless you've tried unsuccessfully, after substantial efforts, to get it on the market.

Assuming you're ready for publicity, one way to get it (at a price) is to hire a public-relations or marketing research firm to promote your invention for you. There are many reputable firms who can come up with many creative and valuable ideas for a fee. However, since the cost of public-relations services is very high, I don't recommend it unless you can bear the cost without difficulty.

Many magazines will feature new ideas free if you send them a clear, understandable, professional-quality photo or drawing of your invention, plus a brief, clear, and understandable description of it. They may even write a full-length feature about your invention if they think it's interesting enough. Suitable magazines are *Popular Science, Mechanics Illustrated, Popular Electronics, Better Homes and Gardens, Pageant, Parade, Playboy, This Week, True Story, Jet, Outdoor Life, House and Garden, House Beautiful, Outdoor Living, Changing Times, McCall's, Apartment Life, Argosy,* and *Sunset.* You can obtain the addresses of those you think are relevant from *Ulrich's International Periodicals Directory* in your local library.

The magazine *Advertising Age* has a feature called "Idea Marketplace" in each issue in which they publicize new inventions gratis. Write to them at Crown Communications, Inc., 740 Rush Street, Chicago, IL 60611, sending a picture and brief description of your invention. Thomas Publications, 1 Pennsylvania Plaza, New York, NY 10119, has a bimonthly called *Technology Mart* that offers a similar service, as does *Dental X Change,* http://dentalXchange.com, and the "Form + Function" column of the *Wall Street Journal,* by John Pierson.

Review the trade magazines in the field of your invention for other ideas.

Nolo also publishes an excellent book, *Marketing Without Advertising,* by Michael Phillips and Salli Rasberry; its title is self-explanatory.

Other sources of publicity and possible sale or licensing opportunities are exhibits, trade fairs, and business shows. I don't recommend that you use these, since I've heard only a few success stories from exhibitors. On the other hand, I have heard of many more cases where foreign or domestic manufacturers copy good inventions and hope to make a quick killing or avoid any pertinent patents. But if you feel that you may get a bite from this type of exposure, try one—the cost is usually a few hundred dollars. You'll be given a table or booth, or equivalent space to demonstrate your invention at the fair or show. Naturally, your exhibit should be attractive and interesting, and it is preferable to have a working model or very good literature available in connection with your invention. There are exhibition-service companies that will prepare a display exhibit for you for a fee. Also, several of the Contingent-Fee Invention Brokers listed above have exhibition areas. The following site lists over 50,000 trade shows held annually in the U.S.: www.tscentral.com.

Don't overlook the media (radio, TV, newspapers, and magazines) as an excellent source of free publicity, which most experts say is the best kind. Many local radio and TV stations feature talk shows whose hosts are always looking for interesting guests; some stations even have shows in which new inventors can demonstrate or discuss their inventions. One syndicated show is *Million Dollar Idea* (www.milliondollarideashow.com). To find other shows and get on them, call your local stations, ask what talk shows they have and which might be interested in interviewing an inventor with a hot new product, and who the appropriate producers are. Then send the producers a press kit or letter describing your invention and why it and you would be of interest to the show's listeners.

One of the best ways to get media publicity (and concomitant interviews) is to dream up or pull a stunt. For example, if you've invented a new bicycle drive mechanism, you might enter and win a local bike race, or sponsor some type of contest (which you can win!).

Lastly, don't overlook a new phenomenon—invention stores that sell newly invented products at retail. One is the New Products Showcase at the Irving Mall in Irving, Texas. Also, there are a number of Sharper Image- and Nature Co.-like stores that sell dozens of new gadgets and are always looking for new ones to scoop their competition.

6. The Premium Marketing Route

If you can't get a manufacturer or distributor to take your invention, try offering it as a premium to accompany a related product that is already on the market. For example,

one television magazine show featured a girl, Abbey Mae Fleck, 8, of St. Paul, Minnesota, who invented a great plastic hanger to suspend bacon in a microwave oven so that the grease dripped away while it cooked. However, none of the manufacturers of plastic microwave accessories would bite (their loss!). So ingenious Abbey approached a bacon company and got them to offer her MAKIN BACON® via a discount coupon on their bacon packages. The result: an instant success! The bacon company's investment was minimal, yet it profited handsomely by providing a way to cook its bacon dryly. And Abbey got her commercial distribution. Abbey's story also shows that creativity has no age limits.

7. The Celebrity Endorsement Route

If a product bears a celebrity's name or endorsement, people will be far more likely to buy it. So, getting a celebrity to endorse it is often a key to instant success. Consider George Foreman's Lean, Mean Grilling Machine griller. Without the champ's endorsement and name it might not have been a fabulous success. Celebrity endorsements are particularly useful if you have a sporting goods invention, such as a golf club. To get a celebrity endorsement, first perfect and get your product ready for market. Prepare suitable sales and promotional materials, with photos, and then approach the celebrity you feel would do your baby justice. While you'll have to share a good portion of your profits, you'll find that your chances of success will be almost assured if you have a good product and can get a famous celebrity to endorse and name it.

K. Summary

After filing a patent application, try to get your invention on the market; don't wait until your patent issues. Since it can take a long time to license an invention, perseverance and patience are essential.

There are seven routes to profit from an invention and they involve using a marketing intermediary, manufacturing and/or marketing your invention yourself, or licensing your invention to a company. Most inventors use the latter.

Don't use a fee-based intermediary unless they can demonstrate that many of their clients have made more money than they paid the intermediary.

The best way to sell or license an invention is to demonstrate a working model. Find prospective manufacturers in stores, catalogues, and trade magazines. Larger companies will require that you sign a waiver (giving up all rights except patent rights) before they will look at your invention. You may have better luck with companies that are smaller and geographically close to you. These companies usually communicate in a more direct manner, avoid the NIH syndrome, and often don't require a waiver.

If you want to manufacture and/or distribute the invention yourself you may need financing and a business plan.

There are many ways to get publicity for your invention including premium marketing and celebrity endorsements. ■

Chapter 12

Going Abroad

Inventor's Commandment #21

Foreign Filing: Don't file your invention in any foreign country unless you're highly confident it has extremely strong commercial potential there or unless someone else will pay the costs. File a Patent Cooperation Treaty (PCT) application or file directly in Convention (major industrial) countries within one year of your earliest U.S. filing date (regular or Provisional Patent Application) and in non-Convention countries before the invention becomes publicly known. Don't file abroad until you receive a foreign-filing license or until six months after your U.S. filing date.

A. Introduction

By now you've gotten your U.S. application on file and have taken steps to have your invention manufactured and distributed in anticipation of receiving a patent. Your next step will be either to file in one or more other countries (this chapter) or to deal with the first substantive response by the USPTO (called an "Office Action") to your application (Chapter 13).

If you've already received your first Office Action from the USPTO, you'll have a pretty good idea of the patentability of your invention and, consequently, your chance of getting foreign patents abroad. (If you want to help determine your chances of getting foreign patents, see Chapter 10, Section P, to see how to get your U.S. application examined earlier.)

Why file your patent application in other countries? Simply because a U.S. patent will give you a monopoly in the U.S. only. If you think your invention is important enough to be manufactured or sold in large quantities in any other countries, so that you want to create a monopoly there, you'll have to go through the considerable effort and expense of foreign filing in order to eventually get a patent in each desired foreign country. Otherwise, anyone in a foreign country where you have no patent will be able to make, use, and sell your invention with impunity. However, if you have a U.S. patent they won't be able to bring it into the U.S. without infringing your U.S. patent.

This chapter doesn't give you the full, detailed instructions necessary to file abroad. That would take another book. Instead, my mission is to alert you to the basic procedures for foreign filing, so that you won't lose your opportunity to do so through lack of information. However, once you decide to foreign file, you'll probably need some professional guidance, notwithstanding the availability of other resources (discussed in Section M of this chapter) that will answer most of your questions.

The most important points you can learn from this chapter are presented in Inventor's Commandment #21 at the beginning of the chapter. It states (a) don't foreign file in any foreign country unless you're highly confident your invention has extremely strong commercial potential there, (b) don't foreign file until you get a foreign-filing license (see Section H, below) or until six months has elapsed from your U.S. filing date, (c) you must do any desired filing in non-Convention countries (see Section F, below) before you publish or sell the invention, and (d) you must file a Patent Cooperation Treaty application or file in all other countries (Convention countries—see Section B, below) within one year of your earliest U.S. filing date (regular or Provisional Patent Application (PPA)).

Prior to discussing the ins and outs of foreign filing, it's important that you familiarize yourself with several important treaties and arrangements. As I'll explain in detail below, most countries are treaty members of the "Paris Convention," which gives you the full benefit of your filing date in your home country, provided you file in a foreign Convention country within one year (Section B, below). Also, most of the countries of Europe have joined the European Patent Convention, which has created a single patent office—the European Patent Office (EPO—Section D, below)—to grant European patents that are good in all member countries provided they're registered and translated in each country. Lastly, most industrialized countries are also members of the PCT—Patent Cooperation Treaty—which enables applicants to file a relatively economical international application in their home country within one year of their home-country filing date. The PCT gives applicants up to a 30-month delay and enables them to have a search, and optimally an examination, performed before making an expensive filing abroad (Section E). Let's discuss these areas in detail.

U.S. patent applications are published 18 months after the earliest claimed filing date, unless the applicant files a Nonpublication Request (NPR) at the time of filing, stating that the application will not be filed abroad. If you do file an NPR and then file abroad, you must revoke the NPR and notify the PTO of the foreign filing within 45 days (use PTO Form PTO/SB/36).

B. The Paris Convention and the One-Year Foreign Filing Rule

The most important thing to know about foreign filing is the International Convention for the Protection of Industrial Property. Most people in the patent field call it the "Paris Convention" or simply "the Convention." The majority of industrialized nations of the world are parties to this international treaty, which was entered into in Paris in 1883 and has been revised many times since. Generally, the Paris Convention governs almost all reciprocal patent filing rights.

For the purpose of this chapter, there's only one thing you need to know about the all-important Paris Convention: If you file a patent application (regular or PPA) in any one member jurisdiction of the Paris Convention (such as the U.S.), you can file a corresponding application in any other member jurisdiction (such as the U.K., Japan, the EPO, the PCT, Australia, etc.), within one year of your earliest filing date—six months for designs. Your application in each foreign jurisdiction will be entitled to the filing date of your U.S. application (regular or PPA) for purposes of overcoming prior art. ("Jurisdiction" refers to any country or group of countries that have joined under a treaty such as the EPO, PCT, or AIPO (the African Intellectual Property Organization).)

You do have to claim "priority" of your original application. If you fail to file any foreign applications under the Convention within the one-year period, you can still file after the one-year period in Convention jurisdictions, provided you haven't sold, published, or patented your invention yet. However, any such late application won't get the benefit of your original U.S. filing date, so any relevant prior art that has been published in the meantime can be applied against your applications. Put differently, once you miss the one-year deadline, your foreign application won't be entitled to the filing date of your original application. Rather, it becomes a non-Convention application, even in Convention countries. Also, once your U.S. application issues, it's too late to foreign file anywhere (unless you file within the one-year period)—that is, if you file a Convention application.

All jurisdictions that are members of the Paris Convention are indicated in Fig. 12A, where the most popular jurisdictions for foreign filing are indicated in boldface.

C. Other Priority Treaties Similar to the Paris Convention

There are three other priority treaties that operate similarly to the Paris Convention—that is, the member or signatory countries have reciprocal priority rights in each others' countries. For example, the U.S. has entered into treaties with the Republic of China (Taiwan), India, and Thailand, so that applicants who file a U.S. application can file corresponding applications in each of these countries within one year and obtain the benefit of their U.S. filing date, and vice versa. These treaties are indicated in Fig. 12A.

D. European Patent Office/Europäisches Patentamt/Office européen des brevets (EPO)

The European Patent Office (EPO) (www.european_patent _office.org) is a separate and vast trilingual patent office in Munich, across the Isar River from the famous Deutsches Museum. There is also a facility in The Hague, Netherlands. The EPO grew out of the earlier formation of the European Union (EU, formerly EEC), and the economic integration that resulted. Member nations of the EEC are also members of a treaty known as the European Patent Convention (EPC). Under the EPC you can make one patent filing in the EPO, whose main branch is at Ehrhardstrasse 27, D-8000, München 2, Germany. If this filing matures into a European patent, it will, when registered in whatever individual member countries you select, cover your invention in these selected countries. And since the EPC is, in turn, considered

the same as a single country (a jurisdiction) under the Paris Convention and the PCT, your effective EPO filing date will be the same as your original U.S. filing date, so long as you comply with the one-year foreign filing rule. In other words, filing in the EPO allows you to kill many birds with one stone.

Once your application is on file, the EPO will subject it to a rigorous examination, including an opposition publication 18 months after filing. (See Chapter 13.) Even though you'll have to work through a European agent, patent prosecution before the EPO is generally smoother than in the PTO, because the examiners are better trained (all speak and write three languages fluently) and because they actually take the initiative and suggest how to write your claims to get them allowed. If your application is allowed, you'll be granted a European patent that lasts for 20 years from your filing date (provided you pay maintenance fees in the member countries you've selected). Your patent will be valid automatically in each member country of the EPC that you've designated in your application, provided that you register it in and file translations in each country and appoint an agent there.

⚠ Filing in the EPO is extremely expensive for U.S. residents, and you'll have to pay an annuity to the EPO each year your application is on file there until it issues. Thereafter, you'll have to pay annuities in each member country in which you've registered your Europatent. Therefore, as I suggest in Section I, below, you should not file for a Europatent unless you're extremely confident your invention will be commercially successful there, or unless someone else, such as a European licensee, is paying the freight.

All member countries of the EPO are indicated in Fig. 12A. The member countries have agreed to establish a community patent for all of Europe by 2006.

E. The Patent Cooperation Treaty (PCT)

The PCT is another important treaty to which most industrial countries are a party. Under the Patent Cooperation Treaty (PCT), which was entered into in 1978, U.S. residents can file in the U.S. and then make a single international filing in the USPTO within the one-year period. This can cover all of the PCT jurisdictions, including the European Patent Office (EPO). Eventually, you must file separate or "national" applications in each PCT jurisdiction (including the EPO) where you desire coverage. These separate filings, which must be translated for non–English-speaking juris-

dictions, must be made for most countries within 30 months after your U.S. filing date.

If you file a PCT application, the USPTO will make a patentability search of your invention and will give you an indication of its patentability. If you want an actual examination of your invention to see what claims are allowable or rejected and to prosecute the application and revise claims, elect Chapter II of the PCT by 19 months after your U.S. filing date. Except for the single international filing, the PCT affords you a 30-month extension in which to file in most PCT countries or the EPO.

Also, you can file your first application under the PCT and then file in any PCT jurisdiction (including the U.S.) within 30 months from your PCT filing date. You should take this route if you've filed a PPA and you've decided to foreign file by one year after your PPA filing date. Further, since the PCT is a member of the Paris Convention, if you file with the PCT first, you can file in any non-PCT Convention jurisdiction within one year from your PCT filing date. As stated, after you file your PCT application, you'll receive a "search report" citing any pertinent references against your application. If you elect Chapter II of the PCT (optional) you'll receive an "examination report," which allows or rejects the claims of your application on the cited references. A list of PCT jurisdictions is indicated in Fig. 12A. All PCT jurisdictions are bound by Chapter I (searching part) and Chapter II (examination part). (Note that all PCT members are members of the Paris Convention, but not vice versa.)

The PCT is administered by the World Intellectual Property Organization (WIPO), www.wipo.int, whose main mailing address is listed in Section M.

F. Non-Convention Countries

There are several countries (generally nonindustrial) that aren't parties to any Convention. These are indicated in Fig. 12A.

Filing isn't common in most of these countries, but if you do want to file in any of them, you may do so at any time, provided:

a. Your invention hasn't yet become publicly known, either by your publication, by patenting, by public sale, or by normal publication, in the course of prosecution in a foreign jurisdiction (the PCT and the EPO publish 18 months after filing), and

b. You've been given a foreign-filing license on your U.S. filing receipt (see Section H, below) or six months has elapsed from your U.S. filing date.

I won't discuss filing in non-Convention countries in detail, except to note that if you do wish to file in any, you

Country or Jurisdiction	Paris Cnvn.	EPO	PCT	Pan Am Cnvn.
Albania	■		■	
Algeria	■		■	
Antigua & Barbuda	■		■	
Argentina	■			
ARIPO *	■		■	
Armenia°	■		■	
Australia	■		■	
Austria	■	■	■	
Azerbaijan°	■		■	
Bangladesh	■			
Barbados	■		■	
Belarus°	■		■	
Belgium	■	■		
Belize	■		■	
Bolivia	■			
Bosnia-Herzegovina	■		■	
Botswana	■		■	
Brazil	■		■	
Bulgaria	■	■	■	
Burundi	■			
Canada	■		■	
Chile	■			
China, Mainland[1]	■		■	
China, Taiwan△				
Colombia	■		■	
Congo	■			
Costa Rica	■		■	■
Comoros	■		■	
Côte d'Ivoire	■			
Croatia	■		■	
Cuba	■		■	
Cyprus	■	■	■	
Czech Republic	■	■	■	
Denmark	■	■	■	
Dominica	■		■	
Dominican Republic	■			
Ecuador	■		■	■
Egypt	■		■	
El Salvador	■			
Equatorial Guinea	■		■	
Estonia	■	■	■	
Ethiopia				
European Pat. Off.	■	■	■	
Finland	■	■	■	
France	■	■	■	■
Gambia	■		■	
Georgia	■			
Germany	■	■	■	
Ghana	■		■	
Greece	■	■	■	
Grenada	■			
Grenadines	■		■	
Guatemala	■			■
Guinea-Bissau	■			
Guyana	■			
Haiti	■			
Holy See	■			
Honduras	■			
Hungary	■		■	
Iceland	■		■	
India△	■		■	
Indonesia	■		■	
Iran	■			
Iraq	■			
Ireland	■	■	■	
Israel	■		■	
Italy	■	■	■	
Jamaica	■			
Japan	■		■	
Jordan	■			
Kazakhstan°	■		■	
Korea, North	■		■	

⚠ The PCT organization (WIPO) is a member of the Paris Convention.

* African Regional Industrial Property Organization: Ghana, Kenya, Malawi, Sudan, and Uganda.

° Also can be covered by Eurasian Patent from Eurasian Patent Office in Moscow.

[1] Includes Hong Kong

△ Separate priority treaties between United States and Taiwan, India, and Thailand.

† African Intellectual Property Organization: Common patent system for African countries: Benin, Burkina Faso, Cameroon, Central African Republic, Chad, Congo, Côte d'Ivoire, Gabon, Guinea, Mali, Mauritania, Niger, Senegal, and Togo.

Fig. 12A—Memberships in Patent Conventions

Country or Jurisdiction	Paris Cnvn.	EPO	PCT	Pan Am Cnvn.
Korea, South	■		■	
Kuwait				
Kyrgyzstan°	■		■	
Lao Dem. Rep.	■			
Latvia	■		■	
Lebanon	■			
Lesotho	■		■	
Liberia	■		■	
Libya	■			
Liechtenstein	■	■	■	
Lithuania	■		■	
Luxembourg	■	■	■	
Macedonia	■		■	
Madagascar	■		■	
Malaysia	■			
Malta	■			
Mauritania	■		■	
Mauritius	■			
Mexico	■		■	
Moldova, Republic of	■		■	
Monaco	■	■	■	
Mongolia	■		■	
Morocco	■		■	
Mozambique	■		■	
Namibia	■		■	
Netherlands	■	■	■	
New Zealand	■		■	
Nicaragua	■		■	■
Niger	■		■	
Nigeria	■			
Norway	■		■	
OAPI †	■		■	
Oman	■		■	
Pakistan				
Panama	■			
Papua New Guinea	■		■	
Paraguay	■			
Peru	■			
Philippines	■		■	
Poland	■		■	
Portugal	■	■	■	
Qatar	■			
Romania	■		■	
Russian Federation°	■		■	
Rwanda	■			
St. Kitts & Nevis	■			
Saint Lucia	■		■	
St. Vincent & Grenadines			■	
San Marino	■			
Seychelles	■		■	
Sierra Leone	■		■	
Singapore	■		■	
Slovak Republic	■	■	■	
Slovenia	■		■	
South Africa	■		■	
Spain	■	■	■	
Sri Lanka	■		■	
Sudan	■			
Suriname	■			
Swaziland	■		■	
Sweden	■	■	■	
Switzerland	■	■	■	
Syria	■		■	
Tajikistan°	■		■	
Tanzania	■		■	
Thailand△				
Togo	■		■	
Tonga	■			
Trinidad & Tobago	■		■	
Tunisia	■		■	
Turkey	■	■	■	
Turkmenistan°	■		■	
Ukraine	■		■	
United Arab Emirates	■			
United Kingdom	■	■	■	
United States	■		■	
Uruguay	■			
Uzbekistan	■		■	
Venezuela	■			
Vietnam	■		■	
Yugoslavia	■		■	
Zambia †	■			
Zimbabwe	■		■	

Fig. 12A—Memberships in Patent Conventions (cont'd)

should do so in exactly the same manner as you would for an individual filing in a Convention country (see Section K, below). However, you won't need a certified copy of your U.S. application since you won't be able to obtain priority (the benefit of your U.S. filing date).

G. Never Wait Until the End of Any Filing Period

As stated, you have one year after you file your U.S. application (PPA or RPA) to file foreign Convention patent applications (and be entitled to your U.S. filing date) in the PCT, the EPO, or any other jurisdiction that's a member of the Paris Convention. You also have 30 months after you file a U.S. application to file in the individual PCT countries, including the EPO, provided you filed a PCT application. You have one year, if you file under the PCT first, to file in non-PCT Convention countries or 20 months (30 months under Chapter II) to file in the PCT countries, respectively. However, you should never wait until the end of any of these periods. You should normally make your decision and start to take action about two or three months before the end of the period. This is to give you and the foreign agents time to prepare (or have prepared) the necessary correspondence and translations and to order a certified copy, if needed, of your U.S. application. So mark your calendar in advance accordingly. (While you shouldn't wait until the very end of the one-year period, you shouldn't file until near the end, since there's no advantage in filing early, unless you need an early patent—for example, because you have a foreign infringement.)

H. The Early Foreign Filing License or Mandatory Six-Month Delay

Normally, the official filing receipt that you get after filing your U.S. application (Chapter 13, Section A) gives you express permission from the PTO to file abroad. This permission usually will be printed on your filing receipt, as follows: "If required, Foreign Filing License Granted 12/14/2004." However, if your filing receipt fails to include a foreign filing license (only inventions with possible military applications won't include the license), you aren't allowed to foreign file on your invention until six months following your U.S. filing date. What's the reason for this? To give the U.S. government a chance to review your application for possible classification on national security grounds. You probably won't be af-

fected by any of this, as most applications get the foreign filing license immediately and, in any case, there is usually no good reason to file before six months after your U.S. filing. If your situation is different, however, and your filing receipt doesn't include a license, see a patent lawyer (Chapter 6, Section F). If your invention does have military applications, not only will you fail to get a foreign filing license on your filing receipt, but after you receive the receipt, you may receive a Secrecy Order from the PTO. This will order you to keep your invention secret until it's declassified, which often takes 12 years. Your patent can't issue till then, but the government may compensate you if they use your invention in the meantime. You can foreign file an application that is under a secrecy order, but it's complicated; see a patent lawyer who has experience in this area.

I. Don't File Abroad Unless Your Invention Has Very Good Prospects in Another Country

Because patent prosecution and practice in other countries is relatively complicated and extremely expensive, you should not file applications abroad unless:

- A significant market for products embodying the invention is *very* likely to exist, or
- *Significant* commercial production of your invention is *very* likely to occur, or
- You've already located a foreign licensee or there is someone else willing to pay for the foreign filing.

It's been my experience that far too many inventors file abroad because they're in love with their invention and feel it will capture the world. Unfortunately, this almost never happens. Almost all inventors who do file abroad never recoup their investment—that is, they usually waste tens of thousands of dollars in fees and hardly ever derive any royalties, let alone enough royalties to cover their costs. Thus, as a general rule, I suggest that you file in another country only if you feel that you're:

- very likely to sell at least $500,000 worth of products embodying your invention there, if you're selling it yourself, or
- very likely to earn at least $100,000 in royalties from sales of your invention there by others, or
- associated with a licensee or sales representative there who contracts to pay you royalties with a substantial advance or guarantee, or who will pay for your foreign filing in that country.

In addition to the high initial cost of foreign filing, you will have to pay substantial expenses to obtain foreign patents and maintenance fees each year to keep them in force.

Note that even if an infringement occurs in a country where you didn't file, it still is not worth paying for foreign filing there, unless the infringement is substantial enough to justify the expense of filing, getting the patent, paying the maintenance fees, and the uncertainties of licensing and litigation.

The U.S., with its approximately 300 million people, provides a huge marketplace that should be a more-than-adequate market from which to make your fortune, especially if it's your first invention. In comparison, most foreign countries are relatively insignificant. For example, Switzerland, Lebanon, and Israel are each smaller in size than San Bernardino County in California and smaller in population than Los Angeles County; Canada has fewer people than California. In other words, filing in the U.S. usually gives you ten to 50 times more bang for your buck than filing abroad, which costs ten to 50 times as much anyway.

J. The Patent Laws of Other Countries Are Different

Despite the Paris Convention and other treaties covering patent applications, and except for Canada, whose patent laws and practice are practically identical to ours, almost all countries have some differences from the U.S. in their substantive patent laws and practices. These differences have been reduced under the GATT treaty, but some that still exist are as follows:

- In the U.S., once an application is examined and allowed, the patent issues without any further proceedings. However, most foreign countries have an opposition proceeding under which the application is published and anyone who believes the invention isn't patentable can cite additional prior art to the patent office in order to block the patent.
- In the U.S. the patent must be applied for in the name of the actual inventor, but in most foreign countries any assignee (usually the inventor's employer-company) can apply in its own name.
- Many smaller countries (for example, Belgium and Portugal) don't conduct novelty examinations on applications that are filed there directly (not through the EPO), but instead simply issue a patent on every application filed and leave it up to the courts (in the event of an infringement) to determine whether the invention was novel and unobvious.
- Some jurisdictions (the EPO, France, Germany, Italy, Australia, the Netherlands) require the payment of

annual maintenance fees while the application is pending. But if you file in these countries (except Australia) through the EPO, no individual country fees are due until the European patent issues and is registered in each country. However, annual EPO fees are due until the Europatent issues.
- Most foreign countries don't have the one-year grace period the U.S. has. Thus you must get an effective filing date in most countries (either by actual filing there or by filing in the U.S. and then filing a corresponding Convention application there within one year) before publication of the invention. Most foreign countries consider any publication in any country as prior art, but some recognize only publications in their country as prior art. Some countries allow an exhibit at a recognized trade show, provided the application is filed within six months.
- Some countries such as Italy don't grant patents on drugs and some don't grant patents on computer programs or business methods.
- If two different applicants file respective patent applications on the same invention, virtually every country will award a patent to the first to file, a simple, economical, and easy-for-a-layperson system. However, the U.S. and the Philippines award the patent to the "first to invent," a system that requires an expensive, complicated, and lawyer-conducted trial proceeding called an interference (see Chapter 13).
- In Japan, the filing and translation fees are very high. Then, examination must be separately requested within seven years, requiring another stiff fee. After examination is requested, it takes about three years before the Japanese Patent Office, which is understaffed, gets around to it. Getting the application allowed is very difficult. However, it will be given more respect than in the U.S. That is, competitors will be far less likely to infringe or challenge it. Nevertheless, Japanese courts tend to interpret patents narrowly.

K. The Ways to File Abroad

Until several years ago, there was only one way to foreign file, namely, to file a separate application in each country in which you wished to file. As this was a cumbersome and expensive process, many of the countries got together to simplify things. Now there are five basic approaches to filing abroad in Convention countries. You may end up using different approaches for different countries, or the same approach for all. The chart below, Fig. 12B, summarizes these alternatives. The lettered routes in the explanation

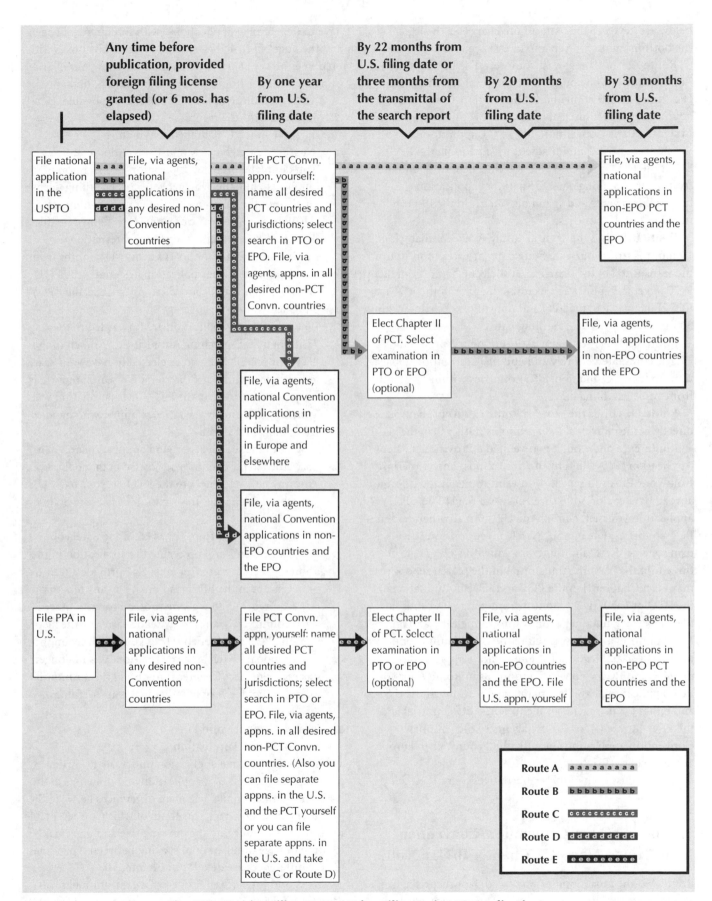

Fig. 12B—Foreign Filing Routes (After Filing Basic U.S. Application)

below are keyed to the paths in the chart (see the legend at the bottom right of the chart). In essence, the routes are:

Route A: This is the most common. File in U.S. Then file in non-Convention countries before publication or sale. (For more information about filing in non-Convention countries, see Section F, above.) Then, within one year, under the Paris Convention, file a PCT application to cover the PCT countries and jurisdictions (including the EPO). Select the PTO or EPO for the search. Then, by 30 months from your U.S. filing date, file national applications (you'll have to hire agents and spend big bucks) in the EPO and non-EPO PCT countries.

Route B: This is the same as Route A, except that within 19 months from your U.S. filing date, or three months from the transmittal of the search report, elect Chapter II of the PCT to get the application examined, either in the PTO or EPO. Finally, file in the EPO and non-EPO countries within 30 months from your U.S. filing date.

Route C: This is the same as Route A, except that the PCT is eliminated entirely and you file Convention applications in the EPO and non-EPO countries within 12 months from your U.S. filing date.

Route D: This is the same as Route C, except that you file directly in the individual EPO countries (rather than the EPO).

Route E: In addition, if you've filed a Provisional Patent Application (PPA), and by the time almost one year elapses from your PPA's filing date you want to file in the U.S. and abroad, you can do so in three basic ways: (1) File a PCT application yourself, naming the U.S. and all other desired PCT countries. File in non-PCT Convention countries using agents. By 22 months from your PPA filing date or three months from the transmittal of the search report, you may elect Chapter II of the PCT and select examination in the PTO or EPO. By 30 months from your PPA filing date, file, via agents, national applications in the EPO and non-EPO countries and file yourself in the U.S., claiming priority of your PCT application. (2) File separate applications in the U.S. and PCT yourself. Continue as in Route A for your PCT application. (3) File separate applications in the U.S. and either (a) use agents to file in non-EPO countries and the EPO (Route C), or (b) use agents to file national Convention applications in individual countries in Europe and elsewhere (Route D).

Let's discuss each of these alternatives in more detail.

1. Route A: Non-Convention/Convention (PCT and Non-PCT/Chapter II/National)

Route A is the most popular way to go. Not surprisingly, it's also the cheapest way to go in the short run, since you won't have to file national applications (with foreign patent agents and the huge expense they entail—indicated by boxes with bold lines on the chart) until 30 months from your U.S. filing date. Under Route A, you file in the U.S. first and then go abroad through the PCT, insofar as possible. Here's how it works for U.S. inventors:

- First file in the U.S. in the usual manner.
- Next file directly in any non-Convention countries you desire, before your application or invention is published, but after you get your foreign-filing license or six months has elapsed from your U.S. filing date.
- Then, before one year from your U.S. filing date, file a PCT request form and a separate "international application" with the USPTO within 12 months from your filing date. The application designates the PCT member countries or jurisdictions (such as the EPO) in which you desire coverage.
- The request and application are forwarded to the "International Searching Authority" (a branch of the PTO) or the EPO (if you've elected to have your search made there) where an "international search report" is prepared. If you select the PTO, the examination will generally be done by the same examiner who handles your U.S. application.
- Copies of the search report and application are then forwarded to the countries designated in the application. Cite any new references to the PTO on your basic U.S. case through another Information Disclosure Statement.
- Within 30 months from your U.S. filing date, you must hire agents and prosecute the application in the individual countries. You must also provide a translation (except in the EPO) and must pay any fees that are required. While separate prosecution is required in each country, it's commonly made easier by the fact that the PCT member countries generally rely on the international search and examination. It is no longer necessary to elect Chapter II to obtain the 30-month delay, except for certain individual country filings.

a. How to Prepare and File an International Application

To file an international application under the PCT, first prepare your original U.S. application and drawings in the A4 international format. The main differences between the PCT and U.S. national formats (both of which are acceptable for U.S. applications) are the drawing size and margins, location of page numbers, and spacing between typed lines. (These differences are detailed in Chapter 10.)

The World Intellectual Property Organization has software ("PCT-Easy") that enables you to pay reduced fees and automates the process of completing the PCT filing forms. Download it from http://pcteasy.wipo.int/en/index.html.

If you want to fill in paper A4 forms, obtain and complete a multipage "Request" (Form PCT/RO/101) and transmittal letter (Form PTO 1382) from the PTO's website (www.uspto.gov). Click Patents, then click PCT. The form can also be obtained from Box PCT, Commissioner for Patents, Washington, DC 20231, Tel. 703-305-3257 (Fax 703-305-3230). Ask for the latest fees when you call, or you can find these in the last *Official Gazette* on the PTO's website. Complete the forms (full instructions and examples are attached), requesting the PTO to prepare a certified copy of your U.S. application for use with your PCT application, and attach a copy of your application in PCT (A4) format (with drawings) and a CCPF or check payable to the Commissioner for Patents for the international application filing fees as computed on the Fee Calculation Sheet—the last page of the Request form.

b. PCT Fees

The fee for a certified copy of your U.S. application is listed in Appendix 4, Fee Schedule. The PCT fees frequently vary due to exchange rate fluctuations. They're composed of several parts as follows:

- Transmittal Fee
- Search Fee: (a) if you haven't already filed in the U.S. (that is, you filed your first application in the PCT, rather than the U.S.—very rare—see Section 6, below); (b) if you've already filed in the U.S. (the usual case); and (c) if you want to use the EPO as your searching authority (recommended)
- International Fee (Country designation fees are no longer required since all possible countries are automatically designated.)

A common course of action is to designate the EPO and Japan with an EPO search. You should designate the EPO as your searching authority if you intend to file there since they generally do a better search than the USPTO and you'll save money and time in the EPO later. But be warned: Sometimes the EPO does such a good search that you might have to abandon both your U.S. and EPO applications. If any foreign patent office cites a new reference against your application, be sure to cite it in your U.S. application by filing it with a supplemental IDS and PTO-1449. (See Chapter 10, Section N.)

As of 2004 Feb 12, applicants can file a PCT application online at the International Bureau (WIPO) in Geneva (rather than the USPTO). Full instructions and software are at www.wipo.int/pct-safe.

c. How to File PCT and Non-PCT Convention Applications

To file the PCT application, mail the Transmittal Letter, Request, copy of your application and drawings (both on A4 size), and CCPF or check to: Mail Stop PCT, Commissioner for Patents, P.O. Box 1450, Alexandria, VA 22313-1450, which, as mentioned, is a designated receiving office for the International Bureau. Like Convention applications, the international (PCT) application should be filed within one year of your U.S. filing date, also known as the priority date.

I advise filing the PCT application at least a month before the anniversary of your U.S. filing date, so you'll have time to correct any serious deficiencies. But you can mail the PCT application as late as the last day of the one-year period from your U.S. filing date if you use Express Mail and complete the Express Mail Certification on page 1 of the Transmittal Letter. (Never use a plain Certificate of Mailing (see Chapter 13, Section H) for any PCT correspondence.)

To file any non-PCT Convention applications, use a foreign patent agent in each country you select to prepare an appropriate application. The easiest way to do this is to send the agent a copy of your U.S. application and ask what else is needed. The requirements vary from country to country, but special drawings in each country's format will always be needed. You can have your foreign agent prepare these, or you can have these prepared yourself at lesser cost by the same companies that make drawings for U.S. divisional applications. (See discussion of "Divisional Applications" in Chapter 14, Section D.) Also, the agent will send you a power of attorney form that you'll have to sign and sometimes get notarized, certified by your county clerk, and legalized by the consulate of the country to which the form is being sent. Also you'll generally need a certified copy of your U.S. application; this can be obtained from the PTO. (See Appendix 4, Fee Schedule.) The cost for filing a foreign application in each individual country is about $1,000 to $5,000, depending on the country, the length of your application, and whether a translation is required.

If you wish to correspond directly with the foreign patent agents yourself, you'll first have to get the name of a patent agent in each country. See Section M, below.

d. What Happens to Your International Application?

You'll receive a filing receipt and separate serial number for your international application, and the application will eventually be transmitted for filing to the countries (including the EPO) you've designated on your request form. If you make any minor errors in your PCT application, the PCT Department of the USPTO will give you a month to correct them.

e. Search Report

When you receive your PCT search report (either from the PTO or EPO), you can comment on it and amend your claims if necessary, but no extended prosecution or negotiation is permitted.

⚠ If the search report cites any new references, be sure to cite these to the PTO by way of a supplemental IDS; see Chapter 10, Section N, and Chapter 13, Section A4.

f. National Stage

Within 30 months from your U.S. filing date, whether or not you elect Chapter II, you must hire an agent in Europe (get one in London or Munich) and file an EPO application based on your PCT application. Also, you must have an agent in each non-EPO PCT country (such as Japan or Australia) in which you wish to file and get national applications on file in these countries. Expect to pay very stiff fees.

As mentioned, each of the separate countries and the EPO will rely to a great extent on the international examination they'll receive from the International Bureau. (In most cases this will be the EPO search or an adoption of the U.S. search.) Thus, one advantage of the PCT approach is that you'll save much of what used to be the agonizing, extremely expensive job of separately and fully prosecuting an application in each country in which you elected to file.

2. Route B: Elect Chapter II of PCT If You Want an International Examination

Route B is the same as Route A, except that instead you elect Chapter II of the PCT before filing your national applications. You have, as indicated, 22 months from your U.S. filing date or three months from the transmittal of the search report, to do this.

Get the forms (PCT/IPEA/401) from the PTO's site or the PCT department of the PTO, and also get the latest fees for Chapter II. If you select the EPO to do the examination, you must file the papers with the EPO in Munich (address in Section D, above) and pay the fee in Deutschmarks. You'll get an examination report where claims will actually be allowed or rejected. You can amend your application once and even interview your examiner.

You file your EPO and non-EPO applications in the same way you did under Route A—that is, you elect agents, send them copies of all of your papers, and tell them you want to file national applications in their countries based upon your U.S. and PCT applications. Route B will cost more than Route A since you incur the expense of Chapter II of the PCT.

3. Route C: Convention Applications in EPO and Non-EPO Countries

Under Route C, you bypass the PCT entirely and file, through agents, national convention applications in the EPO and non-EPO countries within 12 months of your U.S. filing date. This is the cheapest way to go in the long run if you wish to file in several European countries. An EPO filing, while expensive, is generally considered cheaper than separate filings if:

a. Two or more non–English-speaking countries are involved (for example, it's cheaper to file in the EPO than to file separate applications in France and Germany), or

b. The U.K. and more than one non-English country is involved. Conversely, it's cheaper to file separate applications in the U.K. and Germany, for instance, than to go through the EPO.

As mentioned, to file a Convention application in the EPO you'll have to go through a European patent agent, unless you have an address in one of the EPO countries, in which case you can do it yourself. Correspondence with the EPO must be in English if your application is based on your U.S. case.

Including the agent's fee, expect to spend a stiff fee to get your application on file and examined in about six countries. (See Appendix 4, Fee Schedule.) Additional large fees will be incurred for prosecution (getting your application approved once it's filed) and issuance. Then you'll have to arrange to get translations and individual agents for the respective countries you designate. For more information, write to the EPO for a copy of *How to Get a European Patent* (address in Section D, above).

4. Route D: Convention Applications in Individual Countries

Here you bypass both the PCT and the EPO. It's not a wise idea to bypass the EPO unless you want to file in just two countries in Europe—in which case it's usually cheaper to make individual filings rather than go through the EPO. This is the simplest way to go, on the charts, although it can get very complex and involve a lot of parallel correspondence and paperwork, since you'll have to make simultaneous prosecutions in each country. Filing is effected by sending a certified copy of your U.S. application to a patent agent in each country and instructing the agent to file a Convention application based upon your U.S. application. The agent will tell you what else is needed.

5. Route E: PPA Filed

If you've filed a PPA (see Chapter 3), your choices and procedures are the same as Routes A to D, except that at each stage there's another national country in which you can file: the U.S.A. If you've filed a PPA, I recommend you file in the U.S., separately, by one year after you file your PPA, because it's simpler and somewhat cheaper. However, if you want to delay your U.S. filing, you can name the U.S. in your PCT application when you file your PCT application within one year after your PPA's filing date. You can then file your U.S. national application by 30 months after your PPA date. Your U.S. application should be identical to a "regular" U.S. application, except that you should add the following sentence to the PAD (Form 10-2) to get the benefit of your PCT filing date: "I hereby claim foreign priority benefits under 35 USC 119 of PCT patent application, Ser. No. _____, Filed 200___; which in turn claims priority of provisional patent application Ser. Nr. _____ filed _____."

6. File the PCT Application First

Although not listed on the chart because it's not a very popular method, if you haven't filed a PPA you can file a PCT application first (before you file anything) and then file in the U.S. and PCT countries (including the EPO) through the PCT. File in the non-PCT Convention countries through the Convention.

If you haven't filed a PPA and you know for certain, before you file anywhere, that you'll want to file in the U.S. and at least one foreign PCT country, then you can save some fees and effort by filing the PCT application first, before you file in the U.S. In your PCT application you must designate the U.S. and any foreign PCT countries (including the EPO) you desire. Then, within one year of your PCT filing date, you should file Convention applications, based upon your PCT application, in any non-PCT country.

Within 30 months of your PCT filing date, file separately (changing priority of your PCT application) in each country or jurisdiction you've designated in your PCT application, including the U.S. and the EPO. Then order (from the PTO) a certified copy of your PCT application and file this within a few months after your U.S. filing date.

Whether you're filing in a PCT or non-PCT jurisdiction based upon a PCT filing, your foreign patent agents will tell you what you'll need to file PCT-based applications in their countries; allow at least two months before the 20- or 30-month deadline to give them (and you) time to prepare the applications and translations, if necessary.

L. Rescind Any Nonpublication Request

When you filed your U.S. application, you had the opportunity to file a Nonpublication Request (NPR) (see Form 10-7). If you filed an NPR, you must file a rescission of this Request with the PTO within 45 days of filing your foreign application. You must file the rescission regardless of whether you are filing directly in a foreign country or using a PCT application. If you do not file the rescission, the PTO will strike your U.S. application.

To make the rescission, complete and file Form PTO/SB/36, available on the PTO's website. If you don't have Internet access, you can use Form 13-1, but title it "Request to Rescind Previous Nonpublication Request." Remove the sentence stating "In response to Office Letter …" and substitute the following statement: "Applicant has foreign filed the above application on or about [date] and therefore hereby rescinds the previously filed Nonpublication Request under 35 USC 122(b)." Remember to complete or include a Certificate of Mailing at the end of the rescission as in Form 13-2. (If you forget to rescind the NPR within 45 days of your foreign filing your application is technically abandoned but you may revive it by a petition under Rule 136(6), accompanied by a stiff fee.)

After notification, the PTO will schedule publication of your application 18 months after your U.S. filing date (or as soon as possible after the 18-month period). You will have to pay a fee for publication when you pay your issue fee.

M. Resources to Assist in Foreign Filing

There are a number of resources to assist you in foreign filing your patent application. Let's look at them separately.

1. Foreign Patent Agents

As I've mentioned, if you desire to file abroad you'll almost certainly need to find a foreign patent agent who's familiar with patent prosecution in the countries where you desire protection. (In most countries, patent professionals are called "agents" rather than attorneys. As in the U.S., foreign agents are licensed to represent clients before their patent office, but not their courts.) Your best bet is to find one through a U.S. patent attorney (see Chapter 6, Section F), as most are associated with one or more patent agents in other major countries.

If you don't know a U.S. patent attorney or someone who's familiar with foreign patent agents, there are several other ways to obtain the names.

One is to look in the telephone directory of the city where the patent office of the foreign country is located. Most large libraries have foreign telephone directories.

Another simple way is to inquire at the consulate of the country; most foreign countries have consulates in major U.S. cities and these should have a list of patent agents.

A third way is to use the Internet, for example, by entering "patent agent [name of country]" in a search engine.

A fourth possibility is to look in the *Martindale-Hubbell Law Directory* (in any law library or at www.martindale.com), which lists some foreign patent agents in each country.

A fifth possibility is to hire a local patent attorney to do the work for you, although this involves an intermediary's costs. Because of the complicated nature of foreign filing, many patent attorneys even use their own intermediaries, namely, specialized patent-law firms in New York, Chicago, or Los Angeles, which handle foreign filing exclusively.

A sixth possibility is to hire a British firm of patent agents to do all your foreign filing. The reason for this is that they speak fairly good English and they're familiar with foreign filing. This would be especially appropriate if you're filing with the EPO, but most German agents in Munich, although not as fluent in English, have the compensating advantage of their physical proximity to the EPO.

Whichever way you find your foreign patent agent, be careful, since many foreign agents are bound by a minimum fee schedule, which is sometimes exorbitant. Also, keep in mind that some foreign patent agents—like their U.S. counterparts—are incompetent or inclined to overcharge.

2. Written Materials

As you've gathered by now, filing abroad can become very complicated. If you want to learn more, and get the latest information (if the print date of this book is old), including the laws of each country, see *Patents Throughout the World*, by Greene (Clark Boardman). This book is revised annually, so be sure you have the most recent version. Also, you can call the consulate of any country to get information on their patent laws. For more information on how to utilize the PCT, "The PCT Applicant's Guide," "Basic Facts," and other instructive materials and forms are available online at http://www.wipo.int and from the PCT Department of the USPTO. The World Intellectual Property Organization (Post Office Box 18, 1211 Geneva 20, Switzerland) administers the PCT. (For more information on the EPO, see Section D, above.)

Bonne chance et au revoir!

N. Summary

A U.S. patent only provides a monopoly in the United States, so it is necessary to file for corresponding foreign patents in any other countries in which you want offensive rights. Foreign filing is very expensive and few inventors who foreign file ever recoup their investment, so an inventor should foreign file the application in a country only if the invention has extremely strong commercial potential there.

Various conventions govern foreign filing. The Paris Convention grants anyone who files a basic application in any member country the benefit of the basic filing date in any other country where a corresponding application is filed within one year.

The European Patent Office enables one to file a single patent application and get a European patent that is valid in any European country, provided the Europatent is registered in and translated for each country.

The Patent Cooperation Treaty (PCT) enables a U.S.-resident inventor who has filed a patent application in the PTO to file a PCT application in the USPTO within one year and have it searched and examined to determine patentability and delay filing of national stage applications in foreign jurisdictions for 30 months from the U.S. filing date.

Other countries, such as the Republic of China and Thailand, have individual treaties with the U.S. that work similarly to the Paris Convention.

An inventor who files a U.S. application must wait six months before foreign filing, unless the PTO grants a foreign filing license, which it usually grants on the filing receipt. The laws of other countries are different from the U.S. in certain respects—for example, some countries have no interferences, no one-year grace period, and no patents on drugs. Some countries have maintenance fees during pendency, hold opposition proceedings, and companies can apply for patents in the name of the company or an assignee.

There are several routes for filing abroad, but most inventors file in the U.S. first, then file a PCT application within a year, then file national-stage applications within 30 months of the U.S. filing date. An inventor can file a PCT application in the USPTO by completing the PCT forms and filing an A4 copy of the application with the appropriate fees.

If an inventor files a U.S. application with a Nonpublication Request, the inventor must revoke this within 45 days of any foreign filing. It is necessary to hire a foreign patent agent in any jurisdiction where a national-stage application is to be filed. ■

Chapter 13

Getting the PTO to Deliver

Inventor's Commandment #22

Never admit or state anything negative about your invention on the record (in writing), since anything negative you admit will be used against you later by an adversary.

Inventor's Commandment #23

Whenever you have a patent application pending, you must be available to receive Office Actions (letters) from the PTO and you must respond to every OA within the time it allots, since your application will go abandoned if you don't file a timely response.

Inventor's Commandment #24

You may never add any "new matter" (technical information not in the application as filed) to any patent application.

Inventor's Commandment #25

In order to answer properly an Office Action from the PTO, you must respond to each and every point (objection or rejection) in the OA, either by suitable argument or by complying as required.

Inventor's Commandment #26

When drafting an amendment in response to the first Office Action, do your very best job. Include a complete response, all available arguments for patentability, and the narrowest and most comprehensive claims possible, since the next OA will almost certainly be made final, foreclosing any future substantive changes unless you pay another filing fee.

You can file a lawsuit against anyone for anything. Whether you can prove your case and win is, of course, a very different matter.

Similarly, anyone can file a patent application on anything. But getting the Patent and Trademark Office (PTO) to issue you a patent is, of course, a very different matter.

This chapter tells you how to get the PTO to deliver, assuming your invention meets the standards of patentability (Chapter 5). This material is sure to seem confusing the first time you read it. A little familiarity with the process, however, should do a world of good when it comes to your understanding. Sections A to N of this chapter apply to utility patent application except as noted in the design prosecution section (Section P).

A. What Happens After Your Patent Application Is Filed

It will be helpful to review exactly what will occur after your patent application is filed.

1. Receipt Postcard

After sending your patent application to the PTO, you'll receive your receipt postcard back in about two to four weeks. It will have a bar code sticker with a date and an eight-digit number—for example, "U.S. Patent & TM Office, 22 August 2000; 09/801,666." The date is the "deposit" date (date of receipt), and the number is the serial number (sometimes called "application number") of your application. As stated in Chapter 11, Section G, you should keep your serial number and filing date confidential unless a prospective manufacturer has shown serious interest and asks for this information—for example, because you're about to enter into a license or sale agreement.

2. Official Filing Receipt

About one to three months later (if you followed my instructions in Chapter 10) you should receive an official filing receipt. This is a sheet containing the following:
- the name(s) of the inventor(s)
- the title of your patent application
- the examining group to which your application has been assigned
- the filing date and serial number of your application
- the number of claims (total and independent)

- the filing fee you paid
- your name and address
- the words "Small Entity" if you filed as a small entity, and
- the words "Foreign Filing License Granted [date]" if the invention hasn't been militarily classified (most won't be).

Check all of this information carefully; it's what's entered into the PTO's data-processing system about your application. If the filing receipt has any errors, indicate the error on the filing receipt and send a copy or fax it to the Office of the Initial Patent Examination (OIPE) whose numbers will be on the filing receipt—but, if not, see the number in Appendix 5, Mail, Telephone, Fax, and Email Communications With the PTO. Request a new filing receipt.

Assuming you've done everything properly—as explained in Chapter 10—your patent application is technically pending once you receive your Express Mail receipt from the Post Office clerk. However, the actual filing receipt makes it official and shows that it's actually recorded in the PTO.

You may continue to label your invention and any descriptive literature "Patent Pending," or "Patent Applied For." They have the same meaning. Note that it's a criminal offense to use the words "patent applied for" or "patent pending" in any advertising when there's no active, applicable regular or provisional patent application on file.

If for any reason you didn't comply with an item on the checklist in Chapter 10, so that your application hasn't been filed properly (for example, your check bounced, you didn't pay enough for the filing fee, or you forgot to sign the PAD (Form 10-1)), you won't get the filing receipt. Instead, the Application Branch of the PTO will send you a deficiency notice telling you what's needed and what surcharge (fine) you'll have to pay for the error of your ways. Once you comply with the deficiency notice (they usually give you a month), you'll get your filing receipt a few weeks later.

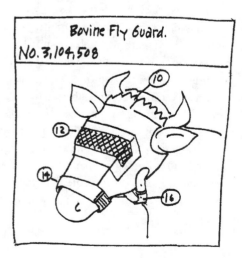

> ## If You Receive a Foreign Filing License
>
> The words "Foreign Filing License Granted" on your filing receipt mean that you can foreign file at any time, rather than waiting six months. However, you still should wait until approximately nine months have passed before considering filing abroad in Convention countries. This will allow time for you to receive a possible Office Action, so you'll have better information about patentability and to accumulate additional commercial information on your invention. You should file abroad in non-Convention countries before you sell or publish details of the invention.

3. Patent Pending Status

The patent pending period begins when your regular patent application or provisional patent application is filed and lasts until the patent issues. During the patent pending period, your rights depend upon whether you have filed a Nonpublication Request (NPR). If you have not filed an NPR, the PTO will publish your regular patent application 18 months after the filing date. Once it is published, you obtain provisional rights that allow you to obtain royalties from an infringer for activities that occurred from the date the infringer gets actual notice of the published application. (You can provide actual notice to the infringer by sending a copy of the published application by certified mail, return receipt requested.) You must wait until after the patent issues to request these "patent pending" royalties. If the patent does not issue, you cannot obtain any royalties.

If, at the time of filing your application, you filed an NPR, your application will not be published prior to issuance and you will have no offensive rights during the patent pending period. In other words, if it is not published prior to issuance, anyone can freely make, use, sell, and offer your invention for sale during the entire pendency period.

In general, a potential infringer won't copy a device that it knows is patent pending. This is because the infringer would have to take the chance that a patent will later be issued and you'll use your patent to enforce your monopoly—that is, stop any further production and marketing. In this case, the money the infringer would have to spend on expensive tooling will have been wasted. (If you're willing to license the infringer under your patent, the infringer's tooling outlay will be worthwhile, but few infringers will be willing to take this chance.) Another reason for marking a device "patent pending" is to show that you have given notice to potential infringers, thereby giving you the right to obtain treble damages and attorney fees (after your patent issues) for willful infringement.

After your application is filed, you may publish articles on your invention without loss of any legal rights in the U.S. or foreign Convention countries (see Chapter 12), but you'll lose rights in non-Convention countries (Chapter 12). However, it's not desirable to reveal details of your invention to potential competitors at this early stage, especially since your application may not become a patent.

4. Send in Your Information Disclosure Statement (IDS)

If you haven't done so already, after receiving your official filing receipt send in your Information Disclosure Statement as discussed in Chapter 10, Section N, together with a PTO/SB/08 form and copies of any non-U.S. patent references you listed on the form. Remember that the PTO wants the IDS to be filed within three months of the application's filing date. Don't forget to print your serial number and filing date on the forms.

If you don't file the IDS within three months of your filing date, or before your first Office Action, or within three months after entry into the "national" stage for references cited in foreign applications, the PTO will still consider it. However, you must file it *before* a final action or a notice of allowance is sent, and (1) pay a "Late IDS Fee" (see Appendix 4, Fee Schedule), or (2) include a certificate as follows:

"Each item of information contained in this Information Disclosure Statement (IDS) was cited in a communication from a foreign patent office in a counterpart foreign patent application not more than three months prior to the filing of such IDS, or no item of information contained in this IDS was cited in a communication from a foreign patent office in a counterpart foreign patent application, or, to my knowledge after making reasonable inquiry, was known to any individual designated in 37 CFR 1.56(c) (inventor, attorney, assignee, etc.) more than three months prior to the filing of such IDS."

You can even file the IDS after a final action or notice of allowance is sent, but before you pay the issue fee. However, you *must* include the above certificate, a petition requesting consideration of the IDS, and a petition fee—see Fee Schedule.

If you send in an IDS and later discover any additional references—for example, in the course of foreign prosecution —you must bring these to the attention of the PTO through a supplemental IDS. (Don't send an IDS for any references the examiner cites in your U.S. case; these will automatically be listed, along with those which you cited, on the patent.)

5. First Office Action

About six months to two years after the filing date (patent prosecution is mostly a waiting game) you'll receive a communication from the PTO known as a "first Office Action" (OA), sometimes called an "official letter." It consists of forms and a letter from the examiner in charge of your application, describing what is wrong with your application and why it cannot yet be allowed. (Rarely will an application be allowed in the first OA.)

Specifically, the OA may:
- reject claims
- list defects in the specification and/or drawings
- cite and enclose copies of prior art that the examiner believes shows your invention is either:
  (a) not novel, or
  (b) obvious, and/or
- raise various other objections.

The PTO no longer sends U.S. patent references with OAs. You must download the patent references from the Internet or send for them by mail. The PTO has a batch downloading procedure under its PAIR system.

To find out approximately when you'll receive the first OA from the PTO, you can call the clerk of the examining group where your application has been assigned. The name of this group will be typed on your filing receipt. PTO phone numbers change, but are listed on the PTO website, in Appendix 5, and are published irregularly in the *Official Gazette* (OG). Each issue of the OG also gives date status information for patent applications in each examining group. Also, you can call the PTO's main number (see Appendix 5, Mail, Telephone, Fax, and Email Communications With the PTO) to find the telephone number of your group.

6. Response to First Office Action

Every OA itself will specify an interval, usually three months (extendable, for a fee, up to six months) from the date the OA was mailed, within which you must file a response. Your response must take whatever action is necessary to overcome the objections and rejections listed in the OA. The response you file is technically called an "amendment" (assuming it contains any changes), or a "response" (assuming it doesn't contain any changes). The entire process of correspondence (Office Actions and amendments) to and from the PTO is known as "patent application prosecution," although no one is "prosecuted" in the usual sense. I show you how to draft your response in Section F, below.

7. Second/Final Office Action

About two to six months after you file your first amendment, you'll receive a second OA from the PTO; this will usually be designated a "final" OA by the PTO. A final OA is supposed to end the prosecution stage before the examiner. However, as we'll see later, this is far from true. In other words, a "final action" is rarely final. Again, you have three months to reply.

8. Notice of Allowance

Assuming you submit what is necessary to get your application in condition for allowance, you'll be sent a Notice of Allowance, indicating that all of your claims are allowed and that an issue fee (and publication fee if the application was published) is due within three months. (Sometimes you'll get a "Notice of Allowability" before or with the formal allowance; this merely states that your claims are all allowed, the Notice of Allowance will be sent, and whether formal drawings are due.)

9. Issue Fee and Issue Notification

Several months after you pay the issue fee (see Appendix 4, Fee Schedule) and file formal drawings (if you didn't do so before), you'll receive an Issue Notification from the PTO, indicating the forthcoming issue date and number of your patent.

10. Receipt of Official Patent Deed

Shortly after the date your patent issues, you'll receive your official "Letters Patent" or deed from the PTO. Any printed copies of the patent that you've ordered will arrive in a separate envelope.

B. General Considerations During Patent Prosecution

Patent application prosecution is generally more difficult than the preparation of the initial application. Assuming that you're going to handle the prosecution phase pretty much on your own, I recommend that you keep the following general considerations in mind.

1. The PTO Can Write Claims for You

As I mentioned in Chapter 9 (claims drafting), you can ask the PTO to write one or more claims for you if you wish. Then you can either accept this claim or amend it if you think you can get it past the examiner. You should generally have several sets of varied claims (one independent and several dependent per set) to cover your invention fully.

2. Consultation With a Patent Professional Might Be Wise

You might wish to consult with a patent expert at this point of the proceedings. Paying $200–$1,000 (if you use a "discount" patent attorney—see Chapter 6) to have an expert amend your claims and argument (which is usually what's required) may prove to be relatively cheap in the long run if you can afford the expense now. As you review the following, often dense, material, remember that expert outside help is available.

3. Intervals Are Approximate

Except for official periods, such as the three-month period for response to an OA or to pay the issue fee, the dates and times I've given in this chapter are only approximate and are gleaned from recent experience. They can vary quite widely, depending on conditions in the PTO at the time you file your patent application. You have to be patient. If you don't receive any communication from the PTO for a long time, say over a year after you file your application, you should check the latest *Official Gazette* for the status of the cases in your group. Also, if it's over six months after you file an amendment, you should make a call, or send a letter, to the examiner or examining group to determine the status of your case. (If you are willing to submit a lot of paperwork, install software, and so forth, you can access the PTO's "Private PAIR" system, which enables you to see a docket sheet and all of the papers for your patent application on the PTO's website. The amount or work involved to get on Private PAIR probably isn't justified unless you have several applications on file. To get on Private PAIR, see the instructions in Chapter 10, Section I, or in Section D, below.)

4. You'll Be Able to Correct Technical Errors

Don't worry too much about minor technical errors (except for dates—see next consideration) when dealing with the

PTO. If you make one, you'll be given an opportunity to correct it. The PTO has so many rules and regulations that even patent attorneys who deal with them all the time can't remember them all. Also, the PTO is flexible in giving do-it-yourself (pro se) applicants opportunities to correct nondate errors that don't affect the substance of the application.

5. Dates Are Crucial

Every OA that you receive from the PTO will specify an interval by which you must reply to the OA. If you fail to reply in the time the PTO allots you, the penalty is draconian: your application will go abandoned, although it can be revived at a price. (See Section Q, below.) Thus, you should write the due date for response to every OA promptly on the OA and on your calendar and heed it carefully. If you're not the type who can faithfully heed due dates, you must do something about this—for example, by hiring a methodical friend to bug you. You can even turn the whole job of prosecution over to a patent attorney. If you miss a crucial date, you'll find that the PTO is a cruel and unforgiving bureaucracy. However, as stated, you can usually pay to revive applications that go abandoned for lateness in responding—see Section Q.

6. Situations Not Covered

If any situation occurs that isn't covered in this book, and you can't find the answer by looking in the *Rules of Practice* or *Manual of Patent Examining Procedure* (see Section 10, below, for how to obtain these), call the PTO, consult an attorney or agent, or use common sense and do what you would expect to be the logical thing to do in such a situation.

Newly Discovered Reference: For example, suppose that after you've filed your patent application you find a prior-art reference that considerably narrows what you thought your invention to be. You should bring this to the attention of the PTO by way of another (supplemental) IDS and PTO/SB/08, and submit an amendment substituting narrower claims that avoid the reference. Remember that you have a continuing duty to disclose all material information about your invention to the PTO.

Embodiment Changes: If you discover that an embodiment of your invention doesn't work, delete it from your application. (See Section E, below, for how to do this.) If you discover a new embodiment of your invention that supersedes the present embodiments, file a continuation-in-part application. (See Chapter 14.)

Small Entity Changes: If you license or assign your application to a large entity (or such a license is terminated

or your application is reassigned back to you), you should send a letter to the PTO asking that your small-entity status be canceled (or send in a letter to establish SE status).

Change of Address: If you change your address, you should send a change of address form (use Form PTO/SB/81 on the PTO's site) or an appropriate letter (caption as in Form 13-1 but headed "Change of Applicant's Address") to the PTO.

PTO Mistakes: If the examiner cites a prior-art reference against your application that is later than your filing date, obviously the examiner made an error (this happens occasionally). You should call or write to bring it to the examiner's attention so that a new Office Action can be issued. If the PTO fails to send you a copy of a non–U.S. patent reference that it has cited against you, send an appropriate paper (captioned as in Form 13-1) headed "Request for Copy of Missing Reference" to the PTO. If a part of the OA doesn't make sense, or a part seems to have been omitted, send an immediate "Request for Clarification of Office Action."

Finally, as a wise person said, "Don't be afraid to ask dumb questions: they're easier to handle than dumb mistakes."

Bureaucratic Static: The examiner may object to something in your application if it's unusual or irregular, even if it's otherwise proper and harmless. This is the result of bureaucratic attitudes—that is, examiners like others in government sometimes have a tendency to rigidly enforce a "standard" administrative procedure. The remedy is to explain to the examiner that what you have done is proper and to respectfully challenge the examiner to provide a specific reason for the objection and a suggestion for correction. The next paragraph shows how I responded to an examiner who objected when I typed "stateless" in the citizenship blank of the declaration form, even though the applicant was stateless; the examiner did not repeat the objection again.

"The Objection to the Declaration: The Office Action objected to the Declaration since it listed the citizenship of the applicant as "stateless." The Examiner required a new declaration. Applicant does not understand this objection, the legal basis therefor, or what remedial action the Examiner would like on any new declaration. Applicant's citizenship is indeed "stateless." In the past, applicant's representative has filed other patent applications for various stateless individuals. He always listed their citizenship as "stateless" and all of these cases went on to patent without ever before encountering any objection. Therefore applicant respectfully submits that the "stateless" entry is proper.

• Applicant is willing to file a new declaration if the Examiner still desires, but he doesn't know what the

Examiner would like applicant to enter in the Citizenship blank in lieu of "stateless." If the Examiner continues the objection, applicant respectfully requests that the Examiner explain what specifically he objects to about the "stateless" entry, the legal basis for the objection, and exactly what replacement entry Examiner would like in any new declaration. Thereupon applicant will be pleased and eager to comply. Note that applicant cannot enter any specific country in the Citizenship blank since he is not a citizen of any country."

7. Standards of Patentability Vary Widely

While I've tried to give the proper standards of patentability in this book (see Chapter 5), what actually happens when your application is examined will vary, depending upon the personality, whims, training, and current emotions of the examiner assigned to handle it. Most examiners adhere to the basic standards of patentability outlined here and are competent, knowledgeable, and occasionally helpful when it comes to telling you what to do to put the case in condition for allowance. Unfortunately, some examiners are very new and inexperienced, new to the U.S. and unfamiliar with English, incompetent or superficial, mean and vindictive, lacking sufficient mental capacity to comprehend a true advance in the art, ignorant in the field or art being examined, or lacking in the requisite sensitivity to appreciate the huge financial and work burdens their acts might impose on applicants. This can sometimes lead them to make arbitrary, irrational rulings and deny patents that should be granted or vice versa. Services have deteriorated everywhere in recent years, but especially in the PTO.

The solution to the problem with an unreasonably tough or inexperienced examiner is to, first, be persistent. Go to the PTO (or hire a patent attorney to go) to interview your examiner. If necessary, appeal. Appealing is a powerful weapon against a tough examiner. Examiners don't like to write answers to appeal briefs since these take a lot of time. Also, they usually must have an appeal conference with two other examiners, and it looks bad on their record if they get reversed.

The problem with an easy examiner is that your allowed application might not stand up in court (should this ever become necessary). Accordingly, if you believe that your examiner is not rigorous enough (for instance, all your claims are allowed in the first Office Action), make especially sure yourself that at least some of your claims are clearly patentable. That is, they should define a novel enough invention to withstand a court challenge. (See Chapter 15.)

It may help to know that examiners themselves have to contend with two opposing forces. On the one hand,

they're expected to dispose of (allow or get the applicant to abandon) a certain number of cases. However, on the other hand, they're subject to a quality review program to make sure they're not too lenient.

Note that even if you have a great invention that is clearly patentable, but you haven't claimed it properly, many U.S. PTO examiners, unlike their counterparts in the European Patent Offices, won't volunteer help or constructive suggestions or try to assist you. They'll simply reject your claims or make a requirement and leave it to you to figure out how to do what's necessary to remedy the situation. Thus, it's up to you to claim and fight for what's rightfully yours. Never automatically accept any examiner's rejection.

8. Don't Take Rejection Personally

If the examiner rejects your claims, don't take such a rejection as a condemnation of you personally. The examiner doesn't know you and is thus merely rejecting your claims and not you. In other words, a rejection of your claims just means one examiner, at one point, feels that your claims are not different enough from the prior art or clear enough to be allowed. You still are a good and worthwhile person and your innovation may still be patentable with revised claims, or if you successfully argue over the rejection.

9. Dealing With the PTO Can Be Frustrating and Unfair

Dealing with the PTO, as with any other government agency, can sometimes be a very difficult, time-consuming, and frustrating experience. I could spend a whole chapter listing the errors and mistakes I've encountered recently, but one example will suffice. I once filed an application for an inventor whose last name was "Loe." The filing receipt

came back with the name "Lee." After several letters and calls with no response, a "corrected" filing receipt arrived with the name spelled "Leo." After a few more calls and much frustration, a correct filing receipt finally arrived. Put succinctly, dealing with the PTO is not like dealing with Federal Express. All I can tell you is to be philosophical, scrupulously check your correspondence with the PTO to make sure they get it right, and persist in correcting errors when they occur.

The Unlevel Playing Field

When you mail a paper
To the PTO,
Make sure it's signed and dated
Or you're in for woe.

Also make sure it's sent
Before the deadline set.
And include the proper fees
Or you'll incur a debt.

All pages should be present
And serial numbers exact
With a certificate of faxing
Or adversely they'll react.

Their rules are very stringent.
If you make a teeny error,
Their penalties are draconian,
Designed to instill much terror.

But if the goof is theirs
They can lose your entire file!
They never are rebuked—
So play their game and smile!

As far as the unfairness goes—there are many situations when you deal with the PTO (and the IRS) where you'll find an inherent unfairness due to no reciprocity. For example, while you have to reply to an OA when the PTO tells you to, they can reply to you whenever they get around to it. Your patent term will be extended to give you a minimum of 17 years of coverage provided the delay wasn't your responsibility. While you have to make your claims and specification clear, grammatical, and free of spelling errors, you'll often find that the correspondence you receive from the PTO doesn't meet these standards. While you have to pay a stiff fine if you forget to sign your check or make some other inadvertent error, the PTO never is liable, no

matter how negligent they are. In other words, you're playing on an unlevel field. There's nothing you can do about this unfairness except, again, to be philosophical and resign yourself to accept the rules of the game before you play.

As stated, the PTO is staffed by many young, inexperienced examiners who often are not closely supervised, yet have tremendous power over the fate of your application. Often they are negative and it is difficult to convince them of an invention's value. The only solutions are to go in for a personal interview (or have a DC-area attorney do it), to persevere by filing an RCE (see Chapter 14), or to appeal.

One inventor was so frustrated that he sued his examiner and the PTO for negligence. The judge said, "This is the sad tale of an inventor frustrated by the bureaucratic mindset and Byzantine workings of the PTO." While he won in trial court, the appellate court reversed, holding that examiners are not legally responsible for their actions.

10. PTO Reference Books

During patent prosecution, you may need to refer to the MPEP, the PTO's *Rules of Practice,* and/or the patent statutes. All can be viewed on or obtained from the PTO's website and the latter two can be obtained from regional government bookstores in paperbound forms. Also, all three can be obtained from the GPO, and the CASSIS CD-ROMs at any PTDL. The PTO's patent rules are given the prefix number "1." to distinguish them from trademark rules "2." and copyright rules "3." For example, Patent Rule 111, referred to later in this chapter, is officially identified as Title 37 of the Code of Federal Regulations, Section 1.111, or in legal citation form, 37 CFR 1.111. The *Manual of Patent Examining Procedure* (MPEP), which is often referred to as the "examiner's bible," covers almost any situation you can encounter in patent prosecution and contains the patent rules and statutes. It's an expensive, large, loose-leaf volume with about four megabytes of text, but you can view and print any part (or all of it) from the PTO's Internet site.

11. Never Make Negative Statements on the Record

When dealing with the PTO, you should never say or write anything that derogates your invention, and you should never admit that any prior-art reference shows (includes) any feature of your invention. Admittedly, this advice may be very difficult to follow in some situations, but it's extremely important that you comply with it. Why? The PTO puts all correspondence into your official file (called your "file wrapper"), and if you get into litigation, your adversary will use any negative admission against you or your patent. Thus, if you always anticipate that your patent may later be involved in litigation, you'll do a much better job in the prosecution phase. This is so important that I've made it Inventor's Commandment #22, at the beginning of this chapter.

12. Remember Your Continuing Duty to Disclose Material Information

As explained in Chapter 10, Section N, you have a duty to disclose all material information, such as relevant prior art, known to you that bears on the patentability of your invention. This duty is normally fulfilled when you send in your IDS and PTO/SB/08(A&B) with the application or three months thereafter. However, if you discover any additional information later, you must send in a supplemental IDS and PTO/SB/08(A&B). However, you do not have to (and shouldn't) admit or state anything negative about your invention, even if what you disclose is very close to your invention. Of course, if you find a prior-art reference that you feel is so close that you believe your invention is not patentable, you should abandon your application.

13. The PTO Can Request Search Information and Literature

In connection with your continuing duty to disclose, above, the PTO can now require, under Rule 105, that any applicant supply any search information and literature which the applicant knows of, which the applicant used to draft the application, or which the examiner can use to examine the application properly. This may include a form paragraph or letter in your application requesting this. If you receive such a Request, comply with it, but don't include any information that you already included with your IDS.

14. Be Available to Answer Office Actions

As mentioned, you'll normally be required to respond to a PTO Office Action within three months. If an OA is sent while you're away or unavailable and you fail to reply to it, your application will, as stated in Section 5, above, be considered abandoned. Thus, I've provided Inventor's Commandment #23, at the beginning of this chapter, to give you ample warning. If you will be unavailable for an extended period while your application is pending, you should empower a patent attorney to handle it for you or arrange to have your mail forwarded by a reliable friend or

relative. Unfortunately, the PTO won't allow you to appoint a layperson to represent you, unless you can show strong need exists; see PTO Rule 342 and write to the Chairman, Committee on Enrollment, at the PTO.

15. Consider Foreign Filing

About eight to ten months after you file your patent application, you should consider whether you want to file for coverage in other countries, as stated in Inventor's Commandment #21 (Chapter 12). Foreign filing is extremely expensive, time-consuming, and arduous, so do it only if you have a very important, innovative invention or a foreign licensee who will pay the freight. There are international conventions or agreements among most countries that entitle you to the benefit of your U.S. filing date on any foreign applications you file within one year after you file your U.S. regular or provisional application. (Refer back to Chapter 12 to see how to file for a patent in other countries.)

16. You Can Call and Visit Your Examiner

If you have any questions about your application, or any reference that is cited against it, you are permitted to call, and/or make an appointment with and visit, the examiner in charge of your application. Your examiner's telephone number will be listed on official letters that you receive from the PTO. However, usually only one, or at most two, applicant-initiated interviews are permitted. So save this privilege for when you really need it. If you have an interview, you must summarize its substance (unless the examiner does so) in the next amendment. An interview is often a very valuable way to get a difficult case allowed, since communication is greatly enhanced when you and the examiner can discuss your differences and reach an understanding through the give and take and multiple feedback loops an interview permits. Also, it's harder to say "no" directly to a person face-to-face. Lastly, an interview provides an excellent opportunity to bring in and demonstrate a working prototype or sample of the invention to the examiner; this is usually an excellent persuader. However, I recommend that you try to avoid calling or interviewing any examiner on Fridays, since, like most of us, they're likely to be less attentive then. An excellent guide for negotiating with examiners is presented by Examining Group Director A.L. Smith at p. 168 of the 1990 February *Journal of the Patent and Trademark Office Society*. (This is available in most academic and business libraries as well as in Patent Depository libraries.)

Sometimes your examiner will call you, offering to allow the application if some changes are made in the application.

If the changes are minor you can agree to them on the spot. But if the changes are substantive and involve the claims, I suggest you tell the examiner you would like to study them for a day or two and will call back. You should study the proposed changes carefully. If they would unduly narrow the claims, try to formulate and suggest some less restrictive changes which are still allowable.

17. Working on Commercial Model

If you have a working or commercial model of your invention, it's usually desirable to show or send this (or literature on it) to your examiner. This may make the examiner a believer in your invention, its operability, its advantages, and its commercial success. If your invention is out on the market and has had commercial success, you should submit a Declaration Under Rule 132 with exhibits attesting to such success and explaining why such success is a result of the novel features of your invention. The Supreme Court has specifically stated that the PTO must consider such commercial success when deciding on patentability—see MPEP §1504.03.

18. No New Matter Can Be Added to Your Application

Virtually every inventor I've ever dealt with has asked me, at one time or another, about adding a new development or embodiment of their invention to their pending application. I must always answer in the negative. This is because once your application is filed, the PTO's Rule 118 prohibits you from adding any "new matter" to it. (New matter consists of any technical information, including dimensions, materials, parts, values, arrangements, connections, methods, etc., that was not present in your application as originally filed.) This prohibition makes sense since, if patent applicants were permitted to add continuing improvements and changes to

their applications, the date of invention, and what was invented when, would be too difficult to determine.

Because of this widespread misconception, and because of the frequency with which PTO examiners must object when "pro se" (no attorney) applicants add new matter, I made this prohibition the subject of Inventor's Commandment #24, at the beginning of this chapter.

If you do want to add any new developments to your application, consider a special type of supplementary application (termed a "continuation-in-part application" or CIP and covered in Chapter 14) or, if your improvement is really significant, an independent, subsequent patent application.

New matter should be distinguished from prior art that may be discovered after an application has been filed. You are obligated to inform the PTO about any newly discovered, relevant prior art. (See Section 6, above.) Such prior art doesn't form part of your specification, nor does it affect the nature of your invention. Rather, it provides the PTO with more information by which to judge your invention for patentability. Also note that if you submit new claims that are broader, narrower, or different, the PTO does not consider them new matter, unless the new claims contain new information that was not originally present in the application.

19. Official Dates Are When the PTO Receives Your Submission

Every paper that you send to or receive from the PTO has an official date. This is the date on which it was mailed from or received by the PTO. You should put your actual date of mailing on anything you send to the PTO, but the date of the PTO's "Received" stamp on your paper will be the "official" date of the paper. If you send in your application by Express Mail with an EM Certification (see Chapter 10), the PTO will stamp it as of the date you express mailed it, even though they receive it one to three days later. This is because, under PTO Rule 10, they consider your local post office their agent to receive your correspondence, provided you use EM.

Fax Now Available; Email Is Coming

All responses, including amendments, petitions, appeals, and elections (but not applications, PCT papers, fees, or drawings) should now be filed by fax. Faxed papers should include, "I certify I have transmitted this paper by fax to the Patent and Trademark Office at [#] on [date]." The PTO will consider the paper as having been filed on the date of transmission or the next business day if you fax it on a nonbusiness day. Keep your signed original and your machine's record of successful transmission. Many of the PTO's fax machines will now automatically fax back a "fax received" receipt. (The PTO's main fax numbers are in Appendix 5, Mail, Telephone, Fax, and Email Communications With the PTO.)

The PTO has announced that it is providing email addresses and Internet access to many of its employees. Email communications may be used for minor matters, such as status requests, minor corrections in a paper, notification that a communication has been sent, etc., but not major papers, such as amendments and patent applications. Email addresses will be available on Office Actions and on the PTO's website (www.uspto.gov). However, since email is not a secure form of communication and the PTO is obligated to preserve all patent applications in secret, PTO employees are not allowed to send email containing any sensitive information unless you specifically authorize this. If you are willing to receive email from the PTO containing sensitive information about your application, you must file the following statement in your application: "Recognizing that Internet communications are not secure, I hereby authorize the PTO to communicate with me concerning any subject matter of this application by electronic mail. I understand that a copy of these communications will be made of record in the application file." Similarly, you should print out and put in your file a copy of all email communications you receive from the PTO.

20. Know Who Has the Ball

To use an analogy drawn from the game of football, during patent prosecution the "ball" (burden of action) will always be either on your side or the PTO's. If you just sent in your case, the ball will be with the PTO until they return your postcard, send you an official filing receipt, and send you a first Office Action. It doesn't go back to your side until that first OA. Once they send the first OA, you have the ball and must usually take action within three months. Once you file an amendment, the PTO has the ball again, and so on. You should always know the status of your case—that is, whose side has the ball.

21. Reread Appropriate Chapters

When you respond to an OA, you should go back and reread the chapter that covers the issue you need to address. For example, if a claim is rejected for prolixity, reread Chapter 9 (drafting claims). If claims are rejected on prior-art grounds, reread Chapter 5. If your specification or drawings aren't in proper form, reread Chapters 8 and 10.

22. Respond to Each and Every Point in the Office Action

A typical OA will contain several criticisms (termed "objections" and/or "rejections"), such as drawing objections, specification objections, claim rejections for indefiniteness, and claim rejections based upon prior art. You must, as stated in Inventor's Commandment #25, at the beginning of this chapter, respond to each and every criticism in your next amendment or your amendment will be considered nonresponsive. (You'll usually be given two weeks to complete the amendment.) A suitable response can be an argument against the criticism or some action to eliminate the criticism—for example, by canceling claims, amending the specification, supplying new drawings, or substituting different claims and arguing that the substituted claims are patentable over the prior art cited.

23. Form Paragraphs

Your actual Office Action, unlike the sample below, will usually include several form paragraphs that quote statutes or rules. Examiners love to use such form paragraphs. Therefore, don't assume, if you receive an Office Action with numerous form paragraphs that quote basic statutes and rules, that you've been singled out or that your application is substandard: all attorneys get OAs with these form paragraphs as well. Also, the form paragraphs that the examiner chose may sometimes be inapplicable or only partially applicable. If so, courteously point this out in your response.

24. Preliminary and Supplemental Voluntary Amendments

In addition to the "regular" amendments discussed in this chapter (sent in response to an OA), you can also file a voluntary Preliminary Amendment before your first OA to correct any errors in the specification or claims, or narrow or broaden the claims. Also, you may file a Supplemental Amendment (after you file a regular amendment, but before the next OA) to correct any errors or omissions in your Amendment. However, remember the rule against adding any new matter to your patent application. Also, you aren't allowed to amend your application after allowance or after a final action, unless the examiner authorizes it—see Section J, below. The examiner must consider the Supplemental Amendment, provided he or she has not already responded to your first amendment.

Effective June 2000, the patent term for any invention will be extended in the event of certain delays caused by the PTO in the course of the patent prosecution process. Every patent is guaranteed an in-force period of at least 17 years provided you did not delay unduly on your side.

25. Double Patenting Obviousness Rejections

If the PTO rejects a claim of your application under Section 103 for obvious-type double patenting on an earlier patent that you own and it is not early enough to be prior art against your application, you can disqualify the earlier patent as prior art. You should submit a terminal disclaimer with a fee (see Chapter 14, Section I) and a declaration stating that the patent is owned by you and has the same inventor (Rule 130).

26. Eighteen-Month Publication

If you haven't filed a Nonpublication Request (see Chapter 10), your application will be published on the PTO's website 18 months after filing (if it's still pending) and anyone can order or download and print out a copy of your application. Anyone will then be able to cite prior art against your application if they think your claims are not patentable. (PTO Rule 99.) I advise you of this so that you will be aware of the fact that, even if the PTO allows your application, they can change their mind and still reject it if someone cites better prior art than your examiner found.

27. *Festo* Considerations

As indicated in Chapter 9, you should have drafted a full spectrum of claims (from broad to specific) which cover every aspect of your invention and all possible permutations. The reason is because of the Supreme Court's decision in *Festo v. Shoketsu*, which holds essentially that the Doctrine of Equivalents (DoE—see Chapter 15) can be used to broaden any claim that was amended during prosecution provided (a) the equivalent was unforeseeable at the time the application was filed, or (b) the equivalent is not related to the way the claim is amended. However, if the court cannot determine the reason for the amendment, the DoE cannot be used. By submitting a full spectrum of claims, at least some of them will stand a good chance of being allowed in the prosecution stage without amendment, thereby preserving your full DoE rights for those claims. During the prosecution stage, you should try, if at all possible, not to amend any claims, or to amend as few as possible. If you have to amend any claims, state the reason for the amendment.

28. Rejection v. Objection

Office actions may contain (either or both) two types of disapproval or criticism of various parts of your application. It's useful to know the difference so that you can use these terms correctly in writing your amendment and in case you have to appeal.

A *rejection* is made by an examiner to a substantive claim deficiency, such as a lack of patentability of a claim over a prior-art reference or indefiniteness in the claim. An *objection* is made to a nonclaim defect, such as an unclear drawing or a misspelling in the specification, or to a nonsubstantive claim matter, such as a dependent claim which is allowable in substance, but which can't be allowed because it's dependent upon a rejected independent claim.

You have to fix or successfully argue over either type of disapproval (rejection or objection) to get the application allowed; the only practical difference is that a *rejection* that can't be overcome must be appealed, while an *objection* that can't be overcome must be petitioned (unless it's associated with a rejection).

C. A Sample Office Action

Now that you have an overview of the patent application prosecution process and the general principles that apply to it, it's time to get more concrete. Fig. 13A, below, shows a sample OA in an imaginary patent application. A study of

UNITED STATES DEPARTMENT OF COMMERCE
Patent and Trademark Office
Address : COMMISSIONER OF PATENTS AND TRADEMARKS
Washington, D C. 20231

SERIAL NUMBER	FILING DATE	FIRST NAMED APPLICANT	ATTORNEY DOCKET NO.
07/345,678	1998 Aug 9	LeRoy Inventor	

Portia Barrister
1237 Chancery Lane
Puyallup, WA 98371-3841

Received
1998 Oct 14
P.B.

EXAMINER	
HEYMAN, J	
ART UNIT	PAPER NUMBER
2540	3

DATE MAILED: 1998 Oct 9

This is a communication from the examiner in charge of your application.

COMMISSIONER OF PATENTS AND TRADEMARKS

Response Due 1999 Jan 9 P.B.

[✓] This application has been examined   [ ] Responsive to communication filed on _____   [ ] This action is made final.

A shortened statutory period for response to this action is set to expire __3__ month(s), __0__ days from the date of this letter.
Failure to respond within the period for response will cause the application to become abandoned. 35 U.S.C. 133

Part I   THE FOLLOWING ATTACHMENT(S) ARE PART OF THIS ACTION:

1. [✓] Notice of References Cited by Examiner, PTO-892.   2. [✓] Notice re Patent Drawing, PTO-948.
3. [ ] Notice of Art Cited by Applicant, PTO-1449   4. [ ] Notice of Informal Patent Application, Form PTO-152
5. [ ] Information on How to Effect Drawing Changes, PTO-1474   6. [ ] _____

Part II   SUMMARY OF ACTION

1. [✓] Claims ___1-7___ are pending in the application.

    Of the above, claims _____ are withdrawn from consideration.

2. [ ] Claims _____ have been cancelled.

3. [ ] Claims _____ are allowed.

4. [✓] Claims ___1-7___ are rejected.

5. [ ] Claims _____ are objected to.

6. [ ] Claims _____ are subject to restriction or election requirement.

7. [✓] This application has been filed with informal drawings which are acceptable for examination purposes until such time as allowable subject matter is indicated.

8. [ ] Allowable subject matter having been indicated, formal drawings are required in response to this Office action.

9. [ ] The corrected or substitute drawings have been received on _____. These drawings are [ ] acceptable;
    [ ] not acceptable (see explanation).

10. [ ] The [ ] proposed drawing correction and/or the [ ] proposed additional or substitute sheet(s) of drawings, filed on _____.
    has (have) been [ ] approved by the examiner. [ ] disapproved by the examiner (see explanation).

11. [ ] The proposed drawing correction, filed _____, has been [ ] approved. [ ] disapproved (see explanation). However,
    the Patent and Trademark Office no longer makes drawing changes. It is now applicant's responsibility to ensure that the drawings are
    corrected. Corrections **MUST** be effected in accordance with the instructions set forth on the attached letter "INFORMATION ON HOW TO
    EFFECT DRAWING CHANGES", PTO-1474.

12. [ ] Acknowledgment is made of the claim for priority under 35 U.S.C. 119. The certified copy has [ ] been received [ ] not been received

    [ ] been filed in parent application, serial no. _____; filed on _____.

13. [ ] Since this application appears to be in condition for allowance except for formal matters, prosecution as to the merits is closed in
    accordance with the practice under Ex parte Quayle, 1935 C.D. 11; 453 O.G. 213.

14. [ ] Other

PTOL-326 (Rev. 7 - 82)   **EXAMINER'S ACTION**

Fig. 13A/1—Sample Office Action

Serial No. 07/345,678   -2-

Art Unit 254

The drawing is objected to under Rule 1.83(a) in that all the features recited in the claims are not shown. See Claims 1 and 2 regarding the "electronic counter means" and "first and second solid state counters."

The specification is objected to under Rule 1.71(b) as inadequate. In particular, there is insufficient information regarding the "counter," "counter memory," and how the counter controls the illumination of the lights. Applicant is required to amplify the disclosure in this regard without the introduction of new matter, 608.04 MPEP.

Claims 1-7 are rejected under 35 U.S.C. § 112, 1st. paragraph, as based on an insufficient disclosure. See above.

Insofar as adequate, Claims 1-6 are rejected under 35 U.S.C. § 102(b) as fully anticipated by Ohman. Ohman shows an electronic cribbage board counter that fully meets these claims. See Fig. 1. The microprocessor 300 shown in Fig. 3 inherently includes the counter means of Claims 1 and 2.

Claim 7 is rejected under 35 U.S.C. § 112, ¶ 2. The term "said LCD readout" lacks proper antecedent basis in parent independent claim 1 as claim 1 recites only an "LCD monitor."

Fig. 13A/2—Sample Office Action

Claim 7 is rejected under 35 U.S.C. § 103 as unpatentable over Ohman in view of Morin. Ohman shows an electronic cribbage board counter, as stated. Morin shows an LCD tally monitor. It would be obvious to substitute Morin's LCD tally monitor for Ohman's mechanical readout, since the substitution of LCD readouts for mechanical readouts is an expedient well known to those skilled in the art. See column 13, lines 34-41 of Morin, which indicate that in lieu of the LCD readout shown, other types of readouts may be used.

No claim is allowed.

The remaining art cited shows other electronic board games containing the claimed structure. Note Morin, which shows the details of a computer as containing first and second counter means.

Any inquiry concerning this communication should be directed to Examiner Heyman at telephone number 703-557-4777, Fax number 703-872-9314.

Heyman/EW

98/10/09

John S. Heyman

Examiner

Group Art Unit 254

Fig. 13A/3—Sample Office Action

FORM PTO-892	U.S. DEPARTMENT OF COMMERCE PATENT AND TRADEMARK OFFICE	SERIAL NO. 07/345,678	GROUP ART UNIT 254	ATTACHMENT TO PAPER NUMBER	3
NOTICE OF REFERENCES CITED		APPLICANT(S) LeRoy Inventor			

U.S. PATENT DOCUMENTS

*		DOCUMENT NO.	DATE	NAME	CLASS	SUBCLASS	FILING DATE IF APPROPRIATE
	A	4 3 6 8 5 1 6	1/1983	Morin	377	5	
	B						
	C						
	D						
	E						
	F						
	G						
	H						
	I						
	J						
	K						

FOREIGN PATENT DOCUMENTS

		DOCUMENT NO.	DATE	COUNTRY	NAME	CLASS	SUB-CLASS	PERTINENT SHTS. DWGS	PP. SPEC.
	L	8 1 0 1 7 6 6	6/1981	International P.U.B. (ACT)	Ohman	273	148R	5	21
	M	1 1 9 5 0 0 1	10/1985	Canada	Mah	273	148R	3	14
	N	2 1 7 3 4 0 6	10/1986	Gr. Britain	Armstrong	273	148R	3	6
	O								
	P								
	Q								

OTHER PRIOR ART (Including Author, Title, Date, Pertinent Pages, Etc.)

R	
S	
T	
U	

EXAMINER J.S. Heyman	DATE 4-1-200X	

* A Copy of this reference is not being furnished with this office action.
(See Manual of patent Examining Procedure, section 707.05(a).)

Fig. 13A/4—Notice of References Cited

Rcd 95028

Form PTO 948 (Rev. 10-93)   U.S. DEPARTMENT OF COMMERCE - Patent and Trademark Office   Application No. **07/883567**

NOTICE OF DRAFTSPERSON'S PATENT DRAWING REVIEW

PTO Draftspersons review all originally filed drawings regardless of whether they are designated as formal or informal. Additionally, patent Examiners will review the drawings for compliance with the regulations. Direct telephone inquiries concerning this review to the Drawing Review Branch, 703-305-8404.

The drawings filed (insert date) **9/27/95** are
A. _____ not objected to by the Draftsperson under 37 CFR 1.84 or 1.152.
B. __✓__ objected to by the Draftsperson under 37 CFR 1.84 or 1.152 as indicated below. The Examiner will require submission of new, corrected drawings when necessary. Corrected drawings must be submitted according to the instructions on the back of this Notice.

1. DRAWINGS. 37 CFR 1.84(a): Acceptable categories of drawings: Black ink. Color.
   ___ Not black solid lines. Fig(s)_____
   ___ Color drawings are not acceptable until petition is granted.

2. PHOTOGRAPHS. 37 CFR 1.84(b)
   ___ Photographs are not acceptable until petition is granted.

3. GRAPHIC FORMS. 37 CFR 1.84 (d)
   ___ Chemical or mathematical formula not labeled as separate figure. Fig(s)_____
   ___ Group of waveforms not presented as a single figure, using common vertical axis with time extending along horizontal axis. Fig(s)_____
   ___ Individuals waveform not identified with a separate letter designation adjacent to the vertical axis. Fig(s)_____

4. TYPE OF PAPER. 37 CFR 1.84(e)
   ___ Paper not flexible, strong, white, smooth, nonshiny, and durable. Sheet(s)_____
   ___ Erasures, alterations, overwritings, interlineations, cracks, creases, and folds not allowed. Sheet(s)_____

Transparent objectionable Figs 1,3

5. SIZE OF PAPER. 37 CFR 1.84(f): Acceptable paper sizes:
   21.6 cm. by 35.6 cm. (8 1/2 by 14 inches)
   21.6 cm. by 33.1 cm. (8 1/2 by 13 inches)
   21.6 cm. by 27.9 cm. (8 1/2 by 11 inches)
   21.0 cm. by 29.7 cm. (DIN size A4)
   ___ All drawing sheets not the same size. Sheet(s)_____
   ___ Drawing sheet not an acceptable size. Sheet(s)_____

6. MARGINS. 37 CFR 1.84(g): Acceptable margins:

Paper size	
21 cm. X 27.9 cm. (8 1/2 X 11 inches)	21 cm. X 29.7 cm. (DIN Size A4)
2.5 cm. (1")	2.5cm.
.64 cm. (1/4")	2.5 cm.
.64 cm. (1/4")	1.5 cm.
.64 cm. (1/4")	1.0 cm.

   Margins do not conform to chart above
   Sheet(s)_____
   ___ Top (T) ___ Left (L) ___ Right (R) ___ Bottom (B)

7. VIEWS. 37 CFR 1.84(h)
   REMINDER: Specification may require revision to correspond to drawing changes.
   ___ All views not grouped together. Fig(s)_____
   ___ Views connected by projection lines. Fig(s)_____
   ___ Views contain center lines. Fig(s)_____
   Partial views. 37 CFR 1.84(h)(2)
   ___ Separate sheets not linked edge to edge. Fig(s)_____
   ___ View and enlarged view not labeled separately. Fig(s)_____
   ___ Long view relationship between different parts not clear and unambiguous. 37 CFR 1.84(h)(2)(ii) Fig(s)_____
   Sectional views. 37 CFR 1.84(h)(3)
   ___ Hatching not indicated for sectional portions of an object. Fig(s)_____
   ✓ Hatching of regularly spaced oblique parallel lines not spaced sufficiently. Fig(s)_____
   ___ Hatching not at substantial angle to surrounding axes or principal lines. Fig(s) **3**
   ___ Cross section not drawn same as view with parts in cross section with regularly spaced parallel oblique strokes. Fig(s)_____
   ___ Hatching of juxtaposed different elements not angled in a different way. Fig(s)_____
   Alternate position. 37 CFR 1.84(h)(4)
   ___ A separate view required for a moved position. Fig(s)_____

Modified forms. 37 CFR 1.84(h)(5)
   ___ Modified forms of construction must be shown in separate views. Fig(s)_____

8. ARRANGEMENT OF VIEWS. 37 CFR 1.84(i)
   ___ View placed upon another view or within outline of another. Fig(s)_____
   ___ Words do not appear in a horizontal, left-to-right fashion when page is either upright or turned so that the top becomes the right side, except for graphs. Fig(s)_____

9. SCALE. 37 CFR 1.84(k)
   ___ Scale not large enough to show mechanism without crowding when drawing is reduced in size to two-thirds in reproduction. Fig(s)_____
   ___ Indication such as "actual size" or "scale 1/2" not permitted. Fig(s)_____
   ___ Elements of same view not in proportion to each other. Fig(s)_____

10. CHARACTER OF LINES, NUMBERS, & LETTERS. 37 CFR 1.84(l)
   ✓ Lines, numbers & letters not uniformly thick and well defined, clean, durable, and black (except for color drawings). Fig(s)_____

11. SHADING. 37 CFR 1.84(m)
   ___ Shading used for other than shape of spherical, cylindrical, and conical elements of an object, or for flat parts. Fig(s)_____
   ___ Solid black shading areas not permitted. Fig(s)_____

12. NUMBERS, LETTERS, & REFERENCE CHARACTERS. 37 CFR 1.84(p)
   ___ Numbers and reference characters not plain and legible. 37 CFR 1.84(p)(l) Fig(s)_____
   ___ Numbers and reference characters used in conjuction with brackets, inverted commas, or enclosed within outlines. 37 CFR 1.84(p)(l) Fig(s)_____
   ___ Numbers and reference characters not oriented in same direction as the view. 37 CFR 1.84(p)(l) Fig(s)_____
   ___ English alphabet not used. 37 CFR 1.84(p)(2) Fig(s)_____
   ___ Numbers, letters, and reference characters do not measure at least .32 cm. (1/8 inch) in height. 37 CFR(p)(3) Fig(s)_____

13. LEAD LINES. 37 CFR 1.84(q)
   ___ Lead lines cross each other. Fig(s)_____
   ___ Lead lines missing. Fig(s)_____
   ___ Lead lines not as short as possible. Fig(s)_____

14. NUMBERING OF SHEETS OF DRAWINGS. 37 CFR 1.84(t)
   ___ Number appears in top margin. Fig(s)_____
   ___ Number not larger than reference characters. Fig(s)_____
   ___ Sheets not numbered consecutively, and in Arabic numerals, beginning with number 1. Sheet(s)_____

15. NUMBER OF VIEWS. 37 CFR 1.84(u)
   ___ Views not numbered consecutively, and in Arabic numerals, beginning with number 1. Fig(s)_____
   ___ View numbers not preceded by the abbreviation Fig. Fig(s)_____
   ___ Single view contains a view number and the abbreviation Fig. Fig(s)_____
   ___ Numbers not larger than reference characters. Fig(s)_____

16. CORRECTIONS. 37 CFR 1.84(w)
   ___ Corrections not durable and permanent. Fig(s)_____

17. DESIGN DRAWING. 37 CFR 1.152
   ___ Surface shading shown not appropriate. Fig(s)_____
   ___ Solid black shading not used for color contrast. Fig(s)_____

ATTACHMENT TO PAPER NO. **9**   REVIEWER **CBR**   DATE **10/25/95**

Applicant's Copy

Fig. 13A/5—Draftsperson's Drawing Objection Sheet

this example will enable you to deal with your first OA far more effectively. It has been purposely written to include the most common objections and rejections; an actual OA is usually not this complicated and quotes applicable statutes. First let's look at Fig. 13A/1 (p. 1 of the OA).

At the top of the OA, the examiner's name and his examining section (Art Unit 2540) are given. Art Unit 2540 is part of Examining Group 2500. Before that, in the large brackets, are the serial number, filing date, and inventor's name. To the right is the date the OA was mailed; this is its official date.

Below the address of the attorney, the first box that is checked indicates: "This application has been examined," denoting that this is the first OA in this application. If it had been a second and nonfinal OA, the second box, "Responsive to communication filed on [date]," would have been checked; had it been a final OA, the third box, "This action is made final," would have been checked.

The next paragraph indicates that the period for response will expire in three months and that failure to respond will cause the application to be abandoned. Since the OA was mailed 1998-10-9, the period for response expires 1999-1-9. If the last date of the period falls on a Saturday, Sunday, or holiday, the period for response expires on the next business day.

Under "Part I," the check at box 1 indicates that two attachments, a "Notice of References Cited" and a "Notice re Patent Drawing," are part of the OA. A typical Notice of References Cited is shown in Fig. 13A/4, below, and the drawing notice is shown in Fig. 13A/5.

Under "Part II—Summary of Action," the examiner has checked various boxes to indicate what action he has taken with the application. He has rejected all seven claims pending. He has also acknowledged that informal drawings were filed and has indicated that these will be acceptable until allowable subject matter is indicated.

Now it's time to look at Figs. 13A/2 and 13A/3 (pp. 2 and 3 of the OA).

On p. 2 of the Office Action, the examiner gives his specific reasons for rejecting or objecting to the claims.

The first paragraph of p. 2 of the OA objects to the drawings because they fail to show certain features recited in the claims. Remember (Chapter 10) that the drawings must show every feature recited in the claims.

The second paragraph objects to the specification as inadequate. As stated in Chapter 8, the specification must teach, in full, clear, and exact detail, how one skilled in the art would make and use the invention. This is a potentially serious and fatal flaw, since it is not permissible to add new matter (see Section B18, above) to supply the missing description.

In the third paragraph, the examiner rejects all of the claims under Section 112, since they are based on an inadequate specification for reasons stated in the second paragraph.

The fourth paragraph rejects Claims 1 to 6 on the Ohman reference (see Fig. 13A/4—p. 4 of the OA), under Section 102. This means that the examiner feels that these claims contain no novelty over Ohman. The requirement that the claims contain novel physical features was discussed in Chapters 5 and 9.

At the bottom of p. 2 of the OA, the examiner has rejected Claim 7 under Section 112 since a "said" clause in Claim 7 has no proper antecedent in parent, independent Claim 1 from which Claim 7 depends. Remember (Chapter 9) that every "said" clause must contain an identical antecedent earlier in the claim or in a parent claim. Many examiners, especially young ones, lean heavily on any Section 112 defects.

In the last paragraph of p. 2 of the OA (Fig. 13A/2-3), the examiner has rejected Claim 7, under our old and troublesome friend Section 103, as unpatentable over two references. Note that the examiner states what each reference shows and why it would be obvious to combine the teachings of these references. Also note that by using two references, or by relying on Section 103, the examiner has tacitly admitted that this claim has satisfied the novelty (Section 102) requirement. (See Chapter 5, Fig. 5A.)

The examiner next summarizes by stating that no claim is allowed.

Finally he refers to certain other prior art, which he cites but does not apply, to provide background and to put on the record in case he wants to use it later.

The examiner will sign the Office Action at the bottom and list his telephone number and fax above his official name stamp.

Next, we turn to Fig. 13A/4 (the Notice of References Cited). It lists one U.S. and three foreign patents. All of the foreign references will be attached to the OA, except any checked in the column marked with the asterisk(*), which were furnished in a prior Office Action, a prior related application, or were furnished by you in your Information Disclosure Statement. The "Document Number" column generally lists patent numbers. You may have to download the U.S. patents from the Internet.

The date column indicates the date the patent issued, or the document was published. If this date is later than your filing date, the reference is not a good reference against your application, unless it is a U.S. patent filed before your application. In the latter instance, the examiner is supposed to indicate the filing date of the patent reference in the last column.

Finally, note the Notice of Draftperson's Patent Drawing Review (Fig. 13A/5). This sheet comes from the PTO's Drafting Department and has been inserted, since they found several self-explanatory defects in the drawings.

If you've sent in your IDS and PTO-1449 (Chapter 10, Section N), the OA will also include a copy of your PTO-1449, and a list of your references will be included under "References Cited" in the printed patent.

When the PTO cites patents as prior-art references, some inventors react in various illogical ways, as indicated by the following Common Misconceptions:

Common Misconception: The PTO can't cite foreign or non-English patents or other publications against a U.S. patent application.

Fact: As indicated in Chapter 5, any publication, including a patent from anywhere in the world, in any language, is valid prior art against your patent application, provided it was published before your filing date, or before your earliest provable date of invention, up to one year before your filing date.

Common Misconception: An in-force foreign patent that shows or claims your invention will prevent you from making the invention in the U.S.

Fact: A patent of any country is enforceable only within the geographical area of that country and has no enforceability elsewhere. Thus, for example, a French patent is enforceable only in France and has no enforceability or effect in the U.S. However, it is a good prior-art reference in the U.S.

Common Misconception: If an examiner cites an in-force U.S. patent as a prior-art reference against your application, this means that your invention, if manufactured, sold, or used, would infringe this patent.

Fact: The only way you can tell if your invention would infringe any patent is to compare the patent's claims against your invention. Most cited in-force patents would not be infringed by your invention, since their claims are directed to a different invention. Again, examiners hardly ever read claims of patents they cite and the PTO is never concerned with infringements.

Common Misconception: If an examiner cites a very old prior-art reference against your application, it is not as good a reference as an in-force patent or a very recent reference.

Fact: The age of a reference is totally irrelevant, so long as its date is earlier than your filing date or your earliest provable date of invention. (See Chapter 5.)

D. What to Do When You Receive an Office Action

When you receive an OA, don't panic or be intimidated or take it personally. It's common for some examiners to reject all claims, even if the rejections are not valid. This type of rejection is termed a "shotgun" or "shoot-from-the-hip" rejection. Although they shouldn't do so, examiners sometimes do this because of the pressure of work, and sometimes to force you to state more clearly the essence of your invention and its true distinguishing features. You'll find that even if your examiner rejects all of your claims, if you approach your OA in a calm, rational, and methodical manner, as outlined below, you shouldn't have too much difficulty in ultimately getting your patent if your invention meets the legal tests for patentability.

If the PTO Suggests You Get an Attorney

Some examiners insert a form paragraph in an OA, suggesting that you hire a patent attorney, regardless of how well the application is prepared, if there is no attorney of record. This has been done in several cases I prepared, but where I did not appear as the attorney of record. You can safely ignore this form paragraph, unless you feel uncomfortable without an attorney.

1. Record Due Date on Your Calendar and OA, and Mount OA in Your File

After you get your Office Action, write the date you received the OA and the due date of your response right on it (as is done in Fig. 13A/1), and also on your calendar so you don't forget it. You should actually write the date *thrice* on your calendar: once on the date it's actually due, once one week before it's due, and once one month before it's due. If the due date falls on a weekend or holiday, your due date is the next business day. Also, mount the OA in your file (see Inventor's Commandment #17 in Chapter 10) so you won't lose it.

2. Check the References and Review Your Application

Your OA will usually cite prior-art references. Some will be applied against your claims and some will be cited as background as a matter of interest. In either case, the PTO does not send copies of any cited U.S. patent and published patent application references with OAs. They do send copies of cited foreign patents and nonpatent references. If you receive an OA which cites U.S. patent references, you must obtain copies of the cited references yourself. You have several ways to do this: (1) Download them one page at a time for free or order entire patents for a fee from the PTO's website (see Chapter 6, Section N, for instructions), (2) Download complete patents for free (up to six a day) or get them for a fee from Patent Fetcher, (3) Obtain access to the PTO's Private PAIR (Patent Application Information Retrieval) system and download complete U.S. patents cited against your patent application. At present I don't see any significant advantage of getting copies via Private PAIR over the Patent Fetcher system, but it can also be used to file patent applications electronically and view the status of your applications. (Since it is somewhat inconvenient to obtain references, you may wish to obtain paper copies of only those that the PTO has actually applied against your claims and merely review on the monitor those that were cited as being of interest.)

To obtain access to Private PAIR, you must: (1) Obtain a PKI (Public Key Infrastructure) Digital Certificate by completing and mailing to the PTO a notarized application; (2) Obtain a Customer Number by sending or faxing an application to the PTO; (3) Associate your Customer Number with your patent application(s) by completing an Excel spreadsheet and mailing it on a CD to the PTO; (4) Obtain and install the PTO's electronic filing software on your computer. (I strongly advise making a ghost backup of your hard disk and learning how to restore the backup before attempting to install any new software.) The full instructions can be found in the *Official Gazette* at the PTO website. Locate the *Official Gazette* of 2004 May 18, and review Item 18—"Electronic Access To US Patent References" (2004 May 24).

After you obtain copies of the cited references, check all of them carefully to make sure you've received all the correct references listed in the Notice of References Cited. If there's any discrepancy, or if any seem irrelevant, call or write the examiner at once. This call will not count as an interview. (You are usually limited to two interviews.)

If you sent in an IDS and PTO/SB/08, the examiner will send, with your first OA, a copy of your PTO/SB/08, with the blank adjacent each reference initialed to show that the examiner has considered it. If you don't get the PTO/SB/08 back with every reference initialed, check with your examiner. Otherwise, the references you cited on your PTO/SB/08 won't be listed on your patent when it's printed.

Next, read the OA carefully and make a detailed written summary of it so that you'll have it impressed in your mind. After that, reread your application, noting all grammatical and other errors in the specification, claims, and drawings that you would like to correct or improve. Remember, however, that you can't add any "new matter" to your application.

3. Read and Analyze Each Cited Reference, Except Patent Claims

Next, read every applied prior-art reference (except the claims of patent references) completely and carefully. (You don't have to read the nonapplied references carefully, but you should review them to be sure none is more relevant than an applied reference.) Make sure that you take enough time to understand each reference completely, including all of the structure involved and how it works. Write a brief summary of each reference, preferably on the reference itself, even if it has an adequate abstract, in order to familiarize yourself with it in your own words.

Don't Fall Into a Claims Trap. As I mentioned in Chapter 6 in connection with conducting a patentability search, don't read the claims of any patent cited as a reference. Why not? Because the patent has not been cited for what it claims, but rather for what it shows about the prior art. The claims generally only repeat parts of the specification and are not directly relevant to the patent prosecution process, since they are only used to determine whether infringement exists. If you think of cited patents as magazine articles, you'll avoid this "claims trap" that most laypersons fall into.

"Swearing Behind" References: Under the PTO's Rule 131, you can "swear behind" and thus eliminate certain cited references as prior art to your application, provided you can prove that your *date of invention* is earlier than the *effective date* of the reference. (Remember from Chapter 5, Section E, that your *date of invention* is the earliest of (1) your *filing date (regular or PPA)*, (2) your *date of building and testing*, or (3) your *date of conception* followed by *diligence*. The *effective date* of any U.S. patent reference is its *filing date* and the *effective date* of any other reference is its *publication date.)*

If the PTO cites a reference against your application that has an *effective date* later than your *date of invention,* and you can prove your *date of invention* (you'll be able to if you've followed my recording instructions in Chapter 3!), you're in luck: you can swear behind this reference and thereby completely eliminate it from consideration. Typical references that you can swear behind are U.S. patents with *filing dates,* and other publications with *publication dates* earlier than your *filing date* but later than your *date of invention.*

To swear behind such a reference, you must submit a declaration containing facts with attached copies of documents showing that you *built and tested* the invention, or conceived the invention and were thereafter *diligent* in building and testing it, or filing the patent application before the *effective date* of the reference. See MPEP 715 for details.

If you've filed a PPA and need to rely on its filing date, merely refer to it by its Serial Number and Filing Date and point out to the examiner that a reference that the examiner cited is ineffective because you have an earlier effective filing date due to your PPA. Remember, however, that if your PPA didn't disclose your invention completely in accordance with Sec. 112, ¶ 1, you won't be entitled to rely on it.

One-Year Rule and Interference Limitations: Two important limitations exist on your right to swear behind: (1) Because of the "one-year rule" (Chapter 5, Section E), you can't swear behind any reference (U.S. patent or otherwise) with a *publication date* over one year before your *filing date.* (There's no limitation as to how far you can swear back if the reference is a U.S. patent which issued less than one year before your *filing date.*) (2) You can't swear behind a U.S. patent which claims the same invention as yours; the only way you can overcome such a patent is to get into interference with it and win "priority." (See Chapter 15.)

4. Make a Comparison Chart

Next, you'll find it helpful to make a comparison chart showing every feature of your invention across the top of the chart and listing the references down the left-hand side of the chart, as in Fig. 13B.

Features of My Invention

	Pivot arm	Bracket at end of arm	Bracket has screw tightener
References			
A	X	X	
B	X		X

Fig. 13B—Comparison Chart

Be sure to break up your invention so that all possible features of it, even those not already claimed, are covered and listed across the top of the chart. Remember that a feature can be the combination of two known separate features or a new use of an old device. Then indicate, by checking the appropriate boxes, those features of your invention that are not shown by each reference. This chart, if done correctly and completely, will be of tremendous aid in drafting your response to the first OA.

5. Follow the Flowchart

Fig. 13C provides a comprehensive, self-explanatory flowchart for dealing with all prior-art (Sections 102 and 103) rejections. Fig. 13D provides a list of all possible arguments I've found against obviousness rejections. For each claim (or set of claims) rejected, follow the chart and list carefully.

6. Compare Your Broadest Claim With the Cited References for Novelty

If the examiner applies any prior-art references under Section 102, you'll need to deal with the novelty question. However, if the reference is said to apply under Section 103 (obviousness), the examiner is tacitly admitting that you've made it past Section 102—that is, your claimed structure is novel. Therefore, you won't have to go through the full analysis in this section. Instead, review the section briefly, and then concentrate on Section 7.

First, reread your broadest claim to see which features it recites. Remember, only positively recited physical structure or acts count. Then consider whether these physical features distinguish your invention from each reference cited against this claim. Don't pay any attention to the advantages of your

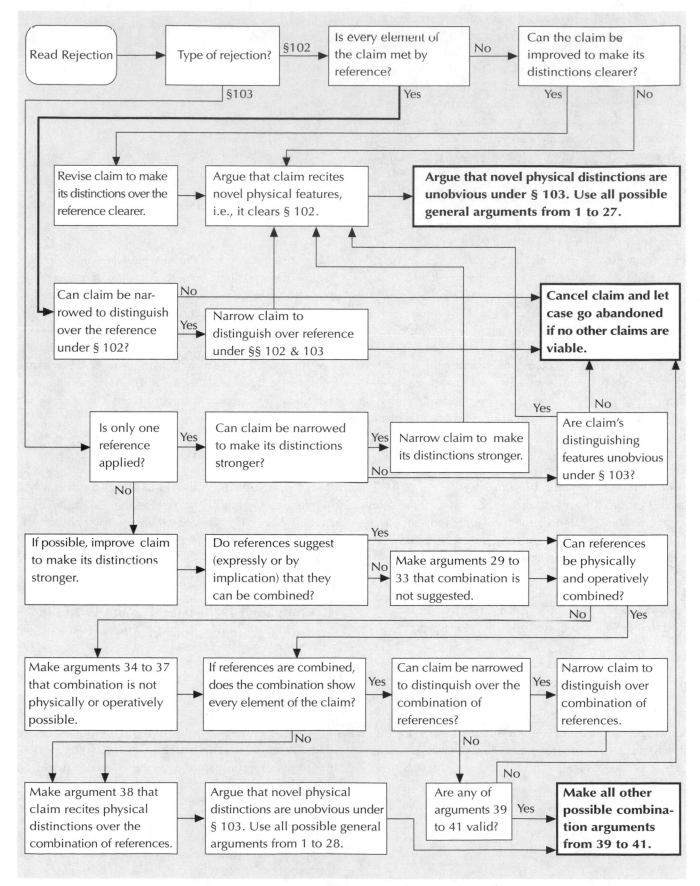

Fig. 13C—Flowchart for Handling Prior-Art Rejections

Part I—General Arguments Against Obviousness

1. **Unexpected Results:** The results achieved by the invention are new, unexpected, superior, disproportionate, unsuggested, unusual, critical, and/or surprising.

2. **Assumed Unworkability:** Up to now those skilled in the art thought or were skeptical that the techniques used in the invention were unworkable or presented an insuperable barrier.

3. **Assumed Insolubility:** Up to now those skilled in the art thought or found the problem solved by the invention to be insoluble—that is, the invention converts failure into success. The failures of prior-art workers indicate that a solution was not obvious.

4. **Commercial Success:** The invention has attained commercial success. (Prove this by a declaration with supporting documents.)

5. **Unrecognized Problem:** The problem solved by the invention was never before even recognized. The recognition of an unrecognized problem militates in favor of patentability.

6. **Crowded Art:** The invention is classified in a crowded art; therefore, a small step forward should be regarded as significant.

7. **Omission of Element:** An element of a prior-art device has been omitted or a prior-art version has been made simpler without loss of capability.

8. **Unsuggested Modification:** The prior art lacks any suggestion that the reference should be modified in a manner required to meet the claims.

9. **Unappreciated Advantage:** Up to now those skilled in the art never appreciated the advantage of the invention, although it is inherent.

10. **Inoperative References:** The prior-art references that were relied upon are inoperative.

11. **Poor References:** The prior-art references are vague, foreign, conflicting, or very old, and, therefore, are weak and should be construed narrowly.

12. **Ancient Suggestion:** Although the invention may possibly have been suggested by the prior art, the suggestion is many years old, was never implemented, and produced greatly inferior results.

13. **Lack of Implementation:** If the invention were in fact obvious, because of its advantages, those skilled in the art surely would have implemented it by now. That is— the fact that those skilled in the art have not implemented the invention, despite its great advantages, indicates that it is not obvious.

14. **Misunderstood Reference:** The reference does not teach what the examiner relies upon it as supposedly teaching.

15. **Solution of Long-Felt and Unsolved Need:** The invention solves a long-felt, long-existing, but unsolved need.

16. **Commercial Acquiescence:** The invention has been licensed, especially to a competitor.

17. **Professional Recognition:** The invention has been given an award or recognized in a professional publication.

18. **Purchase Offers:** Others, especially accused infringers, have tried to purchase or take a license under the invention.

19. **Copying by Others:** Others have chosen to copy and implement the invention, rather than using the techniques of the prior art.

20. **Competitive Recognition:** The invention has been copied by an infringer; moreover, the infringer has made laudatory statements about it, or has admitted it is unobvious.

21. **Contrarian Invention:** The invention is contrary to the teachings of the prior art—that is, the invention goes against the grain of what the prior art teaches.

22. **Strained Interpretation:** The examiner has made a strained interpretation of the reference that could be made only by hindsight.

23. **Paper Patent:** The reference is a "paper patent"—that is, it was never implemented or commercialized and therefore should be construed narrowly. (Don't use if reference completely anticipates your invention.)

24. **New Principle of Operation:** The invention utilizes a new principle of operation. Applicant has blazed a trail, rather than followed one.

25. **Inability of Competitors:** Competitors were unable to copy the invention until they were able to learn its details through a publication or reverse engineering a commercial model; this indicates unobviousness.

26. **Solved Different Problem:** Applicant's invention solves a different problem than the reference, and such different problem is recited in the claims. *In re Wright*, 6 USPQ 2d 1959 (1988).

27. **No Convincing Reasoning:** The examiner has not presented a convincing line of reasoning as to why the claimed subject matter as a whole, including its differences over the prior art, would have been obvious.

28. **Reference Isn't From Same Field:** If a cited reference is from a different field than your invention, this factor weighs against its use in a rejection. *In re Oetiker*, 24 USPQ 2d 1443 (Fed. Cir. 1992).

Fig. 13D—Arguments Against Obviousness Rejections (Part I)

Part II—Arguments Also Used When Combination of References Applied

29. **Unsuggested Combination:** The prior-art references do not contain any suggestion (express or implied) that they be combined, or that they be combined in the manner suggested.

30. **References Are Individually Complete:** Each reference is complete and functional in itself, so there would be no reason to use parts from or add or substitute parts to any reference.

31. **References Take Different Approaches:** The references take mutually exclusive paths and reach different solutions to a similar problem. Since they teach away from each other, it would not be logical to combine them.

32. **References Teach Away:** The references themselves teach away (expressly or by implication) from the suggested combination.

33. **Reference Is From Different Field:** One reference is from a very different technical field than that of the invention—that is, it's "nonanalogous art."

34. **Impossible to Combine:** Those skilled in the art would find it physically impossible to combine the references in the manner suggested.

35. **Inoperative Combination:** If they could be combined, the references would produce an inoperative combination.

36. **Modifications Necessary:** It would be necessary to make modifications, not taught in the prior art, in order to combine the references in the manner suggested.

37. **Mutually Exclusive Paths:** The references can't be legally combined because they take mutually exclusive paths to reach different solutions to a problem, and, therefore, by implication each teaches away from combining itself with the other.

38. **Claimed Features Lacking:** Even if combined, the references would not meet the claims.

39. **Synergism:** The whole (that is—the result achieved by the invention) is greater than the sum of its parts (that is—the respective results of the individual references).

40. **Multiplicity of Steps Required:** The combination suggested requires a series of separate, awkward combinative steps that are too involved to be considered obvious.

41. **Multiplicity of References:** The fact that a large number of references (over three) must be combined to meet the invention is evidence of unobviousness.

Fig. 13D—Arguments Against Obviousness Rejections (Part II)

invention, your statements of function, or your "whereby" clauses. Only focus on the novel physical features, including those that are in the form of a means clause followed by a function.

EXAMPLE: "A lever having a threaded end with a counterbalance thereon" is a proper physical recitation that can distinguish your invention from the prior art. The phrase "means for counterbalancing" is a means clause followed by a function and is equivalent to a physical recitation. But "said lever counterbalancing said arm" is a mere statement of result or function and can't be used to distinguish the prior art.

If only one reference has been cited against your broadest claim, consider whether your claim distinguishes over this reference under Section 102 (that is—whether your claimed structure is novel; see Chapter 5, Section E). In other words, are there any features recited in the claim that are not shown in the reference being cited against it? If not, the claim is "fully met" or anticipated by this reference and will have to be narrowed or canceled.

Remember that the examiner is entitled to interpret any claim in any reasonable way against you. That is, if your claims, or any word in one of your claims, has two reasonable interpretations, the examiner is entitled to take the one least favorable to you when determining if your claim has novel physical structure under Section 102. For example, suppose your invention uses a clamp that is halfway between two ends of a rod and a reference shows a clamp near one end of a rod. If your claim recites that the clamp is "intermediate" the ends of the rod, this won't distinguish over the reference since "intermediate" means "between" as well as "in the middle." The remedy? Recite that your claim is "substantially in the middle" of the rod in order to distinguish over the reference under Section 102 (but not necessarily under Section 103).

Suppose the physical features of your claim are all shown in a prior-art reference, but the prior-art reference's physical features are used for a different purpose than yours. For example, you claim "a depression in a wall plate for holding a clock" and the prior art shows a large oil drip pan under a milling machine; this pan literally constitutes "a plate with a depression." Thus your claim literally "reads on" the prior art, but your claimed elements are directed to a different purpose than the elements of the prior-art reference. Unfortunately, the rejection is valid: you'll have to narrow the claim, or consider claiming your structure as a "new use" invention. (See Chapters 5 and 8.)

Sometimes, even though a claim recites a limitation that is novel, the examiner will overlook the limitation. In order to force the examiner to consider the limitation, it will help to rewrite the limitation in a stronger, separate, more prominent clause in its own paragraph—that is, change "a series of beads" to "a plurality of beads, said plurality of beads being connected in series to form a chain of said plurality of beads."

7. Analyze Novel Features for Unobviousness

If the claim recites (or has been amended to recite) novel features, consider whether these are unobvious over the reference cited against it. All possible reasons for arguing unobviousness are listed in Fig. 13D (Part I). When you use any reasons from this chart, you should not merely copy the reason, as I've seen some inventors do. Rather, you must state facts in support of each reason you use. For example, if you select Reason 1 (Unexpected Results) after stating that your novel claimed structure produces new and unexpected results, state precisely what they are—such as that it does a job faster or more reliably.

If you consider the features of your invention obvious, you'll have to narrow the claim, either by adding more features from your specification or from narrower (dependent) claims (refer to Fig. 13C, above) or by reciting the existing features more narrowly.

8. If References Are Cited in Combination Against Your Broadest Claim

If two or more references have been cited in combination against your broadest claim, refer to Fig. 13D (Part II) to see whether the examiner has a point.

You should especially consider reasons 29 to 33— that is, ask yourself whether it is proper to combine these references in the manner that the examiner has done. Also note that when you use any of the reasons of Fig. 13D, you should not merely state the applicable reason, but also supporting facts that pertain to your invention.

9. Does the Combination Disclose Subject Matter of Your Broadest Claim?

Assuming that the references are combined (whether or not they can be), ask yourself if the combination discloses the subject matter of your claim (Reason 37). If not, are the distinctions in your claim patentable under Section 103 (Reasons 1–28 and 39–41)? Also ask yourself whether there are any other errors in the examiner's logic or reasoning.

10. If Your Claims Are Rejected Under Section 112 of the Patent Laws

If your claim has been rejected under Section 112—a very common occurrence, even for patent attorneys—the examiner feels that the language of your claim is not clear or proper. For example, a very common rejection is for failure to supply an antecedent for a "said xxxx" phrase. This is easy to fix. Either positively recite the missing antecedent earlier in the claim or in a referent claim which the claim depends from, or rewrite the phrase to eliminate the "said." If the examiner makes any other type of Section 112 rejection, try to work out alternative language that will obviate this rejection. Alternatively, you can ask the examiner to write clear claims for you. (See Section F2i, below.)

11. What to Do If You Disagree With the Examiner

If you believe your broadest claim is patentable over the prior art and that there is a serious flaw in the examiner's logic, it is theoretically permissible to "stand pat"—that is, leave the claim as it is and argue its patentability in your response. It can be desirable to do this to emphasize the rightness of your position if the examiner is very wrong. If you do file a reply to an OA without changing the specification or claims, your reply is technically not an "amendment," so call it a "response."

In most situations, I advise you not to stand pat, since it's difficult psychologically for the examiner to back down. In other words, it's easier to get the examiner to change directions slightly than to make an about turn. Thus, to save the examiner's ego, it's best to try to make some amendment to the claim, even if it's insignificant.

"Treat all persons you deal with as if they had a sign around their neck reading, 'Make Me Feel Important.'"

—**Mary Kay Ash**

12. Making Amendments Without Narrowing Scope of Claim

It's usually possible to make amendments to a claim that don't narrow its scope. For example, you can recite that a member, which of necessity must be elongated, *is* elongated. By doing this, you have amended the claim without narrowing your scope of coverage. Also, in the electronic field, you can state that a circuit is energized by a direct-current source. For almost any claim you can add a "whereby" clause to the claim stating the function of the mechanism of the claim, and you can add a longer preamble stating in more detail (but not in narrower language) the environment of your invention. The important thing is to add some words to the claim(s), even if you already believe they distinguish over the prior art under Sections 102 and 103, in order to show that you're meeting the examiner part way.

13. Amending Your Claim When You Agree With the Examiner

If you believe your broadest claim isn't patentable as written, and you agree with all or part of the examiner's rejection, you'll have to narrow the claim by adding physical or structural limitations, or by narrowing the limitations already present, in the manner outlined in Chapter 9, or by canceling the broadest claim(s) and making a dependent claim the new independent claim.

Here are some suggestions on how to approach the amendment of your claims:

a. Look for the physical feature(s) in Fig. 13B that constitute the essence of why your invention can be distinguished from the prior art. Then try to put this essence into your claim. Note that you should amend the main claim so as to distinguish physically over the references under Section 102. The physical distinctions should also be significant enough to define structure that is unobvious under Section 103. Merely reciting a single descriptive word will usually not be enough. For example, "Manifold" may not distinguish over a single pipe (even though it should), but reciting "a pipe with a plurality of outlets" will be explicit enough to do the trick. Save your actual reasons as to why the physical distinctions are unobvious for your remarks or for a "whereby" clause at the end of the claim. ("Whereby" clauses can state the advantages of the invention in a relatively informal manner, without as much concern for antecedents, etc.)

b. Don't make your main claim narrower than necessary. Often you can find the limitation you are looking for in one or more dependent claims. (To see how to combine a dependent claim with an independent claim, see Chapter 9, Section J.)

c. Show your invention and the cited references to friends or associates; often they can readily spot the distinguishing essence of your invention. (Remember to use the Nondisclosure Agreement (Form 3-1) if you are maintaining the invention as a trade secret in the patent prosecution phase.)

d. After you've narrowed your main independent claim so that it distinguishes over the prior art cited by the patent examiner, and you feel the distinguishing features are patentable under Section 103 (that is, they're unobvious), do the same for all your other independent claims.

e. If you've changed any independent claims, change your dependent claims so that they completely and correctly correspond in language and numbering with your main claim. If you incorporate a limitation from a dependent claim into your main claim, cancel the dependent claim. This is because the dependent claim will no longer be able to add anything to narrow the independent claim. You may also think of other, narrower dependent claims to replace those that you've canceled; refer to the comparison chart to be sure you've claimed every feature.

Computer Tip. One way to be sure the language of your dependent claims corresponds with that of your independent claim is to use a computer with a word-processing program with a "windows" function, so that you can display both claims on your monitor simultaneously. In this way, you'll be able to compare both claims easily.

f. You should write the narrowest possible claims you're willing to accept, since it will be difficult to amend again if your amended claims are rejected next time around. See Section J on final Office Actions.

g. Be sure all of the less-important specific features of your invention are recited in your amended dependent claims.

h. Try to distinguish by adding quantitative or relative, rather than qualitative, recitations to your claims, since these carry far more weight. For example, say "a rod at least one meter long" or "a rod that is longer than said post" not "a rod of great length" (or "strength").

Changing Claim Language or Invention

If you have to amend your claims to define over the prior art, you should, of course, try to keep them as broad as possible and worded appropriately to cover your invention in its latest and most likely commercial embodiment. If you change the design of your invention from that shown and described in your application, this will not prejudice you so long as your claims are still broad enough to cover the new design. Judges recognize that designs frequently change as inventions mature. If your design changes by a great amount, consider filing a CIP or a new application. (See Chapter 14.)

14. Plan an Outline of Your Response

Indicate in pencil on a copy of your application, or on separate sheets, the amendments you intend to make to your specification, your claims, your drawing, and your remarks. The "remarks" section of your amendment (as shown in Fig. 13E, below) should consist of:

1. a brief summary of all your amendments
2. a discussion of any technical (Section 112) rejections and how you overcame them
3a. a review of the first prior-art rejection made by the examiner
3b. a review of your invention, emphasizing its novelty
3c. a review of the reference(s) cited by the examiner
3d. a summary of how you changed the independent claims of this rejection, quoting your changes, and a request for reconsideration of the examiner's position
3e. a statement as to how your independent claims under this rejection recite novel subject matter over the reference under Section 102 if one reference was cited
3f. a statement of why the references can't legally be combined, if more than one reference was cited
3g. a statement that even if the references were to be combined, the claims would still recite novel subject matter over the combination, if more than one reference was cited
3h. a statement that the novel features of the claim are unobvious, using all possible arguments from Fig. 13D
3i. a discussion of dependent claims under this rejection, indicating that they are independently patentable
4. repeat steps 3a through 3i for each additional prior-art rejection, but don't repeat any text, just refer to it above

5. any request for aid you may wish to make under MPEP 707.07(j) requesting the examiner to write claims, and
6. a conclusion.

See Section F, below, for specifics on drafting your remarks.

At this point, read Fig. 13E, a sample successful amendment from an actual case (now a patent) to see the format customarily used. Continue to refer to Fig. 13E throughout the next four sections of this chapter.

E. Format for Amending the Specification and Claims

Form 13-1 in Appendix 7 provides the initial part of your amendment. Copy the text from this form into a new file on your word processor.

Fill in the serial number, filing date, your name, title of your application, and the examiner's name and examining unit or group art unit. The date on which you actually mail the amendment goes after "date," and the date of the office letter goes at the space indicated in the first paragraph. Put an appropriate letter (A, B, etc.) after "Amendment" to indicate which amendment it is (your first, second, etc.). Then immediately after the "In response to..." sentence, list the sections of your application (Drawings, Specification, and/or Claims, and Remarks) and their page numbers in the manner indicated below. (You should not format your amendment in the form of a personal letter to the examiner, as I have seen some inventors do.)

1. Changes to Specification

If you're going to make any changes to the specification, provide the heading "SPECIFICATION:" on a new page after the sentence printed on Form 13-1. Then indicate the specific paragraphs (or sections) in your application that you want to replace and provide replacement paragraphs marked to indicate deletions by ~~strikethroughs~~ and additions by underlining. If you are deleting five characters or fewer, you may indicate the deletion by double brackets (e.g., "[[claim]]") instead of strikethroughs. If you are deleting a short item, such as a number or punctuation mark, it's better to delete and replace extra portions of the text for clarity (e.g., "[lever 4 and bracket 5] lever 6 and bracket 5"). See the second page of the sample amendment below. (You may refer to paragraphs to be replaced by number, e.g., "Paragraph [0005]," if you numbered the paragraphs when you filed the application.) (Chapter 10.)

Provide 1" top margin (omitted here) to allow space for mounting hole punching.

In The United States Patent and Trademark Office

Appn. Number: 07/910,721
Appn Filed: 2001 Jan 27
Applicants: Nira Schwartz, Arie Shahar, and Richard Woods
Title: Templates and Unique Histogram Analysis
Examiner/GAU: Yon J. Couso/2872

San Francisco, 2003 Jun 23 Mon

AMENDMENT A

Mail Stop Non-Fee Amendments
Commissioner for Patents
P.O. Box 1450
Alexandria, VA 22313-1450

Sir:

In response to the Office Action Mailed 2002 Mar 23, please amend the above application as follows:

SPECIFICATION: Amendments to the specification begin on page 2 of this Amendment.

CLAIMS: Amendments to the claims begin on page 3 of this amendment.

DRAWINGS: A statement explaining the drawing amendments begins on page 7 of this Amendment.

REMARKS: Remarks begin on page 7 of this Amendment.

SPECIFICATION:

Title: Replace with following new title—Inspection Method Using Multiple Template Images, [Templates And Unique Histogram Analysis]

Page 3, last paragraph (extends to page 4), replace with the following new paragraph:

In accordance with one embodiment of the invention, a scanning system uses a plurality of lamps on a rotating carousel which has arms extending radially outward to form a rim.

Page 10, last paragraph (extends to page 11), replace with the following new paragraph:

Lamp 18 has a collimated beam and does not significantly affect photo-cell 20 [trigger photocell 20].

Page 11, after the last paragraph, add the following new paragraph:

Carousel 22 has a photocell 38 on its bottom.

Fig. 13E/1—Sample "Regular" Amendment

CLAIMS: *The following is a listing of all claims in the application with their status and the text of all active claims.*

1.-36. (CANCELED)

37 (CURRENTLY AMENDED) A method for inspecting products that move on a production line for defects, marks, and dimensional accuracy with the use of a sensor and a processing unit having a memory, comprising:

(a) providing and saving in said memory a plurality of computer-generated artificial template images having a plurality of predetermined coordinates and addresses mapped within said memory, said plurality of computer generated artificial template images together defining a full template image.

(b) assigning a plurality of predetermined gray levels to each of said plurality of computer-generated artificial template images.

(c) creating a respective plurality of histogram vectors of said plurality of computer-generated artificial template images, each of said histogram vectors having values which are correlated to said coordinates and addresses mapped within said memory.

(d) creating a product image by sensing one of [said] a plurality of products with [said] a sensor, said product image comprising a multiplicity of pixels with intensity levels expressed as a plurality of respective gray levels.

(e) modifying said product image to produce a modified product image by converting said plurality of gray levels of said product image to a plurality of modified gray levels.

(f) creating a plurality of additional gray levels by mathematically combining said plurality of modified gray levels with said plurality of predetermined gray levels so that said plurality of additional gray levels are different from

said plurality of modified gray levels or said plurality of predetermined gray levels, and

(g) analyzing said plurality of computer-generated artificial template images, said modified product image, and said plurality of additional gray levels for production inspection.

38. (PREVIOUSLY PRESENTED) The method of claim 37, further including creating said additional gray levels by superposing said modified product image onto said template images by summing gray levels assigned to memory locations of said product image and said full template image, so as to produce a summation which represents a superposed image, and saving said summation in said memory.

39. (PREVIOUSLY PRESENTED) The method of claim 38, further including creating a histogram vector of said superposed image.

40. (PREVIOUSLY PRESENTED) The method of claim 39 wherein said creating said histogram of said superposed image is done so that said histogram vector is compressed

41. (PREVIOUSLY PRESENTED) The method of claim 39 wherein said creating of histogram vector of said superposed image is done by including gray levels that are smaller than the highest gray level of said computer-generated artificial template images so that said histogram vector is truncated.

42. (PREVIOUSLY ADDED) The method of claim 39, further including comparing values of said histogram vectors of said superposed image with those of said histogram vectors of said computer-generated artificial template image.

Fig. 13E/2—Sample "Regular" Amendment

Appn. Number 07/910,721 (Schwartz et al.) GAU 3303 Amnt. A contd. 5 of 19

43. (PREVIOUSLY PRESENTED) The method of claim 39, further including analyzing said histogram vectors of said superimposed image by its discontinuities to indicate dimensions in numbers of pixels.

44. (PREVIOUSLY PRESENTED) The method of claim 39, further including analyzing any new gray-level values which appear in said histogram vectors of said superposed image and were absent in said histogram of said computer-generated artificial template image.

45. (PREVIOUSLY PRESENTED) The method of claim 39, further including analyzing said histogram vectors of said superposed image by its discontinuities to detect, size, and map said defects in numbers of pixels.

46. (PREVIOUSLY PRESENTED) The method of claim 39, further including counting the number of pixels equal to gray levels in said histogram vector and saving the count in memory.

47. (PREVIOUSLY PRESENTED) The method of claim 39, further including analyzing said histogram vectors of said superposed image by its discontinuities to detect marks and express their size in numbers of pixels.

48. (PREVIOUSLY PRESENTED) The method of claim 37 wherein said modifying said product image to produce a modified product image is performed by converting said gray levels of said product image to modified gray levels which are higher than said gray levels of said full template image minus the lowest gray level of said computer-generated artificial template images.

Appn. Number 07/910,721 (Schwartz et al.) GAU 3303 Amnt. A contd. 6 of 19

49. (PREVIOUSLY PRESENTED) The method of claim 37, further including creating a superposed image by superposing said modified product image onto said template image by summing gray levels assigned to memory locations of said product image and said computer-generated artificial template images, and saving the results of summation in said memory.

50. (PREVIOUSLY PRESENTED) The method of claim 37 further including creating a truncated histogram vector of said superposed image by including gray levels that are smaller than the highest gray levels of said computer-generated artificial template image.

51. (PREVIOUSLY PRESENTED) The method of claim 37, further including creating a compressed histogram vector of said superimposed image.

52. (PREVIOUSLY PRESENTED) The method of claim 37 wherein said products are printed circuit boards.

53. (PREVIOUSLY PRESENTED) The method of claim 37, further including modifying the number of said template images to one.

54. (NEW) The method of claim 37 wherein said providing and saving in memory is done so that full template image has a size equal to a line created by a plurality of said pixels.

Fig. 13E/3—Sample "Regular" Amendment

Appn. Number 07/910,721 (Schwartz et al.) GAU 3303 Amnt. A contd. 7 of 19

DRAWINGS:

The attached sheet (sheet 1/4) of drawings includes changes to Fig. 2 and replaces the original sheet 1/4 with Figs. 1 and 2. In Fig. 2 previously omitted reference number 13 has been added. The attached sheet (sheet 3/4) of drawings includes corrections to Fig. 5 and replaces original sheet 3/4 with Figs. 5 and 6. The attached red-marked sheet 3/4 indicates in red the corrections made to Fig. 5.

Appn. Number 07/910,721 (Schwartz et al) GAU 3303 Amnt. A contd. 8 of 19

REMARKS—General

By the above amendment, Applicants have amended the title to emphasize the novelty of the invention. They have amended the drawings as indicated to correct a missing reference number and to make minor corrections to Fig. 5.

Also applicants have rewritten all claims to define the invention more particularly and distinctly so as to overcome the technical rejections and define the invention patentably over the prior art.

The Objection To The Specification And The Claims Rejection Under § 112

The specification was objected to under § 112 since it was said to fail to teach how processor 106 works and there was no description as to how the plurality of template images were related to an inspection machine.

Applicants request reconsideration and withdrawal of this objection since it is not necessary to teach how prior-art processor 106 works, and since the specification teachs how the plurality of template images relate to an inspection machine.

First, note heat processor 106 is a known prior-art item of commerce, made and sold by the company indicated on p. 9 of the specification. There is no requirement that a patent application teach how such a prior-art machine works—only how to make and use the invention claimed. The present clearly teaches how to make and use the invention with processor 106. The present system uses processor 106 in a new manner and the present specification clearly teaches in detail how to use it as part of and in the practice of the invention on pp. 13 to 23.

Note that cited prior patent 5,204,911 to Schwartz and Shahar shows the same processor 106 in Fig 12 and discusses how it works under the discussion of Fig. 12—see cols. 13 and 14. Thus the structure and operation of processor 106 was prior art and was well known prior to applicants' filing date.

As to how the plurality of template images are related to an inspection machine, the specification clearly shows this as follows:

Fig. 13E/4—Sample "Regular" Amendment

P. 5 of the specification states that Fig 2 shows a plurality of template images related to an inspection machine and that Fig 3 is a histogram of a template image of Fig 2. This is done in the inspection machine.

P. 13 of the specification discusses the histogram vector of Fig 3 and how it is saved in compressed form. This is done in the inspection machine.

Pp. 13-16 discuss how an image of the product to be inspected is obtained and stored and how the gray levels of the product image are modified by the look-up tables. This is done in the inspection machine.

Pp. 16-18 discuss how the template images are superposed with the product image; this is also done in the inspection machine.

Pp. 18-21 discuss how the histogram of Fig 6 is built from the superposed image, again using the inspection machine.

Pp. 21 to 23 discuss how the machine of Fig 7 of the invention uses the histogram of Fig. 6 to complete the inspection.

Thus the present specification clearly and completely teaches how to make and use the invention in general, and how the template images are related to an inspection machine in particular.

Accordingly applicants submit that the specification does comply with § 112 and therefore request withdrawal of this objection.

The Rejection Of Claim 19 on Hashim and Gaborski Overcome

The last O.A. rejected independent claim 19 on Hashim and Gaborski. Claim 19 has been rewritten as new claim 37 to define patentably over these references, and any combination thereof. Applicants request reconsideration of this rejection, as now applicable to claim 37, for the following reasons:

(1) There is no justification, in Hashim and Gaborski, or in any other prior art separate from applicants' disclosure, which suggests that these references be combined, much less be combined in the manner proposed.

(2) The proposed combination would not be physically possible or operative.

(3) Even if Hashim and Gaborski were to be combined in the manner proposed, the proposed combination would not show all the novel physical features of claim 37.

(4) These novel physical features of claim 37 produce new and unexpected results and hence are unobvious and patentable over these references.

The References and Differences of the Present Invention Thereover

Prior to discussing the claims and the above four points, applicants will first discuss the references and the general novelty of the present invention and its unobviousness over the references.

Hashim creates an image of a product, but modifies the image of the product using a transformation function. Hashim, col. 2, ll. 60-65. Applicants modify the product image using a different transformation function. Hashim modifies the gray levels in his template to either value 0 or value B related to threshold T (col. 2, l. 57, to col. 3, l. 22). Thus Hashim's procedure modifies the gray levels according to a value and not according to coordinates. There Hashim's procedure of gray-level modification does not enable preselected coordinates and addresses to be mapped inside any template image. Further it does not assign preselected gray levels to any preselected coordinates and addresses. Hashim creates a histogram to be used as a tool for modifying gray levels of his template images (col. 2, l. 57, to col. 3, l. 22). However his histogram cannot be used for evaluation of product dimensions or as an indication of any coordinate values, as can applicants' histogram.

Gaborski's template is composed of vertical lines which are spread apart. There are not coordinates mapping the bars inside the template by assigning preselected gray levels to them, as in applicant's invention. Gaborski creates a histogram to be used as a tool for inspection of maximum correlation between template image and product image. His histogram vector does not contain information about the product's coordinates and dimensional measurements, as applicants' histogram vector will supply.

Fig. 13E/5—Sample "Regular" Amendment

The last O.A. notes that Hashim's system does the following:

(1) creates template images.

(2) creates product images.

(3) creates additional gray levels.

(4) modifies the additional gray levels to prevent ambiguity.

However in general, to create a group of gray levels (A') that are different than gray levels of another group ('B') and the gray levels of still another group ('C'), the procedure of creating the gray levels of group 'A' must take into account the values of the gray levels of groups 'B' and 'C' to prevent ambiguity. Hashim does not do this, but applicants do.

When Hashim creates (modifies) his gray levels [step (4) above] he considers only gray levels within the image that he modifies (Hashim, col. 2, l. 57 to col. 3, l. 18). He does not consider nor is he aware of the gray levels of step (1) above when he performs his modification step (4). Therefore, he cannot have any assurance that ambiguity is prevented. Whatever algorithm he uses to operate on the equalized histogram, this is then scanned to ascertain the positions of the edges (col. 3, ll. 10 to 18); it is NOT done to prevent ambiguity.

With regard to the compression of the histogram vectors, applicants perform this for the first time. Until now no one ever thought of compressing histogram vectors and suggested same, much less actually did it. Applicants' method identifies and maps coordinates using gray levels. Using this: one may create a very long histogram vector, or a large number of short histograms. By compressing the histogram vector, applicants save valuable processing time and storage space. As stated, this procedure was not done before, so neither it nor its concomitant advantages were known or appreciated.

Hashim and Gaborski Do Not Contain Any Justification to Support Their Combination, Much Less in the Manner Proposed

With regard to the proposed combination of Hashim and Gaborski, it is well

known that in order for any prior-art references themselves to be validly combined for use in a prior-art § 103 rejection, *the references themselves* (or some other prior art) must suggest that they be combined. E.g., as was stated in In re Sernaker, 217 U.S.P.Q. 1, 6 (C.A.F.C. 1983):

"[P]rior art references in combination do not make an invention obvious unless something in the prior art references would suggest the advantages to be derived from combining their teachings."

That the suggestion to combine the references should not come from applicant was forcefully stated in Orthopedic Equipment Co. v. United States, 217 U.S.P.Q. 193, 199 (C.A.F.C. 1983):

"It is wrong to use the patent in suit [here the patent application] as a guide through the maze of prior art references, combining the right references in the right way to achieve the result of the claims in suit [here the claims pending]. Monday morning quarterbacking is quite improper when resolving the question of nonobviousness in a court of law [here the PTO]."

As was further stated in Uniroyal, Inc. v. Rudkin-Wiley Corp., 5 U.S.P.Q.2d 1434 (C.A.F.C. 1988), "[w]here prior-art references require selective combination by the court to render obvious a subsequent invention, there must be some reason for the combination other than the hindsight gleaned from the invention itself ... *Something in the prior art must suggest the desirability and thus the obviousness of making the combination*." [Emphasis supplied.]

In line with these decisions, recently the Board stated in Ex parte Levengood, 28 U.S.P.Q.2d 1300 (P.T.O.B.A.&I. 1993):

"In order to establish a *prima facie* case of obviousness, it is necessary for the examiner to present *evidence*, preferably in the form of some teaching, suggestion, incentive or inference in the applied prior art, or in the form of generally available knowledge, that one having ordinary skill in the art

Fig. 13E/6—Sample "Regular" Amendment

would have been led to combine the relevant teachings of the, applied references in the proposed manner to arrive at the claimed invention.... That which is within the capabilities of one skilled in the art is not synonymous with obviousness.... That one can *reconstruct and/or explain* the theoretical mechanism of an invention by means of logic and sound scientific reasoning does not afford the basis for an obviousness conclusion unless that logic and reasoning also supplies sufficient impetus to have led one of the ordinary skill in the art to combine the teachings of the references to make the claimed invention.... Our reviewing courts have often advised the Patent and Trademark Office that it can satisfy the burden of establishing a *prima facie* case of obviousness only by showing some objective teaching in either the prior art, or knowledge generally available to one of ordinary skill in the art, that 'would lead' that individual 'to combine the relevant teachings of the references.' ... Accordingly, an examiner cannot establish obviousness by locating references which describe various aspects of a patent applicant's invention without also providing evidence of the motivating force which would impel one skilled in the art to do what the patent applicant has done."

In the present case, there is no reason given in the last O.A. to support the proposed combination, other than the statement "both references teach histogram template." However the fact that both references teach a histogram template is not sufficient to gratuitously and selectively substitute parts of one reference (Gaborski's template library) for a part of another reference in order to meet applicants' novel claimed combination.

The O.A. noted (p. 5) that the combination of Hashim and Gaborski produces an advantage (broadens system performance). Applicants submit that the fact that the combination produces advantages militates in favor of *applicants* because it proves that the combination produces new and unexpected results and hence is unobvious.

As stated in the above Levengood case,

"That one can reconstruct and/or explain the theoretical mechanism of an invention by means of logic and sound scientific reasoning does not afford the basis for an obviousness conclusion unless that logic and reasoning also supplies sufficient impetus to have led one of ordinary skill in the art to combine the teachings of the references to make claimed invention."

Applicants therefore submit that combining Hashim and Gaborski is not legally justified and is therefore improper. Thus they submit that the rejection on these references is also improper and should be withdrawn.

Applicants respectfully request, if the claims are again rejected upon any combination of references, in accordance with M.P.E.P. § 706.02, that the Examiner include a explanation, in accordance with Ex parte Clapp, 27 U.S.P.Q. 972 (P.O.B.A. 1985), and Ex parte Levengood, supra, a "factual basis to support his conclusion that would have been obvious" to make the combination.

Even If Hashim and Gaborski Were to be Combined in the Manner Proposed, the Proposed Combination Would Not Show All of the Novel Physical Features of Claim 37

However even if the combination of Hashim and Gaborski were legally justified, claim 37 would still have novel (and unobvious) physical features over the proposed combination. In other words, applicant's invention, as defined by claim 37, comprises much more than merely substituting a plurality of templates for one template.

Specifically, clauses (a) and (b) of claim 37 clearly distinguish applicant's template histogram from Gaborski's and Hashim's, or any possible combination thereof, since these clauses recite:

"(a) providing and saving in said memory a plurality of computer-generated artificial template images, each of said plurality of computer-generated artificial template images having a plurality of predetermined coordinates and addresses mapped within said memory, said plurality of computer-

Fig. 13E/7—Sample "Regular" Amendment

generated artificial template images together defining a full template image.

(b) assigning a plurality of predetermined gray levels to each of said plurality of computer-generated artificial template images."

Neither Hasim nor Gaborski show these feature because neither of their systems assign specific gray levels to any predetermined coordinates and addresses, as applicants' system does.

By assigning specific gray levels to predetermined coordinates and addresses, correlated to addresses, applicants' system causes the histogram vectors of clause (c) to have values correlated to addresses, a feature that is missing in ordinary histogram vectors, such as those of Hashim and Gaborski. Thus Hashim and Gaborski also lack the feature of clause (c), i.e.:

"(c) creating a respective plurality of histogram vectors of said plurality of computer-generated artificial template images, each of said histogram vectors having values which are correlated to said coordinates and addresses mapped within said memory."

Clause (f) also clearly distinguishes over Gaborski and Hashim since it recites:

"(f) creating a plurality of additional gray levels by mathematically combining said plurality of modified gray levels with said plurality of preselected gray levels so that said plurality of additional gray levels are different from said plurality of modified gray levels or said plurality of preselected gray levels."

Neither Hashim nor Gaborski create any additional gray levels by mathematically combining the plurality of modified gray levels with the plurality of preselected gray levels so that the additional gray levels are different from the modified gray levels and the preselected gray levels.

As stated above, when Hashim creates his gray levels [step(4) above] he considers only gray levels within the image that he modifies (Hashim, col. 2, l. 57 to col. 3

l. 18). He does not consider nor is he aware of the gray levels of step (1) above while his modification step (4) above is performed.

Therefore, he cannot have any assurance that ambiguity is prevented and he does not combine any previous gray levels to arrive at his additional gray levels.

Thus applicants submit that their invention is much more than merely substituting a plurality of templates for one template and that claim 37 clearly recites novel physical subject matter which distinguishes over any possible combination of Hashim and Gaborski.

The Novel Physical Features of Claim 37 Produce New and Unexpected Results and Hence Are Unobvious and Patentable Over These References Under § 103

Also applicants submit that the novel physical features of claim 37 are also unobvious and hence patentable under § 103 since they produce new and unexpected results over Hashim and Gaborski, or any combination thereof.

These new and unexpected results are the ability of applicants' system to locate addresses and coordinates in memory by referring to the gray levels in the histogram vectors. This in turn results in higher-speed image processing for detecting defects and making dimensional measurements. Applicants' system therefore is vastly superior to that of either Hashim and Gaborski, or any possible combination thereof. The novel features of applicants' system which effect these differences are, as stated, clearly recited in claim 37.

The Dependent Claims Are a Fortiori Patentable Over Hashim and Gaborski

New dependent claims 38 to 54 incorporate all the subject matter of claim 37 and add additional subject matter which makes them a fortiori and independently patentable over these references.

Claim 38 additionally recites

"creating said additional gray levels by superposing said modified product

Fig. 13E/8—Sample "Regular" Amendment

Appn. Number 07/910,721 (Schwartz et al.) GAU 3303   Amnt. A contd.   17 of 19

image onto said template images by summing gray levels assigned to memory location of said product image and said full template image, so as to produce a summation which represents a superposed image, and saving said summation in said memory."

This is entirely foreign to Hashim and Gaborski, or any combination thereof since, as stated, the systems of these references do not sum any gray levels of the product image and the full template image. Hashim modifies the product image using a transformation function, rather than by summing. Gorborski does not sum either.

Claim 39 further adds "creating a histogram vector of said superposed image." Again this is clearly foreign to Hashim and Gaborski.

Claims 40, 41, 50, and 51 further add that the histogram vector is compressed or truncated. As stated above, this feature is novel with applicant and produces new and unexpected results—the saving of processing time and storage space. The last O.A. stated that it would be obvious to compress the histogram vector "in order to **increase** the processing time." [Emphasis added.] As stated, compressing the vector **saves or decreases**, rather than increases, processing time. This is an important and significant advantage. Applicants request reconsideration of the statement that compression would be obvious since they submit that the facts prove that it is (a) novel, and (b) produces valuable new, improved, and unexpected results proves that it is unobvious.

Claim 42 recites comparing values of the histogram vectors of the superposed image with those of the histogram vectors of said computer-generated artificial template image. Neither Hashim nor Gaborski looks for maximum correlation.

Claims 43, 45, and 47 recite analyzing the histogram vectors of the superposed image by its discontinuities to indicate dimensions in numbers of pixels. Neither Hashim nor Gaborski do this: Hashim analyzes discontinuities in the product image itself.

Appn. Number 07/910,721 (Schwartz et al) GAU 3303   Amnt. A contd.   18 of 19

Claim 44 recites analyzing any new gray-level values which appear in the histogram vectors of the superposed image and were absent in the histogram of the computer-generated artificial template image. Neither Hashim nor Gaborski do this: Hashim analyzes new gray levels for threshold levels in order to modify the product image.

Claim 46 recites counting the number of pixels equal to gray levels in the histogram vector and saving the count in memory. Neither Hashim nor Gaborski count pixels in the product image.

Claim 48 recites converting the gray levels of the product image to modified gray levels which are higher than the gray levels of the full template image minus the lowest gray level of the computer-generated artificial template images. Neither Hashim nor Gaborski convert gray levels while preventing ambiguity of gray levels: Hashim converts gray levels "to ascertain the positions of edges." Hashim, Col. 3, 1. 12

Claim 49 recites creating a superposed image by superposing the modified product image onto the template image by summing gray levels assigned to memory location of the product image and the computer-generated artificial template images, and saving the results of the summation in memory. Neither Hashim nor Gaborski do this: Gaborski creates multiplications of the product image and the template image. However his template image is different from applicants' template and his product image is modified differently from applicants' product image.

Claim 53 recites modifying the number of said template images to one. Neither Hashim nor Gaborski do this.

Claim 54 recites that the providing and saving memory is done so that the full template image has a size equal to a line created by a plurality of the pixels. Neither Hashim nor Gaborski deal with an image size of one line.

Accordingly applicants submit that the dependent claims are a fortiori patentable and should also be allowed.

Fig. 13E/9—Sample "Regular" Amendment

Appn. Number 07/910,721   (Schwartz et al.)   GAU 3303   Amnt. A contd.   19 of 19

CONCLUSION

For all the above reasons, applicants submit that the specification and claims are now in proper form, and that the claims all define patentably over the prior art. Therefore they submit that this application is now in condition for allowance, which action they respectfully solicit.

Conditional Request for Constructive Assistance

Applicants have amended the specification and claims of this application so that they are proper, definite, and define novel structure which is also unobvious. If, for any reason this application is not believed to be in full condition for allowance, applicants respectfully request the constructive assistance and suggestions of the Examiner pursuant to M.P.E.P. § 2173.02 and § 707.07(j) in order that the undersigned can place this application in allowable condition as soon as possible and without the need for further proceedings.

Very respectfully,

Nira Schwartz
Nira Schwartz

Arie Shahar
Arie Shahar
————Applicants Pro Se

Richard Woods
Richard Woods

Enc: New sheets 1/4 and 3/4 of drawings and a copy of sheet 3/4 marked in red to indicate the corrections to Fig. 5.

950 Parker Street
Berkeley, CA 94710

Tel. (510) 549-1976; Fax (510) 548-5902

Certificate of Facsimile Transmission. I certify that on the date below I will fax this paper (including Appendix) to GAU 2872 of the U.S. Patent and Trademark Office at 703-872-9319.

2003 Jan. 23

Nira Schwartz

Fig. 13E/10—Sample "Regular" Amendment

When your amendment is received, the clerk of the examining group will make each change in red ink in handwriting on the official copy of your application in the manner you direct. Thus, you should ensure that there is no ambiguity in your amendments.

Be sure that your amendments to the specification don't contain any "new matter." (See Section B18, above.)

If you want to make a large number of amendments to the specification, it's better to submit an entirely retyped specification, called a "substitute specification." To file a substitute specification you must submit an entirely new specification with the changes made in clean copy form, plus a comparison specification with each change highlighted so the examiner can verify that you haven't added any new matter. Also, you must certify that the substitute specification doesn't contain any new matter; see MPEP 608.01(q) for instructions.

2. Amendments to Claims

If you want to amend your claims, start on a new page with the following heading and text:

CLAIMS: Please amend the claims according to the status designations in the following list, which contains all claims that were ever in the application, with the text of all active claims.

The number and status of each claim that is now or was ever in the application must be indicated by providing one of the seven parenthetical expressions, below, after the claim number. (I've indicated the meaning of each parenthetical expression.)

A. (ORIGINAL) The claim has the same number and content as originally filed.

B. (CURRENTLY AMENDED) The claim has the same number as originally or later filed, but is marked up to make amendments (additions and ~~deletions~~) to it.

C. (PREVIOUSLY PRESENTED) The claim was previously amended in marked-up form. It is now typed in clean copy form with the same number as before.

D. (CANCELED) The claim has been or is currently being canceled. Its text is not typed here.

E. (WITHDRAWN) The claim is directed to a nonelected invention, so it is no longer active and is not typed. (It may be submitted in a divisional application.)

F. (NEW) The claim is new and is typed with a new number.

G. NOT ENTERED (The claim was previously submitted after a final action but the examiner refused to enter it.)

You must list all claims in numerical order, regardless of what action you're taking with them; you may not group all deleted claims together unless they're consecutive. See the example below.

For canceled and not entered claims, you should provide only the number and status, but not the claim's text. You should provide the number, status, and claim text for every active (currently under examination) claim. (Fortunately word processors with a copy function allow rapid entry.)

You must present the text of all active claims in clean copy form, except for claims that are being currently amended; use the CURRENTLY AMENDED format for the latter.

Which format should you use to amend claims—CURRENTLY AMENDED or NEW?

I recommend that you use the CURRENTLY AMENDED (marked-up) format if you are making minor changes only to the claim, and/or if you want to point out to the examiner just how you're amending the claim. Use ~~strikethroughs~~ to show deletions and underlining to show additions—the same as for specification amendments. As with specification amendments, if you are deleting five characters or fewer, you may indicate the deletion by double brackets (e.g., "[[lever]]") instead of strikethroughs. If you are deleting a short item, such as a number or punctuation mark, it's better to delete and replace extra portions of the text for clarity (e.g., "[lever 4 and bracket 5] lever 6 and bracket 5").

If you are making any major changes to the claim or prefer to present it in clean copy form, as I usually do and as is done in all foreign countries, I recommend that you use the NEW format: Type the status expression (CANCELED) after the number of the old claim or claims that you're replacing and retype the claim with a new number (use the next highest number) followed by the status expression (NEW), followed in turn by the text of the claim in clean copy form. Include all the changes that you care to make.

Don't forget to re-present all other active claims (those that you're not currently amending) in clean copy form with their statuses indicated.

Here's an example of a claim listing for an amendment:

CLAIMS: Please amend the claims according to the status designations in the following list, which contains all claims that were ever in the application, with the text of all active claims.

1-5 (CANCELED)

6. (ORIGINAL) A bucket made of nylon.

7. (WITHDRAWN) A bucket with a carrying strap.

8. (PREVIOUSLY PRESENTED) *A bucket with a handle.*

9. (CANCELED)

10. (CURRENTLY AMENDED) A bucket with a <u>blue</u> ~~green~~ handle and a round and oval bottom.

11. (WITHDRAWN) A bucket with a bottom hole.

12. (CANCELED)

13. (NEW) A bucket with sides and a bottom which are both made of plastic.

F. Drafting the Remarks

Next, add the "remarks" portion of your amendment starting on a new page. Some general rules for drafting remarks that I'll state first may seem strange, but they're the customary practice, and to deviate substantially may make the examiner feel uncomfortable and take a negative attitude toward your invention.

1. General Rules for Drafting Remarks

Rule 1: As stated before, when writing your remarks observe Inventor's Commandment #22 by never admitting that any prior art anticipates or renders any part of your invention obvious. Similarly, never derogate your invention or any part of it.

Rule 2: Never get personal with the examiner. If you must refer to the examiner, always use the third person. For example, never state "You rejected…"; instead, state "The Examiner [note the capitalization] has rejected…." Better yet, state "The Office Action rejects…" or "Claim 1 was rejected…." Never, never address the examiner by name (do list the examiner's name the caption), and never make your amendment a "Dear Mr. [Examiner's Name]" letter. See the sample amendment of Fig. 13E, above, for how it's done.

Rule 3: If there's an error in the OA, refer to the error in the OA, and don't state that the examiner made the error. Even if you find the examiner made a completely stupid error, just deal with it in a very formal way, keep emotions and personalities out of your response, and don't invalidate the examiner. Remember, you've probably made some stupid errors in your life also, and you wouldn't want your nose rubbed in them. It is okay to respectfully challenge an examiner who you feel is wrong. For example, "If this rejection is repeated, applicant respectfully requests that the examiner explain where, in the references themselves, or in the art, there is a suggestion that they be combined."

Rule 4: When referring to yourself, always refer to yourself in the third person as "Applicant" and never as "I."

Rule 5: Stick to the issues in your remarks. Be relevant and to the point and don't discuss personalities or irrelevant issues. Never antagonize the examiner, no matter how much you'd like to. It's improper, and, if you turn the examiner against you, it can considerably narrow the scope of claims that are ultimately allowed.

Rule 6: Use only the legally relevant, logical arguments that are listed in Fig. 13D. Don't use arguments which, although plausible, aren't legally relevant or logical. Among these are: (1) stating that your invention is superior to a prior patented device (§ 103) without first stating that your claims recite novel hardware over the prior patent (§ 102); (2) that a cited patent shouldn't have been granted or has less novelty than yours (the PTO isn't bound to repeat its past mistakes); and (3) that you spent a lot of time and/or effort to come up with the invention. Also, some inventors have actually telephoned the patentee-inventor of a cited patent. This is a futile exercise, since there's nothing a patentee can do to help you; a patent speaks for itself. As a further example, if the examiner says pages 11 and 12 of your specification don't provide a clear description of the invention, tell why these pages do the job; don't simply explain how it works without reference to these pages.

Rule 7: Whenever you write any new claims or make any additions to a present claim, you must tell why the claim was amended and how the amendments distinguish over the prior art the examiner has cited under Sections 102 and 103. Follow Inventor's Commandment #7 from Chapter 5, repeated below, and Patent Rule 111(b) and (c):

Inventor's Commandment #7

To evaluate or argue the patentability of any invention, use a two-step process: a) First determine what novel features (§ 102) the invention has over the closest prior-art reference(s)—novelty can be a new physical (hardware) feature, a new combination or rearrangement of two separate old features, or a new use of an old feature; and b) Then determine if the novelty produces any new and unexpected results or otherwise indicates unobviousness (§ 103).

(b) In order to be entitled to reexamination or reconsideration, the applicant must make request therefor in writing, and must distinctly and specifically point out the supposed errors in the examiner's action; the applicant must respond to every ground of objection and rejection in the prior Office Action (except that request may be made that objections or

requirements as to form not necessarily to further reconsideration of the claim be held in abeyance until allowable subject matter is indicated), and the applicant's action must appear throughout to be a bona fide attempt to advance the case to final action. A general allegation that the claims define a patentable invention without specifically pointing out how the language of the claims patentably distinguish them from the references does not comply with the requirements of this section.

(c) In amending an application in response to a rejection, the applicant must clearly point out the patentable novelty that the applicant thinks the claims present in view of the state of the art disclosed by the references cited or the objection made. The applicant must also show how the amendments avoid such references or objections.

Rule 8: If you do disagree and think the OA was wrong, you must state exactly why you disagree. If you agree that a claim is obvious over the prior art, don't admit this in your response (see Inventor's Commandment #22); simply cancel the claim and don't give any reason for it, or if you must comment, state merely that it has been canceled in view of the coverage afforded by the remaining claims. However, if you amend any claim be sure to state why you are amending it to preserve your rights to use the DoE later; see Section A27 above.

Rule 9: Make a careful, complete, and convincing presentation, but you don't have to overly agonize about words or minutiae. The reality is that many examiners don't read your remarks or else skim through them very rapidly. This is because they're generally working under a quota system, which means they have to dispose of (finally reject or allow) a certain number of cases in each fiscal quarter. Thus, the examiners are under time pressure and it takes a lot of time to read remarks. It's important to cover all the substantive points in the Office Action and to deal with every objection and rejection. If you do make an error, as stated, the PTO will almost always give you an opportunity to correct it, rather than forcing you to abandon your application.

Two good ways to make sure your examiner reads and (hopefully) understands your points and reasons are to liberally sprinkle your amendment with boldfaced "arguing" headings which themselves tell your whole story (as is done in the sample amendment of Fig. 13E), and to keep your paragraphs short and inviting. For example, some arguing headings might be, "Briskin Does Not Show Any Elongated Lever," "Claim 1 Clearly Defines Over Warner Under Section 102," "Ihara Could Not Be Operatively Combined With Harolde," and "Applicant's Rasterizer Produces New and Unexpected Results Over Hearsh."

Rule 10: If possible, thank or praise the examiner if you can find a reason to do so with sincerity—for example, "Applicant thanks the Examiner for the clear and understandable Office Action." Examiners get criticized and told they're all wet so often that they'll welcome any genuine, deserved praise.

Rule 11: Don't emphasize your beliefs; they're considered irrelevant. For example, don't say "Applicant *believes* this invention is patentable." Rather say, "Since the claims define novel structure that produces new and unexpected results as described above, Applicant *submits* that such claims are clearly patentable."

Rule 12: Although it's okay to state *briefly* why your invention is superior to that of the reference(s), the main thrust of your argument should be a two-part legal argument that tells (a) how your invention, as claimed, differs from the reference(s), and (b) why these differences are important. Again, see Inventor's Commandment #7 above.

You may wonder whether it makes sense to put much effort into your remarks even though the chances are great they won't be carefully read. My opinion is that it does, because you never know. Think of your effort as a kind of insurance against being the one in five (or whatever) whose remarks are in fact subjected to close scrutiny.

Although it's difficult, I recommend that you do the best job you possibly can in Amendment A, since it will probably be the last chance you get to amend your claims in this application. This is so important and is violated so often, that I've made it Inventor's Commandment #26, at the beginning of this chapter. After you draft your amendment, I suggest that you wait a few days and come back and review it again, pretending that you're the examiner. This will probably give you important insights and enable you to improve it further.

2. How to Draft Your Remarks

Your remarks should first provide a brief positive summary of what you've done to the specification and claims. For example, you can start off with a summary as follows: "Applicant has amended the specification and claims to put this application in full and clear condition for allowance. She has amended the specification editorially and to correct those errors noted by the Examiner. Also she has rewritten claims 1 to 5 as new Claims 13 to 18 to more particularly

define the invention in a patentable manner over the cited prior art." Then briefly summarize what each claim recites, as is done in Fig. 13E, above. If the drawing has been objected to, state that it will be corrected after allowance. If you want to make a voluntary amendment to the drawing, refer to the drawing amendment explanation on page one of the amendment (Fig. 13E/1), include a drawing amendment on a separate drawing amendment page (Fig. 13E/4), and attached replacement sheets and a red-marked sheet indicating the changes, if necessary. See Section G, below, for more information. Then include a separate section for each rejection in the amendment.

a. Restate First Rejection

After providing a positive heading for the first rejection of the OA (for example, "The New Claims Overcome the Rejection on Jones and Smith"), restate this rejection. For example, "The Office Action rejected Claims 1 to 5 as unpatentable over Jones in view of Smith." The examiner, thus oriented, saves the time it would take to reread the OA.

b. Review Each Reference Relied on in the Rejection

One or two sentences for each is sufficient. For example: "Reference A (Smith patent 1,234,567) shows a ... [and so forth]."

c. Specifically Describe Any Claim Changes and Argue Section 102 and Then Section 103

Discuss specifically how and why the claim in question has been amended and how it recites structure that physically distinguishes over the references under Section 102. The flowchart of Fig. 13C gives the specifics as to how to do that. For example, *"Claim 1, now rewritten as new Claim 5, recites ...." This language distinguishes over Smith and Jones under Section 102 because Smith does not show [etc.] and Jones does not show {etc].")* (I find it helpful to keep the claim I'm discussing displayed in one window of my computer monitor while I type my remarks in another window. Often I need to amend the claim to distinguish further over a reference under Section 102 as I write the remarks.)

Then, once you've established the novelty of your claim(s), show why the novel features are unobvious and patentable—for example, "These distinctions are submitted to be of patentable merit under Section 103 because [discuss new results that flow from your novel structure, giving as many reasons as you can from Fig. 13D, Part 1, and your completed Form 4-2]."

Using a 102/103 Approach

You must use a 102/103 approach even if your claim was rejected on Section 102 alone. This 102/103 approach is useful if you don't understand the examiner's reasoning. That is, rather than try to figure out what the examiner was trying to say, or questioning the examiner, simply put forth a detailed, cogent 102/103 argument. This will usually win the day, or at worst, reframe the issues in your favor.

I can't emphasize enough that you should discuss how your invention, *as claimed*, distinguishes over—that is, has novel physical features not shown in—the reference, not how the reference differs from your invention, and not, at this stage, why your invention is better than the reference. Remember that under Section 112, a means plus a function is considered a physical recitation.

The following jingle may help you remember this important rule:

> *Never argue what's not in your claim*
> *You'll miss the mark and may lose the game.*

Also be logical in your arguments. For example, if you're claiming B and a reference shows A and B, don't argue that A is no good. Also, don't argue that a reference should be taken lightly—that is, it's a "paper patent," because its invention was never put into commercial use—unless you're absolutely sure of your facts and the reference isn't a dead ringer for your invention.

d. Refute Any Improper Combination of References

If a combination of several references has been cited against your claim, first state why the combination cannot properly be made and then discuss your distinctions under Section 103. For example: *The combination of Smith's lever with Jones's pedal mechanism is submitted to be improper because neither Smith nor Jones suggests such a combination, and one skilled in the art would have no reason to make such a combination. That is, the fact that Smith shows a specific lever does not suggest that his lever can be used with Jones's pedal mechanism, especially since Jones shows his own workable lever. Moreover, the combination could not be made physically because the lever of the Smith type would not fit in or work with Jones's pedal mechanism because…. However, even if the combination could be made, Claim 1 distinguishes because the combination does not show* [here quote language], *and these distinctions are patentable under Section 103 because* [discuss new results and give as many reasons as you can from Fig. 13D and Form 4-2].

If the references themselves don't suggest that they should be combined (Reasons 29–33 in Fig. 13D), you can use the arguments and cases from pp. 8 and 9 of Fig. 13E; this is a very common defect in many current rejections and the cases cited give powerful arguments.

e. Note Secondary Factors of Unobviousness

If your invention has achieved any commercial success or has won any praise, this is relevant, and you should mention it here. If possible, submit copies of advertisements for your invention, copies of industry or trade praise, sales figures, a commercially sold sample, etc. These things reify the invention (that is, make it a "fait accompli") and impress most examiners. If you are submitting any evidence of commercial success, you should do it with a declaration with attached exhibits stating how the invention has achieved commercial success and how such success is related to the novel features of the invention. See Fig. 10S and the next section for the *format* (not the substance) of such a declaration.

f. Draft Any Needed Declaration Under Rule 132 to Refute Technical Points Raised by Examiner

If you want to challenge any technical points raised by the examiner, such as proving that your invention works in a superior manner to a reference, that two references can't be combined, or that a cited reference works in a far inferior way to yours, you or an expert in the field should do the necessary research and make the necessary tests (including building and testing a model of the cited reference) and then submit a "Declaration Under Rule 132." The Declaration should have a caption as in Form 13-1 and an appropriate heading, such as "Rule 132 Declaration Regarding Inferior Performance of Elias Patent." The body of the Declaration should start,

> *Jane Inventor declares as follows:*
> 1. *I am the inventor [or I am a mechanical engineer (state education, experience, and awards)] in the above patent application.*

Then, in numbered paragraphs, detail your technical facts and/or reasons, including tests you made, etc., but state facts, not conclusions or arguments. Whenever you make any legal declaration or affidavit (as opposed to a brief or remarks), heed the words of the immortal Joe Friday, of television's *Dragnet* fame: "Just the facts, ma'am." You can attach and refer to "exhibits"—that is, documents in support of your arguments.

Then conclude with a "declaration paragraph," as in the last paragraph of Form 10-1 (that states "I hereby declare…") and sign and date the declaration.

Similarly, if you want to mention any additional factors relating to your invention, such as commercial success or copying by an infringer, which are relevant to patentability, you can submit a similar Rule 132 declaration. You can attach relevant "Exhibits," such as a prototype, a commercial sample, advertising, or sales reports. As stated, working models usually make believers out of negative examiners.

g. Request Reconsideration

Request reconsideration of the rejection(s) and allowance of the claim: "Therefore applicant submits that Claim 5 is allowable over the cited references and solicits reconsideration and allowance."

If you have dependent claims that were rejected, treat these in the same manner. Since a dependent claim incorporates all the limitations of the parent claim, you can state that the dependent claim is patentable for the same reasons given with respect to the parent claim, and then state that it is even more patentable because it adds additional limitations, which you should discuss briefly.

h. Respond to Rejections Under Section 112 for Lack of Clarity or Conciseness

If a technical rejection has been made (under Section 112), discuss how you've amended your claim and why your new claim is clear and understandable.

i. Request Claim-Drafting Assistance From PTO

Once again, I emphasize that if you feel you have patentable subject matter in your application but have difficulty in writing new claims, you can request that the examiner write new claims for you pursuant to MPEP Section 707.07(j). Your remarks are the place to do this. For example, state, "Therefore Applicant submits that patentable subject matter is clearly present. If the Examiner agrees but does not feel that the present claims are technically adequate, applicant respectfully requests that the examiner write acceptable claims pursuant to MPEP 707.07(j)." If the examiner writes any claims for you, don't rest on them unless you're sure that the broadest one is as broad as the prior art permits, using the criteria above and in Chapter 5. Remember, if you are dissatisfied with the examiner's claims, you can once again submit your own claims, you can submit the examiner's claims with whatever amendments you choose, or you can interview the examiner to discuss the matter. You should request claim drafting assistance when you file, or after the first OA, not after a final OA.

j. Repeat the Above for Any Other Rejections in the Office Action

After you've covered and hopefully decimated the first rejection in the manner discussed in Subsections a to i, above, then do the same for each additional rejection—that is, provide a separate heading for the rejection, review the rejection, review the reference(s), review your new claims, discuss why they distinguish under Section 102, then why the novel features are patentable under Section 103, and request reconsideration and allowance.

k. Discuss Nonapplied References

If a reference of interest has been cited but not applied against any claim, state that you've reviewed it but that it doesn't show your invention or render it obvious.

l. Acknowledge Allowed or Allowable Claims.

Often the examiner will allow some claims, or indicate that certain claims would be allowed if amended in a certain way or rewritten in independent form. You should acknowledge this statement and if necessary, tell how you handled it—for example, "Applicant acknowledges the allowance of claims 1 to 7 with appreciation," or "Applicant has rewritten claim 13 (indicated to contain allowable subject matter) in independent form as new claim 26."

m. Conclusion

Last, provide a conclusion that should repeat and summarize—for example, *"For all the reasons given above, applicant respectfully submits that the errors in the specification are corrected, the claims comply with Section 112, the claims define over the prior art under Section 102* [briefly repeat why]*, and the claimed distinctions are of patentable merit under Section 103 because of the new results* [repeat them briefly again] *provided. Accordingly, applicant submits that this application is now in full condition for allowance, which action applicant respectfully solicits."* Then add the closing, "Very respectfully," followed by your signature, typewritten name, your address, and telephone number on the left-hand side. If you have a co-inventor(s), all of you must sign the amendment.

n. Do Your Very Best Job

It's important to do your very best job in your first amendment, since it's the only full opportunity you'll get to answer the examiner's position. I suggest that after writing the amendment, you have a friend read it or you come back to it after a few days and read it from the viewpoint of your examiner. As stated in Inventor's Commandment #26, make sure your amendment in response to the first OA is complete, carefully crafted, and includes all arguments and the narrowest claims possible, since the next OA will be final.

G. Drawing Amendments

If your Office Action includes any objections to the drawing(s), you must correct these before the case can issue and usually as soon as allowable subject matter is indicated. In addition, if you want to make any voluntary amendments to any Fig(s) of the drawings, you must now make these by submitting a copy of the sheet with the Fig(s) marked in red with the changes, and a replacement sheet with the changes made in black.

To deal with any drawing objections by the examiner or the Drafting Department, first include or check the listing paragraph on page 1 (contents page) of your amendment (see Fig 13E/1) as follows:

"DRAWINGS: A statement explaining the drawing amendments made by this amendment begins on page *[state page]* of this amendment."

Then, on the appropriate DRAWINGS page of the amendment, state that you have attached a replacement sheet with the drawing objections corrected (see Fig. 13E/4). Although not necessary, I prefer to refer briefly to the corrected sheets at the beginning of the Remarks (Fig 13E/5). To make the corrections correct your Bristol board or Mylar film originals, or make new CAD originals, and file new, good xerographic (or CAD output) copies. All lines must be crisp, black, and sharp, and all objections on the drawing objection sheet must be corrected.

List the sheets as an enclosure at the end of the amendment (Fig 13E/10) and attach new (corrected) sheets to the amendment for substitution for your original drawings. (Attach the new drawing sheets with a paper clip—do not staple them.) Be sure to put your name, Serial Number, and Examination Group on the back of any replacement drawing sheets in case they're lost in the PTO; this information should not show through to the front. (Note: You should not fax replacement drawing sheets to the PTO since the transmission quality is inadequate; you will have to mail any amendment containing replacement drawing sheets.)

If the examiner allows you to defer correction of the drawings until after subject matter is allowed or after allowance, you should do so promptly after you receive an indication of allowable subject matter or a Notice of Allowance. This will give the PTO's drawing checkers time to review your corrected drawings and let you know if they're still improper within the statutory three-month period to pay the issue fee. If your corrected drawings aren't approved, the PTO will give you until the end of the three-month period, or an additional 15 days, to file proper drawings.

If *you* find any errors in your drawings, you should voluntarily make any necessary (nonrequired) amendments or corrections. Formerly the PTO required that you obtain approval in advance, but now you may go right ahead and file replacement sheets. If the examiner or the PTO's drawing checkers disapprove of the changes they will notify you.

To make a voluntary drawing amendment, use the above procedure, except that you should also add a red-marked copy of the drawing indicating the changes you are making. That is, include or check the DRAWINGS listing paragraph on the contents page (1) of your amendment (see Fig 13E/1). Then on the appropriate DRAWINGS page of the amendment state that you have attached a replacement sheet with the drawing changes and a copy of the drawing with the changes indicated in red (see Fig 13E/4). Again, I also like to refer briefly to the corrected sheets at the beginning of the Remarks (Fig 13E/4).

Make the changes and attach new, good copies of the changes sheets. List the sheets as an enclosure at the end of the amendment (Fig 13E/10) and attach red-marked sheets and new (corrected) sheets to the amendment for substitution for your original drawings.

If you want to send any replacement drawing sheets separately from an amendment, or with your issue fee transmittal, use Form 13-1. Check the box on this form if you are also including a copy of any sheets marked in red to indicate any changes.

Remember that the PTO prohibits the addition of any new matter to the drawings. However, you may correct obvious errors, such as a reversed diode, a missing reference numeral, or a missing line. I recommend that you keep a file copy of every version of every drawing sheet in case you ever have to refer to any sheet before changes.

H. Typing and Faxing the Amendment

The amendment should be typed with double- or 1.5 line-spacing on letter-size or A4 paper with 1.5-inch top and 1-inch left, right, and bottom margins. I often number my paragraphs and, as stated, include plenty of boldface or underlined "arguing" headings—for example, "The Elias Patent Fails to Show Any Schmitt Trigger." The PTO prefers you to fax the amendment, but if you mail the amendment, don't forget to keep an identical copy of your amendment mounted in your file; the PTO won't return any paper you send them, although they will make a copy of any paper or record for the per-sheet photocopy charge in the Fee Schedule. Again, I recommend using a word processor or typing the amendment on easily erasable paper on which you can readily make corrections. If you mail it, don't forget the postcard. The signatures of all inventors must be on the copy you send to the PTO.

Documents With Copies of Signatures Now Okay

The PTO now accepts documents which contain a copy of any required signature, provided you retain a copy of the document with an original signature, in case it's ever needed. (Original signatures are required only on (a) documents involving the registration of an attorney or agent and (b) certified copies.)

After your signature, add a "Certificate of Facsimile Transmission" (preferable) or a "Certificate of Mailing" (don't use Express Mail) as follows:

Certificate of Facsimile Transmission

I certify that on the date below I will fax this communication, and attachments if any, to Group _____ of the Patent and Trademark Office at the following number: (703) _____.

Date: _____

Inventor's Signature: _____

Certificate of Mailing

I hereby certify that this correspondence, and attachments, if any, will be deposited with the United States Postal Service by First Class Mail, postage prepaid, in an envelope addressed to "Box Non-Fee Amendments, Commissioner for Patents, P.O. Box 1450, Alexandria, VA 22313-1450" on the date below.

Date: _____

Inventor's Signature: _____

Only one inventor needs to sign this certification. If you mail this certificate, you can fax or mail your amendment even at 23:59 on the last day of your response period —it doesn't have to go out on the day it's mailed. Even if you're mailing the amendment two months ahead of time you should use the Certificate anyway, since if the amendment is lost in the mail, causing your application technically to go abandoned, you can get it revived easily by filing a declaration stating the full facts and enclosing a photocopy of the amendment with the Certificate of Mailing—see PTO

Rule 8(b). If you use mail, don't forget to attach a postcard to your amendment reading as in Fig. 13F.

Amendment A (5 pp) plus amended and red-marked copies of sheet 2/4 of drawings in Application of John A. Novel, Ser. Nr. 999,999, filed 200X Jan. 9, received today:

Fig. 13F—Back of Receipt Postcard for Amendment

Draft Amendments May Be Faxed for Discussion

Applicants may now send a proposed amendment for discussion to "sound out" and negotiate with the examiner. Mark the amendment "DRAFT" or "PROPOSED AMENDMENT," do not sign it, and fax it to the examiner. Then call the examiner in a few days to discuss the amendment by phone or visit the examiner personally. You still must file a regular, signed amendment by the due date to avoid abandonment.

Make sure your amendment won't cause the total number of claims of your application to exceed 20, or the number of independent claims to exceed three. Otherwise, you'll have to pay an additional claims fee (expensive and usually not advisable, since three independent and 20 total claims should be more than adequate).

I. If Your Application Is Allowable

Hopefully, your first amendment will do the trick and the examiner will decide to allow the case. If so, you'll often be sent a Notice of Allowability and/or a formal Notice of Allowance (N/A), the latter accompanied by an Issue Fee transmittal form. You have a statutory period of three months to pay the issue fee (and to pay any publication fee if you haven't requested nonpublication); the three-month period is not extendable and forms are self-explanatory. Be sure to send in a receipt postcard with your issue fee transmittal. You can also place an advance order for printed copies of your patent (a space is provided on the issue fee transmittal form) at this time; and the minimum order is ten. However,

Checklist for Sending In a Regular Amendment

Before you mail your amendment, please check the following list carefully to be sure that the amendment's complete and properly done.

☐ A01. You have responded to each point in the OA.

☐ A02. You have responded to any needed drawing objection.

☐ A03. You have re-proofed the specification and have made any needed corrections.

☐ A04. You have amended the prior-art portion of the specification to account for any significant new prior art (optional).

☐ A05. You have not included any new matter in any amendments to the specification.

☐ A06. You have checked all new claims against the checklist in Chapter 9.

☐ A07. All claims recite structure which is physically different from every cited reference (Section 102).

☐ A07-A. You have presented the amendment in the pro-scribed format: (a) a list of contents is on page 1, (b) the Specification and Drawing Amendments (if any) start on respective new pages, (c) the Claim Amendments (if any) start on a new page, (d) the Remarks start on a new page, (e) the specification is amended by replacing whole paragraphs with words to be deleted struck through and words to be added underlined, (f) all claims that were ever in the application are listed in numerical order, (g) the number of every claim is followed by one of the seven required parenthetical expressions (Original, Currently Amended, Previously Presented, Canceled, Withdrawn, New, and Not Entered), (h) for Canceled and Withdrawn claims, only the claim number without the text is provided, and (i) for claims in the Currently Amended format, words to be deleted are struck through and words to be added are underlined.

☐ A08. The physically different structure in every claim is sufficiently different to produce new and un-expected results or otherwise be considered unobvious (Section 103).

☐ A09. The case includes several very narrow dependent claims with a variety of phraseologies so that you won't have to present them for the first time if the next action is made final.

☐ A10. The wording in the remarks is clear, grammati-cally correct, and understandable.

☐ A11. The remarks are written in short paragraphs with ample "arguing" headings.

☐ A12. The patentability of all new claims is argued with respect to the references, using a two-part approach: (a) The claim has physical distinctions over the references under Section 102; (b) The claimed physical distinctions produce new and unexpected results or are otherwise unobvious under Section 103.

☐ A13. You have included all possible arguments for unobviousness (Fig. 13D).

☐ A14. A request for claim-drafting assistance under MPEP 707.07(j) has been made, if desirable.

☐ A15. The amendment is 1.5 or double-spaced with an ample top margin for punching mounting holes.

☐ A16. The last page of the amendment includes your name, address, and phone number.

☐ A17. If the amendment will cause the case to have over 20 total or over three independent claims, the proper additional fee is included (if not pre-viously paid).

☐ A18. The amendment is signed and dated (no pencil) by all applicants.

☐ A19. An identical file copy of the amendment has been made if you are mailing the amendment.

☐ A20. The amendment is being faxed or mailed on time or includes a properly completed Petition to Extend with the proper fee included.

☐ A21. A Certificate of Faxing or Mailing is typed in the amendment.

☐ A22. All pages are complete and present.

☐ A23. A receipt postcard is attached to the amend-ment, if you are mailing it.

☐ A24. The envelope is properly stamped and addressed to "Mail Stop Non-Fee Amendments, Commissioner for Patents, P.O. Box 1450, Alexandria, VA 22313-1450." If you are sending any money with your amendment, omit "Box Non-Fee Amendments." If you're faxing the amendment, make sure you have the correct fax number for your examiner's group and you feed your pages carefully.

the printed copies aren't necessary, as you can make photo-copies from your patent deed. You can order copies separately or download them from the PTO or Patent Fetcher websites (see Chapter 6, Section I2). Also, be sure to fill in the Certificate of Mailing or Faxing on the Issue Fee Transmittal. If your application was published 18 months after filing you will also have to pay the PTO publication fee. The fee is included on your Issue Fee transmittal form. You will receive a "Notice of Patent Term Adjustment" with your N/A. Usually the patent term will not be extended, but if the PTO delayed in responding to an amendment or you had to appeal, you will get a commensurate adjustment.

When you receive your N/A, make any needed drawing corrections at once (see Section G, above) and review the application and drawings once again very carefully to make sure everything is correct, logical, grammatical, and so on. If you want to make any amendments at this time, you can still do so, provided they don't affect the substance of the application. Generally, only grammatical changes are permitted after the N/A. The format of the amendment should be similar to that of Fig. 13-E, except that the first sentence should read, "Pursuant to Rule 312, applicant respectfully requests that the above application be amended as follows:"

Then make any amendments to your specification and claims in the previously used format. Under "Remarks," discuss the amendments, stating that they are not matters of substance and noting that they will require very little consideration by the examiner.

If you've amended your claims in any substantial way during prosecution, after the Notice of Allowance is received you should also file a Supplemental Declaration (Form 13-3) to indicate that you've invented the subject matter of the claims as amended and that you know of no prior art that would anticipate these claims. Sometimes when a case is allowed the examiner will include a "Reasons for Allowance" section. You should review this carefully to

be sure the reasons aren't too narrow since this may adversely affect the scope of your patent. If the reasons are too narrow, you should submit a rebuttal statement to neutralize the examiner's statement.

Prior to sending in the issue fee, you should go through the following checklist:

Checklist for Paying an Issue Fee
☐ A01. You made all needed drawing corrections and enclosed any needed formal drawings.
☐ A02. You have made any needed specification or claim amendments (PTO Rule 312).
☐ A03. You have properly completed and signed the Issue Fee Transmittal Form.
☐ A04. You have filed a completed Supplemental Declaration if you have made any significant claim changes during prosecution.
☐ A05. You have enclosed a check, or if paying by credit card, a completed Form PTO-2038 for the issue fee.
☐ A06. You have attached a receipt postcard, properly stamped, and addressed, if you are mailing the issue fee.
☐ A07. You have completed a certificate of mailing or faxing on the Notice of Allowance.
☐ A08. You are faxing or mailing the papers by the due date (no extensions allowed).
☐ A09. If you are mailing the papers you have made a file copy of all issue fee transmittal papers.

You must make the drawing corrections and submit the new drawings by mail within the three-month period. Obviously you should do so as early as possible so you'll have time to make revisions in case they aren't approved.

Once your issue fee is received, your application goes to the Government Printing Office and no further changes are permitted.

Several months after the issue fee is paid, you may receive an Issue Notification Form, which will indicate the number of your patent and the date it will issue, usually a week or so after you receive the receipt. A few days after your patent issues, you'll receive the deed, or letters patent, and, separately, any additional printed copies you've ordered. (See Chapter 15, Section H, for a discussion of maintenance fees.)

J. If Your First Amendment Doesn't Result in Allowance

If your first amendment doesn't place the application in condition for allowance, the examiner will usually make the next OA final. However, if the second OA cites any new references, it won't be made final unless the examiner had to dig out the new references to meet some new limitations in your amended claims. If your second OA isn't made final, you should respond to it in the same manner as you responded to the first OA. However, if the second OA is called final—and it usually will be—note the provisions of Rules 113 and 116, which govern what happens after a final action is sent:

Rule 113—Final Rejection or Action

(a) On the second or any subsequent examination or consideration, the rejection or other action may be made final, whereupon applicant's response is limited to appeal in the case of rejection of any claim (Rule 191), or to amendment as specified in Rule 116. Petition may be taken to the Commissioner in the case of objections or requirements not involved in the rejection of any claim (Rule 181). Response to a final rejection or action must include cancellation or appeal from the rejection of, each claim so rejected, and, if any claim stands allowed, compliance with any requirement or objection as to form.

(b) In making such final rejection, the examiner shall repeat or state all grounds of rejection then considered applicable to the claims in the case, clearly stating the reasons therefor.

Rule 116—Amendments After Final Action

(a) After final rejection or action (Rule 113) amendments may be made canceling claims or complying with any requirement of form that has been made, and amendments presenting rejected claims in better form for consideration on appeal may be admitted; but the admission of any such amendment or its refusal, and any proceedings relative thereto shall not operate to relieve the application from its condition as subject to appeal or to save it from abandonment under Rule 135.

(b) If amendments touching the merits of the application be presented after final rejection, or after appeal has been taken, or when such amendment might not otherwise be proper, they may be admitted upon a showing of good and sufficient reasons why they are necessary and were not earlier presented.

These rules mean, in effect, that "final" isn't final after all. It's just that the rules shift a bit. If you want to continue prosecuting your patent application after a final OA, you must take one of the following actions:

1. Narrow, cancel, or fix the claims *as specified by the examiner.*
2. Argue with and convince the examiner to change position.
3. Try a further amendment narrowing the claims.
4. Appeal to the Board of Appeals and Patent Interferences (BAPI).
5. File a continuation application (see Chapter 14).
6. Petition the PTO Commissioner.
7. Abandon the application.

Let's examine these options in more detail.

1. Comply With Examiner's Requirements

If the examiner indicates that the case will be allowed if you amend the claims in a certain way, for example, if you cancel certain claims or add certain limitations to the claim, and you agree with the examiner's position, you should submit a complying amendment similar to the previously discussed amendment. However, instead of stating, "Please amend the above application as follows:" (Form 13-1), state "Applicant requests that the above application be amended as follows:" This is because the clerk won't enter any amendments after a final OA unless the examiner gives permission.

Generally, no other amendments after a final OA are permitted unless you can show very good reasons why they weren't presented earlier. If your amendment changes the claims in the manner required by the examiner to get them allowed, this will clearly entitle it to entry. You should file your complying amendment as soon as possible, since you have to get the case in full condition for allowance within the three-month period, plus any extensions you've bought. If you file an after-final amendment near the end of the three-month period and the examiner agrees that it places the application in condition for allowance, but the period has expired, you'll have to buy an appropriate extension (Form 13-4): a case can't be allowed when it's technically abandoned. If you file an amendment or argument and it doesn't convince the examiner to allow your case, the examiner will send you an "advisory action," telling you why, and the three-month period will continue to run.

2. Convince the Examiner

You can try to convince the examiner to change position, either by written argument, by phone, or in person. Phone and personal interviews are especially effective because of the multiple feedback loops and give-and-take they provide in a short period. Also, it's more difficult to say no when facing someone, as any salesperson will tell you. Try to come to some agreement to get the case allowed. This is often an excellent, effective choice, especially if you have a friendly examiner and you're willing to compromise. Do this as soon as possible so you'll have time to appeal or file a continuation application, if necessary. (See Chapter 14, Section B.)

3. Amendment After Final Rejection

You can try a further amendment, narrowing your claims, or submitting other claims, provided you raise no new issues. If the examiner agrees that the amendment narrows or changes the claims sufficiently to place the case in condition for allowance, the examiner will authorize its entry and allow the case. Otherwise, the examiner will send you an "advisory action," reiterating the examiner's former position, and you'll still have the opportunity to exercise the other choices. Even if the examiner doesn't want to enter the amendment because it raises new issues, the advisory action will state whether the amendment will be entered for purposes of appeal. The examiner will enter it for appeal if it places the case in better condition for appeal and neither raises any new issues nor requires further search or consideration.

You should fax (preferable) or mail any amendment after final as soon as possible. The PTO will try to reply to After-Final amendments within one month if you do the following with a *red marker*: (1) mark the upper right of p.1 of your amendment "RESPONSE UNDER 37 CFR 1.116—EXPEDITED PROCEDURE—EXAMINING GROUP NUMBER [insert #]," (2) address the envelope and the amendment "Box AF, Commr. of Pats... [etc.]," and (3) write "BOX AF" in the lower left of envelope. The PTO now has special fax numbers for after-file amendments; see the last page of the OA, Appendix 5, or the PTO website.

If you do send in an amendment after a final OA, you should head it "Amendment Under Rule 116," and request (not direct) that the case be amended as follows to place it in condition for allowance. Also comply with the following checklist.

Checklist for Sending an After-Final Amendment

☐ A01. You have completed all points on the checklist for "regular" amendments, except point A09.

☐ A02. The amendment requests (rather than directs) entry of the amendment.

☐ A03. The claim changes or cancellations either comply with the examiner's requirements or otherwise narrow or revise the claims to obviate the outstanding rejections.

☐ A04. The remarks state and justify why the claim changes, if any, were not presented before.

☐ A05. The claims don't contain any new limitations or radical changes that would raise new issues.

☐ A06. The amendment is being faxed or sent in as soon as possible after final action.

☐ A07. The first page of the amendment and the envelope (if the amendment is being mailed) are marked in red as indicated above.

4. Appeal

If you don't see any further way to improve the claims, and if you believe the examiner's position is wrong, you can appeal a final or secondary rejection (not objection) to the BAPI (Board of Appeals and Patent Interferences), a tribunal

THIS IS A VERY STRONG APPEAL MR. HODGEKISS BUT I'M AFRAID....

of senior examiners or administrative law judges in the PTO. To appeal, you must:

- File a notice stating that you appeal to the BAPI from the examiner's final action.
- Enclose an appeal fee. (See Appendix 4, Fee Schedule.)
- File an appeal brief in triplicate if by mail, or a single copy if by fax, describing your invention and claims in issue and arguing the patentability of your claims. This brief is due within two months after you file your notice of appeal and must be in a specific format specified by the Rules.
- Enclose a brief fee.
- If you desire it, request an oral hearing and enclose a further hearing fee (see Appendix 4, Fee Schedule). If you want an oral hearing, you'll have to travel to the PTO in Arlington, Virginia, or ask for a telephone hearing, and
- As always, include a Certificate of Mailing and postcard or Certificate of Faxing with all correspondence.

For information on how to comply with the appeal procedure, see PTO Rules of Practice 191 to 198.

After you file an appeal brief, the examiner must file a responsive brief (termed an "Examiner's Answer") to maintain the rejection. To do this, the examiner (and usually two other examiners) must take another good, hard look at your case. Often this review will result in changing the examiner's mind. More commonly, the examiner will maintain the rejection and file an Examiner's Answer. You may then file a reply brief to respond to the Examiner's Answer.

If you do have a hearing, you will be allowed 20 minutes for oral argument. Sometimes the examiner attends; if so, 15 minutes will be allowed for the examiner's presentation.

If the Board disagrees with the examiner, it will issue a written decision, generally sending the case back with instructions to allow the case. If it agrees with the examiner, its decision will state why it believes your invention to be unpatentable. The Board upholds the examiner in about 65% of the appeals.

If the Board upholds the examiner and you still believe your invention is patentable, you can take a further appeal within 60 days of the date of the BAPI's decision to the Court of Appeals for the Federal Circuit (CAFC). The CAFC is located in Washington, but sometimes sits in local areas. If the CAFC upholds the PTO, you can even request the United States Supreme Court to hear your case, although the Supreme Court rarely hears patent appeals. (See Chapter 15, Section M, for more on the CAFC.)

Under the new GATT law, as indicated, patents expire 20 years from the filing date of the patent application, but the PTO will extended this term up to five years if delay occurs due to an appeal to the BAPI, the CAFC, or because of an interference. (35 USC 154.)

Appeal briefs aren't easy to write, so I suggest you consult professional help if you want to appeal.

If the examiner has issued a ruling on a matter other than the patentability of your claims—for example, has refused to enter an amendment or has required the case to be restricted to one of several inventions—you have another option. Although you can't appeal from this type of decision you can petition the Commissioner of Patents and Trademarks to overrule the examiner. (See Section 6, "Petitions to the Commissioner," below.)

Appealing to Extend Your Patent's Term

If you want to obtain the maximum term possible for your patent, and three years have elapsed since the filing date of your application (or the filing date of any parent applications if it's a divisional or continuation —see Chapter 14), I recommend that you appeal after the second Office Action if the case is still under rejection, even if your second Action is not a final Action. Why? As stated, under the new laws, your patent will expire 20 years from your first filing date, regardless of when your patent issues. However, the PTO must extend this 20-year term (for up to five more years) from the date you file an appeal until the date of a final decision on appeal, except that if any portion of the appeal period occurs within three years of your filing date, this will not be counted in extending the expiration date (Rule 701).

Thus any time you take to negotiate with the examiner or file another amendment will shorten your patent's term. However, if three years have elapsed after your first filing date, you can avoid this shortening and actually extend your patent's term by filing an appeal and doing any negotiation or filing any amendments while your appeal is pending. If you can't get the examiner to allow the case, just follow through with the appeal by filing a brief and fee within two months after the date you file the notice of appeal. If you do get the examiner to allow the case while it's on appeal, just file a notice withdrawing the appeal; your patent's term will be extended for the time your appeal was active.

5. File a Continuation Application or Request Continued Examination

If you want to have your claims reviewed further in another round with the examiner, you can file a new "continuation application" or request continued examination in the same application.

Filing a continuation application is a relatively simple procedure involving writing new claims, paying a new filing fee, and sending in a special form requesting that a continuation application examination be prepared. (See Chapter 14 for how to do this.) As explained in Chapter 14, if you file a "regular" continuation application with a new copy of the specification, drawings, and formal papers (Rule 53(b)), you'll receive a new serial number and filing date for the purpose of your patent's duration, but you'll be entitled to the benefit of the filing date of your original application for the purpose of determining the relevancy of prior art. Your application will be examined all over again with the new claims.

If you file a Request for Continued Examination (RCE) (Rule 114)(preferable) you won't have to file a new copy of the specification or drawings and you won't receive a new serial number or filing date. You simply file an RCE form, pay another filing fee, and submit another amendment. (See Chapter 14.)

You must actually file the continuation application or RCE before the end of the three-month period or any extensions you buy. (See Section Q, below.) You should not use a Certificate of Mailing (CM). According to the PTO's Rules (8 and 10), a CM isn't effective when an application is being filed; you must actually get it physically on file before the other case goes abandoned. The best way to do this is to fax an RCE or use Express Mail with an Express Mail certificate (Chapter 10, Section L, and Chapter 14, Section B).

6. Petitions to the Commissioner for Nonsubstantive Matters

The Commissioner of Patents and Trademarks has power to overrule almost anyone in the PTO or any objection made by an examiner. (The BAPI has jurisdiction over rejections and objections if they're associated with a rejection. See Rules 181-183.) Thus, if the examiner has made an objection that you think is wrong or if you think you've been treated unfairly or illegally, you can petition the Commissioner to overrule a subordinate. For example, if the PTO's application branch (OIPE) has made a ruling regarding your patent application, such as that it's not entitled to the filing date you think you're entitled to (but not

a rejection of your claims), you can petition the Commissioner to overrule this ruling.

If you petition the Commissioner for any reason, you must do so promptly after the occurrence of the event forming the subject matter of the petition, and you must make your grounds as strong and as complete as possible. Generally, most petitions must be accompanied by a verified showing and fee. A verified showing is a statement signed by you and either notarized or containing a declaration such as that in the paragraph of Form 10-1 (that starts "I hereby declare...."). (The petition fee is indicated in Appendix 4, Fee Schedule.)

7. Abandon Your Application

You must take any action in response to a final OA within the three-month period for response or any time extensions you buy (see Section Q, below); otherwise the application will go abandoned. That is, you must either appeal, file a continuation application, or get the examiner to allow your application within the period for response. However, if you're going to file an amendment or an argument, you should do it as soon as possible, preferably within one month, so the examiner's reply will reach you in time for you to take any further needed action within the three-month period.

If all claims of your application are rejected in the final OA, and you agree with the examiner and can't find anything else patentable in your application, you'll have to allow the application to become abandoned, but don't give up without a fight or without thoroughly considering all factors involved.

If you do decide to allow your application to go abandoned, it will go abandoned automatically if you don't file a timely reply to the final action, since the ball's in your court. You'll be sent a Notice of Abandonment advising you that the case has gone abandoned because you failed to reply to an outstanding Office Action.

If you do abandon the application, that doesn't mean that you've abandoned the invention. If your invention has a unique shape and it hasn't been made available to the public, offered for sale, or sold more than a year ago, consider filing a design patent application on it. Even if a utility or design patent isn't available, it may still be commercially viable; consider trade secret or trademark protection. (See Chapter 7 for more information.)

K. Interferences

An interference is a proceeding conducted by the PTO (a Patent Interference Examiner and the BAPI). An interference is instituted to determine priority of inventorship—that is, who will get the patent when two or more inventors are claiming the same invention.

The PTO generally institutes an interference when they discover two patent applications claiming the same invention. However, since the PTO is such a large, complex, and populous organization, and since its employees do not always do perfect work, they sometimes make mistakes. Thus they may allow an application that should have been involved in an interference with another application to issue as a patent without declaring an interference.

If this occurs and then an examiner or other patent applicant sees the patent and believes it claims the same invention as a pending application, an interference can be declared with the patent, provided the issued patent has not been in force for more than one year.

How is the interference instituted by you, the applicant, if you believe that you, rather than someone else, deserves the patent? Simple. You merely copy (present) the claims of the in-force patent in your application, informing the patent examiner about the patent from which you copied the claims, and showing the examiner how such claims are supported in your application. Remember, you must copy the claims of any patent within one year after it issues.

Monitoring Patent Applications

If you really want to do a bang-up job of patent prosecution, you should find the class and subclass of your patent application (you can find this by calling the clerk of the examining division to which your application is assigned) and then monitor all patents which issue in the class/sub while your application's pending. If you find a patent that claims the same invention as yours, you should get interference with it by copying its claims in your application (see above). If you find a patent that is relevant prior art to your invention, you should cite it via a supplemental IDS (see Section B6 above).

On the other hand, if you've been granted a patent, be aware that there may be other patent applicants whose applications contain the same invention as yours. All such applicants have one year from your patent's date of issuance to copy your claims in their applications to get their application into interference with your patent.

Procedurally, an interference is a very complex proceeding, which would take another book of this size to cover. Unless you have an exceptional grasp of patent law and formal advocacy techniques, definitely seek help from a patent attorney who's experienced in trial work. Unlike some of the other situations where I've recommended professional help, representation in an interference proceeding is usually very costly, usually running $10,000 to $25,000 or more.

Despite the need for professional help should an interference occur, there's much you can do on your own to help your case. The Boy Scout motto will do nicely here: Be prepared. If your application is one of the 2% that becomes involved in interference, sufficient advance preparation will go a long way toward helping your case. As I stressed in Chapter 3:

- Record all steps in your invention development (conception, building, and so on) carefully. (Inventor's Commandment #1)
- Be diligent in building, testing, and recording your invention—unless you've filed a Provisional Patent Application (PPA) and are relying on that filing as your priority date. (Inventor's Commandment #2)
- File a patent application promptly.

Who wins an interference? As briefly stated in Chapter 5, the winner in an interference will not necessarily be the first to file a patent application on the invention. Rather, the first inventor to "reduce the invention to practice" (file a patent application or build and test the invention) will prevail, *unless* the other party conceives the invention first and has been diligent in effecting a reduction to practice. This means that the typical interference involves lots of testimony and introduction of documents by both sides, all for the purpose of proving priority. It's this trial-like aspect of the interference that virtually necessitates professional help.

Although there are certain advantages to the U.S.'s "first to invent" system, all other countries, except the Philippines, have a "first to file" system, which eliminates interferences and their attendant tremendous expense, complexity, and time delays. Some have called the interference laws a "patent attorney's relief act." If you agree, write your Congressperson or have your inventors' club launch an effort to simplify this area of the law.

L. Statutory Invention Registration (SIR)

If you intend to abandon your application, but want to prevent anyone else from ever getting a valid patent on your invention, you can have an abstract and one drawing figure of your application published in the OG—Patents (see Chapter 6 and

Appendix 2, Resources: Government Publications, Patent Websites, and Books of Use and Interest) and have your application printed like a patent. This is called "converting your application to a Statutory Invention Registration (SIR)." For the reasons stated in Chapter 14, Section G, I strongly recommend against ever using a SIR.

M. If Your Application Claims More Than One Invention

Often patent applications claim several embodiments of an invention, and the PTO will regard these embodiments as separate inventions. The PTO will thus require you to "restrict" the application to just one of the inventions. The theory is that your filing fee entitles you to have only one invention examined.

Also, if two of your claims are directed to the same invention, but the examiner feels that the two claims are directed to subject matter that is classified in two separate subclasses (see Chapter 6), the examiner can require you to restrict the application—that is, to elect one set of claims for prosecution.

Another situation in which restriction may be required occurs when your application contains both method and apparatus claims. Even when both sets of claims are directed to the same invention, examiners often consider them two separate inventions and require you to elect either the method or the apparatus claims.

Generally speaking, it's very difficult to successfully "traverse" (argue against) a PTO-imposed restriction. Fortunately, it's possible to file a second application (called a divisional application—see Chapter 14) if you think pursuing the nonelected claims is worth the cost (new filing fee) and if present indications are that your divisional application will comprise allowable subject matter. You can file the divisional application any time until your first (parent) application issues, and your divisional application will be entitled to the filing date of your parent application. However, you should file any divisional application(s) as soon as possible since, under the new GATT law, any patent that issues on the divisional application will expire 20 years from the filing date of the *original* application in the chain.

One way to overcome a requirement for restriction is to add or include a "linking" claim in your application. If a linking claim is found allowable, the examiner will drop the restriction requirement. A linking claim is one that includes features of both inventions. For example, product and process claims can be linked by a claim to the product made by the process. While details of linking claims are found in

MPEP 809.03, I recommend that you seek professional help in this area, since the rules are complex.

Another, related situation occurs when you claim several embodiments or "species" of one invention. In the first OA, the examiner may require you to elect claims to one species for purpose of examination; this is to facilitate the search. If you don't get any generic claim allowed—that is, a claim that covers all of your different species—you'll be allowed to claim only the elected species; you can file divisional applications on the nonelected species. (In this case, the PTO will consider each species to be a separate invention.) If you do get a generic claim allowed, you'll be allowed to claim a reasonable number of different species of the invention (Rule 146).

N. The Public May Cite Additional Prior Art Against Your Published Patent Application

Most other countries have a practice under which they permit the public to see pending and allowed applications before they issue in order to give the public a chance to cite prior art or otherwise object to the allowance of the application. This practice has now been implemented in the U.S. by the 18-month publication system. This means, among other things, that you give up the confidentiality of your invention. Copies of any published application can be obtained by any member of the public who wants to download or order them; anyone can then cite prior art against your application upon payment of a fee.

I advised you to file an NPR (see Chapter 10), because of the disadvantages of publicity (the cost, the delay, the possibility of more examination, the possibility of fatally damaging prior art being cited against your application, and the loss of any trade secret rights in the application which you could otherwise maintain if the application is not allowed). However, an application that is published and survives the process will be a stronger patent. Also, a published patent application can be used to recover damages from infringers for infringing activity during the pendency of your application. See Chapter 15, Section J.

How to Cite Prior Art Against a Pending Application of Another Patent

If you know of any prior adverse information against a published patent application of another and you want to bring this to the attention of the examiner to prevent the application from issuing, you can cite the art against such application. Use the caption of Form 13-1, filling in as much information as possible, and head the paper "Citation of Prior Art." List, enclose, but do not explain the relevance of the prior art. Be sure to cite the application's Serial Number and the name of the applicant. Don't forget the Prior-Art Citation Fee (see Appendix 4).

O. NASA Declarations

If your invention relates to aerospace, the PTO will send you a form letter (PTOL-224) with your filing receipt or after your application is allowed. The letter will state that because your invention relates to aerospace, you'll have to file a declaration stating the "full facts" regarding the making of your invention. This is to be sure NASA has no rights in it. If you don't file the declaration, you won't get a Notice of Allowance. Fortunately, the PTO now includes a declaration form for you to fill out. Check the appropriate blanks, indicating that you made the invention on your own time, and with your own facilities, and materials, and not in performance of any NASA contract, if this is the case.

P. Design Patent Application Prosecution

Design patent application prosecution is much simpler than regular patent application prosecution, and, armed with the instructions of this chapter, you'll find it to be duck soup. Design patent application prosecution will never require anything but the most elementary changes to the specification and claim; the examiner will tell you exactly what to do. (Make the amendments in the manner specified in Sections E1 and E2.)

To be patentable, the *appearance* of your design, as a whole, must be unobvious to a designer of ordinary skill over the references (usually earlier design patents) that the examiner cites. If your design has significant differences over the cited prior art, it should be patentable; if not, you'll have to abandon your application, as there's no way to narrow or change the substance of the claim or drawings of a design patent application. If the examiner rejects your design as obvious over one or more references, you should use the 102-then-103 attack as explained in Sections F and J and Inventor's Commandment #7 for utility patent applications —that is, point out the differences in your design and then argue their importance and significance, albeit from an aesthetic viewpoint. To reject a design claim on two or more references, one must look basically like the claimed design. (*In re Harvey*, 29 U.S.P.Q. 2d 1206 (Fed.Cir. 1993).)

If your design case is allowed, you must pay an issue fee (see Appendix 4, Fee Schedule), which makes the design patent effective for a term of 14 years from its date of issue. There are no maintenance fees for a design patent. You can convert a design application to a utility application, or vice versa, by filing a continuing application under 35 USC 120. However a design patent application may not claim priority of a PPA.

Q. What to Do If You Miss or Want to Extend a PTO Deadline

If you miss any PTO deadline—for example, the three-month period to reply to an OA—your application technically becomes abandoned, but you can buy an automatic extension. If your application goes abandoned, or if you want more time to reply to an OA, it can be "revived" or extended in any of three following ways:

- buying an extension
- petition to Revive if delay was "unavoidable"
- petition to Revive if delay was avoidable but unintentional.

Let's look at these separately and in more detail.

1. Buy an Extension Before the Six-Month Period Ends (Rules 136(a) and 17(a)-(d))

Most substantive OAs give you three months from their mailing date to reply. Most nonsubstantive OAs (e.g., a requirement for restriction to one of two inventions) allow only one month. If you don't reply within your designated period, you can send in your reply at any time up to the end of the sixth month by buying an extension of up to five months (if it won't carry you over six months) at the prices indicated in the Fee Schedule. To buy an extension in this manner, simply mail your reply (amendment) by the last day of the extension month, together with a "Petition for Extension of Time under 37 CFR 1.136(a)" (PTO/SB/22 or Form 13-4), completed as necessary, and a check or credit card charge. It is not necessary to apply in advance. Make sure you include a Certificate of Faxing or Mailing on your amendment. You should calculate your total number of months from the date of the OA; don't add your extension months to your original due date. For example, assume your OA gave a one-month period to reply and was mailed 2003 May 21 so that your period originally expired 2003 Jun 23 since 2003 Jun 21 was a Saturday. You want to buy a five-month extension. Your total period is then six months from May 21—that is, to 2003 Nov 21—not five months from Jun 23. You should mail your response, petition for extension, and petition fee, which is very high, by midnight Nov 21. It does not have to go out or be postmarked by Nov 21. Remember that by statute you can't extend any response period beyond six months. Also, you can't buy an extension to send in your issue fee; the three-month statutory period from the Notice of Allowance is not extendable.

2. Petition to Revive If Delay Was "Unavoidable" (Rule 137(a))

If you failed to send in your amendment or issue fee within the regular three-month period and your delay was "unavoidable"—for example, you never received the OA, you had a death in the family that precluded your drafting an amendment, you suffered a severe illness, or your home burned down—you can petition to revive the application. The fee is indicated in the Fee Schedule and you should file three papers: (a) your reply, (b) a petition to revive, and (c) a declaration. The petition (use Form PTO/SB/61 or make your own petition using the heading of Form 13-1) should petition to revive the above application, state that the delay was unavoidable because (give the reason), as explained in the attached declaration. The declaration (use heading of Form 13-1 and make the last paragraph the same as that of Form 10-3) should state in detail the specific facts that caused the delay. Use numbered paragraphs and start it as follows:

A.B. declares as follows:

1. I am the applicant in the above application.

Then, give your reasons in short, specific, numbered, factual paragraphs. Refer to and attach copies of any documents you feel are relevant. Your petition and paper must be promptly filed after you become aware of the abandonment. If your petition under this paragraph is denied, you can still petition under the next paragraph if you do so within three months.

3. Petition to Revive If Delay Was Avoidable but Unintentional (Rule 137(b))

If you failed to send in your amendment or issue fee within the three-month period and your delay was "avoidable but unintentional"—such as, you merely dropped the ball, or misinterpreted the time to reply to the OA—you can still petition to revive the application, albeit at a much higher cost. You should file three papers:
- your reply
- a petition to revive (use PTO/SB/64 or write your own, making it the same as the petition in the preceding paragraph, except state the delay was "unintentional"), and
- a declaration similar to that of the preceding paragraph, except you need merely state that the abandonment was unintentional (no reason is needed—the stiff fee (see Fee Schedule) is ample).

R. Summary

After your application is filed, you will receive a receipt postcard in a few weeks and an official filing receipt soon after that, usually with a foreign filing license that permits you to file abroad before six months has elapsed.

Check the information in the filing receipt carefully and apply for any needed corrections. Your application is now "patent pending" and you can release details if necessary without undue risk. Be sure to file an IDS within three months.

When you receive a first Office Action check it carefully and be sure to respond in the time allotted or any extensions you buy. After you respond you'll receive a second and usually final Office Action or a notice of allowance.

If you didn't file an NPR when you filed the application your application will be published on the PTO's website 18 months after filing and the public can cite new prior art against your application. If the case is allowed you'll have to pay an issue fee and then will receive the patent deed.

During prosecution you can ask the examiner to write claims for you if the invention is patentable. Note that standards of patentability vary widely and the PTO can be unfair, so you should argue against and appeal any rejection you feel is improper.

It's important to avoid making any negative statements on the record, comply with your continuing duty to disclose material information about the invention, avoid amending your claims unless necessary, and consider foreign filing within one year of your filing date. It's often useful to call or visit your examiner. You are not allowed to add any new matter to your application, but you must respond to every point in any Office Action.

To respond to an Office Action first review your application, then the cited references, and then decide what is novel and unobvious about your invention and consider amending the claims to define over the prior art if necessary. When drafting your remarks in the amendment, go through the flowchart and use possible arguments for patentability. Be sure to separate your arguments into novelty and unobvious parts and distinguish between physical novelty and new results.

The PTO requires a specific format for an amendment, with each section starting on a new page and a listing of every claim that was ever in the application. Follow the specific rules for drafting remarks.

Fax your amendment rather than mail it, unless it includes new drawing sheets. If you receive a final action your only options are to appeal, amend the claims as required, interview the examiner to come to an agreement, try a further amendment without raising new issues, file a full or RCE continuation application, or abandon the application. You can petition the Commissioner for nonsubstantive matters.

Design patent application prosecution is similar to utility prosecution, except that the design must be unobvious in the aesthetic sense. If you miss a PTO deadline, you can buy an extension, or petition to revive if the delay was unavoidable or unintentional. ■

Chapter 14

Your Application Can Have Children

A. Available Extension Cases

As we saw in Chapter 13 (application prosecution), the patent laws and PTO rules allow you to do much more than either get a patent or abandon your patent application. In this sense, perhaps, a patent application can best be understood by comparing it to a family tree, as shown in Fig. 14A, which shows all of the different extensions you may file.

The Basic Application is like a parent, and just as a parent has children, the parent application can be used to produce offshoots. Depending upon the situation, the parent application is called by many names (for example, "parent," "prior," "basic," or "original" application), while the offshoot applications are referred to as "daughter," "continuation," "divisional," "reissue," "independent," or "substitute" applications. If there are several successive extensions, the Basic Application is called the "grandparent" or "great-grandparent" application and the latest-filed application can be called a "granddaughter," "great-granddaughter," "continuation-of-a-continuation," etc., application.

Note that some extensions come from the bottom point of the Basic Application (BA) or the basic patent. These are "sequential" extensions since they replace the BA or its patent.

Other extensions come from the sides of the BA; these are "parallel" extensions since they can exist in addition to the BA or its patent.

The various extensions, starting from the upper left and proceeding down, then the middle and down, etc., are as follows:

- **Division:** Suppose your examiner held that your BA covered two or more inventions, and required you to "restrict" it to one of these inventions. To cover the other, "non-elected" invention you'll have to file a separate application on it. You do this by filing a divi-

sional application. Your divisional application gets the benefit of the filing date of your BA, but also expires 20 years from your BA's filing date. Your divisional patent can be in addition to your original patent.

- **Continuation:** Suppose your examiner sends you a final Office Action (OA), and you want to get another round with the examiner on the same claims, or to try a new and different set of claims. You can do this by filing a new application that "continues" your original application. The continuation application gets the benefit of the filing date of your original application but also expires 20 years from your BA's filing date. A continuation patent can be in addition to your original patent, but it must claim a different invention to avoid double patenting.

- **Request for Continuing Examination (RCE):** Moving down from the top of the middle column of the chart, you will see the RCE box. An RCE is closely allied with the continuation application and enables you to purchase another round with the examiner in the same application. Note from the chart that the RCE is like a detour or second chance on the path to a patent. The RCE replaces the BA.

- **Reissue:** If you've received an original patent, but you want to revise the claims of the patent or correct significant errors in the specification for some valid reason, you should file a reissue application. As indicated, your reissue patent takes the place of your original patent.

- **CIP:** Moving up to the top of the right column, if you've improved your basic invention in some material way during the pendency of your application, and you want to obtain specific claims to the improvement, you should file a continuation-in-part (CIP) application (right side of chart). As indicated, your CIP patent can exist with your original patent, or your CIP application can replace your BA.

- **Substitute:** Suppose you abandon your application and later refile a new application on the same invention. The new application, as indicated by the broken line, has no copendency or continuity with the original application. It is called a substitute application. Of course, no patent on your original application is possible.

- **Independent:** If you've made a major improvement in your basic invention that uses new concepts and can really stand by itself, you should file an independent application. An independent application is entirely separate from your BA, although you may refer to your BA in the independent.

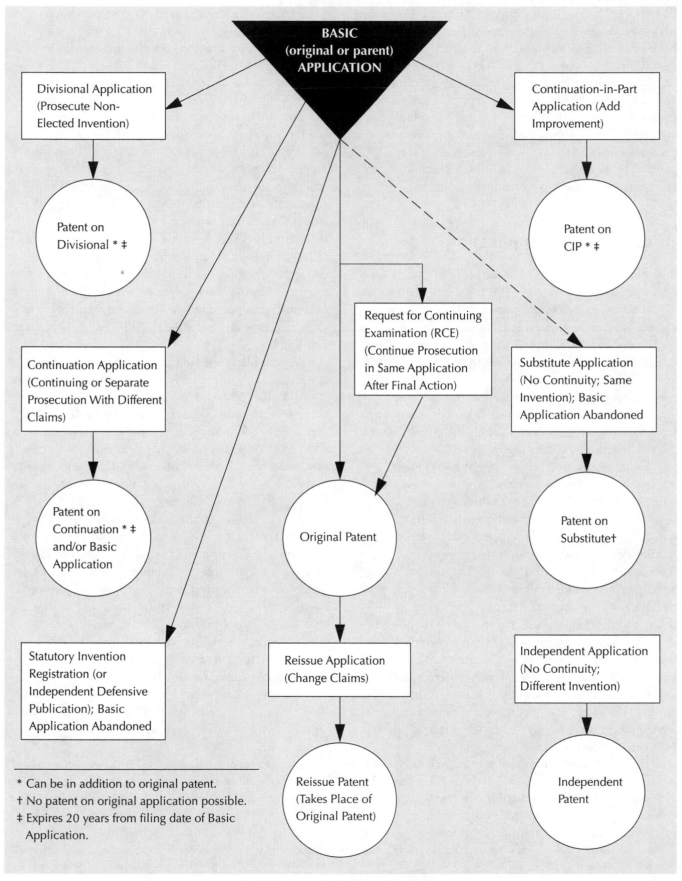

Fig. 14A—Available Extension Cases

Now that I've identified the major types of extensions, it's time to examine each one in more detail. Before we do, however, here's a word of advice. As suggested in Chapter 13, the types of problems that will occasion your using the information in this chapter may make it appropriate for you to at least consult with an expert prior to making a decision. In other words, before you decide to file a continuation, etc., you should seriously consider seeing a patent lawyer. Also note that, of necessity, the chart is abbreviated (it doesn't cover extensions of extensions), so rely primarily on the text, rather than the chart.

B. Continuation Applications

A continuation application is concisely defined in the *Manual of Patent Examining Procedure* (MPEP), Section 201.07, as "a second application for the same [or similar] invention claimed in a prior nonprovisional [regular] application and filed before the original [the prior application] becomes abandoned or patented." Note that both the original application and continuation can issue as separate patents. However they cannot claim the same invention since this would violate the double-patenting rule that prohibits two patents on the same invention. Thus, I added "[or similar]" after "same" to expand the PTO's definition.

A continuation application is almost always filed in response to a final rejection when an applicant wants to have another round with the examiner, either to try again to get the existing claims allowed or try new claims. If you don't file a continuation within the response period (three months unless extended for a fee), you give up your right to file it at all. An applicant can also file a continuation after an original application is allowed and before it issues to patent in order to get a parallel patent with a somewhat different set of claims to a similar invention. In this case the continuation is somewhat like a divisional, except that the continuation covers a similar, rather than a different, invention. If the claims of the continuation aren't patentably different from those of the original, the applicant must file a terminal disclaimer (TD) in the continuation so that the second patent won't run longer than the original patent.

If you think that it's inconsistent for the PTO to allow you to continue prosecuting claims to an invention after it has supposedly declared an Office Action "final," a word of explanation is in order. As stated in Chapter 13, "final" has a special, unusual meaning. A "final" action doesn't mean that the examiner has given the final word on your invention, but merely has decided to cut off your right to freely change your claims in your current application. In other words, you've gotten as many go-arounds as they're going to give you for your filing fee.

An historical explanation will make it even clearer. Up to the "old" days when I worked in the PTO (early '60s), patent prosecution proceeded at a leisurely pace. The PTO (then the PO) allowed examiners to send four or five OAs before they had to issue a final action. Examiners issued a final OA only after an issue had been clearly defined and reached, or if it was a fourth or fifth OA. However, in the late 1960s the PTO instituted a "compact prosecution" practice. Under this practice the examiner is almost always supposed to make the second OA final. The purpose of this change was to obtain more income for the PTO (a continuation application gets the PTO an additional filing fee), to reduce the amount of work the PTO performed, and to shorten the backlog of pending applications.

However, two OAs are often not enough to adequately define the invention, reach an issue with the examiner, and complete the prosecution in a proper manner. Therefore, continuation applications and RCEs (see next section) are often filed, especially since the RCE process has been made very simple.

You must file a continuing application like a regular application. The procedure is governed by 35 USC 120 and the PTO's Rule 53(b).

A continuation application must cover the same or a similar invention as the parent or Basic Application (BA). The BA can either be abandoned or can issue after a continuation is filed. The continuation application is entitled to the benefit of the filing date of the parent or prior application for purposes of overcoming prior art.

You can also file a continuation of a continuation. In fact, it's theoretically possible to file an unlimited sequence of continuation applications. But note that if an issue has been reached in a parent application, the examiner can, and often will, make the first OA final in a continuation application or will make the next OA final after a continuation is filed. In other words, a continuation application will be quickly rejected unless you truly come up with a different slant on or definition of your invention that was not previously considered by the PTO.

If you want to delete any inventors when you file a continuation, you may do so by including a simple request on a separate form. All inventors named in the prior application should sign the form.

As with a regular application, you'll receive your postcard back with the filing date of (and a new serial number for) your continuation. Thereafter, you'll receive the first Office Action in due course.

If the claims that are finally allowed in a continuation application, or divisional application (see Section D, below), differ significantly from the claims originally presented in the parent application, file a Supplemental Declaration (Form 13-3) before or when you pay the issue fee.

Filing a continuation application is very similar to filing a regular, original application. You must prepare the continuation like an original application as in Chapter 10. I.e., provide a complete new copy of the specification and claims, and drawings. You should amend the specification at the beginning (under "CROSS-REFERENCE TO RELATED APPLICATIONS") with the following sentence: "This is a continuation of application Ser. Nr.___/_____, Filed _____, now abandoned [or now patent Nr. _____ [fill in later], granted _____ [fill in later]]." Rewrite the claims as you want them and number them from number 1. Prepare and sign a new patent application declaration (PAD—Form 10-1). Fill out a Patent Application Transmittal—Form 10-2 and a Fee Transmittal—Form 10-3 as before, except you should also fill out Block 18 in Form 10-2 to refer to the parent case. Don't forget the postcard, as always. You must get the continuation application on file while the parent case is pending, so make sure you mail it to allow enough mailing time, or you can use Express Mail with Form 10-2 as explained in Chapter 10. (Don't use a Certificate of Mailing.) Your continuation will receive a new serial number and filing date, but it will be entitled to the filing date of the parent case.

You also have to file an IDS cover letter (Form 10-5) and the actual IDS Forms (10-6) (use a photocopy), but you don't have to file the references again if your IDS cover letter refers to the IDS in the prior case. Just type the following on Form 10-5:—"Pursuant to Rule 98(d), the references listed on attached Forms SB/08(A&B) are not enclosed since these were supplied in the parent case, Ser. Nr. ___/_____."

Changing Examiners. If you feel that the examiner in your parent case was unduly tough, it may be possible to get a different examiner in your continuation case by claiming your invention differently. The examining division to which a patent application is assigned is determined by the class and subclass to which the application

is assigned. The class and subclass is in turn determined by the subject matter of the narrowest (longest or most specific) claim in the case.

EXAMPLE: Suppose you've invented a new gear for a bicycle and the narrowest claim of your parent case recites the fine details of the gear per se. Your case will be assigned to an examining division in the "gear" arts. If your "gear" examiner is a hardnose, you'll probably be able to get it into bicycles, a different examining division, by adding the bicycle to your narrowest claim. You can do this by providing a "bicycle" preamble for the claim (see Chapter 9) or by actually reciting other parts of the bike in the body of the claim. If your narrowest claim is directed to a bike, your whole case will be classified in the bike division, and you'll have a different examiner.

Obviously, this maneuver can't be done in every instance. You should do some research on the PTO's Examining Division art assignments (see the "Patent Examining Corps" page of any recent *Official Gazette*) to make sure your end run around a particular examiner will work. Lastly, in an effort to get a new examiner, it also helps to change the title of your invention to one that is commensurate with your revised narrowest claim. For example, change "Gear with Anti-Backlash Pawl" to "—Bicycle Pedal Drive Gear—."

Changing examiners is one of several situations where I believe a consultation with a patent attorney or agent may be called for, due to the artsy nature of claims drafting. (See Chapter 6, Section F.)

20-Year Term. Under the new GATT Law, effective 6/95, if you file an RCE or continuation application (or a continuation of a continuation) and get a patent on your RCE application or continuation, the patent will expire 20 years after the filing date of your first, original, or parent application. So it behooves you to file any RCE application or continuation as soon as possible and to prosecute it diligently if you don't want your monopoly to be shorter than the former 17-year term. Since any extension (continuation, division, or CIP) will expire 20 years from the filing date of its parent case, before filing any extension, consider whether you'll really need to rely upon the parent case's filing date. If you're certain that no adverse prior art has issued since the parent's filing date, you can have any new case expire 20 years from its filing date (rather than from the filing date of the original case) if your new case doesn't claim priority of your original case, i.e., if you file it as a regular patent application, rather than as an extension.

C. Request for Continued Examination (RCE)

Requesting a Continued Examination (RCE) of an existing application has the same effect as filing a continuation application but without going through the paperwork of filing a new application. The applicant simply sends in a form, pays another filing fee, and continues prosecuting the same application. Prosecution continues as if there were no final action. In other words, filing an RCE is a way of buying your way out of a final action so you can continue prosecution for one or two more go-arounds, as in the old days.

In order to file an RCE, prosecution in the application must be "closed"—that is, the last OA must have been a final action, a notice of allowance, or some other action closing prosecution. Also, the application must be a regular utility application (not a PPA or design application). When a patent issues on an RCE, the heading of the patent will not indicate that it's based on the RCE.

When you file an RCE, the PTO uses your same file jacket, papers, Serial Number, and filing Date. The procedure is covered by the PTO's Rule 114 and the RCE Transmittal Form (Form 14-1/PTOSB/30).

To file an RCE, simply do the following:
- complete Form 14-1
- attach a check or CCPF (Form 10-4) for a new application filing fee (large or small entity—see Appendix 4, Fee Schedule)
- attach an amendment containing the new claims you desire to prosecute or check the appropriate block on Form 14-1 if you want to have your Amendment under Rule 116 entered, and
- as always, attach a receipt postcard (see Chapter 10) if you are mailing the RCE.

You must fax or mail your RCE before the period for response to the final rejection expires or before any extensions you've bought expire. (For an explanation of purchasing extensions, see Chapter 13.) As is the case with an amendment, you can fax or mail your RCE request on the last day of the period for response if you complete the Certificate of Mailing section at the bottom of Form 14-1. Since you're not filing a new application, you don't have to use Express Mail and you don't have to get the RCE on file before the period expires. Fax the papers to your examining group or mail to Mail Stop RCE, P.O. Box 1450, Alexandria, VA 22313-1450.

You don't have to file a new IDS when you file an RCE.

For the Amendment, complete Form 13-1 exactly as you would do with a regular amendment. Then proceed as usual: cancel the old claims and insert the new claims in the normal amendment manner, numbered in sequence after the highest numbered claim of the prior application. Under "Remarks," you should state, "The above new claims are submitted to be patentable over the art of record for the following reasons." Then give your reasons and arguments in the same manner as you would for a regular amendment, as explained in Chapter 13.

Be sure to include all the claims you desire in the amendment, since the next OA after the RCE is filed may be made final if the examiner doesn't cite any new prior art. As with a regular application, you'll receive your postcard back with the filing date of your RCE but no new serial numbers. After that, you'll receive the next Office Action.

If the claims that are finally allowed in either an RCE, continuation, or a divisional application (see Section D, below) differ significantly from the claims you originally presented in the parent application, you should file a Supplemental Declaration (Form 13-3) before or when you pay the issue fee.

Note that Divisional and CIP applications must be filed like a regular application under Rule 53(b). They cannot be filed via an RCE.

D. Divisional Applications

Now let's turn our attention to the divisional application.

A divisional application or "division" is "a later application for a distinct or independent invention, carved out of a pending application and disclosing and claiming only subject matter disclosed in the earlier or parent application" (MPEP 201.06). You should file a divisional application when (1) the PTO decides that two separate or distinct inventions have been claimed in the parent application (not permitted, since your filing fee entitles you to get only one invention examined), (2) you've agreed to restrict the parent application to the set of claims to one of the inventions, and (3) you want to get a patent on the other, non-elected invention. You don't have to file a divisional application on the other invention, and should do so only if you think it's important enough to justify the expense of a separate patent and you think it may be patentable. Divisional applications are so called because they cover subject matter that is "divided out" of the parent case.

A divisional application is entitled to the filing date of the parent case for purposes of overcoming prior art. The parent application of a divisional application can either issue as a patent or become abandoned if you feel the parent is not patentable over the prior art. The divisional must be filed as a complete new application under Rule 53(b), and, like the Rule 53(b) continuation application, will receive its own serial number and filing date for PTO administrative purposes. A patent issuing on a divisional application will show the serial number and filing date of the parent application; this will be the divisional's effective filing date. But remember that the divisional application must be filed while the parent is pending. Also note that you can file a division of a continuation application, and a continuation of a divisional application. (Definitely consult an expert if you get into these murky waters.)

Whether or not you're abandoning the parent case you'll have to proceed under Rule 53(b). File a complete copy of the divisional application, including an Application Transmittal (Form 10-2), Fee Transmittal (Form 10-3), filing fee, drawings (see below), specification, claims, and abstract, PAD (Form 10-1), and postcard. Optionally, you may also file a Preliminary Amendment. Everything should be the same as if you were filing a completely new application (use the checklist in Chapter 10), with the following exceptions:

a. Add the following sentence to the specification under "CROSS-REFERENCE TO RELATED APPLICATIONS": "This is a division of application Ser. Nr. ____/_____, Filed 200_____, now abandoned [or now patent Nr. _____ *[fill in later]*, granted _____ *[fill in later]*.]" Also you should amend the specification, either directly on the copy of the specification you file, or by a Preliminary Amendment. Remove any matter directed exclusively to the embodiment or invention of the parent case, and make any editorial amendments you desire or which you've made in the parent case.

b. When you complete the Patent Application Transmittal (Form 10-2) fill out Block 18 to refer to the parent case and to indicate you're filing a divisional.

c. Delete any nonapplicable figures from the drawings—that is, any figures directed exclusively to the embodiment of the parent case. Make sure your specification and drawings conform to each other.

d. You also have to file an IDS transmittal letter (Form 10-5) and the actual IDS Forms (10-6) (use a photocopy), but you don't have to file any references again if your IDS cover letter refers to the IDS in the prior case. Just type the following on Form 10-5: "Pursuant to Rule 98(d), the references listed on attached Forms SB/08(A&B) are not enclosed since these were supplied in the parent case, Ser. Nr. ____/_____."

To supply drawings for a parallel divisional case (the parent case will be issuing), you have three choices:

a. If you've made formal Mylar film or Bristol board originals of your drawings, you can file very good xerographic copies of these for your divisional's formal drawings.

b. You can file rough xerographic copies as informal drawings and file formal drawings later, as explained in Chapter 10.

c. If you've made CAD drawings, print out a new copy.

To supply drawings for a replacement divisional case (the parent case will be abandoned), you have four choices: the three above choices (a, b, and c) for the parallel divisional case. Also, you can request (use a separate letter) that the drawings be transferred from the parent case, which is being abandoned, to the divisional case.

If you want to delete any inventors when you file a division, you may do so by including a simple request on a separate form. All inventors named on the prior application should sign.

Double Patent Warning. You're not permitted to obtain two patents on the same invention. If you do, it's called "double patenting," (DP), a situation in which both patents may be held invalid. However, if in your parent case the examiner required you to restrict the application to one of several inventions, there's a special statute (35 USC 121) that helps you. This statute states that if you file your divisional(s) on the non-elected invention(s) after a requirement for restriction, you can do so with total immunity from DP. However, if the examiner didn't require you to restrict, and you're filing your divisional "voluntarily," you must be sure that it's to a clearly different invention than that claimed in the parent case. Otherwise, both patents can be held invalid for DP.

Once again, I recommend that you consult with a patent attorney in the event you (or the PTO) decide that a divisional application is indicated.

20-Year Term Warning. The 20-year term warning for continuation applications in Section B also applies to divisional applications.

E. Continuation-in-Part and Independent Applications

As defined in MPEP 201.08, "a continuation-in-part" (CIP) is an application filed during the lifetime of an earlier application by the same applicant, repeating some substantial portion or all of the earlier application and adding matter not disclosed in the earlier application. CIP applications are not common; they're used whenever you wish to cover an improvement of your basic invention, for example, if you've discovered a new material or a better design. (Remember, you can't add these to a pending application because of the proscription on "new matter" discussed in Chapter 13 and mandated by Rule 121(f).

I discuss the various CIP situations, below.

Generally, the parent application should be allowed to go abandoned when a CIP is filed. However, if you do want the parent application to issue, you must be sure that the claims of the CIP application are patentably different—that is, they define subject matter which is unobvious over that of the parent application. Otherwise the CIP and parent application patent can both be held invalid for double patenting, unless you file a terminal disclaimer. (See Section I, below.)

The advantage of a CIP application over a separate application is that the CIP is entitled to the filing date of the parent application for all subject matter common to both applications. Also, you need pay issue and maintenance fees for only one case. However, if any claims of the CIP cover subject matter unique to the CIP, such claims are entitled to the filing date of the CIP only.

If your "improvement" of your Basic Application is different enough to be unobvious over the basic invention, you can file an entirely separate, independent application, rather than a CIP. However, it's usually better to use a CIP application, since the common subject matter gets the filing date of the parent application.

EXAMPLE 1: Suppose you've invented a bicycle gear with a new shape. You've claimed this shape in a patent application, which I'll call the parent application. After you file the parent application, your research shows you that the gear works much more quietly if it's made of a certain vanadium alloy (VA). The VA isn't patentable over the invention of the parent case and your parent case's claims cover the gear no matter what material it's made of. However, since the VA works much better, you'd like to add a few dependent claims specifically to cover a gear made of the VA. In this way, if there's an infringer who copies your gear made of the VA, you can show the judge that the infringer is infringing your specific as well as your broad claims. Also, you will have specific claims to VA to fall back on if your broad claims are held invalid. You can't add the VA to the specification or the claims of the parent case, since it would be verboten "new matter." The solution: file a CIP, describing the VA in the specification, keep all of the original claims, and add a few dependent claims that recite that the gear is made of VA. To avoid any possibility of double patenting, you should abandon the parent case or file a terminal disclaimer (see Section I), since the VA isn't patentable over the invention of the parent case. For purposes of clearing the prior art, your broad claims to the gear shape per se will get the benefit of the parent case's filing date. However, the claims to the gear made of the VA will be entitled only to the later filing date of the CIP.

EXAMPLE 2: On the other hand, suppose your gear shape works well, but you've come up with a related, but nonobvious different shape that works better. That is, the new shape is patentable over the invention of the parent case. You should file a CIP with claims to the new shape and continue to prosecute the parent case to a patent. The CIP's claims generally will be entitled to only the CIP's filing date. However, their CIP status will entitle you to refer back to the parent's filing date to show when you came up with the underlying concept common to the parent and CIP gears. This will be useful in case the CIP is ever involved in litigation or an interference.

EXAMPLE 3: Lastly, suppose your gear shape works well, but you come up with an unrelated, and nonobvious different shape that works better. You should file a new, independent application, not related to the "parent," with claims to the new gear shape. The two applications would be entirely separate.

You can file a CIP of a continuation or divisional application or vice versa in either case. It's also theoretically possible to file an unlimited number of successive CIP applications to cover successive improvements. There have been rare cases where inventors have filed chains of CIPs with as many as eight or more applications, each of which issued into a patent.

If you are abandoning the parent case, you may claim whatever you want in the CIP, provided that the specification supports the claims. Only those claims that are supported by the specification of the parent case will be entitled to the filing date of the parent case. If the claims of the CIP are patentably different from those of the parent case, and the parent case issues, you don't need to file a terminal disclaimer. If the claims of the CIP are not patentably different from those of the parent case, you must file a terminal disclaimer to avoid double patenting.

You must use the same procedure (Rule 53(b)) as outlined above for filing a divisional when the parent case will issue, except substitute or check "continuation-in-part" for "divisional" in the Transmittal Letter (Form 10-2) and specification.

Don't forget the filing fee and postcard. Also use the checklist in Chapter 10. The new subject matter in the CIP and any claims directed to it will be entitled to the CIP's filing date, not the filing date of the parent case.

As with continuation and divisional applications, you also have to file an IDS cover letter (Form 10-5) and the actual IDS Forms (10-6) (use a photocopy). However, you don't have to file the references again if your IDS cover letter refers to the IDS in the prior case. Just type the following on Form 10-5:

Pursuant to Rule 98(d), the references listed on attached Forms SB/08(A&B) are not enclosed since these were supplied in the parent case, Ser. Nr. ____ /_____.

If you want to delete any inventors when you file a CIP, you may do so by including a simple request on a separate form. All inventors named on the prior applications should sign.

If you're filing an independent application (rather than a CIP), do it in the usual manner (see Chapters 8 through 10), except that you can add the following sentence to the CROSS-REFERENCE TO RELATED APPLICATION part of specification:

This application is related to application Ser. Nr. ____/_____, Filed _____, now patent Nr. _____, granted _____.

If you want to abandon any parent case, you can do so in a separate letter or by not responding to an Office Action.

⚠️ **20-Year Term Warning.** The 20-year term warning for continuation applications in Section B also applies to CIP applications.

F. Reissue Applications

As stated in MPEP 201.05, "a reissue application is an application for a patent that takes the place of an unexpired patent that's defective in some one or more particulars." Parts 1400 to 1401.12 of the MPEP discuss reissue applications extensively. Suppose you've received a patent and believe that the claims are not broad enough, that they're too broad (you've discovered a new reference), or that there are some significant errors in the specification. To remedy this, you can file an application to get your original patent reissued at any time during its term. (See "If You Want to Broaden the Claims by Reissue.") The reissue patent will take the place of your original patent and expire the same time as the original patent would have expired.

To file a reissue application you must:

- Reproduce the entire specification of the original application (a copy of the printed patent pasted one

---

If You Want to Broaden the Claims by Reissue

If you wish to broaden the claims of your patent through a reissue application, you must do so within two years from the date the original patent issued. Moreover, anyone who manufactures anything between the issue dates of the original patent and the reissue patent that infringes the broadened but not the original claims is entitled to "intervening rights." These preclude a valid suit against this person for infringement of the reissue patent's broadened claims. (35 USC 251, 252.)

EXAMPLE: Suppose you invent a new gear shape and get a patent, but unfortunately you included an unnecessary limitation in your independent claims as filed, namely they all recite that the gear is made of carbon steel. If you discover your error within a two-year period after your patent's issue date, you can file an application to reissue the patent with broader claims—that is, claims that specify only the gear's shape and not its material. Your patent will be reissued with the broader claims. However, suppose that an infringer (Peg) made gears with your inventive shape, but out of aluminum, between the date of your original and reissue patents. Peg's aluminum gears would not infringe the claims of your original patent, but they would infringe the broader claims of the reissue. Nevertheless, Peg can continue to make her aluminum gears with impunity since she has "intervening rights" by virtue of her manufacture of the aluminum gears in the interim.

Note that a reissue can't be filed to "recapture" subject matter you deliberately gave up in the original case. In the example above, suppose that in your original case you simply recited "a gear" in the claims, but during prosecution you added that the gear was made of nylon to define over the prior art. Since this was a deliberate, conscious act, you aren't permitted to eliminate the "carbon steel" limitation (and thus "recapture" your broader claims) in a reissue.

column per page is acceptable), putting brackets around matter to be canceled and underlining matter to be added. When the reissue patent issues, it will include the brackets and underlining.

- Supply a request for a title report on the original patent (see Fee Schedule for amount) and offer to surrender the original patent deed.
- Provide a declaration stating you believe the original patent to be wholly or partially inoperative or invalid and referring to and discussing at least one error in the patent. See Patent Rules 171-179.

Reissue patents are relatively rare and are identified by the letters "RE" followed by a five-digit number, for example, "Patent RE 26,420."

Although the procedure has been somewhat simplified recently, it is still relatively complicated, so I suggest that you consult a patent lawyer if you are interested in filing a reissue.

Reissue Warning. If you file a reissue, all of the claims of your original patent will be examined and can be rejected. Thus you should consider whether you want to take this chance before filing a reissue.

G. Statutory Invention Registration (SIR) and Defensive Publications

Suppose you've filed a U.S. application and for some reason don't wish it to issue as a patent, or can't obtain a patent on it. However, you want to be absolutely sure that no one else will ever be able to obtain a patent on it. This can occur if you're manufacturing a product embodying the invention. You can elect to have an abstract of your application published in the *Official Gazette* and have your entire application published like a patent. This purely defensive procedure is called a "Statutory Invention Registration" (SIR). It will cause your invention to become a prior-art reference, effective as of its filing date. The SIR will thus preclude anyone else from obtaining a patent on the invention, provided no one else filed an application on the invention before yours. Your application will then be printed and published like a patent, but you won't have any monopoly rights. (You will retain the right to revive your application and get into interference if a patent or application is discovered that claims your invention.) If you do choose to convert your application to an SIR, follow PTO Rules 293-297 and 17(n) or (o).

I don't recommend use of the SIR procedure because of the generally higher fee required—it's cheaper to publish your own book about your invention or to list it with an invention register. One such invention register is ITD, Inc., P.O. Box 371-0371, Tinley Park, IL 60477. Others are Technotec, 8100 34th Ave. South, Minneapolis, MN 55440 (about $160); *Research Disclosure Magazine*, Industrial Opportunities, Ltd., Homewell, Havant, Hampshire, PO9 1EF, UK (about $100), the IBM *Technical Disclosure Bulletin*; Tel. 914-742-6274 or Fax 914-742-5826, and for online publishing, you can publish the details of your invention on your own website, or use an Internet publishing service such as IP.com, Inc., 150 Lucius Gordon Drive, West Henrietta, NY 14586, www.ip.com, Tel. 716-427-8180; Fax 716-427-8183. If you use your own website, your publication should be a good defense if any later-filed patents are asserted against you, but if you use a service, the patent examiners are more likely to search it and use it to reject any such later-filed patents. If you have your invention published this way, the effective date of publication will be later than your filing date. However, the cost is generally much less and the later date won't make any difference unless someone has filed on the same invention before you publish it.

H. Substitute Applications

The term "substitute" is defined in MPEP 201.09 as "an application that is in essence a duplicate of an application by the same applicant that was abandoned before the filing date of the later case." A substitute (also called a "re-file") can be filed for the same purpose that you can file a continuation, division, or CIP. That is, you can file a substitute to continue prosecution that you didn't complete, to cover a different invention, or to cover an improvement invention.

I hope you never have to file a substitute application, since it doesn't get the benefit of the filing date of the earlier case. This is because it wasn't filed while the earlier case was pending. Thus any prior art that issues after the filing date of the earlier case and before the filing date of the substitute case is good against the substitute case. Suppose, however, that you somehow abandon your application (not your invention) and you can't successfully petition the Commissioner of Patents to revive the application (see Chapter 13). You still may be able to cover your invention by filing a substitute application, assuming significant prior art hasn't been published in the meantime.

There are no special forms or procedures for filing a substitute application; just file it like you would a regular patent application, except that you can add a reference in the specification to the prior case. As stated, you won't get the benefit of your prior case's filing date. However, the date of the parent case may be useful if you ever have to swear behind a reference (see Chapter 13) or prove earlier conception and/or reduction to practice, such as in case of an interference. (See Chapter 13, Section K.) If your substitute application issues into a patent, the patent will expire 20 years from the filing date of the substitute.

I. Double Patenting and Terminal Disclaimers

Double patenting (DP) is a situation that exists when one person or entity obtains two patents on the same invention, or on two inventions that are not patentably distinct. It's very important to avoid DP, since both patents can be held invalid by a court. Also, if the PTO sees that you have two applications pending that aren't patentably distinct, they will reject them on the grounds of potential DP. Thus, you must always be aware of the DP trap whenever you file a second case on any invention.

There are two types of DP: statutory DP and obviousness-type DP.

In statutory DP, the two patents cover the same invention. This situation is prohibited by 35 USC 101, which says that "Whoever discovers any new and useful [invention] … may obtain a patent therefor …." This means that an inventor may obtain only one patent for an invention, not two patents. Statutory-type double patenting is absolutely prohibited and cannot be overcome by a terminal disclaimer.

In obviousness-type DP, an inventor obtains two patents on respective inventions which are not identical, but which are also not different enough to be considered unobvious over each other. This situation is prohibited by judicial decisions, because a second patent will usually extend the inventor's monopoly beyond the expiration date of the first patent. However, obviousness-type DP can be overcome by filing a terminal disclaimer (TD) in the later application so that any patent issuing on it will not extend beyond the expiration date of the first patent and to ensure that both patents will continue to be owned by the same entity. (Rules 130(b) and 321(b).) Also, obviousness-type DP can be avoided if your examiner has required restriction. As explained in Section D, above, under "Double Patent Warning," a special statute (35 USC 121) states that you have total immunity from DP if you file a divisional after the examiner required restriction.

Under a TD, you agree to give up the terminal (end) period of your second patent so that both patents will expire on the same date, and will continue to be commonly owned, thereby eliminating the harm to the public interest (extension of monopoly beyond normal term or prohibiting a second patent that is not patentably different from issuing to a different entity) of double patenting. Although I don't provide instructions on preparing and filing TDs (the practice is tricky) I want to make you aware of their exist-ence so you'll know what options are available and when to consult an attorney. If you feel brave enough to venture into this area alone, TD forms and the filing fees are available on the PTO's website.

J. Summary

A patent applicant can file a number of possible extensions from an original, parent, or base patent application. If the base application has two or more inventions and is restricted to only one of these inventions, a *divisional application* may be filed to cover the other invention. If you've gotten a final action in the base application and want to submit new claims and continue prosecution, you may file a *continuation application* or a *request for a continuing application (RCE)*. If you develop an improvement on the invention of the base application and want to claim it specifically and still keep the filing date of the base application for the base invention, you may file a *continuation-in-part application (CIP)*. The divisional, continuation, RCE, and CIP all get the benefit of the filing date of the base application, but also expire 20 years from the base application.

If you come up with a substantially different improvement or new invention, it's best to file an *independent application*. If you get a patent and discover an error in it, such as claims that are too narrow, you can file a *reissue application* to have the patent reissued. The reissue patent takes the place of the original patent and expires when the original patent would have expired. You cannot use a reissue patent to claim (recapture) subject matter that you voluntarily gave up in the original case; any reissue with broader claims must be filed within two years from the original patent and is subject to the intervening rights statute.

If you can't get or don't want to get a patent on an invention, but want to prevent someone else from getting a patent on it, you can *defensively publish* your application privately or convert your application to a *Statutory Invention Registration (SIR)*. A SIR is relatively expensive to file, but can be converted back to a regular application in case of an interference and it is prior art as of its filing date.

If you abandon your application and want to file on it again, you will have to file a *substitute* application; such an application has no connection to the base application. No one may legally receive two patents for the same invention since this would constitute statutory *double patenting*. Also no one may legally receive two patents for two inventions that are not patentably different since this would constitute *obviousness-type double patenting*. However *obviousness-type double patenting* can be avoided by filing a terminal disclaimer so that the two patents will expire at the same time. ∎

Chapter 15

After Your Patent Issues: Use, Maintenance, and Infringement

> ### Inventor's Commandment #28
>
> Once your patent issues, check it for printing errors, consider patent marking if you manufacture a product covered by the patent, be alert for infringements, and pay three maintenance fees (3.0 to 3.5, 7.0 to 7.5, and 11.0 to 11.5 years after issue) to keep it in force.

A. Issue Notification

Several months after you pay the issue fee (Chapter 13), you'll receive an Issue Notification. This will indicate the number and issue date of your patent (commonly within two weeks after you receive the notice). On the issue date, which will usually be a Tuesday, the patent will be granted, published, and mailed to you so that several days later you'll receive your patent deed (also called "letters patent"). This consists of a copy of your patent on stiff paper, a fancy jacket, seal, and ribbon. You'll also receive (separately) the printed copies of your patent if you ordered them when you paid your issue fee. The *Official Gazette—Patents*, which is usually published electronically only on the Tuesday of grant, will list the highlights of your patent.

B. Press Release

You may wish, when you learn the number and date of your patent, to prepare a press release about it. See any book on advertising to learn how to prepare a press release; it should cover the six facets of reporting:

> *"I had six honest serving men*
> *They taught me all I knew;*
> *Their names were WHERE and WHAT and WHEN*
> *And WHY and HOW and WHO."*
>
> **—Rudyard Kipling**

Make your headline and text simple and short (250 words maximum), yet interesting and catchy—for example, "Midgeville Inventor Gets Patent on Jam-Free Bike Mechanism." Be conversational; don't use jargon or technical language. Type on only one side of the paper, double spaced, and include your name, address, phone number, and "For Immediate Release" at the top. If you have more than one page, number and type "more" at the bottom of each page (except the last) and staple the pages together. Type "30" or "###" at the end. If you have an interesting or important invention, send a letter or copy of your PR (as soon as you get the issue notice) to N.Y. Times Patent Columnist, 229 West 43d St., New York, NY 10036, and States News Service, Fax 202-737-1851. They may mention your patent in their regular column when your patent issues. Also send the PR to your local papers and trade magazines (each with a copy of your patent) on the day you get the patent. You can make extra copies of your patent from the deed, the printed copies, or download them from the Internet (see Chapter 6 for more on obtaining patent copies). One source for getting publicity is Publicity Goldmine (www.publicitygoldmine.com).

C. Check Your Patent for Errors

First, proofread your patent carefully, preferably aloud with a friend or coworker. Carefully examine the information in the heading of the patent—serial number, filing date, title, your name, etc.—to make sure all is correct. Then read the patent word for word and compare it with the application in your file as amended during the prosecution phase.

If you find errors, you have several possible courses of action.

1. If the Errors Aren't Significant

If the errors aren't significant, that is, if the meaning you intended is obvious and clear, the PTO won't issue a Certificate of Correction, but you should make the error of record in the PTO's file of your patent. To do this, simply write a "make-of-record" letter to be put in the file of your patent, listing the errors you found. This letter should be captioned similarly to Form 15-1 with the patent number, issue date, and patentee(s) name(s) and should be headed, "Make-of-Record Letter for Errors in Printed Patent." It should then list all the errors in the patent.

2. Certificate of Correction

If any of the errors you discover are significant, that is, if the meaning is unclear because of a wrong reference numeral, missing or transposed words, failure to include a significant amendment, any errors in the claims, etc., you may obtain a Certificate of Correction. If the errors are the fault of the printer, the PTO will issue the Certificate of Correction free. If the errors are your fault, that is, they appear in your file as well as in the printed patent, you still can get a Certificate of Correction. However, the error must be of a clerical or minor nature and must have occurred in good faith. Examples are a wrong reference numeral or an omitted line or word. (The fee for a Certificate of Correction to fix your error is listed in Appendix 4, Fee Schedule.) To obtain a Certificate of Correction (printer's fault or yours), do the following:

Step 1: Fill out Forms 15-1 and 15-2. In Form 15-1 (the request letter), insert the patent number, issue date, patentee(s), Ser. Nr., filing date, and the date you mailed the form. Check paragraph 2 if the error is the fault of the PTO; check paragraph 3 and insert the amount from the Fee Schedule if the error is your fault.

In either case (whether you checked paragraph 2 or 3), in paragraph 4 list the places in the application file where the errors occurred and explain who was at fault; for example:

"4. Specifically, on p. 4, line 12, of the specification, applicant erroneously typed '42' instead of '24' and neither applicant nor the examiner detected this error during prosecution."

or

"4. Specifically, on p. 4, line 12, of the specification, the reference numeral '24' has been erroneously printed by the GPO in the patent as '42' instead of '24.'"

Step 2: Complete the caption of Form 15-2 with the patent number, issue date, and inventor(s). (The PTO also furnishes carbon sets of the Certificate of Correction form gratis.) In the body of Form 15-2, make the necessary corrections as if you were making an amendment (see Chapter 13) to the actual printed patent; for example:

"Col. 3, line 54, change 'the diode' to —varistor 23—."

Put your return address and the patent number on the bottom of Form 15-2.

Step 3: Send one copy of completed Form 15-1 and *two* copies of completed Form 15-2 to the PTO with a receipt postcard, and a check for the correct amount if the error was your fault. You'll get an approved copy of your Form 15-2 back in several months and the PTO will affix copies of it to the copies of your patent that it maintains in its storage facilities and will include the Certificate as the last page of the patent on its Internet site.

D. Patent Number Marking

If you already have sales blurbs promoting your invention, change them to indicate that your invention is "patented" rather than "patent pending." If you, or a licensee of yours, is manufacturing a product embodying the invention, you should consider marking your product with the patent number.

A section of the patent laws (35 USC 278) states that products embodying a patented invention may be marked with the legend "Pat." or "Patent," followed by the patent number. If you make or sell products embodying your invention that are properly marked, you can recover damages from any infringers you sue from the date you began marking, whether they see your notice or not. If you make or sell products but don't mark them with your patent number, or mark them "Patented" without the number, your rights are reduced and you can recover damages only from the date you notify the infringer of infringement, or from the date you file suit against the infringer, whichever is earlier.

You should do the actual marking on the product itself, on its package, or by means of a label affixed to the product.

Suppose you don't manufacture any product embodying the invention, or if the invention relates to a process that's not associated with a product and hence can't be marked. In these cases you can recover damages from an infringer for the entire period of infringement without marking.

The disadvantage of patent marking is that any sophisticated person who wants to copy your product can easily see the number of your patent, order the patent, read its claims, and attempt to design around the claims of your patent. If you don't mark your product, the potential infringer can still probably get this same information, but only through a lot more expense and effort. In other words, by not marking you may depend in part on human inertia to protect your invention from being copied. Many companies, therefore, favor *not* marking their patented products, or simply marking them "Patented" without including the number. They rely on their own familiarity with the field to enable them to quickly spot and promptly notify any infringer of the existence of the patent.

E. Advertising Your Patent for Sale

If you still haven't licensed or sold your invention by the time your patent issues, you can advertise the availability of your patent for license or sale on the Internet or in one or more of several publications, such as:

- *Patent Official Gazette,* Commissioner for Patents, P.O. Box 1450, Alexandria, VA 22313-1450
- *The International Invention Register,* P.O. Box 547, Fallbrook, CA 92028
- *The Wall Street Journal, U.S.A. Today,* local newspapers in large cities, etc.

Contact the publications for listing information and fees. The Internet provides many opportunities for advertising your invention and many sites provide methods for listing inventions for sale or license including *The Patent Café* (www.patentcafe.com), Cool License (www.coollicense.com), and *Inventor's Digest* (www.inventorsdigest.com). Contact these sites for more information.

However, the number of patentees who make successful contacts by advertising their patents is relatively low. Your chances of a successful nibble will be far greater if you use the targeted, individual approach described in Chapter 11.

F. What Rights Does Your Patent Give You?

Now that you've actually obtained a patent, you'll undoubtedly want to know exactly what rights you receive under it. While I've indicated that a patent provides a monopoly on the manufacture, use, and sale of your invention that expires 20 years from the filing date of your application, I'll now specifically discuss what this means in the real world.

1. Enforceable Monopoly Against Manufacture, Use, Sale, Offer for Sale, Importing, Etc.

The grant of a patent gives you, or any person or entity to whom you "assigned" (legally transferred) your patent or patent application, a monopoly on the invention *defined by the claims of the patent*. The monopoly begins with the patent's date of issuance and expires 20 years from the date you filed your application (or the first application in the chain if your patent issued from a division, continuation, or continuation-in-part). (For applications issuing before 1995 Jun 8, the term is 17 years from issuance, and for applications filed before this date and issuing thereafter, the term is the greater of the 17- or 20-year term. The PTO will extend any term if you encountered a delay due to FDA processing of a new drug or medical device application, had to appeal or prosecute an interference, or had your application placed under a secrecy order. (35 USC 154-156.)) If the PTO published your patent application—usually 18 months after filing (unless you requested earlier publication)—and you actually notified an infringer of your patent application, you can recover damages from the infringer from the actual date of notification. (35 USC 154(d).)

Your monopoly gives you the right (35 USC 271) to bring a valid suit against anyone who does any of the following during the term of your patent:

1. Makes, uses, offers to sell, sells, or imports the invention defined by the claims of your patent. (There is a DNA exemption which is too complicated to cover here. See 35 USC 271(c)(1).) Note also the medical exemption discussed in Section 3, below.
2. Files a new drug application on your invention in the U.S.
3. If your U.S. patent covers a process, imports a product made abroad by your patented process.
4. Induces infringement of your patent.
5. Offers to sell, sells, or imports a material component of your patented machine or process made especially for use in infringement of your patent and not a staple article of commerce with substantial non-infringing use; or
6. Supplies in or from the U.S. a substantial portion of the components of your patented machine for assembly outside of the U.S.

You can use your ownership of the patent to obtain value in any of seven ways:

1. Sell the patent outright.
2. License others to make, use, and/or sell the patented invention in return for royalties under a variety of conditions, subject to the antitrust laws mentioned in the note below. (See Chapter 16 for a more detailed discussion about the sale and licensing of patent rights.)
3. Use your patent to create a monopoly by preventing anyone else from making, using, or selling the

invention. In this case you would manufacture the invention yourself (or have it manufactured for you) and charge more than you'd have to in a competitive situation. Xerox did this in the early days of photocopiers and Polaroid and Sony do it now with their instant film, cameras, and the one-gun Trinitron CRT. In other words, a patent will give you the right (within limits) to fix the price of your product—a capitalist's dream!

4. If accused of patent infringement, you may be able to assert your patent against the other patent holder and generate a cross-licensing arrangement to avoid paying royalties or having to stop infringing.

5. You can tout your patent in advertising.

6. You can use a patent as a publication (as of its filing date) to prevent others from patenting the same thing.

7. While a patent does not give you any immunity from infringing others' patents, if you are manufacturing anything and another patent holder charges you with infringement, you can sometimes use the patent to (a) show that your products are separately patentable and thus are not direct copies, and (b) prevent the infringer from using the doctrine of equivalents.

Extending the Effectiveness of Your Patent

If you want to continue to make money from your creativity after your patent expires, you should plow back some of your royalties or proceeds from the sale of the patent for research. In this way you can invent further developments and improvements, and thereby get more and later patents so as effectively to extend your monopoly beyond its relatively short term. You can even file a new patent application on the improvements when you invent them, but withhold the introduction of products with the improvements until you've milked the market with the basic products. DuPont did this with its *Teflon* and *Teflon II*.

Antitrust Note. Occasionally, companies or individuals who own a patent or manufacture a patented invention use their patent to extend their monopoly in ways that the antitrust laws prohibit. For example, compulsory package licensing, compulsory price fixing, and other practices that impose undue restraints on free trade all violate the antitrust laws. This is very rarely a

problem for the independent inventor but can occasionally raise problems for large corporations. For a discussion of antitrust law as it affects the use of patents, go to any law library and look for any books on patent-antitrust law. One text is *Antitrust Law Handbook 1999*, by William C. Holmes (West 1999). Also look under the heading "Patents," subhead, "antitrust," in any legal encyclopedia, such as *Corpus Juris Secundum*.

2. Property Rights

The law considers a patent to be personal property that its owner can sell, give away, or otherwise dispose of. It can even be seized by your judgment creditors, just like your car, a share of stock, or any other item of personal property. Although it's personal property, the actual patent deed you receive from the PTO has no inherent value; thus you need not put it in your safe-deposit box or take any steps to preserve it against loss. Your ownership of the patent is recorded in the PTO (just like the deed to your house is recorded by your county's Recorder of Deeds). If you lose the original deed, you can download copies, or the PTO will sell you copies of the printed patent (certified if you desire) and/or certified copies of a title report showing that you're the owner.

3. Medical Procedure Exemption

A few years ago, one physician sued another for infringement of a patented ophthalmic surgery technique. This upset the medical establishment, which used its considerable clout to get a federal statute enacted which exempts health care providers (for instance, doctors, nurses, and hospitals) from liability for performing medical procedures covered by in-force patents. (35 USC 287(c).) In view of this statute, it no longer makes sense to patent medical procedures, as such. However, the statute still allows patent owners to sue health care providers for any activity that infringes a patent on (a) a device, (b) a drug, (c) the use of a drug, or (d) a biotechnology invention.

While well-intentioned, most patent practitioners believe that this medical proceedings exemption statute stifles innovation. An example will show why. A client of mine invented a new and promising ophthalmic technique that would help sight-impaired persons. He needed funding to develop it. When he asked me to prepare a patent application on it, I told him about the new law. He realized that even if he got a patent, he would not be able to enforce it against any medical practitioners who used the technique. He also realized that any patent he got would be worthless.

Since it would not pay to develop it unless he could get a proprietary position, he dropped it and the world will not have the benefit of his potentially valuable innovation. Thus, many people with impaired vision who could have been helped will have to live with their impairment.

G. Be Wary of Offers to Provide Information About Your Patent

Soon after being awarded a patent, a client of mine received an offer by mail, advising that an "article" about her patent was published and offering to send her a copy of the article for $3.95. After anxiously sending in her money, she received the "article," a photocopy of a page from the PTO's *Official Gazette,* showing the usual main drawing figure and claim of her patent! Fortunately she was able to obtain a refund by threatening to call in the FTC and postal inspectors, but you may not be so lucky; new rackets originate all the time.

Another offer very frequently received by patentees, usually about a year or more after their patent issues, comes as a postcard, such as the following:

Important Notice

To: *Owners of U.S. Patent # 4688283*
                                            Assignor

Our search of your U.S. patent shows the ____[#]____ most recent patents, issued after your patent, that the U.S. Patent Office has classified identically or cross-referenced in the same class and subclass as your patent.

You may want to determine if your patent dominates the later patents, the activity of competitors, and the latest state of the art.

For each of the later-issued patents we will send you the patent no., an abstract, a drawing, plus address-information on the inventor, and/or the owner or manufacturer for $1.00 each, plus a service charge of $60.00 if you **return THIS CARD** (or a copy) with your payment of $96.00. Make check or money order to _____**(Name)**_____ payable on a **U.S. Bank.**

Or send $60.00 for a list of later patent numbers.

                             CD 60

1-2-3-4-1   *Providing Patent Information Since 1976*   1-2-3-4-2

Fig. 15A—Postcard Offer of Dubious Value

I believe this offer has marginal utility to most inventors, and at a very high cost. I wouldn't accept the offer, since almost all patents in which earlier patents are cited as references are very different and extremely unlikely to be of any value to the owner of the earlier patent. You can obtain an enhanced version of the same service at a lower cost by using the Delphion or MicroPatent computer search service in Chapter 6. Look under "Patents which cite this patent." These services will provide you with a list of *all* patents that have issued after yours, which cite your patent as a reference.

A third offer is the "Patent Certificate." This offer is sent to many patentees in an official-looking letter from Washington, marked "U.S. Patent Certificate," "For Official Use Only" (next to the postage stamp), and "Important Patent Information." In reality, it's from a private company that wants to sell you a nicely framed version of your patent. Needless to say, this product is of no official value.

A fourth offer, definitely of questionable value, also comes on a postcard that states something similar to the following: "Our search of your patent has located X companies that manufacture, market, or sell products in a field allied to your invention." It offers to sell you the names of the X companies for a stiff fee, usually about $80. If you want to find the names of the companies that are in a similar field, I strongly advise that you save your money. Instead take a trip to a store or library where you'll find plenty of suitable companies for free. (Use the techniques outlined in Chapter 11.)

A fifth offer is to include you in a compendium of inventors, such as a "Who's Who" of inventors, or an offer to sell you such a volume with your name included. Definitely not worth it, unless you like your ego stroked for a price.

A sixth recent scam comes in the form of an email to a patentee. The email states that it comes from a Japanese industrialist who is seeking to buy patents that cover inventions he can manufacture. A client traced back the email and found that the sender really is a grafter based in Nigeria.

As a patentee, you may receive other offers along the lines of the foregoing. Be sure to investigate and think about it carefully (or ask a trusted advisor) before you follow up on any offer.

H. Maintenance Fees

In 1983, a law was passed under which the PTO instituted a maintenance fee (MF) system. While MFs are new to the U.S., their use had been commonplace in most countries for decades. Under the U.S. MF system, your patent, when granted, will subsist in force for 20 years from the filing date of its application, provided three maintenance fees are paid.

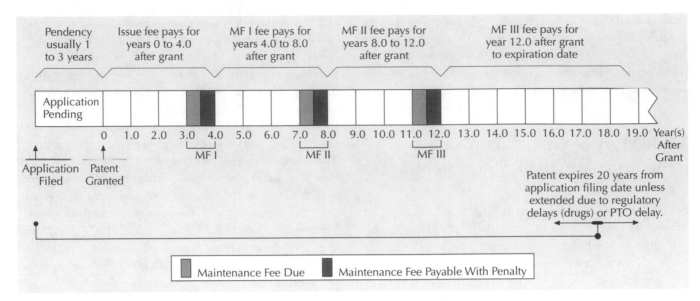

Fig. 15B—Maintenance Fee Timing Chart

If you don't pay any MFs, your patent will expire four years from grant. If you pay a first MF between years 3.0 and 3.5 from grant, the PTO will extend the patent to expire eight years from grant. If you pay a second (much higher) MF between years 7.0 and 7.5, the PTO will extend the patent to expire 12 years from grant. And if you pay a third and final (much higher yet) MF between years 11.0 and 11.5, the PTO will extend the patent to expire 20 years from filing. This information is presented in Fig. 15B, an MF timing chart. The adjustable arrow indicates that the expiration date varies, depending upon the length of pendency of the application.

To help you remember when to pay your MFs, I've provided an MF Reminder Sheet as Form 15-3; a sample is completed in Fig. 15C. You should copy this sheet and fill it out in ink—except write the year of MF I (three years after issue) in pencil on the top line and leave the last three columns in the table blank. Put the sheet at the end of your current year's calendar. Keep moving it ahead to the end of each new year's calendar at the end of each year, until the third year after issue when the fee is due. Write that the MF is due on the appropriate date on your calendar for the third year. Fill in the last three columns in the table. When you pay the first fee and receive your receipt statement, change the year at the top of the sheet to the seventh year after issue and repeat the process.

As indicated in Fig. 15B, if you forget to pay any fee during its normal six-month payment period, you can pay it in the six-month period (grace period) following its normal six-month payment period. However, as always, whenever you miss a PTO date you must pay a penalty or surcharge (see Appendix 4, Fee Schedule). If you pay a maintenance fee in the grace period, infringers do not acquire "intervening rights"—see below.

If you forgot to pay a maintenance fee in the normal and grace periods, the patent will expire at the end of the grace period. However, an expired patent can be revived on petition if you show, by declaration, that the delay was "unavoidable" (Rule 378(b)), or "unintentional" (Rule 378(c)).

An "unavoidable" petition (PTO/SB/65) must provide facts showing that you took reasonable care and steps to pay the fee in a timely manner but were unable to do so. An example of an unavoidable delay might be that your house burned down and as a result all your records were lost. You must accompany the petition by the MF, the MF transmittal letter, and the "unavoidable" fee (see Appendix 4, Fee Schedule).

An "unintentional" petition (PTO/SB/66) must merely state the nonpayment was unintentional. You must accompany the petition by the MF, the MF transmittal letter, and a very high "unintentional" fee (see Appendix 4, Fee Schedule). You must file the petition within two years after the end of the grace period. (See Chapter 13, Section Q, for how to prepare such a petition and declaration.)

If any infringement occurred or was prepared for after the patent expired and before it was revived—either with an unavoidable petition or an unintentional petition—the infringer has "intervening rights." This means that the infringer can continue any infringing activity performed in the lapse period as if the patent were not revived. (35 USC 41(c).)

The easiest way to pay an MF is with a credit card through the PTO's website. Go to the PTO website (www.uspto.gov) and click "Access Financial Services." Next, click "USPTO Office of Finance Home Page," then, click "Pay Patent Maintenance Fees." At this point you must enter the patent

Maintenance Fee Reminder

Next fee due: <u>2002</u> / <u>7</u> / <u>16</u>
                             yr   mo   date
(Write year in pencil and change after each payment)

Patent Nr.: <u>5,032,015</u>   Issued: <u>1995/7/16</u>

Application Serial Nr.: <u>07/427,862</u>   Filed: <u>93/1-/27</u>

Title: <u>"Shower Mirror with Valve"</u>

Patentee(s) (Inventor[s]/Applicant[s]): <u>T.R. Christianson</u>

Assignee(s) (if any): <u>ShowerTek, Inc.</u>

Expires <u>13/10/27</u>   (if all three maintenance fees are paid).[1]

☒ Small entity status was filed in application or patent.
   (If not, large entity fees[2] must be paid.)

Maintenance Fee Number	Fee Due From:	To:	Sent Form & Check [4]	Amount	Received Receipt Statement
I. Due 3.0 - 3.5 YAI [3]	98/ 7 / 16	99/ 1 / 16	99/ 8/ 16	$ 320	99/ 9/ 15
II. Due 7.0 - 7.5 YAI	02/ 7/ 16	03/ 1 / 16	02/ 8/ 12	$ 1,020	02/ 9/ 14
III. Due 11.0 - 11.5 YAI	06/ 7/ 16	07/ 1 / 16	/ /	$	/ /

Notes:

1. Expiration is 20 years from filing date of application for applications filed after 1995 Jun 7; 17 years from issue date for patents issuing before 1995 Jun 8; and the greater of 17– or 20–year term for patents issuing after 1995 Jun 7 and filed before 1995 Jun 8, provided you pay all three maintenance fees.

2. Please check all fee amounts before paying, since PTO fees change often.

3. YAI = Years After Issue date.

4. Send or make Internet payment at least a month before due date to allow time to take corrective action before entering grace (penalty) period in case PTO does not accept payment.

Fig. 15C—Maintenance Fee Reminder (Form 15-3 in Appendix 7)

number and the application serial number. You can find out how much is currently due by clicking "Retrieve Fees to Pay" or you can view the payment dates by clicking "View Payment windows." After that, click "Pay Using Credit Card" and complete the form by supplying your credit card information. The PTO will present a Maintenance Fee Statement (receipt) on the website showing receipt of payment. Print out the Statement for your records.

If you don't want to pay the fee online, use Form 15-4 or PTO/SB/45 to pay the maintenance fees. Complete every blank in the form including the serial number of the application, or the PTO won't accept your fee and the delay may carry you into the grace period, costing you a surcharge. (If you've assigned or licensed your patent to a large entity, check "large entity" on Form 15-4 and pay the large-entity fee.) If the PTO accepts your maintenance fee, they'll send you a Maintenance Fee Statement to this effect. Anyone can sign Form 15-4. Note that the address for payment is different than the usual address.

If you use the Certificate of Mailing at the end of the form, you can send in the fee on the last day of the period. If the last day of the period falls on a Saturday, Sunday, or holiday, it's extended to the next business day. And don't forget a postcard! Of course, if you feel, at any time a maintenance fee is due, that your invention's prospects have become nil, you shouldn't pay the fee. In this case, your patent will expire as indicated above.

The PTO won't accept a maintenance fee before its due period and usually sends you an MF reminder only after the due period expires, when you're in the six-month grace (penalty) period. They also usually send you a Notice of Patent Expiration if you don't pay the fee in either the regular or grace periods. The PTO publishes the numbers of lapsed patents in the *Official Gazette* and on its website. If you move, you must notify the PTO of your new address with a separate letter or PTO/SB/123 sent to Mail Stop Post Issue, Commissioner for Patents, P.O. Box 1450, Alexandria, VA 22313-1450; otherwise the PTO will send your MF receipt to your old address (even if you put your new address on your MF transmittal).

I. Legal Options If You Discover an Infringement of Your Patent

As stated in the Inventor's Commandment at the beginning of this chapter, once you get a patent you should monitor all products in its field and be alert for any infringement. If you find an infringer, you may wish that the earth would shake, the skies thunder, and a mighty lightning bolt would come down and vaporize the miscreant. Failing this, you might wish that you could present details of the infringement to the PTO and they will get on a white horse, ride out to the infringer, and strike them down with the sword of justice. In fact, nothing will happen and the infringement will continue unless you affirmatively do something about it. Although some inventors think that the PTO plays a role in infringement situations, nothing could be further from the truth. Rather, the PTO is in the business of simply issuing patents and doing whatever ancillary functions are necessary. The patent owner must assume the full burden for stopping the infringer and obtaining damages.

If you haven't yet licensed or manufactured your invention, you may find some solace in an infringement of your patent, since it shows that your invention has at least made it in the marketplace. Keep in mind that well over 90% of patents never attain commercial success. Here, viewed broadly, are the steps you can take to complete the last step and get the remuneration you deserve:

- Ask the infringer to stop infringing and pay you compensation for the past infringement.
- Ask the infringer to pay you compensation for past infringement and royalties for future activity.
- Ask the infringer to buy your patent for a sum that will cover past infringement and the present value of future activity.
- If you're a manufacturer and the infringer has a patent of interest to you, exchange licenses with the infringer.
- Sue the infringer in federal court in the district where the infringer resides or has committed infringement (in the event your request is unsuccessful). If your suit is successful, you will be awarded damages and will also get an injunction, precluding the infringer from using your invention in the future, during the remaining term of the patent.

Damages will be equivalent to a reasonable royalty you could have gotten had you licensed the patent or the profits the infringer made. In exceptional cases—if the infringer's conduct was flagrant or in bad faith—you may also be able to recover attorney fees and triple damages. Sometimes damages can be based upon the infringer's profits. Patent infringement damages and fees sometimes can even exceed the infringer's gross sales. The injunction is an order signed by a federal court, which, if violated, can subject the violator to contempt-of-court sanctions, including imprisonment and fines.

J. What to Do About Patent Infringement

Let's now take a closer look at what to do if your patent is infringed.

Step 1: Obtain Details of the Infringement

If you discover what you believe to be an infringement of your patent, obtain as many details and particulars about the infringing device or process and infringer as possible. To do this, procure service manuals, photographs, actual samples of the infringing device, advertisements, product-catalogue sheets, etc., plus details of the individual or company that is committing the infringement.

Step 2: Compare Your Broadest Claim With Infringing Device

I have encountered many inventors, who, after being awarded a patent, somehow get the notion that it covers everything in the field, no matter what the claims recite. Of course, you'll know this isn't true if you understood the purpose of claims, discussed at the beginning of Chapter 9. A patent covers only what the claims recite, plus their equivalents and contributory components (see Steps 3 and 4, below). Thus you must compare your patent's claims with the physical nature of the infringing device or process.

To infringe your patent, the device in question must physically have or perform all of the elements contained in the main or broadest claims of your patent. Even if the infringing device has additional elements, it will still infringe. For example, if your claim recites three elements, A, B, and C, and the infringing device has these three elements, it will infringe. If it has four elements, A, B, C, and D, it will still infringe. But if the infringing device has only two of the three elements, A and B, it won't infringe. Similarly, if the supposed infringing device has three elements A, B, and C′, it won't infringe, provided element C of your claim doesn't read on element C′ of the supposed infringing device. A patent claim is, in effect, a little statute that says, "If each and every one of the following elements is met, infringement occurs. If not all of the elements are met, there is no infringement. If more than all elements claimed are present, infringement still occurs."

To analyze infringement, you should make a claim chart with two columns. Break the first independent claim (#1) into its elements, each one in a respective block in the left column. In each corresponding block in the right column write a brief narrative stating why you feel the corresponding element in the left column is met by the infringing device. Refer to an attached drawing or exhibit. You need do only one independent claim that you believe to be infringed, but if you can do all independent claims, that's best. If the other independent claims differ substantially from claim 1, you should definitely do them. Below is a sample claim chart.

Claim 1 of Smith Patent x,xxx,xxx	Peel-O-Matic Device
1. A device for peeling potatoes, comprising:	The Peel-O-Matic device (POMD) is designed to peel potatoes tSee description on package (Exhibit A) which states, "Peels all produce faster." A potato is an item of produce.
a handle with a series of finger grips,	The POMD has a handle with a series of finger grips as can be seen in the lower part of the photo on the package (Exhibit A).
a head attached to said handle,	The POMD has a head attached to its handle as shown in Exhibit A.
said head having an elongated blade,	The head includes an elongated blade as also shown in Exhibit A.
said elongated blade having a longitudinal slot,	The elongated blade of the POMD has a longitudinal slot as also shown in Exhibit A.
said longitudinal slot having a pair of elongated, sharpened edges on opposite sides of said slot, said edges facing each other,	The longitudinal slot of the POMD has a pair of elongated, sharpened edges on opposite sides of the slot and these edges face each other as clearly shown in Exhibit A.
whereby said device may be securely held in one's hands by said handle without slipping and may be used to peel potatoes using said sharpened edges of said slot.	The POMD device can be held securely by its handle due to its finger grips and the sharpened edges of its slot may be used to peel potatoes.

You don't need to do the dependent claims at this time. Remember that each dependent claim incorporates all of the limitations of its referent claim(s) (the claim it refers to and any claim(s) the referent claim(s) refer to). Also, each dependent claim is considered independently (after the limitations of the referent claim(s) are incorporated) of its referent claim(s), even if its referent claim(s) is held invalid.

Moreover, even if your patent has 50 claims, you need prove that only one claim is infringed to prove infringement; your damages do not depend upon the number of claims that are infringed. And even if your claims don't literally read on the infringing device, there are still two ways you may be able to bag the infringer: the "doctrine of equivalents" and the "doctrine of contributory infringement."

Step 3: Apply the Doctrine of Equivalents

The law, recognizing that humans aren't perfect, formerly provided an out if the essence of an invention was copied, but the claims weren't literally infringed. Under the doctrine of equivalents (DoE), even if each element of a patent's claim is not literally met by an element of the device, so long as the element of the device is the "equivalent" of the claimed element, the device can still infringe that element. A device element is equivalent if it performs the same function in the same way to achieve the same result as the claim element, or the role of the device element is substantially the same as that of the claim element. However, the DoE was severely limited by the U.S. Supreme Court on 2002 May 28 in *Festo v. Shoketsu*, 535 U.S. 722 (2002). Under *Festo*, if the patentee amends a claim in any way during prosecution to make it allowable (this is almost always the case), the DoE can't be used with that claim unless the patentee can show that the narrowing amendment did not surrender the particular equivalent in question—that is, if the particular equivalent is not related to the way the claim was amended or was not foreseeable at the time. Also, if the court can't determine the reason for the amendment, the DoE will not be available.

Even without *Festo*, the DoE did not apply if "file wrapper estoppel" (also known as "prosecution history estoppel") exists—that is, the claim element was amended during prosecution to define over prior art.

EXAMPLE: Minerva Murgatroid of San Francisco has a patent on a mechanism for bunching broccoli. Its main claim recites the mechanism, including a recitation that the broccoli is banded with a wire-reinforced paper band. She didn't claim the band more broadly because she didn't read Chapter 9 and think to do so, this being the only type of band that would work at the time she got the patent.

A few years later, LeRoy Phillips of Philadelphia discovers a plastic broccoli band that will work just as well as Minerva's wire-reinforced band. He makes broccoli-banding machines and sells them, with his plastic bands, to Fred Farmer, who uses them to band broccoli on his farm in Fresno. Minerva can sue either LeRoy in Philadelphia or Fred in Fresno. Even though her main claim doesn't literally read on LeRoy's machine—that is, describe all of its physical elements—she can win the infringement suit using the DoE, provided she didn't amend her claims during prosecution so as to invoke the *Festo* doctrine. LeRoy's plastic band is equivalent in structure, function, and result to the wire and paper band, the band material being a relatively minor change that won't get LeRoy or Fred off the hook.

However, suppose during prosecution of her patent application before the PTO, Minerva originally had broad claims to any type of band but then narrowed them to the wire-reinforced paper band to avoid a prior-art reference. In this situation Minerva is subject to the doctrine of file wrapper estoppel and may not use the DoE to rebroaden her claim. Even if Minerva merely amended her claims to make them clearer, under the *Festo* doctrine, she can't use the DoE.

The Negative Doctrine of Equivalents

There's a rarely used converse of the doctrine of equivalents, the so-called negative doctrine of equivalents. Under this, even if your claims literally read on the infringing device, but the infringing device has a different structure, function, or result than your invention, the device may be held not to infringe.

Step 4: Consider Whether a Contributory Infringement Has Occurred

If your claims don't read on the infringing device, but the infringing device is a specially made component that's only useful in a machine covered by your patent, the infringer may be liable under the doctrine of contributory infringement.

EXAMPLE: In the example above, LeRoy makes an entire broccoli-banding machine like Minerva's, except that he doesn't sell or supply any bands. Minerva's claims don't literally read on LeRoy's machine since her claims recite the band. Nevertheless, Minerva can bag Fred under the doctrine of contributory infringement, since his broccoli-banding machine is useful only in the machine of Minerva's patent claim and since it has no other noninfringing use.

Under new legislation, if a patent holder sues to enforce a method or process claim, a defendant can escape liability if the defendant built and commercially used the invention more than one year before the patent application filing date. 35 USC 273.

Step 5: Find a Patent Attorney

When you first reasonably suspect that an infringement is occurring, you should promptly consult with a patent attorney. (See Chapter 6, Section F.) This is because you'll need to embark on a course of action that is very difficult for the nonlawyer to perform in its entirety. Unfortunately, the cost is high, and it's difficult to get a patent attorney to take this type of case on a contingent fee (you pay them only if you win). This means you'll have to pay the attorney up front (or at least partially up front). It depends on the complexity of your case, but an initial retainer of $20,000 would be typical. However, if you've got a very strong case and if the infringer is solvent (would be good for the damages if you win), it's possible that you may find an attorney who will take your case on a contingent-fee basis. If you do get an attorney to do this, you still may have to pay the out-of-pocket costs through trial; these can run as high as $100,000, so be sure you can afford them. See Section T for sources of patent litigation financing and contingent-fee attorneys.

If, as will usually happen, you can't get a contingent-fee arrangement, you should be prepared for a shock: patent trial attorneys generally charge about $350 to $700 per hour, and a full-blown infringement suit can run to hundreds or even thousands of hours' work, most of it before trial! The American Intellectual Property Law Association, a trade group for patent attorneys, estimates the median cost of patent infringement actions for each side is $280,000 up to trial, and $518,000 through trial. You should be sure that your damages, if you win, will make this worthwhile. Also, be sure the defendant can pay any judgment you obtain. And don't depend on getting attorney fees or triple damages; these are awarded only in "exceptional cases"—that is, those where the defendant's conduct was flagrant.

Of course, what's sauce for the goose is sauce for the gander: an infringer will usually have the same fee burden, and may be inclined to settle if your attorney writes a few letters and he or she thinks you're serious about suing. A substantial number of cases are in fact settled before suit is even brought and most are settled before trial.

The material in the following steps is not intended to help you do your own patent infringement litigation. It would take a big book just to get you started. However, it will give you an overview of what's involved so that you can play an active role in deciding on your course of action and, if a lawsuit is brought, helping your attorney bring its prosecution to a successful conclusion.

Step 6: Write a Letter

The first step to follow in the event an infringement has occurred is to write a letter. This letter can:

• Ask the infringer to stop infringing your patent and to pay you royalties for past activity, or
• Offer the infringer a license under your patent for future activity and again ask for a settlement for the past. Remember, any infringer is a potential licensee, so don't make war right away.

As is often the case, the letter may go unanswered, or your demands may not be acceded to. If so, you'll have to sue for patent infringement if you want to recover damages or an injunction. Also, if your letter creates a reasonable apprehension that you will sue them, the infringer can sue you in an inconvenient location to have your patent declared invalid under what is known as a "declaratory judgment action." To prevent this, don't threaten to sue, but instead offer the infringer a license.

Step 7: Act Promptly

The statute of limitations for patent infringement is six years, which means you cannot recover damages that occurred more than six years back from the date you filed suit. However, despite this rather lengthy limitations period, it's important that you not wait six years, but act rapidly once you become aware of an infringement. Otherwise, the infringer may reasonably argue that it continued to infringe because you appeared not to be concerned. Your inactivity may prevent you from collecting the bulk of the damages you would otherwise be entitled to. This would occur under the legal doctrines known as *estoppel* and *laches,* which generally mean that a court won't award you damages if your action (or lack of action in this case) in some way brought them about.

If you're selling a product embodying the invention and you failed to mark it with the patent number (see Section D, above), the six-year term of damages can be considerably shortened as a practical matter by application of the patent-marking statute (35 USC 287). On the other hand, you can bring suit even after your patent has expired and still go back six years during the time the patent was in force (again, provided that you had some valid reason for delaying your action).

Step 8: Who Should Be Sued?

Obviously, you can sue any manufacturer who makes, uses, sells, imports, or offers for sale any device or practices any process covered by the claims of your patent. You must bring suit against the manufacturer where (1) it has a place of business, and (2) has committed an act of infringement. (If you have a process patent which covers a process used abroad to make a device that is imported into the U.S., under a new statute, the device will be considered to infringe.)

You can also sue the retailer or ultimate purchaser of the invention (including a private individual) as well as the manufacturer. Suits against the retailer or customer are sometimes brought in order to find a court that's favorable, or at least geographically close, to the patent owner. If a suit is brought against the retailer or customer of a patented invention, under the Uniform Commercial Code the manufacturer of the patented invention must step in and defend or reimburse the customer's suit. If your infringer is an out-of-state manufacturer and you can sue its local retailer, it puts a tremendous burden on the manufacturer to defend at a distance.

Lastly, don't be afraid to take on a big company simply because they have more resources to defend a patent infringement suit than you have to prosecute it. You have the right to a jury trial (see Section O, below), which helps equalize the odds.

Note that if you assert patent rights, your opponent may cite prior art including (a) any publication, including a patent, that was published before your filing date, or (b) a U.S. patent that was filed on any date before your filing date. If this prior art anticipates or renders your invention obvious, it will defeat your right to sue unless you can prove

(1) you conceived the invention before the date of (a) or (b) and you were diligent in filing you patent application or building and testing the invention, or (2) you built and tested the invention before (a) or (b).

See the article, "The Truth About Patent Litigation for Patent Owners Contemplating Suit," by Vanderburg, at p. 331 of the *Journal of the Patent and Trademark Office Society* for 1991 April.

If the Infringer Has a Government Contract

If the infringer of your patent is a company or individual who's making products embodying your invention under a government contract, you can sue only the government in the Court of Claims in Washington. You can't sue the company and you can't sue in your local jurisdiction. Moreover, you can't get an injunction prohibiting the company from manufacturing your invention, since the infringing device may be useful for national defense. In other words, we have compulsory licensing of any patent that covers an invention used by the government. You can, however, recover damages and interest.

Step 9: Consider Stopping Importation of the Infringing Device

If a device covered by your invention is being imported into the U.S. and the effect of such importation is to harm or prevent the establishment of a U.S. industry, or restrain or monopolize trade in the U.S., you can bring a proceeding before the International Trade Commission to have the device stopped at the port of entry. This proceeding can be brought in addition—or as an alternative—to any other legal action. While such a proceeding is complex and expensive, it provides a remedy that is extremely powerful. The pertinent statute is 19 USC 1337(a), and two articles about ITC actions can be found in the *Journal of the Patent Office Society* for 1979 Mar., p. 115, and 1984 Dec., p. 660.

Step 10: Consider Ordering a Customs Survey

As an economical alternative to suing or filing an ITC action, you can order the U.S. Customs Service to make an import survey for two, four, or six months (cost: $1,000, $1,500, or $2,000, respectively) to determine the address of any importer whose goods appear to infringe. While such a survey will not stop any importation, it will provide you with valuable information and will delay the infringing goods, thereby burdening the importer. Write to Commissioner of Customs, Attn.: IPR Branch, Room 2104, U.S. Customs Service, 1301 Constitution Ave., Washington, DC 20229, for an import survey application.

If You Discover an Infringement During Pendency

You may recover a reasonable royalty for an infringement during the pendency of your application, but you must wait until the patent issues to sue for such royalties and the royalty will only be applicable to infringements that occur after the publication of the application. You must also notify the infringer of the published patent application (PubPA) and the infringing device or process must be substantially identical to the invention as claimed in the PubPA. 35 USC 154(d). The royalty you receive will be applicable to any infringements that occur after the publication of the application.

If you filed a Nonpublication Request, you should rescind it in order to have your application published so that you can take advantage of this "royalties before issuance" statute. If you discover the infringement well before the normal 18-month-after-filing publication date, you may request that the application be published earlier than 18 months by requesting same and paying the publication fee. Rule 219 (37 CFR 01.219.)

Design Patent Infringement

If you have a design patent, infringement is determined by the "eyeball" method: the drawings of the design patent are first compared with the prior art to determine the scope or novelty of the design invention. Then, with this in mind, they're compared with the accused infringing design to see if it incorporates the innovative essence or novelty of the design and whether an ordinary observer would thereby be deceived into purchasing the accused device, supposing it to be the patented device. As in most evidentiary trials, both sides will call in their "hired guns" (experts) to testify for their side; the trier of fact (jury or judge) will decide which side's experts are more convincing.

K. Product Clearance (Can I Legally Copy or Make That?)

This is the other side of the coin: Here I'll assume that, instead of having your own invention, you're interested in copying the invention or product of someone else or making a new product that you feel may be covered by someone else's patent. What can you legally do and how do you find out?

1. Common Misconceptions

Before giving you the applicable rules and information, first I want to dispel some widespread misconceptions so you'll start from neutral territory.

Common Misconception: If you make an identical copy of a device or circuit, you can be validly sued for infringement, even if the copied device is not patented.

Fact: You are free to copy any device or circuit, even to the minutest detail, so long as you do not infringe any applicable patent, trademark, or copyright, and so long as you don't copy any features that have a "secondary meaning." (See Chapter 1, Section R.)

Common Misconception: If a product is not marked "Patented" and it does not have a patent number, you are free to copy the product, since the law requires patented products to be marked with the legend "Patented" and the patent number.

Fact: Patented products don't have to be marked as such: See "Patent Number Marking" (Section D).

Common Misconception: If a product that you intend to make is shown in the drawing of another's patent, you would be an infringer of that patent if you made the product.

Fact: Only the claims of a patent determine infringement. (See Chapters 9, 13, and Section J, above.)

Common Misconception: That which you do in your own home or for your own personal use will not infringe a patent that is otherwise applicable.

Fact: While "home infringement" may be difficult to detect, nevertheless it is a form of infringement that is legally actionable and can subject the infringer to paying damages and/or an injunction prohibiting further infringement.

Common Misconception: If you change a patented product a fixed percentage, say 20%, you won't be an infringer.

Fact: The amount you'll have to change a patented product to avoid infringement is not subject to quantitative analysis, but rather is determined by the breadth of the patent's claims. (See Section J, above.)

2. Find Out If There's an Applicable Patent and Whether You Will Infringe It

Suppose you do want to manufacture a specific product or perform a specific process commercially, and you have some reason to believe it may be covered by an in-force patent or pending application. How can you find out whether you can proceed without infringing the patent in the process, or without infringing a patent that will issue in the future?

Unfortunately, there is no way to be 100% sure, because no search can cover pending patent applications. However I can give you some pretty specific instructions and guidelines.

If the process or product you wish to duplicate is already manufactured or used, look at the product, the literature accompanying it, and the packing material, to see if any patent number is given. If you can get the patent number, download it from the PTO website (see Chapter 6, Section L) or order the patent from the PTO or a private service. If the patent issued before 1995 Jun 8, it expired (or expires) 17 years from issue; if it issued after 1995 Jun 8, it expires 20 years from its filing date, or the filing date of any parent cases from which it originated, whichever is sooner. Here's a rough guide that will help you make a rough determination as to when any patent issued: Patent #1 issued in 1836; #100,000 in 1870; #500,000 in 1893; #1,000,000 in 1911; #1,500,000 in 1924; #2,000,000 in 1935; #2,500,000 in 1950; #3,000,000 in 1961; #3,500,000 in 1970; #4,000,000 in 1977; #4,500,000 in 1985; #5,000,000 in 1991; #5,500,000 in 1996; #6,000,000 in 1999; #6,500,000 in 2001; and #6,800,000 in 2004.

If the patent is in force, things usually aren't as bad as they seem. Often a patent that supposedly covers a product in reality may cover only a minor aspect of the product (such as the housing) that is easy to design around. Sometimes the patent doesn't cover the product at all: How can you be sure? The only way is to read its claims carefully, diagramming them if necessary, to know exactly what they cover. (See Section J, above.) If what you want to manufacture is not covered by the claims, and if you feel there is no other patent on the item you wish to manufacture, you are free to do so.

If the product or process you wish to manufacture is simply marked "Patented" and carries no number, your task is more difficult. You can write to the company, asking for the number and date of their patent, or whether their patent is in force, but they're not bound to answer, and you'll have tipped your hand by communicating with them.

You can have a (relatively cheap) search made in the PTO or on its website of all of the patents issued to the company in question (see Chapter 6, Section L). But there is no guarantee that this will uncover the manufacturer, since the patent may not be owned by the company in question; the manufacturer may simply be a licensee. The best way to determine whether an in-force patent is applicable is to make a search in the relevant classes and sub-classes of the PTO (see Chapter 6), have someone make the search for you, or search on the Delphion or PTO sites. The search should seek to find any patent on the invention in question. This will involve a greater expenditure of time or money, but at least you will be fairly certain of your position. If, however, there is a patent pending on the product or process, there is no way to obtain any details, even if the manufacturer marks the product "patent pending"; thus, not all risks can be eliminated.

If the product or process you wish to manufacture has been known or used in the marketplace for over 17 years, you can be pretty sure that no in-force patent will be applicable, or that even if one is applicable, it is just about to expire anyway.

If you can't find any U.S. patents and the product or process is relatively new, you shouldn't feel free to copy it, because it may be the subject of a pending patent application. It's not possible to search pending U.S. patent applications, since they're kept secret unless they are published 18 months after filing. You can search published U.S. applications and you can often find some pending U.S. applications by searching for published corresponding foreign applications, which are all published 18 months after filing. (To search published foreign applications, use one of the database searching services listed in Chapter 6, Section L.) Also, if the probable owner of a patent application you want to research has been selling the product under a trademark, such as "the Zorch widget," investigate the item in the PTO (trademark applications are not kept secret) to obtain the date of first use of the trademark in the United States. It's likely that the filing date of any patent application is just before the date of first trademark use.

If you find an applicable in-force patent or patent application, and you don't think you can break it, avoid it, or get a license at a reasonable royalty, consider designing around the patent or using older (nonpatented) technology.

3. What to Do If an In-Force Patent Is Applicable

If there is an in-force patent applicable, and you still wish to manufacture the product, you have several alternatives:

• Although I don't advise it, some companies manufacture or use the product or process and hope that the patentee won't catch them. When they do this, they usually follow a good accounting practice, by keeping reasonable royalty reserves (see Chapter 16 for what is a reasonable royalty) in case they're ever caught. Also, they usually analyze the patent, or have a patent attorney do so, to see if there are any good defenses to show that they were not a "willful" infringer, since willful infringers may be subject to triple damages or attorney fees in a lawsuit. They must always be aware that the patent owner may discover the infringement, and sue them, and get an injunction prohibiting further manufacturing. Although the idea of manufacturing without a license may seem deceitful, risky, and inadvisable, it is done frequently in the U.S. (but not commonly in Japan). The infringer simply takes the full-speed-ahead-and-damn-the-torpedoes attitude and hopes to be able to negotiate a favorable settlement or break the patent if caught.

• You can ask the patent owner for a license to manufacture under the in-force patent. However, here you take the risk, if you aren't familiar with the patent owner's practices, of being refused a license. Moreover, you'll have shown your hand, so that if you do manufacture, the patent owner will be looking out for you and will certainly sue or accuse you of willful infringement in short order.

• You can make an extended validity search to try to "break" the patent. You should use a professional, experienced searcher to do this and should expect to spend a thousand or more dollars in order to make the widest and most complete search possible. Also, you should order a copy of the PTO's file of the patent (see Fee Schedule for cost) to see if there are any weaknesses or flaws in the patent that are not apparent from the printed patent itself. Again, the services of an experienced attorney should be employed here, because breaking patents requires a highly skilled practitioner. If the attorney feels that the patent can be invalidated or is not infringed, you can have them write a "green-light letter" to you, explaining in detail why it would not be likely that you would be liable for infringing the patent. This letter can show you are not a willful infringer and thus avoid treble damages or attorney fees if you are sued.

• If you find highly relevant prior art, you can bring it to the attention of the patent owner and ask it to disclaim or dedicate the patent to the public. Or, you can send the art to the PTO to be put in the file of the patent (35 USC 301) or apply to have the patent reexamined (35 USC 302; see Section N, below).

Defending Against Method (Process) Claims

Effective November 1999, if you are commercially using a method or process that has been patented by someone else and your use preceded the patent's filing date by more than one year, you have an absolute defense against an infringement charge. However, this defense is personal to you and will generally not invalidate the patent. (35 USC 273.)

• Your last alternative is to review the claims of the patent and then try to design around them. Often you will find that the claims of a patent, upon analysis, have one or more limitations that can be eliminated in your product or process so that you can make the patented invention even cheaper than the patentee. Alternatively, you can design around one of the elements of the patent, make an improved device, and get your own patent on it. Remember, if you don't infringe the independent claims, you won't have to worry about the dependent claims. (See Chapters 9 and 13, and Section J, above.)

4. If No In-Force Patent Is Applicable

Unless there is an in-force patent covering an item, anyone is free to make and manufacture identical copies of it, provided:

• One doesn't copy the trademark of the product
• The shape of the product itself is not considered a trademark (such as the shape of the *Fotomat* huts), and
• You don't copy "secondary meaning" features. (See Chapter 1.)

If you buy a product from another in the course of business, your vendor is obligated to indemnify you for any such infringement under the Uniform Commercial Code. However, you can be sued for infringement and be liable for damages. (Hopefully, your vendor will be around to reimburse you.) You can also be subject to an injunction ordering you not to infringe any more.

One manufacturer's effort to copy a small hardware item by having it manufactured cheaply in the Orient backfired. He sent the item overseas with instructions to make several thousand identical copies of the item. Since he didn't give any further instructions, the Oriental manufacturer did as instructed, manufacturing and shipping back several thousand copies of the item, including a faithful copy of the embossed trademark of the manufacturer's competitor. The manufacturer then had to spend significant money obliterating the trademark, thereby losing his entire profit in the process.

L. Citing Prior Art Against Patent Applications and Patents

Suppose you're aware of prior art that would affect a patent or patent application and you want to make the PTO or the public aware. Perhaps you want to get the art in the file of your own patent or application to get it behind you and show your good faith and put forth your arguments as to why it doesn't invalidate your claims. Or maybe you are manufacturing (or contemplating manufacturing) something based on the invention and you don't want someone to get a patent on it. Or possibly you just want to do it as a public service to prevent an improper patent from issuing or cast a cloud on a patent you know was improperly issued. How do you apprise the PTO or the public of this prior art?

There are five ways that you can cite prior art relevant to your own or someone else's patent or patent application.

1. Passive citation against your own patent application (Rule 97)
2. Passive citation against a published patent application (Rule 99)
3. Protest against a pending application (Rule 291)
4. Passive citation against a patent (Rule 501)
5. Reexamination (Rules 510 and 902).

Let's examine each of these in more detail:

1. Passive Citation Against Your Own Patent Application (Rule 97)

As part of your "duty of disclosure" under Rule 97 you are required to provide an Information Disclosure Statement (IDS) in which you cite prior art that you are (or become) aware of, against your own application. (I include it here for the sake of completeness. For more information, see Chapter 10, Section N.) Once your patent issues, this obligation ends, although it would be considered highly improper to sue on a patent that you know is invalid.

2. Passive Citation Against a Published Patent Application (Rule 99)

Under Rule 99, anyone can cite prior art against a published patent application. The PTO will enter the citation in the application file if it includes a fee (see Appendix 4, Fee Schedule), a list of the citations, and a copy of each citation. (The relevant portions of non-English citations must be translated.) A copy of the citation must be sent to (served upon) the applicant. The person making the citation should not explain the relevance of the citations.

3. Protest Against a Pending Application (Rule 291)

Under Rule 291, anyone can protest any pending application before it has been published or allowed. The protest must be filed with the PTO and a copy must be served upon the applicant. If the protestor does not know the address of the applicant, they must file two copies with the PTO. If the protest is made on the basis of prior art, it must include a list of the prior art, copies of the art, and an explanation of the relevance of each citation. (The relevant portions of non-English citations must be translated.) If the protest is made on some other basis, such as fraud or improper inventorship, it will be put in the file without any further action. The protest should identify the application as completely as possible. No fee is required and the PTO will not communicate further with the protestor, except to return the usual postcard if one is included with the protest. If you don't know the serial number, filing date, and/or name of the inventor (the usual case), you should identify the application with as much information as you can.

4. Passive Citation Against a Patent (Rule 501)

Under Rule 501, anyone can cite prior art in the file of a patent. (If the patentee makes the citation, it must include an explanation of the pertinence of the art and how the claims differ from the art.) The person making the citation can make it anonymously and should send copies to the PTO and the patentee, or should file it in duplicate with the PTO. No fee is required.

5. Reexamination (Rules 510 and 902)

Anyone can cite newly discovered prior art against a patent and have it reexamined. There are two types of reexamination, ex parte (one party) under Rules 510 et seq., and inter partes (two parties) under Rules 902 et seq. As reexamination procedures are relatively complicated and expensive, I suggest you consult an attorney if you want to institute a reexamination.

M. The Court of Appeals for the Federal Circuit (CAFC)

Full-blown patent infringement suits are very expensive and can cost each side hundreds of thousands, and even millions, of dollars in attorney fees, travel, and deposition expenses, witness fees, and telephone and secretarial expenses. Also, patent litigation can take one to ten years to complete. Thus, litigation favors wealthy or large corporations, which are far better equipped to defend and maintain patent infringement suits than a single individual. In the past, if you discovered an infringement, it was usually to your advantage not to sue and to accept a settlement that was less than you thought you were owed. In short, "gold ruled the law."

The pendulum recently has swung back a good deal in favor of the patent owner, however, primarily because of several important statutory and common-law changes. One of these is the Court of Appeals for the Federal Circuit (CAFC). All patent appeals, both from the PTO's refusal to grant a patent and from judgments in infringement suits brought in the U.S. District Courts around the country (federal trial courts are where patent infringement actions are first brought and decided), are now heard by the CAFC. It is headquartered in Washington, DC, but it sometimes travels around the U.S. to hear appeals in major cities. This means that one court decides all appeals and thus creates a body of legal interpretation that's uniform. Previously, appeals were decided by the various Circuit Courts of Appeal covering the area of the country where the U.S. District Court was located, with a resulting patchwork quilt of inconsistent decisions.

One happy result of the uniformity brought by the CAFC has been the upholding of more patents and higher damage awards for infringement. While, as mentioned, patent infringement lawsuits and trials must still be brought and conducted in local U.S. District Courts, all of these courts are bound to follow the more pro-patentee decisions of the CAFC (under principles of common-law precedent).

Another pro-patentee change is the greater availability of a most powerful weapon—the preliminary injunction. Formerly, courts would grant a preliminary injunction (a court order prohibiting the infringer from continuing the infringing activity) only if it appeared that, beyond question, the patentee would win. Now all the patentee need prove is a "reasonable likelihood of success."

N. Using the Reexamination Process to Reduce the Expense of Patent Infringement Suits

Another valuable statutory change is the reexamination process (35 USC 302) in which the PTO can be asked to reexamine any in-force patent to determine whether prior art newly called to its attention knocks out one or more of the patent's claims. How does this help the patent holder? Suppose the patent holder decides to go after an infringer. Very soon after the first demand letter is sent, or suit is filed, the infringer will make a search and tell the patent holder of prior art that the infringer feels invalidates one or more claims in the patent. Formerly, if it still thought its patent was valid, the patent holder had to push ahead with an expensive patent infringement lawsuit and hope that the U.S. District Court judge (who is often unfamiliar with patent principles) would decide its way instead of for the infringer.

Now, instead of leaving the matter up to the judge, anyone can request a reexamination by the PTO. The party requesting the reexamination can participate in the reexamination process, and has the right to appeal any decision in favor of the patentee. The PTO will reexamine the claims in light of the prior art and either issue a certificate of patentability, or unpatentability. In the case of the former, this opinion will weigh almost conclusively in favor of the patent holder in any ensuing litigation and quite often will lead to a favorable settlement beforehand. In the event the latter occurs (certificate of unpatentability), the unpatentable claims will be canceled automatically by the PTO. While this will not result in victory for the patent holder, it will save time and money that otherwise would have been spent haggling in court.

The reexamination process can also be used to your advantage if you're accused of infringement. By obtaining a PTO certification that the patent holder's claims are unpatentable over the prior art, you may save yourself an expensive defense in court.

To institute a reexamination of any patent, anyone can file a request, together with the patent number, prior art, and the fee. (See Fee Schedule.) The fee appears huge, but is small compared with the expense of litigation. If the PTO feels that the prior art is relevant, it will conduct the reexamination. The reexamination can be conducted ex parte (only the requester can file briefs) or inter partes (both sides can file a brief setting forth their arguments). If the PTO feels the newly cited art isn't relevant, it will terminate the proceeding and refund a large part of the fee.

O. Jury Trials

Juries love patent holders and have awarded very large damages in patent infringement actions, especially where an individual patent holder has sued a large corporation. Thus, if you sue on a patent, always demand a jury trial: most juries love injured individual inventors and usually award more than a judge will. Be aware, however, that the Supreme Court in *Markman v. Westview Instruments, Inc.,* 116 S.Ct. 1384 (1996), has recently removed juries' powers to interpret claims and hence reduced their power to decide the issue of infringement.

P. Arbitration

Instead of a lawsuit, if both parties agree, the entire infringement dispute can now be submitted to arbitration. In this case, an arbitrator, usually a patent attorney or retired judge, will hear from both sides in a relatively informal proceeding. The arbitrator will adjudicate the patent's validity, infringement, etc. The arbitrator's fee (about $10,000 to $50,000 and up) is far cheaper than the cost of a regular lawsuit complete with depositions, formal interrogatories, and other formal proceedings. In addition, it's much faster. The arbitrator must file the award with the PTO. The American Arbitration Association is frequently used and has rules for arbitration of patent disputes, but the parties can use any arbitrator(s) they choose.

Q. How Patent Rights Can Be Forfeited

Patents and their claims can be and often are retroactively declared invalid or unenforceable by the PTO or the courts for various reasons, such as:

- Relevant prior art that wasn't previously uncovered (Chapter 6)
- Public use or sale of the invention prior to the filing date of the patent application (Chapter 5, Section E)
- Misuse of the patent by its owner—for example, by committing antitrust violations, and
- Fraud on the PTO committed by the inventor—for example, by failing to reveal relevant facts about the invention and the prior art (Chapter 10, Section H).

In addition to losing your patent rights, you may discover that what you thought was a broad claim is so narrow as to be virtually useless. Generally, you'll discover this when your airtight infringement action goes down the drain when the PTO or the judge declares your patent noninfringed.

Most people are surprised to learn that patents, although duly and legally issued, can be declared invalid, nonenforceable, or noninfringed. In other words, a patent isn't the invincible weapon many believe it to be. Rather, a patent can be defeated if it has weaknesses or if it isn't used in the proper manner. Still, 50% of patents that get to court are upheld. In addition, the percentage of patents that are treated as valid is higher than the court statistics indicate, since they don't count the many patents that don't get to court because the infringers saw the impossibility of invalidating them or didn't want to spend the $250,000 or more necessary to fight the patent.

An accused infringer of a patent can avoid liability (that is—defend against the infringement action) in three different ways:

- By showing that the claims of the patent aren't infringed
- By showing that the patent isn't enforceable, or
- By showing that the patent is invalid.

With regard to the first, noninfringement has already been covered above in Section J.

Under the second, a patent can be declared nonenforceable if the owner of the patent has misused the patent in some way or has engaged in some illegal conduct that makes it inequitable for the owner to enforce the patent. Some examples of conduct that will preclude enforceability of a patent are:

- False marking (marking products with patent numbers that don't cover the product marked)
- Illegal licensing practices, such as false threats of infringement
- Various antitrust violations, such as package licensing
- Extended delay in bringing suit, which works to the prejudice of the accused infringer, and
- Fraud on the PTO, such as withholding a valuable reference from your Information Disclosure Statement, or failing to disclose the full and truthful information about your invention in your patent application. (See Inventor's Commandment #15 in Chapter 10.)

Third, the validity of the patent being sued on can be challenged by:

- Prior-art references that the PTO didn't discover or use properly
- Proof that the specific machine covered by the patent is inoperable
- A showing that disclosure of the patent is incomplete, that is, it doesn't teach one skilled in the art to make and use the patented invention
- A showing that the claims are too vague and indefinite under Section 112, or
- A showing that the patent was issued to the wrong inventor, etc.

As you can imagine, the subjects of patent nonenforce-ability and invalidity are also complex and difficult. In fact, it has been said that if enough money is spent, almost any patent can be "broken." However, patents are respected in many quarters and, as stated, billions of dollars change hands in the United States each year for the licensing and sale of patent rights.

R. Your Patent Is Subject to Interference for One Year

For one year following the issuance of your patent, you are potentially subject to losing it if another inventor who has a pending application on the same invention can get the PTO to declare an interference. If the other inventor wins "priority" in the interference—that is, the PTO finds that the other inventor "reduced the invention to practice" (built and tested it or filed a patent application) before you, or conceived it first and was diligent in effecting a reduction to practice—you'll effectively lose your patent or any claims in issue. While conflicts between patent applications and in-force patents are relatively uncommon, they do occur, due to the failure of the examiner to spot the interfering application before your patent issues. (See Chapter 13, Section K, for more on this.)

S. Tax Deductions and Income

I include this brief section because, unfortunately, most inventors give no thought whatever to taxes, either with regard to the money they spend to get their patents, or to the money they make when they sell or license their patents. I say "unfortunately" because the government will effectively subsidize your patent expenses by allowing you to deduct them. Because of space limitations, I can't provide a full guide to all of the patent-tax rules, but here are the basics. You should consult a tax professional or the IRS for the final word:

1. You can legally deduct your patent and invention expenses (i.e., the cost of this book, patent searches, drafting and attorney fees, PTO fees, technical research, models, experimentation and testing, up to $25,000 of depreciable property, etc.) if the IRS considers that your inventing constitutes a trade or business. If you buy depreciable property above the $25,000 limit, you must depreciate this over its useful life. If you meet the trade or business test, you're in luck: You can deduct any net Schedule-C loss against your other (ordinary) income. However if the IRS considers that your inventing is a hobby (that is, you're a dilettante) they will allow you to deduct your patent and invention expenses only against any income that you receive from the hobby. What do you have to do to meet the trade or business test? The taxman will consider that you have engaged in a trade or business if you can show that you have been serious, diligent, and have spent substantial time on your invention activities. In other words, Uncle Sam will give you a passing grade if you kept careful records, had a model made, did prior-art and marketing research, made substantial efforts to sell or license the invention, acted in a businesslike manner, etc.

2. If you license your invention on a nonexclusive basis (see Chapter 16), you haven't given away all of your rights, so your royalties are considered ordinary income. Report on Schedule C or Schedule E.

3. If you sell all of your patent rights, or grant a full exclusive license, the IRS considers that you've sold it all; your receipts or royalties, even though received over a long number of years, are considered capital gains; report on Schedule D.

T. Patent Litigation Financing

Because of the high cost of litigation, cost assistance (at a price) is now available from several companies. Lloyds of London (www.lloyds.com) and Intellectual Property Insurance Services Corp. (www.infringeins.com), 10503 Timberwood Circle, Ste. 114, Louisville, KY 40223, 800-537-7863, write policies directly. These companies will, in return for an annual premium, reimburse part or all of the cost of patent enforcement litigation, up to the policy limit. You can even begin coverage while your patent application is pending. However, some companies may have a less-than-optimum rating and some may require you to jump through difficult hoops, such as getting an infringement and validity opinion from an independent attorney, before they will reimburse your expenses.

Below are some companies that finance contingent-fee patent litigation. Carefully investigate any company before engaging them. Also, as stated, most litigating attorneys will take on contingent-fee litigation if the defendant has a deep pocket and the patent is strong and clearly infringed. Below are just a few of the many litigating patent attorneys who have handled contingent-fee litigation:

• Enpat, Inc., 407-725-7066, 1901 S. Harbor City Blvd., Suite 600, Melbourne, FL 32901 (www.enpat.com)

- General Patent Corporation International, 845-368-4000, 75 Montebello Rd., Suffern, NY 10901-3740 (www.patentclaim.com)
- Patent Enforcement And Royalties Ltd. 800-827-0992, 500-6 Adelaide Street East, Toronto, Ontario, Canada, M5C 1H6 (www.PearlLtd.com)
- Costello, John P., Esq., 916-441-2234, 331 J Street, Suite 200, Sacramento, CA 95814 (patents@cwnet.com)
- Freiburger, Thomas M., Esq. 415-781-0310, 650 California St., 25th Floor, San Francisco, CA 94108
- Hosteny, Joe, Esq., 312-236-0733, Niro, Scavone, Haller, & Niro, 181 West Madison, Suite 4600, Chicago, IL 60602 (jhosteny@hosteny.com)
- DiPinto & Shimokaji, 1301 Dove St., Suite 480, Newport Beach, CA 92660, 949-223-0838, (shimokaji@dsattorenys.com)
- ThinkFire Services USA, Ltd., Perryville Corporate Park III, 53 Frontage Road, P.O. Box 4013, Clinton, NJ 08809, Phone: 908-713-3800, Fax: 908-713-3838, (info@thinkfire.com)
- America Invents, Presidio of San Francisco, 220 Halleck Street, #G100, P.O. Box 29150, San Francisco, CA 94129, tel. 866-36-INVENT, (www.AmericaInvents.com).

Also, if you're sued for patent infringement, your own general liability insurance may reimburse you for the cost of defending the suit; see the article about this at p. 527 of the *Journal of the Patent and Trademark Office Society* for 1991 July.

U. Summary

After you pay the issue fee, the PTO will print your patent and send you an Issue Notification and then the deed in a few months. It may be helpful to prepare a press release or advertise your patent for sale at this time. Check your patent for printing or other errors and obtain a Certificate of Correction if necessary. If the error is yours, the PTO charges a fee for issuing a Certificate. If you or a licensee is manufacturing a product under the patent, consider marking the product with the patent number. If you mark you can recover damages from infringers from the date you started marking, but they will have easy access to your patent number and may be more inclined to break your patent or design around it. A patent is intangible personal property that gives you a monopoly on the invention covered by the claims (so long as maintenance fees are paid), against anyone who makes, uses, sells, imports, etc., the invention. You can profit from a patent by selling or licensing it or using it to exclude others to create a monopoly (with higher prices) for yourself. However patents on medical procedures are no longer enforceable against health care providers. Patentees get offers for goods or services, but most are of no value.

Be sure to pay the three maintenance fees to keep your patent in force: The first is due 3.0 to 3.5 years after issue (YAI), the second 7.0 to 7.5 YAI, and the third 11.0 to 11.5 YAI. If you neglect to pay any fee in the due period you may pay it in a grace period (next six months) with a surcharge and thereafter if the delay was unintentional (two-year limit) or unavoidable. However if you pay it after the grace period any infringer will acquire intervening rights.

If you discover an infringer the PTO will not help you; you must contact and sue the infringer. First get details of the infringing product, compare your claims to verify infringement (be aware of the doctrine of equivalents and contributory infringement), write a letter, and sue in court or with the ITC if necessary.

To determine if you can make a product it is usually necessary to make a subject-matter search for applicable in-force patents. If an in-force patent is applicable you can design around the patent, ask for a license, or try to break the patent.

There are five ways to cite prior art against patent applications and patents:

- The usual IDS citation against your own patent application
- Citation against a published patent application of another
- Protest against any pending application
- Citation in the file of a patent
- File a request for reexamination (ex parte or inter parties)—reexamination can be used to invalidate a patent if new prior art is discovered.

All patent appeals must go to the Court of Appeals for the Federal Circuit, which is often pro-patentee. Juries no longer have the power to interpret patent claims, but they can otherwise be pro-patentee. Arbitration is an alternative to patent infringement lawsuits. Patent rights can be forfeited in various ways, e.g., if relevant prior art or a prior public use or sale is discovered, the patent is misused, or the patentee committed fraud on the PTO by not citing prior art that it knew of.

Up to one year after your patent issues anyone with a pending application on the same invention can get into interference with your patent. Patent expenses can be deducted from ordinary income if you're a serious inventor, or otherwise just against royalties. Insurance is available to finance patent litigation and companies and attorneys are available to finance patent infringement litigation on a contingency basis. ■

Chapter 16

Ownership, Assignment, and Licensing of Inventions

Inventor's Commandment #29

File the patent application in the names of all actual inventors, but no one else. To transfer part or the entire ownership of an application or patent, the inventor-applicant(s) must sign an *assignment,* and to give permission to practice a claimed invention, they must use a *license agreement.*

Inventor's Commandment #30

If a patent has several owners, absent any agreement to the contrary the law permits any owner to practice the invention without accounting to any other owners. All joint owners should consider signing a Joint Owners' Agreement requiring cooperation and sharing of any profits from the patent.

In the simplest possible situation, a single inventor invents something, obtains a patent on it, manufactures it, and markets it directly to the public for the full period that the patent remains in force. In most instances, things are not that simple. Two or more people may be involved in the conception of the invention, and many more in its development and marketing. A business may want to use the invention and be willing to pay large royalties for the privilege. Employees and employers may disagree over who owns a particular invention that was developed at least partially on company time or with company materials or facilities. Thus, the entire question of invention ownership and utilization can become complex.

In this chapter, I outline some of the ways to deal with these various ownership questions and the common agreements that are used in the process. However, because the subject of invention ownership, licensing, and transfer is complicated, you'll probably want to retain a lawyer, if only to review your plans and paperwork.

A. The Property Nature of Patents

Before I begin explaining who owns an invention, it might be helpful to review exactly what patent ownership means. Think of a patent as a valuable property right. This right, as I've stressed elsewhere in this book, gives you the right to exclude others from manufacturing, using, selling, and importing your invention. This means that you have, in effect, an enforceable legal monopoly on the invention for the in-force period of the patent. If you do grant a company permission to use your invention, the law terms this permission a "license." As with most other intangible economic rights—such as the right to operate a business, the right to withdraw money from a bank account, and the right to vote stock in a corporation—patent rights, or a portion of them, can be sold to others, or licensed for a particular use over a particular period of time.

An invention has virtually no economic value to its inventor unless it is patented, sold, or licensed as a trade secret, or has some other intellectual property coverage (See Chapter 1, Sections G to S). Sales of nonpatented inventions or inventions protected under trade secret law are difficult to make. For that reason, patent ownership and invention ownership often amount to the same thing.

B. Who Can Apply for a Patent?

As stated in Chapter 10, Section F, only the true inventor(s) can apply for a patent. As mentioned in Chapter 1, when it comes to eligibility to apply for a patent, the status of the applicant(s)-inventor(s) makes no difference, so long as each is a true inventor. That is, an applicant can be of any nationality, sex, age, or even incarcerated, insane, or deceased. (Insane and deceased people can apply for patents through a legal representative.)

What happens to patent ownership if more than one person is involved in a particular invention? If other people are involved in the inventing stage, they're considered joint or co-inventors. Most often, the trick is to determine what type of activity constitutes invention. For instance, suppose one person came up with the concept of the invention, while the other merely built and tested it—that is, did not contribute any inventive concepts but merely did what any skilled artisan or model maker could do. In this situation the second person is not a co-inventor. Similarly, financiers, or others who provided business advice, but not technical input, should not be listed as co-inventors.

On the other hand, suppose one person came up with the idea for an invention and a model maker then came up with valuable suggestions and contributions that went beyond the skill of an ordinary model maker or machinist and made the invention work far better. In this situation both people should be named as co-inventors on the patent application (see Chapter 10, Section F), provided the model maker's contribution is present in at least one claim.

The PTO and the courts don't recognize degrees of inventorship. Thus, the order in which the inventors are named on a patent application is legally irrelevant, although the first-named inventor will be more prominent in the printed patent.

If the joint applicants invented different parts of the claimed invention, they should keep accurate records as to what part each invented. That way, if one inventor's part is dropped later in the prosecution, they can change the named inventors. For this purpose I have provided Form 16-1, Joint Applicants—Statement of Respective Contributions, (see Appendix 7). I strongly recommend that all inventors complete this form whenever two or more people apply for a patent.

Completing this form is straightforward: enter the title of the application or invention, then fill out each inventor's contribution in the right-hand blocks. Have each inventor sign and date in the left-hand column adjacent to their contribution. Each inventor should keep a copy of the form (don't file it with the PTO) and refer to it later—for example, if the claims are changed in any way so that one inventor's contribution is no longer claimed, the inventors should remove that inventor from the application. See Patent Rules 48 and 324. Joint inventors need not have worked together either physically or at the same time, and each need not have made the same type or amount of contribution. To qualify as a co-inventor, as stated, an inventor need merely have contributed something to at least one claim of the application, even if it's a dependent claim.

Another problem sometimes arises when two or more persons work on an invention, but not all of them are named as applicants in the patent application. Disputes regarding inventorship with the omitted inventor(s) sometimes arise later. For example, a model builder may later come back, after an application is filed, and claim to have been wrongfully excluded as a joint applicant. As I stated in Chapter 3, the best way to avoid such problems is for all inventors to keep a lab notebook—that is, a technical diary, which faithfully records all developments and is frequently signed by the inventor(s) and witnesses. In that way the complaining model builder can be answered by positive proof from the true inventor(s). Also using the Consultant's Work Agreement (Form 4-3) will eliminate many potential disputes. Absent such documentation, or agreement, expensive disputes can arise, with only vague memories to deal with.

It's important to include in your application all the inventors who are true inventors and to exclude those who aren't inventors. If it is discovered later that your inventorship is incorrect, and that the mistake resulted from bad faith, your patent can be held invalid, although this rarely happens. (If you do discover that the wrong inventor(s) is (are) named on a patent or patent application, this can be corrected under Patent Rules 48 or 324.)

Common Misconception: If you want to make your financier a 50% owner of your invention, it is okay to do this by filing the patent application in both of your names.

Fact: A U.S. patent application must be filed in the name(s) of the true inventor(s) only. There are several legitimate ways to convey an interest in your invention to a noninventor. (See Sections E and G, below.)

Common Misconception: If you came up with a bare idea for a valuable invention and your associate "took your ball and ran with it"—that is, built and tested the invention after hundreds of hours of work leading to final success, then your associate must be named as a co-inventor with you.

Fact: As stated above, only the true inventor(s)—that is, the one(s) who came up with the inventive concepts recited in the claims—should be named as applicant(s). An associate who did only what any model maker would have done should not legally be named as co-inventor, no matter how much work was involved. On the other hand, if your associate contributed inventive concepts that made the invention workable, and that are recited in one or more claims, then the associate should be named as a joint inventor with you.

Changing Inventorship

If you find that the incorrect inventors are named in a patent application or patent, for example, due to a change in the subject matter claimed, or discovery of an earlier error, you can correct inventorship by following the procedures under PTO Rule 48 (patent applications) or Rule 324 (patent). At least one original inventor must always be retained, that is, it is not possible to change inventorship so that all inventors in the application as originally filed are changed.

C. Joint Owners' Agreement

Problems commonly arise in situations where there are two or more inventors or owners of a patent application or patent. These include questions as to who is entitled to commercially exploit the invention, who is entitled to any financial shares, what type of accounting must be performed on partnership books, etc. Fortunately, most of these predictable problems can be ameliorated, if not completely prevented from arising, by the use of a Joint Owners' Agreement (JOA).

The JOA is also desirable because a federal statute (35 USC 262) provides that either of the joint owners of a patent may make, use, or sell the patented invention without the consent of and without accounting to (paying) the other joint owner(s). This statute seems unfair, since it can work a severe hardship on one joint owner in either of two ways:

1. If one joint owner exploits and derives income from the patent while pushing the other aside, the passive joint owner will not be rewarded for any inventive contribution (if an inventor) or any capital contribution (if an investor—that is, someone who has bought part of the patent).

2. If one joint owner works hard to engineer and develop a market for the patented product, the other joint owner can step in as a competitor without compensating the engineer or marketing pathmaker for the efforts accomplished.

The JOA that I provide as Form 16-2 prevents these results from occurring and also accomplishes the following:

- Prohibits any joint owner from exploiting the patent without everyone's consent, except that if there is a dissenter, a majority can act if consultation is unsuccessful.
- Provides that in case of an equally divided vote, the parties will select an arbiter, whose decision shall control.
- Provides that disputes are to be resolved by mediation or binding arbitration if mediation fails.
- Provides that the parties shall share profits proportionately, according to their interests in expenditures and income, except that if one party does not agree to an expenditure, the other(s) can advance the amount in question, subject to double reimbursement from any income.
- Provides that if an owner desires to manufacture or sell the patented invention, that owner must pay a reasonable royalty to all other owners, including the manufacturing owner.

You should not regard this agreement as cast in stone, but merely as one solution to an unfair statute. You may ignore, modify, add to, or replace this agreement with any understanding you wish, so long as you're aware of the problems of Section 262, as paraphrased above.

The manner of completing the JOA of Form 16-2 is straightforward. Fill it in after or concurrently with an assignment (Section E, below) or a joint patent application (Chapter 10). Fill in the names and respective percentages owned by each at the top of the form, identify the patent application (or patent) next, and have each joint owner sign and date the end of the form. As with all agreements, each joint owner should get and preserve an original signed copy. The JOA should not be filed in the PTO.

⚠️ Time and space do not allow me to freely explain the possible ramifications of each paragraph in the JOA, or the many possible variations that might be more appropriate to your situation. If you want to be sure that your joint owners' agreement accurately reflects your needs, consult a patent attorney.

D. Special Issues Faced by the Employed Inventor

Many inventors are employed in industries that are at least somewhat related to the inventing they do on their own time. Such inventors naturally have a strong desire to learn what rights, if any, they have on inventions that they make during their employment, both on their own time and when they are on the job. This complex subject is covered in detail in *Who Owns Innovation? The Rights and Obligations of Employers and Employees*, by Spanner (Dow Jones Irwin 1984). I'll just cover the high points here.

Generally, the rights and obligations of employed inventors are covered by the Employment Agreement (EA) they sign with their employer—that is, the EA prevails—unless it conflicts with state law. (See below.) Below is an example (Fig. 16A) of a typical EA.

If you have *no* EA, it is possible that an employer may own rights to your employee-created invention under the "employed to invent" doctrine. How does this rule apply? If you are employed—even without a written employment agreement—to accomplish a defined task, or are hired or directed to create an invention, your employer will own all rights to the subsequent invention. This doctrine is derived from a Supreme Court ruling that stated, "One employed to make an invention, who succeeds, during his term of service, in accomplishing that task, is bound to assign to his employer any patent obtained." *Standard Parts Co. v. Peck*, 264 U.S. 52 (1924). Generally, most companies prefer to use an EA because it is more reliable and easier to enforce than this implied agreement.

If you have no EA and are not employed to invent, you'll own all your inventions, subject to the employer's extensive "shop rights" (that is, a right to use the invention solely for

Agreement

varian

IN CONSIDERATION of my employment or the continuance of my employment by VARIAN ASSOCIATES, I agree as follows:

1.   For the purpose of this Agreement the term "the Company" shall include VARIAN ASSOCIATES, its subsidiaries and/or its affiliates in which VARIAN ASSOCIATES now or hereafter during the term of this Agreement owns more than twenty percent of the stock eligible to vote for directors and the assignees and licensees of VARIAN ASSOCIATES, its subsidiaries and affiliates.

2.   I agree that all information and know-how, whether or not in writing, of a private, secret or confidential nature concerning the Company's business affairs, including its inventions, products, processes, projects, developments, and plans are and shall be the property of the Company, and I will not disclose the same to unauthorized persons or use the same for any unauthorized purposes without written approval by an officer of the Company, either during or after the term of my employment, until such time as such information has become public knowledge. I also agree to treat all U. S. Government classified information and material in the manner specified by applicable Government regulations.

3.   I agree that all files, letters, memos, reports, sketches, drawings, laboratory notebooks or other written material containing matter of the type set forth in paragraph 2 above which shall come into my custody or possession shall be and are the exclusive property of the Company to be used by me only in the performance of Company duties and that all such records or copies thereof in my custody or possession shall be delivered to the Company upon termination of my employment.

4.   I agree that my obligation not to disclose or to use proprietory or confidential information of the types set forth in paragraphs 2 and 3 above also extends to such types of information of customers of the Company or suppliers to the Company who may have disclosed or entrusted such information to the Company or me in the course of business.

5.   I hereby assign and agree to assign to the Company or its designee all my right, title and interest in and to all inventions, improvements, discoveries or technical developments, whether or not patentable, which I, solely or jointly with others, may conceive or reduce to practice during the term of my employment and which are conceived or first actually reduced to practice (a) in the utilization by the Company of my services in a technical or professional capacity in the areas of research, development, marketing, management, engineering or manufacturing, or (b) pursuant to any project of which I am a participant or member and that is either financed or directed by the Company, or (c) at the Company's expense, in whole or in part.   All other inventions, improvements, discoveries or technical developments shall remain my property.

6.   I agree to promptly disclose to and to cooperate with the Company or its designee, both during and after employment, with respect to the procurement of patents for the establishment and maintenance of the Company's or its designee's rights and interests in said inventions, improvements, discoveries or developments, and to sign all papers which the Company may deem necessary or desirable for the purpose of vesting the Company or its designee with such rights, the expense thereof to be borne by the Company.

7.   Since I am to assign to the Company certain inventions which I may conceive or first actually reduce to practice after I enter the employ of the Company, I have listed below all those inventions which I own at this time and which I believe should be brought to the attention of the Company to avoid future misunderstandings as to ownership.

8.   I agree that I will make no claim for pecuniary award or compensation under the provisions of the Atomic Energy Act of 1954, as amended, with respect to any invention or discovery made or conceived by me, solely or jointly with others, in the course of or under any contracts that the Company now has or may have pertaining to work for the Atomic Energy Commission during the term of my employment.

DATE _____   EMPLOYEE _____

DATE _____   WITNESS _____

PRIOR INVENTIONS OWNED BY EMPLOYEE
(PLEASE USE REVERSE SIDE IF MORE SPACE IS REQUIRED)

_____

_____

_____

_____

111-1-3 R 1/69

Fig. 16A—Typical Employment Agreement

the employer's business, without paying the employee) on inventions made using company time, facilities, or materials.

If you *have* an EA, it will almost certainly require that you assign (legally transfer) to your employer all inventions, that are:

1. Made during the term of employment. (Note that Form 16A asks you to list all inventions you owned prior to employment; those are excluded from the agreement.)
2. Related to the employer's existing or contemplated business
3. Made by using the employer's time (that is, the time for which the employee is paid), facilities, or materials, or
4. Made as a result of activity within the scope of the employee's duties.

Note that under items 1, 2, and 4, even if an employee makes an invention at home, on the employee's own time, the employer still can be entitled to ownership.

Also, you'll usually be bound to disclose *all* inventions to the employer (so the employer can determine if they're assignable). Lastly, most EAs will require you to keep your employer's trade secrets confidential during and after your employment. Some states, such as California, have enacted statutes (Calif. Labor Code, Sections 2870 et seq. and 2860) prohibiting the employer from requiring the employee to sign any EA that is broader than the foregoing. For example, under such statutes the employee can't be made to turn over all inventions, no matter where and when made, to the employer. Similarly, the employer is prohibited from providing an EA that states that everything an employee acquires from the employer (except salary) belongs to the employer.

> **EXAMPLE:** Griselda is an engineer employed by Silicon Valley Chips (SVC) to design integrated circuits. Griselda's EA requires her to disclose to SVC all inventions made during the term of her employment at SVC and to assign to SVC all inventions which relate to integrated circuits or SVC's business, or which she makes using SVC's time, facilities, or materials. While employed, Griselda invents a new toilet valve at home in her workshop. The toilet valve is clearly outside the scope of SVC's business and therefore, Griselda owns it totally. However, she should disclose the valve to SVC (regardless of whose time it was invented on). Later, Griselda, while still employed but on vacation, is cogitating about an integrated circuit design problem she had last week at work. She comes up with a valuable, less-expensive integrated circuit passivation technique. Since this invention relates to SVC's business, SVC owns it and Griselda must disclose it to SVC and sign any patent application and assignment on it that SVC requests.

If the invention is clearly within the scope of the EA, or is in a gray area, I still recommend first disclosing it to the employer. If the employer isn't interested in the invention after reviewing it, the employee can apply for a release, a document under which the employer reassigns or returns the invention to the employee. (The employer may retain a "shop right" under the release—that is, a nontransferable right to use the invention for its own purposes and business only.)

If the invention is in the gray area and the employer wants to exploit the invention, the employee can then try to negotiate some rights, such as a small royalty, or offer to have the matter decided by arbitration. Failing this, a lawsuit may be necessary, but I favor employees disclosing "gray-area" inventions so that a cloud of ownership uncertainty will not engulf their invention.

Most EAs also require the invention-assigning employee to keep good records of inventions made and to cooperate in signing patent applications, giving testimony when needed, even after termination of employment. Most companies give the employee a small cash bonus, usually from one to several thousand dollars or more, when the employee signs a company patent application. This bonus is not in payment for the signing (the employee's wages are supposed to cover that) but to encourage employees to invent and turn in invention disclosures on their inventions. Some employers, such as Lockheed, give their inventor-employees a generous cut of the royalties from their invention, and some will even set up a subsidiary entity (partly owned by the employee-inventor) to exploit the invention. Most, however, prefer to reward highly creative employees via the salary route.

Legislation has been proposed and engineering organizations have sought to expand the rights of the employed inventor. One of these proposals is to change the U.S. to the German system, where employees own their inventions but usually assign them to their employers in return for a generous cut, such as 20% of the profits or royalties.

E. Assignment of Invention and Patent Rights

Suppose you're an employed inventor and you make an invention on your employer's time and your employer wants to file a patent application on it. Under the law, every patent application must be filed in the name(s) of the true inventor(s). This raises a problem. If it's filed in your name, how will the employer get ownership? Since inventions, patent applications, and patents aren't tangible things like a car, money, or goods, you can't transfer ownership by mere

Assignment of Invention and Patent Application

For value received, __Roberta Ann Brisken_____ ,

of __Merion Station, PA_____

(hereinafter ASSIGNOR), hereby sells, assigns, transfers, and sets over unto __Rotten Kid Enterprises, Inc.__

of __Marcus Hook, PA_____

and her or his successors or assigns (hereinafter ASSIGNEE) __100__% of the following: (A) ASSIGNOR'S right, title, and interest in and to the invention entitled " __Poetry Therapy Systems_____

_____ "

invented by ASSIGNOR; (B) the application for United States patent therefor, signed by ASSIGNOR on __2004 Jan 1_____ ,U.S. Patent and Trademark Office Serial Number __10/123,456_____ ,

filed __2004 Jan 5_____ ; (C) any patent or reissues of any patent that may be granted thereon; and (D) any applications which are continuations, continuations-in-part, substitutes, or divisions of said application. ASSIGNOR authorizes ASSIGNEE to enter the date of signature and/or Serial Number and Filing Date in the spaces above. ASSIGNOR also authorizes and requests the Commissioner for Patents to issue any resulting patent(s) as follows: __0_____% to ASSIGNOR and __100_____% to ASSIGNEE. (The singular shall include the plural and vice versa herein.)

ASSIGNOR hereby further sells, assigns, transfers, and sets over unto ASSIGNEE, the above percentage of ASSIGNOR'S entire right, title, and interest in and to said invention in each and every country foreign to the United States; and ASSIGNOR further conveys to ASSIGNEE the above percentage of all priority rights resulting from the above-identified application for United States patent. ASSIGNOR agrees to execute all papers, give any required testimony, and perform other lawful acts, at ASSIGNEE'S expense, as ASSIGNEE may require to enable ASSIGNEE to perfect ASSIGNEE'S interest in any resulting patent of the United States and countries foreign thereto, and to acquire, hold, enforce, convey, and uphold the validity of said patent and reissues and extensions thereof, and ASSIGNEE'S interest therein.

In testimony whereof ASSIGNOR has hereunto set its hand and seal on the date below.

Roberta Ann Briskin _____

_____

State: __Pennsylania_____

County: __Montgomery_____

Subscribed and sworn to before me __1 January_____ , 200 __4__ .

Nellie Notary _____
Notary Public

SEAL

My commission expires 2004 Aug 9

Fig. 16B—Completed Assignment Form (Form 16-3A in Appendix 7)

delivery, or even by mere delivery with a bill of sale or receipt. To make a transfer of ownership in the arcane patent world, you must sign an "assignment"—a legal document that the law will recognize as effective to make the transfer of ownership.

An assignment for transferring ownership of an invention and its patent application is provided as Form 16-3A (Appendix 7). (I recommend that you do not use the PTO's assignment form, PTO/SB/15, since it doesn't cover foreign rights and requires notarization.) A cover sheet and fee must be submitted to the PTO with any assignment to be recorded; the cover sheet is provided as Form 16-3B (PTO-1595), and the fee is listed in Appendix 4, Fee Schedule. A completed assignment is shown in Fig. 16B.

As indicated, employed inventors ("assignors") usually make full assignments (transfer of 100% of the invention and its patent application) to their employers ("assignees"). They do this because they have agreed, in their EA, to assign all inventions they make within the scope of their employment to their employer. In these cases the assignee is usually a corporation.

A partial assignment (transfer of less than 100%) is usually made where the assignee (the person getting the transferred interest) has financed all or part of the patent application.

The assignment document presented here, like the Joint Owners' Agreement, is but one of many possible alternatives. If you use it, you may want to change a number of provisions to fit your situation. Also, keep in mind my cautionary note regarding the Joint Owner's Agreement, that is, a consultation with a patent attorney is advisable if you wish to fully understand how this agreement will affect your rights. For example, where there will be many owners of the patent application, the percentage interest of each should be specifically listed in the last sentence of paragraph 1.

To complete the assignment do the following:

Lines 1-3: Insert the names of the assignors (the inventor patent applicants) on lines 1 and 2 of the first paragraph after "received," and insert their cities and states of residence after "of" on line 3.

Lines 4-6: Do the same for the assignee on line 4.

Line 7: Put the percentage of the patent rights being assigned (normally 100%).

Lines 8-9: Put the title of the invention on line 7.

Lines 10-12: Put the date the patent application was signed (sometimes termed "executed" in the law) on line 11. If the application has already been filed, also put the serial number of the patent application on line 11 and put the filing date on line 12. Put the percentages owned by the assignor and assignee in the penultimate line of this paragraph.

Each assignor should sign and date the assignment. If the assignment is to be used abroad, have two witnesses sign and date the bottom two lines to make it recordable abroad. The PTO no longer requires notarization.

F. Record Your Assignment With the PTO

To be fully effective, the assignment must be recorded in the PTO, just as the deed to your house must be recorded with your county clerk. If the assignment is not recorded, and the assignors make a subsequent (fraudulent) assignment to a different assignee who is unaware of the first assignment, the second assignee's rights will prevail over those of the first assignee if the second assignee records the assignment first. (Lawyers call this a "race arrangement" since the assignee who prevails is the one who wins the race to the PTO.) This means any assignee should record the assignment as soon as possible after it's signed. To do this, merely send or fax or email the assignment and cover sheet to the PTO with a recording fee (see Appendix 4, Fee Schedule). The PTO will record the assignment by making a copy of it and the cover sheet, and return the recorded assignment and cover sheet and a record sheet listing the assignment data to the person requesting recording. This process is similar to what your county's recorder did with the deed to the building in which you're living or working. To email an assignment you must first make a PDF or TIFF

copy of the signed assignment (you'll need a scanner for this). You'll also need a credit card to pay the recordal fee. Once you're ready, follow the online instructions at www.uspto.gov/ebc/index.html, Click "File Assignments Online," then click "Access EPAS Forms," then "Start" and follow the instructions. You don't need a cover sheet since the system will ask you for the necessary information.

If the assignment has been made before the patent application is filed, it is permissible to send the assignment in with the application and have it recorded at that time (see Chapter 10, Section O). However, you must fill in the date the application was signed (executed) on the assignment and cover sheet. (You won't be able to insert the serial (application) number or filing date since you don't know those yet.) However, even if the assignment is signed before filing, I prefer to wait until I can add the filing date and application (serial) number to it before sending it in for recording. This will connect it to the application in an unequivocal way. If you send in the assignment after you file the application, fax or mail the assignment, the cover sheet, a CCPF or check (mail only) for the fee to (Fax: 703-306-5995) or to "Mail Stop Assignment, Commissioner for Patents, P.O. Box 1450, Alexandria, VA 22313-1450." If you mail the papers, don't forget the usual receipt postcard.

G. Licensing of Inventions— An Overview

Usually, the owner of a patent application or patent needs to allow others to make and sell the patented invention. Inventors, after all, are rarely also manufacturers. When an inventor gives another permission to manufacture and market an invention in exchange for compensation (such as a royalty or flat payment), it is, as stated, done with a document termed a "license." It is essential that a license agreement be written and signed by the inventor or owner of the patent or patent application (the licensor) and the manufacturer (the licensee). Here are just a few major considerations and terms that can be written into a license agreement:

1. The proposed licensee can buy an option from you (the licensor) under which you give it the exclusive (or nonexclusive) right to obtain a license under your patent application or patent within a fixed time, say two years. The payment for this option can be merely the company's agreement to research and develop your invention (this is a typical arrangement), or it can involve a cash payment. The general rule is that the more you receive up front, the more seriously the licensee will view and promote your invention.

2. As noted, if you grant the company a license, the license can be *exclusive,* under which you agree to license only the company and no one else. Alternatively, it can be *nonexclusive,* under which you license them but also have the right to license others. Exclusive licenses are more common, since manufacturers want to have a monopoly. Nonexclusive licenses are usually used where a very valuable invention exists and several manufacturers want licenses to get into the business. For example, Pilkington Brothers, the great British glass company, granted many nonexclusive licenses under its float glass patents.

3. The license, if granted, can be for the life of the patent, or just for a limited term, say five years, with an option to renew for succeeding five-year terms.

4. The license can require the payment of an advance that may be recoverable against royalties, or may it be in addition to royalties. You, of course, want to get as much money at the beginning as possible under the old "bird-in-the-hand" theory.

5. The license can require the payment of minimum annual royalty payments during each year of its existence. This is usually done when an exclusive license is granted.

6. The license rights can be transferred ("assigned") by your licensee to another manufacturer, or any such assignment can be prohibited. From your point of view, it's a good idea to try to get a provision included in the agreement prohibiting assignment without your approval.

There are hundreds of other, less important, considerations in licensing, which I won't discuss here. Licensing, as you may have gathered by now, is a difficult, complex subject, and one that requires knowledge as well as negotiation skill. Unfortunately, most invention licensing agreements tend to be tailor-made by large corporations to protect their interests. To date, no good self-help law book deals with the ins and outs of doing this. However, I refer to several standard patent law treatises in Appendix 2, Resources: Government Publications, Patent Websites, and Books of Use and Interest.

It's important to realize that even though you can make a great invention, prepare a patent application on it, and sell it to a manufacturer, you may not be able to represent yourself adequately in negotiating a license agreement unless you're familiar with licensing and adept at business. It's therefore often wise to hire a patent lawyer to review any contract that is offered to you. You'll find this will probably cost several hundred dollars or more, but the money will be well spent, especially if you have a potentially good deal in the offing.

In fact, most reputable companies would prefer that you be represented by an attorney when you negotiate a license agreement and often give you money to pay an attorney. The reason for this is that an agreement between an unrepresented inventor and a much larger company is likely to be interpreted against the company by the courts. If the inventor is represented by an experienced lawyer, the courts will tend to treat the parties equally if a dispute later arises.

H. Universal License Agreement

If you do feel confident enough to represent yourself, and you're the type of person who can go through a long license agreement with nit-picking skill and then competently negotiate with corporate pros, more power to you. Start your quest by referring to the Universal License Agreement in Appendix 7 (Form 16-4). This agreement can be used to exclusively or nonexclusively license your invention as well as to license know-how. It can also be used to grant a potential licensee an option to evaluate your invention for a given period in return for a payment. As I've said, most companies will either prefer their own license agreement or make one up from scratch, but you can use the Universal License Agreement for purposes of comparison.

Do you find the agreement long and complex? So do I. To deal with it easily, it's best to consider each of its parts separately. The sample shown (Fig. 16C) is for the first page of an exclusive license with an option grant and a know-how license.

Part 1: The licensor is the party, usually the inventor, who does the licensing, while the licensee is the party who is licensed—that is, given permission to use the invention, patent, know-how, etc.

The Patent Royalty rate is the percentage rate the licensee pays for use of the patent. I made this rate low (2%) purposely, since a know-how license has been granted at a rate of 3% for an overall (total) royalty of 5%. It's usually to an inventor's advantage to license know-how, as well as patent rights, and to make the know-how rate as high a proportion of the total rate as possible. This is because patents can be held invalid and can only be licensed for a limited term (the duration of the patent application plus the approximately 18-year term of the patent), usually a total of about 19 years; whereas a know-how license can extend indefinitely.

A licensing fee (advance) is customarily paid to the licensor upon signing the agreement as a reward for past work. In the agreement, the licensing fee is computed as an estimate of the first year's sales by multiplying (a) the Patent Royalty Rate by (b) the Estimated First Year's Sales in Units by (c) the Estimated Unit Price in dollars. Again, it's usually in the inventor's interest to get as large a signing bonus as possible, and not to have this money be set off against later royalty payments.

The "Exclusive" box is checked, indicating that only the licensee will be entitled to make, use, or sell the invention. If the "Nonexclusive" box is checked, the licensor will be able to license others, and the licensee and the licensor will be able to make, use, and sell the invention. The title, serial number, and filing date of the patent application are identified next.

The "Minimum Number of Units to Be Sold to Compute Minimum Annual Royalty" (whether or not they are actually sold) is provided to ensure that the licensor receives an adequate income from the licensee inasmuch as he can't, under an exclusive license, license others to derive more income. This minimum annual royalty has been computed on the basis of a minimum annual number of units to be sold (rather than a fixed dollar amount) to give the licensor the benefit of inflation in unit price. While the manufacturer can cut the price of the licensed product and thereby reduce its royalty payments to you, it's generally not in its interest to do this, since it will be reducing its profits as well. However, if you want protection against this possibility, you can substitute a fixed dollar amount for the minimum annual royalty.

For the privilege of obtaining an option to exclusively evaluate the invention for the Option Term, an Option Premium (a one-time cash payment) has been paid to the licensor.

The Know-How Royalty Rate is stated and is added to the Patent Royalty Rate to get the total, or Running Royalty Rate.

Part 2: The effective date of the agreement is the date when the last signature is made.

Part 3: Here the Recitals provide the reasons or premises for the agreement. The recitals simply state that the licensor has an invention, a patent application, and possibly know-how, and the licensee desires to evaluate licensor's invention (if an option has been granted) and to make, use, and sell the licensed invention.

Part 4: This covers the parties' rights if an option has been granted. In this case, the regular license grant doesn't take effect yet, but the licensee has the exclusive right to investigate the invention for the option term indicated in Part 1. If the investigation is favorable, the licensee will exercise its option and the patent license grant of Part 5 will take effect. If not, the option will not be exercised and all rights will revert to the licensor and the licensor will get the results of the licensee's investigation of the invention.

Part 5: This contains the actual license grant. This comes into play immediately if the invention is licensed or if an

Universal License Agreement

1. Parties and Summary of Terms:

Parties: This agreement is between:

Licensor: _Henry Beresofsky_ ,

of _Chernegov, Ukraine_ .

Licensee: _Chernobyl Reactor Works, Inc._ ,

of _Russian Hill, CA_ .

Summary: Type of License: ☒ Exclusive ☐ Nonexclusive

Invention Title: _Perpetual Energy Machine_ .

Patent Application Ser. Nr.: _07/123,456_ , Filing Date: _200X Aug 9_

If Exclusive License, minimum number of units to be sold to compute Minimum Annual Royalty (MAR): _____

MARs start first quarter of _200X_ .

☒ Option Granted: Premium $_5,000_ For term of: (months) _18_

Patent Royalty Rate _2.00_ % ☒ Know-How Licensed: Know-How Royalty Rate: _3.00_ %

Total Royalty Rate (Patent Royalty Rate plus Know-How Royalty, if applicable): _5.00_ %.

Estimated 1st year's sales (units): _200_ x Estimated Unit Price $_1,000.00_

x Total Royalty Rate _5.00_ % = Licensing Fee $_10,000.00_

2. Effective Date: This agreement shall be effective as of the latter of the signature dates below written and shall be referred to as the Agreement of such date.

3. Recitals:

A. **LICENSOR** has developed an invention having the above title and warrants that LICENSOR has filed a patent application on such invention in the U.S. Patent and Trademark Office, which patent application is identified by the above title, Serial Number, and Filing Date. LICENSOR warrants that licensohas full and exclusive right to grant this license on this invention and LICENSOR'S patent application. If the "Know-How Licensed" box above is checked, LICENSOR has also developed know-how in connection with said invention and warrants that LICENSOR owns and has the right to license said know-how.

B. **LICENSEE** desires, if the "Option Granted" box above is checked, to exclusively investigate LICENSOR'S above invention for the term indicated. If said "Option Granted" box is not checked, or if said box is checked and LICENSEE investigates LICENSOR'S invention for the term indicated and such investigation is favorable, LICENSEE desires to make, use, and sell the products embodying such invention and covered by the claims of LICENSOR'S patent application and any patent(s) issuing thereon (hereinafter "Licensed Product").

4. If Option Granted: If the "Option Granted" box above is checked, then (A) the patent license grant of Part 5 below shall not take effect except as defined in this part, and (B) LICENSOR hereby grants LICENSEE, for the option premium stated above, an exclusive option to investigate LICENSOR'S invention for the term indicated above, such term to commence from the date of this Agreement. LICENSOR will furnish LICENSEE with all information and know-how (if any) concerning LICENSOR'S invention in LICENSOR'S possession. LICENSEE will investigate LICENSOR'S invention for operability, costing, marketing, etc. LICENSEE shall report the results of its investigation to LICENSOR at any time before the end of the option term. If LICENSEE'S determination is favorable, it may thereupon exercise this option and the patent license grant of Part 5 below shall become effective. If LICENSEE'S determination is unfavorable, then said option shall not be

Fig. 16C—Completed First Page of Universal License Agreement (Form 16-4 in Appendix 7)

option is granted or if the option is granted and exercised. Remember, if an option is granted, the actual license isn't granted until the option is exercised. The license granted (exclusive or nonexclusive) gives the licensee the right to make, use, and sell the Licensed Product in the U.S., and it includes any derivative applications and patents (see Chapter 14). If the "know-how" box of Part 1 has been checked, then know-how is also licensed.

Part 6: Know-how is covered in this part. If know-how is licensed, then the licensor is obligated to communicate all of its know-how to the licensee within one month, plus provide up to 80 hours of consultation to the licensee, with travel and other expenses paid by licensee. The licensor disclaims any guarantee that the know-how is workable. The know-how royalty is to be paid for three years and thereafter for so long as the licensee enjoys a U.S. competitive market share of at least 15%. This means that the licensor can enjoy know-how royalty payments indefinitely, provided its know-how was valuable enough to give the licensee a market share of over 15% after three years have passed.

Part 7: This concerns royalties and is the heart of the agreement.

Subpart A: If a Licensing Fee is paid; it's an advance against future royalties. If the estimated Licensing Fee has been computed inaccurately (Part 1) then an adjustment is made when royalties are paid. (Note: It is permissible to draft an agreement whereby the licensing fee is a one-time payment and not an advance against royalties.)

Subpart B: The running royalty is covered and is paid quarterly, within one month after the end of each quarter, together with a report of the sales made in the quarter.

Subpart C: The minimum annual royalty (MAR) is to be paid if an exclusive license has been granted. The MAR payment is computed using the royalty rate times the minimum number of units of Part 1. Minimum annual royalties start as also stated in Part 1. If the minimum number of units is not sold in any year, the licensee must pay the appropriate makeup difference to the licensor with its payment for the fourth quarter.

Subpart D: If the minimum is not paid by licensee, either due to lack of sufficient sales or licensee's choice, then the license grant will be converted to a nonexclusive one, and the licensor can immediately license others.

Subpart E: If the license is or becomes nonexclusive, then the licensor may not grant more favorable terms to any other licensee.

Subpart F: Patent royalties are not due after the patent expires, or if it is declared invalid, or if no patent is granted.

Subpart G: Late payments earn interest at 10%.

Subpart H: The "Net Factory Sales Price," on which royalties are based, is the factory selling price, less shipping, insurance, taxes, etc., if billed separately. If the units are imported, then the importer's gross selling price is the basis for royalties. The royalty paid on returns is deductible against future royalties.

Part 8: This requires the licensee to keep full records for at least two years after each payment, so that the licensor can verify the royalty payments.

Part 9: Here the licensee's sublicensees are bound by all of the terms of the agreement and the licensee must notify the licensor if it grants sublicenses. A licensee will usually grant a sublicense when it has the licensed product made for it by a contracting company.

Part 10: This simply states the parties' responsibilities for patent prosecution.

Subpart A: Requires the licensor to pay for prosecution of the U.S. patent application, together with the patent maintenance fees that are payable after the patent issues. If the licensor intends to abandon the patent application, it must notify the licensee at least two months in advance to give it the opportunity to take over.

Subpart B: The licensor may file for patent coverage abroad, but if it doesn't do so, then the licensee may do so. If licensor wants to license any foreign licensees, it has to give the licensee the opportunity of first refusal.

Subpart C: If the licensee takes over the U.S. patent prosecution, and is successful, then it can reduce its royalties by 25%, and can deduct its patent prosecution expenses. If the licensee elects to file abroad, then the royalty rate on foreign sales is 50% of the U.S. rate, less foreign prosecution expenses.

Part 11: This requires the licensee to mark products sold with the legend "patent pending" while the patent application is pending and with the patent number (see Chapter 15) after the patent issues.

Part 12: This states that if the patent is infringed, the licensor can sue to enforce its patent rights. If it doesn't choose to do so, the licensee may do so. If the licensee sues, it can keep 75% of this recovery, less costs of the suit.

Part 13-A: This clause states that licensor doesn't guarantee that its patent is valid or that it has any particular scope (breadth).

Part 13-B: This clause states, in effect, that if someone is injured by the patented product, the licensor is not liable.

Part 14: This clause states that the term or maximum duration of the agreement shall be until the last patent of licensor expires, unless know-how is licensed, in which case Part 6 governs the term.

Part 15: This clause covers the situations when the parties may terminate the agreement before the term expires. Under Subparts A and B, the licensor may terminate the agreement if the licensee defaults in making royalty payments, or if it ever declares bankruptcy. Subpart C, the antishelving clause, is very important. This protects the licensor in case the licensee stops production for 1.5 years, or doesn't start production within 1.5 years from the date the license agreement is signed. In these cases, the licensor can terminate the agreement.

Clauses like this one (and others) are designed to put teeth into the agreement to deter the licensee from defaulting: it is not enough to make a fair agreement; all agreements should also be structured to ensure the other party's performance by giving an incentive for performance, or a penalty for nonperformance.

Part 16: This clause states how and where notices under the agreement are to be sent.

Part 17: This clause provides that if the parties have any dispute, they shall submit the matter to mediation. If mediation can't resolve the dispute, the parties must submit the dispute to binding and final arbitration. In no case will the dispute go to a court for resolution, since litigation is extremely expensive and thus works to the detriment of the independent inventor.

Part 18: This clause allows the licensor to assign (legally transfer) its rights to anyone without permission, but the licensee needs advance permission of licensor to assign the licensee's rights unless it makes an assignment to its successor in business.

Part 19: This clause specifies that the laws of licensor's state shall govern interpretation of the agreement. Normally, state law on the interpretation of contracts doesn't vary much, but since a licensor is usually at an economic disadvantage, I've given it the benefit here. Also, it specifies that any lawsuit on the agreement shall be brought in licensor's county.

Part 20: This states that neither party shall take any action that hampers the rights of the other and that both parties shall engage in good faith and fair dealing. This clause is supposed to be read into any agreement, but I've expressly stated it in order to increase cooperation and reduce disputes.

Part 21: This states that in case of any mistake in the agreement, it shall be rectified to conform to the parties' intentions. The clause is designed to save a misdrafted agreement that otherwise might be thrown out.

Part 22: This makes it clear the agreement supersedes prior or concurrent oral, or prior written, understandings.

Part 23: This one states that the parties have carefully read the agreement and have consulted, or have been given an opportunity to consult, counsel and that each has received a signed original. This makes a challenge to the agreement more difficult.

All that remains is to sign and date the agreement. Each party should get an original, ink-signed copy.

Again, I remind you that while the Universal License Agreement incorporates most of the customary terms and covers many common licensing situations, it probably won't be appropriate for your situation without some modification. Obviously, if your arrangement won't fit within the terms of this agreement, or if you don't like any of the "fixed" terms, such as the 80 hours of consultation (Clause 6), the 15% market share (Clause 6), compulsory arbitration (Clause 17), etc., you should propose changes, or hire an expert to help you.

I. How Much Should You Get for Your Invention?

Many inventors seem to believe that patents are almost always licensed at a royalty rate of 5%. The 5% royalty generally means that you get 5% of the money received by the factory for its sales of the item embodying your invention. This is sometimes termed 5% of the "ex-factory" price. This assumption is simply not true. While 5% is often used as a starting point in many license negotiations, very few licenses are granted at this rate. I've seen them run from 0.1% to 15% of the factory price of licensed hardware items (as high as 30% of the retail price for software).

As you've guessed, many factors affect the royalty rate. Obviously, the more desirable your invention is to the licensee, the better royalty you'll get, subject to industry norms. Here's a list of some factors that militate in favor of increasing the royalty rate. Use as many of these as possible in your negotiations:

1. sales volume
2. selling price
3. low competition
4. profit margin
5. ingeniousness and novelty of product
6. amount of development work inventor has done
7. degree to which invention pervades product
8. size of licensed territory
9. amount of services or materials and parts or tooling inventor furnishes
10. absence of competition between licensee and licensor
11. degree of respect in field for patents
12. difficulty of licensee's avoiding patent—that is the strength of the patent
13. difficulty of making agreement
14. cost savings to licensee
15. reputation of inventor, if any
16. anticipated life of product

17. low start-up costs to produce invention

18. number of patents or patent applications you have

19. willingness of consumers to pay a premium price for the product

20. whether the product can be sold at lower cost than its competition, and

21. a higher up-front payment will reduce the rate and vice versa.

Of course, your bargaining skill will transcend all of these considerations. As business negotiating seminar leader C.L. Karrass says: "In business, you don't get what you deserve—you get what you negotiate." An excellent guide to negotiating is "Take It or Leave It—The Only Guide to Negotiating You'll Ever Need," *Inc. Magazine*, August, 2003.

Also the custom of the industry will dominate—for example, toys usually get an exclusive royalty rate of 2.5% to 4%, medical products 6% to 7%, and software inventions up to 10% and sometimes more. An exclusive license will entitle you to about 50% more than a nonexclusive license.

If your licensee doesn't want to pay the rate you ask, a good technique is to accept the lower rate they're willing to pay. However, add a proviso stating that the rate will be increased to the rate you want if "x" number of units are sold.

Instead of a negotiated percentage, some experts advocate getting a royalty equivalent to "one-third of the manufacturer's profit." This means that the company will take its selling price for your invention, say $10, subtract its cost of manufacture, including overhead, say $7, and give you one-third of the difference—that is, $1 = $1/3$ of its $3.00 profit. This type of royalty is often enticing to a manufacturer since the company only contemplates parting with a portion of its profit, not paying a fixed sum per item, whether the particular product turns out to be profitable or not. If your licensee is willing to accept this type of royalty, you can substitute this language in the Universal Agreement. But, if you do so, be sure you include an auditing right (such as Clause 8) to ensure that you can verify its cost of manufacture.

Lump Sum Payment

If you're offered a single lump-sum payment for all your rights (this is rare), should you take it, and if so, how much should you get? To answer the first question, only you can decide if a relatively large bird in the hand is worth more than a potential (but by no means assured) stream of smaller, but aggregately heavier, birds in the bush over the years. To grapple with the second question, estimate the potential sales of your invention for the life of your patent application (one to three years), plus the term of the patent (approximately 18 years), then apply your royalty to this figure. Be willing to take half of this as a single payment lump sum for a fully paid-up license.

For example, suppose you expect your widget to be sold for the next 20 years (two years during patent pendency, and 18 years during life of patent), for an average factory price of 50 cents and an average yearly quantity of 150,000 units, and that a patent royalty of 5% is fair. Applying the formula, the substitute lump-sum payment for your royalty would be 0.5 x 19 x 150,000 x $0.05, or $35,625. If you are offered much less than this, it could very well be unwise to sell.

Don't make Mary Jacobs's mistake. She invented the bra (out of two hankies and a ribbon) and was able to sell her patent for $15,000 in 1914. Although this was a princely sum then, she practically gave it away since

(as you know) her invention soon took hold and her patent eventually was worth $15 *million*!

The disadvantage with the alternative lump-sum calculation is that it's very hard to estimate anything about what will happen in the next 20 years. Will sales go up or down? Will the product become obsolete or even more popular? Will competition affect its price, etc.? These are just some of the imponderables and unknowables, so, as stated, be extremely careful before selling your rights for a single lump-sum payment.

⚠️ If you do have an opportunity to sell your invention, you should use the assignment form (Form 16-3A), changing "For value received" at the beginning of the form to "In exchange for $_____." For obvious reasons, make sure you actually receive the money by certified check or money order before you sign. Do not, under any circumstances, assign your patent in return for a series of payments. If your assignee defaults in the payments, you'll be left without your patent or your money, but with a big legal headache—getting your patent back. If someone wants to buy your patent for a series of payments, see a lawyer or legal forms book and make a suitable license with an agreement to assign only after all payments have been made.

J. Summary

All actual inventors must be named in the patent application, provided each contributed something to at least one claim. Financiers, advisors, model makers, or others that did not contribute any inventive concepts should not be named as inventors. If the claims of a patent application are changed, inventorship should be reviewed and changed if necessary. Use Form 16-1 in Appendix 7 to preserve each inventor's contribution.

Under patent law statute, any joint owner of a patent can practice the invention without paying any other inventor. To guarantee that all inventors receive compensation if the invention is commercialized, use the Joint Owners' Agreement—Form 16-2.

An employed inventor's rights are usually governed by an Employment Agreement, which mainly requires the employee to assign to the employer all inventions that are made in the course of the employer's business, use the employer's, time, facilities, or materials, or are within the scope of the employee's duties. Employees who are hired to invent have a common law obligation to assign inventions made in the scope of their duties. Other inventions are the property of the employee, but the employment agreement may require the employee to notify the employer about them.

A patent application and a patent are intangible personal property and part or full ownership must be transferred by an assignment, which should be recorded in the PTO to prevent a subsequent, fraudulent assignment.

To collect royalties for use of an invention, an inventor (licensor) should make a licensing agreement with the manufacturer (licensee). The main considerations are the amount of any up-front payment, whether the license is exclusive or nonexclusive, and the royalty rate. It's advantageous to license know-how as well as patent rights. The Universal License Agreement (Form 16-4) covers most situations, but the terms must be negotiated. Factors affecting the royalty rate are the strength of the patent, the amount of design work already done, the anticipated sales volume, the profit margin, the field of the invention, etc. Never assign a patent or application for a series of payments; always get full payment at the time of assignment. ∎

Appendix 1

Abbreviations Used in *Patent It Yourself*

Throughout *Patent It Yourself* (PIY) I've used many abbreviations to save space and to spare you the tedium of repeatedly reading long phrases like "Manual of Patent Examining Procedure." I've tried to define each abbreviation the first time I've used it and again if I've used it at a location remote from the first usage. However, in case I've failed to define any abbreviation adequately, here's a list of (hopefully) all the abbreviations I've used in PIY:

A&ARTP	Attorneys and Agents Registered to Practice		EA	Employment Agreement
AF	After Final		EEC	European Economic Community
AIPO	African Intellectual Property Organization		EM	Express Mail
BA	Basic Application		EPC	European Treaty Convention
BAPI	Board of Appeals & Interferences		EPO	European Patent Office
BBS	Bulletin Board System		FDA	Food and Drug Administration
BNA	Bureau of National Affairs		FWC	File-Wrapper-Continuing
BRS	Bibliographic Research Services		GATT	General Agreement on Tariffs and Trade
CAD	Computer-Aided Drafting		GPO	Government Printing Office
CAFC	Court of Appeals for the Federal Circuit		IC	Inventors' Commandment
CASSIS	Classification And Search Support Information System		IDS	Information Disclosure Statement
			ITC	International Trade Commission
CCPF	Credit Card Payment Form		JOA	Joint Owners' Agreement
CFR	Code of Federal Regulations		JPTOS	*Journal of the Patent and Trademark Office Society*
CIP	Continuation-in-Part			
CM	Common Misconception; Certificate of Mailing		KISS	Keep It Simple, Stupid
CTRP	Constructive Reduction to Practice		MAR	Minimum Annual Royalty
D	Design Patent		MDC	Multiple Dependent Claim
DDP	Disclosure Document Program		MF	Maintenance Fee
DOE	Department of Energy; Doctrine of Equivalents		MPEP	*Manual of Patent Examining Procedure*
DP	Double Patenting		N/A	Notice of Allowance
DPED	Domestic Priority Establishing Document		N&UR	New and Unexpected Results

NCC	Non-Convention Country		RCE	Request for Continued Examination
NIH	Not Invented Here		RPA	Regular Patent Application
N(N)C	Normally (Non-) Conductive		RTP	Reduced to Practice
NPR	Nonpublication Request		S	Solution
OA	Office Action		SBA	Small Business Administration
OG	*Official Gazette*		SD	Supporting Declaration
OIPE	Office of Initial Patent Examination		SE	Small Entity
P	Problem		SED	Small-Entity Declaration
PA	Prior Art		SIR	Statutory Invention Registration
PAD	Patent Application Declaration		SPO	Shadow Patent Office
PCT	Patent Cooperation Treaty		SSM	Statutory Subject Matter
PDF	Portable Document Format		TD	Terminal Disclaimer
PDL	Patent Depository Library		TM	Trademark
PGL	Paranoia, Greed, Laziness		TN	Trade Name
PPA	Provisional Patent Application		TS	Trade Secret
Pre-Ex	Preliminary to Examination		UC	Unfair Competition
PTDL	Patent and Trademark Depository Libraries		UCC	Uniform Commercial Code
PTMS	Petition To Make Special		USC	United States Code
PTO	Patent and Trademark Office (U.S.)		VA	Vanadium Alloy
PubPA	Published Patent Application			

■

Appendix 2

Resources: Government Publications, Patent Websites, and Books of Use and Interest

It has been said that knowing where to look is half the battle of knowing the law. With this in mind, this section is provided to help you avoid having to hire a patent lawyer in case you encounter any situations or problems which this book does not cover. I've also provided a number of resources and publications I feel will be of interest to inventors and other creative people.

A. Government Publications

In addition to being available in paper-bound publications, most of the publications below are now available on the Internet at the PTO website (www.uspto.gov) and on CD-ROMs, which are updated quarterly and which may be read on the computer in any Patent and Trademark Depository Library. (See list of libraries in Chapter 6.)

Annual Index of Patents. Issued yearly in two volumes: *Patentees* and *Titles of Inventions.* U.S. Government Printing Office (GPO), Washington, DC 20402. Comes out long after the end of year to which it pertains—for instance, in September. Available on line at www.uspto.gov.

Attorneys and Agents Registered to Practice Before the U.S. Patent and Trademark Office. Annual. GPO. Contains alphabetical and geographical listings of all attorneys and agents.

Index to Classification. Loose-leaf. Contains all subclasses and cross-references arranged alphabetically. Available online at www.uspto.gov.

Manual of Classification. GPO. Loose-leaf. Contains 300 search classes for patents arranged numerically, together with subclasses in each class. Available online at www .uspto.gov.

Manual of Patent Examining Procedure (MPEP). Revisions issued several times per year. GPO. Called "the patent examiner's bible," the MPEP provides answers to most questions about patent prosecution. Available online at www.uspto.gov.

Patent Laws (Title 35 of U.S. Code). The federal statute governing patents (available at the PTO's website under MPEP).

Rules of Practice in Patent Cases (Title 37, Code of Federal Regulations). GPO. Revised annually. The PTO's Rules of Practice. Paper version is a must for all who prosecute their own patent applications. Paper version is almost always incomplete due to frequent rule changes. Look in

Official Gazette (especially the first volume each year) for later rules. Available online at www.uspto.gov.

B. Patent Websites

Below are three groups of patent links. The first group provides sources of information for inventors, the second group includes resources on patent law and intellectual property law, and the third provides patent searching databases. As with all Internet links, we cannot guarantee the continued accuracy of any of these sites.

1. Inventor Resources

DaVinci Design Resource (www.uspatentinfo.com). Provides information and resources that may be helpful to the inventor in building a prototype of an invention and provides basic information about patents, copyrights, trademarks, and trade secrets.

Intellectual Property Owners (IPO) (www.ipo.org). An association that serves owners of patents, trademarks, copyrights, and trade secrets. It is the sponsor of the National Inventor of the Year Award. Write to them at Intellectual Property Owners, 1255 23rd St. NW, Suite 850, Washington, DC 20037. Phone: 202-466-2396; Fax: 202-466-2893; or email: info@ipo.org.

Invention Convention (www.inventionconvention.com). The National Congress of Inventor Organizations (NCIO) and its executive director, Stephen Paul Gnass, maintain this invention website that includes links, trade show information, and advice for inventors. National Congress of Inventor Organizations, 727 North 600 West, Logan, UT, 84321. Phone 801-753-0888.

InventNet Forum (www.inventnet.com). Provides an online forum and mailing list if you wish to contact other inventors.

Inventor's Bookstore (www.inventorhelp.com). Offers condensed reports and other guidance for inventors.

Inventor's Digest Online (www.inventorsdigest.com). Publishes online information and a print publication for independent inventors ($27/year for six issues). Includes articles on new inventions, licensing, and marketing, and advertisements from reputable inventor promotion companies.

Minnesota Inventors Congress (www.invent1.org). One of the oldest and most respected inventor organizations.

National Technology Transfer Center (NTTC) (www.nttc.edu) at Wheeling Jesuit University. Helps entrepreneurs and companies looking to access federally funded research and development activity at U.S. universities: 316 Washington Avenue, Wheeling, WV 26003, 800-678-6882, Fax: 304-243-4388, technology@nttc.edu.

Nolo (www.nolo.com). Patent, copyright, trade secret, and trademark resources and products and updates of David Pressman's *Patent It Yourself.*

Patent Café (www.patentcafe.com). An inventor resource maintained by inventor and entrepreneur Andy Gibbs. It lists inventor organizations and related links and provides information on starting an inventor organization.

Patent Law Links (www.patentlawlinks.com). Provides links to everything "patent" on the Internet.

PTO Independent Inventor Resources (www.uspto.gov/web/offices/com/iip/indextxt.htm). In 1999, the PTO established a new office aimed at providing services and support to independent inventors. The PTO expects to eventually offer seminars and expanded educational opportunities for inventors. For more information, call: 800-PTO-9199 (800-786-9199) or 703-308-HELP.

Ronald J. Riley's Inventor Resources (www.inventored.org). Comprehensive links and advice for inventors.

United Inventors Association (UIA) (www.uiausa.org). A national inventors' organization. For more information, write to P.O. Box 23447, Rochester, NY 14692-3347, 716-359-9310; Fax: 716-359-1132, email: UIAUSA@aol.com.

2. Patent Law and Intellectual Property Law Websites

Copyright Office (www.loc.gov/copyright). The Copyright Office has numerous circulars, kits, and other publications that can help you, including one on searching copyright records. These publications and application forms can be obtained by writing to the Copyright Office at Publication Section, LM-455, Copyright Office, Library of Congress, Washington, DC 20559. Most Copyright Office publications can be downloaded directly from the Copyright Office website. Frequently requested Copyright Office circulars and announcements are also available via the Copyright Office's fax-on-demand telephone line at 202-707-9100.

European Patent Office (EPO) (www.european-patent-office.org/online). Agency that implements the European Patent Convention—a simplified method of acquiring a patent among member nations—by granting "regional" European patents that are automatically valid in each European Patent Convention member country.

Fedlaw (http://fedlaw.gsa.gov). Source of federal law links with a thorough collection of intellectual property statutes, case law, and readings.

Government Printing Office (www.access.gpo.gov/#info). Searchable source for U.S. Code of Federal Regulations, Congressional Record, and other Government Printing Office products and information.

Intellectual Property Mall (www.ipmall.fplc.edu). IP links and information.

Internet Patent News Service (www.bustpatents.com). Source for patent news, information about searching, and patent documents, news about patents, and information about bad patents, software, and business methods.

Legal Information Institute (http://lii.law.cornell.edu). Intellectual property links and downloadable copies of statutes and cases.

Patent & Trademark Office (PTO) (www.uspto.gov). Offers a number of informational pamphlets, including an introduction to patents ("General Information About Patents") and an alphabetical and geographical listing of patent attorneys and agents registered to practice before the PTO ("Directory of Registered Patent Attorneys and Agents Arranged by States and Countries"). The PTO also has an online searchable database of patent abstracts (short summaries of patents). For purposes of patent searching, this database is an excellent and inexpensive first step in the searching procedure. Most patent forms can be downloaded from the PTO website, as can many important publications including the *Manual of Patent Examining Procedures, Examination Guidelines for Computer-Related Inventions*, and *Disclosure Document Program.* For a catalogue listing all the products and services available from the PTO online and off, call 800-PTO-9199 and ask for the "U.S. Patent and Trademark Office Products and Services Catalog."

PCT Applicant's Guide (www.wipo.int). PCT information and software for facilitating completion of the PCT forms is available through the PCT's website.

Trademarks (www.uspto.gov). Trademarks are examined and registered by a division of the PTO. An introductory pamphlet about trademarks ("General Information About Trademarks") and information about the operations of the Patent and Trademark Office are available from the

Superintendent of Documents, Government Printing Office, Washington, DC 20402, or from the PTO's website at www.uspto.gov. This site includes the relevant applications and trademark office forms. You can write to the Commissioner for Trademarks, 2900 Crystal Drive, Arlington, VA 22202-3515.

3. Patent Searching Online

Here are several organizations that offer computer searching of patent records and a description of their services. Several of the "for fee" databases also provide foreign patent information.

U.S. Patent & Trademark Office (www.uspto.gov/patft/index.html). Free online full-text searchable database of patents and drawings that covers the period from January 1976 to the most recent weekly issue date (usually each Tuesday). In order to view the drawings, your computer must be able to view TIFF files. The PTO's site is linked to a source that provides a free downloadable TIFF reader program. For faster searching there is also a Bibliographic Database that contains only the text of each patent without drawings.

Delphion (www.delphion.com). Fee-based online searchable database with full text searching capability for patents issued from 1974 to the present.

Foreign Patent Searching (http://patent.search-in.net). Information on searching foreign patents.

IP Search Engine (www.ipsearchengine.com). Uses "concept" searching that is more complete than Boolean logic.

LexPat (www.lexis-nexis.com). Commercial database of U.S. patents searchable from 1971 to the present. In addition, the LEXPAT library offers extensive prior-art searching capability of technical journals and magazines.

MicroPatent (www.micropatent.com). Commercial database of U.S. patents searchable from 1836 to the present. Users must first set up an account. Also offers delivery of patent copies dating back to 1790 by U.S. mail, fax, and email.

PatBase (www.patbase.com). A new database that can search back to the 1800s through many countries' patents.

PatMax (www.patentmax.com). Another commercial patent database.

QPAT (www.qpat.com) and Questel/Orbit (www.questel.orbit.com). Both of these commercial services access the QPAT database, which includes U.S. patents searchable

from 1974 to the present and full-text European A (1987-present) and B (1991-present) patents.

Nolo's Legal Encyclopedia

Nolo's website (www.nolo.com) features an extensive Legal Encyclopedia that includes a section on intellectual property. You'll find answers to frequently asked questions about patents, copyrights, trademarks, and other related topics; as well as sample chapters of Nolo books and a wide range of articles. Simply click on "Legal Encyclopedia" and then on "Patents, Copyright & Trademark."

Nolo Books on Intellectual Property

Nolo, the publisher of this book, also publishes a number of other titles on intellectual property, including:

- *Copyright Your Software,* by Stephen Fishman
- *How to Make Patent Drawings Yourself,* by Jack Lo and David Pressman
- *Inventor's Guide to Law, Business & Taxes,* by Stephen Fishman
- *License Your Invention,* by Richard Stim
- *Nolo's Patents for Beginners,* by David Pressman and Richard Stim
- *Nondisclosure Agreements: Protect Your Trade Secrets & More,* by Richard Stim and Stephen Fishman
- *Patent Pending in 24 Hours,* by Richard Stim and David Pressman
- *Patent Searching Made Easy,* by David Hitchcock
- *Patent, Copyright & Trademark: An Intellectual Property Desk Reference,* by Richard Stim
- *Web and Software Development: A Legal Guide,* by Stephen Fishman
- *The Copyright Handbook,* by Stephen Fishman.
- *The Inventor's Notebook,* by Fred Grissom and David Pressman
- *The Public Domain: How to Find & Use Copyright-Free Writings, Music, Art & More,* by Stephen Fishman
- *Trademark: Legal Care for Your Business & Product Name,* by Stephen Elias.

C. Books of Use and Interest

Below are lists of books and magazines that may be of special interest to inventors, including general interest books, business books, and books relating to self-improvement. Many of these books may out of print or available only in libraries. You can often acquire out-of-print books from online booksellers, such as Amazon.com, Powells.com, and Bookfinder.com.

I provide comment where the title of the book or source isn't self-explanatory. Most books that can't be found in a general or business library may be found in a law library. (Most county courthouses and law schools have law libraries.) Prices aren't indicated since they change frequently. This list isn't exclusive by any means. If you browse in your bookstore or a patent depository or law library, you'll find many other valuable books.

1. Patent Books, Magazines, and a Museum Relating to Patents, Inventions, and Trademarks

American Heritage of Invention and Technology, P.O. Box 5338, Harlan, IA 51593-2838. A beautiful, artistic, and interesting magazine.

The Catalyst, by Harness, Charles R., Esq. Pocket Books, New York. Science fiction story involving a patent attorney, an invention, and an interference.

Complete Guide to Making Money With Your Ideas and Inventions, by Paige, R.E. Barnes & Noble, New York, NY. Excellent guide to invention marketing.

CompuMark Directory of U.S. Trademarks. Thomson & Thomson, Quincy, MA. Available in search libraries.

Edison, The Man Who Made the Future, by Clark, R.W. Putnam, New York.

The Existential Pleasures of Engineering, by Florman, S.C. St. Martins, 1976. A brilliant, eloquent panegyric of technology; a crushing blow to Reich, Mumford, Rozak, et al.

Eureka! The Invention and Innovation Newsletter, 156 Columbia Street West, Waterloo, Ontario N2L 3L3. A quarterly inventor publication primarily for Canadian inventors.

The Firefly Visual Dictionary, by Corbel and Archambault, Firefly Books 2002

How to Become an Inventor, by Daniels, J.R. (e-book, www.booklocker.com.)

Idea Marketplace, P.O. Box 131758, Staten Island, NY 10313, Phone: 800-IDEA-MRK ($14.95/year/6 issues). A semimonthly magazine covering issues of interest to inventors.

Inventing: How the Masters Did It. Moore Pub., Durham, NC.

The Inventor's Bible: How to Market and License Your Brilliant Ideas, by Docie, R.L. Sr., Ten Speed Press, Berkeley, CA.

Inventor's Digest, 30 Union Wharf, Boston, MA 02109 (for more information, see "Inventor Resources," above).

Inventure Place, 221 So. Broadway, Akron, OH 44308, Tel. 216-762-4463. A museum of inventors and inventions.

Man of High Fidelity: Edwin Howard Armstrong, by Lessing, L. Lippincott, Philadelphia, PA. Biography of the inventor of frequency modulation; he committed suicide because of the delays and difficulties of patent litigation against the large radio companies, but his widow eventually collected millions in settlements.

Marketing Your Invention, by Mosley, Jr., Thomas E. Upstart Publishing, Chicago, IL. Another excellent guide to invention marketing.

Millions From the Mind, by Tripp, A.R. Teletyano Press 2003.

The National Inventors Hall of Fame. *Biographies of Inductees*. NIHF Foundation, Room 1D01, Crystal Plaza 3, 2001 Jefferson Davis Hwy., Arlington, VA 22202. Free.

One Day at Kitty Hawk, by Walsh, J.E. Crowell, New York, NY. The story of the development and sale of rights to the airplane.

Patently Female—Stories of Women Inventors, by Vare, E.A., and Ptacek, G. Wiley. A great history of female inventors.

Trademark Register of the United States. Annual. Trademark Register, Washington Bldg., Washington, DC 20005. Lists all registered trademarks by subject matter classes.

Will It Sell? How to Determine If Your Invention Is Profitably Marketable (Before Wasting Money on a Patent), by White, James E. (www.willitsell.com.)

2. Publications Relating to Business

Apollo Handbook of Practical Public Relations, by Adams, A.B. Apollo Editions, New York, NY. How to get publicity.

Applied Sciences and Technology Index. H.W. Wilson Co., Bronx, NY 10452. Lists engineering, scientific, and industrial periodical articles by subject

Bacon's Publicity Checker—Magazines; Bacon's Publicity Checker—Newspapers. Annual. Bacon Pub. Co., Chicago, IL. Classifies all sources of publicity.

Business Plans That Win $$$: Lessons From the MIT Enterprises Forum, by Rich, S.R., & Gumpert, D. Harper & Row.

California Manufacturers Register. Annual. 1115 S. Boyle Ave., Los Angeles, CA 90023.

Conover Mast Purchasing Directory. Conover Mast, Denver, CO 80206. Annual. Three volumes. Manufacturers listed alphabetically and by products. Also lists trademarks.

Dun & Bradstreet Reference Book. Six issues per year. Lists three million businesses in the United States and Canada. D&B also publishes specialized reference books and directories, such as *Apparel Trades Book* and *Metalworking Marketing Directory.*

The Entrepreneur's Manual. Brown, D. Ballantine.

Gale Directory of Publications and Broadcast Media. Annual. Ayer Press, Philadelphia, PA 19106. Lists United States newspapers and magazines geographically.

Getting to Yes; Negotiating Agreements Without Giving In, by Fisher, R., & Ury, W. Penguin.

Guide to American Directories. B. Klein Pubs., New York, NY. Lists directories by industry, profession, and function.

How to License Your Million Dollar Idea, by Reese, H. (Wiley 2002).

How to Market a Product for Under $500! by Dobkin, J. Danielle Adams Pub., Box 100, Merion Station, PA 19066.

How to Write a Business Plan, by McKeever, M., Nolo.

Innovation and Entrepreneurship, by Drucker, P. Harper & Row. How any organization can become entrepreneurial.

International Yellow Pages. R.H. Donnelley Corp., New York, NY 10017. Similar to local Yellow Pages, but provides foreign business listings.

Licensing Royalty Rates, by Batters, G. J., and Grimes, C. W. (Aspen 2004). Details royalty rates for 1,500 products and services and ten major categories.

MacRae's Blue Book. MacRae's Blue Book Co., Hinsdale, IL 60521. Sources of industrial equipment, products, and materials. Also lists trademarks.

Marketing Without Advertising, by Phillips, M., & Rasberry, S. Nolo.

The Partnership Book, by Clifford, D., & Warner, R. Nolo.

Pratt's Guide to Venture Capital Sources. Venture Economics, Inc.

R & D Partnerships, by Petillon, L.R., & Hull, R.J. Clark Boardman.

Thomas Register of American Manufacturers. Thomas Pub. Co., New York, NY 10001. Eleven volumes. Similar to *Conover Mast Directory* above.

Ulrich's International Periodicals Directory. R.R. Bowker Co., New York, NY 10036. Lists periodicals by subject.

Up Your Own Organization, by Dible, D.M. Entrepreneur Press, c/o Hawthorn Books, New York, NY. How to start and finance a business.

Young Inventors, A Kit for Competition Organizers, by Huta, Y. Inventors of the Future Project, P.O. Box 19405, Washington, DC 20030.

D. Books Relating to Self-Improvement

I believe that the real key to success and happiness, in inventing as well as life, lies principally within each individual's own mind. A positive, optimistic attitude, hard work and perseverance, the willingness to take full responsibility for

one's own destiny, and living and thinking mainly in the present time—rather than luck, inherited abilities, and circumstances—are principally responsible for success and happiness. I have therefore provided a list of books whose main purpose is to prime you with the attitude to secure such success and happiness so that you'll be able to use *Patent It Yourself* as effectively as possible.

Explorations in Awareness, by Bois, S. Harper & Row. Break through mental blocks and preconceptions.

Higher Creativity—Liberating the Unconscious for Breakthrough Insights, by Harman, W., & Rheingold, H. J.P. Tarcher.

Language in Thought and Action, by Hayakawa, S.I., and A.R. Harcourt Brace Jovanovich.

Levels of Knowing & Existence, by Weinberg, H. Harper & Row. A new approach that answers many questions.

A New Guide to Rational Living, by Ellis, A., and Harper, R.A. Wilshire Book Co., Los Angeles, CA.

The Pleasure Trap, Mastering the Hidden Force that Undermines Health & Happiness, by Lisle, D. J., Ph.D., and Goldhamer, A., D.C. (Healthy Living Publications, Sumnertown, TN 2003) How to recognize and overcome the distracting and often destructive pursuit of pleasure and focus on happiness instead.

People in Quandries, by Johnson, W. Harper & Row. Classic book on emotional problem solving.

The Psychology of Self-Esteem, by Branden, N. Nash. Los Angeles, CA.

Three Minute Therapy: Change Your Thinking, Change Your Life, by Edelstein, M. R., Ph.D. (Glenbridge Publishing, Denver, CO 1997). Rapidly applied techniques for overcoming problems and focusing on your goals.

303 of the World's Worst Predictions, by Coffey, W. Tribeca Communications, Inc.

Your Erroneous Zones, by Dyer, W.W. Funk & Wagnalls, New York, NY. ∎

Appendix 3

Glossaries

Section A contains a glossary of words used to describe parts and functions of inventions. Section B contains a glossary of patent terms and their definitions as used in patent law.

A. Glossary of Useful Technical Terms

This Glossary[1] provides a list of useful words to describe the hardware, parts, and functions of your invention in the specification and claims. The most esoteric of these words are briefly defined. While some definitions are similar, this is due to space limitations; all words have nuances in meanings.

If you're looking for a word to describe a certain part, look through the list for a likely prospect and then check a dictionary for its precise meaning. If you can't find the right word here, look in your search patents, in *What's What* or another visual dictionary, or in a thesaurus. If you can't find an appropriate word, you'll probably be able to get away with "member" or "means-plus-a-function" language. Also, for new fields, you may invent words, preferably using Latin or Greek roots, as Farnsworth did with "television," or by extending the meaning of words from analogous devices (e.g., "base" for a part of a transistor). Very technical or specialized fields have their own vocabulary (e.g., "catamenial" in medicine, "syzygy" in astronomy); look in appropriate tutorial texts for these. The words are grouped loosely by the following functions:

1. Structure
2. Mounting and Fastening
3. Springs
4. Numbers
5. Placement
6. Voids
7. Shape
8. Materials and Properties
9. Optics
10. Fluid Flow
11. Electronics
12. Movement
13. Rotation/Machine.

---

[1] Expanded and used with kind permission and thanks from a list originally prepared by Louis B. Applebaum, Esq., of Newport, R.I.

1. Structure

annulus (ring)

apron

apse (dome)

arbor (shaft)

arm

bail (arch wire)

band

barrel

bascale (seesaw)

base

beam
  —cantilever
  —simple

belt

bib

blade

blower

board

bob (hanging weight)

body

bollard (thick post)

boom

boss (projection)

bougie (body-insertion member)

boule (pear-shaped)

branch

breech (back part)

bunker

caisson

canard (front wing)

carriage

case

channel

charger (shallow dish)

chase

chord

cincture (encircling band)

clew (sail part)

column

configuration

container

conveyor

cornice (horiz. top of structure)

cover

cupola (projection)

cylinder

dasher (plunger, churn)

derrick

detent

device

dibble (pointed tool)

die

disparate (dissimilar)

diversion

doctor blade (scraper)

dog (holder)

drum

echelon (staggered line)

element

enclosure

fence (stop on tool)

felly (rim of spoked wheel)

fillet (narrow strip)

fin

finger

finial (ornament)

flange

fluke (triangular part)

flute (groove on shaft)

frame

fret

frit (vitreous substance)

frustrum (cut-off area)

furcate (branch)

futtock (curved ship timber)

gaff (hook, spar)

gauge

generatrix (path traced)

gnomon (sundial upright)

graticulate (squares)

grommet

groove

gusset (triangular insert)

handle

head

header (base, support conduit)

homologous

horn

housing

hub

jacket

jaw

jib (crane arm)

knocker (clapper)

lagging (support)

ledger (horizonal support)

leg

lip

list (margin strip)

lobe

magazine

mandrel (tapered axle)

manifold

marge (edge)

marginate (w/margin)

medium

member

mullion (dividing strip)

nacelle (pod)

napiform (turnip-shaped)

neck

obcordate (heart shaped)

object

outcrop

panel

parietal (wall)

particle

partition

piece

piston

placket (slit in garment)

platform

plug

plunger

pontoon

portion

post

pounce (fine powder)

projection

purlin (horiz. rafter support)

putlog (horiz. support above ledger)

race

raceway

rank (row, series, range)

rib

riddle (sieve)

riffles (obstructions)

ring

rod

sash (frame)

screed (guide strip)

scroll

sear (catch)

shell

shoe

shoulder

skeleton

sleeve

sluice (channel)

snare

snorkel

spar (pole, support)

spline (projection on shaft)

spoke

sprag (spoke stop)

spur

stanchion

station

stay

stem

stent (stretcher)

step

stepped

stile (dividing strip)

stop

strake (ship plank)

strip

strut

tang (shank, tool)

tare (net weight)

tine

tip

tongue

trace (pivoted rod)

tracery (scrolling)

track

trave (crossbar)

truss
tuft
turret
tuyere (air pipe)
upright
vang (guy)
volar (palm, sole)
wall
ward (ridge or notch)
warp
woof (weft)
ziggurat (pyramid with
    terraces)

2. Mounting & Fastening

attach
billet (tip of belt)
bolt
bonnet
braze
busing
cable
camber
caster
clamp
cleat (reinforcer)
clevis (U-shaped pin)
colligate (bound together)
connection
couple
coupling
cribbing (support)
demountably
docking
dowel
engage
fay (join tightly)
ferrule (barrel)
ferruminate (attach, solder)
fix
funicular (ropelike)
gib (holding member)
gland (sliding holder)
guy wire
harp (lamp shade support)

hold
holder
hook
imbricate (regular overlap)
joint
    —universal
keeper
key
latch
lock
lug
matrix
mount
nail
nut
pin
plinth (base)
pricket (holding spike)
pylon (support)
ribband (holds ribs)
rivet
scarf (notched joint)
screw
seam
seat
secure
set
sheathed
sliding
snare/loop
solder
spike
springably
support
toe-in
thill (horse joinder stake)
thrust
weld

3. Springs

air
bias
    —element
coil
compressed
elastic

expanded
helical
    —compression
    —tension
leaf
press
relaxed
resilient
springably
torsional
urge

4. Numbers

argument
caboodle (collection,
    bunch)
compound
congeries (collection,
    aggregation)
difference
dividend
divisor
equation
formula
index
lemma
minuend
modulo
multiplicand
multiplicity
multiplier
plurality
power
product
quotient
remainder
sheaf
subtrahend
variable

5. Placement (Relation)

adjacent
aft
aligned

angle
aposition (facing)
array
attached
axial
bottom
close
complementary
concentric
contiguous
contracted
course
crest
disposed
distal
divided
edge
engaged
equitant (overlap in two
    ranks)
evert (inside out)
extended
external
face
fiducial (reference)
film
fore
horizontal
imbricate (overlapping
    series)
incline
integral
intermediate
internal
interposed
juxtaposed
layer
located
lower
mating
meshing
mesial (between)
normal

oblique

obtuse

offset

open

opposed

overlapping

parallel

perpendicular

pitched

positioned

projecting

prolapsed (out of place)

proximal

proximate

raked (pitched)

reference

removable

resting

rim

row

sandwich

section

slant

spacer

staggered

superimposed

supported

surface

surrounding

symmetrical

tilt

top

ubiety (located in a place)

vernier (9:10 gauge)

vertical

6. Voids

aperture

bore

cavity

chamber

concavity

cutout

dimple

duct

embrasure (slant opening)

engraved

filister (groove)

foramen (opening)

fossa (depression)

furrow (groove)

gain (notch)

gap

groove

hole

hollow

infold

intaglinated (engraved)

invaginate (enclosed, turned in)

lumen (bore of tube)

lunette (crescent opening)

mortise (cutout)

nock (notch on arrow)

notch

opening

orifice

passage

placket (garment slit)

polled (dehorned)

rabbet (groove)

raceway

recess

rifling (spiral groove)

separation

slit

slot

spandrel (triangular gap above arch side)

sulcus (groove)

ullage (lost liquid)

via (path)

void

wicket (small door or gate)

7. Shape

acclivity (slope)

acicular (needle-shaped)

agonic (no angle)

annular

anticline (peak)

applanation

arch

arcuate

barrel

bevel

bifurcated (2 branches)

bight (bend)

botryoidal (like a bunch of grapes)

bucket

buckled

chamfer (beveled)

channel

circular

coin

concave

congruent (same shape)

conical

convex

convoluted (curled in)

corner (inside, outside)

corrugated

crest

crimp

crispate (curled)

cup

cusp (projection)

cylinder

depression

dihedral (two-faced)

direction

disc

dome

draw (depression)

drawing (pulling out)

elliptical

fairing (streamlined)

fin

flange

fold

fork

fossa (groove)

fundus (base)

furcate (branched)

goffer (ridges or pleats)

helical

hook

incurvate (curved in)

invaginate (sheathed, folded in)

line

lobe

lozenge (diamond-shaped)

lune (crescent)

mammilated (nipple-shaped)

navicular (boat-shaped)

notch

oblate (flattened)

oblong

ogive (pointed arch)

orb (globe)

oval

parabolic

parallelogram

plane

prolate (cigar-shaped)

rectangular

reticulated (gridlike)

rhomboid (nonequal adjacent sides)

rhombus (equal adjacent sides)

rick-rock

rill (long narrow valley)

round

salient (standing out)

serrated

setaceous (bristlelike)

sheet

shelf

sinusoidal

skive (shaven)

slab

spall (broken chips)

spherical

spica (overlapping reverse spirals)

square

stamped

striated (grooved or ridged)

swaged (flattened)

swale (depression)

syncline (V-shaped)

taper terminus (end)

tesselated (tiled)

topology (unchangeable geometry)

tortuous (twisting)

tram (on wheels)

trefoil (three-leaved)

triangular

trihedral (3-sided)

trough

tubular

tumescence (detumescence)

turbinate (top/spiral shaped)

twist

upset (distorted)

vermiculate (worm-eaten)

volute (spiral)

wafer

web

wedge

whorl (spiral)

xyresic (razor-sharp)

8. Materials & Properties

adhesive

alluvial (sand or clay deposited by water)

concrete

cork

dappled (spotted)

denier (gauge)

dense

elastic

enlarged

fabric

fiber

flexible

foraminous

frit (fused glass)

haptic (sense of touch)

humectant (moistener)

insulation

intenerate (soften)

liquid

material

metal

nappy

opaque

pied (splotched)

placer (glacial deposit)

plastic

porous

prill

refractory

resilient

rigid

rubber

sand

screen

shirred (gathered)

smectic (cleaning)

stratified (layered)

strong

sturdy

translucent

transparent

wood

xerotic (dry)

9. Optics

aniseikonic (unequal sizes)

astigmatic

bezel

bulb

—fluorescent

—incandescent

fresnel

lamp

light

—beam

—ray

opaque

parallax (change in direction)

pellicle

pellucid (clear)

reflection

refraction

schlieren (streaks)

translucent

transmission

transparent

window

10. Fluid Flow

accumulator

afferent (to center)

aspirator

bellows

bibb (valve)

bung (hole or stopper)

cock (valve)

conduit

confluent (flow together)

connector

convection

cylinder

—piston

—rod

dashpot

diaphragm

discharge

dispenser

efferent (away from center)

filter

fitting

flue

gasket

hose

hydraulic

medium

navicular (like boat)

nozzle

obturator (blocker)

outlet

pipe

plunger

poppet (axial valve)

port

—inlet

—outlet

pump

—centrifugal

—gear

—piston

—reservoir

—seal

—siphon

—tank

—vane

sparge (spray)

sprue (vent tube)

suctorial (sucking)

sufflate (inflate)

swash (channel barrier)

tube

valve

—ball

—check

—control

—gate

—shutoff

wattle (intertwined wall)

weir (dam)

wicket (gate or door)

11. Electronics

adder

amplifier

astable

capacitance

clipping

conductor

contact

control element

demodulator
diode
electrode
electromagnet
filament
flip flop
gate (AND, OR, etc.)
impedance
inductance
insulator
integrated circuit
laser
lead
light emitting diode
line cord
liquid crystal
maser
memory
motor
multiplier
multivibrator
oscillator
pixel (CRT spot)
power supply
raster
read-and-write memory
read-only memory
resistance
sampling
Schmitt trigger
shift register
Shottky diode
socket
solenoid
switch
terminal
thermistor
transformer
transistor
triode
valve
varistor
wire
Zener diode

12. Movement

alternate
articulate (jointed)
avulsion (tear away)
cam
compression
cyclic
detent (click)
downward
draft (pull)
drag
drift pin
drill
eccentric
emergent
epicyclic (on circle)
equilibrate (bring into
  equilibrium)
escapement
extensible
extrude
grinding
impact
inclined plane
inertia
interval
lag
lead
lever
linkage
  —parallel
longitudinal
machine
meeting
nutate (to and fro)
pressing
propelling
pulverize
sagging
sequacious (regular)
severing
shuttle (to & fro member)
skive (peel)
slidable

snub (stop)
straight line
  —motion
terminating
toggle
torque
traction
transverse
traversing
triturate (grind to powder)
trochoid (roll on circle)
urging
vibrating
wedge

13. Rotation/ Machine

antifriction
  —ball
  —needle
  —roller
  —tapered
arbor (shaft)
bell crank
brake
  —band
  —disk
  —shoe
bushing
cam
chain
clevis (circular holder)
clutch
  —centrifugal
  —one-way
  —sprag (stop)
  —toothed
cog (tooth)
connecting rod
crank arm
drive
  —belt
  —pulley
  —sheave
  —toothed

flexible coupling
friction
fulcrum
gear
  —bevel
  —crown
  —internal
  —noncircular
  —pinion
  —right angle
  —spur
  —wheel
  —worm
gin (hoist, pile driver,
  pump)
guide
gudgeon (axle)
intermittent
  —escapement
  —geneva
  —pawl
  —pendulum
  —ratchet
jack
journal
mandrel
orbit
pinion (small wheel)
pintle (axle)
pivot
pulley
radial
radius bar
screw
seal
sheave (pulley)
spindle
sprocket
swash (wobble) plate
tappet (valve cam)
trunnion
variable speed
vertiginous (turning)
ward (ridge or notch)
winch
yoke

B. Glossary of Patent Terms

abstract a concise, one-paragraph summary of the patent. It details the structure, nature, and purpose of the invention. The abstract is used by the PTO and the public to quickly determine the gist of what is being disclosed.

abandonment 1. allowing a pending, active patent application to be removed from the PTO's active files and treated as if the inventor has given up all claims to a patent on the invention. An inventor can expressly abandon an application by letter or allow an application to go abandoned by not timely replying to an office action. 2. treating an invention as if the inventor has lost all interest in exploiting it, usually by not developing it or by not filing a patent application on it for a very long time.

actual damages (also known as compensatory damages) in a lawsuit, money awarded to one party to cover actual injury or economic loss. Actual damages are intended to put the injured party in the position he was in prior to the injury.

answer a written response to a complaint (the opening papers in a lawsuit) in which the defendant admits or denies the allegations and may provide a list of defenses.

best mode the inventor's principal and preferred method of embodying the invention.

Board of Appeals and Patent Interferences (BAPI) a tribunal of judges at the PTO that hears appeals from final Office Actions.

cease and desist letter correspondence from the owner of a proprietary work that requests the cessation of all infringing activity.

clear and convincing proof evidence that is highly probable and free from serious doubt.

complaint papers filed with a court clerk by the plaintiff to initiate a lawsuit by setting out facts and legal claims (usually called causes of action).

compositions of matter items such as chemical compositions, conglomerates, aggregates, or other chemically significant substances that are usually supplied in bulk (solid or particulate), liquid, or gaseous form.

conception the mental part of inventing, including how an invention is formulated or how a problem is solved.

confidentiality agreement (also known as a nondisclosure agreement) a contract in which one or both parties agree not to disclose certain information.

continuation application a new patent application that allows the applicant to re-present an invention and get a second or third bite at the apple. The applicant can file a new application (known as a "continuation") while the original (or "parent") application is still pending. A continuation application consists of the same invention, cross-referenced to the parent application and a new set of claims. The applicant retains the filing date of the parent application for purposes of determining the relevancy of prior art.

Continuation-in-Part (CIP) less common than a continuation application, this form of extension application is used when a portion or all of an earlier patent application is continued and new matter (not disclosed in the earlier application) is included. CIP applications are used when an applicant wants to present an improvement but is prevented from adding a pending application to it because of the prohibition against adding "new matter."

Continuing Prosecution Application (CPA) a patent application that is like a continuation application in effect, but no new application need be filed. The applicant merely pays another filing fee, submits new claims, and files a CPA request form. CPAs can only be used for applications filed prior to 2000 May 29. Applications after that date must use the Request for Continued Examination.

contributory infringement occurs when a material component of a patented invention is sold with knowledge that the component is designed for an unauthorized use. This type of infringement cannot occur unless there is a direct infringement. In other words, it is not enough to sell infringing parts; those parts must be used in an infringing invention.

copyright the legal right to exclude others, for a limited time, from copying, selling, performing, displaying, or making derivative versions of a work of authorship such as a writing, music, or artwork.

counterclaim a legal claim usually asserted by the defendant against an opposing party, usually the plaintiff.

Court of Appeals for the Federal Circuit (CAFC) the federal appeals court that specializes in patent appeals. If the Board of Appeals and Patent Interferences rejects an application appeal, an applicant can further appeal to the CAFC within 60 days of the decision. If the CAFC upholds the PTO, the applicant can request the United States Supreme Court hear the case (although the Supreme Court rarely hears patent appeals).

date of invention the earliest of the following dates: (a) the date an inventor filed the patent application (provisional or regular), (b) the date an inventor can prove that the invention was built and tested in the U.S. or a country that is a member of the North American Free Trade Association (NAFTA) or the World Trade Organization (WTO), or (c) the date an inventor can prove that the invention was conceived in a NAFTA or WTO country, provided the inventor can also prove diligence in building and testing it or filing a patent application on it.

declaratory relief a request that the court sort out the rights and legal obligations of the parties in the midst of an actual controversy.

deposit date the date the PTO receives a patent application.

deposition oral or written testimony of a party or witness and given under oath.

design patent covers the unique, ornamental, or visible shape or design of a nonnatural object.

divisional application a patent application used when an applicant wants to protect several inventions claimed in the original application. The official definition is "a later application for a distinct or independent invention, carved out of a pending application and disclosing and claiming only subject matter disclosed in the earlier or parent application" (MPEP 201.06). A divisional application is entitled to the filing date of the parent case for purposes of overcoming prior art. The divisional application must be filed while the parent is pending. A divisional application can be filed as a CPA.

Doctrine of Equivalents (DoE) a form of patent infringement that occurs when an invention performs substantially the same function in substantially the same manner and obtains the same result as the patented invention. A court analyzes each element of the patented invention separately. Under a recent Supreme Court decision, the DoE must be applied on an element-by-element basis to the claims.

double patenting when an applicant has obtained a patent and has filed a second application containing the same invention, the second application will be rejected. If the second application resulted in a patent, that patent will be invalidated. Two applications contain the same invention when the two inventions are literally the same or the second invention is an obvious modification of the first invention.

embodiment a physical version of an invention as described in a patent application; a patent application may describe several embodiments of an invention, but is supposed to state the one that the inventor considers the **best mode** as of the filing date; see **ramification**.

enhanced damages (treble damages) in exceptional infringement cases, financial damages may be increased, at the discretion of the court, up to triple the award for actual damages (known as "enhanced damages").

examiner's answer a brief submitted by a patent examiner in response to an applicant's brief in an appeal to the PTO's Board of Patent Appeals and Interferences.

exclusive jurisdiction the sole authority of a court to hear a certain type of case.

exhaustion (see "first sale doctrine").

ex parte (Latin: one party only) refers to legal proceedings where only one party is present or represented.

experimental use doctrine a rule excusing an inventor from the one-year bar provided that the alleged sale or public use was primarily for the purpose of perfecting or testing the invention.

file wrapper estoppel (or prosecution history estoppel) affirmative defense used in patent infringement litigation that precludes the patent owner from asserting rights that were disclaimed during the patent application process. The term is derived from the fact that the official file in which a patent is contained at the Patent and Trademark Office is known as a "file wrapper." All statements, admissions, correspondence, or documentation relating to the invention are placed in the file wrapper. Estoppel means that a party is prevented from acting contrary to a former statement or action when someone else has relied to his detriment on the prior statement or action.

final office action the examiner's response to the applicant's first amendment. The final Office Action is supposed to end the prosecution stage but a "final action" is rarely final.

first Office Action (sometimes called an "official letter" or "OA") response from the patent examiner after the initial examination of the application. It is very rare that an application is allowed in the first Office Action. More often, the examiner rejects some or all of the claims.

first sale doctrine (also known as the exhaustion doctrine) once a patented product (or product resulting from a patented process) is sold or licensed, the patent owner's rights are exhausted and the owner has no further rights as to the resale of that particular article.

generic (genus) an entire group or class, or a group of related items or species.

grace period a period in which an action may be taken even though the normal period for taking action has passed.

indirect infringement occurs either when someone is persuaded to make, use, or sell a patented invention without authorization (inducing infringement); or when a material component of a patented invention is sold with knowledge that the component is designed for an unauthorized use (contributory infringement). An indirect infringement cannot occur unless there is a direct infringement. In other words, it is not enough to sell infringing parts; those parts must be used in an infringing invention.

infringement an invention is infringing if it is a literal copy of a patented invention or if it performs substantially the same function in substantially the same manner and obtains the same result as the patented invention (see "doctrine of equivalents").

injunction a court order requiring that a party halt a particular activity. In the case of patent infringement, a court can order all infringing activity be halted at the end of a trial (a permanent injunction) or the patent owner can attempt to halt the infringing activity immediately, rather than wait for a trial (a preliminary injunction). A court uses two factors to determine whether to grant a preliminary injunction: (1) Is the plaintiff likely to succeed in the lawsuit? and (2) Will the plaintiff suffer irreparable harm if the injunction is not granted? The patent owner may seek relief for a very short injunction known as a temporary restraining order or TRO, which usually only lasts a few days or weeks. A temporary restraining order may be granted without notice to the infringer if it appears that immediate damage will result—for example, that evidence will be destroyed.

interference a costly, complex PTO proceeding that determines who will get a patent when two or more applicants are claiming the same invention. It is basically a method of sorting out priority of inventorship. Occasionally an interference may involve a patent that has been in force for less than one year.

inter partes (Latin: between parties) refers to legal proceedings where all parties to the action are represented.

interrogatories written questions that must be answered under oath.

invention any new article, machine, composition, or process or new use developed by a human.

jury instructions explanations of the legal rules that the jury must use in reaching a verdict.

lab notebook a system of documenting an invention that usually includes descriptions of the invention and novel features; procedures used in the building and testing of the invention; drawings, photos, or sketches of the invention; test results and conclusions; discussions of any known prior-art references; and additional documentation such as correspondence and purchase receipts.

literal infringement occurs if a defendant makes, sells, or uses the invention defined in the plaintiff's patent claim. In other words, the infringing product includes each and every component, part, or step in the patented invention. It is a literal infringement because the defendant's device is actually the *same* invention in the patent claim.

machine a device or things used for accomplishing a task; usually involves some activity or motion performed by working parts.

magistrate an officer of the court, who may exercise some of the authority of a federal district court judge, including the authority to conduct a jury or nonjury trial.

manufactures (sometimes termed "articles of manufacture") items that have been made by human hands or by machines; may have working or moving parts as prime features.

means-plus-function clause (or means for clause) a provision in a patent claim in which the applicant does not specifically describe the structure of one of the items in the patent and instead describes the function of the item. Term is derived from the fact that the clause usually starts with the word "means."

new matter any technical information, including dimensions, materials, etc., that was not present in the patent application as originally filed. An applicant can never add new matter to an application (PTO Rule 118).

new-use invention a new and unobvious process or method for using an old and known invention.

nonobviousness a standard of patentability that requires that an invention produce "unusual and surprising results." In 1966, the U.S. Supreme Court established the steps for determining unobviousness in the case of *Graham v. John Deere*, 383 U.S. 1 (1966).

Notice of Allowance a document issued when the examiner is convinced that the application meets the requirements of patentability. An issue fee is due within three months.

objection a disapproval made by an examiner to a nonsubstantive matter, such as an unclear drawing or dependent claim having a rejected claim.

objects and advantages a phrase used to explain "what the invention accomplishes." Usually, the objects are also the invention's advantages, since those aspects are intended to be superior over prior art.

Office Action (OA, also known as Official Letter or Examiner's Action) correspondence (usually including forms and a letter) from a patent examiner that describes what is wrong with the application and why it cannot be allowed. Generally, an OA will reject claims, list defects in the specifications or drawings, raise objections, or cite and enclose copies of relevant prior art demonstrating a lack of novelty or nonobviousness.

on-sale bar prevents an inventor from acquiring patent protection if the application is filed more than one year from the date of sale, use, or offer of sale of the invention in the United States.

one-year rule a rule that requires an inventor to file a patent application within one year after selling, offering for sale, or commercially or publicly using or describing an invention. If an inventor fails to file within one year of such occurrence the inventor is barred from obtaining a patent.

patent a grant from a government that confers upon an inventor the right to exclude others from making, using, selling, importing, or offering an invention for sale for a fixed period of time.

patent application a set of papers that describe an invention and that are suitable for filing in a patent office in order to apply for a patent on the invention.

Patent Application Declaration (PAD) a declaration that identifies the inventor or joint inventors and provides an attestation by the applicant that the inventor understands the contents of the claims and specification and has fully disclosed all material information. The PTO provides a form for the PAD.

patent misuse a defense in patent infringement that prevents a patent owner who has abused patent law from enforcing patent rights. Common examples of misuse are violation of the antitrust laws or unethical business practices.

patent pending (also known as the "pendency period") time between filing a patent application (or PPA) and issuance of the patent. The inventor has no patent rights during this period. However, when and if the patent later issues, the inventor will obtain the right to prevent the continuation of any infringing activity that started during the pendency period. If the application has been published by the PTO during the pendency period and the infringer had notice, the applicant may later seek royalties for these infringements during the pendency period. It's a criminal offense to use the words "patent applied for" or "patent pending" (they mean the same thing) in any advertising if there's no active, applicable regular or provisional patent application on file.

patent prosecution the process of shepherding a patent application through the Patent and Trademark Office.

Patent Rules of Practice administrative regulations located in Volume 37 of the Code of Federal Regulations (37 CFR § 1).

pendency period (see patent pending).

permanent injunction a durable injunction issued after a final judgment on the merits of the case; permanently restrains the defendant from engaging in the infringing activity.

Petition to Make Special an applicant can, under certain circumstances, have an application examined sooner than the normal course of PTO examination (one to three years). This is accomplished by filing a "Petition to Make Special" (PTMS), together with a Supporting Declaration.

plant patent covers plants that can be reproduced through the use of grafts and cuttings (asexual reproduction).

power of attorney a document that gives another person legal authority to act on your behalf. If an attorney is preparing an application on behalf of an inventor, a power of attorney should be executed to authorize the patent attorney or agent to act on behalf of the inventor. The power of attorney form may be combined with the PAD.

prima facie (Latin: on its face) at first sight, obvious.

prior art the state of knowledge existing or publicly available either before the date of an invention or more than one year prior to the patent application date.

process (sometimes referred to as a "method") a way of doing or making things that involves more than purely mental manipulations.

Provisional Patent Application (PPA) an interim document that clearly explains how to make and use the invention. The PPA is equivalent to a reduction to practice (see below). If a regular patent application is filed within one year of filing the PPA, the inventor can use the PPA's filing date for the purpose of deciding whether a reference is prior art. In addition to an early filing date, an inventor may claim patent pending status for the one-year period following the filing of the PPA.

ramification a version or variation of an invention that is different from a main version or **best mode**.

reduction to practice the point at which the inventor can demonstrate that the invention works for its intended purpose. Reduction to practice can be accomplished by building and testing the invention (actual reduction to practice) or by preparing a patent application or provisional patent application that shows how to make and use the invention and that it works (constructive reduction to practice). In the event of a dispute or a challenge at the PTO, invention documentation is essential in order to prove the "how and when" of conception and reduction to practice.

reissue application an application used to correct information in a patent. It is usually filed when a patent owner believes the claims are not broad enough, the claims are too broad (the applicant discovered a new reference), or there are significant errors in the specification. In these cases, the applicant seeks to correct the patent by filing an application to get the applicant's original patent reissued at any time during its term. The reissue patent will take the place of the applicant's original patent and expire the same time as the original patent would have expired. If the applicant wants to broaden the claims of the patent through a reissue application, the applicant must do so within two years from the date the original patent issued. There is a risk in filing a reissue application because all of the claims of the original patent will be examined and can be rejected.

rejection a disapproval made by an examiner to a substantive matter such as a claim which is deemed obvious over the prior art.

repair doctrine affirmative defense based on the right of an authorized licensor of a patented device to repair and replace unpatented components. It also includes the right to sell materials used to repair or replace a patented invention The defense does not apply for completely rebuilt inventions, unauthorized inventions, or items that are made or sold without authorization of the patent owner.

reply a brief submitted by a patent applicant in response to an examiner's answer.

request for admission request for a party to the lawsuit to admit the truthfulness of a statement.

Request for Continued Examination (RCE) a paper filed when a patent applicant wishes to continue prosecuting an application that has received a final **Office Action**. Filing the RCE with another filing fee effectively removes the final action so that the applicant can submit further amendments, for example, new claims, new arguments, a new declaration, or new references.

request for production of documents the way a party to a lawsuit obtains documents or other physical evidence from the other side.

reverse doctrine of equivalents (or negative doctrine of equivalents) a rarely used affirmative defense to patent infringement in which, even if there is a literal infringement, the court will excuse the defendant's conduct if the infringing device has a different function or result than the patented invention. The doctrine is applied when the allegedly infringing device performs the same function in a substantially different way.

sequence listing an attachment to a patent application used if a biotech invention includes a sequence listing of a nucleotide or amino acid sequence. The applicant attaches this information on separate sheets of paper and refers to the sequence listing in the application (see PTO Rule 77). If there is no sequence listing, the applicant states "Non-applicable."

small entity a status that enables small businesses, independent inventors, and nonprofit companies to pay a reduced application fee. There are three types of small entities: (1) independent inventors, (2) nonprofit companies, and (3) small businesses. To qualify, an independent inventor must either own all rights, or have transferred—or be obligated to transfer—rights to a small business or nonprofit organization. Nonprofit organizations are defined and listed in the Code of Federal Regulations and usually are educational institutions or charitable organizations. A small-entity business is one with fewer than 500 employees. The number of employees is computed by averaging the number of full- and part-time employees during a fiscal year.

species one of a group of related individual items collectively subordinate to a genus.

specification a patent application disclosure made by the inventor and drafted so that an individual skilled in the art to which the invention pertains could, when reading the patent, make and use the invention without needing further experiment. A **specification** is constructed of several sections. Collectively, these sections form a narrative that describes and distinguishes the invention. If it can later be proved that the inventor knew of a better way (or "best mode") and failed to disclose it, that failure could result in the loss of patent rights.

statute of limitations the legally prescribed time limit in which a lawsuit must be filed. In patent law there is no time limit (statute of limitations) for filing a patent infringement lawsuit, but monetary damages can only be recovered for infringements committed during the six years prior to the filing the lawsuit. For example, if a patent owner sues after ten years of infringement, the owner cannot recover monetary damages for the first four years of infringement. Despite the fact that there is no law setting a time limit, courts will not permit a patent owner to sue for infringement if the owner has waited an unreasonable time to file the lawsuit ("laches").

Statutory Invention Registration (SIR) a document that allows an applicant who abandons an application to prevent anyone else from getting a valid patent on the same invention. This is accomplished by converting the patent application to a SIR.

statutory subject matter an invention that falls into one of the five statutory classes: process (method), machine, article of manufacture, composition, or a "new use" of one of the first four.

substitute application essentially a duplicate of an abandoned patent application. (See MPEP § 201.09.) The disadvantage of a substitute application is that the applicant doesn't get the benefit of the filing date of the previously abandoned patent application, which could be useful, because any prior art occurring after the filing date of the earlier case can be used against the substitute case. If the applicant's substitute application issues into a patent, the patent will expire 20 years from the filing date of the substitute.

successor liability responsibility for infringement that is borne by a company that has purchased another company that is liable for infringements. In order for successor liability to occur, there must be an agreement between the companies to assume liability, a merger between the companies, or the purchaser must be a "continuation" of the purchased business. If the sale is made to escape liability and lacks any of the foregoing characteristics, liability will still attach.

summons a document served with the complaint that tells the defendant he has been sued, has a certain time limit in which to respond, and must appear in court on a stated date.

temporary restraining order (TRO) a court order that tells one party to do or stop doing something—for example to stop infringing. A TRO is issued after the aggrieved party appears before a judge. Once the TRO is issued, the court holds a second hearing where the other side can tell his story and the court can decide whether to make the TRO permanent by issuing an injunction. The TRO is often granted *ex parte* (without allowing the other side to respond), and for that reason is short in duration and only remains in effect until the court has an opportunity to schedule a hearing for the preliminary injunction.

traverse to argue against.

tying a form of patent misuse in which, as a condition of a transaction, the buyer of a patented device must also purchase an additional product. For example, in one case a company had a patent on a machine that deposited salt tablets in canned food. Purchasers of the machine were also required to buy salt tablets from the patent owner. A party that commits patent misuse may have its patent invalidated, may have to pay monetary damages, or both.

utility patent the main type of patent, which covers inventions that function in a unique manner to produce a utilitarian result.

verified statement a statement made under oath or a declaration. A false verified statement is punishable as perjury.

vicarious liability legal responsibility that results when a business such as a corporation or partnership is liable for infringements committed by employees or agents. This liability attaches when the agent acts under the authority or direction of the business, an employee acts within the scope of employment, or the business benefits from, or adopts or approves the infringing activity.

voir dire *("speak the truth")* process by which attorneys and judges question potential jurors in order to determine whether they may be fair and impartial. ■

Appendix 4

Fee Schedule

⚠ These fees are good as of 2004 December 8, but fees change periodically and other changes are in the works. Thus, you should check with the PTO, 703-308-HELP, its PCT Office, 703-308-3257, its website (www.uspto.gov), or the Nolo website, www.nolo.com, before paying this fee. If you underpay any fee, the PTO imposes a stiff surcharge. (If you overpay any fee, the PTO will send you a refund (refund must be requested if under $25).) The USPTO's new filing fee is broken into three parts (filing, search, and examination). These fees are itemized on the Fee Transmittal Form (PTO/SB17), but since the total must be paid at the time of filing, the listing below includes only the total fee. Two fees separated by a slash refer to large entity/small entity; a single fee applies to both entities. PTO fees are listed in order for the patenting process.

Service or Item	Fee ($)	Form/Chapter
PTO Fees (Rule)		
Disclosure Document, filing (21(c))	10	3-3
Printed Copy of Patent or Patent Order Coupon Utility/Design; Also for Copy of SIR (19(a))	3	Ch. 6
Copy of Plant Patent in Color/Utility With Color Drawings (19(a))	15	
Application Filing Fees:		
Utility Patent (incl. search and exam fees) (16(a))	1,000/500	10-1, 14-1
Utility Patent Electronic Filing (incl. search and exam fees)	1,000/425	
Design Patent (incl. search and exam fees) (16(f))	430/215	10-8
Plant Patent (incl. search and exam fees) (16(g))	660/330	Ch. 10
Provisional Patent Appn., Filing (16(r))	200/100	Ch. 3
Prov. Appn. Late Filing Fee or Cover Sheet (16(l))	50/25	Ch. 3
Prov. Appn. Correct inventors or convert RPA to PPA (17(q))	50	Ch. 3
Fee for Each Independent Claim Over Three (16(b))	200/100	10-1, 14-1
Fee for Each Claim Over 20 (Independent or Dependent) (16(c))	50/25	Ch. 10
Surcharge—Multiple Dependent Claims in Any Application (16(d))	360/180	Ch. 10
Surcharge If Filing Fee or Declaration Late (16(e))	130/65	Ch. 10
Recording Assignment per Application or Patent Involved (21(h))	40	10-1
Surcharge If Any Check Bounces (21(m))	50	Ch. 10

Service or Item	Fee ($)	Form/Chapter
Petitions to Commissioner:		
To Accept Color Drawings (17(k)), Regarding Inventorship	130	Ch. 10
Maint. Fees, Interferences, Foreign Filing Licenses, Access to		
Records, Foreign Priority Papers, and misc.	130	Ch. 13
Amendments After Issue Fee, Defer/Withdraw a Case		
From Issue (17(k,l))	130	10-7
To Make Application Special (where fee required) (17(l))	130	Ch. 10
Expedited Examination of Design Application (Rocket Docket) (17(k))	900	Ch. 10
Petition to Revive Abandoned Appn.:		
Unavoidable Delay (17(l))	500/250	Ch. 13
Unintentional Delay (17(m))	1,500/750	Ch. 13
Extensions to Reply to Office Actions:		
1st Month (17(a))	120/60	13-5
2nd Month (17(b))	450/225	13-5
3rd Month (17(c))	1,020/510	13-5
4th Month (17(d))	1,590/795	13-5
5th Month (17(d)) (no extension over six months)	2,160/1,080	13-5
Certified Copy Patent Application as Filed (19(b))	25	Ch. 12
Late IDS Fee (before or after final action) (17(p))	180	Ch. 13
Appeal to Board of Appeals & Pat. Intrfs.:		
Filing Notice of Appeal (17(b)) or Brief (17(c))	500/250	Ch. 13
Oral Hearing (17(g))	1,000/500	Ch. 13
Application Issue Fees:		
Utility Patent (18(a))	1,400/700	Ch. 13
Utility Patent Publication Fee (18(d))	300	Chs. 8-10, 13
Prior Art Citation Fee Against Published Appn. (17(p))	180	Ch. 13
Design Patent (18(b))	800/400	Ch. 13
Plant Patent (18(c))	1,100/550	Ch. 13
Certificate to Correct Patent (Applicant's Mistake) (20(a))	100	15-1
Reexamination Fee Ex Parte (20(c))	2,520	Ch. 15
Reexamination Fee Inter Partes (20(c)(2))	8,800	
Utility Patent Maintenance Fees:		
I (3.5 years—pays for yrs 4 thru 8) (20(e))	900/450	15-3
II (7.5 years—pays for yrs 9 thru 12) (20(f))	2,300/1,150	15-3
III (11.5 years—pays for yrs 13 thru 17) (20(g))	3,800/1,900	15-3
Late Charge (in 6-month grace period) (20(h))	130/65	15-3
Petition to Revive (after patent expires)—unintentional delay (20(i))	1,640	Ch. 15
Petition to Revive (after patent expires)—unavoidable delay (20(i))	700	Ch. 15
Certified Copy of File & Contents—Issued Patent (19(b)(2)) up to 400 pp.	200	Ch. 15

Service or Item	Fee ($)	Form/Chapter
Certified Copy of Patent Assignment Record (19(b)(3))	25	Ch. 14
Disclaimer of Claims or Terminal Part of Term of Patent (20(d))	130/65	
Dedication of Entire Term or Terminal Part of Term of Patent	No charge	

Other Fees

Trademark Application Filing (in PTO)	335	Ch. 1
Trademark Application Filing (in California)	70	Ch. 1
Copyright Application Filing (in Copyright Office)	30	Ch. 1
Filing a European or Japanese Pat. Appn., incl. agent's fee, approx.	5,000-7,000	Ch. 12

PCT Fees (Always check just before filing; these fees change frequently)

Transmittal Fee	300	Ch. 12
Search Fees:		
In U.S. PTO		
—no corres. prior U.S. appn. filed	1,000	Ch. 12
—corres. prior U.S. appn. filed	300	Ch. 12
In European Patent Office	1,920	Ch. 12
International Fees:		
Basic (First 30 Pages)	1,134 *	Ch. 12
Each Additional Sheet Over 30	12	Ch. 12
Chapter II Fees:		
Handling Fee	160	Ch. 12
Examination Fee		
In U.S. PTO (assuming a patent search is done by the U.S. PTO, as described in Chapter 1)	600	Ch. 12

* $1,053 if PCT-EASY software used.

Appendix 5

Mail, Telephone, Fax, and Email Communications With the PTO

A. Patent and Trademark Office Mail Addresses

Special Boxes for Patent Mail

If you are sending mail in any of the "Type of Mail" categories below to the PTO, add the appropriate Mail Stop below as the first line of your address as indicated. If your mail does not fall into one of these categories, e.g., an amendment with a fee for extra claims, simply address it using just the last three lines of the address below.

> Mail Stop _____
> Commissioner for Patents
> P.O. Box 1450
> Alexandria, VA 22313-1450

Mail Stop	Type of Mail
Mail Stop AF	Amendments and other responses after final rejection, other than an appeal brief.
Mail Stop Amendment	Information disclosure statements, drawings, and replies to Office Actions in patent applications
Mail Stop Appeal Brief-Patents	Appeal briefs.
Mail Stop Assignment	Assignments (with cover sheets).
Mail Stop Certificate	Requests for Certificates of Correction.
Mail Stop DD	Disclosure Documents or materials related to the Disclosure Document Program.
Mail Stop EBC	Mail for the Electronic Business Center
Mail Stop Expedited Design	Initial filing of design applications accompanied by a request for expedited examination ("Rocket Docket").
Mail Stop Express Abandonment	Requests for abandonment of a patent application pursuant
Mail Stop Issue Fee	All communications following the receipt of a Notice of Allowance and Fee(s) Due, and prior to the issuance of a patent.
Mail Stop M	Maintenance fee correspondence, excluding maintenance fee payments.
Mail Stop PCT	Mail related to international applications filed under the Patent Cooperation Treaty.
Mail Stop Petition	Petitions to be decided by the Office of Petitions including petitions to revive and petitions to accept late payment of issue or maintenance fees.
Mail Stop PGPUB	Correspondence regarding publication of patent applications, including request for early publication and rescission of nonpublication request.
Mail Stop Post Issue	In patented files: requests for changes of address, powers of attorney.

Mail Stop	Type of Mail
Mail Stop RCE	Requests for continued examination under 37 CFR 1.114.
Mail Stop Ex Parte Reexam	Requests for Reexamination for original request papers only.
Mail Stop Inter Partes Reexam	Requests for Inter Partes Reexamination.
Mail Stop Reissue	All new and continuing reissue application filings.
Mail Stop Sequence	Submission of computer-readable form (CRF) for applications with sequence listings, when the CRF is not being filed with the application.

Payments of maintenance fees in patents not submitted electronically over the Internet at www.uspto.gov should be mailed to United States Patent and Trademark Office, P.O. Box 371611, Pittsburgh, PA 15250-1611.

Federal Government Holidays: The PTO is closed on weekends and the following holidays: New Year's Day, M.L. King Day, Presidents' Day, Memorial Day, Independence Day, Labor Day, Columbus Day, Veterans' Day, Thanksgiving, and Christmas. If any action falls due on a holiday or weekend, it is due on the next open-for-business day.

B. Patent and Trademark Office Telephone, and Faxes

All numbers are in area code 703 but are changing to area code 571. These numbers change often, so check current listings at the USPTO online Yellow Pages (www.uspto.gov/web/info/asubject.htm) or check the first *Official Gazette* of the year (or a later edition if it contains a new list).

Check for Updated Phone Listings

The following list shows the various departments in the PTO. Note, however, that most of the PTO's phone numbers have changed to new numbers in the 571 area code. As this edition went to press, the PTO's phone numbers have not been updated on its website. Until the PTO's site is updated, the best way to get the number of anyone or any department in the PTO is to call the PTO's General Information number, 800-786-9199.

Service or Department	Telephone	Fax
Advance Orders of Patent Soft Copies, Non-Receipt	703-305-8263	703-305-4372
After Publication	703-308-9401 Ext.200	
After Registration	703-308-9500	
General Information	703-308-9000	

Appeals

Board of Patent Appeals and Interferences	703-308-9797	

Service or Department	Telephone	Fax
Initial Patent Examination	703-308-1202	703-308-7751
Patent Cooperation Treaty (PCT)–General Information	703-305-3257	703-305-2919
Provisional Applications for Patent, General Information	800-786-9199 703-308-4357	703-305-7786
Reexamination, General Information	800-786-9199 703-308-4357	703-305-7786
Status Inquiry of Allowed Applications	703-308-6789	703-308-5065
Status Inquiry of Pending Applications	703-305-1801	
Statutory Invention Registrations (SIRs)	703-306-4200	
Assignment Division	703-308-9723	
Copies of Recorded Documents	703-308-9726 800-972-6382	703-305-8759
Recording Changes Affecting Title	703-308-9723	
Assistance Center, Patent (PAC)	800-786-9199 703-308-4357	703-305-7786
Board of Patent Appeals and Interferences	703-308-9797	703-308-7953
Certificates of Correction, Patents	703-305-8309	703-308-6672
Certification Services	703-308-9726 800-972-6382	703-308-7048
Attorney Roster	703-306-4097	
Issued Patents for File Records (Office of Public Records)	703-308-9726	
Issued Patents for Maintenance Fee Notification	703-308-5069	
Complaints Regarding Invention Promotion Firms	866-767-3848	703-306-5570
Advance Orders, Non-Receipt (Patent Copies)	703-305-8263	703-305-4372
Copies of Patent and Trademark Office Documents (Certified and Uncertified)	703-308-9726 800-972-6382	703-308-7048
Foreign Patents	703-308-1076	
Correction of Applications for Patent	703-305-9285	
Disclosure Document Program	703-308-0900	
Drawing Corrections, Patents	703-305-8404	
Federal Protective Service	202-708-1111	
To Obtain a Copy of the Fee Schedule	800-786-9199 703-308-4357	703-305-7786
Maintenance	703-308-5068 703-308-5069	703-308-5077
Maintenance Fee Status Inquiry (Automated Voice Response System)	703-308-5392 703-308-5393	
Refunds	703-305-4229	703-308-6778
To Order Files for Self-Service Copying, Patent	703-308-2733	
PTO-Provided Copies	703-308-9726	703-308-7048

Service or Department	Telephone	Fax
Abandoned Patent Application File Histories	703-308-2733	
Patented File Histories	703-308-2733	
Pending Patent Applications	703-308-2733	
Patent	703-308-1202	703-746-9195
Foreign Patents Copies	703-308-1076	703-308-1000
Reference Assistance	703-308-1076	
Translations	703-308-0881	703-308-0989
Forms	800-786-9199 703-308-4357	703-305-7786
Patent Cooperation Treaty (Help Desk)	703-308-4129	
Information Directory (to request a copy)	800-786-9199 703-308-4357	703-305-7786
Initial Patent Examination, Office of	703-308-0910	703-305-9822
Customer Service	703-308-1202	703-308-7751
Inspection of Patent Files	703-308-2733	
Inventors Assistance Program	800-786-9199	703-305-8825
Journal of the Patent and Trademark Office Society (JPTOS) Send email to: jptos.org	n/a	703-519-7449
License to File Abroad (Request to file a patent application abroad) See Director, Technology Center 3600		703-306-4187
Licensing and Review (Secrecy Orders)	703-306-5771	
Licensing and Sale Notices in *Official Gazette*	703-305-8263	703-305-4372
To purchase, call the Superintendent of Documents (Government Printing Office)	202-512-1800	202-512-2250
Manual of Patent Examining Procedure (MPEP)	703-305-8850	703-305-8825
Content questions	703-305-8813	703-305-8825
To Purchase a Paper Copy or Subscribe to a Print Publication of the MPEP, call the Superintendent of Documents (Government Printing Office)	202-512-1800	202-512-2250
To Purchase MPEP on DVD-ROM	703-306-2600	703-306-2737
Notice of Appeal	703-308-9797	
PatentIn Software *See* PatentIn Software Program Support (SIRA)	703-308-4212	
Sequence Listing Submissions	703-308-4216	
Official Gazette Notices, Patent	703-305-8263	703-305-4372
Official Gazette, Patents (eOG:P) on CD-ROM	703-306-2600	703-306-2737
Official Searches (lost patent or trademark files)	703-305-1801	
Patent and Trademark Office Documents .... (Certified or Uncertified)	703-308-9726 800-972-6382	703-308-7048
Patent and Trademark Depository Library Program (PTDLP)	703-308-5558	703-306-2654

Service or Department	Telephone	Fax
Patent Application Information Retrieval (PAIR) Technical Support	703-305-3028	
Patent Assistance Center (PAC)	800-786-9199 703-308-4357	703-305-7786
PCT Operations Receptionist	703-305-3165	703-305-3230
Director of Operations	703-308-2674	703-305-3230
PCT Help Desk	703-305-3257	703-305-2919
Office of PCT Legal Administration	703-305-0045	703-308-6459
Patent Court Appeals, Inquiries	703-305-9035	
Patent Electronic Business Center Customer Service Center	703-305-3028	
Patent File Archive	703-308-9726 800-972-6382	
Patent Filing Receipt	703-308-2733	
Patent Grant, Non-Receipt	703-305-8263	703-305-4372
Patent Products on Magnetic Tape	703-306-2600	703-306-2737
Patent Programs Control, Office of	703-305-9182	703-308-5548
Patent Publication, Office of	703-305-8263	703-305-4372
Patent Quality Review, Office of	703-305-3125	703-308-7132
Patent Statistics	703-306-2600	703-306-2737
Patent Subclass Listing, Purchase of (list of all patent numbers in a subclass)	703-306-2600	703-306-2737
Patent Subclass Subscription (copies of every patent issued every Tuesday for a particular subclass)	703-305-8263	
Patent Technology Monitoring Division	703-306-2600	703-306-2737
Patented Files	703-308-2733	
Technical Assistance	703-306-4119	
Central Reexamination Unit	703-306-2892	
General Questions	703-305-9282	
Reexamination Petitions	703-305-9282	
Reexamination Pre-Processing	703-308-9692	703-308-7751
Refunds	703-305-4229	703-308-6778
General	703-308-1076	703-308-1000
Biotechnology/Chemical Library	703-308-4478	703-308-4496
EIC1700	703-308-4483	703-308-5095
EIC2100	703-308-5174	703-306-5509
EIC2600	703-305-4071	703-305-5443
EIC2800	703-306-5419	703-308-6097
EIC3600	703-308-4211	703-306-5758
EIC3700	703-305-5932	703-305-5915

Service or Department	Telephone	Fax
Foreign Patents	703-308-1076	703-308-1000
Lutrelle F. Parker Sr. Memorial Law Library	703-308-5300	703-308-5095
Translations	703-308-0881	703-308-0989
Search and Information Resources Administration (SIRA)	703-306-3104 703-308-5192	703-305-0854
Patent Public Search Room	703-305-4463	
Patent File Archive	703-308-2733	
Patent Search and Image Retrieval Facility	703-308-6001	
Public Training (Automated Systems)	703-308-3040	
Public User IDs	703-305-4463	
Sequence Listing Submissions (STIC–CRF)	703-308-4212	703-308-4221
Sequence Rules	703-308-4216	
Simultaneous Issuances	703-305-8283	
Solicitor, Office of	703-305-9035	
Freedom of Information Act Requests	703-305-9035	
Special Program Law Office	703-305-9285	703-308-6916
Status Issued Patents	703-308-2733	
Patent Applications	703-308-2733	
Status of Patent Files in Official Search	703-305-1801	
Statutory Invention Registrations (SIRs)	703-306-4177	
Subclass Listing, Purchase of (list of all patent numbers in a subclass)	703-306-2600	703-306-2737

Subscription Information

CD-ROM Products	703-306-2600	703-306-2737
MPEP on CD-ROM	703-306-2600	703-306-2737
MPEP (Paper Version) *See* Government Printing Office	202-512-1800	
Official Gazette, Patents (eOG:P) on CD-ROM	703-306-2600	703-306-2737
Patent Subclass (copies of every patent issued every Tuesday for a particular subclass)	703-305-8263	
Terminal Disclaimers	703-305-8408	
TTY Questions	703-305-7785	
Under Secretary of Commerce for Intellectual Property and Director of the United States Patent and Trademark Office	703-305-8600	703-305-8664
USPTO Contact Center (formerly General Information Services Division)	800-786-9199 703-308-4357	703-305-7786
Video Conference Center	703-308-9660	703-308-9698

■

Quick-Reference Timing Chart

The following is a summary of some of the more important timing intervals that apply in intangible property law. This list is not intended to be comprehensive, and certain exceptions may be applicable, so check the pertinent parts of this book, or with a patent attorney, if you have a special situation or need more precise advice.

From the date of first publication, offer of sale, sale, or public or commercial use (excluding experimental use) of anything embodying an invention, one must file a U.S. utility, design, or plant patent application within .... 1 year.

From the date of filing a PPA, to get the benefit of its filing date, one must file a utility patent application and corresponding foreign applications within .... 1 year.

To preserve foreign-filing rights in Convention Countries, one must not sell or publicly disclose details of an invention until ....after U.S. filing date.

To preserve foreign-filing rights in Non-Convention Countries (NCCs), one must not publicly disclose or sell invention until .... after filing date in NCC.

From the PTO's mailing date, unless an extension is purchased, or unless a shorter date is set, one must file a response to most office actions within .... 3 months.

The maximum statutory time to reply to an Office Action, provided extensions are bought, is .... 6 months.

Unless a Nonpublication Request has been filed, or unless it has issued or is abandoned, every patent application is published .... 18 months after filing.

The full term of a utility or plant patent is measured from the filing date and is ....20 years.

The full term of a design patent is measured from the issue date and is .... 14 years.

From the date of issue (grant) the issue fee will keep a utility patent in force for the first .... 4 years.

From the issue date of a patent, the patentee must file a reissue application that attempts to broaden the claims within .... 2 years.

From the issue date of a patent, an applicant in a pending application who wants to get
into interference with the patent must copy the patent's claims in their application within .... 1 year.

Timely payment of Maintenance Fee I (between year 3.0 and 3.5, or 3.5 and 4.0
with late charge) will keep a utility patent in force for another .... 4 years.

Timely payment of Maintenance Fee II (between year 7.0 and 7.5, or 7.5 and 8.0
with late charge) will keep a utility patent in force for another .... 4 years.

Timely payment of Maintenance Fee III (between year 11.0 and 11.5, or 11.5
and 12.0 with late charge) will keep a utility patent in force until expiration,
which occurs .... 20 years after filing.

For works not made for hire, the copyright term is .... author's life + 70 years.

For works made for hire, the copyright term is the shorter of .... 95 years from publication or
120 years from creation.

To get statutory damages and attorney fees, one must apply to register a
copyright before infringement begins or within .... 3 months of publication.

A California state trademark registration lasts for .... 10 years.

A U.S. (federal) trademark registration lasts for .... 10 years.

State and U.S. trademark registrations can be renewed .... in perpetuity.

If kept secret, and provided it's not discovered independently, a trade secret
will be enforceable against those who discover it illegally .... in perpetuity.

Unless a foreign filing license has been granted, after filing a U.S. patent application,
before foreign filing a patent application, you must wait .... 6 months.

From the U.S. filing date, to obtain priority of a utility patent application, one must
file a foreign Convention application (PCT, EPO, or industrial countries) within .... 1 year.

From the U.S. filing date, to obtain priority of a design patent application, one must
file a foreign Convention application (PCT, EPO, or industrial countries) within .... 6 months.

One must file a foreign Non-Convention application
(most nonindustrial countries) .... before invention becomes publicly known.

From the U.S. filing date, after filing a PCT application, if a patent in
the foreign jurisdiction is desired, one must file abroad within .... 30 months.

From the U.S. filing date, after filing a PCT application, if
examination in the U.S. PTO or the European Patent Office
is desired (Chapter II), one must file a request within .... 22 months or 3 months from search report.

■

Appendix 7

Tear-Out Forms

Form numbers indicate the chapters in which the forms are discussed; for example, Form 10-7 is discussed in Chapter 10. Some of these forms differ from the corresponding PTO versions due to the fact that I have simplified them and added warnings. However, both versions are perfectly acceptable. The PTO forms also have a Burden-Hour Statement, which you need not include on any forms you send to the PTO. The tear-out versions of these forms are 8" wide but may be used for PTO purposes if you copy them on to 8.5"-wide paper. (Place a white backing over the form to avoid a black edge on the side.)

Nondisclosure Agreement

1. **Parties.** This Disclosure Agreement (the "Agreement") is entered into by and between _____ _____, ("Disclosing Party") and _____, ("Receiving Party") for the purpose of preventing the unauthorized disclosure of Confidential Information (as defined below).

   The parties agree to enter into a confidential relationship with respect to the disclosure of certain proprietary and confidential information ("Confidential Information").

2. **Definition of Confidential Information.** For purposes of this Agreement, "Confidential Information" shall include the following: _____

   _____

   _____

   _____

   _____

   _____

   _____

   _____

   "Confidential Information" shall also include all information or material, written or oral, that has or could have commercial value or other utility in the business in which Disclosing Party is engaged.

   [Receiving Party should check the box and initial the appropriate choice, below.]

   Receiving Party:

   ☐ has received the above Confidential Information from Disclosing Party (_____).

   ☐ understands that Disclosing Party will immediately send the above Confidential Information to Receiving Party upon Disclosing Party's receipt, from Receiving Party, of a signed copy of this Agreement (_____).

   ☐ will show the above materials to Receiving Party on _____ (date) but will keep such Confidential Information in Disclosing Party's possession (_____).

3. **Loan of Tangible Copies of Confidential Information.** In the event that Disclosing Party furnishes physical or tangible copies of any of the Confidential Information to Receiving Party, Receiving Party acknowledges and agrees that these materials are furnished under the following conditions: (a) these materials are loaned to Receiving Party solely for purposes of evaluation and review; (b) these materials shall be treated consistent with the Receiving Party's obligation for Confidential Information under this Agreement; (c) Receiving Party may not copy or otherwise duplicate these materials; and (d) Receiving Party shall return to Disclosing Party any and all such material (including but not limited to records, notes, and other written, printed, or tangible materials) in its possession pertaining to Confidential Information immediately if Disclosing Party requests it in writing.

4. **Exclusions From Confidential Information.** Receiving Party's obligations under this Agreement do not extend to information that is: (a) publicly known at the time of disclosure or subsequently becomes publicly known through no fault of the Receiving Party; (b) discovered or created by the Receiving Party before disclosure by Disclosing Party; (c) learned by the Receiving Party through legitimate means other than from the Disclosing Party or Disclosing Party's representatives; or (d) is disclosed by Receiving Party with Disclosing Party's prior written approval.

5. **Obligations of Receiving Party.** Receiving Party shall hold and maintain the Confidential Information in strictest confidence for the sole and exclusive benefit of the Disclosing Party. Receiving Party shall carefully restrict access to Confidential Information to employees, contractors, and third parties as is

reasonably required and shall require those persons to sign nondisclosure restrictions at least as protective as those in this Agreement. Receiving Party shall not, without prior written approval of Disclosing Party, use for Receiving Party's own benefit, publish, copy, or otherwise disclose to others, or permit the use by others for their benefit or to the detriment of Disclosing Party, any Confidential Information.

6. **Time Periods.** The nondisclosure provisions of this Agreement shall survive the termination of this Agreement and Receiving Party's duty to hold Confidential Information in confidence shall remain in effect until the Confidential Information no longer qualifies as a trade secret or until Disclosing Party sends Receiving Party written notice releasing Receiving Party from this Agreement, whichever occurs first.

7. **Miscellaneous.** Nothing contained in this Agreement shall be deemed to constitute either party a partner, joint venturer, or employee of the other party for any purpose. If a court finds any provision of this Agreement invalid or unenforceable, the remainder of this Agreement shall be interpreted so as best to effect the intent of the parties. This Agreement expresses the complete understanding of the parties with respect to the subject matter and supersedes all prior proposals, agreements, representations, and understandings. This Agreement may not be amended except in a writing signed by both parties. The failure to exercise any right provided in this Agreement shall not be a waiver of prior or subsequent rights. This Agreement and each party's obligations shall be binding on the representatives, assigns, and successors of such party. Each party has signed this Agreement through its authorized representative.

Receiving Party: _____
(Print Name of Organization or Individual)

By: _____ Date: _____/_____/_____
(Signature)

_____
(Print Name and Title, if any)

Disclosing Party: _____
(Print Name of Organization or Individual)

By: _____ Date: _____/_____/_____
(Signature)

_____
(Print Name and Title, if any)

OTHER PERSONS WITHIN RECEIVING PARTY'S ORGANIZATION OBTAINING ACCESS TO CONFIDENTIAL INFORMATION:

Signature: _____ Date: _____/_____/_____

Print Name: _____

Signature: _____ Date: _____/_____/_____

Print Name: _____

Signature: _____ Date: _____/_____/_____

Print Name: _____

Invention Disclosure

Sheet _____ of _____

Inventor(s): _____

Address(es): _____

Title of Invention: _____

To record **Conception,** describe 1. Circumstances of conception, 2. Purposes and advantages of invention, 3. Description, 4. Sketches, 5. Operation, 6. Ramifications, 7. Possible novel features, and 8. Closest known prior art. To record **Building and Testing,** describe: 1. Any previous disclosure of conception, 2. Construction, 3. Ramifications, 4. Operation and Tests, and 5. Test results. Include sketches and photos, where possible. Continue on additional identical copies of this sheet if necessary; inventors and witnesses should sign all sheets.

Inventor(s): _____ Date: _____ / _____ / _____

_____ Date: _____ / _____ / _____

The following understand, have witnessed, and agree not to disclose the above confidential information:

_____ Date: _____ / _____ / _____

_____ Date: _____ / _____ / _____

Date: _____

Box DD
Commissioner for Patents
P.O. Box 1450
Alexandria, VA 22313-1450

Request for Participation in Disclosure Document Program

Disclosure of _____
Your Name(s)

Entitled: _____
Title of Disclosure

Sir:

Attached is a copy of a disclosure of my above-entitled invention (consisting of _____
sheets of written description and _____ separate drawings or photos), $_____
by ☐ check or money order or ☐ Credit Card Payment Form (PTO Form PTO-2038).

The undersigned respectfully requests that this disclosure be accepted and retained for two
years (or longer if it is later referred to in a paper filed in a patent application) under the
Disclosure Document Program and that the enclosed postcard be date stamped, numbered,
and returned.

The undersigned understands that (1) this disclosure document is neither a patent application
nor a substitute for one, (2) its receipt date will not become the effective filing date of a later-
filed patent application, (3) it will be retained for two years and then destroyed unless it is
referred to in a patent application, (4) this two-year retention period is not a "grace period"
during which a patent application can be filed without loss of benefits, (5) in addition to this
document, proof of diligence in building and testing the invention, and/or filing a patent
application on the invention, may be vital in case of an interference, and in other situations,
(6) if such building and testing is done, signed, and dated, records of such should additionally
be made and these should be witnessed and dated by disinterested individuals (not the PTO),
and (7) if any public use or sale of the invention is made in the U.S., or any publication is
made anywhere, no valid patent can be granted on the invention unless a patent application
is filed on it within one year of any such public use, sale, or publication, regardless of the
filing date of this Disclosure Document.

Very respectfully,

_____   _____
Signature of Inventor   Signature of Joint Inventor

_____   _____
Print Name   Print Name

_____   _____
Address   Address

_____   _____

Enclosures:
As stated above

In the United States Patent and Trademark Office

Serial Number: _____

Appn. Filed: _____

Applicant(s): _____

Appn. Title: _____

Examiner/GAU: _____

Disclosure Document Reference Letter

Date: _____

Commissioner for Patents
P.O. Box 1450
Alexandria, VA 22313-1450

Sir:

A disclosure document as identified below was previously filed in the Patent and Trademark Office. As this disclosure relates to the above patent application, applicant(s) request that this Disclosure Document be retained and referenced to the above application.

Disclosure Document Title: _____

Disclosure Document Number: _____

Disclosure Document Filing Date: _____

Very Respectfully,

_____ | _____
Signed Name | Signed Name

_____ | _____
Printed Name, First Applicant | Printed Name, Joint Applicant

_____ | _____
Address of First Applicant | Address of Joint Applicant

_____ | _____

In the United States Patent and Trademark Office

Mail Stop Provisional Patent Application   Mailed 200_____

Commissioner for Patents

P.O. Box 1450

Alexandria, VA 22313-1450

Sir:

Please file the enclosed Provisional Patent Application (PPA) papers listed below under 37 C.F.R. § 1.53(b)(2).

Each of the undersigned understands:

A. This PPA is not a substitute for a Regular Patent Application (RPA), cannot be converted to an RPA, cannot get into interference with an RPA of another person, cannot be amended, will not be published, cannot claim any foreign priority, and will not mature into a patent;

B. If an RPA referring to this PPA is not filed within one year of the filing date of this PPA, this PPA will be worthless and will be destroyed;

C. Any desired foreign Convention applications (including PCT applications) based upon this PPA *must* be filed within one year of the filing date of this PPA;

D. This PPA *must* contain a written description of the invention, and of the manner and process of making and using it, in such full, clear, concise, and exact terms as to enable any person skilled in the art to which it pertains, or with which it is most nearly connected, to make and use the same, and shall set forth the best mode contemplated by the inventor of carrying out his invention. 35 U.S.C. § 112, ¶ 1. Otherwise this PPA will be worthless.

E. Any RPA will be entitled to claim the benefit of this PPA only if such RPA names at least one inventor of this PPA and this PPA discloses such inventor's invention, as claimed in at least one claim of the RPA, in the matter provided in Item D above.

Inventor # 1, Name: _____

Legal Residence: _____

Inventor # 2, Name: _____

Legal Residence: _____

Title of Invention: _____

☐ Specification, sheets: _____   ☐ Drawing(s), sheets:_____

☐ Check or Credit Card Payment (use PTO-2038) for $_____ for   ☐ small entity
    ☐ large entity filing fee

☐ Return Receipt Postcard Addressed to Inventor # 1.

Very respectfully,

_____   _____
Signature of Inventor # 1   Signature of Inventor # 2

_____   _____
Print Name of Inventor # 1   Print Name of Inventor # 2

_____   _____
Telephone Number of Inventor # 1   Telephone Number of Inventor # 2

_____   _____
Address (Send Correspondence Here)   Address

_____   _____

_____   _____

Express Mail Label #_____; **Date of Deposit 200**_____

Positive and Negative Factors Evaluation

Inventor(s): _____   Invention: _____

_____

Factor	Weight (−100 to +100)	Factor	Weight (−100 to +100)
1. Cost	_____	31. Miscellaneous	_____
2. Weight	_____	32. Long Life Cycle	_____
3. Size	_____	33. Related Product Addability	_____
4. Safety/Health	_____	34. Satisfies Existing Need	_____
5. Speed	_____	35. Legality	_____
6. Ease of Use	_____	36. Operability	_____
7. Ease of Production	_____	37. Development	_____
8. Durability	_____	38. Profitability	_____
9. Repairability	_____	39. Obsolescence	_____
10. Novelty	_____	40. Incompatibility	_____
11. Convenience/Social Benefit/ Mechanization	_____	41. Product Liability Risk	_____
12. Reliability	_____	42. Market Dependence	_____
13. Ecology	_____	43. Difficulty of Distribution	_____
14. Salability	_____	44. Service Requirements	_____
15. Appearance	_____	45. New Tooling Required	_____
16. Viewability	_____	46. Inertia Must Be Overcome	_____
17. Precision	_____	47. Too Advanced Technically	_____
18. Noise	_____	48. Substantial Learning Required	_____
19. Odor	_____	49. Difficult to Promote	_____
20. Taste	_____	50. Lack of Market	_____
21. Market Size	_____	51. Crowded Field	_____
22. Trend of Demand	_____	52. Commodities	_____
23. Seasonal Demand	_____	53. Combination Products	_____
24. Difficulty of Market Penetration	_____	54. Entrenched Competition	_____
25. Potential Competition	_____	55. Instant Anachronism	_____
26. Quality	_____	56. Prototype Availability	_____
27. Excitement	_____	57. Broad Patent Coverage Available	_____
28. Markup	_____	58. High Sales Anticipated	_____
29. Inferior Performance	_____	59. Visibility of Invention in Final Product	_____
30. "Sexy" Packaging	_____	60. Ease of Packaging	_____

TOTAL _____

Signed: _____   Date: _____

Inventor(s)

Positive and Negative Factors Summary

Inventor(s):_____   Invention:_____

_____   _____

List Factors With Positive Values	**Weight**	**List Factors With Negative Values**	**Weight**
_____	_____	_____	_____
_____	_____	_____	_____
_____	_____	_____	_____
_____	_____	_____	_____
_____	_____	_____	_____
_____	_____	_____	_____
_____	_____	_____	_____
_____	_____	_____	_____
_____	_____	_____	_____
_____	_____	_____	_____
_____	_____	_____	_____
_____	_____	_____	_____
_____	_____	_____	_____
_____	_____	_____	_____
_____	_____	_____	_____
_____	_____	_____	_____
_____	_____	_____	_____
_____	_____	_____	_____
_____	_____	_____	_____
_____	_____	_____	_____
_____	_____	_____	_____
_____	_____	_____	_____
_____	_____	_____	_____
_____	_____	_____	_____

Positive Total _____   Negative Total _____

NET (Positive Total less Negative Total): _____

Signed: _____   Date: _____
_____Inventor(s)_____

Consultant's Work Agreement

1. **Parties:** This Work Agreement is made between the following parties:

    Name(s): _____

    Address(es): _____

    _____

    (hereinafter Contractor), and

    Name(s): _____

    Address(es): _____

    _____

    (hereinafter Consultant).

2. **Name of Project:** _____

    _____

    _____

3. **Work to Be Performed by Consultant:** _____

    _____

    _____

    _____

4. **Work/Payment Schedule:** _____

    _____

    _____

5. **Date:** This Agreement shall be effective as of the latter date below written.

6. **Recitals:** Contractor has one or more ideas relating to the above project and desires to have such project developed more completely, as specified in the above statement of Work. Consultant has certain skills desired by Contractor relating to performance of the above Work.

7. **Performance:** Consultant will perform the above work for Contractor, in accordance with the above-scheduled Work/Payment Schedule and Contractor will make the above scheduled payments to Consultant. Any changes to the Work to Be Performed or the Work/Payment Schedule shall be described in a writing referring to this Agreement and signed and dated by both parties. Time is of the essence of this Agreement, and if Consultant fails to perform according to the above work schedule, contractor may (a) void this agreement and pay consultant 50% of what would otherwise be due, or (b) require that Consultant pay contractor a penalty of $_____ per day.

8. **Intellectual Property:** All intellectual property, including trademarks, writings, information, trade secrets, inventions, discoveries, or improvements, whether or not registrable or patentable, which are conceived, constructed, or written by Consultant and arise out of or are related to work and services performed under this agreement, are, or shall become and remain, the sole and exclusive property of Contractor, whether or not such intellectual property is conceived during the time such work and services are performed or billed.

9A. **Protection of Intellectual Property:** Contractor and Consultant recognize that under U.S. patent laws, all patent applications must be filed in the name of the true and actual inventor(s) of the subject matter sought to be patented. Thus if Consultant makes any patentable inventions relating to the above project, Consultant agrees to be named as an applicant in any U.S. patent application(s) filed on such invention(s). Actual ownership of such patent applications shall be governed by clause 8.

9B. **Disclosure:** Consultant shall promptly disclose to Contractor in writing all information pertaining to any intellectual property generated or conceived by Consultant under this Agreement. Consultant hereby assigns and agrees to assign all of Consultant's rights to such intellectual property, including patent rights and foreign priority rights. Consultant hereby expressly agrees, without further charge for time, to do all things and sign all documents deemed by Contractor to be necessary or appropriate to invest in intellectual property, including obtaining for and vesting in Contractor all U.S. and foreign patents and patent applications which Contractor desires to obtain to cover such intellectual property, provided that Contractor shall bear all expenses relating thereto. All reasonable local travel time and expenses shall be borne by Consultant.

10. **Trade Secrets:** Consultant recognizes that all information relating to the above Project disclosed to Consultant by Contractor, and all information generated by Consultant in the performance of the above Work, is a valuable trade secret of Contractor and Consultant shall treat all such information as strictly confidential, during and after the performance of Work under this Agreement. Specifically Consultant shall not reveal, publish, or communicate any such information to anyone other than Contractor, and shall safeguard all such information from access to anyone other than Contractor, except upon the express written authorization of Contractor. This clause shall not apply to any information which Consultant can document in writing is presently in or enters the public domain from a bona fide source other than Consultant.

11. **Return of Property:** Consultant agrees to return all written materials and objects received from Contractor, to deliver to Contractor all objects and a copy (and all copies and originals if requested by Contractor) of all written materials resulting from or relating to work performed under this Agreement, and not to deliver to any person, organization, or publisher, or cause to be published, any such written material without prior written authorization.

12. **Conflicts of Interest:** Consultant recognizes a fiduciary obligation to Contractor arising out of the work and services performed under this agreement. Accordingly, Consultant will not offer services to or perform services for any competitor, potential or actual, of Contractor for the above Project. Consultant will not perform any other acts which may result in any conflict of interest by Consultant, during and after the term of this Agreement.

   [Check one]
   ☐ Consultant represents to Contractor that prior to this agreement, Consultant has not made and does not own any inventions relating to the above Project.
   ☐ Consultant has made or does own inventions relating to this Project and has provided a list of such inventions on a separate sheet incorporated in this Agreement by reference.

13. **Mediation and Arbitration:** If any dispute arises under this Agreement, the parties shall negotiate in good faith to settle such dispute. If the parties cannot resolve such dispute themselves, then either party may submit the dispute to mediation by a mediator approved by both parties. If the parties cannot agree to any mediator, or if either party does not wish to abide by any decision of the mediator, they shall submit the dispute to arbitration by any mutually acceptable arbitrator, or the American Arbitration Association (AAA). If the AAA is selected, the arbitration shall take place under the auspices of the nearest branch of such to both parties. The costs of the arbitration proceeding shall be borne according to the decision of the arbitrator, who may apportion costs equally, or in accordance with any finding of fault or lack of good faith of either party. The arbitrator's award shall be nonappealable and enforceable in any court of competent jurisdiction.

14. **Governing Law:** This Agreement shall be governed by and interpreted under and according to the laws of the State of _____.

15. **Signatures:** The parties have indicated their agreement to all of the above terms by signing this Agreement on the respective dates below indicated. Each party has received an original signed copy hereof.

Contractor: _____   Date: _____

Consultant: _____   Date: _____

Searcher's Worksheet

Sheet _____ of _____

Inventor(s): _____

Invention Description (use keywords and variations): _____

_____

_____

Selected Search Classifications

Class/Sub	Description	Checked	Comments
_____	_____	_____	_____
_____	_____	_____	_____
_____	_____	_____	_____
_____	_____	_____	_____
_____	_____	_____	_____
_____	_____	_____	_____
_____	_____	_____	_____

Patents (and Other References) Thought Relevant

Patent #	Name or Country	Date	Class/Sub	Comment
_____	_____	_____	_____	_____
_____	_____	_____	_____	_____
_____	_____	_____	_____	_____
_____	_____	_____	_____	_____
_____	_____	_____	_____	_____
_____	_____	_____	_____	_____
_____	_____	_____	_____	_____
_____	_____	_____	_____	_____
_____	_____	_____	_____	_____
_____	_____	_____	_____	_____
_____	_____	_____	_____	_____
_____	_____	_____	_____	_____
_____	_____	_____	_____	_____
_____	_____	_____	_____	_____
_____	_____	_____	_____	_____

Searcher: _____   Date: _____

Drawing Reference Numerals Worksheet

PART NAME		PART NAME	
10		84	
12		86	
14		88	
16		90	
18		92	
20		94	
22		96	
24		98	
26		100	
28		102	
30		104	
32		106	
34		108	
36		110	
38		112	
40		114	
42		116	
44		118	
46		120	
48		122	
50		124	
52		126	
54		128	
56		130	
58		132	
60		134	
62		136	
64		138	
66		140	
68		142	
70		144	
72		146	
74		148	
76		150	
78		152	
80		154	
82		156	

PTO/SB/01 (09-04)
Approved for use through 07/31/2006. OMB 0651-0032
U.S. Patent and Trademark Office; U.S. DEPARTMENT OF COMMERCE
Under the Paperwork Reduction Act of 1995, no persons are required to respond to a collection of information unless it contains a valid OMB control number.

DECLARATION FOR UTILITY OR DESIGN PATENT APPLICATION (37 CFR 1.63)

Attorney Docket Number	
First Named Inventor	
	COMPLETE IF KNOWN
Application Number	
Filing Date	
Art Unit	
Examiner Name	

☐ Declaration Submitted With Initial Filing   **OR**   ☐ Declaration Submitted after Initial Filing (surcharge (37 CFR 1.16 (e)) required)

I hereby declare that:

Each inventor's residence, mailing address, and citizenship are as stated below next to their name.

I believe the inventor(s) named below to be the original and first inventor(s) of the subject matter which is claimed and for which a patent is sought on the invention entitled:

(Title of the Invention)

the specification of which

☐   is attached hereto

OR

☐   was filed on (MM/DD/YYYY) _____ as United States Application Number or PCT International

Application Number _____ and was amended on (MM/DD/YYYY) _____ (if applicable).

I hereby state that I have reviewed and understand the contents of the above identified specification, including the claims, as amended by any amendment specifically referred to above.

I acknowledge the duty to disclose information which is material to patentability as defined in 37 CFR 1.56, including for continuation-in-part applications, material information which became available between the filing date of the prior application and the national or PCT international filing date of the continuation-in-part application.

I hereby claim foreign priority benefits under 35 U.S.C. 119(a)-(d) or (f), or 365(b) of any foreign application(s) for patent, inventor's or plant breeder's rights certificate(s), or 365(a) of any PCT international application which designated at least one country other than the United States of America, listed below and have also identified below, by checking the box, any foreign application for patent, inventor's or plant breeder's rights certificate(s), or any PCT international application having a filing date before that of the application on which priority is claimed.

Prior Foreign Application Number(s)	Country	Foreign Filing Date (MM/DD/YYYY)	Priority Not Claimed	Certified Copy Attached? YES	NO
			☐	☐	☐
			☐	☐	☐
			☐	☐	☐
			☐	☐	☐

☐   Additional foreign application numbers are listed on a supplemental priority data sheet PTO/SB/02B attached hereto.

[Page 1 of 2]

This collection of information is required by 35 U.S.C. 115 and 37 CFR 1.63. The information is required to obtain or retain a benefit by the public which is to file (and by the USPTO to process) an application. Confidentiality is governed by 35 U.S.C. 122 and 37 CFR 1.11 and 1.14. This collection is estimated to take 21 minutes to complete, including gathering, preparing, and submitting the completed application form to the USPTO. Time will vary depending upon the individual case. Any comments on the amount of time you require to complete this form and/or suggestions for reducing this burden, should be sent to the Chief Information Officer, U.S. Patent and Trademark Office, U.S. Department of Commerce, P.O. Box 1450, Alexandria, VA 22313-1450. DO NOT SEND FEES OR COMPLETED FORMS TO THIS ADDRESS. **SEND TO: Commissioner for Patents, P.O. Box 1450, Alexandria, VA 22313-1450.**
If you need assistance completing the form, call 1-800-PTO-9199 and select option 2.

Form 10-1: Patent Application Declaration

PTO/SB/01 (09-04)
Approved for use through 07/31/2006. OMB 0651-0032
U.S. Patent and Trademark Office; U.S. DEPARTMENT OF COMMERCE
Under the Paperwork Reduction Act of 1995, no persons are required to respond to a collection of information unless it contains a valid OMB control number.

DECLARATION — Utility or Design Patent Application

Direct all correspondence to:	☐ The address associated with Customer Number:		OR ☐	Correspondence address below

Name

Address

City	State	ZIP

Country	Telephone	Fax

I hereby declare that all statements made herein of my own knowledge are true and that all statements made on information and belief are believed to be true; and further that these statements were made with the knowledge that willful false statements and the like so made are punishable by fine or imprisonment, or both, under 18 U.S.C. 1001 and that such willful false statements may jeopardize the validity of the application or any patent issued thereon.

NAME OF SOLE OR FIRST INVENTOR: ☐ A petition has been filed for this unsigned inventor

Given Name (first and middle [if any])	Family Name or Surname

Inventor's Signature	Date

Residence: City	State	Country	Citizenship

Mailing Address

City	State	Zip	Country

NAME OF SECOND INVENTOR: ☐ A petition has been filed for this unsigned inventor

Given Name (first and middle [if any])	Family Name or Surname

Inventor's Signature	Date

Residence: City	State	Country	Citizenship

Mailing Address

City	State	Zip	Country

☐ Additional inventors or a legal representative are being named on the _____ supplemental sheet(s) PTO/SB/02A or 02LR attached hereto.

Form 10-1: Patent Application Declaration

PTO/SB/05 (09-04)
Approved for use through 07/31/2006. OMB 0651-0032
U.S. Patent and Trademark Office. U.S. DEPARTMENT OF COMMERCE
Under the Paperwork Reduction Act of 1995, no persons are required to respond to a collection of information unless it displays a valid OMB control number.

UTILITY PATENT APPLICATION TRANSMITTAL

(Only for new nonprovisional applications under 37 CFR 1.53(b))

Attorney Docket No.	
First Inventor	
Title	
Express Mail Label No.	

APPLICATION ELEMENTS
See MPEP chapter 600 concerning utility patent application contents.

ADDRESS TO: **Commissioner for Patents**
P.O. Box 1450
Alexandria VA 22313-1450

1. ☐ **Fee Transmittal Form** (e.g., PTO/SB/17)
(Submit an original and a duplicate for fee processing)

2. ☐ **Applicant claims small entity status.**
See 37 CFR 1.27.

3. ☐ **Specification** [*Total Pages_____*]
Both the claims and abstract must start on a new page
(For information on the preferred arrangement, see MPEP 608.01(a))

4. ☐ **Drawing(s)** (35 U.S.C. 113) [*Total Sheets _____*]

5. **Oath or Declaration** [*Total Sheets _____*]
a. ☐ Newly executed (original or copy)
b. ☐ A copy from a prior application (37 CFR 1.63(d))
(for continuation/divisional with Box 18 completed)
   i. ☐ DELETION OF INVENTOR(S)
      Signed statement attached deleting inventor(s)
      name in the prior application, see 37 CFR
      1.63(d)(2) and 1.33(b).

6. ☐ **Application Data Sheet.** See 37 CFR 1.76

7. ☐ **CD-ROM or CD-R** in duplicate, large table or
Computer Program (*Appendix*)
☐ Landscape Table on CD

8. **Nucleotide and/or Amino Acid Sequence Submission**
(if applicable, items a. – c. are required)
a. ☐ Computer Readable Form (CRF)
b. Specification Sequence Listing on:

   i. ☐ CD-ROM or CD-R (2 copies); or
   ii. ☐ Paper

c. ☐ Statements verifying identity of above copies

ACCOMPANYING APPLICATION PARTS

9. ☐ **Assignment Papers** (cover sheet & document(s))

   Name of Assignee_____

   _____

10. ☐ **37 CFR 3.73(b) Statement** ☐ **Power of**
(when there is an assignee) **Attorney**

11. ☐ **English Translation Document** (*if applicable*)

12. ☐ **Information Disclosure Statement** (PTO/SB/08 or PTO-1449)
☐ Copies of citations attached

13. ☐ **Preliminary Amendment**

14. ☐ **Return Receipt Postcard** (MPEP 503)
(Should be specifically itemized)

15. ☐ **Certified Copy of Priority Document(s)**
(if foreign priority is claimed)

16. ☐ **Nonpublication Request** under 35 U.S.C. 122(b)(2)(B)(i).
Applicant must attach form PTO/SB/35 or equivalent.

17. ☐ **Other:**_____

_____

18. If a CONTINUING APPLICATION, *check appropriate box, and supply the requisite information below and in the first sentence of the specification following the title, or in an Application Data Sheet under 37 CFR 1.76:*

☐ Continuation ☐ Divisional ☐ Continuation-in-part (CIP) of prior application No.: ....

Prior application information: Examiner _____ Art Unit: _____

19. CORRESPONDENCE ADDRESS

☐ The address associated with Customer Number: [_____] **OR** ☐ Correspondence address below

Name	
Address	

City		State		Zip Code	
Country		Telephone		Fax	

Signature		Date	
Name (Print/Type)		Registration No. (Attorney/Agent)	

This collection of information is required by 37 CFR 1.53(b). The information is required to obtain or retain a benefit by the public which is to file (and by the USPTO to process) an application. Confidentiality is governed by 35 U.S.C. 122 and 37 CFR 1.11 and 1.14. This collection is estimated to take 12 minutes to complete, including gathering, preparing, and submitting the completed application form to the USPTO. Time will vary depending upon the individual case. Any comments on the amount of time you require to complete this form and/or suggestions for reducing this burden, should be sent to the Chief Information Officer, U.S. Patent and Trademark Office, U.S. Department of Commerce, P.O. Box 1450, Alexandria, VA 22313-1450. DO NOT SEND FEES OR COMPLETED FORMS TO THIS ADDRESS. **SEND TO: Commissioner for Patents, P.O. Box 1450, Alexandria, VA 22313-1450.**
If you need assistance in completing the form, call 1-800-PTO-9199 and select option 2.

Form 10-2: Patent Application Transmittal

PTO/SB/17 (12-04v2)
Approved for use through 07/31/2006. OMB 0651-0032
U.S. Patent and Trademark Office; U.S. DEPARTMENT OF COMMERCE
Under the Paperwork Reduction Act of 1995, no persons are required to respond to a collection of information unless it displays a valid OMB control number

FEE TRANSMITTAL
For FY 2005

Effective on 12/08/2004.
Fees pursuant to the Consolidated Appropriations Act, 2005 (H.R. 4818).

☐ Applicant claims small entity status. See 37 CFR 1.27

TOTAL AMOUNT OF PAYMENT | ($)

Complete if Known

Application Number	
Filing Date	
First Named Inventor	
Examiner Name	
Art Unit	
Attorney Docket No.	

METHOD OF PAYMENT (check all that apply)

☐ Check   ☐ Credit Card   ☐ Money Order   ☐ None   ☐ Other (please identify):_____

☐ Deposit Account   Deposit Account Number:_____   Deposit Account Name:_____

For the above-identified deposit account, the Director is hereby authorized to: (check all that apply)

☐ Charge fee(s) indicated below   ☐ Charge fee(s) indicated below, **except for the filing fee**

☐ Charge any additional fee(s) or underpayments of fee(s)   ☐ Credit any overpayments
   under 37 CFR 1.16 and 1.17

WARNING: Information on this form may become public. Credit card information should not be included on this form. Provide credit card information and authorization on PTO-2038.

FEE CALCULATION

1. BASIC FILING, SEARCH, AND EXAMINATION FEES

Application Type	FILING FEES Fee ($)	Small Entity Fee ($)	SEARCH FEES Fee ($)	Small Entity Fee ($)	EXAMINATION FEES Fee ($)	Small Entity Fee ($)	Fees Paid ($)
Utility	300	150	500	250	200	100	_____
Design	200	100	100	50	130	65	_____
Plant	200	100	300	150	160	80	_____
Reissue	300	150	500	250	600	300	_____
Provisional	200	100	0	0	0	0	_____

2. EXCESS CLAIM FEES

Fee Description	Fee ($)	Small Entity Fee ($)
Each claim over 20 (including Reissues)	50	25
Each independent claim over 3 (including Reissues)	200	100
Multiple dependent claims	360	180

Total Claims	Extra Claims	Fee ($)	Fee Paid ($)
_____ - 20 or HP =	_____ x	_____ =	_____

HP = highest number of total claims paid for, if greater than 20.

Indep. Claims	Extra Claims	Fee ($)	Fee Paid ($)
_____ - 3 or HP =	_____ x	_____ =	_____

HP = highest number of independent claims paid for, if greater than 3.

Multiple Dependent Claims

Fee ($)	Fee Paid ($)
_____	_____

3. APPLICATION SIZE FEE

If the specification and drawings exceed 100 sheets of paper (excluding electronically filed sequence or computer listings under 37 CFR 1.52(e)), the application size fee due is $250 ($125 for small entity) for each additional 50 sheets or fraction thereof. See 35 U.S.C. 41(a)(1)(G) and 37 CFR 1.16(s).

Total Sheets	Extra Sheets	Number of each additional 50 or fraction thereof	Fee ($)	Fee Paid ($)
_____ - 100 =	_____ / 50 =	_____ (round **up** to a whole number) x	_____ =	_____

4. OTHER FEE(S)

Non-English Specification, $130 fee (no small entity discount)

Fees Paid ($)
_____

Other (e.g., late filing surcharge): _____
_____

SUBMITTED BY

Signature		Registration No. (Attorney/Agent)	Telephone
Name (Print/Type)			Date

This collection of information is required by 37 CFR 1.136. The information is required to obtain or retain a benefit by the public which is to file (and by the USPTO to process) an application. Confidentiality is governed by 35 U.S.C. 122 and 37 CFR 1.14. This collection is estimated to take 30 minutes to complete, including gathering, preparing, and submitting the completed application form to the USPTO. Time will vary depending upon the individual case. Any comments on the amount of time you require to complete this form and/or suggestions for reducing this burden, should be sent to the Chief Information Officer, U.S. Patent and Trademark Office, U.S. Department of Commerce, P.O. Box 1450, Alexandria, VA 22313-1450. DO NOT SEND FEES OR COMPLETED FORMS TO THIS ADDRESS. **SEND TO: Commissioner for Patents, P.O. Box 1450, Alexandria, VA 22313-1450.**

If you need assistance in completing the form, call 1-800-PTO-9199 and select option 2.

Form 10-3: Fee Transmittal

United States Patent and Trademark Office
Instructions for Completing the Credit Card Payment Form

Credit Card Information

- Enter all credit card information including the payment amount to be charged to your credit card and remember to sign the form. The United States Patent and Trademark Office (USPTO) cannot process credit card payments without an authorized signature.

- The USPTO does **not** accept debit cards or check cards that require use of a personal identification number as a method of payment.

Credit Card Billing Address

- Address information is required for credit card payment as a means of verification. Failure to complete the address information, including zip/postal code, may result in the payment not being accepted by your credit card institution.

Request and Payment Information

- Provide a description of your request based on the payment amount. For example, indicate the item as "basic filing fee" (patent) *or* "first maintenance fee" (patent maintenance fee) or "application for registration" (trademark) *or* "certified copy of a patent" (other fee).

- Indicate the nature of your request by the type of fee you wish to pay: Patent Fee, Patent Maintenance Fee, Trademark Fee or Other Fee. Complete information for each type of fee as applicable to identify the nature of your request. Indicate only one type of fee per form.

- If you are requesting and paying a fee based on a previously filed patent or trademark application, indicate the application/serial number, patent number or registration number that is associated with your request. "Other Fee" is used to request copies of patent and trademark documents, certified copies, assignments, and other information products.

- IDON numbers are assigned by the USPTO for customers ordering patent and trademark information and products specified as "Other Fee" on the order form. If you have been assigned an IDON number from a previous customer order, include it with your request.

- For more information on USPTO fees and amounts, refer to the current fee schedule at http://www.uspto.gov. To request a copy by mail, contact the USPTO General Information Services Division at (800) 786-9199 or (703) 308-4357.

Important Information

- The USPTO will not include the Credit Card Payment Form among the patent or trademark records open for public inspection. Failure to use the Credit Card Payment Form when submitting a credit card payment may result in the release of your credit card information.

- Information on mailing addresses is available at http://www.uspto.gov (click-on the "Site Index" tab, "Mailing Addresses" link). You may also contact the USPTO General Information Services Division for additional information, or to request a copy of the *Basic Facts about Patents* or *Basic Facts about Trademarks* information booklet by calling (800) 786-9199 or (703) 308-4357.

United States Patent and Trademark Office
Instructions for Completing the Credit Card Payment Form

Under the Paperwork Reduction Act of 1995, no persons are required to respond to a collection of information unless it displays a valid OMB control number.

United States Patent and Trademark Office
Credit Card Payment Form
Please Read Instructions before Completing this Form

Credit Card Information

Credit Card Type: ☐ Visa   ☐ MasterCard   ☐ American Express   ☐ Discover

Credit Card Account #:

Credit Card Expiration Date:

Name as it Appears on Credit Card:

Payment Amount: $ (US Dollars):

Cardholder Signature:	Date:

Refund Policy: The Office may refund a fee paid by mistake or in excess of that required. A change of purpose after the payment of a fee will not entitle a party to a refund of such fee. The office will not refund amounts of $25.00 or less unless a refund is specifically requested, and will not notify the payor of such amounts (37 CFR § 1.26). Refund of a fee paid by credit card will be issued as a credit to the credit card account to which the fee was charged.
Service Charge: There is a $50.00 service charge for processing each payment refused (including a check returned "unpaid') or charged back by a financial institution (37 CFR § 1.21 (m)) .

Credit Card Billing Address

Street Address 1:

Street Address 2:

City:

State/Province:	Zip/Postal Code:

Country:

Daytime Phone #:	Fax #:

Request and Payment Information

Description of Request and Payment Information:

☐ Patent Fee	☐ Patent Maintenance Fee	☐ Trademark Fee	☐ Other Fee
Application No.	Application No.	Application No.	IDON Customer No.
Patent No.	Patent No.	Registration No.	
Attorney Docket No.		Identify or Describe Mark	

If the cardholder includes a credit card number on any form or document other than the Credit Card Payment Form, the United States Patent and Trademark Office will not be liable in the event that the credit card number becomes public knowledge.

Form 10-4: Credit Card Payment Form

In the United States Patent and Trademark Office

Serial Number: _____

Appn. Filed: _____

Applicant(s): _____

Appn. Title: _____

Examiner/GAU: _____

Mailed: _____

At: _____

Information Disclosure Statement Cover Letter

Commissioner for Patents
P.O. Box 1450
Alexandria, VA 22313-1450

Sir:

Attached is a completed Form PTO/SB/08(A&B) and copies of any non-U.S. patent references cited thereon. Following are comments on any non-English-language references pursuant to Rule 98:

Very respectfully,

Applicant(s):_____

_____

Enc.: PTO/SB/08(A&B)

c/o:_____

_____

_____

Telephone: _____

Certificate of Mailing

I certify that this correspondence will be deposited with the United States Postal Service as first class mail with proper postage affixed in an envelope addressed to: "Commissioner for Patents, P.O. Box 1450, Alexandria, VA 22313-1450" on the date below.

Date: 200_____ _____, Applicant

PTO/SB/08A (08-03)
Approved for use through 07/31/2006. OMB 0651-0031
U.S. Patent and Trademark Office; U.S. DEPARTMENT OF COMMERCE
Under the Paperwork Reduction Act of 1995, no persons are required to respond to a collection of information unless it contains a valid OMB control number.

Substitute for form 1449/PTO

INFORMATION DISCLOSURE STATEMENT BY APPLICANT

(Use as many sheets as necessary)

Sheet ___ of ___

Complete if Known

Application Number	
Filing Date	
First Named Inventor	
Art Unit	
Examiner Name	
Attorney Docket Number	

U. S. PATENT DOCUMENTS

Examiner Initials*	Cite No.[1]	Document Number Number-Kind Code[2] *(if known)*	Publication Date MM-DD-YYYY	Name of Patentee or Applicant of Cited Document	Pages, Columns, Lines, Where Relevant Passages or Relevant Figures Appear
		US-			
		US-			
		US-			
		US-			
		US-			
		US-			
		US-			
		US-			
		US-			
		US-			
		US-			
		US-			
		US-			
		US-			
		US-			
		US-			
		US-			
		US-			
		US-			

FOREIGN PATENT DOCUMENTS

Examiner Initials*	Cite No.[1]	Foreign Patent Document Country Code[3]¯Number[4]¯Kind Code[5] *(if known)*	Publication Date MM-DD-YYYY	Name of Patentee or Applicant of Cited Document	Pages, Columns, Lines, Where Relevant Passages Or Relevant Figures Appear	T[6]

Examiner Signature		Date Considered	

*EXAMINER: Initial if reference considered, whether or not citation is in conformance with MPEP 609. Draw line through citation if not in conformance and not considered. Include copy of this form with next communication to applicant. [1] Applicant's unique citation designation number (optional). [2] See Kinds Codes of USPTO Patent Documents at www.uspto.gov or MPEP 901.04. [3] Enter Office that issued the document, by the two-letter code (WIPO Standard ST.3). [4] For Japanese patent documents, the indication of the year of the reign of the Emperor must precede the serial number of the patent document. [5] Kind of document by the appropriate symbols as indicated on the document under WIPO Standard ST.16 if possible. [6] Applicant is to place a check mark here if English language Translation is attached.

This collection of information is required by 37 CFR 1.97 and 1.98. The information is required to obtain or retain a benefit by the public which is to file (and by the USPTO to process) an application. Confidentiality is governed by 35 U.S.C. 122 and 37 CFR 1.14. This collection is estimated to take 2 hours to complete, including gathering, preparing, and submitting the completed application form to the USPTO. Time will vary depending upon the individual case. Any comments on the amount of time you require to complete this form and/or suggestions for reducing this burden, should be sent to the Chief Information Officer, U.S. Patent and Trademark Office, P.O. Box 1450, Alexandria, VA 22313-1450. DO NOT SEND FEES OR COMPLETED FORMS TO THIS ADDRESS. **SEND TO: Commissioner for Patents, P.O. Box 1450, Alexandria, VA 22313-1450.**

If you need assistance in completing the form, call 1-800-PTO-9199 (1-800-786-9199) and select option 2.

Form 10-6A: Information Disclosure Statement

PTO/SB/08B (08-03)
Approved for use through 07/31/2006. OMB 0651-0031
U.S. Patent and Trademark Office; U.S. DEPARTMENT OF COMMERCE
Under the Paperwork Reduction Act of 1995, no persons are required to respond to a collection of information unless it contains a valid OMB control number.

Substitute for form 1449/PTO	**Complete if Known**	
INFORMATION DISCLOSURE STATEMENT BY APPLICANT *(Use as many sheets as necessary)*	Application Number	
	Filing Date	
	First Named Inventor	
	Art Unit	
	Examiner Name	
Sheet [ ] of [ ]	Attorney Docket Number	

NON PATENT LITERATURE DOCUMENTS

Examiner Initials*	Cite No.[1]	Include name of the author (in CAPITAL LETTERS), title of the article (when appropriate), title of the item (book, magazine, journal, serial, symposium, catalog, etc.), date, page(s), volume-issue number(s), publisher, city and/or country where published.	T[2]

Examiner Signature		Date Considered	

*EXAMINER: Initial if reference considered, whether or not citation is in conformance with MPEP 609. Draw line through citation if not in conformance and not considered. Include copy of this form with next communication to applicant.

1 Applicant's unique citation designation number (optional). 2 Applicant is to place a check mark here if English language Translation is attached.
This collection of information is required by 37 CFR 1.98. The information is required to obtain or retain a benefit by the public which is to file (and by the USPTO to process) an application. Confidentiality is governed by 35 U.S.C. 122 and 37 CFR 1.14. This collection is estimated to take 2 hours to complete, including gathering, preparing, and submitting the completed application form to the USPTO. Time will vary depending upon the individual case. Any comments on the amount of time you require to complete this form and/or suggestions for reducing this burden, should be sent to the Chief Information Officer, U.S. Patent and Trademark Office, P.O. Box 1450, Alexandria, VA 22313-1450. DO NOT SEND FEES OR COMPLETED FORMS TO THIS ADDRESS. **SEND TO: Commissioner for Patents, P.O. Box 1450, Alexandria, VA 22313-1450.**

If you need assistance in completing the form, call 1-800-PTO-9199 (1-800-786-9199) and select option 2.

Form 10-6B: Information Disclosure Statement

PTO/SB/35 (09-04)
Approved for use through 07/31/2006. OMB 0651-0031
U.S. Patent and Trademark Office; U. S. DEPARTMENT OF COMMERCE
Under the Paperwork Reduction Act of 1995, no persons are required to respond to a collection of information unless it displays a valid OMB control number.

NONPUBLICATION REQUEST UNDER
35 U.S.C. 122(b)(2)(B)(i)

First Named Inventor	
Title	
Attorney Docket Number	

I hereby certify that the invention disclosed in the attached application **has not and will not be** the subject of an application filed in another country, or under a multilateral agreement, that requires publication at eighteen months after filing.

I hereby request that the attached application not be published under 35 U.S.C. 122(b).

_____
Signature

_____
Date

_____
Typed or printed name

_____
Registration Number, if applicable

_____
Telephone Number

This request must be signed in compliance with 37 CFR 1.33(b) and submitted with the application **upon filing.**

Applicant may rescind this nonpublication request at any time. If applicant rescinds a request that an application not be published under 35 U.S.C. 122(b), the application will be scheduled for publication at eighteen months from the earliest claimed filing date for which a benefit is claimed.

If applicant subsequently files an application directed to the invention disclosed in the attached application in another country, or under a multilateral international agreement, that requires publication of applications eighteen months after filing, the applicant **must** notify the United States Patent and Trademark Office of such filing within forty-five (45) days after the date of the filing of such foreign or international application. **Failure to do so will result in abandonment of this application (35 U.S.C. 122(b)(2)(B)(iii)).**

This collection of information is required by 37 CFR 1.213(a). The information is required to obtain or retain a benefit by the public which is to file (and by the USPTO to process) an application. Confidentiality is governed by 35 U.S.C. 122 and 37 CFR 1.11 and 1.14. This collection is estimated to take 6 minutes to complete, including gathering, preparing, and submitting the completed application form to the USPTO. Time will vary depending upon the individual case. Any comments on the amount of time you require to complete this form and/or suggestions for reducing this burden, should be sent to the Chief Information Officer, U.S. Patent and Trademark Office, U.S. Department of Commerce, P.O. Box 1450, Alexandria, VA 22313-1450. DO NOT SEND FEES OR COMPLETED FORMS TO THIS ADDRESS. **SEND TO: Commissioner for Patents, P.O. Box 1450, Alexandria, VA 22313-1450.**

If you need assistance in completing the form, call 1-800-PTO-9199 (1-800-786-9199) and select option 2.

Form 10-7: Nonpublication Request

In the United States Patent and Trademark Office

Serial Number: _____

Appn. Filed: _____

Applicant(s): _____

Appn. Title: _____

Examiner/GAU: _____

Mailed: _____

At: _____

Request Under MPEP 707.07(j)

Mail Stop Non-Fee Amendments
Commissioner for Patents
P.O. Box 1450
Alexandria, VA 22313-1450

Sir:

The undersigned, pro se applicant(s), respectfully requests that if the Examiner finds patentable subject matter disclosed in this application, but feels that Applicant's present claims are not entirely suitable, the Examiner draft one or more allowable claims for applicant, pursuant to MPEP 707.07(j).

Very respectfully,

_____   _____
Signature of Inventor # 1   Signature of Inventor # 2

_____   _____
Address   Address

_____   _____

_____   _____
Telephone   Telephone

In the United States Patent and Trademark Office

Serial Number: _____

Appn. Filed: _____

Applicant(s): _____

Appn. Title: _____

Examiner/GAU: _____

Mailed: _____

At: _____

Petition to Make Special

Commissioner for Patents
P.O. Box 1450
Alexandria, VA 22313-1450

Sir:

Applicant hereby respectfully petitions that the above application be made special under MPEP Sec. 708.02 for the following reason; attached is a declaration in support thereof:

I. ☐ Manufacturer Available;*

II. ☐ Infringement Exists;*

III. ☐ Applicant's Health Is Poor;

IV. ☐ Applicant's Age Is 65 or Greater;

V. ☐ Environmental Quality Will Be Enhanced;

VI. ☐ Energy Savings Will Result;

VII. ☐ Recombinant DNA Is Involved;*

VIII. ☐ Special Procedure: Search Was Made;*

IX. ☐ Superconductivity Is Advanced;

X. ☐ Relates to HIV/AIDS or Cancer;*

XI. ☐ Counters Terrorism.*

*☐ Also attached, since reason I, II, VII, VIII, X, or XI has been checked, is the $_____ Petition Fee pursuant to Rules 102 and 17(i).

Very respectfully,

Applicant(s): _____

_____

Attachment(s): Fee if indicated and supporting Declaration

Applicant(s): _____

_____

c/o: _____

_____

_____

Telephone: _____

Certificate of Mailing

I certify that this correspondence will be deposited with the United States Postal Service as first class mail with proper postage affixed in an envelope addressed to: "Commissioner for Patents, P.O. Box 1450, Alexandria, VA 22313-1450" on the date below.

Date: 200_____   _____, Applicant

Design Patent Application—Preamble, Specification, and Claim

Mail Stop Design
Commissioner for Patents
P.O. Box 1450
Alexandria, VA 22313-1450
Sir:

PREAMBLE:

The petitioner(s) whose signature(s) appear on the declaration attached respectfully request that Letters Patent be granted to such petitioner(s) for the new and original design set forth in the following specification. The filing fee of $_____, _____ sheets of drawings, a patent application declaration, fee transmittal, a credit card payment form or check, and a return receipt postcard are attached.

SPECIFICATION:

The undersigned has (have) invented a new, original, and ornamental design entitled "_____" of which the following is a specification. Reference is made to the accompanying drawings which form a part hereof, the figures of which are described as follows:

CROSS-REFERENCE TO RELATED APPLICATIONS:

STATEMENT REGARDING FEDERALLY SPONSORED RESEARCH:

DRAWING FIGURES:

FEATURE DESCRIPTION:

CLAIM: I (We) Claim:
The ornamental design for a _____, as shown and described.

Express Mail Label # (_____) ; **Date of Deposit 200**_____

PTO/SB/18 (09-04)
Approved for use through 06/30/2003. OMB 0651-0032
U.S. Patent and Trademark Office; U.S. DEPARTMENT OF COMMERCE
Under the Paperwork Reduction Act of 1995, no persons are required to respond to a collection of information unless it displays a valid OMB control number.

DESIGN PATENT APPLICATION TRANSMITTAL

(Only for new nonprovisional applications under 37 CFR 1.53(b))

Attorney Docket No.	
First Named Inventor	
Title	
Express Mail Label No.	

ADDRESS TO:
Commissioner for Patents
P.O. Box 1450
Alexandria, VA 22313-1450

DESIGN V. UTILITY: A "design patent" protects an article's ornamental appearance (e.g., the way an article looks) (35 U.S.C. 171), while a "utility patent" protects the way an article is used and works (35 U.S.C. 101). The ornamental appearance of an article includes its shape/configuration or surface ornamentation upon the article, or both. Both a design and a utility patent may be obtained on an article if invention resides both in its ornamental appearance and its utility. For more information, see MPEP 1502.01.

APPLICATION ELEMENTS
See MPEP 1500 concerning design patent application contents.

1. [ ] Fee Transmittal Form *(e.g., PTO/SB/17)*
   (Submit an original, and a duplicate for fee processing)

2. [ ] Applicant claims small entity status.
   See 37 CFR 1.27.

3. [ ] Specification   [*Total Pages* _____]
   (preferred arrangement set forth below, MPEP 1503.01)
   - Preamble
   - Cross References to Related Applications
   - Statement Regarding Fed sponsored R & D
   - Description of the figure(s) of the drawings
   - Feature description
   - Claim (only one (1) claim permitted, MPEP 1503.03)

4. [ ] Drawing(s) *(37 CFR 1.152)* [*Total Sheets* _____]

5. Oath or Declaration   [*Total Pages* _____]

   a. [ ] Newly executed (original or copy)

   b. [ ] A copy from a prior application (37 CFR 1.63(d))
      (for continuation/divisional with Box 16 completed)
      DELETION OF INVENTOR(S)
      i. [ ] Signed statement attached deleting inventor(s) named in the prior application, see 37 CFR 1.63(d)(2) and 1.33(b)

6. [ ] Application Data Sheet. See 37 CFR 1.76

ACCOMPANYING APPLICATION PARTS

7. [ ] Assignment Papers (cover sheet & document(s))

8. [ ] 37 CFR 3.73(b) Statement   [ ] Power of Attorney
   (when there is an assignee)

9. [ ] English Translation Document *(if applicable)*

10. [ ] Information Disclosure Statement (IDS) PTO/SB/08 or PTO-1449
    [ ] Copies of foreign patent documents, publications, & other information

11. [ ] Preliminary Amendment

12. [ ] Return Receipt Postcard (MPEP 503)
    (Should be specifically itemized)

13. [ ] Certified Copy of Priority Document(s)
    (if foreign priority is claimed)

14. [ ] Request for Expedited Examination of a Design Application (37 CFR 1.155) (NOTE: Use "Mail Stop Expedited Design"

15. [ ] Other:

16. If a CONTINUING APPLICATION, *check appropriate box, and supply the requisite information below and in the first sentence of the specification following the title, or in an Application Data Sheet under 37 CFR 1.76:*

[ ] Continuation   [ ] Divisional   [ ] Continuation-in-part (CIP) of prior application No.: _____

Prior application information: Examiner _____ *Art Unit:* _____

17. CORRESPONDENCE ADDRESS

[ ] The address associated with Customer Number: [_____]   **OR**   [ ] *Correspondence address below*

Name	
Address	

City		State		Zip Code	
Country		Telephone		Fax	

Signature		Date	
Name (Print/Type)		Registration No. (Attorney/Agent)	

This collection of information is required by 37 CFR 1.53(b). The information is required to obtain or retain a benefit by the public which is to file (and by the USPTO to process) an application. Confidentiality is governed by 35 U.S.C. 122 and 37 CFR 1.11 and 1.14. This collection is estimated to take 12 minutes to complete, including gathering, preparing, and submitting the completed application form to the USPTO. Time will vary depending upon the individual case. Any comments on the amount of time you require to complete this form and/or suggestions for reducing this burden, should be sent to the Chief Information Officer, U.S. Patent and Trademark Office, U.S. Department of Commerce, P.O. Box 1450, Alexandria, VA 22313-1450. DO NOT SEND FEES OR COMPLETED FORMS TO THIS ADDRESS. **SEND TO: Commissioner for Patents, P.O. Box 1450, Alexandria, VA 22313-1450.**
If you need assistance in completing the form, call 1-800-PTO-9199 and select option 2.

Form 10-11: Design Patent Application Transmittal

PTO/SB/27 (09-04)
Approved for use through 07/31/2006. OMB 0651-0031
U.S. Patent and Trademark Office; U.S DEPARTMENT OF COMMERCE
Under the Paperwork Reduction ACT of 1995, no persons are required to respond to collection of information unless it displays a valid OMB control number.

REQUEST FOR EXPEDITED EXAMINATION OF A DESIGN APPLICATION (37 CFR 1.155)	Application Number	
	Filing Date	
	First Named Inventor	
	Title	
	Atty Docket Number	

ADDRESS TO:

MAIL STOP EXPEDITED DESIGN
COMMISSIONER FOR PATENTS
P.O. Box 1450
Alexandria, VA 22313-1450

This is a request for expedited examination of a design application under 37 CFR 1.155.

NOTE: If the Request made by this form accompanies original application papers, include form PTO/SB/18 "Design Patent Application Transmittal" or its equivalent.

A preexamination search was conducted. The field of search was:

_____

_____

_____

Related applications: _____

If not previously filed for the above-identified application, the following items required by 37 CFR 1.155 are enclosed:

- Formal drawings (see 37 CFR 1.84).
- The fee set forth in 37 CFR 1.17(k).
- An information disclosure statement in compliance with 37 CFR 1.98.

_____	_____
Signature	Date
_____	_____
Typed or printed name	Registration Number, if applicable
_____	
Telephone Number	

WARNING: Information on this form may become public. Credit card information should not be included on this form. Provide credit card information and authorization on PTO-2038.

This collection of information is required by 37 CFR 1.155. The information is required to obtain or retain a benefit by the public which is to file (and by the USPTO to process) an application. Confidentiality is governed by 35 U.S.C. 122 and 37 CFR 1.11 and 1.14. This collection is estimated to take 6 minutes to complete, including gathering, preparing, and submitting the completed application form to the USPTO. Time will vary depending upon the individual case. Any comments on the amount of time you require to complete this form and/or suggestions for reducing this burden, should be sent to the Chief Information Officer, U.S. Patent and Trademark Office, U.S. Department of Commerce, P.O. Box 1450, Alexandria, VA 22313-1450. DO NOT SEND FEES OR COMPLETED FORMS TO THIS ADDRESS. **SEND TO: Commissioner for Patents, P.O. Box 1450, Alexandria, VA 22313-1450.**

If you need assistance in completing the form, call 1-800-PTO-9199 and select option 2.

Form 10-12: Request for Expedited Examination of a Design Application

In the United States Patent and Trademark Office

Serial Number: _____

Appn. Filed: _____

Applicant(s): _____

Appn. Title: _____

Examiner/GAU: _____

Mailed: _____

At: _____

Amendment _____

Commissioner for Patents
P.O. Box 1450
Alexandria, VA 22313-1450

Sir:

In response to the Office Letter mailed _____, 20_____, please amend
the above application as follows:

☐ SPECIFICATION: Amendments to the specification begin on page _____ of this amendment.

☐ DRAWINGS: Amendments to the drawings are discussed on page _____ of this amendment.

☐ CLAIMS: Amendments to the claims begin on page _____ of this amendment.

☐ REMARKS begin on page _____ of this amendment.

In the United States Patent and Trademark Office

Serial Number: _____

Appn. Filed: _____

Applicant(s): _____

Appn. Title: _____

Examiner/GAU: _____

Mailed: _____

At: _____

Submission of Corrected Drawings

Commissioner for Patents
P.O. Box 1450
Alexandria, VA 22313-1450
Attn: Chief Draftsperson

Sir:

New drawing sheet(s) (_____) for the above application is/are enclosed, corrected as necessary. Please substitute this/these for the corresponding sheet(s) on file.

☐ A copy of sheet(s) _____ is attached and is marked in red to indicate the changes being made.

Very respectfully,

Applicant(s):_____

_____

c/o:_____

_____

_____

Telephone: _____

Certificate of Mailing

I certify that this correspondence will be deposited with the United States Postal Service as first class mail with proper postage affixed in an envelope addressed to: "Commissioner for Patents, P.O. Box 1450, Alexandria, VA 22313-1450."

Date: 200_____   _____, Applicant

In the United States Patent and Trademark Office

Serial Number: _____

Appn. Filed: _____

Applicant(s): _____

Appn. Title: _____

Examiner/GAU: _____

Mailed: _____

At: _____

Supplemental Declaration
(for Use After Close of Prosecution or With Continuation-in-Part Application)

As an applicant in the above-identified application, I declare as follows:

1. If only one inventor is named below, I am a sole inventor, and if more than one inventor is named below, I am a joint inventor with the inventor(s) named below of the subject matter of the above-identified application.

2. I have reviewed and understand the contents of the specification and claims, as originally filed, and as amended by the amendment(s) dated _____.

3. I believe that I, and the other inventor(s) named below if more than one inventor is named below, am the original and first inventor or inventors of the subject matter which is claimed and for which a patent is sought.

4. I acknowledge the duty to disclose information which is material to the examination of the application in accordance with 37 C.F.R. Section 1.56(a), and if this oath accompanies or refers to a continuation-in-part application, I acknowledge the duty to disclose material information as defined in 37 C.F.R. Section 1.56(a) which occurred between the filing date of the prior application and the national or PCT international filing date of the continuation-in-part application.

5. I hereby declare that all statements made herein of my own knowledge are true and that all statements made on information and belief are believed to be true, and further that these statements were made with the knowledge that willful false statements and the like so made are punishable by fine or imprisonment, or both, under Section 1001 of Title 18 of the United States Code, and that such willful false statements may jeopardize the validity of the application, any patent issuing thereon, or any patent to which this verified statement is directed.

_____

Signature of Inventor

_____

Printed Name of Inventor

_____

Date

_____

Signature of Joint Inventor

_____

Printed Name of Joint Inventor

_____

Date

PETITION FOR EXTENSION OF TIME UNDER 37 CFR 1.136(a) FY 2005 *(Fees pursuant to the Consolidated Appropriations Act, 2005 (H.R. 4818).)*	Docket Number (Optional)
Application Number	Filed
For	
Art Unit	Examiner

This is a request under the provisions of 37 CFR 1.136(a) to extend the period for filing a reply in the above identified application.

The requested extension and fee are as follows (check time period desired and enter the appropriate fee below):

		Fee	Small Entity Fee	
☐	One month (37 CFR 1.17(a)(1))	$120	$60	$_____
☐	Two months (37 CFR 1.17(a)(2))	$450	$225	$_____
☐	Three months (37 CFR 1.17(a)(3))	$1020	$510	$_____
☐	Four months (37 CFR 1.17(a)(4))	$1590	$795	$_____
☐	Five months (37 CFR 1.17(a)(5))	$2160	$1080	$_____

☐ Applicant claims small entity status. See 37 CFR 1.27.

☐ A check in the amount of the fee is enclosed.

☐ Payment by credit card. Form PTO-2038 is attached.

☐ The Director has already been authorized to charge fees in this application to a Deposit Account.

☐ The Director is hereby authorized to charge any fees which may be required, or credit any overpayment, to Deposit Account Number _____. I have enclosed a duplicate copy of this sheet.

WARNING: Information on this form may become public. Credit card information should not be included on this form. Provide credit card information and authorization on PTO-2038.

I am the   ☐ applicant/inventor.

☐ assignee of record of the entire interest. See 37 CFR 3.71.
     Statement under 37 CFR 3.73(b) is enclosed (Form PTO/SB/96).

☐ attorney or agent of record. Registration Number _____

☐ attorney or agent under 37 CFR 1.34.
     Registration number if acting under 37 CFR 1.34 _____

_____	_____
Signature	Date
_____	_____
Typed or printed name	Telephone Number

NOTE: Signatures of all the inventors or assignees of record of the entire interest or their representative(s) are required. Submit multiple forms if more than one signature is required, see below.

☐ Total of _____ forms are submitted.

Form 13-4: Petition for Extension of Time

PTO/SB/30 (09-04)
Approved for use through 07/31/2006. OMB 0651-0031
U.S. Patent and Trademark Office; U.S. DEPARTMENT OF COMMERCE
Under the Paperwork Reduction Act of 1995, no persons are required to respond to a collection of information unless it contains a valid OMB control number.

Request for Continued Examination (RCE) Transmittal

Address to:
Mail Stop RCE
Commissioner for Patents
P.O. Box 1450
Alexandria, VA 22313-1450

Application Number	
Filing Date	
First Named Inventor	
Art Unit	
Examiner Name	
Attorney Docket Number	

This is a Request for Continued Examination (RCE) under 37 CFR 1.114 of the above-identified application.
Request for Continued Examination (RCE) practice under 37 CFR 1.114 does not apply to any utility or plant application filed prior to June 8, 1995, or to any design application. See Instruction Sheet for RCEs (not to be submitted to the USPTO) on page 2.

1. **Submission required under 37 CFR 1.114** Note: If the RCE is proper, any previously filed unentered amendments and amendments enclosed with the RCE will be entered in the order in which they were filed unless applicant instructs otherwise. If applicant does not wish to have any previously filed unentered amendment(s) entered, applicant must request non-entry of such amendment(s).

a. ☐ Previously submitted. If a final Office action is outstanding, any amendments filed after the final Office action may be considered as a submission even if this box is not checked.

i. ☐ Consider the arguments in the Appeal Brief or Reply Brief previously filed on _____

ii. ☐ Other _____

b. ☐ Enclosed

I. ☐ Amendment/Reply   iii. ☐ Information Disclosure Statement (IDS)

ii. ☐ Affidavit(s)/ Declaration(s)   iv. ☐ Other _____

2. **Miscellaneous**

a. ☐ Suspension of action on the above-identified application is requested under 37 CFR 1.103(c) for a period of _____ months. (Period of suspension shall not exceed 3 months; Fee under 37 CFR 1.17(i) required)

b. ☐ Other _____

3. **Fees** The RCE fee under 37 CFR 1.17(e) is required by 37 CFR 1.114 when the RCE is filed.

a. ☐ The Director is hereby authorized to charge the following fees, or credit any overpayments, to Deposit Account No. _____. I have enclosed a duplicate copy of this sheet.

i. ☐ RCE fee required under 37 CFR 1.17(e)

ii. ☐ Extension of time fee (37 CFR 1.136 and 1.17)

iii. ☐ Other _____

b. ☐ Check in the amount of $ _____ enclosed

c. ☐ Payment by credit card (Form PTO-2038 enclosed)

WARNING: Information on this form may become public. Credit card information should not be included on this form. Provide credit card information and authorization on PTO-2038.

SIGNATURE OF APPLICANT, ATTORNEY, OR AGENT REQUIRED

Signature		Date	
Name (Print/Type)		Registration No.	

CERTIFICATE OF MAILING OR TRANSMISSION

I hereby certify that this correspondence is being deposited with the United States Postal Service with sufficient postage as first class mail in an envelope addressed to: Mail Stop RCE, Commissioner for Patents, P. O. Box 1450, Alexandria, VA 22313-1450 or facsimile transmitted to the U.S. Patent and Trademark Office on the date shown below.

Signature		
Name (Print/Type)		Date

This collection of information is required by 37 CFR 1.114. The information is required to obtain or retain a benefit by the public which is to file (and by the USPTO to process) an application. Confidentiality is governed by 35 U.S.C. 122 and 37 CFR 1.11 and 1.14. This collection is estimated to take 12 minutes to complete, including gathering, preparing, and submitting the completed application form to the USPTO. Time will vary depending upon the individual case. Any comments on the amount of time you require to complete this form and/or suggestions for reducing this burden, should be sent to the Chief Information Officer, U.S. Patent and Trademark Office, U.S. Department of Commerce, P.O. Box 1450, Alexandria, VA 22313-1450. DO NOT SEND FEES OR COMPLETED FORMS TO THIS ADDRESS. **SEND TO: Mail Stop RCE, Commissioner for Patents, P.O. Box 1450, Alexandria, VA 22313-1450.**
If you need assistance in completing the form, call 1-800-PTO-9199 and select option 2.

Form 14-1: Request for Continued Examination (RCE) Transmittal

PTO/SB/30 (09-04)
Approved for use through 07/31/2006. OMB 0651-0031
U.S. Patent and Trademark Office; U.S. DEPARTMENT OF COMMERCE
Under the Paperwork Reduction Act of 1995, no persons are required to respond to a collection of information unless it contains a valid OMB control number.

Instruction Sheet for RCEs
(not to be submitted to the USPTO)

NOTES:

An RCE is not a new application, and filing an RCE will not result in an application being accorded a new filing date.

Filing Qualifications:
The application must be a utility or plant application filed on or after June 8, 1995. The application cannot be a provisional application, a utility or plant application filed before June 8, 1995, a design application, or a patent under reexamination. See 37 CFR 1.114(e).

Filing Requirements:
Prosecution in the application must be closed. Prosecution is closed if the application is under appeal, or the last Office action is a final action, a notice of allowance, or an action that otherwise closes prosecution in the application (e.g., an Office action under *Ex parte Quayle*). See 37 CFR 1.114(b).

A submission and a fee are required at the time the RCE is filed. If reply to an Office action under 35 U.S.C. 132 is outstanding (e.g., the application is under final rejection), the submission must meet the reply requirements of 37 CFR 1.111. If there is no outstanding Office action, the submission can be an information disclosure statement, an amendment, new arguments, or new evidence. See 37 CFR 1.114(c). The submission may be a previously filed amendment (e.g., an amendment after final rejection).

WARNINGS:

Request for Suspension of Action:
All RCE filing requirements must be met before suspension of action is granted. A request for a suspension of action under 37 CFR 1.103(c) does <u>not</u> satisfy the submission requirement and does not permit the filing of the required submission to be suspended.

Improper RCE will NOT toll Any Time Period:

Before Appeal - If the RCE is improper (e.g., prosecution in the application is not closed or the submission or fee has not been filed) and the application is not under appeal, the time period set forth in the last Office action will continue to run and the application will be abandoned after the statutory time period has expired if a reply to the Office action is not timely filed. No additional time will be given to correct the improper RCE.

Under Appeal - If the RCE is improper (e.g., the submission or the fee has not been filed) and the application is under appeal, the improper RCE is effective to withdraw the appeal. Withdrawal of the appeal results in the allowance or abandonment of the application depending on the status of the claims. If there are no allowed claims, the application is abandoned. If there is at least one allowed claim, the application will be passed to issue on the allowed claim(s). See MPEP 1215.01.

See MPEP 706.07(h) for further information on the RCE practice.

Form 14-1: Request for Continued Examination (RCE) Transmittal

In the United States Patent and Trademark Office

Patent No.: _____

Issued: _____

Patentee(s): _____

Ser. Nr.: _____

Filed: _____

Request for Certificate of Correction

Date: _____

Commissioner for Patents
P.O. Box 1450
Alexandria, VA 22313-1450

Sir:

    1. The above patent contains significant error, as indicated on the attached Certificate of Correction form (submitted in duplicate). These errors arose at the respective places in the application file indicated below.

☐ 2. Such error arose through the fault of the Patent and Trademark Office, therefore patentee requests that the Certificate be issued at no cost.

☐ 3. Such error arose through the fault of patentee(s). A check or CCPF for $_____ for the fee is enclosed. Such error is of a clerical or minor nature and occurred in good faith and therefore patentee requests issuance of the Certificate of Correction.

    4. Specifically,

Very respectfully,

_____   _____
Patentee   Co-Patentee

Encs.

_____   _____
Address

_____   _____

(_____)   – _____
Phone

PTO/SB/44 (04-04)
Approved for use through 04/30/2007. OMB 0651-0033
U.S. Patent and Trademark Office; U.S. DEPARTMENT OF COMMERCE
Under the Paperwork Reduction Act of 1995, no persons are required to respond to a collection of information unless it displays a valid OMB control number.
(Also Form PTO-1050)

UNITED STATES PATENT AND TRADEMARK OFFICE
CERTIFICATE OF CORRECTION

PATENT NO.   :

DATED   :

INVENTOR(S) :

It is certified that error appears in the above-identified patent and that said Letters Patent is hereby corrected as shown below:

MAILING ADDRESS OF SENDER: PATENT NO._____

No. of additional copies

This collection of information is required by 37 CFR 1.322, 1.323, and 1.324. The information is required to obtain or retain a benefit by the public which is to file (and by the USPTO to process) an application. Confidentiality is governed by 35 U.S.C. 122 and 37 CFR 1.14. This collection is estimated to take 1.0 hour to complete, including gathering, preparing, and submitting the completed application form to the USPTO. Time will vary depending upon the individual case. Any comments on the amount of time you require to complete this form and/or suggestions for reducing this burden, should be sent to the Chief Information Officer, U.S. Patent and Trademark Office, U.S. Department of Commerce, P.O. Box 1450, Alexandria, VA 22313-1450. DO NOT SEND FEES OR COMPLETED FORMS TO THIS ADDRESS. **SEND TO: Attention Certificate of Corrections Branch, Commissioner for Patents, P.O. Box 1450, Alexandria, VA 22313-1450.**

If you need assistance in completing the form, call 1-800-PTO-9199 and select option 2.

Form 15-2: Certificate of Correction

Maintenance Fee Reminder

Next fee due: _____/_____/_____
                        yr   mo   date

(Write year in pencil and change after each payment)

Patent Nr.: _____   Issued: _____

Application Serial Nr.: _____   Filed: _____

Title: _____

Patentee(s) (Inventor[s]/Applicant[s]): _____

Assignee(s) (if any): _____

Expires _____(if all three maintenance fees are paid).[1]

☐ Small entity status was filed in application or patent.
  (If not, large entity fees[2] must be paid.)

Maintenance Fee Number	Fee Due From:	To:	Sent Form & Check [4]	Amount	Received Receipt Statement
I. Due 3.0 - 3.5 YAI [3]	/ /	/ /	/ /	$	/ /
II. Due 7.0 - 7.5 YAI	/ /	/ /	/ /	$	/ /
III. Due 11.0 - 11.5 YAI	/ /	/ /	/ /	$	/ /

Notes: _____

_____

_____

_____

_____

_____

_____

_____

_____

_____

1. Expiration is 20 years from filing date of application for applications filed after 1995 Jun 7; 17 years from issue date for patents issuing before 1995 Jun 8; and the greater of 17– or 20–year term for patents issuing after 1995 Jun 7 and filed before 1995 Jun 8, provided you pay all three maintenance fees.

2. Please check all fee amounts before paying, since PTO fees change often.

3. YAI = Years After Issue date.

4. Send or make Internet payment at least a month before due date to allow time to take corrective action before entering grace (penalty) period in case PTO does not accept payment.

In the United States Patent and Trademark Office

Patent No.: _____

Issued: _____

Patentee(s): _____

Ser. Nr.: _____

Filed: _____

Submission of Maintenance Fee

United States Patent and Trademark Office
P.O. Box 371611
Pittsburgh, PA 15250-1611

Sir:

Enclosed is the following maintenance fee for the above patent: this fee is for a ☐ large entity ☐ small entity, since small-entity status was filed in connection with the above application and small-entity status is still proper.

☐ 3.5 yr fee; $ _____; due 3.0 to 3.5 yrs after issue; covers yrs 4.0 thru 8.0.

☐ 7.5 yr fee; $ _____; due 7.0 to 7.5 yrs after issue; covers yrs 8.0 thru 12.0.

☐ 11.5 yr fee; $_____; due 11.0 to 11.5 yrs after issue; covers yrs 12.0 thru expiration.

☐ Also enclosed is a surcharge of $ _____ (total enclosed $ _____) since this
   fee is being filed in the six-month grace period after the above due period.

Very respectfully,

_____
Either Patentee/Assignee

_____
Address

_____

(_____) _____ – _____
Phone

Certificate of Mailing or Faxing

I certify that I will ☐ mail this correspondence with the U.S. Postal Service as First Class Mail in an envelope addressed to "United States Patent and Trademark Office, P.O. Box 371611, Pittsburgh, PA 15250-1611" ☐ fax this correspondence to the U.S. Patent and Trademark Office, at 703-308-5077 on the date below.

Date: 200_____   _____ , Patentee

 www.nolo.com   **Form 15-4: Submission of Maintenance Fee**   Page 1 of 1

Joint Applicants—Statement of Respective Contributions

The parties to this statement are Joint Applicants (JAs) to the invention or patent application entitled:

"_____"

We recognize that a patent application or patent can be held invalid if:

- a person is named as a JA without having contributed to at least one claim or
- a true joint inventor is not named as a JA.

We also recognize and agree that if the patent claims in any patent application based on the invention are altered so that the listing of any JA is inappropriate, that JA should be removed from the patent application.

In order to keep the contributions of the JAs in order and preserve them, we hereby record each JA's contributions as follows:

Joint Applicant	**Contribution**

Signature: _____ _____

Print Name: _____ _____

Date: _____ _____

_____

_____

_____

_____

Signature: _____ _____

Print Name: _____ _____

Date: _____ _____

_____

_____

_____

_____

Joint Owners' Agreement

This agreement is made by and between the following parties who, by separate assignment or as joint applicants, own the following respective shares of the invention, patent application, or patent identified below:

_____ _____ of _____, _____%,

_____ _____ of _____, _____%,

_____ _____ of _____, _____%.

Invention Title: _____

Patent Application Ser. Nr.: _____, Filed: _____

Patent Nr.: _____, Issued: _____

Applicants: _____

_____

The above patent application data is to be filled in as soon as it becomes available if the application has not yet been filed.

The parties desire to stipulate the terms under which they will exploit this invention and patent application and therefore agree as follows:

1. **No Action Without Everyone's Consent:** None of the parties to this agreement shall license, use, make, or sell the invention or application, or take any other action, other than normal prosecution, without the written consent and cooperation of the other party or parties (hereinafter "parties") to this agreement, except as provided below. Any action so taken shall be committed to a writing signed by all of the parties, or as many parties as consent, with copies to all other parties.

2. **Decisions:** In case any decision must be made in connection with the invention or the patent application, including foreign filing, appealing from an adverse decision in the Patent and Trademark Office, or any opportunity to license, sell, make, or use the invention or application, the parties shall consult on such opportunity and a majority decision shall control. In the event the parties are equally divided, the matter shall be decided in accordance with Paragraph 5 below. After a decision is so made, all parties shall abide by the decision and shall cooperate fully by whatever means are necessary to implement and give full force to such decision. However, if an offer is involved and there is time for any parties to obtain a better or different offer, they shall be entitled to do so and the decision shall be postponed for up to one month to allow such other parties to act.

3. **Proportionate Sharing:** The parties to this agreement shall share, in the percentages indicated above, in all income from, liabilities, and expenditures agreed to be made by any decision under Part 2 above in connection with the invention or patent application. In case a decision is made to make any expenditure, as for foreign patent application filing, exploitation, etc., and a minority or other parties opposes such expenditure or is unable to contribute his or her proportionate share, then the others shall advance the minority or other parties' share of the expenditure. Such others shall be reimbursed by the minority or other parties by double the amount so advanced from the minority or other parties' proportionate share of any income received, provided such income has some reasonable connection with the expenditure. No party shall be entitled to reimbursement or credit for any labor unless agreed to in advance by all of the parties hereto.

4. **If Any Parties Desire to Manufacture, Etc.:** If any parties who do not constitute all of the parties to this agreement desire to manufacture, distribute, or sell any product or service embodying the above invention, they may do so with the written consent of the other parties under Part 1 above. The cost of the product or service shall include, in addition to normal profit, labor, commission, and/or overhead, etc., provision for a reasonable royalty which shall be paid for the term of the above patent application and any patent which may issue thereon. Such royalty shall be determined before any action is taken under this part and as if a valid patent on the invention had been licensed to an unrelated exclusive licensee (or a nonexclusive licensee if the patent is licensed to others) in an arm's-length transaction. Such royalty shall be distributed to all of the parties hereto according to their proportionate shares and on a quarterly basis, accompanied by a written royalty report and sent within one month after the close of each calendar quarter.

5. **In Case of Dispute:** In case any dispute, disagreement, or need for any decision arises out of this agreement or in connection with the invention or patent application, and the parties cannot settle the matter or come to a decision in accordance with Paragraph 2, above, the parties shall first confer as much as necessary to settle the disagreement; all parties shall act and compromise to at least the degree a reasonable person would act. If the parties cannot settle their differences or come to a decision on their own, they shall submit the dispute or matter to mediation by an impartial third party or professional mediator agreed to by all of the parties. If the parties cannot agree on a mediator, or cannot come to an agreement after mediation, then they shall submit the matter to binding arbitration with a mutually acceptable arbitrator or the American Arbitration Association. The arbitrator shall settle the dispute in whatever manner he or she feels will do substantial justice, recognizing the rights of all parties and commercial realities of the marketplace. The parties shall abide by the terms of the arbitrator's decision and shall cooperate fully and do any acts necessary to implement such decision. The costs of the arbitrator shall be advanced by all of the parties or in accordance with Part 3 above and the arbitrator may make any allocation of arbitration costs he or she feels is reasonable.

6. **Nonfrustration:** No party to this Agreement shall commit any act or take any action which frustrates or hampers the rights of another party under this Agreement. Each party shall act in good faith and engage in fair dealing when taking any action under or related to this Agreement.

Signature

Date

Signature

Date

Signature

Date

Assignment of Invention and Patent Application

For value received, _____ ,

_____

of _____

_____

(hereinafter ASSIGNOR), hereby sells, assigns, transfers, and sets over unto _____

_____

of _____

and her or his successors or assigns (hereinafter ASSIGNEE) _____% of the following: (A) ASSIGNOR'S

right, title, and interest in and to the invention entitled "_____

_____ "

invented by ASSIGNOR; (B) the application for United States patent therefor, signed by ASSIGNOR on

_____ ,U.S. Patent and Trademark Office Serial Number _____ ,

filed _____ ; (C) any patent or reissues of any patent that may be granted

thereon; and (D) any applications which are continuations, continuations-in-part, substitutes, or divisions

of said application. ASSIGNOR authorizes ASSIGNEE to enter the date of signature and/or Serial Number

and Filing Date in the spaces above. ASSIGNOR also authorizes and requests the Commissioner for

Patents to issue any resulting patent(s) as follows: _____% to ASSIGNOR and _____%

to ASSIGNEE. (The singular shall include the plural and vice versa herein.)

ASSIGNOR hereby further sells, assigns, transfers, and sets over unto ASSIGNEE, the above percentage
of ASSIGNOR'S entire right, title, and interest in and to said invention in each and every country foreign
to the United States; and ASSIGNOR further conveys to ASSIGNEE the above percentage of all priority
rights resulting from the above-identified application for United States patent. ASSIGNOR agrees to
execute all papers, give any required testimony, and perform other lawful acts, at ASSIGNEE'S expense,
as ASSIGNEE may require to enable ASSIGNEE to perfect ASSIGNEE'S interest in any resulting patent of
the United States and countries foreign thereto, and to acquire, hold, enforce, convey, and uphold the
validity of said patent and reissues and extensions thereof, and ASSIGNEE'S interest therein.

In testimony whereof ASSIGNOR has hereunto set its hand and seal on the date below.

_____   _____
Signature   Date

_____   _____
Signature   Date

Witnessed by:

_____   _____
Signature   Date

_____   _____
Signature   Date

Form **PTO-1595** (Rev. 06/04)
OMB No. 0651-0027 (exp. 6/30/2005)

RECORDATION FORM COVER SHEET
PATENTS ONLY

To the Director of the U.S. Patent and Trademark Office: Please record the attached documents or the new address(es) below.

1. **Name of conveying party(ies)/Execution Date(s):**	2. **Name and address of receiving party(ies)**
	Name: _____
	Internal Address: _____
	_____
Execution Date(s)_____	Street Address: _____
Additional name(s) of conveying party(ies) attached? ☐ Yes ☐ No	_____

3. Nature of conveyance:

☐ Assignment   ☐ Merger

☐ Security Agreement   ☐ Change of Name

☐ Government Interest Assignment

☐ Executive Order 9424, Confirmatory License

☐ Other_____

City: _____

State: _____

Country:_____Zip:_____

Additional name(s) & address(es) attached? ☐ Yes ☐ No

4. Application or patent number(s):

☐ This document is being filed together with a new application.

A. Patent Application No.(s)   B. Patent No.(s)

Additional numbers attached? ☐ Yes ☐ No

5. Name and address to whom correspondence concerning document should be mailed:

Name:_____

Internal Address:_____

_____

Street Address:_____

_____

City: _____

State:_____Zip:_____

Phone Number:_____

Fax Number:_____

Email Address:_____

6. Total number of applications and patents involved: [ ]

7. Total fee (37 CFR 1.21(h) & 3.41) $_____

☐ Authorized to be charged by credit card

☐ Authorized to be charged to deposit account

☐ Enclosed

☐ None required (government interest not affecting title)

8. Payment Information

a. Credit Card   Last 4 Numbers _____
                 Expiration Date _____

b. Deposit Account Number _____

   Authorized User Name _____

9. Signature:

_____   _____
Signature   Date

_____
Name of Person Signing

Total number of pages including cover sheet, attachments, and documents: [ ]

Documents to be recorded (including cover sheet) should be faxed to (703) 306-5995, or mailed to:
Mail Stop Assignment Recordation Services, Director of the USPTO, P.O.Box 1450, Alexandria, V.A. 22313-1450

Form 16-3B: Recordation Form Cover Sheet

Guidelines for Completing Patents Cover Sheets (PTO-1595)

Cover Sheet information must be submitted with each document to be recorded. If the document to be recorded concerns both patents and trademarks separate patent and trademark cover sheets, including any attached pages for continuing information, must accompany the document. All pages of the cover sheet should be numbered consecutively, for example, if both a patent and trademark cover sheet is used, and information is continued on one additional page for both patents and trademarks, the pages of the cover sheet would be numbered from 1 to 4.

Item 1. Name of Conveying Party(ies).

Enter the full name of the party(ies) conveying the interest and the execution date(s) of the document. It is preferable to use the name of the month, or an abbreviation of that name, in order that confusion over dates is minimized. If there is insufficient space, enter a check mark in the "Yes" box to indicate that additional information is attached. The name of the additional conveying party(ies) should be placed on an attached page clearly identified as a continuation of the information Item 1. Enter a check mark in the "No" box, if no information is contained on an attached page.

Item 2. Name and Address of Receiving Party(ies).

Enter the name and full address of the first party receiving the interest. If there is more than one party receiving the interest, enter a check mark in the "Yes" box to indicate that additional information is attached. Enter a check mark in the "No" box, if no information is contained on an attached page.

Item 3. Nature of Conveyance.

Place a check mark in the appropriate box describing the nature of the conveying document. If the "Other" box is checked, specify the nature of the conveyance.

Item 4. Application Number(s) or Patent Number(s).

Indicate the application number(s), and/or patent number(s) against which the document is to be recorded. National application numbers must include both the series code and a six-digit number (e.g., 07/123,456), and international application numbers must be complete (e.g., PCT/US91/12345).

Enter a check mark in the appropriate box: "Yes" or "No " if additional numbers appear on attached pages. Be sure to identify numbers included on attached pages as the continuation of Item 4. Also enter a check mark if this Assignment is being filed with a new application.

Item 5. Name and Address of Party to whom correspondence concerning the document should be mailed.

Enter the name and full address of the party to whom correspondence is to be mailed.

Item 6. Total Applications and Patents involved.

Enter the total number of applications and patents identified for recordation. Be sure to include all applications and patents identified on the cover sheet and on additional pages.

Block 7. Total Fee Enclosed.

Enter the total fee enclosed or authorized to be charged. A fee is required for each application and patent against which the document is recorded.

Item 8. Payment Information.

Enter either the last four digits of your credit card and expiration date or the deposit account number and authorized user name to authorize charges.

Item 9. Signature.

Enter the name of the person submitting the document. The submitter must sign and date the cover sheet. Enter the total number of pages including the cover sheet, attachments, and document.

Universal License Agreement

1. **Parties and Summary of Terms:**

Parties: This agreement is between:

Licensor: _____,

of _____.

Licensee: _____,

of _____.

Summary: Type of License: ☐ Exclusive ☐ Nonexclusive

Invention Title: _____.

Patent Application Ser. Nr.: _____, Filing Date: _____

If Exclusive License, minimum number of units to be sold to compute Minimum Annual

Royalty (MAR): _____

    MARs start first quarter of _____.

☐ Option Granted: Premium $_____ For term of: (months)_____

Patent Royalty Rate _____% ☐ Know-How Licensed: Know-How Royalty Rate: _____%

Total Royalty Rate (Patent Royalty Rate plus Know-How Royalty, if applicable): _____%.

Estimated 1st year's sales (units): _____ x Estimated Unit Price $_____

    x Total Royalty Rate _____%   = Licensing Fee $_____

2. **Effective Date:** This agreement shall be effective as of the latter of the signature dates below written and shall be referred to as the Agreement of such date.

3. **Recitals:**

   A. **LICENSOR** has developed an invention having the above title and warrants that LICENSOR has filed a patent application on such invention in the U.S. Patent and Trademark Office, which patent application is identified by the above title, Serial Number, and Filing Date. LICENSOR warrants that LICENSOR has full and exclusive right to grant this license on this invention and LICENSOR'S patent application. If the "Know-How Licensed" box above is checked, LICENSOR has also developed know-how in connection with said invention and warrants that LICENSOR owns and has the right to license said know-how.

   B. **LICENSEE** desires, if the "Option Granted" box above is checked, to exclusively investigate LICENSOR'S above invention for the term indicated. If said "Option Granted" box is not checked, or if said box is checked and LICENSEE investigates LICENSOR'S invention for the term indicated and such investigation is favorable, LICENSEE desires to make, use, and sell the products embodying such invention and covered by the claims of LICENSOR'S patent application and any patent(s) issuing thereon (hereinafter "Licensed Product").

4. **If Option Granted:** If the "Option Granted" box above is checked, then (A) the patent license grant of Part 5 below shall not take effect except as defined in this part, and (B) LICENSOR hereby grants LICENSEE, for the option premium stated above, an exclusive option to investigate LICENSOR'S invention for the term indicated above, such term to commence from the date of this Agreement. LICENSOR will furnish LICENSEE with all information and know-how (if any) concerning LICENSOR'S invention in LICENSOR'S possession. LICENSEE will investigate LICENSOR'S invention for operability, costing, marketing, etc. LICENSEE shall report the results of its investigation to LICENSOR at any time before the end of the option term. If LICENSEE'S determination is favorable, it may thereupon exercise this option and the patent license grant of Part 5 below shall become effective. If LICENSEE'S determination is unfavorable, then said option shall not be

exercised and no patent license grant shall take effect, all rights hereunder shall revert to LICENSOR, LICENSEE shall deliver to LICENSOR all results of its investigations for LICENSOR'S benefit, and LICENSEE shall promptly return to LICENSOR all know-how (papers and things) received from LICENSOR or generated by LICENSEE in its investigations.

5. **Patent License If Option Exercised or If Option Not Granted:** If the "Option Granted" box above is checked and LICENSEE has investigated LICENSOR'S invention and such investigation is favorable and LICENSEE has exercised its option, or if said box is not checked, then LICENSOR hereby grants to LICENSEE, subject to the terms and conditions herein, a patent license of the type (Exclusive or Nonexclusive) checked above. Such patent license shall include the right to grant sublicenses, to make, have made, use, and sell the Licensed Product throughout the United States, its territories, and possessions. Such patent license shall be under LICENSOR'S patent application, any continuations, divisions, continuations-in-part, substitutes, reissues of any patent from any of such applications (hereinafter and hereinbefore LICENSOR'S patent application), any patent(s) issuing thereon, and if the "Know-How Licensed" box is checked above, any know-how transferred to LICENSEE.

6. **If Know-How Licensed:** If the "Know-How" box above is checked, LICENSOR shall communicate to LICENSEE all of LICENSOR'S know-how in respect of LICENSOR'S invention within one month after the date of this Agreement and shall be available to consult with LICENSEE, for up to 80 hours, with respect to the licensed invention and know-how. All travel and other expenses of LICENSOR for such consultation shall be reimbursed by LICENSEE within one month after LICENSOR submits its voucher therefor. LICENSOR makes no warranty regarding the value, suitability, or workability of such know-how. The royalty applicable for such know-how shall be paid, at the rate indicated above, for a minimum of three years from the date of this Agreement if no option is granted, or for three years from the date of exercise if an option is granted and exercised by LICENSOR, and thereafter for so long as LICENSEE makes, uses, or sells Licensed Products and has a share in the United States for of at least 15% of the competitive market for Licensed Products.

7. **Royalties:**
   A. **Licensing Fee:** Unless the "Option Granted" box above is checked, LICENSEE shall pay to LICENSOR, upon execution of this Agreement, a nonrefundable Licensing Fee. This Licensing Fee shall also serve as an advance against future royalties. Such Licensing Fee shall be computed as follows: (A) Take the Total Royalty Rate in percent, as stated above. (B) Multiply by LICENSEE'S Estimate of Its First Year's Sales, in units of Licensed Product, as stated above. (C) Multiply by LICENSEE'S Estimated Unit Price of Licensed Product, in dollars, as stated above. (D) The combined product shall be the Licensing Fee, in dollars, as stated above. When LICENSEE begins actual sales of the Licensed Product, it shall certify its Actual Net Factory Sales Price of Licensed Product to LICENSOR in writing and shall either (1) simultaneously pay LICENSOR any difference due if the Actual Net Factory Sales Price of Licensed Product is more than the Estimated Unit Price, stated above, or (2) advise LICENSOR of any credit to which LICENSEE is entitled if the Actual Net Factory Sales Price of Licensed Product is less than the above Estimated Unit Price. In the latter case, LICENSEE may deduct such credit from its first royalty remittance to LICENSOR, under subpart B below. If an option is granted and exercised under Part 4 above, then LICENSEE shall pay this Licensing Fee to LICENSOR if and when LICENSEE exercises its option.

B. Royalty: If the "Option Granted" box above is not checked, or if said box is checked and LICENSEE has exercised its option under Part 4, LICENSEE shall also pay to LICENSOR a Total Royalty, at the rate stated above. Such royalty shall be at the Patent Royalty Rate stated in Part 1 above, plus, if the "Know-How Licensed" box above is checked, a Know-How Royalty at the Know-How Royalty Rate stated above. Said Total Royalty shall be computed on LICENSEE'S Net Factory Sales Price of Licensed Product. Such Total Royalty shall accrue when the Licensed Products are first sold or disposed of by LICENSEE, or by any sublicensee of LICENSEE. LICENSEE shall pay the Total Royalty due to LICENSOR within one month after the end of each calendar quarter, together with a written report to LICENSOR of the number of units, respective sales prices, and total sales made in such quarter, together with a full itemization of any adjustments made pursuant to subpart F below. LICENSEE'S first report and payment shall be made within one month after the end of the first calendar quarter following the execution of this Agreement. No royalties shall be paid by LICENSEE to LICENSOR until after the Licensing Fee under subpart A above has been earned, but LICENSEE shall make a quarterly report hereunder for every calendar quarter after the execution hereof, whether or not any royalty payment is due for such quarter, except that if an option is granted, LIC-ENSEE shall not make any royalty reports until and if LICENSEE exercises its option.

C. Minimum Annual Royalties: If the "Exclusive" box above is checked, so that this is an exclusive license, then this subpart C and subpart D shall be applicable. But if the "Nonexclusive" box is checked above, then these subparts C and D shall be inapplicable. There shall be no minimum annual royalties due under this Agreement until the "Year Commencing," as identified in Part 1 above. For the exclusivity privilege of the patent license grant under Part 5 above, a Minimum Annual Royalty shall be due beginning with such royalty year and for each royalty year ending on the anniversary of such royalty year thereafter. Such Minimum Annual Royalty shall be equal to the Patent Royalty which would have been due if the "Minimum Number of Units [of Licensed Product] to Be Sold to Compute Minimum Annual Royalty" identified in Part 1 above were sold during such royalty year. If less than such number of units of Licensed Product are sold in any royalty year, then the Patent Royalty payable for the fourth quarter of such year shall be increased so as to cause the Patent Royalties paid for such year to equal said Minimum Annual Royalty. If an option is granted under Parts 1 and 4, then no Minimum Annual Royalties shall be due in any case until and if LICENSEE exercises its option.

D. If Minimum Not Paid: If this part is applicable and if sales of Licensed Product in any royalty year do not equal or exceed the minimum number of units identified in Part 1 above, LICENSEE may choose not to pay the Minimum Annual Royalty under subpart C above. In this case, LICENSEE shall so notify LICENSOR by the date on which the last royalty for such year is due, i.e., within one month after any anniversary of the date identified in Part 1 above. Thereupon the license grant under Part 4 above shall be converted to a nonexclusive grant, and LICENSOR may immediately license others under the above patent.

E. Most Favored Licensee: If this license is nonexclusive, or if it becomes nonexclusive under subpart D above, then (a) LICENSOR shall not grant any other license under the above patent to any other party under any terms which are more favorable than those which LICENSEE pays or enjoys under this Agreement, and (b) LICENSOR shall promptly advise LICENSEE of any such other grant and the terms thereof.

F. **When No Royalties Due:** No Patent Royalties shall be due under this Agreement after the above patent expires or if it is declared invalid by a court of competent jurisdiction from which no appeal can be taken. Also, if LICENSOR'S patent application becomes finally abandoned without any patent issuing, then the Patent Royalty under this Agreement shall be terminated as of the date of abandonment. Any Know-How Royalties under Part 6 above shall continue after any Patent Royalties terminate, provided such Know-How Royalties are otherwise due under such Part 6.

G. **Late Payments:** If any payment due under this Agreement is not timely paid, then the unpaid balance shall bear interest until paid at an annual rate of 10% until the delinquent balance is paid. Such interest shall be compounded monthly.

H. **Net Factory Sales Price:** "Net Factory Sales Price" is defined as the gross factory selling price of Licensed Product, or the U.S. importer's gross selling price if Licensed Product is made abroad, less usual trade discounts actually allowed, but not including advertising allowances or fees or commissions paid to employees or agents of LICENSEE. The Net Factory Sales Price shall not include (1) packing costs, if itemized separately, (2) import and export taxes, excise and other sales taxes, and customs duties, and (3) costs of insurance and transportation, if separately billed, from the place of manufacture if in the U.S., or from the place of importation if manufactured abroad, to the customer's premises or next point of distribution or sale. Bona fide returns may be deducted from units shipped in computing the royalty payable after such returns are made.

8. **Records:** LICENSEE and any of its sublicensees shall keep full, clear, and accurate records with respect to sales subject to royalty under this Agreement. The records shall be made in a manner such that the royalty reports made pursuant to Part 7B can be verified. LICENSOR, or its authorized agent, shall have the right to examine and audit such records upon reasonable notice during normal business hours, but not more than twice per year. In case of any dispute as to the sufficiency or accuracy of such records, LICENSOR may have any independent auditor examine and certify such records. LICENSEE shall make prompt adjustment to compensate for any errors or omissions disclosed by any such examination and certification of LICENSEE'S records. If LICENSOR does not examine LICENSEE'S records or question any royalty report within two years from the date thereof, then such report shall be considered final and LICENSOR shall have no further right to contest such report.

9. **Sublicensees:** If LICENSEE grants any sublicenses hereunder, it shall notify LICENSOR within one month from any such grant and shall provide LICENSOR with a true copy of any sublicense agreement. Any sublicensee of LICENSEE under this Agreement shall be bound by all of the terms applying to LICENSEE hereunder and LICENSEE shall be responsible for the obligations and duties of any of its sublicensees.

10. **Patent Prosecution:**

A. **Domestic:** LICENSOR shall, at LICENSOR'S own expense, prosecute its above U.S. patent application, and any continuations, divisions, continuations-in-part, substitutes, and reissues of such patent application or any patent thereon, at its own expense, until all applicable patents issue or any patent application becomes finally abandoned. LICENSOR shall also pay any maintenance fees which are due on any patent(s) which issue on said patent application. If for any reason LICENSOR intends to abandon any patent application hereunder, it shall notify LICENSEE at least two months in advance of any such abandonment so as to give LICENSEE the opportunity to take over prosecution of any such application and maintenance of any

patent. If LICENSEE takes over prosecution, LICENSOR shall cooperate with LIC-
ENSEE in any manner LICENSEE requires, at LICENSEE'S expense.

   B. Foreign: LICENSOR shall have the opportunity, but not the obligation, to file
   corresponding foreign patent applications to any patent application under subpart A
   above. If LICENSOR files any such foreign patent applications, LICENSOR may
   license, sell, or otherwise exploit the invention, Licensed Product, or any such
   foreign application in any countries foreign to the United States as it chooses, provided that LICENSOR must give LICENSEE a right of first refusal and at least one
   month to exercise this right before undertaking any such foreign exploitation. If
   LICENSOR chooses not to file any corresponding foreign applications under this
   part, it shall notify LICENSEE at least one month prior to the first anniversary of the
   above patent application so as to give LICENSEE the opportunity to file corresponding foreign patent applications if it so chooses.

   C. If Licensee Acts: If LICENSEE takes over prosecution of any U.S. patent application
   under subpart A above, and LICENSEE is successful so that a patent issues, then
   LICENSEE shall pay LICENSOR royalties thereafter at a rate of 75% of the royalty
   rate and any applicable minimum under Part 7C above and LICENSEE shall be
   entitled to deduct prosecution and maintenance expenses from its royalty payments.
   If LICENSEE elects to prosecute any foreign patent applications under subpart B
   above, then LICENSEE shall pay LICENSOR royalties of 50% of the royalty rate
   under Part 7 above for any applicable foreign sales, less all foreign prosecution and
   maintenance expenses incurred by LICENSEE.

11. **Marking:** LICENSEE shall mark all units of Licensed Product, or its container if direct
    marking is not feasible, with the legend "Patent Pending" until any patent(s) issue from
    the above patent application. When any patent(s) issue, LICENSOR shall promptly
    notify LICENSEE and thereafter LICENSEE shall mark all units of Licensed Product
    which it sells with proper notice of patent marking under 35 U.S.C. Section 287.

12. **If Infringement Occurs:** If either party discovers that the above patent is infringed, it
    shall communicate the details to the other party. LICENSOR shall thereupon have the
    right, but not the obligation, to take whatever action it deems necessary, including the
    filing of lawsuits, to protect the rights of the parties to this Agreement and to terminate
    such infringement. LICENSEE shall cooperate with LICENSOR if LICENSOR takes any
    such action, but all expenses of LICENSOR shall be borne by LICENSOR. If LICENSOR
    recovers any damages or compensation for any action it takes hereunder, LICENSOR
    shall retain 100% of such damages. If LICENSOR does not wish to take any action
    hereunder, LICENSEE shall also have the right, but not the obligation, to take any such
    action, in which case LICENSOR shall cooperate with LICENSEE, but all of LICENSEE'S
    expenses shall be borne by LICENSEE. LICENSEE shall receive 75% of any damages or
    compensation it recovers for any such infringement and shall pay 25% of such dam-
    ages or compensation to LICENSOR, after deducting its costs, including attorney fees.

13. **Disclaimer and Hold Harmless:**

    A. Disclaimer of Warranty: Nothing herein shall be construed as a warranty or
    representation by LICENSOR as to the scope or validity of the above patent applica-
    tion or any patent issuing thereon.

    B. Product Liability: LICENSEE shall hold LICENSOR harmless from any product
    liability actions involving Licensed Product.

14. **Term:** The term of this Agreement shall end with the expiration of the last of any
    patent(s) which issues on LICENSOR'S patent application, unless terminated sooner for

any reason provided herein, or unless know-how is licensed, in which case the terms of Part 6 shall cover the term of this Agreement.

15. **Termination:** This Agreement may be terminated under and according to any of the following contingencies:

   A. **Default:** If LICENSEE fails to make any payment on the date such payment is due under this Agreement, or if LICENSEE makes any other default under or breach of this Agreement, LICENSOR shall have the right to terminate this Agreement upon giving three months' written Notice of Intent to Terminate, specifying such failure, breach, or default to LICENSEE. If LICENSEE fails to make any payment in arrears, or otherwise fails to cure the breach or default within such three-month period, then LICENSOR may then send a written Notice of Termination to LICENSEE, whereupon this Agreement shall terminate in one month from the date of such Notice of Termination. If this Agreement is terminated hereunder, LICENSEE shall not be relieved of any of its obligations to the date of termination and LICENSOR may act to enforce LICENSEE'S obligations after any such termination.

   B. **Bankruptcy, Etc.:** If LICENSEE shall go into receivership, bankruptcy, or insolvency, or make an assignment for the benefit of creditors, or go out of business, this Agreement shall be immediately terminable by LICENSOR by written notice, but without prejudice to any rights of LICENSOR hereunder. This paragraph shall not apply so long as LICENSEE continues to pay royalties on time under Part 7, subpart B or C.

   C. **Antishelving:** If LICENSEE discontinues its sales or manufacture of Licensed Product without intent to resume, it shall so notify LICENSOR within one month of such discontinuance, whereupon LICENSOR shall have the right to terminate this Agreement upon one month's written notice, even if this Agreement has been converted to a nonexclusive grant under Part 7D above. If LICENSEE does not begin manufacture or sales of Licensed Product within one and one-half years from the date of this Agreement or the date of its option exercise if an option is granted, or, after commencing manufacture and sales of Licensed Product, discontinues its manufacture and sales of Licensed Product for one and one-half years, LICENSOR shall have the right to terminate this Agreement upon one months' written notice, unless LICENSEE can show that it in good faith intends and is actually working to resume or begin manufacture or sales, and has a reasonable basis to justify its delay. In such case LICENSEE shall advise LICENSOR in writing, before the end of such one-and-one-half-year period, of the circumstances involved and LICENSEE shall thereupon have up to an additional year to resume or begin manufacture or sales. It is the intent of the parties hereto that LICENSOR shall not be deprived of the opportunity, for an unreasonable length of time, to exclusively license its patent if LICENSEE has discontinued or has not commenced manufacture or sales of Licensed Product. In no case shall LICENSOR have the right to terminate this Agreement if and so long as LICENSEE is paying LICENSOR minimum annual royalties under Part 7C above.

16. **Notices:** All notices, payments, or statements under this Agreement shall be in writing and shall be sent by first-class certified mail, return receipt requested, postage prepaid, to the party concerned at the above address, or to any substituted address given by notice hereunder. Any such notice, payment, or statement shall be considered sent or made on the day deposited in the mails. Payments and statements may be sent by ordinary mail.

17. **Mediation and Arbitration:** If any dispute arises under this Agreement, the parties shall negotiate in good faith to settle such dispute. If the parties cannot resolve such dispute themselves, then either party may submit the dispute to mediation by a mediator approved by both parties. The parties shall both cooperate with the mediator. If the parties cannot agree to any mediator, or if either party does not wish to abide by any decision of the mediator, then they shall submit the dispute to arbitration by any mutually acceptable arbitrator. If no arbitrator is mutually acceptable, then they shall submit the matter to arbitration under the rules of the American Arbitration Association (AAA). Under any arbitration, both parties shall cooperate with and agree to abide finally by any decision of the arbitration proceeding. If the AAA is selected, the arbitration shall take place under the auspices of the nearest branch of the AAA to the other party. The costs of the arbitration proceeding shall be borne according to the decision of the arbitrator, who may apportion costs equally, or in accordance with any finding of fault or lack of good faith of either party. The arbitrator's award shall be non-appealable and enforceable in any court of competent jurisdiction.

18. **Assignment:** The rights of LICENSOR under this Agreement shall be assignable or otherwise transfer-rable, in whole or in part, by LICENSOR and shall vest LICENSOR'S assigns or transferees with the same rights and obligations as were held by LICENSOR. This Agreement shall be assignable by LICENSEE to any entity that succeeds to the business of LICENSEE to which Licensed Products relate or to any other entity if LICENSOR'S permission is first obtained in writing.

19. **Jurisdiction and Venue:** This Agreement shall be interpreted under the laws of LICENSOR'S state, as given in Part 1 above. Any action related to this Agreement shall be brought in the county of LICENSOR'S above address; LICENSEE hereby consents to such venue.

20. **Nonfrustration:** Neither party to this Agreement shall commit any act or take any action which frustrates or hampers the rights of the other party under this Agreement. Each party shall act in good faith and engage in fair dealing when taking any action under or related to this Agreement.

21. **No Challenge:** LICENSEE has investigated the validity of LICENSOR'S patent and shall not challenge, contest, or impugn the validity of such patent.

22. **Rectification:** In case of any mistake in this Agreement, including any error, ambiguity, illegality, contradiction, or omission, this Agreement shall be interpreted as if such mistake were rectified in a manner which implements the intent of the parties as nearly as possible and effects substantial fairness, considering all pertinent circumstances.

23. **Entire Agreement:** This Agreement sets forth the entire understanding between the parties and supersedes any prior or contemporaneous oral understandings and any prior written agreements.

24. **Signatures:** The parties, having carefully read this Agreement and having consulted or having been given an opportunity to consult counsel, have indicated their agreement to all of the above terms by signing this Agreement on the respective dates below indicated. LICENSEE and LICENSOR have each received a copy of this Agreement with both LICENSEE'S and LICENSOR'S original ink signatures thereon.

Licensor: _____ Date: _____

Print Licensor's Name: _____

Licensee: _____ Date: _____

Print Licensee's Name: _____

Appendix 8

Forms Available at the PTO Website

Maintenance Fee Unintentionally Delayed—Petition to Accept Late	PTO/SB/66
Multiple Dependent Claim Fee Calculation Sheet	PTO/SB/07
Nonpublication Request	PTO/SB/35
Nonpublication Request, Request To Rescind, + Not. of For. Filing	PTO/SB/36
Oral Hearing before Board of Patent Appeals & Interf., Request for	PTO/SB/32
Order Form For Service or Document—Charge to CCPA	PTO/SB/91
Patent Application (Utility) Transmittal	PTO/SB/05
Patent Application Declaration (Additional Inventors)	PTO/SB/02
Patent Application Fee Transmittal	PTO/SB/17
Petition Fee Transmittal	PTO/SB/17p
Petition for Extension of Time under 37 CFR 1.136(b)	PTO/SB/23
Plant Patent Application Declaration	PTO/SB/03
Plant Patent Application Transmittal	PTO/SB/19
Prior Art Citation in a Patent File	PTO/SB/42
Reexamination, Ex Parte, Request for	PTO/SB/57
Reexamination, Inter Partes, Request for	PTO/SB/58
Reissue Application Declaration	PTO/SB/51
Reissue Application, Supplemental Declaration to Correct Errors	PTO/SB/51S
Reissue Application—Consent of Assignee	PTO/SB/53
Reissue Patent Application Fee Transmittal	PTO/SB/56
Reissue Patent Application Transmittal	PTO/SB/50
Reissue Patent Application, Statement re Loss of Original Patent	PTO/SB/55
Request for Continued Examination (RCE) Transmittal	PTO/SB/30
Revival of Abandoned Appn.—Failure to Notify of Foreign Filing	PTO/SB/64a
Statutory Invention Registration, Request for	PTO/SB/94
Supplemental Declaration for Utility or Design Patent Application	PTO/SB/04
Terminal Disclaimer to Accompany Petition (No Period Specified)	PTO/SB/63
Terminal Disclaimer to Accompany Petition (Period Specified)	PTO/SB/62
Terminal Disclaimer—Double Patenting Rejection on Pending Appn.	PTO/SB/25
Terminal Disclaimer—Double Patenting Rejection on Prior Patent	PTO/SB/2
Transmittal Form for General Use	PTO/SB/21
Unavoidably Abandoned Application, Petition for Revival	PTO/SB/61
Unintentionally Abandoned Application, Petition for Revival	PTO/SB/64
Utility or Design Patent Application Declaration	PTO/SB/01

Index

unusual, detailing in application, 8/6
See also Method (process) claims; Method (process) patents
Margins
of amendment, 13/45
of application, 10/15
of drawings, 10/5, 10/9
Marketability. *See* Commercial viability evaluation; Test marketing
Marketing of invention, 11/2–15
alternative routes for, 11/3–6
brochures for, 10/8
with celebrity endorsement, 11/14
correspondence with prospect, 11/11
decision making for, 7/4–8, 7/9–10, 7/12
ease of, 4/8
finding manufacturers/distributors, 11/7–8
to government agencies, 11/13
Inventor's Commandments for, 11/2
with manufacture/distribution by inventor, 7/8–11, 11/6, 11/12–14, 15/6
need for, 4/2
NIH (Not Invented Here) syndrome and, 11/8
patent number marking and, 15/4, 15/14, 15/15, 15/16, 15/20
in patent pending period, 10/36, 11/2–3, 11/9, 11/10, 11/11
perseverance in, 11/3
as premium, 11/14
presentation to prospect, 11/10–11
publicity and, 11/13–14, 15/3
simultaneous, to several companies, 11/11
summary, 11/14–15
timing of, 11/2–3
venture capitalist and, 11/12
waiver of manufacturer, 7/5–6, 11/8–10, 11/11
working model for, 11/6–7, 11/10–11
See also Assignment; Commercial use or sale of invention; Licensing; Manufacturers; Sale of patent rights; Test marketing
Marketing research firm, 11/4, 11/13
Market novelty, 7/7
Markush group claims, 9/15
Materials
alternative embodiments or ramifications and, 8/5, 8/23
terms for, Appendix 3
trademarked, 8/8–9, 8/21
unusual or novel, 8/6, 8/20, 8/27, 9/27
See also Parts of invention
Means clauses, 9/13–14
in additional set of claims, 9/27
broad claims containing, 9/10, 9/18, 9/19, 9/20

dependent claims and, 9/23, 9/25
labeling of means in, 9/22
law regarding, 9/4
minor ramifications and, 8/23
require combination of elements, 9/10
response to Office Action and, 13/26
in software claims, 9/14
support in specification for, 9/14, 9/17, 9/27
Media exposure, 11/14, 15/3
Medical devices, 8/23, 15/5, 15/6
explaining in specification, 8/22
need for, 2/5
royalties for, 16/14
Medical procedures, 5/6, 15/6
Meditation, to stimulate creativity, 2/4, 2/8
Mental processes, patentability and, 1/9, 5/8
Metal parts. *See* Machine shops
Method (process) claims, 9/5–7
with apparatus (machine) claims, 9/21, 9/27, 9/28, 13/54
dependent, 9/24, 9/28
gerunds in, 9/21, 9/27
interconnections of elements in, 9/18
Method (process) patents, 5/4, 5/5–7
embodiments of, 8/5
flowcharts for, 8/13
infringement of
abroad, 15/5, 15/14
filing date and, 15/13, 15/17
machine patents and, 5/7
novelty of, 5/15
prior user's rights and, 7/10
ramifications of, 8/5, 8/23
specification for, 8/19
Metric dimensions, 8/27
Microfiche, computer program on, 8/3, 8/22
Microfilm, in PTDL search, 6/37, 6/38, 6/40
Microorganisms, 5/9, 8/8. *See also* Bacteria
MicroPatent, 6/42, 6/49
searching patents citing your patent, 15/7
Military applications, 12/7, 13/5
Mindware, 2/8
Model maker, 3/7, 4/12, 11/6
as co-inventor, 16/2, 16/3
See also Building and testing; Machine shops; Scale model; Working model (prototype)
Molecular diagrams, 8/13
Money order, to Commissioner for Patents, 10/24
Monopoly
from exclusive license, 16/9, 16/12, 16/14
under patent law, 15/5–6, 16/2
See also Intellectual property (IP)

CATALOG

...more from Nolo

BUSINESS	PRICE	CODE
Becoming a Mediator: Your Guide to Career Opportunities	$29.99	BECM
Business Buyout Agreements (Book w/CD-ROM)	$49.99	BSAG
The CA Nonprofit Corporation Kit (Binder w/CD-ROM)	$59.99	CNP
Consultant & Independent Contractor Agreements (Book w/CD-ROM)	$29.99	CICA
The Corporate Minutes Book (Book w/CD-ROM)	$69.99	CORMI
Create Your Own Employee Handbook (Book w/CD-ROM)	$49.99	EMHA
Dealing With Problem Employees	$44.99	PROBM
Deduct It! Lower Your Small Business Taxes	$34.99	DEDU
The Employer's Legal Handbook	$39.99	EMPL
Everyday Employment Law	$29.99	ELBA
Federal Employment Laws	$49.99	FELW
Form Your Own Limited Liability Company (Book w/CD-ROM)	$44.99	LIAB
Hiring Independent Contractors: The Employer's Legal Guide (Book w/CD-ROM)	$34.99	HICI
How to Run a Thriving Business: Strategies for Success & Satisfaction	$19.99	THRV
Home Business Tax Deductions: Keep What You Earn	$34.99	DEHB
How to Create a Noncompete Agreement (Book w/CD-ROM)	$44.95	NOCMP
How to Form a California Professional Corporation (Book w/CD-ROM)	$59.99	PROF
How to Form a Nonprofit Corporation (Book w/CD-ROM)—National Edition	$44.99	NNP
How to Form a Nonprofit Corporation in California (Book w/CD-ROM)	$44.99	NON
How to Form Your Own California Corporation (Binder w/CD-ROM)	$59.99	CACI
How to Form Your Own California Corporation (Book w/CD-ROM)	$34.99	CCOR
How to Get Your Business on the Web	$29.99	WEBS
How to Write a Business Plan	$34.99	SBS
Incorporate Your Business	$49.99	NIBS
The Independent Paralegal's Handbook	$34.99	PARA
Leasing Space for Your Small Business	$34.95	LESP
Legal Guide for Starting & Running a Small Business	$34.99	RUNS
Legal Forms for Starting & Running a Small Business (Book w/CD-ROM)	$29.99	RUNSF
Marketing Without Advertising	$24.00	MWAD
Mediate, Don't Litigate	$24.99	MEDL
Music Law (Book w/CD-ROM)	$39.99	ML
Nolo's Guide to Social Security Disability	$29.99	QSS
Nolo's Quick LLC	$29.99	LLCQ
Nondisclosure Agreements (Book w/CD-ROM)	$39.95	NAG
The Small Business Start-up Kit (Book w/CD-ROM)	$24.99	SMBU
The Small Business Start-up Kit for California (Book w/CD-ROM)	$24.99	OPEN
The Partnership Book: How to Write a Partnership Agreement (Book w/CD-ROM)	$39.99	PART
Sell Your Business: A Step by Step Legal Guide (Book w/CD-ROM)	$49.99	SELBU
Sexual Harassment on the Job	$24.95	HARS
Starting & Running a Successful Newsletter or Magazine	$29.99	MAG
California Workers' Comp: How to Take Charge When You're Injured on the Job	$34.99	WORK
Tax Savvy for Small Business	$36.99	SAVVY
Workplace Investigations: A Step by Step Guide	$39.99	CMPLN
Working for Yourself: Law & Taxes for the Self-Employed	$39.99	WAGE
Your Crafts Business: A Legal Guide (Book w/CD-ROM)	$26.99	VART
Your Limited Liability Company: An Operating Manual (Book w/CD-ROM)	$49.99	LOP
Your Rights in the Workplace	$29.99	YRW

Prices subject to change.

CONSUMER

	PRICE	CODE
How to Win Your Personal Injury Claim	$29.99	PICL
Nolo's Encyclopedia of Everyday Law	$29.99	EVL
Nolo's Guide to California Law	$24.99	CLAW
Trouble-Free Travel...And What to Do When Things Go Wrong	$14.95	TRAV

ESTATE PLANNING & PROBATE

8 Ways to Avoid Probate	$19.99	PRAV
Estate Planning Basics	$21.99	ESPN
The Executor's Guide: Settling a Loved One's Estate	$34.99	EXEC
How to Probate an Estate in California	$49.99	PAE
Make Your Own Living Trust (Book w/CD-ROM)	$39.99	LITR
Nolo's Simple Will Book (Book w/CD-ROM)	$36.99	SWIL
Plan Your Estate	$44.99	NEST
Quick & Legal Will Book	$16.99	QUIC
Quicken Willmaker: Estate Planning Basics	$49.99	QWMB

FAMILY MATTERS

Child Custody: Building Parenting Agreements That Work	$29.99	CUST
The Complete IEP Guide	$29.99	IEP
Divorce & Money: How to Make the Best Financial Decisions During Divorce	$34.99	DIMO
Do Your Own California Adoption: Nolo's Guide for Stepparents and Domestic Partners (Book w/CD-ROM)	$34.99	ADOP
Get a Life: You Don't Need a Million to Retire Well	$24.99	LIFE
The Guardianship Book for California	$39.99	GB
A Legal Guide for Lesbian and Gay Couples	$29.99	LG
Living Together: A Legal Guide (Book w/CD-ROM)	$34.99	LTK
Medical Directives and Powers of Attorney in California (Book w/CD-ROM)	$19.99	CPOA
Prenuptial Agreements: How to Write a Fair & Lasting Contract (Book w/CD-ROM)	$34.99	PNUP
Using Divorce Mediation: Save Your Money & Your Sanity	$29.99	UDMD

GOING TO COURT

Beat Your Ticket: Go To Court & Win! (National Edition)	$21.99	BEYT
The Criminal Law Handbook: Know Your Rights, Survive the System	$34.99	KYR
Everybody's Guide to Small Claims Court (National Edition)	$26.99	NSCC
Everybody's Guide to Small Claims Court in California	$29.99	CSCC
Fight Your Ticket & Win in Califonia	$29.99	FYT
How to Change Your Name in California	$34.99	NAME
How to Collect When You Win a Lawsuit (California Edition)	$29.99	JUDG
How to Seal Your Juvenile & Criminal Records (California Edition)	$34.95	CRIM
The Lawsuit Survival Guide	$29.99	UNCL
Nolo's Deposition Handbook	$29.99	DEP
Represent Yourself in Court: How to Prepare & Try a Winning Case	$34.99	RYC
Sue in California Without a Lawyer	$34.99	SLWY

HOMEOWNERS, LANDLORDS & TENANTS

California Tenants' Rights	$27.99	CTEN
Deeds for California Real Estate	$24.99	DEED
Dog Law	$21.95	DOG
Every Landlord's Legal Guide (National Edition, Book w/CD-ROM)	$44.99	ELLI
Every Tenant's Legal Guide	$29.99	EVTEN
For Sale by Owner in California	$29.99	FSBO
How to Buy a House in California	$34.99	BHCA
The California Landlord's Law Book: Rights & Responsibilities (Book w/CD-ROM)	$44.99	LBRT
The California Landlord's Law Book: Evictions (Book w/CD-ROM)	$44.99	LBEV
Leases & Rental Agreements	$29.99	LEAR
Neighbor Law: Fences, Trees, Boundaries & Noise	$26.99	NEI
The New York Landlord's Law Book (Book w/CD-ROM)	$44.99	NYLL
New York Tenants' Rights	$27.99	NYTEN
Renters' Rights (National Edition)	$24.99	RENT

	PRICE	CODE

IMMIGRATION

Becoming a U.S. Citizen: A Guide to the Law, Exam and Interview	$24.99	USCIT
Fiancé & Marriage Visas (Book w/CD-ROM)	$44.99	IMAR
How to Get a Green Card	$29.99	GRN
Student & Tourist Visas	$29.99	ISTU
U.S. Immigration Made Easy	$44.99	IMEZ

MONEY MATTERS

101 Law Forms for Personal Use (Book w/CD-ROM)	$29.99	SPOT
Bankruptcy: Is It the Right Solution to Your Debt Problems?	$19.99	BRS
Chapter 13 Bankruptcy: Repay Your Debts	$34.99	CHB
Creating Your Own Retirement Plan	$29.99	YROP
Credit Repair (Book w/CD-ROM)	$24.99	CREP
Getting Paid: How to Collect from Bankrupt Debtors	$29.99	CRBNK
How to File for Chapter 7 Bankruptcy	$34.99	HFB
IRAs, 401(k)s & Other Retirement Plans: Taking Your Money Out	$34.99	RET
Money Troubles: Legal Strategies to Cope With Your Debts	$29.99	MT
Stand Up to the IRS	$24.99	SIRS
Surviving an IRS Tax Audit	$24.95	SAUD
Take Control of Your Student Loan Debt	$26.95	SLOAN

PATENTS AND COPYRIGHTS

The Copyright Handbook: How to Protect and Use Written Works (Book w/CD-ROM)	$39.99	COHA
Copyright Your Software	$34.95	CYS
Domain Names	$26.95	DOM
Getting Permission: How to License and Clear Copyrighted Materials Online and Off (Book w/CD-ROM)	$34.99	RIPER
How to Make Patent Drawings Yourself	$29.99	DRAW
Inventor's Guide to Law, Business and Taxes (Book w/CD-ROM)	$34.99	ILAX
The Inventor's Notebook	$24.99	INOT
Nolo's Patents for Beginners	$29.99	QPAT
License Your Invention (Book w/CD-ROM)	$39.99	LICE
Patent, Copyright & Trademark	$39.99	PCTM
Patent It Yourself	$49.99	PAT
Patent Pending in 24 Hours	$29.99	PEND
Patent Searching Made Easy	$29.95	PATSE
The Public Domain	$34.99	PUBL
Trademark: Legal Care for Your Business and Product Name	$39.99	TRD
Web and Software Development: A Legal Guide (Book w/CD-ROM)	$44.99	SFT

RESEARCH & REFERENCE

Legal Research: How to Find & Understand the Law	$39.99	LRES

SENIORS

Long-Term Care: How to Plan & Pay for it	$21.99	ELD
The Conservatorship Book for California	$44.99	CNSV
Social Security, Medicare & Goverment Pensions	$29.99	SOA

SOFTWARE
Call or check our website at www.nolo.com for special discounts on Software!

LLC Maker—Windows	$89.95	LLP1
PatentEase—Windows	$349.00	PEAS
Personal RecordKeeper 5.0 CD—Windows	$59.95	RKD5
Quicken Legal Business Pro 2005—Windows	$109.99	SBQB5
Quicken WilMaker Plus 2005—Windows	$79.99	WQP5

Special Upgrade Offer
Save 35% on the latest edition of your Nolo book

Because laws and legal procedures change often, we update our books regularly. To help keep you up-to-date, we are extending this special upgrade offer. Cut out and mail the title portion of the cover of your old Nolo book and we'll give you 35% off the retail price of the NEW EDITION of that book when you purchase directly from Nolo. This offer is to individuals only.

Prices and offer subject to change without notice.

Order Form

Name

Address

City

State, Zip

Daytime Phone

E-mail

Our "No-Hassle" Guarantee

Return anything you buy directly from Nolo for any reason and we'll cheerfully refund your purchase price. No ifs, ands or buts.

☐ Check here if you do not wish to receive mailings from other companies

Item Code	Quantity	Item	Unit Price	Total Price

Subtotal	
Add your local sales tax (California only)	
Shipping: RUSH $9, Basic $5 (See below)	
"I bought 3, ship it to me FREE!"(Ground shipping only)	
TOTAL	

Method of payment

☐ Check　　☐ VISA　　☐ MasterCard
☐ Discover Card　　☐ American Express

Account Number

Expiration Date

Signature

Shipping and Handling

Rush Delivery—Only $9

We'll ship any order to any street address in the U.S. by UPS 2nd Day Air* for only $9!

* Order by noon Pacific Time and get your order in 2 business days. Orders placed after noon Pacific Time will arrive in 3 business days. P.O. boxes and S.F. Bay Area use basic shipping. Alaska and Hawaii use 2nd Day Air or Priority Mail.

Basic Shipping—$5

Use for P.O. Boxes, Northern California and Ground Service.

Allow 1-2 weeks for delivery. U.S. addresses only.

For faster service, use your credit card and our toll-free numbers

Call our customer service group
Monday thru Friday 7am to 7pm PST

Phone	1-800-728-3555
Fax	1-800-645-0895
Mail	Nolo
950 Parker St.
Berkeley, CA 94710

Order 24 hours a day @
www.nolo.com

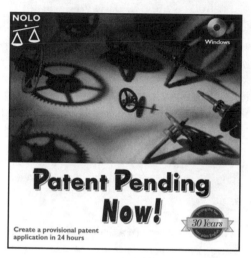

Remember:

Little publishers have big ears.
We really listen to you.

Take 2 Minutes & Give Us Your 2 cents

Your comments make a big difference in the development and revision of Nolo books and software. Please take a few minutes and register your Nolo product—and your comments—with us. Not only will your input make a difference, you'll receive special offers available only to registered owners of Nolo products on our newest books and software. Register now by:

PHONE
1-800-728-3555

FAX
1-800-645-0895

EMAIL
cs@nolo.com

or **MAIL** us
this registration card

fold here

Registration Card

NAME _____ DATE _____

ADDRESS _____

_____

CITY _____ STATE _____ ZIP _____

PHONE _____ E-MAIL _____

WHERE DID YOU HEAR ABOUT THIS PRODUCT? _____

WHERE DID YOU PURCHASE THIS PRODUCT? _____

DID YOU CONSULT A LAWYER? (PLEASE CIRCLE ONE)   YES   NO   NOT APPLICABLE

DID YOU FIND THIS BOOK HELPFUL?   (VERY)   5   4   3   2   1   (NOT AT ALL)

COMMENTS _____

_____

_____

WAS IT EASY TO USE?   (VERY EASY)   5   4   3   2   1   (VERY DIFFICULT)

We occasionally make our mailing list available to carefully selected companies whose products may be of interest to you.

❏   If you do not wish to receive mailings from these companies, please check this box.

❏   You can quote me in future Nolo promotional materials.
     Daytime phone number _____.

PAT 11.0

Nolo in the NEWS

fold here

- -

Place
stamp here

Nolo
950 Parker Street
Berkeley, CA 94710-9867

Attn: | PAT 11.0 |